Best Practices and Strategies for Online Instructors:

Insights From Higher Education Online Faculty

Lori B. Doyle
Concordia University, Irvine, USA

Tanya M. Tarbutton
Concordia University, Irvine, USA

Published in the United States of America by
IGI Global Scientific Publishing
701 East Chocolate Avenue
Hershey, PA, 17033, USA
Tel: 717-533-8845
Fax: 717-533-8661
E-mail: cust@igi-global.com
Website: https://www.igi-global.com

Copyright © 2025 by IGI Global Scientific Publishing. All rights reserved. No part of this publication may be reproduced, stored or distributed in any form or by any means, electronic or mechanical, including photocopying, without written permission from the publisher.
Product or company names used in this set are for identification purposes only. Inclusion of the names of the products or companies does not indicate a claim of ownership by IGI Global Scientific Publishing of the trademark or registered trademark.

Library of Congress Cataloging-in-Publication Data

Names: Doyle, Lori, 1975- editor. | Tarbutton, Tanya, 1973- editor.
Title: Best practices and strategies for online instructors : insights from higher education online faculty / Edited by Lori Doyle, Tanya Tarbutton.
Description: Hershey, PA : IGI Global Scientific Publishing, [2025] | Includes bibliographical references and index. | Summary: "This edited book will serve as a collection of best practices and strategies as described by online faculty working in higher education"-- Provided by publisher.
Identifiers: LCCN 2024047148 (print) | LCCN 2024047149 (ebook) | ISBN 9798369344071 (hardcover) | ISBN 9798369344118 (paperback) | ISBN 9798369344088 (ebook)
Subjects: LCSH: Web-based instruction. | Education, Higher--Computer-assisted instruction. | Internet in higher education. | Distance education.
Classification: LCC LB1028.57 .B47 2025 (print) | LCC LB1028.57 (ebook) | DDC 371.33/44678--dc23/eng/20241017
LC record available at https://lccn.loc.gov/2024047148
LC ebook record available at https://lccn.loc.gov/2024047149

Vice President of Editorial: Melissa Wagner
Managing Editor of Acquisitions: Mikaela Felty
Managing Editor of Book Development: Jocelynn Hessler
Production Manager: Mike Brehm
Cover Design: Phillip Shickler

British Cataloguing in Publication Data
A Cataloguing in Publication record for this book is available from the British Library.

All work contributed to this book is new, previously-unpublished material.
The views expressed in this book are those of the authors, but not necessarily of the publisher.
This book contains information sourced from authentic and highly regarded references, with reasonable efforts made to ensure the reliability of the data and information presented. The authors, editors, and publisher believe the information in this book to be accurate and true as of the date of publication. Every effort has been made to trace and credit the copyright holders of all materials included. However, the authors, editors, and publisher cannot assume responsibility for the validity of all materials or the consequences of their use. Should any copyright material be found unacknowledged, please inform the publisher so that corrections may be made in future reprints.

Table of Contents

Preface xvi

Chapter 1
Beyond the Screen: Cultivating Joy, Creativity, and Well-Being in Online
Learning Environments 1
    Ellen Nicole Beattie, Center for Intentional Learning, USA

Chapter 2
Strategies for Using Online Education in Support of Global Contexts 41
    *Doris Chasokela, National University of Science and Technology,
        Zimbabwe*
    *Lungisani Mpofu, National University of Science and Technology,
        Zimbabwe*

Chapter 3
Fostering Self-Efficacy for Higher Education Online Instructors 73
    *Doris Chasokela, National University of Science and Technology,
        Zimbabwe*
    *Lungisani Mpofu, National University of Science and Technology,
        Zimbabwe*

Chapter 4
Creating and Maintaining Successful Online Learning Environments 109
    Nurul Naimah Rose, Universiti Malaysia Perlis, Malaysia
    Faten Khalida Khalid, Universiti Malaysia Perlis, Malaysia
    Aida Shakila Ishak, Universiti Malaysia Perlis, Malaysia
    Nazifah Hamidun, Universiti Malaysia Perlis, Malaysia
    Nur Farhinaa Othman, Universiti Malaysia Perlis, Malaysia

Chapter 5
Beyond Lectures: The Flipped Learning Model 133
    Elissar Gerges, Zayed University, UAE

Chapter 6
Enhancing Adult Online Learners' Graduate Leadership Experiences
Through the Lens of Care Theory 167
    Carrie M. Grimes, Vanderbilt University, USA

Chapter 7
Implementing Online Project-Based Learning: Opportunities for Social Capital Development 195
    Youmei Liu, University of Houston, USA

Chapter 8
A "Behind the Screens" Look at Humanizing Online Learning Spaces 229
    Crystal Neumann, American College of Education, USA
    Audra Pickett, American College of Education, USA

Chapter 9
Online Teaching Readiness in the Era of Digital Transformation: Challenges and Recommendations 253
    Zhuqing Ding, Georgetown University, USA
    Khalid Alharbi, Georgetown University, USA

Chapter 10
Understanding the Cognitive Constituents of E-Learning 277
    Swati Sharma, Indian Institute of Technology, Jodhpur, India
    Deepak Kumar Saxena, Indian Institute of Technology, Jodhpur, India

Chapter 11
Use of Scaffolding to Promote Engagement and Learning in Asynchronous Online Discussions 313
    Linda Clark Ashar, American Public University System, USA

Chapter 12
Effective Strategies for Teaching Mathematics in Virtual Higher Education Environments 341
    Rocío Rodríguez-Padín, Universidade da Coruña, Spain

Chapter 13
Empowering Educators and Students Through Boundaries 369
    Mary K. Lannon, Purdue University Global, USA
    Holli Vah Seliskar, Purdue University Global, USA
    David Alan White, Purdue University Global, USA

Chapter 14
Successful Teaching in Virtual Classrooms: Strategies for Online Open Elective Educators... 393
    Vishnu Achutha Menon, Institute for Educational and Developmental Studies, India

Chapter 15
The Role of Virtual Classrooms in Realizing Effective Online Learning 415
    Servet Kılıç, Ordu University, Turkey
    Seyfullah Gökoğlu, Bartın University, Turkey

Chapter 16
Using Video Feedback to Create Faculty Presence in the Virtual Classroom .. 443
    Mary Streit, National University, USA
    Madia Levin, National University, USA
    Alycia Harris, National University, USA

Chapter 17
Strategies and Practices for Instructors in Online Open Elective Courses:
Teacher Lessons 471
    Patcha Bhujanga Rao, Jain University, India
    B. G. Guruprasad, Surana Evening College, India
    V. S. Vainik, Jain University, India
    D. Deepak, Jain University, India
    Usha Prabhu, Jain University, India

Chapter 18
Curriculum Design in the Crossroads at Higher Education Institutions (HEIs)
Boosting Quality Assurance: Satelliting Intellectual Property, Innovation -
Legal Landscape 497
    Bhupinder Singh, Sharda University, India
    Christian Kaunert, Dublin City University, Ireland

Compilation of References 527

About the Contributors 643

Index 651

Detailed Table of Contents

Preface xvi

Chapter 1
Beyond the Screen: Cultivating Joy, Creativity, and Well-Being in Online Learning Environments... 1
  Ellen Nicole Beattie, Center for Intentional Learning, USA

Beyond the Screen: Cultivating Joy, Creativity, and Well-Being in Online Learning Environments explores the detrimental impact of stress on college students' mental health and academic performance. The chapter emphasizes the need to shift from traditional pedagogical approaches to a framework prioritizing student well-being. Seligman's PERMA model, encompassing positive emotions, engagement, relationships, meaning, and accomplishment, is a foundation for incorporating positive psychology principles into the online classroom. Infusing playful pedagogy may positively benefit student engagement, student resilience, and the creation of a positive academic classroom culture. The chapter concludes with strategies to foster students' emotional, social, and academic growth.

Chapter 2
Strategies for Using Online Education in Support of Global Contexts 41
  Doris Chasokela, National University of Science and Technology, Zimbabwe
  Lungisani Mpofu, National University of Science and Technology, Zimbabwe

This chapter explores the potential of online education as a powerful tool for supporting global contexts and addressing the diverse educational needs of learners around the world. By harnessing the power of digital technologies, online education offers the potential to break down barriers of geography, culture, and economics that have traditionally limited access to quality education. Through a discussion of key themes and case studies, this chapter aims to provide a comprehensive overview of the strategies and best practices for using online education in support of global contexts. By the end of this chapter, readers will have gained a deeper understanding of how online education can be used to: Improve access to education in underserved communities. Provide personalized learning experiences that cater to diverse learning styles and cultural backgrounds. Facilitate cross-cultural exchange and understanding through global collaboration and virtual exchanges. Leverage technology to create innovative teaching and learning approaches .

Chapter 3
Fostering Self-Efficacy for Higher Education Online Instructors 73
    Doris Chasokela, National University of Science and Technology, Zimbabwe
    Lungisani Mpofu, National University of Science and Technology, Zimbabwe

This book chapter explores the best practices and strategies that can be used by higher education online instructors to foster self-efficacy among their students. Based on insights from higher education online faculty, the chapter discusses how instructors can create a positive learning environment, promote learner autonomy, and provide appropriate levels of support and feedback. It also explores how instructors can use technology to facilitate effective communication and collaboration, and how they can adapt their teaching methods to the unique needs of online learners. Ultimately, the chapter aims to help higher education online instructors create an effective learning experience for their students. The specific strategies and best practices are discussed in the chapter. The chapter outlines particular tools and technologies that can be used to foster self-efficacy, such as discussion forums, collaborative learning tools, and interactive learning activities.

Chapter 4
Creating and Maintaining Successful Online Learning Environments 109
    Nurul Naimah Rose, Universiti Malaysia Perlis, Malaysia
    Faten Khalida Khalid, Universiti Malaysia Perlis, Malaysia
    Aida Shakila Ishak, Universiti Malaysia Perlis, Malaysia
    Nazifah Hamidun, Universiti Malaysia Perlis, Malaysia
    Nur Farhinaa Othman, Universiti Malaysia Perlis, Malaysia

This chapter is about creating and maintaining successful online learning environments emphasizing on the online learning in higher education especially in Malaysia. This chapter will have several segments which will begin with the overview of online learning in Malaysia. It will explore the scenarios of using online learning way back in the year 2000 until recently. Then, some explanations about the Online Collaborative Learning Theory (OCL) may benefit in some ways. The chapter continues with further discussion on the key points such as the access and accessibility, the enhancement of online classroom engagement, building the online learning community and the personalization of learning experience to student tailored to their needs and pace. The future of online learning in Malaysia is highly promising, propelled by emerging trends and opportunities. As technology advances, online learning platforms in Malaysia are expected to integrate increasingly sophisticated tools and features, enhancing the educational experience and expanding opportunities for learners across the nation.

Chapter 5
Beyond Lectures: The Flipped Learning Model 133
    Elissar Gerges, Zayed University, UAE

Despite the robust evidence supporting active learning, it is quite surprising that students complete weeks of lectures before an assignment, the product of their learning, is due. In such classes, learning is assumed to occur as students complete the assigned readings and attend classes without demonstrating their understanding. Alternatively, courses designed based on an active learning approach require students to showcase their learning in various tasks in a collaborative environment. The literature provides a wealth of research studies with empirical evidence of the effectiveness of active learning strategies in enhancing student achievement shifting from didactic teaching to a student-centered environment. This chapter will introduce the Flipped Learning Model as an active learning pedagogy in an online classroom. The flipped learning model aligns with the social constructivist approach as a theoretical framework that underpins active learning. Two active learning strategies will be explored in the flipped classroom context: Jigsaw Groups and Active Reading.

Chapter 6
Enhancing Adult Online Learners' Graduate Leadership Experiences
Through the Lens of Care Theory 167
    Carrie M. Grimes, Vanderbilt University, USA

This chapter aims to provide an in-depth analysis of how instructors can leverage Nel Noddings' care theory (1986, 2002, 2013, 2019) in order to design and deliver learning experiences which support the unique needs of adult online learners who are studying leadership in impactful ways. This chapter will also explore the ways in which online instructors may be seen as facilitators or coaches who use mental models of care theory to anticipate and positively guide relationships within the online learning environment through instructional and advising practices. This chapter will describe how online instructors may strategically use a care theory framework of modeling, dialogue, practice and confirmation to guide adult learners through different stages of the learning experience, in order to contribute to a caring and relational dynamic which drives students' learning outcomes and leadership capacity.

Chapter 7
Implementing Online Project-Based Learning: Opportunities for Social
Capital Development.. 195
    Youmei Liu, University of Houston, USA

This chapter examines the relationship between online Project-Based Learning (PBL) and social capital development, tracing the historical roots of PBL from learning by doing and experiential learning to modern implementations supported by digital platforms. It highlights how PBL, grounded in student-centered, real-world projects, fosters deep learning and critical thinking. As PBL has evolved, the integration of AI technology offers new tools to enhance learning but also introduces ethical challenges that must be carefully managed. The chapter emphasizes that building social capital – through trust, collaboration, and community engagement – is essential for the success of online PBL. It discusses strategies for overcoming the challenges of diverse student backgrounds and real-world complexities, focusing on the importance of ethical AI use and inclusive practices. Ultimately, this chapter underscores the potential of online PBL to not only enhance academic outcomes but also contribute to stronger, more resilient communities through the development of social capital.

Chapter 8
A "Behind the Screens" Look at Humanizing Online Learning Spaces 229
    Crystal Neumann, American College of Education, USA
    Audra Pickett, American College of Education, USA

With recent advances in technology and education, it is important to explore programs, applications, and efforts which assist with interaction and humanizing online learning. Achieving student engagement goals for an online institution were evaluated through observations, document reviews, and narratives highlighting the best practices and achievements from American College of Education (ACE). Techniques ACE uses to promote faculty and student engagement within the online environment will be identified. Get a "behind the screens" look at how online communities can be built by promoting engagement techniques, such as implementing additional software applications, developing digital toolboxes for students, promoting the Diversity, Equity, Inclusion (DEI) Center, implementing a Virtual Student Wellness Center, and embracing the use of Artificial Intelligence (AI). The chapter explores the increasing availability of educational technology useful for engaging student interaction in the classroom.

Chapter 9
Online Teaching Readiness in the Era of Digital Transformation: Challenges
and Recommendations 253
> *Zhuqing Ding, Georgetown University, USA*
> *Khalid Alharbi, Georgetown University, USA*

Digital transformation requires faculty development professionals and decision-makers in higher education to equip faculty and institutions with the skills to enable teaching and learning with technologies in online spaces. This chapter reviews a range of studies on faculty online readiness conducted in the past ten years and proposes a new framework, the Interrelated model of online teaching readiness (IMOTR), providing a new perspective that accounts for the interrelated nature of technological, pedagogical, agentic, and contextual readiness categories and factors. The findings provide insights to help inform faculty development professionals and university decision-makers to design appropriate infrastructure and training needed to prepare faculty to teach online.

Chapter 10
Understanding the Cognitive Constituents of E-Learning 277
> *Swati Sharma, Indian Institute of Technology, Jodhpur, India*
> *Deepak Kumar Saxena, Indian Institute of Technology, Jodhpur, India*

With the rapid development of ICT, E-learning has experienced exponential growth and drastic transformation in past years (Yao et al, 2022). E-learning works on the model of virtual education. There are different formats, like fully online learning, hybrid learning model which uses the combination of in-person and online components, and Massive Open Online Courses (MOOCs) which enable course engagement across the globe. The domain explores innovative pedagogical approaches. This chapter discusses various formats such as fully online courses, blended learning models, and Massive Open Online Courses (MOOCs). It explores innovative pedagogical approaches, popular theories and adaptive technologies to cater to diverse learning styles, based on cognitive science principles. Chapter further highlights e-learning, its growth and transformation due to advancements in Information and Communication Technology (ICT) and important theoretical frameworks to understand the various components of e-learning. At the end of this chapter, challenges and future research directions are discussed.

Chapter 11
Use of Scaffolding to Promote Engagement and Learning in Asynchronous
Online Discussions 313
    Linda Clark Ashar, American Public University System, USA

This chapter per the author proposes scaffolding as a best practice methodology for encouraging student learning and engagement in asynchronous discussions in the online higher education classroom. Grounded in Lev Semyonovich Vygotsky's Zone of Proximal Development and developmental theories that followed, scaffolding techniques harmonize with fundamental learning theories and practices, such as the tripartite Community of Inquiry framework of social, teaching, and cognitive presence. This chapter explains the value of scaffolding as supported by relevant research, and offers illustrative examples of the use of scaffolding to promote engagement and learning in online asynchronous discussions.

Chapter 12
Effective Strategies for Teaching Mathematics in Virtual Higher Education
Environments 341
    Rocío Rodríguez-Padín, Universidade da Coruña, Spain

This chapter provides a comprehensive guide for higher education instructors on effective strategies for teaching mathematics in virtual environments. As the shift to online education accelerates, particularly after the COVID-19 pandemic, educators must adopt evidence-based methods to enhance student learning. The chapter explores key principles of instructional design tailored for online mathematics, focusing on creating interactive and personalized learning experiences. Strategies for fostering student engagement, leveraging educational technologies, and promoting self-regulation are discussed. Additionally, the chapter highlights the importance of formative assessment in virtual settings, emphasizing methods that provide constructive feedback and opportunities for self-assessment. By addressing the challenges and opportunities of online mathematics education, this chapter aims to equip educators with the tools needed to optimize teaching and learning in the digital age.

Chapter 13
Empowering Educators and Students Through Boundaries 369
    Mary K. Lannon, Purdue University Global, USA
    Holli Vah Seliskar, Purdue University Global, USA
    David Alan White, Purdue University Global, USA

Setting and maintaining boundaries is critical to any healthy relationship; this is no less true of the relationship between faculty and students. Education aims to empower students by facilitating their development of independent decision-making, critical thinking, problem-solving, time management skills, accountability, and self-efficacy. This can be done by setting boundaries that balance being accessible to students and providing the space for them to learn, explore, and develop independence. Boundaries also empower faculty by helping to reduce stress, avoid burnout, and promote an appropriate work-life balance. The authors explore research on setting boundaries to promote student success, empower faculty, and promote a healthy learning environment. Recommendations are shared on how to set and maintain boundaries between faculty and students regarding classroom expectations, activities, communications, and grading.

Chapter 14
Successful Teaching in Virtual Classrooms: Strategies for Online Open
Elective Educators.. 393
    Vishnu Achutha Menon, Institute for Educational and Developmental
        Studies, India

The evolution of online education highlights its potential and challenges. It offers flexible, accessible learning opportunities but also underscores the need to address digital divides and provide robust support systems for students and educators. Future directions should focus on utilizing technological advancements, encouraging inclusive practices, and developing innovative pedagogical approaches. Key factors for effective online education include interactive platforms, multimedia content, personalized learning, engaging assessments, and strong support systems. Continuous professional development for educators and community building among students are essential to enhance the online learning experience.

Chapter 15

The Role of Virtual Classrooms in Realizing Effective Online Learning 415
    Servet Kılıç, Ordu University, Turkey
    Seyfullah Gökoğlu, Bartın University, Turkey

As of 2020, with the pandemic occurring worldwide, face-to-face learning activities at all levels, from preschool to higher education, have been moved to online environments. The importance of virtual classes has become more evident when these courses are conducted synchronously or asynchronously. This chapter mentions the roles of virtual classrooms in effectively executing online learning activities. The features of virtual classrooms in the context of teacher, student, and content are included. In this context, we examined widely used virtual classroom platforms such as Adobe Connect, BigBlueButton, Moodle, Zoom, Microsoft Teams, OpenMeetings, Google Meet, Electa, ClassDojo, WizIQ, and Kahoot. These platforms have many standard features, such as video conferencing, screen sharing, image sharing, presentation features, voice and text chat, document sharing, classroom management, lesson planning, and alternative measurement and evaluation tools.

Chapter 16

Using Video Feedback to Create Faculty Presence in the Virtual Classroom .. 443
    Mary Streit, National University, USA
    Madia Levin, National University, USA
    Alycia Harris, National University, USA

The inherent transactional distance in online learning often leads to student feelings of disengagement, disconnection, and anxiety. The increasing reliance on technology exacerbates this issue by eliminating key elements of human communication such as facial expressions and tone of voice. To mitigate these issues, faculty are increasingly turning to video feedback which can enhance the sense of faculty presence. This approach aims to replicate aspects of in-person communication vital to fostering a connected, engaging, and supportive learning environment. This chapter explores the efficacy of video feedback in establishing social, teaching, and cognitive presence as described by the Community of Inquiry Model. Through an examination of recent research on faculty perceptions, the chapter underscores the potential of video feedback to foster a more interactive, engaging, and humanized online learning environment, while also highlighting the need for further faculty training and best practices.

Chapter 17
Strategies and Practices for Instructors in Online Open Elective Courses:
Teacher Lessons 471
    Patcha Bhujanga Rao, Jain University, India
    B. G. Guruprasad, Surana Evening College, India
    V. S. Vainik, Jain University, India
    D. Deepak, Jain University, India
    Usha Prabhu, Jain University, India

The importance of online open elective courses (OOECs) in contemporary education is examined in this study, along with the difficulties teachers have when instructing them. Despite the advantages of OOECs—accessibility, flexibility, range of subjects, and individualized learning—teachers still have challenges in maintaining student engagement, supervising big classes, guaranteeing high-quality assessment systems, overcoming technological problems, and encouraging diversity. This study's primary focus is on the tactics and best practices that educators can use to overcome these obstacles and increase OOEC effectiveness. This work is important because it has the potential to improve the caliber of online education. It responds to the growing need for online education, provides teachers with the resources and information they require to improve student learning outcomes, trains them in research-based techniques, and works in tandem with

Chapter 18
Curriculum Design in the Crossroads at Higher Education Institutions (HEIs)
Boosting Quality Assurance: Satelliting Intellectual Property, Innovation -
Legal Landscape 497
    Bhupinder Singh, Sharda University, India
    Christian Kaunert, Dublin City University, Ireland

Innovation is the key factor boosting economics and international competitiveness, but it takes a long time for a nation to get to the point where innovation becomes the main force. The concept of innovation has to be seen somewhat differently when applied to latecomer nations than it is when applied to leaders. The technology combines textual feedback and machine learning and this approach examines the remarks, viewpoints and assessments of instructors made by students. Also, textual criticism enhances teaching style and provides valuable insights on the effectiveness of instruction. The inputs are recorded by the technology and stored in an authorized database. To assist the teacher see the input, ratings and graphs are provided. This chapter evaluates current econometric research on how changes in IPR policy affect educational growth and comes to research points to the acceleration of education and innovation development with stronger IPR regimes.

Compilation of References 527

About the Contributors 643

Index 651

Preface

In recent years, the landscape of higher education has undergone a dramatic shift, with online learning emerging as a crucial component of academic delivery. For many students and instructors, the virtual classroom has become a primary venue for teaching and learning. As this mode of education continues to evolve, the need for well-prepared, skilled, and innovative online educators has never been greater. This handbook, *Best Practices and Strategies for Online Instructors: Insights From Higher Education Online Faculty*, was created to help bridge the gap between the challenges inherent in online teaching and the opportunities for growth that exist within this dynamic learning environment.

As editors, we, Lori Doyle and Tanya Tarbutton, have had the privilege of working with and learning from countless dedicated and inspiring online instructors at Concordia University Irvine and beyond. Our shared experiences have reinforced the importance of providing educators with both the theoretical foundations and practical tools they need to succeed in this rapidly changing field. This volume is the result of our collective efforts to compile the knowledge, strategies, and best practices that have been tested and refined by experts in the field of online higher education.

Drawing on both scholarly research and real-world experiences, the chapters in this book offer a diverse range of perspectives, approaches, and solutions that address the unique demands of online teaching. Whether you are a seasoned online educator or just beginning your journey in the virtual classroom, you will find valuable insights here to support your professional growth and enhance your teaching practice.

The importance of evidence-based practices in online education cannot be overstated. The research and strategies presented in this book emphasize the need for instructors to engage in thoughtful, reflective teaching while also staying current with emerging trends, tools, and technologies. From fostering student engagement and motivation to designing impactful learning experiences, the contributors to this volume share strategies that have proven successful in real-world online classrooms.

Beyond pedagogy, this handbook also explores the broader context of online higher education. It addresses the challenges faced by faculty in adapting to online teaching, the need for innovative tools and platforms, and the ways in which instructors can create inclusive, accessible, and globally relevant learning environments. Moreover, it offers practical guidance for instructors seeking to sustain long-term success and growth in their online teaching careers.

We believe that this collection will serve not only as a reference for instructors seeking best practices, but also as an inspirational tool to encourage continued innovation and excellence in online education. Our hope is that this book will inspire you, the reader, to reflect on your own teaching practices, to explore new ideas, and to embrace the possibilities of online learning in higher education.

We are grateful to the contributors who have shared their expertise and experiences, and to you, the reader, for your commitment to the ongoing development of online education. It is through the dedication and collaboration of faculty like you that online higher education continues to thrive, creating opportunities for students around the world to engage in transformative learning experiences.

CHAPTER OVERVIEWS

Chapter 1: Beyond the Screen: Cultivating Joy, Creativity, and Well-being in Online Learning Environments

This chapter addresses the critical need to prioritize student well-being in the online classroom. It delves into the impact of stress on student mental health and academic performance, advocating for a shift from traditional pedagogies to frameworks that integrate positive psychology principles. The chapter utilizes Seligman's PERMA model—focusing on positive emotions, engagement, relationships, meaning, and accomplishment—as a foundation for fostering a healthier, more engaging online learning environment. The author explores the potential of playful pedagogy to boost student engagement and resilience, ultimately creating a classroom culture that supports both emotional and academic growth.

Chapter 2: Strategies for Using Online Education in Support of Global Contexts

In this chapter, readers are introduced to the expansive possibilities of online education in addressing global educational needs. The author discusses how online learning can bridge geographical, cultural, and economic divides, thus improving access to quality education. With case studies and practical examples, the chapter explores strategies for creating personalized learning experiences that respect diverse learning styles and cultural backgrounds. Emphasizing cross-cultural exchange, the chapter offers insight into how technology can promote global collaboration and enhance learning approaches that are innovative and inclusive.

Chapter 3: Fostering Self-efficacy for Higher Education Online Instructors

This chapter provides practical strategies for online instructors to foster self-efficacy among their students. The author draws on experiences and research to show how instructors can create a supportive and autonomous learning environment, promoting self-confidence and independence in learners. Topics include providing meaningful feedback, using technology to facilitate communication, and adapting instructional practices to the needs of online learners. Ultimately, the chapter serves as a guide for instructors who want to empower students to take ownership of their learning through thoughtful engagement and strategic support.

Chapter 4: Creating and Maintaining Successful Online Learning Environments

Focusing on the Malaysian context, this chapter offers a comprehensive look at the evolution of online learning in higher education, examining trends, challenges, and opportunities in the region. The author highlights the importance of accessibility, engagement, and personalization in online learning. Drawing from the Online Collaborative Learning Theory (OCL), the chapter explores how building a supportive online learning community and tailoring educational experiences to individual student needs can drive success. It concludes with a look ahead to the future of online education in Malaysia, where technological advancements are poised to further enhance educational opportunities.

Chapter 5: Beyond Lectures: The Flipped Learning Model

This chapter challenges traditional approaches to online learning by introducing the Flipped Learning Model as a powerful alternative to passive lecture-based teaching. Drawing on the social constructivist framework, the chapter explores how active learning strategies like Jigsaw Groups and Active Reading can enhance student engagement and understanding. The chapter argues for a student-centered approach where learning is not just a passive reception of information but an active process involving collaboration, critical thinking, and problem-solving.

Chapter 6: Enhancing Adult Online Learners' Graduate Leadership Experiences through the Lens of Care Theory

Addressing the unique needs of adult learners, this chapter explores how Nel Noddings' Care Theory can be applied in the online classroom to enhance graduate-level leadership education. The author emphasizes the role of online instructors as facilitators and coaches who use a framework of modeling, dialogue, and confirmation to nurture a caring and relational learning environment. Through care-centered practices, instructors can guide adult learners in developing their leadership skills while fostering strong, supportive relationships that contribute to their academic and personal growth.

Chapter 7: Implementing Online Project-Based Learning: Opportunities for Social Capital Development

This chapter explores the intersection of Project-Based Learning (PBL) and social capital development, illustrating how online PBL fosters deep learning, collaboration, and critical thinking. The author examines the evolution of PBL, the role of AI in enhancing learning, and the challenges associated with integrating diverse student backgrounds and real-world complexities. By focusing on trust, collaboration, and community engagement, this chapter underscores how PBL not only improves academic outcomes but also helps build stronger, more resilient online learning communities.

Chapter 8: A "Behind the Screens" Look at Humanizing Online Learning Spaces

Humanizing the online learning experience is the focus of this chapter, which examines the programs and tools that help build engagement and community in virtual classrooms. Highlighting successful strategies at the American College of Education (ACE), the chapter discusses how various technologies—such as diversity and inclusion initiatives, wellness programs, and AI tools—can enhance faculty-student interaction and promote a sense of belonging in the online space. By providing a "behind the scenes" look at these efforts, the chapter offers valuable insights for creating more engaging and personalized online learning environments.

Chapter 9: Online Teaching Readiness in the Era of Digital Transformation: Challenges and Recommendations

This chapter reviews the concept of teaching readiness in the context of digital transformation, proposing a new framework—The Interrelated Model of Online Teaching Readiness (IMOTR). This model takes into account the technological, pedagogical, and contextual factors that influence faculty's preparedness for online teaching. The chapter provides recommendations for faculty development professionals and university administrators to design infrastructure and training that supports online teaching readiness, ensuring faculty are equipped with the necessary skills to succeed in digital environments.

Chapter 10: Understanding the Cognitive Constituents of E-Learning

This chapter explores the cognitive foundations of e-learning, with a particular focus on how various learning formats—such as fully online courses, hybrid models, and MOOCs—can be designed to meet diverse student needs. By integrating cognitive science principles, the chapter highlights how adaptive technologies and innovative pedagogies can improve online learning experiences. The chapter also addresses the growth of e-learning and explores challenges and future research directions in the field, offering a forward-looking perspective on its continued evolution.

Chapter 11: Use of Scaffolding to Promote Engagement and Learning in Asynchronous Online Discussions

Focusing on the power of scaffolding in online education, this chapter provides a detailed exploration of how instructors can use this methodology to enhance engagement and learning in asynchronous discussions. Drawing from Vygotsky's Zone of Proximal Development and the Community of Inquiry framework, the chapter discusses how scaffolding can support students' cognitive, social, and teaching presence in the online classroom. The author shares practical examples and research-backed strategies for using scaffolding to promote deeper learning and stronger student participation in online discussions.

Chapter 12: Effective Strategies for Teaching Mathematics in Virtual Higher Education Environments

Teaching mathematics in virtual environments presents unique challenges, and this chapter provides a comprehensive guide to effective strategies for online math instruction. The chapter discusses the importance of interactive, personalized learning experiences and provides actionable strategies for fostering student engagement in mathematics. Emphasizing formative assessment, self-regulation, and the use of educational technologies, the chapter offers instructors valuable tools to optimize teaching and learning in online math classrooms.

Chapter 13: Empowering Educators and Students Through Boundaries

In this chapter, the authors explore the essential role of boundaries in fostering healthy and productive relationships between educators and students in the online classroom. By examining research on setting boundaries, the chapter offers strategies for maintaining a balance between accessibility and student autonomy. The authors argue that well-defined boundaries help prevent burnout, promote a healthier work-life balance for faculty, and support students' development of critical life skills such as decision-making, time management, and self-efficacy.

Chapter 14: Successful Teaching in Virtual Classrooms: Strategies for Online Open Elective Educators

This chapter addresses the unique challenges faced by instructors teaching online open elective courses (OOECs). The author discusses strategies for maintaining student engagement, managing large online classes, and ensuring high-quality assessments. The chapter also highlights the importance of utilizing technological advancements and fostering an inclusive and supportive learning environment. It serves as a valuable resource for educators seeking to improve the effectiveness of their online open elective courses.

Chapter 15: The Role of Virtual Classrooms in Realizing Effective Online Learning

This chapter examines the growing role of virtual classrooms in facilitating online learning, particularly in the wake of the COVID-19 pandemic. The author explores the features of popular virtual classroom platforms and how they support various aspects of teaching and learning, such as video conferencing, collaborative tools, and content sharing. By focusing on platforms like Zoom, Microsoft Teams, and Moodle, the chapter provides an overview of how these tools can enhance the delivery of online education and improve student engagement.

Chapter 16: Using Video Feedback to Create Faculty Presence in the Virtual Classroom

Asynchronous online learning can often lead to feelings of disengagement and isolation. This chapter explores the use of video feedback as a means to enhance faculty presence and establish a more humanized online learning experience. The chapter highlights research that supports the effectiveness of video feedback in fostering cognitive, social, and teaching presence. It also discusses best practices for using video feedback and the training needed for faculty to maximize its potential in creating an interactive and supportive virtual classroom environment.

Chapter 17: Strategies and Practices for Instructors in Online Open Elective Courses: Teacher Lessons

Focusing on the challenges and strategies of teaching Online Open Elective Courses (OOECs), this chapter explores best practices for overcoming obstacles such as maintaining engagement in large classes, addressing technological issues, and ensuring equitable access to resources. The chapter provides practical advice on creating high-quality learning experiences, utilizing interactive platforms, and supporting diverse learners in OOECs, offering a blueprint for educators to enhance student outcomes and course effectiveness.

Chapter 18: Curriculum Design in the Crossroads at Higher Education Institutions (HEIs) Boosting Quality Assurance: Satelliting Intellectual Property, Innovation- Legal Landscape

This chapter examines the intersection of curriculum design, intellectual property, and innovation within the context of higher education institutions. Focusing on how changes in intellectual property law affect education and innovation, the author discusses the role of technology in enhancing teaching practices and ensuring quality assurance in curriculum design. By highlighting econometric research on IPR policy and educational growth, the chapter offers valuable insights into the evolving landscape of higher education in the digital age.

This compilation of chapters provides educators with a diverse array of insights, practical strategies, and innovative solutions to navigate the complexities of online teaching in higher education. Whether you are teaching leadership, mathematics, or designing curriculum for global contexts, this book offers guidance to help you thrive in the evolving digital classroom.

As we close this volume, it is clear that the future of online higher education is brimming with potential, complexity, and promise. The chapters in *Best Practices and Strategies for Online Instructors: Insights From Higher Education Online Faculty* collectively represent a vast body of knowledge—drawn from both research and real-world experiences—that will help instructors navigate the evolving landscape of virtual teaching. Whether you are a seasoned educator or new to online instruction, we believe that the strategies, tools, and frameworks shared within these pages will provide the insights necessary to enhance your teaching practices, support student success, and foster meaningful, inclusive learning experiences.

The journey of online education is not without its challenges. The shift to digital platforms, the adoption of new technologies, and the diverse needs of students present ongoing hurdles for educators. Yet, as this book demonstrates, these challenges are opportunities in disguise—opportunities to rethink traditional pedagogies, experiment with innovative methods, and embrace new ways of fostering connection, engagement, and deep learning in virtual spaces. The contributors to this volume have shown that by remaining reflective, adaptable, and committed to our students' growth, we can transform online teaching into a vibrant, human-centered practice that thrives in today's digital age.

Importantly, we must not lose sight of the need for balance—balancing the power of technology with the essential human elements of teaching; balancing the demands of efficiency with the need for creativity and engagement; balancing instructor expertise with student agency. In this respect, this handbook serves not only as a practical guide but as a call to action—to inspire instructors to continually evolve, to push boundaries, and to develop online learning environments that reflect the diversity, complexity, and interconnectedness of the world around us.

We are grateful to each contributor for sharing their knowledge and experiences, and to you, the reader, for your commitment to improving your online teaching practice. It is your dedication to lifelong learning and innovation that drives the continued growth of online education, providing students across the globe with opportunities to engage, succeed, and thrive in an ever-changing academic landscape. Together, as a community of educators, we have the power to shape the future of higher education in meaningful and transformative ways.

We hope this book will serve as both a reference and a source of inspiration, encouraging you to reflect on your own teaching journey, to explore new ideas, and to embrace the boundless possibilities of online learning.

Chapter 1
Beyond the Screen:
Cultivating Joy, Creativity, and Well-Being in Online Learning Environments

Ellen Nicole Beattie
https://orcid.org/0009-0004-9912-8721
Center for Intentional Learning, USA

ABSTRACT

Beyond the Screen: Cultivating Joy, Creativity, and Well-Being in Online Learning Environments explores the detrimental impact of stress on college students' mental health and academic performance. The chapter emphasizes the need to shift from traditional pedagogical approaches to a framework prioritizing student well-being. Seligman's PERMA model, encompassing positive emotions, engagement, relationships, meaning, and accomplishment, is a foundation for incorporating positive psychology principles into the online classroom. Infusing playful pedagogy may positively benefit student engagement, student resilience, and the creation of a positive academic classroom culture. The chapter concludes with strategies to foster students' emotional, social, and academic growth.

BEYOND THE SCREEN: CULTIVATING JOY, CREATIVITY, AND WELL-BEING IN ONLINE LEARNING ENVIRONMENTS

The online learning environment has evolved rapidly in recent years, but with this evolution comes a growing recognition of the challenges facing today's students. College students across all disciplines are grappling with unprecedented levels of stress, anxiety, and mental health concerns. As educators, we know these struggles

DOI: 10.4018/979-8-3693-4407-1.ch001

can directly impact student success, engagement, and overall well-being. Yet, there is room for optimism. What if the very nature of how we teach could help alleviate these issues? What if online classrooms could be transformed into spaces that nurture not just intellectual growth, but also joy, creativity, and resilience?

The aim of this chapter is to invite readers to rethink what student engagement in the online learning environment can look like. Moving beyond traditional pedagogical approaches, this chapter will provide an exploration of how integrating well-being, positive emotions, and even play into online academic settings can address students' mental health challenges while fostering a more dynamic and supportive learning experience. This shift not only benefits students' academic performance, but it also helps them become well-rounded individuals, better prepared to thrive in the world beyond graduation.

Preview of the Chapter

The chapter begins by examining the pressing mental health crisis that many of our students face today. With research highlighting alarming rates of stress, anxiety, and disengagement in higher education, it is clear that something must change. But how can online instructors make a difference?

In response, this chapter presents the field of positive psychology—specifically Martin Seligman's PERMA framework—which offers a roadmap for enhancing well-being through positive emotions, engagement, relationships, meaning, and accomplishment. Each of Seligman's components of well-being will be examined through the lens of being applied to the online classroom to create a more engaging, supportive, and enriching learning environment.

Next, the reader will be encouraged to explore playful pedagogy, an approach often associated with early childhood but one that holds untapped potential for online higher education. Readers will discover how infusing play and creativity into teaching can spark curiosity, increase student motivation, and foster deeper learning, even in a digital space.

Finally, practical strategies that one can implement immediately in their online courses will be offered. From fostering social connections and promoting resilience to embedding gamified elements and brain breaks, these evidence-based techniques are designed to elevate students' learning experiences and well-being. By the end of this chapter, readers will have both the theoretical foundation and the practical tools to reimagine the online classroom—not just as a place where content is delivered, but as a space where students can flourish, academically and personally.

MENTAL HEALTH CHALLENGES IN HIGHER EDUCATION

Both traditional and nontraditional college students experience significant stress that can negatively impact their academic performance and well-being. For students aged 18 to 22, who are in the life stage of emerging adulthood, this stress is often amplified by the major life transitions they face, such as changes in living arrangements, relationships, and employment. For nontraditional students, balancing academic demands with work and family responsibilities can create additional burdens. In both cases, the pressures of academic work, financial concerns, and the need to meet higher expectations contribute to heightened stress levels (Matud et al., 2020).

Academic stress is a significant factor, with education being the primary source of stress for 87% of college students surveyed by the American Psychological Association (2020). This includes heavy course loads, financial pressures, and adapting to new academic standards. Studies have shown a clear link between academic stress and poor mental health, which, in turn, affects academic performance (Pascoe et al., 2019; Freire et al., 2016). As many as 60% of college students meet the criteria for at least one mental health condition, according to the 2022–2023 Healthy Mind survey, with rates of depression, anxiety, and suicidality at an all-time high. Alarmingly, many students report that mental health challenges are serious enough to consider dropping out of their programs (Gallup & Lumina Foundation, 2024).

Challenges Specific to Online Education

While the stressors for all college students are high, online students face additional, unique challenges that compound their mental health and academic struggles. Isolation, lack of motivation, and difficulties in managing cognitive load are prominent issues in virtual learning environments. Students in online courses often report feeling socially isolated, deprived of face-to-face interactions that help foster a sense of community (Arrieta et al., 2021). This isolation, coupled with the challenge of balancing academic work and personal life in a virtual setting, can lead to diminished motivation and engagement.

Time management and workload management are particularly difficult in the online context, where students must independently navigate assignments, discussions, and exams without the structure of an in-person schedule (Aboagye et al., 2020). Compounding this, accessibility issues such as poor internet connectivity and limited access to technology can hinder students' ability to participate fully in online classes, exacerbating stress and anxiety (Phiriepa et al., 2023).

Cognitive Load and Design Challenges in Online Learning

The digital nature of online learning also poses cognitive challenges. Cognitive load theory suggests that learning environments should minimize extraneous cognitive load, but online platforms sometimes unintentionally increase it. For example, interactive digital learning experiences, while intended to enhance engagement, can sometimes introduce task-irrelevant distractions that overwhelm students (Skulmowski & Xu, 2021). Striking a balance between engaging digital experiences and a manageable cognitive load is crucial for educators designing online courses. Educators must be mindful not only of the content delivered but also of how it is presented to ensure that students can focus on learning without being overwhelmed.

Impact of the COVID-19 Pandemic on Online Students' Mental Health

The COVID-19 pandemic exacerbated many of these challenges, leading to a dramatic increase in the use of virtual learning platforms. This shift placed additional stress on students, who had to navigate not only complex digital environments but also the psychological effects of prolonged isolation and uncertainty. Many students report that the autonomous nature of online learning has worsened mental health conditions, impairing their ability to concentrate and make effective decisions (Fierro et al., 2020).

Environmental factors, such as inadequate home learning spaces, and technological issues, like unstable internet connections, contribute to the mental and physical toll on students (Ealangov et al., 2022). The demands of balancing personal and academic responsibilities in an online setting—without the usual social interactions or campus resources—have been particularly taxing, and the ongoing impact of socioeconomic uncertainty adds another layer of stress (Salimi et al., 2021).

Addressing Online Learning Challenges

To support online students, institutions must consider targeted strategies, such as improving digital literacy education, enhancing virtual communication to foster a sense of community, and providing robust academic and mental health support. Teaching students to manage cognitive load in digital environments and providing tools to foster motivation and engagement are crucial for improving their learning experiences (Wang, 2024). Moreover, holistic approaches that include offering mental health services and encouraging stress-relieving activities—such as engaging in hobbies, physical activity, and spiritual practices—can help students cope with the demands of online learning (Ealangov et al., 2022).

The Academic Dangers of the Body's Natural Stress Response

Our body's natural stress response, commonly known as the "fight or flight" response, is an adaptive mechanism designed to help us react quickly to threats. This physiological reaction is initiated by the autonomic nervous system, particularly the sympathetic branch, which releases stress hormones like adrenaline and cortisol (Huberman, 2023). These hormones prepare the body for action by increasing heart rate, elevating blood pressure, and redirecting blood flow to essential muscles. While this response is helpful in acute situations, chronic activation due to ongoing stress can lead to negative health outcomes such as weakened immune function, anxiety, and fatigue.

Stress occurs on a spectrum. Research suggests that moderate stress can potentially motivate students to study harder, particularly when framed positively as "eustress" (Khafifah et al., 2023). However, moderate stress can quickly escalate to more detrimental levels of chronic and sustained stress for students. Academic stress has been shown to have significant negative impacts on students' academic performance and well-being. Multiple studies have found a strong inverse relationship between academic stress and performance, with higher stress levels resulting in decreased academic achievement (Sahu et al., 2024; Nepali, 2021). This stress can lead to reduced motivation, increased dropout rates, and mental health issues like depression and anxiety (Nepali, 2021). Gender differences in stress levels have been observed, with female students reporting higher academic stress than males (Sahu et al., 2024). Managing academic stress appears crucial to optimizing student performance and well-being.

The unique challenges faced by online students, such as isolation and increased self-regulation demands, require innovative strategies that foster connection, motivation, and resilience. Looking ahead, the next step is to expand this focus from individual strategies within the online classroom to a broader, institutional vision. Cultivating a well-being-focused culture in higher education will require systemic change, embedding these principles into the very fabric of how educators design courses, support students, and create learning communities. With this foundation in place, the subsequent section will shift attention to how higher education institutions can foster an environment that prioritizes the well-being of all students and educators.

CREATING A WELL-BEING FOCUSED CULTURE IN HIGHER EDUCATION

The mental health crisis among college students, characterized by rising rates of depression, anxiety, and disengagement, demands urgent attention from higher education institutions. The statistics on mental illness, the increasing incidence of campus violence, and dissatisfaction with current mental health interventions highlight the need for a shift in how student well-being is addressed. Institutions can no longer afford to view well-being as peripheral. Instead, they must place it at the core of their educational mission, recognizing that a focus on well-being not only improves student outcomes but also contributes to broader institutional and societal success.

Students who are mentally and physically well demonstrate improved academic performance and are better equipped with essential life skills such as resilience, conflict management, and emotional intelligence. These competencies enable students to engage meaningfully in their academic work and navigate personal and professional relationships effectively, leading to increased retention and graduation rates. Research consistently shows that emotionally healthy students are more likely to persist in their programs and thrive beyond their academic years (Durlak et al., 2011).

The benefits of a well-being-centered approach extend beyond students to faculty and staff. A positive academic culture fosters faculty engagement, reduces burnout, and enhances job satisfaction. Faculty members working in supportive environments are more likely to participate actively in academic discussions, contribute to community activities, and experience greater professional fulfillment (Joshi & Jaffer, 2024; Alsulami & Sherwood, 2020). Additionally, a culture of well-being promotes diversity and inclusivity, both of which are essential for retaining faculty and creating a harmonious work environment (Smith & Costello, 2020). A quality academic culture positively influences faculty collaboration, knowledge sharing, and institutional engagement, benefiting the entire academic community (Herminingsih & Rizki, 2021).

Institutional leaders who prioritize student and faculty well-being contribute to the creation of a socially responsible and equitable academic environment. By reducing stress and promoting social connections, leaders can create an academic culture that fosters inclusivity and supports students' personal, financial, and social challenges. Graduates from institutions that emphasize well-being are more likely to emerge as well-rounded, resilient contributors to the workforce and society.

Recent studies have explored the effectiveness of online well-being programs as tools for supporting students, particularly in the context of increased mental health challenges during the COVID-19 pandemic. While some programs show promise, such as a 7-week wellness intervention that significantly reduced stress and improved perceived wellness (Beauchemin, 2018), others have had mixed results (Villarino et al., 2022). These mixed outcomes suggest the need for more tailored and evidence-based digital health promotion strategies that address the specific needs of online learners. Research has shown that online students report higher rates of chronic illnesses and psychiatric conditions compared to their campus-based peers, emphasizing the importance of digital well-being initiatives (Burcin et al., 2019). Innovative programs based on frameworks like cognitive behavioral therapy and the PERMA model are emerging as cost-effective ways to address these needs, but more research is required to assess their long-term effectiveness (Akmal & Kumalasari, 2021; Villarino et al., 2022).

Incorporating well-being into the core of higher education is not an option but a necessity. Institutional leaders can take proactive steps to create supportive environments that promote resilience, reduce stress, and foster meaningful social connections. By doing so, they can ensure that students, faculty, and the institution as a whole thrive in the evolving landscape of higher education.

THEORETICAL FRAMEWORK: SELIGMAN'S PERMA THEORY

Nearly three decades ago, Martin Seligman, former president of the American Psychological Association, challenged the field of psychology to move beyond a focus on illness and pathology and toward an exploration of human flourishing. This shift birthed the field of positive psychology, which focuses on the elements that make life worth living. Seligman presented this as a shift from addressing problems and deficits to fostering and enhancing the positive qualities already present within individuals. Seligman's (2011) theory of well-being represents a culmination of decades of research and thought. Initially centered around the concept of authentic happiness, his work evolved into a comprehensive framework for understanding human flourishing through the PERMA model. The model identifies five core, independent elements of well-being: positive emotions, engagement, relationships, meaning, and accomplishment. These building blocks are presented not as a singular theory of well-being, but as measurable components that individuals can cultivate independently to enhance overall life satisfaction.

Seligman emphasized that well-being is not a singular construct that can be captured by one measure. Rather, it is a complex, multifaceted concept that requires operationalizing through the distinct elements of PERMA. Each element offers pathways to flourishing:

- Positive emotion (P) refers to the pursuit of joy, gratitude, and other emotions that contribute to feeling good. Positive emotions are subjective but play a critical role in psychological well-being.
- Engagement (E) captures the idea of being fully absorbed in tasks, often leading to a flow state—a concept introduced by Csikszentmihalyi (1988). Engagement is also a subjective experience that can lead to enhanced performance and personal fulfillment.
- Relationships (R) underscore the importance of social connections in human well-being. Seligman (2011) argued that little of what is positive in life is experienced in isolation, making relationships foundational for flourishing.
- Meaning (M) involves the sense of purpose derived from being part of something greater than oneself, whether through work, community, or personal beliefs.
- Accomplishment (A) relates to setting and achieving goals, fostering a sense of pride and fulfillment.

Moreover, PERMA has been adapted into broader contexts, such as organizational settings, where Donaldson et al. (2022) expanded the framework to include physical health, mindset, physical work environments, and economic security—known as the PERMA+4 model. This expanded framework emphasizes the importance of well-being not just for individuals but for creating supportive, high-functioning environments.

In summary, Seligman's PERMA theory offers a robust framework for understanding and enhancing well-being by focusing on five key elements: positive emotions, engagement, relationships, meaning, and accomplishment. By operationalizing these elements, individuals can take actionable steps toward cultivating a flourishing life. The theory's flexibility and adaptability, especially in the PERMA+4 model, extend its relevance to various settings, including education. In the following section, this well-being framework will be applied specifically to the context of online learning, providing strategies for enhancing student engagement, resilience, and success in virtual environments.

APPLYING THE PERMA MODEL TO ONLINE EDUCATION

Over the past decade, enrollment in online university programs has surged, yet the unique health risks and well-being needs of online learners remain underexplored. Research has produced inconsistent findings about the health outcomes of online students. For example, Rohrer et al. (2012) found that a significant proportion of online students were smokers, likely favoring the flexibility of studying at home.

Conversely, Maynard et al. (2015) suggested that being an online student was not directly linked to poor health outcomes. However, Burcin et al. (2019) revealed that online students experience higher rates of chronic illness, mental health issues, and unhealthy behaviors compared to their on-campus counterparts. These studies highlight the need for tailored well-being approaches for online learners.

The application of Seligman's PERMA framework offers a promising avenue for addressing the well-being needs of online students. For instance, PERMA has been shown to mediate the relationship between disability and life satisfaction for students with functional disabilities (Tansey et al., 2018), and it has demonstrated positive correlations with college success factors (Kovich et al., 2022). The framework has also been applied to language learning, where it significantly improved student outcomes in English proficiency compared to traditional methods (Cheng & Chen, 2021). The following sections examine how each PERMA element can be applied to online education to enhance student well-being and academic performance.

Positive Emotions

Positive emotions are a cornerstone of Seligman's PERMA framework and are uniquely crucial in online classroom settings. The online learning environment is often characterized by isolation, and the use of positive emotions can enhance the online educational experience for students and instructors. Wu and Yu (2022) identified that positive achievement emotions, such as enjoyment and pride, generally have a positive effect on motivation, performance, engagement, satisfaction, and achievement in online learning.

Managing Stress Through Positive Emotions

Positive emotions are crucial for managing stress, a common issue among online students. Research has shown that positive emotions can replenish psychological resources, diminish negative emotions, and aid in recovery from stressful experiences (Leger et al., 2020). Since online learning often involves self-regulated tasks, fostering positive emotions can help students manage anxiety and improve their ability to cope with the demands of virtual education. In addition to managing stress, positive emotions significantly influence students' drive to succeed. These emotions help sustain motivation, a crucial factor for academic success in self-directed online learning environments.

Motivation and Academic Success

Positive emotions are also linked to increased motivation and academic behaviors such as attending classes, participating in discussions, and staying on top of assignments (Williams et al., 2013). Given the self-directed nature of online learning, maintaining high levels of motivation is critical. Facilitating opportunities for students to experience joy and accomplishment can lead to sustained engagement. Moreover, positive emotions are not just about immediate motivation; they play a key role in fostering long-term resilience. By building emotional strength, positive emotions help students overcome academic and personal challenges with adaptive coping strategies.

Resilience and Coping Strategies

Building resilience through positive emotions can help students navigate academic and personal obstacles. Gloria and Steinhardt (2016) found that adaptive coping strategies, supported by positive emotions, can reduce the impact of stress and contribute to improved academic outcomes. Online courses that integrate tools for emotional regulation and stress management can help students build resilience.

Engagement

Seligman's PERMA framework includes engagement as a building block of human flourishing. Seligman (2012) described engagement as a state of complete immersion, akin to becoming fully absorbed in the rhythm of music. Seligman's concept of engagement aligns with fellow positive psychology researcher, Csikszentmihalyi's (1988) concept of "flow." Flow is understood as the loss of self-consciousness and complete absorption in an activity. Meyer and Jones (2013) found that when graduate students report feeling flow in online courses, it correlates with their satisfaction with the course. Im and Lee (2021) found that flow in higher learning is associated with reduced learning burnout, and cognitive learning flow is partially mediated by the perceived effectiveness of online learning. Evidence-based strategies to encourage engagement include building interest, focus, and concentration, supporting flow and optimal performance, and developing academic skills. One of the key ways to foster engagement in online learning is by capturing and sustaining students' attention. This can be achieved by connecting course material to students' real-world interests, which in turn helps improve focus and concentration.

Interest, Focus, and Concentration

Online learning environments can easily lead to distractions, making sustained focus a challenge. Research suggests that student interest in course material enhances engagement and concentration (Liu & Jirigela, 2024). Connecting course content to students' real-world goals and interests can foster deeper engagement and encourage students to remain focused during virtual lessons. However, engagement goes beyond merely capturing attention. To create truly immersive learning experiences, fostering a flow state is essential, where students become fully absorbed in their tasks and learning becomes effortless.

Flow and Optimal Performance

Achieving a flow state—where students are fully absorbed in their tasks—can significantly enhance learning outcomes (Mandhana & Caruso, 2023). Online educators can promote flow by designing activities that strike a balance between challenge and skill, encouraging students to lose themselves in the learning process. Beyond promoting flow and immersion, engagement can also serve as a vehicle for skill development. By encouraging research and creative activities, educators can help students deepen their learning and build essential academic competencies.

Skill Development through Engagement

Providing opportunities for students to engage in research and creative pursuits can deepen their learning and develop essential academic skills (Hu, 2008). Encouraging inquiry-based activities in online settings supports problem-solving, critical thinking, and independent research, which are key to success in online education.

Relationships

Strong student-instructor relationships are key to student satisfaction, engagement, and retention (Emde et al., 2020; Smith & Crowe, 2017). These relationships involve knowing students, helping them meet their needs, and fostering a sense of community (Smith & Crowe, 2017; Brown et al., 2022). Effective relationship-building strategies in online environments include sharing, demonstrating care, promoting collaboration, and providing constructive feedback (Brown et al., 2022). Additionally, relationships extend beyond student-instructor interactions to include peer relationships and connections with support services, all contributing to a sense of belonging in the online learning community (Brown et al., 2022). To combat feelings of isolation in online environments, instructors should focus on building positive connections and enhancing interaction. This can be achieved by facilitating connections between course elements, linking conceptual learning to practical applications, connecting student cohorts, and utilizing synchronous tools for interactive atmospheres (Waldow & AuCoin, 2021). Overall, prioritizing relationship-building in online education is crucial for enhancing student learning experiences and outcomes. Evidence-based strategies to build relationships include community-building, collaboration and peer support, and targeted networking. One of the most effective ways to establish strong relationships in online learning environments is through intentional community-building efforts. By fostering a sense of connection, students can feel more supported and engaged.

Building Community

While online learning can often feel isolating, fostering positive relationships is crucial for student success. Jennings (2020) recommended strategies such as building community through humanized courses and maintaining faculty immediacy to enhance social presence. Students who feel supported by their peers and instructors are more likely to engage in the course and persist through challenges. While community-building fosters a sense of belonging, collaboration and peer support are critical for deepening these relationships and providing the social interaction necessary for student success.

Collaboration and Peer Support

Collaboration among students, both formally in group projects and informally through discussions, can provide much-needed social support (Galvin, 2012). Instructors can facilitate collaborative learning by encouraging teamwork and peer support, which is especially important in online environments where face-to-face interaction is limited. Beyond peer collaboration, another powerful tool for building lasting relationships in online education is targeted networking. By connecting students with professionals in their field, online courses can help students develop valuable career connections.

Targeted Networking

The communication and relationship-building skills that students develop in online courses are transferable to other contexts, including professional networking (Wills & Grimes, 2020). Providing opportunities for students to connect with peers and professionals in their field can enhance their future career prospects.

Meaning

Seligman's PERMA theory of well-being includes meaning as a core component to human flourishing. In the online college environment, students may find meaning in their coursework and course activities and assignments. The literature supporting meaning and online learning environments is sparse. Ransdell (2013) found that meaningful posts in online discussions predicted better learning outcomes for adult online students, beyond just overall activity levels. The concept of "calling"—finding purpose and meaning in work—has been identified as potentially important for college students' career development and overall well-being (Adams, 2012). Purpose-driven learning and fostering a sense of belonging are evidence-based strategies to support the construction of meaning in the online classroom. By connecting coursework to personal and professional goals, students can develop a stronger sense of why their education matters.

Purpose-Driven Learning

Students who understand the personal significance of their education are more likely to persist and succeed. Kuh (2016) noted that when students can articulate how their academic work relates to their future goals, they remain committed to learning. Online courses that explicitly connect content to students' long-term aspirations can enhance motivation and engagement. In addition to personal purpose, a sense of belonging plays a critical role in creating meaning for students. Building strong connections within the learning community can deepen their commitment to their studies and to the larger group.

Fostering a Sense of Belonging

Creating meaning in education is also tied to students' sense of belonging. Effective course design and facilitation can help students feel connected to their learning community, fostering shared purpose and trust (Shea, 2019). Online educators should strive to create an inclusive, supportive environment where students feel they are part of something bigger than themselves.

Accomplishment

PERMA's last building block of well-being is accomplishment. Online instructors can help students feel small wins by implementing various strategies to enhance engagement and rapport. Building rapport in asynchronous online courses involves initiating connections early and maintaining them through personalized instruction

(Flanigan et al., 2021). Asynchronous online discussions, or "check-ins," can be used as touchpoints throughout the course to connect with students, understand their circumstances, and provide the necessary support and encouragement (Weems-Landingham & Paternite, 2021). Evidence-based strategies to promote feelings of accomplishment include goal setting for academic confidence and tracking progress to sustain motivation. One of the most effective ways to foster a sense of accomplishment is through goal setting, which allows students to gain confidence as they work toward and achieve academic milestones.

Goal Setting for Academic Confidence

Setting and achieving academic goals is central to building confidence and motivation. In an online learning environment, instructors can facilitate this process by encouraging students to set realistic and achievable goals, as well as providing tools for tracking their progress (Wong et al., 2021). Recognizing accomplishments, even small ones, can boost students' confidence and help them stay committed to their studies. In addition to setting goals, helping students track their progress is crucial in maintaining motivation and a sense of achievement throughout their academic journey.

Tracking Progress to Sustain Motivation

Motivation increases as students see themselves making progress toward long-term goals. Online courses can incorporate tools like progress trackers, badges, or performance dashboards to help students monitor their achievements and stay motivated as they approach their academic objectives.

A Vision for Evidence-Based Change in Online Education

The application of Seligman's PERMA framework to online education offers a promising roadmap for addressing the unique challenges faced by today's online learners. By focusing on the building blocks of well-being—positive emotions, engagement, relationships, meaning, and accomplishment—educators can create a more supportive, motivating, and engaging virtual learning environment. The integration of these evidence-based strategies aims to enhance student resilience, academic performance, and overall well-being, fostering a holistic approach that goes beyond traditional measures of success.

As higher education continues to adapt to the needs of a diverse and increasingly online student population, it is essential for institutions to adopt a vision for change rooted in the latest research and best practices. Embracing strategies that emphasize well-being, connection, and meaningful engagement can transform the online educational experience, leading to greater student satisfaction, reduced dropout rates, and improved learning outcomes. The path forward involves a collective effort from educators, administrators, and institutions to reimagine online learning environments as dynamic spaces that cultivate not just academic success but also human flourishing. This shift toward a more holistic, student-centered approach will empower learners to thrive both academically and personally, preparing them to make meaningful contributions to their communities and the world.

RESILIENCE AND STUDENT ENGAGEMENT: BUILDING A POSITIVE ACADEMIC CULTURE

Resilience plays a pivotal role in student engagement, particularly in online education, where isolation and stress are common. The science of well-being integrates both physical and mental health, with resilience as a key component that allows individuals to adapt to adversity, maintain performance, and thrive despite challenges. Suzanne Kobasa's (1979) concept of psychological hardiness identifies three core factors—commitment, control, and challenge—that help differentiate resilient students from those who struggle under stress. These factors are particularly relevant to online learners, who must often self-motivate, manage learning environments, and adapt to new educational formats.

For online students, developing resilience can improve engagement by encouraging them to find meaning in their studies, view challenges as opportunities for growth, and maintain a sense of control over their academic journeys (Reivich & Shatte, 2002). Building resilience is not just about personality traits; it involves learned behaviors, thoughts, and actions. Dr. Sarah McKay's (2020) model suggests three distinct pathways to building resilience:

1. Bottom-up: Strengthening physical health through exercise, sleep, and nutrition.
2. Outside-in: Cultivating social support, which is vital in often-isolated online learning environments.
3. Top-down: Developing positive thought patterns, emotional regulation, and mindfulness to manage stress.

One effective way to cultivate resilience is by incorporating stress-management techniques, such as controlled breathing exercises, to help students regulate their body's stress response. Neuroscience research shows that techniques like box breathing can quickly reduce anxiety and enhance focus (Huberman, 2023). Engaging students in cognitively challenging yet enjoyable activities can also promote a state of flow, which improves focus, reduces cognitive load, and fosters deeper learning (Csikszentmihalyi, 1988).

Beyond resilience, fostering a positive academic culture that focuses on student engagement is crucial for success in online environments. Research demonstrates that supportive academic environments improve student persistence and performance, particularly for underserved or minority students (Owusu-Agyeman, 2021; Moller et al., 2014). Engagement can be categorized into three core types: behavioral, emotional, and cognitive. Together, they form a foundation for an effective learning experience.

- Behavioral engagement: Behavioral engagement includes the observable actions of an on-task student. It may include participating in course discussions, paying attention, asking questions, and generally aligning with the expectations of the course. In online courses, active participation in online discussions or synchronous sessions, regular logins, and adherence to course guidelines are critical to student success. Course organization significantly influences behavioral engagement and perceived learning outcomes, with behavioral engagement positively affecting emotional and cognitive engagement (Kim, 2022).
- Emotional engagement: Emotional engagement includes the emotion or affect connected to a learning task or environment. Students who display high interest, enjoyment, positive attitude, curiosity, and a sense of belonging are more likely to have high emotional engagement. A positive learning attitude and a sense of belonging foster emotional investment in the course. Strategies like providing regular feedback and holding virtual office hours can create a supportive learning atmosphere. Higher levels of emotional engagement have been shown to have positive effects on cognitive engagement (Kim, 2022).
- Cognitive engagement: Cognitive engagement includes a student's ability to comprehend complex concepts and acquire challenging skills. Students who exhibit high levels of cognitive engagement work beyond the minimum expectations and see the challenge as a motivator. Encouraging deeper intellectual investment through critical thinking, problem-solving, and reflective practices helps students develop a more profound connection to the course material. Implementing active learning strategies, along with technology tools like Mentimeter and Canva, can enhance cognitive engagement in online classes (Azizan, 2023).

Educators can promote engagement through a variety of strategies, such as using collaborative platforms, gamification, and providing personalized feedback. These strategies enhance both emotional and cognitive engagement, creating an online learning environment that supports students' academic achievement and overall well-being.

By combining resilience-building practices with evidence-based engagement strategies, educators can foster a positive academic culture that enhances both student well-being and academic performance. This holistic approach ensures that students not only succeed academically but also develop the resilience needed to thrive in both their studies and future careers.

Connecting Resilience and Engagement to PERMA

The concepts of resilience and student engagement are intricately connected to Seligman's PERMA model, which emphasizes positive emotions, engagement, relationships, meaning, and accomplishment as the building blocks of well-being. Resilience plays a critical role in fostering positive emotions by helping students manage stress and maintain psychological balance in the face of challenges. By building resilience, students are more likely to experience joy, pride, and optimism as they navigate the academic demands of online learning. Engagement, another core element of PERMA, is essential for achieving a state of flow in academic activities, where students become fully immersed and absorbed in their work. Fostering engagement through strategies that promote focus, persistence, and deep cognitive investment aligns with PERMA's focus on achieving personal fulfillment and peak performance. Moreover, by enhancing relationships—whether through peer collaboration or supportive student-instructor connections—students can feel a greater sense of community, which combats the isolation often associated with online learning. Relationships, particularly those built on trust and encouragement, help to build meaning, as students connect their academic efforts to broader personal and professional goals. Finally, fostering accomplishment through goal setting and progress tracking reinforces the achievement aspect of PERMA, giving students a clear sense of direction and fulfillment as they meet their educational milestones.

Ultimately, resilience and engagement serve as practical pathways for realizing the full potential of the PERMA framework in online education. By integrating these elements, educators not only support academic success but also nurture the holistic well-being of their students, preparing them for both personal and professional flourishing.

INVITATION TO TEACH DIFFERENTLY

This chapter has explored why emphasizing well-being is essential to address the growing mental health challenges faced by many college students. By employing Seligman's PERMA framework to integrate the building blocks of human flourishing into online learning, educators can significantly enhance engagement, resilience, and overall performance among online college students. This approach urges higher education institutions to rethink their traditional strategies and consider more holistic methods that align with the needs of today's learners.

The next step is to introduce playful pedagogy as a transformative approach that reimagines educational settings. By doing so, classroom environments can shift the focus from rigid academic structures to creating a dynamic environment that fosters creativity, joy, and engagement—key components that contribute to student well-being.

Playful Pedagogy

Playful pedagogy is not a new concept, but it holds significant potential for revitalizing teaching methods in higher education. In the introduction to *Playful Pedagogies*, the author outlines a vision of education as a "playful exploration and unveiling of relationships with knowledge, each other, and the world" (Holflod, 2022, p. vii). This idea resonates with early educational experiences where learning and fun were seamlessly intertwined. While play is often associated with childhood, it can also serve as a powerful tool for adult learners, fostering a sense of reinvigoration, creativity, and engagement in their educational journey.

Despite its potential, play is frequently undervalued in higher education due to a predominant focus on academic rigor, discipline-specific expertise, and measurable outcomes. However, evidence shows that playful learning strategies can enhance cognitive processes, increase motivation, and reduce stress—factors that are crucial in creating a positive learning environment, particularly in online settings (Forbes, 2021). Research has linked playful learning in higher education to enhanced creativity, collaborative skills, and experiential learning (Holflod, 2022).

Challenging Traditional Views of Higher Education

Play and academia are often seen as opposing forces, with traditional views of higher education emphasizing mastery of content, critical thinking, and professional preparation over creativity and exploration. James (2018) found that some faculty members fear embracing play in academic settings could undermine their professional credibility. Indeed, the demands for research output, measurable student outcomes, and adherence to accreditation standards often make the integration of play seem impractical. Nevertheless, these views need to be challenged, given the mounting evidence supporting playful pedagogy.

Lisa Forbes and David Thomas, advocates of playful learning, argued in their *Professors at Play Playbook* (2023) that creating a playful learning environment can lead to better academic outcomes, higher student satisfaction, and improved mental health (Forbes, 2021). Further, James (2018) identified practical applications of play in research, such as facilitating idea generation, honing decision-making skills, and developing research competencies. These approaches do not detract from academic rigor; instead, they blend intellectual challenge with elements of joy, curiosity, and creativity to enhance learning experiences.

Play and Positive Emotions: Joy, Awe, and Pride

Research suggests that playfulness and playful approaches significantly contribute to building positive emotions and well-being in adults. Playfulness has been shown to have robust positive relationships with various aspects of well-being, including positive emotions, engagement, relationships, and meaning (Farley et al., 2020). In educational settings, playful learning methods foster imagination, innovation, and co-creation, creating moments of joyful discovery in a supportive environment (Heljakka, 2023). Short, self-administered playfulness interventions have been effective in increasing playfulness, enhancing well-being, and reducing depressive symptoms (Proyer et al., 2020).

Positive emotions are a cornerstone of Seligman's PERMA framework. Barbara Fredrickson's broaden-and-build theory of positive emotions posits that these emotions expand awareness, enhance cognitive flexibility, and build long-term psychological, social, and emotional resources (Fredrickson, 2004). Her research highlights ten key positive emotions—joy, gratitude, serenity, interest, hope, pride, amusement, inspiration, awe, and love—that contribute to individual well-being and resilience (Fredrickson, 2013).

These principles are particularly relevant to online education. Research indicates that students who experience positive emotions demonstrate better time management, motivational regulation, and reduced academic procrastination compared to those with neutral or negative emotional profiles (Cheng et al., 2022). Positive emotions in the classroom have also been linked to greater engagement and stronger social connections between students and instructors, enhancing the overall learning experience (Rodríguez-Muñoz et al., 2021; Huang et al., 2019).

The Benefits of Playful Pedagogy in Higher Education

Integrating play into higher education aligns closely with the principles of the PERMA framework, offering several specific benefits for both students and educators:

- Engagement: Playful activities naturally engage students, making learning enjoyable and interactive, which is particularly beneficial in combating disengagement in online courses (Rice, 2009). Collaborative activities within playful pedagogy have been shown to increase student participation and promote sustained engagement (Witkowski & Cornell, 2015).
- Creativity and imagination: Play encourages creative thinking and problem-solving, allowing students to explore solutions in innovative ways that are relevant to real-world challenges (Rice, 2009). This fosters a more dynamic and flexible learning environment.
- Social bonding: Group games and collaborative play activities enhance social interactions, helping online learners build meaningful connections with peers and instructors, which is essential in virtual learning environments (Forbes, 2021).
- Exploration and discovery: Play provides a low-stress space for experimentation and learning from mistakes, which builds resilience and adaptability among students. This aligns with the PERMA elements of meaning and accomplishment, encouraging students to view challenges as opportunities for growth.
- Student-centered learning: Playful pedagogy promotes student agency, allowing learners to take control of their educational journey and make choices that align with their interests and goals (Tidmand, 2021). This approach supports self-directed learning and personal development.

Connecting Play to Adult Learning Principles

Adult learners benefit from practical, relevant, and self-directed learning experiences that align with their professional and personal goals. Playful pedagogy fits well with adult learning principles by incorporating elements of choice, real-life applications, and reflective learning into the educational process (El-Amin, 2020). This strategy empowers adult learners to engage more deeply with content and fosters the critical thinking skills essential for lifelong learning.

Overcoming Skepticism: Evidence-Based Support for Play in Higher Education

While skepticism about the role of play in higher education persists, the evidence supports its integration as a valid educational strategy. Studies indicate that playful learning can reduce stress, improve student satisfaction, and lead to better academic outcomes (Lipson et al., 2022; National College Health Assessment, 2023). Playfulness has also been linked to lower rates of school burnout and increased life satisfaction among university students, mediated by a sense of control over their learning environment (Li et al., 2021). Play has the potential to enhance creativity, promote wellness, and improve graduate employability (Leather et al., 2020).

A Call to Action for Educators

The challenges facing higher education today call for innovative solutions that go beyond traditional teaching methods. Playful pedagogy offers a way to break away from rigid structures, creating a holistic educational experience that prioritizes student well-being, creativity, and engagement. As educators and institutions continue to confront rising rates of student anxiety, disengagement, and isolation, it is essential to reimagine what learning in higher education could look like. By embracing play, we can create a richer, more supportive educational environment that not only enhances academic performance but also fosters well-being and personal growth among students.

STRATEGIES FOR WEAVING POSITIVE EMOTIONS, PLAY, AND WELL-BEING INTO ONLINE INSTRUCTION

This final section offers evidence-based strategies that online faculty can employ to integrate well-being and play into their teaching practices. It emphasizes the importance of adopting research-backed approaches that have been shown to enhance student engagement, resilience, and academic performance. By embracing these strategies, educators have the opportunity to create a vision for change in higher education—one that prioritizes holistic student development and reimagines online learning environments as spaces where creativity, joy, and well-being thrive.

Strategy #1: Championing Student Well-being

Championing well-being in online coursework is crucial for student success and overall educational outcomes. The COVID-19 pandemic has highlighted the importance of addressing students' psychological well-being in online learning environments (Popescu & Dobromirescu, 2021). By prioritizing well-being in online coursework, educators can address the potential negative impacts of isolation and stress on students, ultimately leading to better learning outcomes and overall student satisfaction in virtual educational settings. Breathing techniques and social connection offer two opportunities to champion student well-being.

Teach Breathing Techniques

Incorporating stress-reduction practices and breathing techniques can support students' mental and emotional health. These techniques help students learn to manage stress (long-term and immediate) in positive ways. Breathwork is a time-honored tradition in many cultures and provides students with a valuable life skill. There are YouTube videos of the following breathing techniques that can minimize stress: lion's breath, 4-7-8 breathing, and box breathing. Further, real-time stress management can be taught using the physiological sigh. Stanford neuroscientist and principal investigator of the Huberman Lab, Dr. Andrew Huberman, shared insight into how one can use breathing to change one's mental state. This calming breathing technique involves two short inhalations, ideally through the nose, followed by one extended exhalation, ideally through the mouth. It mirrors a natural sigh and is the most effective and quickest way to induce a sense of calm by activating the parasympathetic nervous system.

Facilitate Social Engagement and Connection Opportunities

Opportunities for social engagement and connection can combat the isolation often felt in online learning environments. For example, synchronous sessions can be offered as virtual meet-ups or interest-based clubs. Not all instructor-student interactions must be focused on content.

Consider hosting a late afternoon Friday "happy hour" where students are encouraged to bring any beverage or snack and informally chat with others. For students, this may be an unfamiliar way to interact with instructors, so do not be discouraged by a slow start and give it time. Foster peer interactions with collaborative discussions and ask students questions to get to know each other. Questions that encourage students to share information about themselves informally work effectively, for example:

- Do you have a favorite time of the day?
- If you have an unexpected "free" day, how would you spend it?
- Who inspires you?

Strategy #2: Foster a Supportive Online Atmosphere

Creating an online environment that radiates warmth, encouragement, and respect is essential for making learners feel valued and supported. While online instructors commonly use course announcements to provide context and clarify assignments (Fendler, 2021), these announcements can also set the tone for a warm and friendly learning environment. Incorporating visual elements like pictures, memes, and varied colors and fonts can make communications more engaging and inviting. If the learning management system supports open announcements, use these as opportunities to invite questions and comments, promoting an interactive and inclusive classroom culture.

Active instructor engagement is crucial, as it models the behaviors and attitudes desired from students. Timely responses to questions and prompt, constructive feedback on assignments not only enhance learning but also strengthen the instructor's presence and connection with students (Martin et al., 2020). Furthermore, designing collaborative spaces within the learning management system allows students to connect, share insights, and build a sense of community, which enhances both peer learning and emotional support.

Personalized messages of encouragement further enrich the online classroom experience (Weru, 2023). From a holistic wellness perspective, instructors might consider sending weekly reminders that emphasize self-care and balance. These messages could include links to accessible, reliable resources, such as articles on improving sleep or positive, uplifting quotes, reinforcing that student well-being is a key priority alongside academic success.

Strategy #3: Apply Principles of Emotional Design

Emotional design in online courses has gained attention for its potential to enhance learner engagement and outcomes. Research suggests that incorporating emotional design elements, such as personalized stories, warm colors, and tender voices, can trigger situational interest and improve learning performance (Endres et al., 2020). The deliberate use of design elements to induce emotional states in learners can lead to increased learning outcomes without significantly adding to cognitive demands (Plass & Hovey, 2021). Use design elements that evoke positive emotions, such as aesthetically pleasing visuals, to enhance the learning experience. Select a calming color palette for course materials and announcements. Soft, warm colors can create a welcoming atmosphere; avoid overly bright whites and harsh colors that cause eye strain. In addition, use a user-friendly layout and navigation elements, ensuring that the layout is intuitive and easy to navigate. Aim for well-organized content, clear headings, and consistent placement of elements to reduce cognitive load and potential for student frustration.

Moreover, diverse multimedia resources should be integrated to cater to diverse students, reducing cognitive strain and increasing material accessibility. High-quality and relevant images, infographics, and illustrations should be incorporated to support the content and add visual appeal. Videos can be used to explain complex concepts and make the learning process more dynamic and fun.

Further, collaborative spaces in the classroom can be included for student interaction. For example, set up a discussion forum where students can informally connect, ask questions, or share insights into the weekly content. Encourage participation in the discussion by using interesting and thought-provoking prompts.

Gamification can enhance learner motivation, retention, and satisfaction in online courses (Eliyas & Ranjana, 2022). Consider badges, points, or other reward systems for students to earn as they work through the course content. These informal gamification elements can add friendly competition or challenges with leaderboards to add an element of fun.

Strategy #4: Enliven Learning Through Games

As previously discussed, incorporating play into the classroom can significantly enhance classroom culture, boost engagement, and improve learning outcomes. Interactive simulations and gamified learning experiences are excellent tools to make education both enlightening and enjoyable. For example, virtual "escape room" activities can be easily created using various online resources, allowing students to solve problems collaboratively and apply course concepts in a fun, engaging way. Additionally, creative icebreakers based on popular games (e.g., *Connections*) can introduce content in an interactive manner. For instance, during a recent doctoral in-residence session, the author designed a *Connections* game on research methodology with four sets of related words, providing a fun and informative way to introduce course content while informally assessing students' prior knowledge.

Strategy #5: Promote Reflective Practices and Personal Growth

Research indicates that reflective activities can significantly enhance online college students' learning outcomes and overall well-being. Reflection within online courses has been shown to deepen students' understanding, identify learning gaps, personalize the educational experience, and foster connections among peers

(Chang, 2019). One effective approach is gratitude journaling, a simple yet impactful intervention that has been found to boost well-being, reduce negative affect, and alleviate stress and anxiety among college students (Tolcher et al., 2022).

To implement these strategies, instructors can guide students in recognizing and articulating their emotional journeys throughout the learning process, promoting mindfulness and self-awareness. By encouraging students to reflect on their progress, challenges, and achievements, educators help them cultivate a deeper connection to their learning. Additionally, creating opportunities for students to share their personal experiences, coping mechanisms, and growth strategies can establish a supportive and collaborative environment, enhancing both individual growth and collective well-being. These practices not only promote academic success but also foster a culture of mutual support and continuous improvement.

Strategy #6: Promote Character Strength Awareness and Utilization

Research shows that character strengths are closely linked to positive well-being and academic success in college students (Bachik et al., 2020). Specific strengths, such as hope and gratitude, have been found to predict academic integration and persistence, particularly among first-year college students (Browning et al., 2018). To foster these strengths, begin courses by guiding students through a strengths assessment, such as the VIA Character Strengths Survey (available online at no cost) to help them identify their core strengths. Encourage students to maintain a reflection journal throughout the course, where they can document their experiences using these strengths and how this practice enhances their engagement and satisfaction.

Incorporate dedicated time for weekly strength reflections, using varied prompts like "What past achievements are you most proud of?" and "What activities energize you in the present?" These prompts help students connect their strengths to their personal and academic lives, fostering a sense of purpose and motivation.

Additionally, review and adapt the assignment structure to allow students to showcase their strengths. Providing flexibility in assignment formats enables students to choose options that align with their unique abilities and interests, enhancing both engagement and creativity. Integrate opportunities for students to engage in strength-spotting, where they identify and comment on strengths in case studies, historical figures, or their peers during presentations. This practice not only builds a sense of community but also reinforces the application of strengths in real-world contexts.

To further promote character strengths, consider incorporating digital badges for various strengths that students can earn when they demonstrate these qualities in class. Allow students to award badges to their peers, fostering a culture of positive reinforcement. Display these badges on student profiles within the learning platform to celebrate achievements and build a sense of pride and accomplishment. This approach encourages students to recognize and actively cultivate their strengths, contributing to a more engaging and fulfilling learning experience.

Strategy #7: Celebrate Achievement

PERMA emphasizes the importance of relationships and accomplishment as key components of human flourishing (Seligman, 2012). In online education, instructors can leverage feedback not only to evaluate but to build meaningful connections with students, demonstrating care and concern through personalized, thoughtful comments. Research suggests that focusing feedback on skill improvement rather than solely on grades can increase student motivation and engagement (Tucker, 2020).

To celebrate and showcase student achievement, create opportunities for students to display their work in virtual spaces, such as online galleries or portfolio pages, where they can upload projects, presentations, or research papers. Recognize excellence beyond traditional grading by introducing badges or awards for categories like outstanding performance, best collaboration, most detailed research, or most creative solution. These awards provide recognition for a variety of skills and contributions, motivating students to strive for excellence in diverse areas.

Additionally, provide detailed, constructive, and personalized feedback on all assignments. While it is important to identify areas for improvement, prioritize highlighting specific strengths and accomplishments. Research shows that specific, positive feedback is more likely to be internalized by students as supportive and meaningful, helping them build confidence and view their achievements as valid and valuable. This approach not only enhances student learning but also fosters a sense of pride and ownership in their work.

Strategy #8: Incorporate Brain Breaks

Incorporating "brain breaks"—short, movement-based activities lasting 2–5 minutes—can be highly effective in minimizing cognitive load and re-energizing students. Research shows that these breaks help re-engage learners, enhance focus, and improve academic performance (Feiler, 2018). Students report positive perceptions of these breaks, valuing the variety, experiential element, and increased engagement they bring to the learning environment (Stapp & Prior, 2018). Brain breaks can include short games, playful activities, or lighthearted conversation sessions that provide a refreshing pause from coursework.

Integrating brain breaks not only aids cognitive function but also addresses the sedentary nature of both online and in-person classroom learning environments. Such activities promote physical movement, helping students reset and focus more effectively when they return to the lesson (Feiler, 2018; Stapp & Prior, 2018). By embracing these strategies, educators can create a dynamic and balanced learning experience that prioritizes both well-being and academic achievement.

Brain breaks can be designed to refresh students' minds and enhance overall engagement, and they can be either physical or mental:

- Physical breaks: Encourage students to stand, stretch, and move around. One might share a short video guide if they are unable to lead the group directly. For synchronous sessions, set an online timer for a quick, five-minute break, prompting students to walk around their environment or do simple stretches.
- Mental breaks: These can involve mindfulness exercises. Incorporate them into synchronous sessions or post them as announcements for students to use when they have time. These activities need not be elaborate; for example, students can close their eyes and focus on their breath, paying attention to surrounding sounds and sensations. Alternatively, search for YouTube videos on progressive relaxation, where students tense and relax different muscle groups to relieve stress.

Incorporate a variety of break types to keep students engaged and energized:

- Cognitive breaks: Offer puzzle breaks or brain teasers related to course content. Examples include riddles, word searches, or problem-solving activities. Trivia quizzes, which can be created using online tools and artificial intelligence, also work well for quick, engaging cognitive breaks.
- Creative breaks: Encourage doodling or drawing, either related to course concepts or just for fun. Prompts like "Draw a scene related to this week's content" or "Draw your favorite animal with a thought bubble summarizing this week's key takeaway" can spark creativity and reinforce learning.
- Social breaks: Use breakout rooms for light, nonacademic discussions. Pose simple "getting to know you" questions or fun debate topics to foster connection. One can also use artificial intelligence tools to generate a list of interesting questions or conversation starters.

By incorporating these diverse brain breaks, educators can enhance students' focus, engagement, and overall academic experience, making learning both effective and enjoyable.

SUMMARY

This chapter offers a comprehensive approach to addressing the mental health and engagement challenges faced by online students today. By applying the principles of Seligman's PERMA framework, educators can transform virtual classrooms into dynamic spaces that promote not only academic success but also holistic well-being. Strategies like playful pedagogy, resilience-building practices, and brain breaks create opportunities for students to engage meaningfully, feel supported, and flourish within their educational journeys. As the landscape of higher education evolves, the integration of these evidence-based approaches ensures that institutions and educators are equipped to foster environments where students thrive both academically and personally. The shift towards a well-being-centered approach in online learning promises to enhance student satisfaction, engagement, and long-term success, paving the way for a more enriched and fulfilling higher education experience.

REFERENCES

Aboagye, E., Yawson, J. A., & Appiah, K. (2020). COVID-19 and e-learning: The challenges of Students in tertiary institutions. *Social Education Research*, 2(1), 1–8. DOI: 10.37256/ser.212021422

Adams, C. M. (2012). Calling and career counseling with college students: Finding meaning in work and life. *Journal of College Counseling*, 15(1), 65–80. DOI: 10.1002/j.2161-1882.2012.00006.x

Alsulami, S. A., & Sherwood, G. D. (2020). The experience of culturally diverse faculty in academic environments: A multi-country scoping review. *Nurse Education in Practice*, 44, 102777. Advance online publication. DOI: 10.1016/j.nepr.2020.102777 PMID: 32252017

American College Health Association. (2023). *National college health assessment.* https://www.acha.org/ncha/data-results/survey-results/

American Psychological Association. (2020). *Stress in America 2020: A national mental health crisis.* https://www.apa.org/news/press/releases/stress/2020/sia-mental-health-crisis.pdf

American Psychology Association. (2012). *Resilience.* https://www.apa.org/topics/resilience

Arrieta, G. S., Calabio, R. C., & Rogel, E. M. (2021). Accompanying students in online learning: Challenges and interventions. *Jurnal Inovatif Ilmu Pendidikan*, 2(2), 106–119. DOI: 10.23960/jiip.v2i2.21787

Azizan, M. T. (2023). Promoting cognitive engagement using technology enhanced book-end method in online active learning strategies. *ASEAN Journal of Engineering Education*, 7(2), 8–16. DOI: 10.11113/ajee2023.7n2.129

Bachik, M. A. K., Carey, G., & Craighead, W. E. (2020). VIA character strengths among U.S. college students and their associations with happiness, well-being, resiliency, academic success and psychopathology. *The Journal of Positive Psychology*, 16(4), 512–525. DOI: 10.1080/17439760.2020.1752785

Beauchemin, J. D. (2018). Solution-focused wellness: A randomized controlled trial of college students. *Health & Social Work*, 43(2), 94–100. DOI: 10.1093/hsw/hly007 PMID: 29490041

Brown, C., Hartnett, M., Ratima, M. T., Forbes, D., Datt, A., & Gedera, D. (2022). Putting whanaungatanga at the heart of students' online learning experiences. In S. Wilson, N. Arthars, D. Wardak, P. Yeoman, E. Kalman, & D.Y.T. Liu (Eds.), *Reconnecting relationships through technology. Proceedings of the 39th International Conference on Innovation, Practice and Research in the Use of Educational Technologies in Tertiary Education, ASCILITE 2022*. Article e22146. DOI: 10.14742/apubs.2022.146

Browning, B. R., Mcdermott, R. C., Scaffa, M. E., Booth, N. R., & Carr, N. T. (2018). Character strengths and first-year college students' academic persistence attitudes: An integrative model. *The Counseling Psychologist*, 46(5), 608–631. DOI: 10.1177/0011000018786950

Burcin, M. M., Armstrong, S. N., Early, J. O., & Godwin, H. (2019). Optimizing college health promotion in the digital age: Comparing perceived well-being, health behaviors, health education needs and preferences between college students enrolled in fully online versus campus-based programs. *Health Promotion Perspectives*, 9(4), 270–278. DOI: 10.15171/hpp.2019.37 PMID: 31777706

Cabrera, V., & Donaldson, S. I. (2023). PERMA to PERMA+4 building blocks of well-being: A systematic review of the empirical literature. *The Journal of Positive Psychology*, 19(3), 510–529. DOI: 10.1080/17439760.2023.2208099

Chang, B. (2019). Reflection in learning. *Online Learning : the Official Journal of the Online Learning Consortium*, 23(1), 95–110. DOI: 10.24059/olj.v23i1.1447

Cheng, M. Y., & Chen, P. (2021). Applying PERMA to develop college students' English listening and speaking proficiency in China. *International Journal of English Language and Literature Studies*, 10(4), 333–350. DOI: 10.18488/journal.23.2021.104.333.350

Cheng, S., Huang, J. C., & Hebert, W. (2022). Profiles of vocational college students' achievement emotions in online learning environments: Antecedents and outcomes. *Computers in Human Behavior*, 138, 107452. Advance online publication. DOI: 10.1016/j.chb.2022.107452

Csikszentmihalyi, M. (1988). The flow experience and its significance for human psychology. In Csikszentmihalyi, M., & Csikszentmihalyi, I. S. (Eds.), *Optimal experience: Psychological studies of flow in consciousness* (pp. 15–35). Cambridge University Press. DOI: 10.1017/CBO9780511621956.002

Donaldson, S. I., van Zyl, L. E., & Donaldson, S. I. (2022). PERMA+4: A framework for work-related wellbeing, performance and positive organizational psychology 2.0. *Frontiers in Psychology*, 12, 817244. Advance online publication. DOI: 10.3389/fpsyg.2021.817244 PMID: 35140667

Durlak, J. A., Weissberg, R. P., Dymnicki, A. B., Taylor, R. D., & Schellinger, K. B. (2011). The impact of enhancing students' social and emotional learning: A meta-analysis of school-based universal interventions. *Child Development*, 82(1), 405–432. DOI: 10.1111/j.1467-8624.2010.01564.x PMID: 21291449

Ealangov, S., Kadir, I. F., Zakaria, N. A., Soppy, A. H., & Mahamod, Z. (2022). Challenges, impacts, and strategies of online learning on mental health of community college students and lecturers. *Online Journal for TVET Practitioners*, 7(2), 53–65. https://penerbit.uthm.edu.my/ojs/index.php/oj-tp/article/view/11207

El-Amin, A. (2020). Andragogy: A theory in practice in higher education. *Journal of Research in Higher Education*, 4(2), 54–69. DOI: 10.24193/JRHE.2020.2.4

Eliyas, S., & Ranjana, P. (2022). Gamification: Is e-next learning's big thing? *Journal of Internet Services and Information Security*, 12(4), 238–245. DOI: 10.58346/JISIS.2022.I4.017

Emde, R. J., Doherty, E. K., Ellis, B., & Flynt, D. (2020). Relationships in online learning experiences. In Kyei-Blankson, L., Ntuli, E., & Blankson, J. (Eds.), *Handbook of research on creating meaningful experiences in online courses* (pp. 140–152). IGI Global., DOI: 10.4018/978-1-7998-0115-3.ch010

Endres, T., Weyreter, S., Renkl, A., & Eitel, A. (2020). When and why does emotional design foster learning? Evidence for situational interest as a mediator of increased persistence. *Journal of Computer Assisted Learning*, 36(4), 514–525. DOI: 10.1111/jcal.12418

Farley, A., Kennedy-Behr, A., & Brown, T. (2020). An investigation into the relationship between playfulness and well-being in Australian adults: An exploratory study. *OTJR (Thorofare, N.J.)*, 41(1), 56–64. DOI: 10.1177/1539449220945311 PMID: 32723209

Feiler, K. E. (2018). Brain breaks go to college. *Pedagogy in Health Promotion*, 5(4), 299–301. DOI: 10.1177/2373379918799770

Fendler, R. (2021). Improving the "other side" to faculty presence in online education. *Online Journal of Distance Learning Administration*, 24(1). https://www.westga.edu/~distance/ojdla/spring241/fendler241.pdf

Detweiler, , K. LDetweiler, , S. L. (2020). Evaluating mental illness among college students: Implications for online students. *Journal of Online Higher Education: Volume*, 4(1).

Flanigan, A. E., Akcaoglu, M., & Ray, E. (2021). Initiating and maintaining student-instructor rapport in online classes. *The Internet and Higher Education*, 53, 100844. Advance online publication. DOI: 10.1016/j.iheduc.2021.100844

Forbes, L. (2021). The process of playful learning in higher education: A phenomenological study. *Journal of Teaching and Learning*, 15(1), 57–73. DOI: 10.22329/jtl.v15i1.6515

Forbes, L., & Thomas, D. (2023). *Professors at play playbook*. Carnegie Mellon Press., DOI: 10.57862/appf-kp25

Freire, C., Ferradás, M. D., Valle, A., Núñez, J. C., & Vallejo, G. (2016). Profiles of psychological well-being and coping strategies among university students. *Frontiers in Psychology*, 7, 1554. Advance online publication. DOI: 10.3389/fpsyg.2016.01554 PMID: 27790168

Gallup & Lumina Foundation. *State of higher education 2024 report*. https://www.gallup.com/analytics/644939/state-of-higher-education.aspx

Galvin, R. (2012). Peer support: Enhancing the online learning experience. *International Journal of Innovation and Learning*, 12(1), 41–53. DOI: 10.1504/IJIL.2012.047309

Gloria, C. T., & Steinhardt, M. A. (2016). Relationships among positive emotions, coping, resilience and mental health. *Stress and Health*, 32(2), 145–156. DOI: 10.1002/smi.2589 PMID: 24962138

Green, Z. A., Faizi, F., Jalal, R., & Zadran, Z. (2021). Emotional support moderated academic stress and mental well-being in a sample of Afghan university students amid COVID-19. *The International Journal of Social Psychiatry*, 68(8), 1748–1755. DOI: 10.1177/00207640211057729 PMID: 34903066

Herminingsih, A., & Rizki, M. (2021). Quality culture to improve knowledge sharing and the positive effect on engagement of academic staff. *Archives of Business Research*, 9(1), 65–74. DOI: 10.14738/abr.91.9578

Holflod, K. (2022). Playful learning and boundary-crossing collaboration in higher education: A narrative and synthesising review. *Journal of Further and Higher Education*, 47(4), 465–480. DOI: 10.1080/0309877X.2022.2142101

Hu, S. (2008). Reinventing undergraduate education: Engaging college students in research and creative activities. *ASHE Higher Education Report*, 33(4), 1–103. DOI: 10.1002/aehe.3304

Huberman, A. (Host). (2023, October 29). Mental health toolkit: Tools to bolster your mood and mental health [Audio podast episode]. In *Huberman Lab*. https://www.hubermanlab.com/episode/mental-health-toolkit-tools-to-bolster-your-mood-mental-health?timestamp=240

Im, H., & Lee, Y. L. (2021). A study of the relationship between learning flow and learning burnout in college online classes. *Journal of Digital Convergence*, 19(6), 39–46. DOI: 10.14400/JDC.2021.19.6.039

Ingram, D. (2012). College students' sense of belonging: Dimensions and correlates (Publication No. 28168034) [Doctoral dissertation, Stanford University]. ProQuest Dissertation and Theses Global. https://purl.stanford.edu/rd771tq2209

James, A. (2021). Play in research? Yes, it is "proper" practice. *Journal of Play in Adulthood*, 3(1), 9–30. DOI: 10.5920/jpa.864

Jennings, C. L. (2020). Enhancing social presence in online courses: Facilitation strategies and best practices. In Thornburg, A., Abernathy, D., & Ceglie, R. (Eds.), *Handbook of research on developing engaging online courses* (pp. 259–276). IGI Global., DOI: 10.4018/978-1-7998-2132-8.ch015

Joshi, R., & Jaffer, S. (2024). Impact of organizational culture on job stress and well-being among higher education faculty. *Educational Administration: Theory and Practice*, 30(5), 13975–13985. DOI: 10.53555/kuey.v30i5.6170

Khafifah, K. A., Hasanah, U., & Zulfa, V. (2023). Hubungan antara stres akademik dengan academic performance pada santri Madrasah Aliyah Pondok Pesantren Al-Hamid [The relationship between academic stress and academic performance of students of Madrasah Aliyah, Al-Hamid Islamic Boarding School] [Jurnal Kesejahteraan Keluarga dan Pendidikan]. *JKKP*, 10(1), 27–37. DOI: 10.21009/JKKP.101.03

Kim, S. H. (2022). Structural relationships among course organization, student engagement and perceived learning outcome in online learning. *Journal of Learner-Centered Curriculum Education*, 22(21), 81–96. DOI: 10.22251/jlcci.2022.22.21.81

Kobasa, S. C. (1979). Stressful life events, personality, and health: An inquiry into hardiness. *Journal of Personality and Social Psychology*, 37(1), 1–11. DOI: 10.1037/0022-3514.37.1.1 PMID: 458548

Kovich, M. K., Simpson, V. L., Foli, K. J., Hass, Z., & Phillips, R. G. (2022). Application of the PERMA model of well-being in undergraduate students. *International Journal of Community Well-being*, 6(1), 1–20. DOI: 10.1007/s42413-022-00184-4 PMID: 36320595

Kuh, G. D. (2016). Making learning meaningful: Engaging students in ways that matter to them. *New Directions for Teaching and Learning*, 145(145), 49–56. DOI: 10.1002/tl.20174

Kumalasari, D., & Akmal, S. Z. (2021). Less stress, more satisfied in online learning during the COVID-19 pandemic: The moderating role of academic resilience. *Psychological Research on Urban Society*, 4(1), 36–44. DOI: 10.7454/proust.v4i1.115

Leather, M., Harper, N. J., & Obee, P. (2020). A pedagogy of play: Reasons to be playful in postsecondary education. *Journal of Experiential Education*, 44(3), 208–226. DOI: 10.1177/1053825920959684

Leger, K. A., Charles, S. T., & Almeida, D. M. (2020). Positive emotions experienced on days of stress are associated with less same-day and next-day negative emotion. *Affective Science*, 1(1), 20–27. DOI: 10.1007/s42761-019-00001-w PMID: 34113848

Li, Y., Hu, F., & He, X. (2021). How to make students happy during periods of online learning: The effect of playfulness on university students' study outcomes. *Frontiers in Psychology*, 12, 12. DOI: 10.3389/fpsyg.2021.753568 PMID: 34690899

Lipson, S. K., Zhou, S., Abelson, S., Heinze, J., Jirsa, M., Morigney, J., Patterson, A., Singh, M., & Eisenberg, D. (2022). Trends in college student mental health and help-seeking by race/ethnicity: Findings from the National Healthy Minds study, 2013-2021. *Journal of Affective Disorders*, 306(1), 138–147. DOI: 10.1016/j.jad.2022.03.038 PMID: 35307411

Liu, K., & Jirigela, W. (2024). Research on innovative music teaching: To stimulate students' interest in learning. *International Journal of New Developments in Education*, 6(1), 26–32. DOI: 10.25236/IJNDE.2024.060105

Mandhana, D. M., & Caruso, V. (2023). Inducing flow in class activities to promote student engagement. *Communication Education*, 72(4), 348–366. DOI: 10.1080/03634523.2022.2158353

Martin, F., Wang, C., & Sadaf, A. (2020). Facilitation matters: Instructor perception of helpfulness of facilitation strategies in online courses. *Online Learning : the Official Journal of the Online Learning Consortium*, 24(1), 28–49. DOI: 10.24059/olj.v24i1.1980

Matud, M. P., Díaz, A., Bethencourt, J. M., & Ibáñez, I. (2020). Stress and psychological distress in emerging adulthood: A gender analysis. *Journal of Clinical Medicine*, 9(9), 2859. Advance online publication. DOI: 10.3390/jcm9092859 PMID: 32899622

Maynard, P. L., Rohrer, J. E., & Fulton, L. (2015). Health-related quality of life among online university students. *Journal of Primary Care & Community Health*, 6(1), 48–53. DOI: 10.1177/2150131914545517 PMID: 25117557

Meyer, K. A., & Jones, S. J. (2013). Do students experience flow conditions online? *Online Learning : the Official Journal of the Online Learning Consortium*, 17(3), 137–148. DOI: 10.24059/olj.v17i3.339

Moller, S., Stearns, E., Mickelson, R., Bottia, M., & Banerjee, N. (2014). Is academic engagement the panacea for achievement in mathematics across racial and ethnic groups? Assessing the role of teacher culture. *Social Forces*, 92(4), 1513–1544. DOI: 10.1093/sf/sou018

Mund, P. (2016). Kobasa concept of hardiness. *International Research Journal of Engineering, IT & Scientific Research*, 2(1), 34–40. https://sloap.org/journals/index.php/irjeis/article/view/243

Nepali, S. (2021). The impact of academic stress on the academic performance of CBSE higher secondary students, with special reference to Ernakulam district. *Quest Journals*, 9(8), 88–94. https://www.questjournals.org/jrhss/papers/vol9-issue8/Ser-3/N09088894.pdf

Owusu-Agyeman, Y. (2021). Experiences and perceptions of academics about student engagement in higher education. *Policy Futures in Education*, 20(6), 661–680. DOI: 10.1177/14782103211053718

Parker, C., Kennedy-Behr, A., Wright, S., & Brown, T. (2022). Does the self-reported playfulness of older adults influence their wellbeing? An exploratory study. *Scandinavian Journal of Occupational Therapy*, 30(1), 86–97. DOI: 10.1080/11038128.2022.2145993 PMID: 36409561

Pascoe, M. C., Hetrick, S. E., & Parker, A. G. (2019). The impact of stress on students in secondary school and higher education. *International Journal of Adolescence and Youth*, 25(1), 104–112. DOI: 10.1080/02673843.2019.1596823

Phiriepa, A., Mapaling, C., Matlakala, F. K., & Tsabedze, W. F. (2023). COVID-19 and online learning: A scoping review of the challenges faced by students in higher institutions during lockdown. *e-Bangi. Journal of Social Sciences and Humanities*, 20(4), 68–80. DOI: 10.17576/ebangi.2023.2004.23

Plass, J. L., & Hovey, C. M. (2021). The emotional design principle in multimedia learning. In Mayer, R. E., & Fiorella, L. (Eds.), *The Cambridge handbook of multimedia learning* (pp. 324–336). Cambridge University Press. DOI: 10.1017/9781108894333.034

Popescu, E., Tătucu, M., & Dobromirescu, V. (2021). Students' well-being in online education in Covid-19 context. *International Journal of Education and Research*, 9(2), 1–10. https://www.ijern.com/journal/2021/February-2021/01.pdf

Ransdell, S. (2013). Meaningful posts and online learning in Blackboard across four cohorts of adult learners. *Computers in Human Behavior*, 29(6), 2730–2732. DOI: 10.1016/j.chb.2013.07.021

Rice, L. (2009). Playful learning. *The Journal for Education in the Built Environment*, 4(2), 94–108. DOI: 10.11120/jebe.2009.04020094

Robertson, I., Cooper, C., Sarkar, M., & Curran, T. (2015). Resilience training in the workplace from 2003 to 2014: A systematic review. *Journal of Occupational and Organizational Psychology*, 88(3), 533–562. DOI: 10.1111/joop.12120

Rodríguez-Muñoz, A., Antino, M., Ruíz-Zorrilla, P., & Ortega, E. (2021). Positive emotions, engagement, and objective academic performance: A weekly diary study. *Learning and Individual Differences*, 92, 102087. Advance online publication. DOI: 10.1016/j.lindif.2021.102087

Rohrer, J. E., Cole, L. J., & Schulze, F. W. (2012). Cigarettes and self-rated health among online university students. *Journal of Immigrant and Minority Health*, 14(3), 502–505. DOI: 10.1007/s10903-011-9564-4 PMID: 22207447

Sahu, P., Kumar, M., Sahu, D., & Chauhan, S. (2024). A correlational study between the level of academic performance and the level of academic stress among young adults. *Revista Review Index Journal of Multidisciplinary*, 4(2), 8–16. DOI: 10.31305/rrijm2024.v04.n02.002

Salimi, N., Gere, B., Talley, W. B., & Irioogbe, B. (2021). College students' mental health challenges: Concerns and considerations in the COVID-19 pandemic. *Journal of College Student Psychotherapy*, 37(1), 39–51. DOI: 10.1080/87568225.2021.1890298

Seligman, M. E. (2011). *Flourish: A visionary new understanding of happiness and wellbeing*. Simon and Schuster.

Shea, P. (2019). A study of student' sense of learning community in online environments. *Online Learning: The Official Journal of the Online Learning Consortium*, 10(1), 35–44. DOI: 10.24059/olj.v10i1.1774

Skulmowski, A., & Xu, K. M. (2021). Understanding cognitive load in digital and online learning: A new perspective on extraneous cognitive load. *Educational Psychology Review*, 34(1), 171–196. DOI: 10.1007/s10648-021-09624-7

Smith, C., & Costello, T. J. (2020). The individual's role in maintaining a positive climate. *Currents in Pharmacy Teaching & Learning*, 12(5), 496–498. DOI: 10.1016/j.cptl.2020.01.006 PMID: 32336443

Smith, Y. M., & Crowe, A. R. (2017). Nurse educator perceptions of the importance of relationship in online teaching and learning. *Journal of Professional Nursing*, 33(1), 11–19. DOI: 10.1016/j.profnurs.2016.06.004 PMID: 28131143

Stapp, A., & Prior, L. (2018). The impact of physically active brain breaks on college students' activity levels and perceptions. *Journal of Physical Activity Research*, 3(1), 60–67. DOI: 10.12691/jpar-3-1-10

Tansey, T. N., Smedema, S. M., Umucu, E., Iwanaga, K., Wu, J., Cardoso, E. D., & Strauser, D. R. (2018). Assessing college life adjustment of students with disabilities: Application of the PERMA framework. *Rehabilitation Counseling Bulletin*, 61(3), 131–142. DOI: 10.1177/0034355217702136

The Healthy Minds Network. *Healthy mind study—Student survey*. https://healthymindsnetwork.org/hms/

Tidmand, L. (2021). Building positive emotions and playfulness. In Kern, M. L., & Wehmeyer, M. L. (Eds.), *The Palgrave handbook of positive education* (pp. 421–440). Springer., DOI: 10.1007/978-3-030-64537-3_17

Tolcher, K., Cauble, M., & Downs, A. (2022). Evaluating the effects of gratitude interventions on college student well-being. *Journal of American College Health*, 72(5), 1321–1325. DOI: 10.1080/07448481.2022.2076096 PMID: 35623017

Trieu, E., & Abeyta, A. (2023). Finding meaning in education bolsters academic self-efficacy. *International Journal of Applied Positive Psychology*, 8(2), 1–21. DOI: 10.1007/s41042-023-00095-5

Trout, I. Y., & Alsandor, D. J. (2020). Graduate student well-being: Learning and living in the US during the COVID-19 pandemic. *International Journal of Multidisciplinary Perspectives in Higher Education*, 5(1), 150–155. DOI: 10.32674/jimphe.v5i1.2576

Tucker, S. Y. (2020). Instructor perceptions of feedback and the best practices: A pilot study. *American Communication Journal*, 22(1). 1–9. https://www.ac-journal.org/wp-content/uploads/2020/11/Instructor-Perceptions-of-Feedback-and-the-Best-Practices-A-Pilot-Study.pdf

Waldow, J. L., & AuCoin, D. (2021). Computer to community. In Fudge, T., & Ferebee, S. (Eds.), *Curriculum development and online instruction for the 21st century* (pp. 1–19). IGI Global., DOI: 10.4018/978-1-7998-7653-3.ch001

Wang, S. (2024). Problems with students' mental health in the context of online learning. *Transactions on Social Science. Education and Humanities Research*, 5, 44–48. DOI: 10.62051/2r8w5b08

Weems-Landingham, V., & Paternite, J. B. (2021). Using asynchronous discussions to improve online student success. *College Teaching*, 71(3), 195–196. DOI: 10.1080/87567555.2021.2008295

Weru, N. (2023). The role of instructors support and feedback on the performance of online and distance learning. *International Journal of Online and Distance Learning*, 4(1), 35–46. DOI: 10.47604/ijodl.2001

Williams, K. H., Childers, C., & Kemp, E. (2013). Stimulating and enhancing student learning through positive emotions. *Journal of Teaching in Travel & Tourism*, 13(3), 209–227. DOI: 10.1080/15313220.2013.813320

Wills, S., & Grimes, R. (2020). Developing relationships in an online environment. *The European Conference on Language Learning 2020: Official Conference Proceedings*. DOI: 10.22492/issn.2188-112X.2020.8

Witkowski, P. L., & Cornell, T. (2015). An investigation into student engagement in higher education classrooms. *InSight: A Journal of Scholarly Teaching, 10*, 56–67. DOI: 10.46504/10201505wi

Wong, J., Baars, M., He, M., Koning, B. B., & Paas, F. (2021). Facilitating goal setting and planning to enhance online self-regulation of learning. *Computers in Human Behavior*, 124, 106913. Advance online publication. DOI: 10.1016/j.chb.2021.106913

Wu, R., & Yu, Z. (2022). Exploring the effects of achievement emotions on online learning outcomes: A systematic review. *Frontiers in Psychology*, 13, 977931. Advance online publication. DOI: 10.3389/fpsyg.2022.977931 PMID: 36160514

Yackle, K., Schwarz, L. A., Kam, K., Sorokin, J. M., Huguenard, J. R., Feldman, J. L., Luo, L., & Krasnow, M. A. (2017). Breathing control center neurons that promote arousal in mice. *Science*, 355(6332), 1411–1415. DOI: 10.1126/science.aai7984 PMID: 28360327

KEY TERMS AND DEFINITIONS

Flow: Flow is a mental state where a person is fully immersed and focused on an activity, often losing track of time. This state of complete absorption and enjoyment usually occurs when the activity is challenging but manageable, leading to high levels of productivity and satisfaction.

Online learning: Online learning is a method of education where students use the internet to attend classes, complete assignments, and interact with teachers and classmates. This can include a variety of formats, such as virtual classrooms, video lectures, and digital resources.

PERMA: The PERMA framework, developed by Martin Seligman, outlines five core elements of well-being: Positive Emotions, Engagement, Relationships, Meaning, and Accomplishment. These elements work together to help individuals flourish, promoting overall happiness, fulfillment, and psychological resilience.

Positive emotions: Positive emotions are feelings that make us feel good, such as happiness, joy, gratitude, love, and excitement. These emotions can improve our overall mood and help us build stronger relationships.

Positive psychology: Positive psychology is a branch of psychology that focuses on the study and promotion of positive aspects of human life, such as happiness, strengths, and virtues. It aims to understand what makes life worth living and how people can thrive.

Resilience: Resilience is the ability to bounce back from difficult situations and adapt to challenges. It involves being able to cope with stress and adversity, and to recover from setbacks stronger and more capable.

Stress: Stress is the body's response to challenging or demanding situations. It can cause physical and emotional strain, and while some stress can be motivating, too much stress can negatively affect our health and well-being.

Well-being: Well-being refers to the state of being comfortable, healthy, and happy. It includes both physical and mental health, as well as a sense of satisfaction with life and the ability to manage stress effectively.

Chapter 2
Strategies for Using Online Education in Support of Global Contexts

Doris Chasokela
https://orcid.org/0009-0001-5983-8508
National University of Science and Technology, Zimbabwe

Lungisani Mpofu
National University of Science and Technology, Zimbabwe

ABSTRACT

This chapter explores the potential of online education as a powerful tool for supporting global contexts and addressing the diverse educational needs of learners around the world. By harnessing the power of digital technologies, online education offers the potential to break down barriers of geography, culture, and economics that have traditionally limited access to quality education. Through a discussion of key themes and case studies, this chapter aims to provide a comprehensive overview of the strategies and best practices for using online education in support of global contexts. By the end of this chapter, readers will have gained a deeper understanding of how online education can be used to: Improve access to education in underserved communities. Provide personalized learning experiences that cater to diverse learning styles and cultural backgrounds. Facilitate cross-cultural exchange and understanding through global collaboration and virtual exchanges. Leverage technology to create innovative teaching and learning approaches .

DOI: 10.4018/979-8-3693-4407-1.ch002

INTRODUCTION

In today's digital world, education is no longer confined to physical classrooms and geographic borders. Online education has opened up unprecedented opportunities for learning and engagement in a global context, transforming the way we think about learning, teaching, and knowledge sharing (Bozkurt, et al. 2020; Salas-Pilco, et al. 2022). Online education provides a platform for educators, students, and scholars from all over the world to interact, collaborate, and learn from each other (Adedoyin & Soykan, 2023; Aduba & Mayowa-Adebara, 2022; Vlachopoulos & Makri, 2019. This global exchange of ideas and perspectives has led to the development of more diverse and inclusive learning environments, fostering innovation and cross-cultural understanding. As online education continues to grow and evolve, it is increasingly important to understand the unique opportunities and challenges that come with global online learning. Dennen and Bong (2018) and Shonfeld, et al. 2021) cite that from cultural differences and language barriers to differences in educational systems and digital access, many factors shape the experience of online education in a global context.

Despite these challenges, the potential of online education to bridge the divide between cultures, nations, and peoples is vast. By promoting understanding and collaboration, online education can help build a more interconnected, informed, and compassionate global community. The global reach of online education is not only transforming the way we learn but also the way we work and communicate. In an era of globalization and digitalization, the demand for new skills, knowledge, and competencies is rapidly increasing, and online education has emerged as a powerful tool for upskilling and reskilling the global workforce. From online degrees and micro-credentials to massive open online courses (MOOCs) and corporate training (Waks, 2019; Resei, et al. 2018; Van der Hijden & Martin, 2023). Online education offers a wide range of opportunities for individuals and organizations to develop the skills and expertise they need to succeed in a rapidly changing world.

As online education continues to expand its reach and influence, it is essential to consider how it can be used in support of global contexts and issues. Some strategies for harnessing the power of online education in support of global contexts are fostering cross-cultural understanding. Online education can create opportunities for students from different cultures and nations to interact, learn from each other, and develop a deeper understanding of global perspectives. This can be achieved through collaborative projects, discussions, and virtual exchanges. Supporting diversity and inclusion in online education provides an opportunity to create more diverse and inclusive learning environments that reflect the full range of human experience. This can be achieved by incorporating diverse voices and perspectives in course materials, fostering respectful and open dialogue, and providing accessible and inclusive learning experiences. Addressing global challenges in online education can be used to raise awareness and develop solutions for pressing global challenges such as climate change, poverty, and inequality. Bridging the digital divide by providing equitable access to online learning opportunities, online education can help bridge the digital divide and ensure that individuals from all backgrounds have access to quality education and training. Encouraging global citizenship in online education can foster a sense of global citizenship by promoting values such as empathy, compassion, and social responsibility. This can be achieved through intercultural communication, service learning, and global volunteer opportunities. Developing language skills in online education can provide opportunities for students to develop their language skills and communication abilities in a global context. This can include offering language courses, encouraging language exchange partnerships, and providing multilingual support for online learning materials. Promoting sustainable development in online education can be used to promote sustainable development by equipping students with the knowledge and skills needed to tackle global challenges such as environmental degradation, resource depletion, and social injustice. Cultivating entrepreneurial and innovative mindsets on online education can help cultivate entrepreneurial and innovative mindsets among students, equipping them with the skills and knowledge needed to drive innovation and economic growth in a global context. Encouraging lifelong learning in online education can support lifelong learning by providing flexible, affordable, and accessible opportunities for individuals to upskill and reskill throughout their careers, contributing to their personal and professional growth in a global context.

Leveraging Technology for Global Collaboration and Virtual Exchange

Technology has opened up new avenues for global collaboration and virtual exchange (Evolve Project Team, 2020; Msekelwa, 2023; Owens & Hite, 2022). This has therefore allowed individuals from around the world to connect and work together in ways that were previously unimaginable. Leveraging the power of technology, online education has emerged as a platform for global collaboration and exchange, enabling students, educators, and organizations to collaborate, share ideas, and develop solutions to global challenges (Chasokela & Ncube, 2024). Virtual exchange programs, online classrooms, and global communication tools have made it possible for learners to connect with peers and experts from diverse backgrounds (O'Dowd, 2016; O'Dowd, 2021; Siergiejczyk, 2020; Szobonya & Roche 2023). This fosters cross-cultural understanding and enriching learning experiences. In a world that is increasingly globalized and interconnected, leveraging technology for global collaboration and virtual exchange has become an essential component of online education.

Ways in which technology can be used to support global collaboration and exchange are virtual exchanges. Online courses and programs can leverage virtual exchange tools, such as video conferencing and collaborative platforms, to facilitate real-time, cross-cultural collaboration between learners from around the world. By using virtual classroom tools, instructors can create global classrooms, allowing students from different countries to learn together, engage in discussions, and work on group projects in real-time. Social media platforms can be used to facilitate global connections and collaborations, enabling learners to share ideas, resources, and projects with peers and professionals across the globe. Collaborative online learning platforms can be used to host collaborative projects and initiatives (Ansell & Gash, 2018; Curtin & Sarju, 2021), allowing learners to work together on real-world challenges and develop solutions with a global perspective. Cloud computing can be used to store, share, and analyze data from diverse sources, supporting global research and collaboration on issues such as climate change, health care, and education. Augmented and virtual reality technologies can be used to create immersive, interactive learning environments that simulate real-world scenarios and promote global understanding and collaboration (Chasokela, 2024; Tshuma & Chasokela, 2024). Artificial intelligence can be used to facilitate global connections and collaborations, analyzing and aggregating data from diverse sources to support research, decision-making, and innovation in a global context. Blockchain technology can be used to create secure, transparent, and decentralized networks for global collaboration and exchange, enabling individuals and organizations to share and verify data without the need for intermediaries (Kremenova & Gajdos, 2019). Global dataspaces, such as the emerging concept of the "Internet of Everything," offer the potential for seamless, real-time integration of data from diverse sources, enabling global collaboration and innovation in new and exciting ways. Big data analytics can be used to support global collaboration and exchange by enabling organizations and researchers to extract insights from large, complex datasets, supporting informed decision-making and innovation on a global scale. Smart city technologies, such as IoT (Internet of Things) and AI (Artificial Intelligence), can be used to support global collaboration and exchange by creating connected, data-driven urban environments that support sustainable development and quality of life on a global scale. Telemedicine technologies, such as teleconferencing and remote monitoring, can be used to support global collaboration and exchange in the medical field, enabling healthcare professionals to diagnose and treat patients across borders, share expertise, and develop new treatments and cures. Drone technology can be used to support global collaboration and exchange in fields such as humanitarian aid, environmental monitoring, and global logistics (Rejeb, Rejeb, et al. 2021; Quamar, et al. 2023). It allows organizations to monitor and respond to global challenges in real-time. Digital twinning technologies can be used to create virtual replicas of real-world objects or systems, enabling global collaboration and exchange in fields such as urban planning, infrastructure development, and engineering. 3D printing technologies can be used to support global collaboration and exchange by enabling organizations to share designs, prototypes, and finished products across borders, promoting innovation and reducing waste in global supply chains. Intelligent automation technologies, such as machine learning and robotics, can be used to support global collaboration and exchange by automating repetitive or labor-intensive tasks, freeing up human resources for more creative and strategic work on a global scale. Virtual conferences and events, such as online seminars, webinars, and trade shows, can be used to support global collaboration and exchange by enabling individuals and organizations to share knowledge, network, and collaborate across borders.

Overcoming Language Barriers and Digital Divides

Language barriers and digital divides are major challenges in the global exchange of knowledge and innovation (Lupac, 2018; Resta & Laferriere, 2015; Vassilakopoulou & Hustad 2023). This further limits the ability of individuals and organizations to collaborate, learn, and innovate on a global scale. Fortunately, technology is rapidly evolving to address these challenges, offering new tools and solutions for overcoming language barriers and digital divides. From real-time translation tools and language learning platforms to low-cost internet connectivity and digital literacy programs, there are a range of innovative solutions available for overcoming these barriers and enabling global collaboration and exchange.

Strategies for overcoming language barriers and digital divides include language machine translation tools, such as Google Translate or Microsoft Translator, which can be used to quickly and effectively translate text, audio, and video content into multiple languages, supporting global communication and collaboration. Online language learning platforms, such as Duolingo and Rosetta Stone, can be used to help learners develop proficiency in foreign languages, supporting global communication and exchange (Mishan, 2022). Creating content in multiple languages, such as websites, social media posts, and educational materials, can help bridge language barriers and promote global understanding and engagement. Offering language training and support, such as ESL (English as a Second Language) classes or foreign language tutoring, can help individuals develop the skills and confidence needed to communicate and collaborate globally. Multilingual staff and teams: Hiring staff who are proficient in multiple languages, or creating multilingual teams, can help organizations better serve global customers and clients, and support global collaboration and exchange. Creating content that is accessible to individuals with disabilities, such as closed captioning for video content or text-to-speech functionality, can help bridge digital divides and promote global inclusion. Low-cost, high-speed internet connectivity, such as Google's Project Loon or Facebook's Internet.org, can help bridge digital divides (Espinoza & Reed, 2018). It provides affordable, reliable access to the internet in underserved areas. Digital literacy programs, such as those offered by the World Wide Web Foundation and the Mozilla Foundation, can help individuals develop the skills and knowledge needed to effectively use technology and access online content. Open educational resources (OER), such as free textbooks, online courses, and instructional materials, can help bridge language and digital divides by providing high-quality, accessible learning resources to individuals around the world. Universal learning design (UDL) principles can be used to design online content and learning experiences that are accessible and engaging for individuals with diverse language and technology backgrounds, promoting global inclusion and collaboration. Mobile learning, or m-learning, can help bridge language and digital divides by providing flexible, affordable, and accessible learning experiences for individuals with limited access to traditional learning environments. Crowdsourcing platforms, such as Kiva and Indiegogo, can help bridge language and digital divides (Gasparro, 2019). This is done by supporting the growth of local initiatives, businesses, and ideas in underserved communities around the world. Localizing online content and experiences, such as website translations or culturally relevant advertising campaigns, can help organizations better engage with global audiences and bridge language and digital divides. Community-based approaches, such as technology hubs or maker spaces, can help bridge digital divides by providing local access to technology, education, and support for individuals in underserved communities. Digital government services can support language and digital equity by providing online access to public services, such as education, healthcare, and social services, in multiple languages and a user-friendly manner. Governments and organizations can leverage data and analytics to better understand and address language and digital divides, using this information to develop targeted policies and interventions that support global inclusion and collaboration. Citizen science projects, such as Foldit and Zooniverse, can help bridge language and digital divides (Curtis, 2018). Individuals are engaged from diverse backgrounds in scientific research and problem-solving, fostering global collaboration and discovery. Incorporating inclusive design principles, such as accessibility, diversity, and usability, into the design of online content and experiences can help create more accessible, inclusive, and engaging global learning environments.

Personalized Learning for Global Learners

In the era of global online education, personalization is key to delivering a high-quality learning experience that meets the unique needs, preferences, and abilities of learners from diverse backgrounds (Maghsudi, et al. 2021; O'Keefeet, al. 2020). Personalized learning approaches, such as adaptive learning technologies and competency-based education, can help global learners tailor their learning experiences to their individual needs and preferences, leading to better engagement, retention, and outcomes. Ways in which personalized learning can support global learners include adaptive learning technology platforms, such as Knewton or Smart Sparrow (Dutta, et al. 2024; Johnson & Samora, 2016; Marienko, et al. 2020. These platforms can be used to personalize learning experiences by adapting content, assessments, and feedback to individual learner needs and progress. Self-paced learning allows learners to progress through course material at their own pace, providing greater flexibility and control over their learning experiences. Competency-based education, also known as mastery learning, focuses on learner outcomes rather than seat time (Amato, 2021; Casey, 2018). It allows learners to progress at their own pace and demonstrate mastery of a skill or topic before moving on. Portfolio-based learning allows learners to create digital portfolios of their work, experiences, and achievements, providing a personalized and flexible way to demonstrate mastery of skills and knowledge in a global context. Peer learning, such as peer-to-peer feedback, group projects, and study groups, can help support personalized learning by providing learners with opportunities to engage in collaborative problem-solving, self-reflection, and skill development. Individualized coaching can support personalized learning by providing learners with personalized feedback, guidance, and support tailored to their individual needs, preferences, and learning styles. Personal learning networks, such as LinkedIn or Twitter, can support personalized learning by allowing learners to connect with peers, experts, and mentors in their field of interest, sharing knowledge, experiences, and resources in a global context. Gamification, or the use of game-based mechanics to engage learners, can help support personalized learning by providing learners with feedback, incentives, and challenges tailored to their interests and learning goals (Bennani, et al. 2022; Pesare, et al. 2016; Saleem, et al. 2022; Hong, et al. 2024). Flipped classrooms, in which learners watch lectures or complete coursework at home and use class time for discussion and problem-solving, can support personalized learning by allowing learners to learn at their own pace and engage in more personalized interactions with peers and instructors. Micro-credentials, such as badges or certificates, can support personalized learning by allowing learners to demonstrate mastery of specific skills or competencies, providing a more tailored and flexible approach to global online education. Project-based learning, in which learners work on real-world problems or projects, can support personalized learning by allowing learners to apply their knowledge and skills in a relevant, authentic context. Blended learning, which combines online and in-person learning experiences, can support personalized learning by allowing learners to tailor their learning experiences to their individual needs, preferences, and schedules. Lifelong learning, which emphasizes ongoing education and skill development, can support personalized learning by providing global learners with the tools and opportunities to continuously grow, adapt, and innovate throughout their lives. Open educational resources, such as open-access journals and open courseware, can support personalized learning by providing learners with free, high-quality educational content that can be adapted to their individual needs and interests. Social-emotional learning, which focuses on the development of skills such as self-awareness, self-management, and empathy, can support personalized learning by helping global learners better understand themselves and their interactions with others, leading to more effective communication and collaboration. Culturally responsive teaching, which incorporates the values, beliefs, and experiences of diverse learners into the learning environment, can support personalized learning by creating a more inclusive and engaging learning experience for global learners. Data analytics, such as learner analytics or learning analytics, can support personalized learning by providing educators and learners with insights into learning behaviors, preferences, and outcomes, enabling more targeted and effective personalized learning experiences. Universal Design for Learning (UDL) principles, which aim to provide multiple means of representation, expression, and engagement for all learners, can support personalized learning by ensuring that global learners with diverse needs, abilities, and preferences have equitable access to high-quality learning experiences.

Pedagogical Innovations in Global Online Education

Pedagogical innovations in global online education refer to the implementation of new and creative teaching approaches, methods, and strategies that enhance the quality, effectiveness, and engagement of online learning experiences on a worldwide scale. These innovations often involve integrating cutting-edge technologies, interactive multimedia resources, collaborative platforms, and adaptive learning tools to create dynamic and personalized learning environments that cater to diverse learners' needs and preferences. By embracing innovative pedagogical practices, online educators can promote active learning, critical thinking, problem-solving skills, and cultural competence, fostering a deeper understanding, interest, and motivation among students in the global online classroom (Hernandez-de-Menendez, et al. 2019; Holmes, et al. 2015; Skenderi, & Skenderi, 2023). Additionally, pedagogical innovations can help address the challenges of distance education, bridge geographical and cultural barriers, and promote accessibility, inclusivity, and lifelong learning opportunities for learners across different countries and regions. Overall, these innovations play a crucial role in shaping the future of online education and advancing the global landscape of teaching and learning in the digital age.

Pedagogical innovations in global online education are crucial for several reasons (Bizami, et al. 2023; Chigbu, et al. 2023; Major, et al. 2020). Firstly, they help address the diverse learning needs and preferences of a global audience, allowing for more personalized and engaging learning experiences. Additionally, these innovations promote inclusivity and accessibility, breaking down geographical and cultural barriers and providing learning opportunities to students worldwide. They also foster the development of 21st-century skills such as critical thinking, problem-solving, collaboration, and digital literacy, which are essential for success in today's interconnected and rapidly changing world. Moreover, pedagogical innovations in global online education can enhance the quality and effectiveness of teaching and learning, leading to improved student outcomes and satisfaction. Overall, these innovations play a vital role in transforming the landscape of education, enabling educators to adapt to the changing needs of learners in an increasingly digital and globalized society. While pedagogical innovations in global online education offer numerous benefits, they also come with various challenges (Adedoyin & Soykan, 2023; Dhawan, 2020; Kebritchi, et al. 2017). Some of the key challenges include access and equity that is global online education initiatives may face barriers in terms of access to technology and internet connectivity, particularly in disadvantaged or remote regions. Ensuring equitable access to online learning opportunities for all learners remains a significant challenge. Maintaining the quality of education in online settings can be challenging, as ensuring effective pedagogy, meaningful engagement, and assessment practices requires intentional design and monitoring. Not all learners, educators, or institutions may possess the necessary digital literacy skills to effectively engage in online education. Addressing digital skills gaps and providing training and support is essential. Global online education initiatives must be inclusive of diverse cultural and linguistic backgrounds, which can present challenges in terms of language barriers, cultural differences, and differing educational norms. Reliable technological infrastructure is essential for the success of online education initiatives. Issues such as connectivity, hardware, software, and cybersecurity can pose significant challenges.

To address these challenges and move forward with pedagogical innovations in global online education, there are strategies that can be considered (Adedoyin & Soykan, 2023; Guardia, et al. 2021; Vu, et al. 2016). Governments, educational institutions, and organizations should invest in reliable technological infrastructure, including internet connectivity, devices, and digital resources, to ensure equitable access to online education. Offer professional development and training programs to enhance digital literacy skills among educators and learners, enabling them to effectively navigate online learning environments. Encourage collaboration and knowledge sharing among educators, institutions, and stakeholders on a global scale to exchange best practices, innovative ideas, and resources in online education. Embrace culturally responsive practices/pedagogical approaches that respect and incorporate diverse cultural and linguistic perspectives in online education initiatives. Establish mechanisms for quality assurance and continuous improvement in online education, including robust assessment practices, feedback mechanisms, and evaluation processes. By addressing these challenges and implementing these strategies, educators and policymakers can advance pedagogical innovations in global online education, promoting inclusive, high-quality, and engaging learning experiences for learners worldwide.

Best Practices for Facilitating Global Citizenship through Online Education

Introducing global citizenship through online education is a powerful way to foster cross-cultural understanding, empathy, and collaboration among learners from diverse backgrounds (Gibson, et al. 2008; Trede, et al. 2013; Goh, 2012). To facilitate global citizenship effectively, educators can employ a range of best practices in online education such as encouraging open dialogue and communication among learners from different cultural backgrounds (Kopish & Marques, 2020). Facilitate discussions that promote understanding, respect, and empathy for diverse perspectives and experiences. Designing collaborative online activities that require learners to work together on projects or assignments, promotes cooperation, problem-solving, and intercultural communication skills (Rummel & Spada, 2005). Introducing learners to global challenges such as climate change, human rights, or global health pandemics. Encourage critical thinking and reflection on these issues and how they impact communities worldwide. Providing opportunities for experiential learning through virtual simulations, case studies, or virtual exchange programs that immerse learners in real-world global contexts (Asad, et al. 2021). Engaging learners in service-learning projects that connect them with local or global communities in need. Encourage reflection on the impact of their actions and the importance of global citizenship (Thomson, et al. 2011). Encouraging learners to share their stories, experiences, and perspectives through multimedia platforms (Kara, et al. 2020). This can help build empathy, understanding, and connections among learners from different cultural backgrounds. Offer resources, training, and activities to develop cross-cultural competencies, such as language skills, intercultural communication, and cultural awareness. Infuse global perspectives into the curriculum across various subjects and disciplines (Svensson & Wihlborg, 2010). Highlight the interconnectedness of global issues and encourage critical thinking about complex global challenges. Facilitate virtual exchanges with learners from different countries or cultures to foster cross-cultural understanding, language skills, and intercultural communication. Encourage learners to reflect on their own identities, biases, and perspectives. Provide opportunities for self-assessment and growth in cultural competence and global citizenship values (Chhatlani, 2023). By incorporating these best practices into online education, educators can effectively facilitate global citizenship and promote intercultural understanding, empathy, and collaboration among learners, preparing them to be responsible and engaged global citizens in an interconnected world.

Online Education in Higher Education 21st-Century Context

In today's 21st-century context, higher education is undergoing a significant transformation, driven by technological advancements, shifting student demographics, and changing workforce needs (Ahmad, 2020; Kukulska-Hulme, 2012). Online education has emerged as a vital component of this transformation, offering unprecedented flexibility, accessibility, and scalability to students worldwide. As online learning platforms and tools continue to evolve, higher education institutions must adapt to meet the demands of digitally savvy students, who expect personalized and engaging learning experiences (McHaney, 2023). Moreover, the rise of online education has also created new opportunities for institutions to expand their reach, increase student enrollment, and improve student outcomes (Chasokela & Mpofu, 2024; Protopsaltis & Baum, 2019). However, this shift also presents challenges, such as ensuring the quality and authenticity of online courses, addressing digital divides, and developing faculty competencies in online teaching (Kundu & Bej, 2021). This chapter explores the current state of online education in higher education, highlighting its benefits, challenges, and implications for the future of higher education. Online education has undergone significant changes over the past two decades from its early days as a complement to traditional face-to-face learning, online education has evolved to become a mainstream delivery model. Today, online courses are no longer seen as an alternative to traditional classes, but rather as an essential component of a comprehensive educational strategy.

Several key drivers have contributed to the growth and adoption of online education in higher education (Al-Adwan & Smedley, 2012). Examples are changing student demographics, including increased enrollment rates among non-traditional students, working professionals, and international students, which have created a demand for flexible and accessible learning options. According to Kumar et al (2021), advances in technology have enabled the development of sophisticated online learning platforms, tools, and infrastructure, making it easier for institutions to deliver high-quality online courses. The rapidly changing workforce requires professionals with skills in emerging technologies, such as data science, artificial intelligence, and cybersecurity (Li, 2022; Ajayi & Udeh, 2024). Online education can help bridge this skills gap and also provide significant cost savings for institutions, students, and employers, making it an attractive option for those seeking affordable education.

Online education offers several benefits to students, institutions, and employers such as allowing students to learn at their own pace and on their schedule (Naidu, 2008). It enables students to access global resources, expertise, and networking opportunities. It can reach students in remote or underserved areas, increasing access to higher education. Online education can also facilitate personalized learning experiences tailored to individual students' needs (Ingkavara, et al., 2022; Zheng, et al., 2022). While online education offers many benefits, it also presents several challenges such as ensuring the quality and authenticity of online courses is a major concern. The digital divide between students with access to technology and those without can exacerbate existing inequalities. Developing faculty competencies in online teaching is essential for delivering high-quality online courses. Maintaining student engagement and motivation in online courses is crucial for academic success. In conclusion, online education is no longer a peripheral aspect of higher education but a vital component of the 21st-century educational landscape. As institutions continue to evolve their online strategies, they must address the challenges and opportunities presented by this rapidly changing landscape. (Palvia, et al. 2018; Paudel. 2021)

Online Education for Global Workforce Development

In today's world, the demand for skilled and adaptable workers has never been more pressing. As global industries and economies continue to evolve, the need for professionals with specialized knowledge and expertise has become a critical factor in driving economic growth and competitiveness (Dhawan, 2020; Adedoyin & Soykan, 2023). Online education has emerged as a vital tool in addressing this need, providing individuals with the skills and training necessary to thrive in an increasingly globalized workforce. By leveraging online education platforms, institutions can reach students from diverse backgrounds and regions, offering a wide range of programs and courses that cater to the evolving needs of the global economy. This has opened up new opportunities for individuals to upskill and reskill, stay ahead of the curve, and become part of a global workforce that is better equipped to tackle the complex challenges of the 21st century (Carta, 2021). In this context, online education plays a vital role in supporting global workforce development by providing accessible, flexible, and high-quality learning experiences that can help bridge skills gaps and meet emerging workforce needs (Li, 2022).

The Role of Online Education in Supporting Global Workforce Development

Online education offers a range of benefits that can help individuals, organizations, and economies thrive. Ways in which online education can support global workforce development are providing individuals with access to learning opportunities that may not have been previously available due to geographical or financial constraints. This can help bridge the skills gap in emerging economies and provide workers with the skills they need to compete in the global market. Delivering at scale, allowing institutions to reach a large number of students quickly and efficiently. This flexibility is particularly important in global workforce development, where companies need to upskill and reskill workers rapidly to stay competitive. Offering customized training programs that cater to the specific needs of industries, companies, and workers. This can help ensure that workers have the skills they need to perform their jobs effectively and efficiently. Being cost-effective than traditional classroom-based education, particularly for companies that need to train large numbers of workers (Sun & Chen, 2026). This can help reduce training costs and improve Return on investment (ROI). Delivering globally, allowing institutions to reach students from diverse backgrounds and regions. This can help promote global collaboration and knowledge sharing, which is critical in today's interconnected world. Helping individuals develop the skills they need to succeed in an increasingly complex and rapidly changing global economy. This can include skills such as data analysis, digital literacy, and language proficiency. Addressing skills gaps in emerging industries such as artificial intelligence, cybersecurity, and renewable energy can help ensure that workers have the skills they need to succeed in these fields (Ahmad, et al. 2021).

Strategies for Addressing Skills Gaps and Emerging Workforce Needs

Potential strategies for addressing skills gaps and emerging workforce needs are to conduct regular skills assessments to identify gaps in the workforce and determine the skills needed to meet emerging workforce needs. Develop training programs that focus on the skills that are in demand, such as data analytics, cybersecurity, and digital marketing. Upskill and reskill workers to ensure that they have the skills needed to succeed in an increasingly complex and rapidly changing global economy. Collaborate with industry partners to identify the skills that are in demand and develop training programs that meet those needs. Foster a culture of continuous learning by providing opportunities for workers to develop new skills and stay up-to-date with the latest technologies and trends. Emphasize soft skills such as communication, teamwork, and problem-solving, which are essential for success in an increasingly complex and rapidly changing global economy. Encourage interdisciplinary learning by providing opportunities for workers to learn from other disciplines and industries. Provide micro-credentials that recognize workers' skills and knowledge in specific areas, such as data analysis or cybersecurity. Develop apprenticeships and mentorship programs that provide workers with hands-on experience and guidance from experienced professionals (Gallup, 2024). Encourage lifelong learning by providing opportunities for workers to continue learning and developing new skills throughout their careers. Addressing skills gaps and emerging workforce needs requires a comprehensive approach that involves developing training programs, upskilling and reskilling workers, collaborating with industry partners, fostering a culture of continuous learning, emphasizing soft skills, encouraging interdisciplinary learning, providing micro-credentials, developing apprenticeships and mentorship programs, encouraging lifelong learning, developing training programs in emerging technologies, focusing on soft skills, emphasizing critical thinking and problem-solving, developing programs in emerging industries, fostering a culture of innovation, developing programs in emerging regions, encouraging collaboration and knowledge sharing, developing programs in emerging technologies, focusing on sustainability and social responsibility, and developing programs in emerging fields. (Ajayi & Udeh, 2024; Singh Dubey, et al., 2022; Shalev, et al., 2020).

The potential for online education to promote global talent development and knowledge sharing

Online education has emerged as a powerful tool for promoting global talent development and knowledge sharing. With the ability to reach a global audience, online education can help bridge the gap between different regions, cultures, and languages, facilitating the exchange of ideas, skills, and knowledge. Some ways in which online education can promote global talent development and knowledge sharing are access to global online education provides access to high-quality education from top institutions around the world, regardless of geographical location or financial constraints (Jackson, 2016). Online education offers diverse learning experiences, including cultural, linguistic, and disciplinary perspectives, which can help students develop a broader understanding of the world. Online education facilitates cross-cultural collaboration among students, educators, and industry professionals, promoting global understanding, cooperation, and innovation.

Ethics and Online Education in Global Contexts

Online education has become a crucial component of global learning and knowledge sharing. As online education continues to expand, it raises important ethical questions about access, equity, and inclusivity. With the rise of massive open online courses (MOOCs), online degree programs, and virtual learning platforms, the global education landscape is evolving rapidly. However, this growth also presents new challenges, such as ensuring the integrity of online assessments, protecting student data privacy, and addressing cultural and linguistic barriers (Gudino Paredes, et al., 2021). Moreover, the increasing reliance on online education has also sparked concerns about the digital divide, where some students may be left behind due to a lack of access to technology or internet connectivity. As educators, policymakers, and technology providers grapple with these complex issues, it is essential to consider the ethical implications of online education in global contexts. This requires a nuanced understanding of the interplay between technology, culture, and society, as well as a commitment to promoting ethical practices that prioritize student well-being, inclusivity, and social responsibility.

The Importance of Ethics in Online Education

As online education continues to grow and evolve, it is essential to prioritize ethics in this field. Ethics in online education refers to the principles and values that guide the design, delivery, and evaluation of online learning experiences (Toprak, et al., 2007). The importance of ethics in online education cannot be overstated, as it has a direct impact on the quality, integrity, and effectiveness of online education. The importance of ethics in online education includes the collection and storage of sensitive student data, such as personal information, academic records, and assessment results (Tzimas & Demetriadis, 2021). Ethics ensure that this data is protected and used responsibly. Online assessments must be designed to ensure their integrity and prevent cheating. Ethics ensure that assessments are fair, valid, and reliable. Online education must be culturally sensitive and inclusive to cater to diverse learners from different backgrounds. Ethics ensure that online learning experiences are respectful and considerate of different cultures. Online education must be accessible and equitable to all students, regardless of their background, location, or abilities. According to Taylor et al. (2022), Ethics ensure that online learning experiences are designed to promote equity and reduce barriers. Online education requires accountability and transparency in the delivery of online learning experiences. Ethics ensure that educators and institutions are accountable for their actions and decisions. Online education requires educators to prioritize student well-being and support to succeed in their online learning experiences. Confidentiality disclosure agreements are required to protect student data and personal information. Digital citizenship by teaching students how to use technology responsibly, ethically, and safely must be promoted by online education (Searson, et al., 2015). Online learning platforms must be designed with ethical considerations in mind, including data privacy, security, and accessibility. Pedagogical integrity must be prioritized in online education ensuring that online learning experiences are designed to promote student learning, engagement, and retention.

Addressing Ethical Challenges in Global Contexts, Such as Data Privacy and Intellectual Property Concerns

There are several ways to address ethical challenges in global contexts, such as (Calia, et al. 2022):

1. Data Privacy and Protection (Lacroix, 2019; Gambs, 2018)
   - Establish and implement data protection regulations that comply with international standards, such as the General Data Protection Regulation (GDPR), CCPA, and PIPEDA.
   - Conduct regular data audits to ensure that data is properly stored, processed, and secured.
   - Use encryption to protect sensitive data and prevent unauthorized access.
   - Notify data subjects in case of a data breach or security incident.
   - Ensure transparency and accountability in data collection, processing, and storage.
2. Intellectual Property (IP) Concerns (Oppenheimer, et al., 2015; Nicholas, et al., 2010).
   - Respect international IP laws and treaties, such as the Berne Convention and the TRIPS Agreement.
   - Establish clear licensing agreements for IP rights, including copyright, patent, and trademark.
   - Obtain informed consent from individuals or organizations before using their IP.
   - Ensure that any use of IP is fair and reasonable, taking into account the interests of all parties involved.
   - Foster collaboration and partnerships with stakeholders to ensure that IP is used responsibly and beneficially.
3. Cultural Sensitivity and Awareness (Zhu & Jesiek, 2020; Calia, et al., 2022).
   - Develop cultural intelligence to understand the nuances of different cultures and avoid cultural misunderstandings.

- Promote diversity and inclusion by considering the perspectives and needs of all stakeholders.
- Be mindful of sensitive content, such as religious or political beliefs, and avoid causing offense or harm.
- Foster collaborative approaches to problem-solving, taking into account the perspectives and expertise of all stakeholders.
- Provide education and training on cultural awareness, sensitivity, and competence.
4. Ethical Decision-Making (Bonde, 2016; Kuntz, et al., 2013)
   - Develop ethical frameworks that guide decision-making in complex situations.
   - Engage with stakeholders to understand their needs, concerns, and expectations.
   - Ensure transparency and accountability in decision-making processes.
   - Foster collaborative governance models that involve stakeholders in decision-making processes.
   - Provide ethics training to employees and stakeholders to ensure that they understand ethical principles and guidelines.
5. International Cooperation (Rizvi, 2019)
   - Establish global ethics standards that are consistent across countries and regions.
   - Foster international cooperation among governments, organizations, and stakeholders to promote ethical practices globally.
   - Develop global governance frameworks that promote ethical practices in international activities.
   - Engage with stakeholders from diverse backgrounds to promote ethical practices globally.
   - Provide capacity-building programs to help countries develop their ethical frameworks and practices.

By addressing these ethical challenges in global contexts, we can promote ethical practices that respect the rights of individuals, organizations, and communities worldwide.

Future Directions for Online Education in a Global Context

As online education continues to transform the landscape of learning, the future directions for online education in a global context hold significant promise in reshaping educational experiences on a global scale (Saykili, 2018). With advancements in technology, and shifting societal norms, the potential for online education to bridge cultural divides, expand access to quality education, and foster cross-cultural collaboration is immense (Shonfeld, et al., 2021). From personalized learning and virtual reality technologies to global partnerships and sustainability initiatives, the future of online education in a global context is poised to revolutionize learning experiences. It also promotes global citizenship and empowers learners to thrive in a rapidly evolving and diverse world.

Several key trends and future directions are shaping the landscape of online education in a global context such as the adoption of artificial intelligence and personalized learning algorithms will enable educators to tailor learning experiences to the individual needs, preferences, and learning styles of each learner, enhancing engagement and outcomes (Bhutoria, 2022; Ayeni, et al., 2024). The integration of virtual and augmented reality technologies offers immersive and interactive learning experiences, enabling learners to engage with content in new and dynamic ways and creating opportunities for global collaboration and cultural exchange (Torres Vega, et al. 2020). The popularity of microlearning, which delivers content in short, focused bursts, continues to grow, allowing learners to access and digest information efficiently, especially in fast-paced global contexts (Moore, 2020). The use of blockchain technology for verifying credentials, certifications, and qualifications in online education will enhance the credibility and trustworthiness of online learning experiences, particularly in a global context (Alam, 2022). Collaboration platforms and social learning tools facilitate global connections and collaboration among learners, educators, and experts from diverse cultural backgrounds, fostering cross-cultural understanding and exchange. The promotion of sustainability and environmental awareness in online education will become more prevalent, addressing global challenges such as climate change and promoting eco-friendly practices and values among learners. The emphasis on lifelong learning will continue to grow, with online education providing flexible and accessible opportunities for individuals to acquire new skills, knowledge, and competencies throughout their lives, regardless of age or location. Online education plays a crucial role in addressing the evolving demands of the global workforce by offering professional development and upskilling opportunities to support career advancement and adaptability in an increasingly globalized and digitalized economy (Darnell, 2020).

Strategies For Educators on How to Incorporate Online Education to Support Global Contexts

Educators play a vital role in preparing students to navigate and contribute to a global society (Rahimi & Oh, 2024). Incorporating online education can serve as a powerful tool to support global perspectives in the classroom. The following strategies outline how a broad group of educators can integrate online learning environments to enhance global awareness and cultural sensitivity among students.

Collaborative Learning Projects:

One effective strategy is to design collaborative online learning projects that connect students with peers from different cultural backgrounds. Platforms such as ePals, Global SchoolNet, and Microsoft Teams facilitate cross-border collaborative projects. For instance, students can work together on a shared research project addressing a global issue, such as climate change or education inequality. Through regular video conferences and shared documents, participants can develop not only content knowledge but also empathy and respect for diverse viewpoints. This active engagement fosters a sense of global citizenship, encouraging students to appreciate and learn from one another's experiences and insights. (Vanoostveen, et al., 2019; Jeremic, et al., 2012)

Virtual Field Trips and Guest Speakers:

Another approach is to leverage technology for virtual field trips and guest lectures. Educators can use tools like Google Earth, YouTube, or specialized educational platforms to take students on virtual tours of historical sites, world landmarks, or cultural festivals. Additionally, inviting guest speakers from various backgrounds to share their experiences and expertise through webinars can enrich the learning experience. This exposure to different cultures enhances students' comprehension of global contexts and fuels their curiosity about the world around them. When educators pre-teach cultural norms and etiquette, they further equip students to engage meaningfully with diverse perspectives. (Stoddard, 2009; Patiar, et al., 2021)

Culturally Relevant Curriculum:

A key strategy for fostering a global mindset is the integration of a culturally relevant curriculum that reflects the diversity of the world. Educators can utilize online resources to access a wealth of multicultural literature, media, and case studies. Online educational platforms like Khan Academy and TED-Ed provide accessible content on global issues, historical events, and cultural practices that allow teachers to design lessons aimed at enhancing students' global awareness. By incorporating materials that represent various cultures and viewpoints, educators can challenge stereotypes and promote critical thinking about global interdependence. (Kumi-Yeboah & Amponsah, 2023; Chuang, et al., 2020)

Development of Digital Literacy Skills:

Finally, as students engage with online content from diverse sources, educators must emphasize the development of digital literacy skills. This includes teaching students how to discern credible sources, evaluate information critically, and respect copyright and intellectual property rights. By emphasizing ethical online practices and responsible digital citizenship, educators prepare students to engage thoughtfully in global conversations, ensuring that they are not only aware of global issues but also equipped to participate in finding solutions. Incorporating online education into the classroom provides a wealth of opportunities for educators to instill global awareness, cultural sensitivity, and digital literacy in their students. By implementing collaborative projects, facilitating virtual experiences, curating culturally relevant resources, and focusing on digital skills, educators can create a more inclusive and globally-minded learning environment. (Statti & Torres, 2020; Rafi, et al., 2019)

CONCLUSION

By incorporating strategies such as intercultural communication, collaboration and teamwork, global issues exploration, and virtual cultural exchanges, educators can create enriching and transformative learning experiences that transcend geographical boundaries and cultural differences. The future directions outlined in the chapter, including personalized learning, virtual reality technologies, sustainable education, and global partnerships, present exciting opportunities to further enhance the impact and reach of online education in a global context. As online education continues to evolve and expand, educators need to embrace these strategies and future directions to empower learners to navigate and thrive in a globalized society, where cultural competence, cross-cultural collaboration, and global citizenship are crucial for success and positive societal impact. Ultimately, by embracing these strategies and leveraging the power of online education in support of global contexts, educators can inspire a new generation of global citizens who are equipped with the knowledge, skills, and values to contribute positively to a more inclusive, interconnected, and sustainable world.

REFERENCES

Adedoyin, O. B., & Soykan, E. (2023). Covid-19 pandemic and online learning: The challenges and opportunities. *Interactive Learning Environments*, 31(2), 863–875. DOI: 10.1080/10494820.2020.1813180

Aduba, D. E., & Mayowa-Adebara, O. (2022). Online platforms used for teaching and learning during the COVID-19 era: The case of LIS students in Delta State University, Abraka. *The International Information & Library Review*, 54(1), 17–31. DOI: 10.1080/10572317.2020.1869903

Ahmad, T. (2020). A scenario-based approach to re-imagining the future of higher education which prepares students for the future of work. Higher Education. *Skills and Work-Based Learning*, 10(1), 217–238. DOI: 10.1108/HESWBL-12-2018-0136

Ahmad, T., Zhang, D., Huang, C., Zhang, H., Dai, N., Song, Y., & Chen, H. (2021). Artificial intelligence in the sustainable energy industry: Status Quo, challenges and opportunities. *Journal of Cleaner Production*, 289, 125834. DOI: 10.1016/j.jclepro.2021.125834

Ajayi, F. A., & Udeh, C. A.Funmilayo Aribidesi AjayiChioma Ann Udeh. (2024). Review of workforce upskilling initiatives for emerging technologies in IT. *International Journal of Management & Entrepreneurship Research*, 6(4), 1119–1137. DOI: 10.51594/ijmer.v6i4.1003

Al-Adwan, A., & Smedley, J. (2012). Implementing e-learning in the Jordanian Higher Education System: Factors affecting impact. International Journal of Education and Development using ICT, 8(1).

Alam, A. (2022). Platform utilizi blockchain technology for eLearning and online education for open sharing of academic proficiency and progress records. In Smart data intelligence [Singapore: Springer Nature Singapore.]. *Proceedings of ICSMDI*, 2022, 307–320.

Amato, C. (2021). *Community college faculty and competency-based education: a grounded theory study* (Doctoral dissertation, Franklin University).

Ansell, C., & Gash, A. (2018). Collaborative platforms as a governance strategy. *Journal of Public Administration: Research and Theory*, 28(1), 16–32. DOI: 10.1093/jopart/mux030

Asad, M. M., Naz, A., Churi, P., & Tahanzadeh, M. M. (2021). Virtual reality as a pedagogical tool to enhance experiential learning: A systematic literature review. *Education Research International*, 2021(1), 7061623. DOI: 10.1155/2021/7061623

Ayeni, O. O., Al Hamad, N. M., Chisom, O. N., Osawaru, B., & Adewusi, O. E. (2024). AI in education: A review of personalized learning and educational technology. *GSC Advanced Research and Reviews*, 18(2), 261–271. DOI: 10.30574/gscarr.2024.18.2.0062

Bennani, S., Maalel, A., & Ben Ghezala, H. (2022). Adaptive gamification in E-learning: A literature review and future challenges. *Computer Applications in Engineering Education*, 30(2), 628–642. DOI: 10.1002/cae.22477

Bhutoria, A. (2022). Personalized education and artificial intelligence in the United States, China, and India: A systematic review using a human-in-the-loop model. *Computers and Education: Artificial Intelligence*, 3, 100068. DOI: 10.1016/j.caeai.2022.100068

Bizami, N. A., Tasir, Z., & Kew, S. N. (2023). Innovative pedagogical principles and technological tools capabilities for immersive blended learning: A systematic literature review. *Education and Information Technologies*, 28(2), 1373–1425. DOI: 10.1007/s10639-022-11243-w PMID: 35919874

Bonde, S., Briant, C., Firenze, P., Hanavan, J., Huang, A., Li, M., Narayanan, N. C., Parthasarathy, D., & Zhao, H. (2016). Making choices: Ethical decisions in a global context. *Science and Engineering Ethics*, 22(2), 343–366. DOI: 10.1007/s11948-015-9641-5 PMID: 25962719

Bozkurt, A., Jung, I., Xiao, J., Vladimirschi, V., Schuwer, R., Egorov, G., Lambert, S., Al-Freih, M., Pete, J., Olcott, D.Jr, & Rodes, V. (2020). A global outlook to the interruption of education due to COVID-19 pandemic: Navigating in a time of uncertainty and crisis. *Asian Journal of Distance Education*, 15(1), 1–126.

Calia, C., Guerra, C., Reid, C., Marley, C., Barrera, P., Oshodi, A. G. T., & Boden, L. (2022). Developing an evidence-base to guide ethical action in global challenges research in complex and fragile contexts: A scoping review of the literature. *Ethics & Social Welfare*, 16(1), 54–72. DOI: 10.1080/17496535.2021.1916830

Carta, F. (2021). Covid pandemic-2019: Upskilling and reskilling pathways to respond to new professional needs imposed by digitalization. In *Edulearn21 Proceedings* (pp. 5641–5650). IATED. DOI: 10.21125/edulearn.2021.1145

Casey, K. (2018). Moving toward Mastery: Growing, Developing and Sustaining Educators for Competency-Based Education. Competency Works Report. *iNACOL)*.

Chasokela, D. (2024). Exploring the Virtual Frontier: AR and VR for Engineering Skills Development. In R. Siva Subramanian, M. Nalini, & J. Aswini (Eds.), *Navigating the Augmented and Virtual Frontiers in Engineering* (pp. 62-81). IGI Global. https://doi.org/10.4018/979-8-3693-5613-5.ch004

Chasokela, D. & Ncube, C. M. (2024). Leveraging Technology for Organizational Efficiency and Effectiveness in Higher Education. In M. Kayyali (Ed.), *Building Organizational Capacity and Strategic Management in Academia* (pp. 381-410). IGI Global. https://doi.org/10.4018/979-8-3693-6967-8.ch014

Chasokela, D. & Mpofu, S. (2024). Towards Addressing 21st-Century Digital Transformation Skills: The Zimbabwean Higher Education Context. In M. Kayyali (Ed.), *Building Resiliency in Higher Education: Globalization, Digital Skills, and Student Wellness* (pp. 424-442). IGI Global. https://doi.org/10.4018/979-8-3693-5483-4.ch022

Chhatlani, C. K. (2023). Review the Role of Holistic Learning in Cultivating Global Citizenship Skills. EIKI Journal of Effective Teaching Methods, 1(2).

Chigbu, B. I., Ngwevu, V., & Jojo, A. (2023). The effectiveness of innovative pedagogy in the industry 4.0: Educational ecosystem perspective. *Social Sciences & Humanities Open*, 7(1), 100419. DOI: 10.1016/j.ssaho.2023.100419

Chuang, H. H., Shih, C. L., & Cheng, M. M. (2020). Teachers' perceptions of culturally responsive teaching in technology-supported learning environments. *British Journal of Educational Technology*, 51(6), 2442–2460. DOI: 10.1111/bjet.12921

Curtin, A. L., & Sarju, J. P. (2021). Students as partners: Co-creation of online learning to deliver high-quality, personalized content. In *Advances in Online Chemistry Education* (pp. 135-163).

Curtis, V. (2018). *Online citizen science and the widening of academia*. Palgrave Macmillan. DOI: 10.1007/978-3-319-77664-4

Darnell, J. D. (2020). *Next evolution of workforce experiential learning for 21st century global access learners*. Pepperdine University.

Dennen, V. P., & Bong, J.Dennen and Bong. (2018). Cross-cultural dialogues in an open online course: Navigating national and organizational cultural differences. *TechTrends*, 62(4), 383–392. DOI: 10.1007/s11528-018-0276-7

Dhawan, S. (2020). Online learning: A panacea in the time of COVID-19 crisis. *Journal of Educational Technology Systems*, 49(1), 5–22. DOI: 10.1177/0047239520934018

Dutta, S., Ranjan, S., Mishra, S., Sharma, V., Hewage, P., & Iwendi, C. (2024, February). Enhancing Educational Adaptability: A Review and Analysis of AI-Driven Adaptive Learning Platforms. In *2024 4th International Conference on Innovative Practices in Technology and Management (ICIPTM)* (pp. 1-5). IEEE. DOI: 10.1109/ICIPTM59628.2024.10563448

Espinoza, D., & Reed, D. (2018). Wireless technologies and policies for connecting rural areas in emerging countries: A case study in rural Peru. *Digital Policy. Regulation & Governance*, 20(5), 479–511. DOI: 10.1108/DPRG-03-2018-0009

Evolve Project Team. (2020). The impact of virtual exchange on student learning in higher education: EVOLVE project report.

Gallup, A. (2024). What We Know About Registered Apprenticeship: A Systematic Review and Synthesis of 30 Years of Empirical Research. *Economic Development Quarterly*, 38(1), 25–39. DOI: 10.1177/08912424231196792

Gambs, S. (2019). Privacy and Ethical Challenges in Big Data. In Zincir-Heywood, N., Bonfante, G., Debbabi, M., & Garcia-Alfaro, J. (Eds.), Lecture Notes in Computer Science: Vol. 11358. *Foundations and Practice of Security. FPS 2018*. Springer., DOI: 10.1007/978-3-030-18419-3_2

Gasparro, K. E. (2019). *Crowdfunding Our Cities: Three Perspectives on Stakeholder Dynamics During Innovative Infrastructure Delivery*. Stanford University.

Gibson, K. L., Rimmington, G. M., & Landwehr-Brown, M. (2008). Developing global awareness and responsible world citizenship with global learning. *Roeper Review*, 30(1), 11–23. DOI: 10.1080/02783190701836270

Goh, M. (2012). Teaching with cultural intelligence: Developing multiculturally educated and globally engaged citizens. *Asia Pacific Journal of Education*, 32(4), 395–415. DOI: 10.1080/02188791.2012.738679

Guardia, L., Clougher, D., Anderson, T., & Maina, M. (2021). IDEAS for transforming higher education: An overview of ongoing trends and challenges. *International Review of Research in Open and Distance Learning*, 22(2), 166–184. DOI: 10.19173/irrodl.v22i2.5206

Gudino Paredes, S., Jasso Pena, F. D. J., & de La Fuente Alcazar, J. M. (2021). Remotely proctored exams: Integrity assurance in online education? *Distance Education*, 42(2), 200–218. DOI: 10.1080/01587919.2021.1910495

Hernandez-de-Menendez, M., Vallejo Guevara, A., Tudon Martinez, J. C., Hernandez Alcantara, D., & Morales-Menendez, R. (2019). Active learning in engineering education. A review of fundamentals, best practices and experiences. [IJIDeM]. *International Journal on Interactive Design and Manufacturing*, 13(3), 909–922. DOI: 10.1007/s12008-019-00557-8

Holmes, M. R., Tracy, E. M., Painter, L. L., Oestreich, T., & Park, H. (2015). Moving from flipcharts to the flipped classroom: Using technology-driven teaching methods to promote active learning in foundation and advanced masters social work courses. *Clinical Social Work Journal*, 43(2), 215–224. DOI: 10.1007/s10615-015-0521-x

Hong, Y., Saab, N., & Admiraal, W. (2024). Approaches and game elements used to tailor digital gamification for learning: A systematic literature review. *Computers & Education*, 212, 105000. DOI: 10.1016/j.compedu.2024.105000

Ingkavara, T., Panjaburee, P., Srisawasdi, N., & Sajjapanroj, S. (2022). The use of a personalized learning approach to implementing self-regulated online learning. *Computers and Education: Artificial Intelligence*, 3, 100086. DOI: 10.1016/j.caeai.2022.100086

Jackson, L. (2016). Globalization and education. In Oxford research encyclopedia of education. DOI: 10.1093/acrefore/9780190264093.013.52

Jeremic, Z., Milikic, N., Jovanovic, J., Brkovic, M., & Radulovic, F. (2012). Using online presence to improve online collaborative learning. [iJET]. *International Journal of Emerging Technologies in Learning*, 7(S1), 7. DOI: 10.3991/ijet.v7iS1.1918

Johnson, D., & Samora, D. (2016). The potential transformation of higher education through computer-based adaptive learning systems. *Global Education Journal*, *2016*(1).

Kara, N., Cubukcuoglu, B., & Elci, A. (2020). Using social media to support teaching and learning in higher education: An analysis of personal narratives.

Kebritchi, M., Lipschuetz, A., & Santiague, L. (2017). Issues and challenges for teaching successful online courses in higher education: A literature review. *Journal of Educational Technology Systems*, 46(1), 4–29. DOI: 10.1177/0047239516661713

Kopish, M., & Marques, W. (2020). Leveraging technology to promote global citizenship in teacher education in the United States and Brazil. *Research in Social Sciences and Technology*, 5(1), 45–69. DOI: 10.46303/ressat.05.01.3

Kremenova, I., & Gajdos, M. (2019). Decentralized networks: The future internet. *Mobile Networks and Applications*, 24(6), 2016–2023. DOI: 10.1007/s11036-018-01211-5

Kukulska-Hulme, A. (2012). How should the higher education workforce adapt to advancements in technology for teaching and learning? *The Internet and Higher Education*, 15(4), 247–254. DOI: 10.1016/j.iheduc.2011.12.002

Kumar, A., Krishnamurthi, R., Bhatia, S., Kaushik, K., Ahuja, N. J., Nayyar, A., & Masud, M. (2021). Blended learning tools and practices: A comprehensive analysis. *IEEE Access : Practical Innovations, Open Solutions*, 9, 85151–85197. DOI: 10.1109/ACCESS.2021.3085844

Kumi-Yeboah, A., & Amponsah, S. (2023). An exploratory study of instructors' perceptions on inclusion of culturally responsive pedagogy in online education. *British Journal of Educational Technology*, 54(4), 878–897. DOI: 10.1111/bjet.13299

Kundu, A., & Bej, T. (2021). COVID-19 response: Students' readiness for shifting classes online. *Corporate Governance (Bradford)*, 21(6), 1250–1270. DOI: 10.1108/CG-09-2020-0377

Kuntz, J. R. C., Kuntz, J. R., Elenkov, D., & Nabirukhina, A. (2013). Characterizing ethical cases: A cross-cultural investigation of individual differences, organizational climate, and leadership on ethical decision-making. *Journal of Business Ethics*, 113(2), 317–331. DOI: 10.1007/s10551-012-1306-6

Lacroix, P. (2019). Big data privacy and ethical challenges. Big Data, Big Challenges: A Healthcare Perspective: Background, Issues, Solutions and Research Directions, 101-111.

Li, L. (2022). Reskilling and upskilling the future-ready workforce for Industry 4.0 and beyond. *Information Systems Frontiers*, 1–16. PMID: 35855776

Lupac, P. (2018). *Beyond the digital divide: Contextualizing the information society*. Emerald Publishing Limited. DOI: 10.1108/9781787565470

Maghsudi, S., Lan, A., Xu, J., & van Der Schaar, M. (2021). Personalized education in the artificial intelligence era: What to expect next. *IEEE Signal Processing Magazine*, 38(3), 37–50. DOI: 10.1109/MSP.2021.3055032

Major, J., Tait-McCutcheon, S. L., Averill, R., Gilbert, A., Knewstubb, B., Mortlock, A., & Jones, L. (2020). Pedagogical innovation in higher education: Defining what we mean. [IJITLHE]. *International Journal of Innovative Teaching and Learning in Higher Education*, 1(3), 1–18. DOI: 10.4018/IJITLHE.2020070101

Marienko, M., Nosenko, Y., & Shyshkina, M. (2020). Personalization of learning using adaptive technologies and augmented reality. *arXiv preprint arXiv:2011.05802*. DOI: 10.31812/123456789/4418

McHaney, R. (2023). *The new digital shoreline: How Web 2.0 and millennials are revolutionizing higher education.* Taylor & Francis. DOI: 10.4324/9781003447979

Mishan, F. (2022). Language learning materials in the digital era. In *The Routledge Handbook of materials development for language teaching* (pp. 17–29). Routledge. DOI: 10.4324/b22783-3

Moore, M. L. (2020). *Qualitative Exploration of Instructional Designers' Use of Microlearning for Formal Workplace Training.* Capella University.

Msekelwa, P. Z. (2023). Beyond The Borders Global Collaboration in Open Distance Education through Virtual Exchanges. *Journal of Knowledge Learning and Science Technology ISSN: 2959-6386 (online), 2*(2), 1-13.

Naidu, S. (2008). Enabling time, pace, and place independence. In *Handbook of Research on Educational Communications and Technology* (pp. 259–268). Routledge.

Nicholas, G., Bell, C., Coombe, R., Welch, J. R., Noble, B., Anderson, J., & Watkins, J. (2010). Intellectual property issues in heritage management: Part 2: Legal dimensions, ethical considerations, and collaborative research practices. *Heritage Management, 3*(1), 117–147. DOI: 10.1179/hma.2010.3.1.117

O'Dowd, R. (2016). Learning from the past and looking to the future of online intercultural exchange. In *Online Intercultural Exchange* (pp. 273–294). Routledge. DOI: 10.4324/9781315678931

O'Dowd, R. (2021). Virtual exchange: Moving forward into the next decade. *Computer Assisted Language Learning, 34*(3), 209–224. DOI: 10.1080/09588221.2021.1902201

O'Keefe, L., Rafferty, J., Gunder, A., & Vignare, K. (2020). *Delivering High-Quality Instruction Online in Response to COVID-19: Faculty Playbook.* Online Learning Consortium.

Oppenheimer, M., LaVan, H., & Martin, W. F. (2015). A framework for understanding ethical and efficiency issues in pharmaceutical intellectual property litigation. *Journal of Business Ethics, 132*(3), 505–524. DOI: 10.1007/s10551-014-2365-7

Owens, A. D., & Hite, R. L. (2022). Enhancing student communication competencies in STEM using virtual global collaboration project-based learning. *Research in Science & Technological Education, 40*(1), 76–102. DOI: 10.1080/02635143.2020.1778663

Palvia, S., Aeron, P., Gupta, P., Mahapatra, D., Parida, R., Rosner, R., & Sindhi, S. (2018). Online education: Worldwide status, challenges, trends, and implications. *Journal of Global Information Technology Management, 21*(4), 233–241. DOI: 10.1080/1097198X.2018.1542262

Patiar, A., Kensbock, S., Benckendorff, P., Robinson, R., Richardson, S., Wang, Y., & Lee, A. (2021). Hospitality students' acquisition of knowledge and skills through a virtual field trip experience. *Journal of Hospitality & Tourism Education*, 33(1), 14–28. DOI: 10.1080/10963758.2020.1726768

Paudel, P. (2021). Online education: Benefits, challenges and strategies during and after COVID-19 in higher education. [IJonSE]. *International Journal on Studies in Education*, 3(2), 70–85. DOI: 10.46328/ijonse.32

Pesare, E., Roselli, T., Corriero, N., & Rossano, V. (2016). Game-based learning and gamification to promote engagement and motivation in medical learning contexts. *Smart Learning Environments*, 3(1), 1–21. DOI: 10.1186/s40561-016-0028-0

Protopsaltis, S., & Baum, S. (2019). Does online education live up to its promise? A look at the evidence and implications for federal policy. Center for Educational Policy Evaluation, 1-50.

Quamar, M. M., Al-Ramadan, B., Khan, K., Shafiullah, M., & El Ferik, S. (2023). Advancements and applications of drone-integrated geographic information system technology—A review. *Remote Sensing (Basel)*, 15(20), 5039. DOI: 10.3390/rs15205039

Rafi, M., JianMing, Z., & Ahmad, K. (2019). Technology integration for students' information and digital literacy education in academic libraries. *Information Discovery and Delivery*, 47(4), 203–217. DOI: 10.1108/IDD-07-2019-0049

Rahimi, R. A., & Oh, G. S. (2024). Rethinking the role of educators in the 21st century: navigating globalization, technology, and pandemics. Journal of Marketing Analytics, 1-16.

Rejeb, A., Rejeb, K., Simske, S., & Treiblmaier, H. (2021). Humanitarian drones: A review and research agenda. *Internet of Things : Engineering Cyber Physical Human Systems*, 16, 100434. DOI: 10.1016/j.iot.2021.100434

Resei, C., Friedl, C., & Zur, A. (2018). MOOCs and entrepreneurship education-contributions, opportunities and gaps. *International Entrepreneurship Review*, 4(3), 151.

Resta, P., & Laferriere, T. (2015). Digital equity and intercultural education. *Education and Information Technologies*, 20(4), 743–756. DOI: 10.1007/s10639-015-9419-z

Rizvi, F. (2019). Global interconnectivity and its ethical challenges in education. *Asia Pacific Education Review*, 20(2), 315–326. DOI: 10.1007/s12564-019-09596-y

Rummel, N., & Spada, H. (2005). Learning to collaborate: An instructional approach to promoting collaborative problem-solving in computer-mediated settings. *Journal of the Learning Sciences*, 14(2), 201–241. DOI: 10.1207/s15327809jls1402_2

Salas-Pilco, S. Z., Yang, Y., & Zhang, Z. (2022). Student engagement in online learning in Latin American higher education during the COVID-19 pandemic: A systematic review. *British Journal of Educational Technology*, 53(3), 593–619. DOI: 10.1111/bjet.13190 PMID: 35600418

Saleem, A. N., Noori, N. M., & Ozdamli, F. (2022). Gamification applications in E-learning: A literature review. *Technology. Knowledge and Learning*, 27(1), 139–159. DOI: 10.1007/s10758-020-09487-x

Saykili, A. (2018). Distance education: Definitions, generations and key concepts and future directions. *International Journal of Contemporary Educational Research*, 5(1), 2–17.

Searson, M., Hancock, M., Soheil, N., & Shepherd, G. (2015). Digital citizenship within global contexts. *Education and Information Technologies*, 20(4), 729–741. DOI: 10.1007/s10639-015-9426-0

Shonfeld, M., Cotnam-Kappel, M., Judge, M., Ng, C. Y., Ntebutse, J. G., Williamson-Leadley, S., & Yildiz, M. N. (2021). Learning in digital environments: A model for cross-cultural alignment. *Educational Technology Research and Development*, 69(4), 1–20. DOI: 10.1007/s11423-021-09967-6 PMID: 33654347

Siergiejczyk, G. (2020). Virtual international exchange as a high-impact learning tool for more inclusive, equitable and diverse classrooms. *European Journal of Open. Distance and E-Learning*, 23(1), 1–17. DOI: 10.2478/eurodl-2020-0001

Singh Dubey, R., Paul, J., & Tewari, V. (2022). The soft skills gap: A bottleneck in the talent supply in emerging economies. *International Journal of Human Resource Management*, 33(13), 2630–2661. DOI: 10.1080/09585192.2020.1871399

Skenderi, F., & Skenderi, L. (2023). Fostering Innovation in Higher Education: Transforming Teaching for Tomorrow. *Knowledge-International Journal*, 60(2), 251–255.

Statti, A., & Torres, K. M. (2020). Digital literacy: The need for technology integration and its impact on learning and engagement in community school environments. *Peabody Journal of Education*, 95(1), 90–100. DOI: 10.1080/0161956X.2019.1702426

Stoddard, J. (2009). Toward a virtual field trip model for social studies. *Contemporary Issues in Technology & Teacher Education*, 9(4), 412–438.

Sun, A., & Chen, X. (2016). Online education and its effective practice: A research review. *Journal of Information Technology Education*, 15, 15. DOI: 10.28945/3502

Svensson, L., & Wihlborg, M. (2010). Internationalizing the content of higher education: The need for a curriculum perspective. *Higher Education*, 60(6), 595–613. DOI: 10.1007/s10734-010-9318-6

Szobonya, P., & Roche, C. M. (2023). Virtual Exchange Experiences Energized by an Educational Technology Paradigm Shift. In *Handbook of Research on Current Trends in Cybersecurity and Educational Technology* (pp. 267–297). IGI Global. DOI: 10.4018/978-1-6684-6092-4.ch016

Taylor, C., Dewsbury, B., & Brame, C. (2022). Technology, equity, and inclusion in the virtual education space. In *Technologies in Biomedical and Life Sciences Education: Approaches and Evidence of Efficacy for Learning* (pp. 35–60). Springer International Publishing. DOI: 10.1007/978-3-030-95633-2_2

Thomson, A. M., Smith-Tolken, A. R., Naidoo, A. V., & Bringle, R. G. (2011). Service learning and community engagement: A comparison of three national contexts. *Voluntas*, 22(2), 214–237. DOI: 10.1007/s11266-010-9133-9

Toprak, E., Ozkanal, B., Kaya, S., & Aydin, S. (2007). What do learners and instructors of online learning environments think about ethics in e-learning? A case study from Anadolu University. In European Association of Distance Teaching Universities Conference.

Torres Vega, M., Liaskos, C., Abadal, S., Papapetrou, E., Jain, A., Mouhouche, B., & Famaey, J. (2020). Immersive interconnected virtual and augmented reality: A 5G and IoT perspective. *Journal of Network and Systems Management*, 28(4), 796–826. DOI: 10.1007/s10922-020-09545-w

Trede, F., Bowles, W., & Bridges, D. (2013). Developing intercultural competence and global citizenship through international experiences: Academics' perceptions. *Intercultural Education*, 24(5), 442–455. DOI: 10.1080/14675986.2013.825578

Tshuma, L. S. & Chasokela, D. (2024). The Rise of Online Learning and the Technological Revolution in Higher Education. In M. Kayyali & B. Christiansen (Eds.), *Insights into International Higher Education Leadership and the Skills Gap* (pp. 447-470). IGI Global. https://doi.org/10.4018/979-8-3693-3443-0.ch017

Tzimas, D., & Demetriadis, S. (2021). Ethical issues in learning analytics: A review of the field. *Educational Technology Research and Development*, 69(2), 1101–1133. DOI: 10.1007/s11423-021-09977-4

Van der Hijden, P., & Martin, M. (2023). *Short courses, micro-credentials, and flexible learning pathways: A blueprint for policy development and action.* International Institute for Educational Planning.

Vanoostveen, R., Desjardins, F., & Bullock, S. (2019). Professional development learning environments (PDLEs) embedded in a collaborative online learning environment (COLE): Moving towards a new conception of online professional learning. *Education and Information Technologies*, 24(2), 1863–1900. DOI: 10.1007/s10639-018-9686-6

Vassilakopoulou, P., & Hustad, E. (2023). Bridging digital divides: A literature review and research agenda for information systems research. *Information Systems Frontiers*, 25(3), 955–969. DOI: 10.1007/s10796-020-10096-3 PMID: 33424421

Vlachopoulos, D., & Makri, A. (2019). Online communication and interaction in distance higher education: A framework study of good practice. *International Review of Education*, 65(4), 605–632. DOI: 10.1007/s11159-019-09792-3

Vu, P., Fredrickson, S., & Moore, C. (Eds.). (2016). *Handbook of research on innovative pedagogies and technologies for online learning in higher education.* IGI Global.

Waks, L. J. (2019). Massive open online courses and the future of higher education. *Contemporary Technologies in Education: Maximizing Student Engagement, Motivation, and Learning*, 183-213.

Zheng, L., Long, M., Zhong, L., & Gyasi, J. F. (2022). The effectiveness of technology-facilitated personalized learning on learning achievements and learning perceptions: A meta-analysis. *Education and Information Technologies*, 27(8), 11807–11830. DOI: 10.1007/s10639-022-11092-7

Zhu, Q., & Jesiek, B. K. (2020). Practicing engineering ethics in the global context: A comparative study of expert and novice approaches to cross-cultural ethical situations. *Science and Engineering Ethics*, 26(4), 2097–2120. DOI: 10.1007/s11948-019-00154-8 PMID: 31721025

KEY TERMS AND DEFINITIONS

Asynchronous Learning: Learning approach that allows students to engage with course materials and participate in discussions at their own pace and time, without the need for real-time interaction with instructors or peers.

Digital Divide: The gap between individuals or communities who have access to digital technologies and resources and those who do not, often leading to disparities in educational opportunities and outcomes.

Digital Literacy: The ability to access, evaluate, and effectively use digital technologies and information to navigate and participate in today's digital society.

Global Citizenship: The idea of having a sense of belonging to a global community, advocating for social justice, human rights, and environmental sustainability, and promoting cross-cultural understanding and cooperation on a global scale.

Global Collaboration: Working together across cultural, geographic, or disciplinary boundaries to address global challenges, foster cross-cultural understanding, and promote cooperation and exchange of ideas.

Global Education: An educational approach that emphasizes the interconnectedness and interdependence of individuals and societies around the world, promoting global awareness, understanding, and engagement.

Language Barriers: Challenges or obstacles that arise from differences in language proficiency, communication styles, and cultural norms, impacting effective communication and collaboration in educational settings.

Multicultural Education: Educational approach that values and incorporates diverse cultural perspectives, experiences, and backgrounds in the curriculum to promote understanding and respect for diverse cultures.

Online Learning: Educational delivery method that uses the internet and digital technologies to facilitate learning outside of a traditional classroom setting, often providing flexibility and accessibility to learners.

Technology-Enhanced Learning: Integrating technology tools and resources into educational practices to enhance learning outcomes and engage learners in interactive and innovative ways.

Virtual Exchange: A form of online collaboration that enables students from different locations to interact, communicate, and collaborate on projects, promoting intercultural dialogue and understanding.

Chapter 3
Fostering Self-Efficacy for Higher Education Online Instructors

Doris Chasokela
https://orcid.org/0009-0001-5983-8508
National University of Science and Technology, Zimbabwe

Lungisani Mpofu
National University of Science and Technology, Zimbabwe

ABSTRACT

This book chapter explores the best practices and strategies that can be used by higher education online instructors to foster self-efficacy among their students. Based on insights from higher education online faculty, the chapter discusses how instructors can create a positive learning environment, promote learner autonomy, and provide appropriate levels of support and feedback. It also explores how instructors can use technology to facilitate effective communication and collaboration, and how they can adapt their teaching methods to the unique needs of online learners. Ultimately, the chapter aims to help higher education online instructors create an effective learning experience for their students. The specific strategies and best practices are discussed in the chapter. The chapter outlines particular tools and technologies that can be used to foster self-efficacy, such as discussion forums, collaborative learning tools, and interactive learning activities.

DOI: 10.4018/979-8-3693-4407-1.ch003

INTRODUCTION

Fostering self-efficacy among higher education online instructors is crucial for ensuring high-quality online learning experiences for students. Self-efficacy refers to an individual's belief in their ability to perform a particular task or achieve a particular goal (Bandura, 1977, 1986, 1997). When fostering self-efficacy among online instructors one can consider clear communication; professional development; peer support; work-life balance; recognition and feedback; leadership support; transparency; autonomy; workflow management; personal growth; student feedback and professional identity. Providing clear and frequent communication to online instructors can help them feel supported and confident in their role. Providing online instructors with opportunities for professional development, such as workshops, webinars, and mentorship, can help them develop new skills and knowledge, boosting their confidence (Johnson, et al., 2019). Facilitating peer-to-peer support networks can help online instructors learn from each other, share best practices, and build their self-efficacy. Encouraging work-life balance for online instructors can help them avoid burnout and maintain their motivation.

Recognizing and providing feedback to online instructors for their efforts and achievements can help them feel valued and appreciated (Prilop, et al., 2021). Providing effective leadership support, including consistent communication and collaborative decision-making, can help online instructors feel supported and valued in their role. Ensuring transparency and clarity in online instructors' roles and responsibilities can help them feel confident and competent in their work. Providing online instructors with autonomy and flexibility in their work can help them feel ownership and control over their work. Providing effective workflow management tools and resources can help online instructors feel organized and productive in their work, supporting their self-efficacy. Encouraging personal growth and development opportunities for online instructors can help them feel challenged and engaged in their work, supporting their self-efficacy (Ventura, et al. 2015). According to Hsia, et al. (2016), collecting and sharing student feedback with online instructors can provide valuable insights into their performance and help them feel supported in their work. Promoting a strong sense of professional identity among online instructors can help them feel confident and competent in their work.

Horvitz, et al. (2015) and Zheng, et al. (2020) posit that fostering self-efficacy among online instructors in higher education is a global concern. Several perspectives on fostering self-efficacy among online instructors in different regions are highlighted. In the United States and Canada, online learning has become increasingly common in institutions of higher learning (Chau, 2010; Picciano, et al., 2010). Many institutions are investing in professional development programs and support services for online instructors to help them feel confident and effective in their work. In

Europe, online learning is also becoming more prevalent in higher education, with many universities and colleges adopting virtual learning platforms and innovative teaching methods (Gaebel, et al., 2018). However, there is still some variation in the level of support and resources provided to online instructors, with some countries investing more heavily in professional development and support services.

In Asia, many countries are investing heavily in online learning, particularly in countries such as China, India, and South Korea (Phan & Coxhead, 2014). In Africa, online learning is less widespread than in other continents due to issues such as limited internet connectivity and access to technology (Faturoti, 2022). However, there is growing interest in online learning, and some countries, such as South Africa and Kenya, are investing in digital infrastructure and online education initiatives. In Latin America, the adoption of online learning in higher education varies across countries, with Brazil, Mexico, and Argentina leading the way in terms of investment and innovation in online education (Salas-Pilco, et al., 2022). In Oceania, Australia and New Zealand have well-developed online learning infrastructure and support for online instructors (Paul et al., 2021). Both countries have invested in professional development programs and resources to support online instructors. In the Middle East, some countries, such as the United Arab Emirates and Qatar, are investing in online learning, while others have more limited resources and infrastructure for online education (Ben Hassen, 2021; Kamel, 2014). Overall, fostering self-efficacy among online instructors in higher education is a global concern that varies across regions, but is increasingly recognized as critical to supporting the success of online learning initiatives.

To foster self-efficacy among higher education online instructors, our methodology is based on a multi-faceted approach that includes assessment, development, support, and evaluation (Pumptow & Brahm, 2021). The first step is to conduct a comprehensive needs assessment to identify the specific challenges and barriers that instructors face in online teaching environments. This assessment may involve surveys, focus groups, and interviews to gather insights into their experiences, technological proficiency, and areas where they feel less confident. Based on this data, one can design targeted professional development programs that address identified gaps, emphasizing pedagogical strategies, technology integration, and best practices for online engagement. Workshops and training sessions incorporate hands-on activities, real-world scenarios, and opportunities for peer collaboration to enhance learning outcomes (Lotrecchiano, et al., 2013). The second component of our roadmap involves establishing mentorship and peer support networks, pairing novice instructors with experienced faculty members to create a culture of knowledge sharing and encouragement. Regular check-ins and collaborative teaching projects can be facilitated to build relationships and foster a sense of community among instructors. This peer mentoring not only boosts individual self-efficacy but also cultivates a supportive environment where best practices in online education are shared and celebrated. According to Ndukwe & Daniel (2020), integrating a systematic feedback mechanism, allows instructors to reflect on their teaching experiences and receive constructive input from peers and students, further enhancing their confidence through actionable insights.

Finally, the effectiveness of our efforts will be evaluated through ongoing assessments of instructor performance and student outcomes, utilizing metrics such as student engagement, course completion rates, and instructor self-reported confidence levels. By iteratively refining the professional development programs and support structures based on feedback, sustainability and growth of self-efficacy among online educators can be ensured. This comprehensive methodology not only aims to empower instructors but also aligns their professional growth with the overarching goal of enhancing student learning experiences in online higher education

Creating A Positive Learning Environment to Foster Self-Efficacy For Higher Education Online Instructors

Creating a positive learning environment is essential for fostering self-efficacy among higher education online instructors (Fong, et al., 2019). By establishing a supportive, collaborative, and empowering atmosphere, instructors are more likely to believe in their capabilities to effectively navigate the challenges of online instruction, engage with students, and facilitate meaningful learning experiences. According to Kutsyuruba, et al. (2019) providing opportunities for professional development, mentorship, and feedback, as well as promoting a culture of continuous improvement and reflection, can help instructors build confidence, motivation, and resilience in their roles. This ultimately enhances their efficacy and effectiveness in the online teaching environment.

To create a positive learning environment among higher education online instructors, there are several strategies to be followed. Building a sense of community among online instructors can help foster collaboration, support, and shared learning experiences (Yilmaz, 2016). Encouraging open and frequent communication among online instructors, students, and support staff can help everyone feel connected and supported, promoting a positive learning environment. Facilitating feedback and constructive criticism among online instructors, students, and administrators can help online instructors feel valued and supported in their work (Hampton, et al., 2020). Celebrating successes, both large and small, can help online instructors feel recognized and motivated in their work. Recognizing and celebrating diversity among online instructors can help create a more inclusive and welcoming learning environment, fostering a sense of belonging (Coombs, 2022). Encouraging resilience among online instructors, such as through mindfulness practices, can help them cope with challenges and setbacks (Yang, 2021). Promoting self-care and work-life balance among online instructors can help prevent burnout and promote well-being. Encouraging innovation and creativity among online instructors can help them feel empowered and engaged in their work. Providing opportunities for professional growth and development, such as mentorship or leadership opportunities, can help online instructors feel motivated and supported in their work. Providing online instructors with access to supportive resources, such as instructional design tools, learning management systems, and online support forums, can help them feel empowered and effective in their work. Promoting reflection and metacognition among online instructors can help them understand their strengths and weaknesses. (Farley & Burbules, 2022; Fong, et al., 2019; Tsai, et al., 2011, Shee and Lip, 2022)

Stakeholders in Charge of Contributing to Creating a Positive Learning Environment

Creating a positive learning environment for higher education online instructors is a shared responsibility between several stakeholders. Online instructors have a primary role in creating a positive learning environment for themselves and their students, by adopting inclusive, engaging, and supportive teaching practices (Chakraborty & Nafukho, 2015). The institution has a responsibility to provide online instructors with the resources, support, and professional development opportunities they need to be successful, in promoting a positive learning environment. Students have a role in creating a positive learning environment by engaging with course material and providing feedback to their instructors, helping to support their self-efficacy. Educational technology providers play a key role in providing the platforms, tools, and resources that online instructors need to deliver high-quality learning experiences, promoting a positive learning environment. Academic administrators are responsible for setting policies and procedures that promote a positive learning environment for online instructors, supporting their self-efficacy and professional development. Professional organizations in higher education can provide opportunities for networking, collaboration, and professional development, contributing to a positive learning environment for online instructors.

Promoting Learner Autonomy

Promoting learner autonomy is a key component of effective online instruction in higher education. According to Hu and Zhang (2017), learner autonomy refers to the ability of students to take charge of their learning, set goals, plan their work, and monitor their progress. There are several key aspects of promoting learner autonomy in online learning such as self-regulation; feedback; collaboration; choice and control; reflection; problem-solving and adaptability (Alt & Naamati-Schneider, 2021; Wong, et al., 2019). Dembo et al., (2013); Onah (2021) and Wong, et al., (2021) cite that developing self-regulation skills, such as time management, organization, and goal-setting, can help students become more independent learners, supporting their autonomy. Providing timely and meaningful feedback to students on their progress and performance can help them understand their strengths and weaknesses, supporting their self-regulation and autonomy. Supporting collaborative learning experiences, such as peer review, group projects, and online discussions, can help students develop their communication and leadership skills, promoting their autonomy. Giving students choice and control over their learning, such as in the selection of course materials, assignments, or learning activities, can support their autonomy and engagement. Encouraging reflection on learning experiences, such as through personal journals, blogs, or online discussion forums, can help students develop self-awareness and metacognition, supporting their autonomy (de Andres Martinez, 2012; DeMink-Carthew, et al., 2020). Incorporating problem-solving activities into online courses can help students develop critical thinking and decision-making skills, supporting their autonomy in learning and decision-making. Supporting adaptable learning experiences, such as through self-paced learning modules or personalized learning pathways, can help students develop the skills and knowledge they need to navigate and succeed in a changing world.

Learner autonomy significantly enhances the self-efficacy of online instructors by fostering an environment where they can empower students to take ownership of their learning. When instructors promote learner autonomy, they encourage students to set their own goals, make decisions about their learning paths, and engage in self-directed tasks. This shift not only boosts students' confidence and critical thinking skills but also allows instructors to observe and support diverse learning strategies and outcomes. As instructors witness their students thriving in an autonomous learning setting, they gain validation and confidence in their teaching abilities, reinforcing their belief in their capacity to facilitate effective learning experiences. Consequently, this positive feedback loop enriches their self-efficacy, motivating them to innovate further in their instructional approaches and invest more in their professional development.

How Instructors Promote Learner Autonomy

Instructors can promote learner autonomy in online learning by implementing several strategies. Instructors can model learner autonomy by demonstrating effective self-regulation, goal-setting, and reflection skills, providing students with examples of how to take charge of their learning (Andrade & Bunker, 2009; Van Laer & Elen, 2023). Providing frequent and meaningful feedback to students on their progress and performance can help them develop self-awareness (Zimmerman, 2012) and self-regulation skills, supporting their autonomy (Clark, 2012; Yan, et al., 2020). Giving students choice and control over their learning experiences, such as in the selection of course materials or projects, can support their autonomy. According to Nevgi, et al. (2006) and Zhang & Cui (2018) encouraging collaborative learning experiences, such as group projects, online discussions, or peer review activities, can help students develop communication and teamwork skills, supporting their autonomy in learning. Incorporating self-assessment activities into online courses, such as quizzes or reflection assignments, can help students develop their ability to identify and address gaps in their knowledge and skills, supporting their autonomy in learning.

Strategies For Promoting Self-Efficacy

Promoting self-efficacy for instructors is a key component of successful online learning experiences in higher education (Stephen & Rockinson-Szapkiw, 2022). When instructors feel confident in their teaching abilities, they are more likely to take initiative, engage in teaching and learning activities, and persevere through challenging tasks. Therefore, it is critical to support instructors' success in online learning environments (Han & Geng, 2023; Stephen & Rockinson-Szapkiw, 2022; Pellas, 2014; Wang, et al., 2013). Several strategies can be in online learning such as encouraging instructors to set specific, achievable goals that can help them develop a sense of competence and progress in their teaching (Schunk, 1990; Pajares, (2012). According to Margolis & McCabe (2003) and Schunk & DiBenedetto, 2022), providing positive reinforcement, such as praise or positive feedback, when students demonstrate progress or achievement in their learning can help them feel more confident and motivated. Providing examples of successful learners and their strategies can help instructors develop a sense of self-efficacy by showing them that success is achievable and providing them with concrete strategies to emulate. Encouraging students to reframe failures as learning opportunities, rather than as evidence of personal inadequacy, can help them develop resilience and persistence in their learning, supporting the instructors' self-efficacy. Encouraging students to use positive self-talk, such as affirmations and visualization techniques, can help them develop a more positive and confident mindset in their learning, supporting the instructors' self-efficacy. Providing support (scaffolding) and resources to help students overcome challenges or difficulties in their learning can help them with the instructors by demonstrating the student's ability to overcome obstacles (Van Dinther, et al., 2011; Vieira, et al., 2021). Incorporating authentic assessments, such as performance-based or portfolio assessments, can help instructors and students demonstrate their knowledge and skills in real-world contexts, reinforcing their sense of self-efficacy (Freire et al. 2020)

Role of Self-Efficacy in Online Learning

Self-efficacy for instructors plays a crucial role in online learning, influencing multiple aspects of student performance and engagement (Wang, et al., 2022). When instructors believe in their ability to succeed in online teaching and learning, they are more likely to actively engage in course activities, seek out social support, employ effective cognitive strategies, and demonstrate resilience and persistence in their learning. Spinks et al. (2022) posit that online learning can be challenging due to its asynchronous and remote nature, which can lead to feelings of isolation or uncertainty among students. However, when instructors have high self-efficacy, they are better equipped to overcome these challenges and succeed in their teaching. By providing constructive feedback, modeling self-efficacy, encouraging collaboration and reflection, offering scaffolding and authentic assessments, and promoting resilience and a growth mindset, instructors can help students develop greater confidence and resilience in their learning. Effective instructors recognize that fostering self-efficacy is not just about teaching content, but also about developing students' ability to take charge of their learning and persevere through challenges. By implementing strategies that support self-efficacy, instructors can create a more positive and productive learning environment for their students.

Technology plays a critical role in online learning, enabling the delivery of course content, assessments, and interactive experiences in a variety of formats (Khan, et al., 2017). Virtual learning environments such as learning management systems, like Blackboard or Moodle, provide a centralized platform for course content, discussions, and assessments (Chasokela, et al. 2024). Technology allows for the creation and delivery of interactive content, such as videos, simulations, and interactive quizzes, which can enhance student engagement and learning outcomes. Online learning platforms can provide analytics and data on student performance and engagement, enabling instructors to make informed decisions about course design and support. Mobile learning has progressed with the widespread adoption of smartphones and other mobile devices, technology has enabled online teaching experiences that are more flexible and accessible, allowing instructors to teach on the go (Berge & Muilenburg, 2013; Brown & Mbati, 2015). According to Lee et al. (2018), technology enables personalized learning experiences. The adaptive learning platforms adjust to individual instructors' needs and preferences. Virtual meeting and conference platforms, such as Zoom or Microsoft Teams, allow instructors and students to communicate and collaborate remotely, enhancing the social aspect of online learning (Chessa & Solari, 2021; Choukaier, 2024). Technology has enabled online tutoring and coaching services, providing additional support and guidance for students in online learning environments (Tshuma & Chasokela, 2024). Virtual and augmented reality technologies can create immersive and interactive learning experiences, helping students develop practical skills and knowledge in a safe and controlled environment. Technology can support accessibility for instructors and students with disabilities, such as text-to-speech tools for visually impaired learners, or captions and transcripts for hearing-impaired learners, making online learning more inclusive and equitable. Technology allows for the use of gamification in online learning, which can engage instructors and students and promote greater motivation and persistence in their studies. (Garcia-Morales et al. 2021)

Using Technology for Communication and Collaboration

Technology plays a very important role among higher education online instructors by providing them with tools and resources that enhance their teaching practices and facilitate student engagement. Through various online platforms, instructors can access a wealth of instructional materials, data analytics, and interactive features that enable them to tailor their teaching strategies to meet diverse learner needs. This technological support not only streamlines the instructional process but also boosts instructors' confidence in their ability to navigate and utilize digital tools effectively. As instructors become adept at integrating technology into their courses, they are more likely to experiment with innovative teaching methods and foster collaborative learning environments. This continuous engagement with technology and adaptation to the online landscape bolsters their self-efficacy, empowering them to embrace challenges and enhance the overall learning experience for their students. Ultimately, technology serves as both a catalyst for growth and a reinforcement of instructors' belief in their capabilities as effective educators in an increasingly digital world.

Technology has revolutionized the way students and instructors communicate and collaborate in online learning environments (Archambault, et al., 2022). From video conferencing and asynchronous forums to project management tools and mobile learning, various digital platforms and tools provide a diverse range of options for engaging and meaningful communication and collaboration. However, the successful implementation of these technologies requires addressing challenges such as the digital divide, technology adoption, cybersecurity risks, and communication barriers, with governments and institutions globally taking various measures to mitigate these challenges (Ma, 2021). Communication and collaboration are critical components of effective online learning experiences, and technology provides a range of tools and platforms to support these activities.

Online learning platforms often include tools for synchronous communication, such as video conferencing, instant messaging, or chat rooms, enabling real-time interaction and collaboration among students and instructors. Online discussion forums, email, and learning management system (LMS) tools allow for asynchronous communication and collaboration, enabling students and instructors to interact and share ideas outside of traditional class time. Tools like Google Docs, Padlet, and Mural enable collaborative editing and brainstorming, supporting real-time group work and knowledge-sharing (Gray & Dunn, 2024). Social media platforms like Twitter, Facebook, and LinkedIn can be used to foster informal communication and community-building among students and instructors, enhancing the sense of connection and belonging in online learning. Video-based communication platforms like Flipgrid and Loom allow instructors and students to create and share short video messages, promoting more personal and engaging communication and collaboration (Hall, et al., 2021; Learning, 2022). Online project management tools, such as Trello or Asana, can help students and instructors stay organized, assign tasks, and track progress in group projects, enhancing collaboration in online learning. Video presentation tools like Prezi, Powtoon, and Canva allow students to create engaging and interactive video presentations, promoting creativity and collaboration in online learning (Artal-Sevilet al., 2018; Stradomska, 2022). Virtual whiteboards online whiteboard platforms, such as Miro and Mural, enable collaborative drawing, brainstorming, and project planning, providing versatile tools. Peer feedback online platforms like Peerceptiv and Turnitin's Feedback Studio provide students with opportunities to provide and receive feedback from their peers, promoting critical thinking and reflective practice in online learning. Online office hours' tools like Zoom and Google Meet allow instructors to host virtual office hours, providing students with one-on-one support and guidance in their learning.

Challenges of the Tools and Platforms Used for Communication and Collaboration

There are several challenges associated with the use of technology-based communication and collaboration tools in online learning (Murphy & Cifuentes, 2001). There is a digital divide and not all students have access to reliable internet or the necessary devices, which can create a digital divide and limit their ability to effectively communicate and collaborate online. Students and instructors may struggle to adopt and adapt to new technologies, leading to frustration or reduced engagement in online learning. The availability of multiple communication and collaboration tools can lead to information overload and communication fatigue among students and instructors, negatively impacting their learning experience. The lack of face-to-face interaction in online learning can create communication barriers, such as miscommunication or lack of non-verbal cues, which can hinder effective collaboration and relationship-building. The increased reliance on online communication and collaboration tools can increase the risk of cyberattacks, data breaches, or other cybersecurity threats, which can compromise the security and privacy of students and instructors. The asynchronous nature of online communication and collaboration can make it difficult for students and instructors to manage their time effectively, leading to delays in project completion or reduced productivity. Online collaboration can be hindered by cultural or language barriers, especially in international or multicultural online learning environments, leading to reduced collaboration and engagement. The rapid pace of online communication can lead to rushed or superficial interactions, reducing the quality and depth of communication and collaboration in online learning. (Buraga, 2019; Daumiller, et al. 2021; Dhawan, 2020; O'Shea, et al. 2015).

Governments and institutions globally have implemented various measures to address the challenges associated with technology-based communication and collaboration in online learning (Maphosa, 2021; Paudel, 2021). On accessibility measures, several countries, such as Brazil and India, have launched initiatives to provide students with affordable internet access, computers, and other digital tools to reduce the digital divide and improve access to online learning (Romero-Hall, 2021; Singh, et al.; 2021). Intergovernmental organizations like UNESCO and the OECD have developed guidelines and resources for online learning, supporting countries in developing effective policies and practices for online learning (Gouedard & Viennet, 2020; Lorente, et al., 2020). Institutions in countries like China and the United Arab Emirates (Rabia & Hazza, 2017). have provided language and cultural support to international students. This has helped the students overcome communication barriers in online learning. Some institutions have adopted alternative communication channels, such as video diaries, podcasts, or virtual field trips, to enhance communication and collaboration in online learning while addressing the limitations of traditional tools.

Africa has taken various steps to address the challenges associated with technology-based communication and collaboration in online learning (Alsuwaida; 2022; Barakabitze, et al., 2019; Chang, et al., 2020). Many African countries have adopted mobile learning as a solution to the lack of reliable internet access and desktop computers, with Kenya, South Africa, and Nigeria leading the way in implementing mobile learning initiatives (Kaliisa & Picard, 2017; Okai-Ugbaje, et al., 2017). Several African countries, including Rwanda and Ghana, have established community learning centers to provide students with access to technology and internet connectivity, enabling them to participate in online learning (Faturoti, 2022). African countries such as Ethiopia, Tanzania, and Senegal have promoted the use of open educational resources (OERs) Adala, 2016). It provides free access to educational materials and resources online, helping to mitigate some of the challenges of online learning. The African Union has launched initiatives, such as the Pan-African e-Network Project, to promote regional cooperation and collaboration in online learning, helping to address communication and cultural barriers in the continent (Froehlich, et al., 2021; Siebrits & van de Heyde, 2019). Some African countries, such as Morocco and Uganda, have implemented bilingual education policies (Hadri, 2022). This has promoted the use of local languages alongside English or French, to overcome language barriers in online learning.

Adapting Teaching Methods for Online Learning

Adapting teaching methods for online learning by instructors is essential to provide students with a rich, engaging, and effective learning experience (Ali et al. 2021; Hossain et al. 2024). With the shift from face-to-face to online learning, instructors must reconsider traditional teaching approaches and embrace student-centered, active learning strategies that promote collaboration, creativity, and critical thinking. Effective online teaching methods include the use of student-centered learning, flipped classrooms, active learning, micro-learning, social learning, gamification, adaptive learning, and UDL principles. According to Roski et al. (2021), universal learning design: (UDL) principles are a set of guidelines for designing learning environments that are accessible and inclusive for all students, regardless of their differences in learning styles, abilities, and backgrounds. The UDL principles were originally developed by researchers at the Center for Applied Special Technology (CAST) and are widely used in the field of education and e-learning (Courtad, 2019; Nieves, et al., 2019; Rao, 2021). The key UDL principles include providing content in different formats (e.g., text, audio, video) to accommodate different learning preferences and abilities (Rao, et al, 2021). Another principle is offering multiple ways for students to express their knowledge and skills, such as through written work, oral presentations, or multimedia projects. Creating engaging and motivating learning experiences by incorporating interactive learning activities, gamification, and personalization. Providing flexible and supportive learning environments that allow students to work at their own pace, adjust the level of challenge, and get the support they need. Respecting and valuing the diversity of learners' backgrounds, cultures, and experiences, and integrating culturally responsive pedagogies into the learning environment. Incorporating ongoing formative and summative assessments to provide timely feedback to students and inform instructional decisions. Last but not least encourages collaboration among students and between students and instructors, fostering a sense of community and belonging within the online learning environment. (Boothe, et al., 2018; Scott, et al., 2017; Van Boxtel & Sugita, 2022)

Adapting teaching methods for online learning is essential to provide students with a high-quality learning experience. The shift from face-to-face to online learning requires instructors to reevaluate their teaching approaches and embrace active learning strategies, such as:

- Student-centered learning: Online learning environments allow students to take ownership of their learning, with instructors serving as facilitators and coaches rather than traditional lecturers (Lee & Hannafin, 2016).
- Flipping the traditional classroom model, where students watch lectures online and use class time for activities and discussions, can increase student engagement and understanding (Gilboy, M. B., et al., 2015).
- Incorporating active learning strategies, such as problem-based learning, simulations, and case studies, can help students develop critical thinking and problem-solving skills.
- Micro-learning: Breaking down complex topics into smaller, more manageable modules or chunks of learning can help students engage more deeply and effectively with the material (Sun, et al., 2015).
- Encouraging students to interact with each other and share their knowledge and experiences can promote social learning, helping students develop skills in teamwork, communication, and collaboration.
- Integrating game-based elements, such as points, badges, and leaderboards, into the online learning experience can increase student motivation and engagement (Saleem, et al., 2022; Sanmugam, et al., 2016).
- Using adaptive learning platforms or personalized feedback tools can help instructors tailor the learning experience to individual student needs and preferences, improving the overall learning outcomes (Peng, et al., 2019).
- Implementing universal design for learning (UDL) principles, such as providing multiple means of representation, action, and expression, can support students with diverse learning needs and preferences in the online learning environment (Nave, 2021).
- Peer-to-peer learning: Assigning students to work together in peer groups or mentor each other can enhance their learning by providing them with opportunities to teach others and receive feedback from their peers (Ahn, et al., 2013).
- Assigning students to work on collaborative projects or case studies can help them develop critical thinking, communication, and problem-solving skills, as well as foster teamwork and cooperation in the online learning environment (Cortazar, et al., 2021).

- Self-directed learning: Encouraging students to take charge of their learning, setting their own goals, and managing their learning pathways, can help them develop autonomy and self-efficacy in online learning (Zhu, et al., 2020).
- Integrating emotional intelligence training and support into the online learning experience can help students develop empathy, self-awareness, and resilience, improving their overall well-being and learning outcomes (Cleary, et al., 2018).
- Personalization: Customizing the learning experience based on individual student needs, interests, and goals can help instructors provide more meaningful and engaging (Alamri, et al., 2020).

Addressing the Unique Needs of Online Instructors

Addressing the unique needs of online instructors is essential for enhancing their effectiveness and ensuring a high-quality educational experience for students, especially in an era where digital learning is becoming increasingly prevalent (Haleem, et al., 2022; Vlachopoulos & Makri, 2019). Online instructors grapple with challenges distinct from their traditional counterparts, which demand a nuanced understanding of both technology and pedagogy (MacKenzie, et al., 2022). For instance, they must navigate a myriad of technology platforms, each with its own set of tools and functionalities, which can be overwhelming and time-consuming. Additionally, adapting pedagogical strategies to suit a virtual environment requires flexibility and creativity; what works in a physical classroom may not translate effectively online. According to Nkomo et. al. (2021) and Burke & Larmar (2021), maintaining student engagement in a digitally mediated space adds another layer of complexity, necessitating the development of interactive activities and fostering a sense of community among students who may never meet face-to-face.

To effectively address these challenges, professional development opportunities tailored specifically for online teaching methodologies are crucial (Shernoff, et al., 2017). These should include comprehensive technology training sessions that not only introduce the tools at their disposal but also offer insights into best practices for utilizing these technologies to enhance learning outcomes. Online instructors can greatly benefit from learning innovative strategies that engage students and promote active participation, such as the use of breakout rooms, discussion boards, and multimedia resources (Kumi-Yeboah, et. al., 2020). Moreover, providing robust support networks through mentorship programs and peer collaboration forums offers online instructors a platform to share best practices, troubleshoot technical issues, and exchange pedagogical strategies. This collaborative environment can significantly reduce feelings of isolation that often accompany online teaching, fostering a sense of community and shared purpose among educators.

Recognizing and proactively addressing the specific challenges faced by online instructors empowers educational institutions to create a more supportive environment that enhances both instructors' professional growth and students' learning experiences. Institutions should also prioritize the promotion of mental well-being through resources geared toward managing the unique pressures of remote teaching (McCallum, 2021). This could involve access to mental health support services, workshops focused on resilience and stress management, and training on work-life balance. Furthermore, offering instructional design assistance can alleviate some of the burdens associated with course creation, allowing instructors to focus more on teaching and connecting with students. By investing in these comprehensive support systems, educational institutions can ensure that online instructors are not only equipped to overcome their challenges but are also able to thrive in their roles, ultimately leading to improved student outcomes and a richer educational experience overall.

The Importance of Evidence-Based Strategies in Online Higher Education by Instructors

The importance of evidence-based strategies in online higher education cannot be overstated, as they serve as the backbone for creating effective and impactful learning experiences for students (Carnahan & Lowrey, 2018). Evidence-based strategies are instructional approaches that have been scientifically tested and validated through rigorous research, and their implementation in the online learning environment is vital for several reasons (Fisher & Newton, 2014). The importance of strategies is:

- They provide a framework for instructors to make informed decisions regarding curriculum design, teaching methods, and assessment practices.
- By relying on empirical data and established practices, instructors can enhance the likelihood of achieving desired student learning outcomes and improve overall course effectiveness.
- This evidence-based approach allows for continuous improvement, as instructors can analyze data from course evaluations and student performance to refine their techniques and materials, leading to higher retention and success rates among online learners.
- Moreover, evidence-based strategies contribute significantly to the development of an inclusive and equitable learning environment, which is essential in online higher education.
- Online classrooms often bring together a diverse student body with varying backgrounds, learning styles, and needs (Vita, 2001).

- Instructors who apply research-backed strategies such as differentiated instruction, formative assessment, and active learning techniques are better equipped to address the multitude of challenges that arise in such a heterogeneous setting (Saini & Corrente, 2024). For instance, the incorporation of formative assessments allows instructors to monitor student understanding in real-time and adjust their teaching in response. This adaptability is critical in ensuring that all students have a fair opportunity to engage with the material and succeed academically.
- Furthermore, leveraging technology in ways that are supported by evidence like using analytics to identify at-risk students enables instructors to intervene promptly, providing the necessary support to help those students stay on track (Liu, et al., 2017).

In addition to enhancing pedagogical effectiveness, employing evidence-based strategies in online higher education fosters greater student engagement and motivation. Research indicates that students are more likely to remain engaged when they perceive their courses as relevant and aligned with their learning goals (Williams, et. al., 2018). Strategies such as collaborative learning, gamification, and real-world problem-solving not only make courses more dynamic but also connect theoretical concepts to practical applications (Sanchez, et al., 2020). These approaches resonate with students, encouraging active participation and a sense of ownership over their educational journey. Furthermore, the use of technology-supported learning tools, such as discussion forums or interactive simulations, can facilitate collaboration and community building among students, enriching their online experience (Ahmed & Opoku, 2022). By prioritizing evidence-based teaching methods, instructors can create stimulating online environments that not only foster deeper learning and critical thinking but also instill a sense of belonging a crucial factor for student retention and satisfaction in higher education.

Ultimately, the integration of evidence-based strategies into online higher education is fundamental in ensuring instructional quality and promoting a positive learning experience for students (Borrego & Henderson, 2014). As the landscape of higher education continues to evolve, particularly with the increasing prevalence of online and hybrid models, the need for robust, research-informed teaching practices grows ever more urgent. Institutions that emphasize the adoption of evidence-based methods empower instructors to deliver courses grounded in proven principles of effective teaching and learning (Rajaram, 2021). This commitment not only elevates the standard of education provided but also prepares students for the complexities of the modern workforce, where adaptability, critical thinking, and collaborative problem-solving are essential skills. As educators in the digital age embrace the importance of these evidence-based strategies, they contribute to building a more effective, accessible, and equitable online education system that benefits students, instructors, and society at large.

Challenges In the Online Classroom And Actionable Steps for Integrating Best Practices

The online classroom presents unique challenges for instructors, many of which stem from the differences in interaction, engagement, and accessibility compared to traditional face-to-face settings (DeCoito & Estaiteyeh, 2022). The significant challenges are:

- Maintaining student engagement and motivation in an environment where distractions are plentiful, and students may feel isolated. According to Blaine (2019), virtual classrooms, instructors often struggle to foster a sense of community among learners who are physically apart. This lack of personal interaction can lead to disengagement, diminished participation in discussions, and, ultimately, lower academic performance. In addition, the absence of non-verbal cues that are readily available in physical classrooms complicates instructors' ability to gauge student understanding and emotional engagement, making it difficult to identify when learners might need additional support (Rosati-Peterson, et. al., 2021).
- Another challenge faced by online instructors is the variability in technology proficiency among students (Scherer, et, al., 2021). While some students may be comfortable navigating online platforms and digital tools, others may lack the necessary skills or access to reliable technology, hindering their ability to participate fully. This digital divide can exacerbate existing inequities in education, leading to frustration for both students and instructors (Clark & Gorski, 2002; Devkota, 2021). Furthermore, faculty members themselves may encounter difficulties mastering the various technologies and tools required to deliver effective online instruction. The quick pace of technological change also means that instructors must continually adapt their teaching methods to incorporate new tools and approaches, which can be overwhelming and time-consuming.

To address these challenges, integrating best practices in online education becomes imperative. One actionable step is to design courses with a strong emphasis on building community and fostering student interaction. Instructors can incorporate synchronous and asynchronous activities that encourage collaboration, such as group projects, discussion boards, and peer feedback sessions (Dailey-Hebert, 2018). Utilizing breakout rooms during live sessions allows for smaller group interactions that can enhance engagement and reduce feelings of isolation. Additionally, instructors can create ice-breaking activities and community-building exercises at the beginning of the course to help students connect and feel more invested in the learning environment.

Another crucial practice is the implementation of varied instructional methods to accommodate the diverse learning styles and technological abilities of students (Cassidy, 2004; Rajaram, 2023). Instructors can enhance course materials with multimedia resources, such as videos, podcasts, and interactive simulations, to appeal to different learning preferences. Providing clear and structured guidance on how to use technology while offering resources for technical support can also promote inclusivity and accessibility. By leveraging a mix of synchronous and asynchronous learning opportunities, instructors can allow students to engage with the material in ways that best suit their individual needs and schedules (Bower, et al., 2015).

Furthermore, regular feedback and formative assessments are essential components of successful online instruction. Instructors should provide ongoing opportunities for students to receive feedback, not only on their assignments but also on their learning experiences (Boud & Molloy, 2013). This could involve using anonymous surveys to collect students' insights and reactions to course content, pace, and delivery methods. By soliciting student feedback, instructors can make real-time adjustments to their teaching strategies, ensuring that they are meeting the needs of all learners. Additionally, utilizing assessment tools that allow for self-reflection can empower students to take ownership of their learning and identify areas where they may need further help.

In summary, while online instructors face significant challenges in the virtual classroom, a strategic approach to integrating best practices can mitigate these issues effectively. By fostering a sense of community, accommodating diverse learning needs, and maintaining open lines of communication through feedback, educators can create dynamic, inclusive learning environments that enhance student engagement and success. As instructors adapt and refine their practices in response to the unique demands of online education, they can not only overcome the obstacles they encounter but also unlock the rich potential of online learning to provide impactful educational experiences for all students.

CONCLUSION

Fostering self-efficacy among higher education online instructors is a crucial component in enhancing their teaching effectiveness and ensuring positive outcomes for their students. Self-efficacy the belief in one's ability to succeed in specific situations plays a significant role in how educators approach their roles, particularly within the unique challenges presented by online learning environments. When instructors possess a strong sense of self-efficacy, they are more likely to embrace innovative teaching strategies, persist through challenges, and maintain a positive attitude toward their instructional practices. Consequently, this confidence translates into enhanced learner engagement, improved course design, and ultimately, better student performance and satisfaction. To cultivate self-efficacy, educational institutions must implement supportive measures that empower online instructors. Professional development programs tailored to the distinctive demands of online teaching should be prioritized, providing educators with the necessary resources, training, and opportunities for skill enhancement. Such programs could focus on pedagogical techniques specific to online learning, technological competencies, and methods for fostering student engagement in a virtual classroom. Additionally, mentorship initiatives can pair novice instructors with experienced colleagues, allowing for knowledge sharing, collaborative problem-solving, and the development of a supportive community. These relationships not only bolster instructors' confidence but also create avenues for peer feedback and affirmation, further reinforcing a sense of competency and efficacy in their teaching roles. Importantly, the creation of an open and supportive institutional culture is fundamental to fostering self-efficacy. Institutions should encourage a growth mindset, where challenges are seen as opportunities for learning rather than insurmountable obstacles. By promoting an environment where experimentation is embraced and failures are viewed as valuable lessons, instructors can feel empowered to take risks in their teaching practices without the fear of harsh judgment. This cultural shift can be reinforced through positive reinforcement, acknowledgment of successes, and the sharing of impactful teaching practices across faculty networks. When educators perceive that their institution values their efforts and is invested in their professional growth, their self-efficacy is bolstered.

In conclusion, fostering self-efficacy among online instructors in higher education holds profound implications not only for instructors themselves but also for the students they teach. By creating a robust support system, offering targeted professional development, and nurturing a positive institutional culture, educational institutions can empower instructors to develop the confidence and skills necessary to navigate the complexities of online teaching. As these instructors grow in their belief in their capabilities, they become more effective educators, leading to richer learning experiences for their students. Ultimately, cultivating self-efficacy is not just about enhancing individual teaching practices; it is about elevating the entire educational experience and creating a thriving online learning community that supports the academic and personal growth of all its members. Through this commitment, higher education can adapt and flourish in an increasingly digital landscape.

REFERENCES

Adala, A. A. (2016). The current state of advancement of Open Educational Resources in Kenya. *UNESCO Institute for Information Technologies in Education. Retrieved from* http://iite. unesco. org/pics/publications/en/files/3214744. pdf

Ahmadi, M. M. (2024). E-Learning for College Students with Disabilities in the UAE: Challenges and Solutions. *The Palgrave Encyclopedia of Disability*, 1-11.

Ahmed, V., & Opoku, A. (2022). Technology supported learning and pedagogy in times of crisis: The case of COVID-19 pandemic. *Education and Information Technologies*, 27(1), 365–405. DOI: 10.1007/s10639-021-10706-w PMID: 34462626

Ahn, J., Weng, C., & Butler, B. S. (2013, January). The dynamics of open, peer-to-peer learning: what factors influence participation in the P2P University? In *2013 46th Hawaii International Conference on System Sciences* (pp. 3098-3107). IEEE. DOI: 10.1109/HICSS.2013.515

Alamri, H., Lowell, V., Watson, W., & Watson, S. L. (2020). Using personalized learning as an instructional approach to motivate learners in online higher education: Learner self-determination and intrinsic motivation. *Journal of Research on Technology in Education*, 52(3), 322–352. DOI: 10.1080/15391523.2020.1728449

Ali, I., Narayan, A. K., & Sharma, U. (2021). Adapting to COVID-19 disruptions: Student engagement in online learning of accounting. *Accounting Research Journal*, 34(3), 261–269. DOI: 10.1108/ARJ-09-2020-0293

Alsuwaida, N. (2022). Online courses in art and design during the Coronavirus (COVID-19) pandemic: Teaching reflections from a first-time online instructor. *SAGE Open*, 12(1), 1–9. DOI: 10.1177/21582440221079827

Alt, D., & Naamati-Schneider, L. (2021). Health management students' self-regulation and digital concept mapping in online learning environments. *BMC Medical Education*, 21(1), 1–15. DOI: 10.1186/s12909-021-02542-w PMID: 33596899

Andrade, M. S., & Bunker, E. L. (2009). A model for self-regulated distance language learning. *Distance Education*, 30(1), 47–61. DOI: 10.1080/01587910902845956

Archambault, L., Leary, H., & Rice, K. (2022). Pillars of online pedagogy: A framework for teaching in online learning environments. *Educational Psychologist*, 57(3), 178–191. DOI: 10.1080/00461520.2022.2051513

Artal-Sevil, J. S., Romero, E., & Artacho, J. M. (2018). Using new multimedia learning technologies: presentation design tools, dynamic animations, interactive maps, visual content and multimedia resources. In *EDULEARN18 Proceedings* (pp. 9617-9627). IATED. DOI: 10.21125/edulearn.2018.2307

Bandura, A. (1977). Self-efficacy: Toward a unifying theory of behavioral change. *Psychological Review*, 84(2), 191–215. DOI: 10.1037/0033-295X.84.2.191 PMID: 847061

Bandura, A. (1986). *Social foundations of thought and action: A social cognitive theory*. Prentice Hall.

Bandura, A., & Wessels, S. (1997). *Self-efficacy*. Cambridge University Press.

Barakabitze, A. A., William-Andey Lazaro, A., Ainea, N., Mkwizu, M. H., Maziku, H., Matofali, A. X., Iddi, A., & Sanga, C. (2019). Transforming African education systems in science, technology, engineering, and mathematics (STEM) using ICTs: Challenges and opportunities. *Education Research International*, 2019(1), 6946809. DOI: 10.1155/2019/6946809

Ben Hassen, T. (2021). The state of the knowledge-based economy in the Arab world: cases of Qatar and Lebanon. *EuroMed Journal of Business, 16*(2), 129-153.

Berge, Z. L., & Muilenburg, L. Y. (Eds.). (2013). *Handbook of mobile learning* (pp. 133-146). Routledge. DOI: 10.1108/EMJB-03-2020-0026

Blaine, A. M. (2019). Interaction and presence in the virtual classroom: An analysis of the perceptions of students and teachers in online and blended Advanced Placement courses. *Computers & Education*, 132, 31–43. DOI: 10.1016/j.compedu.2019.01.004

Boothe, K. A., Lohmann, M. J., Donnell, K. A., & Hall, D. D. (2018). Applying the principles of universal design for learning (UDL) in the college classroom. *The Journal of Special Education Apprenticeship*, 7(3), n3. DOI: 10.58729/2167-3454.1076

Borrego, M., & Henderson, C. (2014). Increasing the use of evidence-based teaching in STEM higher education: A comparison of eight change strategies. *Journal of Engineering Education*, 103(2), 220–252. DOI: 10.1002/jee.20040

Boud, D., & Molloy, E. (2013). Rethinking models of feedback for learning: The challenge of design. *Assessment & Evaluation in Higher Education*, 38(6), 698–712. DOI: 10.1080/02602938.2012.691462

Bower, M., Dalgarno, B., Kennedy, G. E., Lee, M. J., & Kenney, J. (2015). Design and implementation factors in blended synchronous learning environments: Outcomes from a cross-case analysis. *Computers & Education*, 86, 1–17. DOI: 10.1016/j.compedu.2015.03.006

Brown, T. H., & Mbati, L. S. (2015). Mobile learning: Moving past the myths and embracing the opportunities. *International Review of Research in Open and Distance Learning*, 16(2), 115–135. DOI: 10.19173/irrodl.v16i2.2071

Buraga, R. (2019). Students' perspectives on the integration of online collaboration tools for learning. *International Journal of Innovative Technology and Exploring Engineering*, 8(5), 951–955.

Burke, K., & Larmar, S. (2021). Acknowledging another face in the virtual crowd: Reimagining the online experience in higher education through an online pedagogy of care. *Journal of Further and Higher Education*, 45(5), 601–615. DOI: 10.1080/0309877X.2020.1804536

Carnahan, C. R., & Lowrey, K. A. (2018). Facilitating Evidence-Based Practice for Students with ASD. *A Paul H Brookes Publishing Co.*

Cassidy, S. (2004). Learning styles: An overview of theories, models, and measures. *Educational Psychology*, 24(4), 419–444. DOI: 10.1080/0144341042000228834

Chakraborty, M., & Nafukho, F. M. (2015). Strategies for virtual learning environments: Focusing on teaching presence and teaching immediacy. Internet learning, 4(1).

Chang, G. C., Huong, L. T., Moumne, R., ... (2020) COVID-19: a glance at national coping strategies on high-stakes examinations and assessments. *Working Document*. Available at. chrome-extension://efaidnbmnnnibpcajpcglclefindmkaj/ https://en.unesco.org/sites/default/files/unesco_review_of_high-stakes_exams_and_assessments_during_covid-19_en.pdf

Chasokela, D., Shava, G. N., & Mpofu, S. (2024). Challenges and Opportunities of Learning Management System Integration from a Zimbabwean University Perspective. In M. Kayyali (Ed.), *Building Resiliency in Higher Education: Globalization, Digital Skills, and Student Wellness* (pp. 73-98). IGI Global. https://doi.org/10.4018/979-8-3693-5483-4.ch005

Chau, P. (2010). Online higher education commodity. *Journal of Computing in Higher Education*, 22(3), 177–191. DOI: 10.1007/s12528-010-9039-y

Chessa, M., & Solari, F. (2021). The sense of being there during online classes: Analysis of usability and presence in web-conferencing systems and virtual reality social platforms. *Behaviour & Information Technology*, 40(12), 1237–1249. DOI: 10.1080/0144929X.2021.1957017

Choukaier, D. (2024). Enhancing English as A Foreign Language (EFL) Instruction Through Digital Teaching Platforms: Analyzing The Impact of Microsoft Teams, Zoom, And Google Meet On Communication and Participation. *Educational Administration: Theory and Practice*, 30(6), 2404–2418.

Clark, C., & Gorski, P. (2002). Multicultural education and the digital divide: Focus on socioeconomic class background. *Multicultural Perspectives*, 4(3), 25–36. DOI: 10.1207/S15327892MCP0403_6

Clark, I. (2012). Formative assessment: Assessment is for self-regulated learning. *Educational Psychology Review*, 24(2), 205–249. DOI: 10.1007/s10648-011-9191-6

Cleary, M., Visentin, D., West, S., Lopez, V., & Kornhaber, R. (2018). Promoting emotional intelligence and resilience in undergraduate nursing students: An integrative review. *Nurse Education Today*, 68, 112–120. DOI: 10.1016/j.nedt.2018.05.018 PMID: 29902740

Coombs, N. (2022). Embedding Components of the Write on Race Intervention in a Cultural Diversity Course for Pre-Service Teachers, to Increase Cultural Humility, and the Likelihood for Future Implementation of Instructional Strategies Designed to Improve School Climate, Sense of Belonging, and Teacher-Student Relationships for Diverse Students (Doctoral dissertation, University of Missouri-Columbia).

Cortazar, C., Nussbaum, M., Harcha, J., Alvares, D., Lopez, F., Goni, J., & Cabezas, V. (2021). Promoting critical thinking in an online, project-based course. *Computers in Human Behavior*, 119, 106705. DOI: 10.1016/j.chb.2021.106705 PMID: 36571081

Courtad, C. A. (2019). *Making your classroom smart: Universal design for learning and technology. In Smart education and e-learning* (pp. 501-510). Springer Singapore.

Rao, , K. (2021). Inclusive instructional design: Applying UDL to online learning. *The Journal of Applied Instructional Design*, 10(1), 83–97.

Dailey-Hebert, A. (2018). Maximizing interactivity in online learning: Moving beyond discussion boards. *The Journal of Educators Online*, 15(3), n3. DOI: 10.9743/jeo.2018.15.3.8

Daumiller, M., Rinas, R., Hein, J., Janke, S., Dickhäuser, O., & Dresel, M. (2021). Shifting from face-to-face to online teaching during COVID-19: The role of university faculty achievement goals for attitudes towards this sudden change, and their relevance for burnout/engagement and student evaluations of teaching quality. *Computers in Human Behavior*, 118, 106677. DOI: 10.1016/j.chb.2020.106677 PMID: 36570330

de Andres Martinez, C. (2012). Developing metacognition at a distance: Sharing students' learning strategies on a reflective blog. *Computer Assisted Language Learning*, 25(2), 199–212. DOI: 10.1080/09588221.2011.636056

DeCoito, I., & Estaiteyeh, M. (2022). Transitioning to online teaching during the COVID-19 pandemic: An exploration of STEM teachers' views, successes, and challenges. *Journal of Science Education and Technology*, 31(3), 340–356. DOI: 10.1007/s10956-022-09958-z PMID: 35369535

Dembo, M. H., Gubler, J. L., & Lynch, R. (2013). Becoming a self-regulated learner: Implications for web-based education. In *Web-Based Learning* (pp. 185–202). Routledge.

DeMink-Carthew, J., Netcoh, S., & Farber, K. (2020). Exploring the potential for students to develop self-awareness through personalized learning. *The Journal of Educational Research*, 113(3), 165–176. DOI: 10.1080/00220671.2020.1764467

Devkota, K. R. (2021). Inequalities reinforced through online and distance education in the age of COVID-19: The case of higher education in Nepal. *International Review of Education*, 67(1), 145–165. DOI: 10.1007/s11159-021-09886-x PMID: 33678863

Dhawan, S. (2020). Online learning: A panacea in the time of COVID-19 crisis. *Journal of Educational Technology Systems*, 49(1), 5–22. DOI: 10.1177/0047239520934018

Farley, I. A., & Burbules, N. C. (2022). Online education viewed through an equity lens: Promoting engagement and success for all learners. *Review of Education*, 10(3), e3367. DOI: 10.1002/rev3.3367

Faturoti, B. (2022). Online learning during COVID-19 and beyond A human right based approach to internet access in Africa. *International Review of Law Computers & Technology*, 36(1), 68–90. DOI: 10.1080/13600869.2022.2030027

Fisher, K., & Newton, C. (2014). Transforming the twenty-first-century campus to enhance the net-generation student learning experience: Using evidence-based design to determine what works and why in virtual/physical teaching spaces. *Higher Education Research & Development*, 33(5), 903–920. DOI: 10.1080/07294360.2014.890566

Fong, C. J., Dillard, J. B., & Hatcher, M. (2019). Teaching self-efficacy of graduate student instructors: Exploring faculty motivation, perceptions of autonomy support, and undergraduate student engagement. *International Journal of Educational Research*, 98, 91–105. DOI: 10.1016/j.ijer.2019.08.018

Freire, C., Ferradas, M. D. M., Regueiro, B., Rodríguez, S., Valle, A., & Nunez, J. C. (2020). Coping strategies and self-efficacy in university students: A person-centered approach. *Frontiers in Psychology*, 11, 530329. DOI: 10.3389/fpsyg.2020.00841 PMID: 32508707

Froehlich, A., Siebrits, A., Kotze, C., Froehlich, A., Siebrits, A., & Kotze, C. (2021). Towards the Sustainable Development Goals in Africa: Space Supporting African Higher Education. *Space Supporting Africa: Volume 2. Education and Healthcare as Priority Areas in Achieving the United Nations Sustainable Development Goals*, 2030, 1–90.

Gaebel, M., Zhang, T., Bunescu, L., & Stoeber, H. (2018). Learning and teaching in the European higher education area. European University Association asbl.

Garcia-Morales, V. J., Garrido-Moreno, A., & Martín-Rojas, R. (2021). The transformation of higher education after the COVID disruption: Emerging challenges in an online learning scenario. *Frontiers in Psychology*, 12, 616059. DOI: 10.3389/fpsyg.2021.616059 PMID: 33643144

Gilboy, M. B., Heinerichs, S., & Pazzaglia, G. (2015). Enhancing student engagement using the flipped classroom. *Journal of Nutrition Education and Behavior*, 47(1), 109–114. DOI: 10.1016/j.jneb.2014.08.008 PMID: 25262529

Gouedard, P., Pont, B., & Viennet, R. (2020). Education responses to COVID-19: Implementing a way forward.

Gray, L. E., & Dunn, S. D. (Eds.). (2024). *Humanizing Online Teaching and Learning in Higher Education*. IGI Global. DOI: 10.4018/979-8-3693-0762-5

Hadri, O. E. (2022). African Languages Development in Education-Bilingualism and African Languages. *International Journal of Language and Literary Studies*, 4(2), 223–241. DOI: 10.36892/ijlls.v4i2.893

Haleem, A., Javaid, M., Qadri, M. A., & Suman, R. (2022). Understanding the role of digital technologies in education: A review. *Sustainable operations and computers, 3*, 275-285.

Hall, J. A., Widdall, C., & Lei, J. (2021). Preparing for virtual student teaching: A presence experience design case. *TechTrends*, 65(6), 963–976. DOI: 10.1007/s11528-021-00660-2 PMID: 34485993

Hampton, D., Culp-Roche, A., Hensley, A., Wilson, J., Otts, J. A., Thaxton-Wiggins, A., Fruh, S., & Moser, D. K. (2020). Self-efficacy and satisfaction with teaching in online courses. *Nurse Educator*, 45(6), 302–306. DOI: 10.1097/NNE.0000000000000805 PMID: 31972846

Han, J., & Geng, X. (2023). University students' approaches to online learning technologies: The roles of perceived support, affect/emotion, and self-efficacy in technology-enhanced learning. *Computers & Education*, 194, 104695. DOI: 10.1016/j.compedu.2022.104695

Horvitz, B. S., Beach, A. L., Anderson, M. L., & Xia, J. (2015). Examination of faculty self-efficacy related to online teaching. *Innovative Higher Education*, 40(4), 305–316. DOI: 10.1007/s10755-014-9316-1

Hsia, L. H., Huang, I., & Hwang, G. J. (2016). Effects of different online peer-feedback approaches on students' performance skills, motivation and self-efficacy in a dance course. *Computers & Education*, 96, 55–71. DOI: 10.1016/j.compedu.2016.02.004

Hu, P., & Zhang, J. (2017). A pathway to learner autonomy: A self-determination theory perspective. *Asia Pacific Education Review*, 18(1), 147–157. DOI: 10.1007/s12564-016-9468-z

Johnson, K. R., Hewapathirana, G. I., & Bowen, M. M. (2019). Faculty development for online teaching. In *Handbook of research on virtual training and mentoring of online instructors* (pp. 40–55). IGI Global.

Kaliisa, R., & Picard, M. (2017). A systematic review on mobile learning in higher education: The African perspective. *Turkish Online Journal of Educational Technology-TOJET*, 16(1), 1–18.

Kamel, S. (2014). Education in the Middle East: Challenges and opportunities. Business and education in the Middle East, 99-130.

Khan, A., Egbue, O., Palkie, B., & Madden, J. (2017). Active learning: Engaging students to maximize learning in an online course. *Electronic Journal of e-Learning*, 15(2), 107–115.

Kumi-Yeboah, A., Kim, Y., Sallar, A. M., & Kiramba, L. K. (2020). Exploring the use of digital technologies from the perspective of diverse learners in online learning environments. *Online Learning : the Official Journal of the Online Learning Consortium*, 24(4), 42–63. DOI: 10.24059/olj.v24i4.2323

Kutsyuruba, B., Walker, K. D., Stasel, R. S., & Makhamreh, M. A. (2019). Developing resilience and promoting well-being in early career teaching. *Canadian Journal of Education/Revue canadienne de l'éducation*, 42(1), 285-321.

Learning, P. B. (2022). Use of Technology with Problem-Based Learning in Higher Education.

Lee, D., Huh, Y., Lin, C. Y., & Reigeluth, C. M. (2018). Technology functions for personalized learning in learner-centered schools. *Educational Technology Research and Development*, 66(5), 1269–1302. DOI: 10.1007/s11423-018-9615-9

Lee, E., & Hannafin, M. J. (2016). A design framework for enhancing engagement in student-centered learning: Own it, learn it, and share it. *Educational Technology Research and Development*, 64(4), 707–734. DOI: 10.1007/s11423-015-9422-5

Lorente, L. M. L., Arrabal, A. A., & Pulido-Montes, C. (2020). The right to education and ICT during COVID-19: An international perspective. *Sustainability (Basel)*, 12(21), 9091. DOI: 10.3390/su12219091

Lotrecchiano, G. R., McDonald, P. L., Lyons, L., Long, T., & Zajicek-Farber, M. (2013). Blended learning: Strengths, challenges, and lessons learned in an interprofessional training program. *Maternal and Child Health Journal*, 17(9), 1725–1734. DOI: 10.1007/s10995-012-1175-8 PMID: 23291875

Ma, C. (2021). Smart city and cyber-security; technologies used, leading challenges and future recommendations. *Energy Reports*, 7, 7999–8012. DOI: 10.1016/j.egyr.2021.08.124

MacKenzie, A., Bacalja, A., Annamali, D., Panaretou, A., Girme, P., Cutajar, M., Abegglen, S., Evens, M., Neuhaus, F., Wilson, K., Psarikidou, K., & Gourlay, L. (2022). Dissolving the dichotomies between online and campus-based teaching: A collective response to the manifesto for teaching online (Bayne et al. 2020). *Postdigital Science and Education*, 4(2), 271–329. DOI: 10.1007/s42438-021-00259-z

Maphosa, V. (2021). Teachers' perspectives on remote-based teaching and learning in the COVID-19 era: Rethinking technology availability and suitability in Zimbabwe. *European Journal of Interactive Multimedia and Education*, 2(1), e02105. DOI: 10.30935/ejimed/9684

Margolis, H., & McCabe, P. P. (2003). Self-efficacy: A key to improving the motivation of struggling learners. *Preventing School Failure*, 47(4), 162–169. DOI: 10.1080/10459880309603362

Mazzetti, G., Paolucci, A., Guglielmi, D., & Vannini, I. (2020). The impact of learning strategies and future orientation on academic success: The moderating role of academic self-efficacy among Italian undergraduate students. *Education Sciences*, 10(5), 134. DOI: 10.3390/educsci10050134

McCallum, F. (2021). Teachers' wellbeing during times of change and disruption. In *Wellbeing and Resilience Education* (pp. 183-208). Routledge.

Murphy, K. L., & Cifuentes, L. (2001). Using Web tools, collaborating, and learning online. *Distance Education, 22*(2), 285-305.

Ndukwe, , I. GDaniel, , B. K. (2020). Teaching analytics, value and tools for teacher data literacy: A systematic and tripartite approach. *International Journal of Educational Technology in Higher Education*, 17, 1–31.

Nave, L. (2021). Universal design for learning: UDL in online environments: The WHAT of learning. *Journal of Developmental Education*, 44(2), 30–32.

Nevgi, A., Virtanen, P., & Niemi, H. (2006). Supporting students to develop collaborative learning skills in technology-based environments. *British Journal of Educational Technology*, 37(6), 937–947. DOI: 10.1111/j.1467-8535.2006.00671.x

Nieves, L. H., Moya, E. C., & Soldado, R. M. (2019). A MOOC on universal design for learning designed based on the UDL paradigm. *Australasian Journal of Educational Technology*, 35(6), 30–47. DOI: 10.14742/ajet.5532

Nkomo, L. M., Daniel, B. K., & Butson, R. J. (2021). Synthesis of student engagement with digital technologies: A systematic review of the literature. *International Journal of Educational Technology in Higher Education*, 18, 1–26. PMID: 34778529

O'Shea, S., Stone, C., & Delahunty, J. (2015). "I 'feel' like I am at university even though I am online." Exploring how students narrate their engagement with higher education institutions in an online learning environment. *Distance Education*, 36(1), 41–58. DOI: 10.1080/01587919.2015.1019970

Okai-Ugbaje, S., Ardzejewska, K., & Imran, A. (2017). A systematic review of mobile learning adoption in higher education: The African perspective. *i-manager's Journal on Mobile Applications & Technologies, 4*(2), 1-13

Onah, D. F., Pang, E. L., Sinclair, J. E., & Uhomoibhi, J. (2021). An innovative MOOC platform: The implications of self-directed learning abilities to improve motivation in learning and to support self-regulation. *The International Journal of Information and Learning Technology*, 38(3), 283–298. DOI: 10.1108/IJILT-03-2020-0040

Pajares, F. (2012). Motivational role of self-efficacy beliefs in self-regulated learning. In *Motivation and self-regulated learning* (pp. 111–139). Routledge.

Paudel, P. (2021). Online education: Benefits, challenges and strategies during and after COVID-19 in higher education. [IJonSE]. *International Journal on Studies in Education*, 3(2), 70–85. DOI: 10.46328/ijonse.32

Paul, A. R., Aldiab, A., Chattopadhyaya, S., Hossain, A., Tasneem, Z., Haque, N., & Alam, F. (2021). Impact of COVID-19 on Online Education in Developing Countries–An Overview. *International Journal of Engineering Education*, 37(6), 1489–1510.

Pellas, N. (2014). The influence of computer self-efficacy, metacognitive self-regulation, and self-esteem on student engagement in online learning programs: Evidence from the virtual world of Second Life. *Computers in Human Behavior*, 35, 157–170. DOI: 10.1016/j.chb.2014.02.048

Peng, H., Ma, S., & Spector, J. M. (2019). Personalized adaptive learning: An emerging pedagogical approach enabled by a smart learning environment. *Smart Learning Environments*, 6(1), 1–14. DOI: 10.1186/s40561-019-0089-y

Phan, D., & Coxhead, I. (2014). Education in Southeast Asia: Investments, achievements, and returns. In Routledge Handbook of Southeast Asian Economics (pp. 245-269). Routledge.

Picciano, A. G., Seaman, J., & Allen, I. E. (2010). Educational transformation through online learning: To be or not to be. *Online Learning : the Official Journal of the Online Learning Consortium*, 14(4), 17–35. DOI: 10.24059/olj.v14i4.147

Prilop, C. N., Weber, K. E., Prins, F. J., & Kleinknecht, M. (2021). Connecting feedback to self-efficacy: Receiving and providing peer feedback in teacher education. *Studies in Educational Evaluation*, 70, 101062. DOI: 10.1016/j.stueduc.2021.101062

Pumptow, M., & Brahm, T. (2021). Students' digital media self-efficacy and its importance for higher education institutions: Development and validation of a survey instrument. *Technology. Knowledge and Learning*, 26(3), 555–575. DOI: 10.1007/s10758-020-09463-5

Rabia, A., & Hazza, M. (2017). Undergraduate Arab International Students' Adjustment to US Universities. *International Journal of Higher Education*, 6(1), 131–139. DOI: 10.5430/ijhe.v6n1p131

Rajaram, K. (2021). *Evidence-based teaching for the 21st-century classroom and beyond*. Springer Singapore. DOI: 10.1007/978-981-33-6804-0

Rajaram, K. (2023). Future of learning: Teaching and learning strategies. In *Learning Intelligence: Innovative and Digital Transformative Learning Strategies: Cultural and Social Engineering Perspectives* (pp. 3–53). Springer Nature Singapore. DOI: 10.1007/978-981-19-9201-8_1

Rao, K. (2021). Inclusive instructional design: Applying UDL to online learning. *The Journal of Applied Instructional Design*, 10(1), 83–97.

Rao, K., Torres, C., & Smith, S. J. (2021). Digital tools and UDL-based instructional strategies to support students with disabilities online. *Journal of Special Education Technology*, 36(2), 105–112. DOI: 10.1177/0162643421998327

Romero-Hall, E. (2021). Current initiatives, barriers, and opportunities for networked learning in Latin America. *Educational Technology Research and Development*, 69(4), 2267–2283. DOI: 10.1007/s11423-021-09965-8 PMID: 33584078

Rosati-Peterson, G. L., Piro, J. S., Straub, C., & O'Callaghan, C. (2021). A nonverbal immediacy treatment with pre-service teachers using mixed reality simulations. *Cogent Education*, 8(1), 1882114. DOI: 10.1080/2331186X.2021.1882114

Roski, M., Walkowiak, M., & Nehring, A. (2021). Universal design for learning: The more, the better? *Education Sciences*, 11(4), 164. DOI: 10.3390/educsci11040164

Saini, M. A., & Corrente, S. (2024). Educating for change: A meta-analysis of education programs for separating and divorcing parents. *Family Court Review*, 62(3), 512–541. DOI: 10.1111/fcre.12801

Salas-Pilco, S. Z., Yang, Y., & Zhang, Z. (2022). Student engagement in online learning in Latin American higher education during the COVID-19 pandemic: A systematic review. *British Journal of Educational Technology*, 53(3), 593–619. DOI: 10.1111/bjet.13190 PMID: 35600418

Saleem, A. N., Noori, N. M., & Ozdamli, F. (2022). Gamification applications in E-learning: A literature review. *Technology. Knowledge and Learning*, 27(1), 139–159. DOI: 10.1007/s10758-020-09487-x

Sanchez, E., van Oostendorp, H., Fijnheer, J. D., & Lavoue, E. (2020). Gamification. In *Encyclopedia of Education and Information Technologies* (pp. 816–827). Springer International Publishing. DOI: 10.1007/978-3-030-10576-1_38

Sanmugam, M., Zaid, N. M., Abdullah, Z., Aris, B., Mohamed, H., & van der Meijden, H. (2016, December). The impacts of infusing game elements and gamification in learning. In *2016 IEEE 8th International Conference on Engineering Education (ICEED)* (pp. 131-136). IEEE. DOI: 10.1109/ICEED.2016.7856058

Scherer, R., Howard, S. K., Tondeur, J., & Siddiq, F. (2021). Profiling teachers' readiness for online teaching and learning in higher education: Who's ready? *Computers in Human Behavior*, 118, 106675. DOI: 10.1016/j.chb.2020.106675

Schunk, D. H. (1989). Self-efficacy and achievement behaviors. *Educational Psychology Review*, 1(3), 173–208. DOI: 10.1007/BF01320134

Schunk, D. H. (1990). Goal setting and self-efficacy during self-regulated learning. *Educational Psychologist*, 25(1), 71–86. DOI: 10.1207/s15326985ep2501_6

Schunk, D. H., & DiBenedetto, M. K. (2022). Academic self-efficacy. In *Handbook of positive psychology in schools* (pp. 268–282). Routledge. DOI: 10.4324/9781003013778-21

Scott, L. A., Thoma, C. A., Puglia, L., Temple, P., & D'Aguilar, A. (2017). Implementing a UDL framework: A study of current personnel preparation practices. *Intellectual and Developmental Disabilities*, 55(1), 25–36. DOI: 10.1352/1934-9556-55.1.25 PMID: 28181884

Shee, M. Y., & Lip, S. T. (2022). Online learning motivation during Covid-19 pandemic: The role of learning environment, student self-efficacy and learner-instructor interaction. [MJLI]. *Malaysian Journal of Learning and Instruction*, 19(2), 213–249.

Shernoff, D. J., Sinha, S., Bressler, D. M., & Ginsburg, L. (2017). Assessing teacher education and professional development needs for the implementation of integrated approaches to STEM education. *International Journal of STEM Education*, 4(1), 1–16. DOI: 10.1186/s40594-017-0068-1 PMID: 30631669

Siebrits, A., & van de Heyde, V. (2019). Towards the sustainable development goals in Africa: The African space-education ecosystem for sustainability and the role of educational technologies. In *Embedding Space in African Society: The United Nations Sustainable Development Goals 2030 Supported by Space Applications* (pp. 127–180). Springer International Publishing. DOI: 10.1007/978-3-030-06040-4_10

Singh, M., Adebayo, S. O., Saini, M., & Singh, J. (2021). Indian government E-learning initiatives in response to COVID-19 crisis: A case study on online learning in Indian higher education system. *Education and Information Technologies*, 26(6), 7569–7607. DOI: 10.1007/s10639-021-10585-1 PMID: 34177350

Spinks, M. L., Metzler, M., Kluge, S., Langdon, J., Gurvitch, R., Smitherman, M., Esmat, T., Bhattacharya, S., Carruth, L., Crowther, K., Denton, R., Edwards, O. V., Shrikhande, M., & Strong-Green, A. (2023). "This Wasn't Pedagogy, It Was Panic-gogy": Perspectives of the Challenges Faced by Students and Instructors during the Emergency Transition to Remote Learning Due to COVID-19. *College Teaching*, 71(4), 227–243. DOI: 10.1080/87567555.2021.2018395

Stephen, J. S., & Rockinson-Szapkiw, A. (2022). Promoting online student persistence: Strategies to promote online learning self-efficacy. In *Academic Self-efficacy in Education: Nature, Assessment, and Research* (pp. 161–176). Springer Singapore. DOI: 10.1007/978-981-16-8240-7_10

Stradomska, M. (2022). Visual Thinking (VT) in Educational Issues. *Innovative Teaching Methods. Project Management*, 39-54.

Sun, G., Cui, T., Yong, J., Shen, J., & Chen, S. (2015, May). Drawing micro learning into MOOC: Using fragmented pieces of time to enable effective entire course learning experiences. In *2015 IEEE 19th International Conference on Computer Supported Cooperative Work in Design (CSCWD)* (pp. 308-313). IEEE.

Van Boxtel, J. M., & Sugita, T. (2022). Exploring the implementation of lesson-level UDL principles through an observation protocol. *International Journal of Inclusive Education*, 26(4), 348–364. DOI: 10.1080/13603116.2019.1655596

Van Dinther, M., Dochy, F., & Segers, M. (2011). Factors affecting students' self-efficacy in higher education. *Educational Research Review*, 6(2), 95–108. DOI: 10.1016/j.edurev.2010.10.003

Van Laer, S., & Elen, J. (2023). An instrumentalized framework for supporting learners' self-regulation in blended learning environments. In *Learning, Design, and Technology: An International Compendium of Theory, Research, Practice, and Policy* (pp. 575–612). Springer International Publishing. DOI: 10.1007/978-3-319-17461-7_121

Ventura, M., Salanova, M., & Llorens, S. (2015). Professional self-efficacy as a predictor of burnout and engagement: The role of challenge and hindrance demands. *The Journal of Psychology*, 149(3), 277–302. DOI: 10.1080/00223980.2013.876380 PMID: 25590343

Vieira, C., Magana, A. J., Roy, A., & Falk, M. (2021). Providing students with agency to self-scaffold in a computational science and engineering course. *Journal of Computing in Higher Education*, 33(2), 328–366. DOI: 10.1007/s12528-020-09267-7

Vita, G. D. (2001). Learning styles, culture and inclusive instruction in the multicultural classroom: A business and management perspective. *Innovations in Education and Teaching International*, 38(2), 165–174. DOI: 10.1080/14703290110035437

Vlachopoulos, D., & Makri, A. (2019). Online communication and interaction in distance higher education: A framework study of good practice. *International Review of Education*, 65(4), 605–632. DOI: 10.1007/s11159-019-09792-3

Wang, C. H., Shannon, D. M., & Ross, M. E. (2013). Students' characteristics, self-regulated learning, technology self-efficacy, and course outcomes in online learning. *Distance Education*, 34(3), 302–323. DOI: 10.1080/01587919.2013.835779

Wang, Y., Cao, Y., Gong, S., Wang, Z., Li, N., & Ai, L. (2022). Interaction and learning engagement in online learning: The mediating roles of online learning self-efficacy and academic emotions. *Learning and Individual Differences*, 94, 102128. DOI: 10.1016/j.lindif.2022.102128

Williams, K. M., Stafford, R. E., Corliss, S. B., & Reilly, E. D. (2018). Examining student characteristics, goals, and engagement in Massive Open Online Courses. *Computers & Education*, 126, 433–442. DOI: 10.1016/j.compedu.2018.08.014

Wong, J., Baars, M., Davis, D., Van Der Zee, T., Houben, G. J., & Paas, F. (2019). Supporting self-regulated learning in online learning environments and MOOCs: A systematic review. *International Journal of Human-Computer Interaction*, 35(4-5), 356–373. DOI: 10.1080/10447318.2018.1543084

Wong, J., Baars, M., He, M., de Koning, B. B., & Paas, F. (2021). Facilitating goal setting and planning to enhance online self-regulation of learning. *Computers in Human Behavior*, 124, 106913. DOI: 10.1016/j.chb.2021.106913

Yan, Z., Chiu, M. M., & Ko, P. Y. (2020). Effects of self-assessment diaries on academic achievement, self-regulation, and motivation. *Assessment in Education: Principles, Policy & Practice*, 27(5), 562–583. DOI: 10.1080/0969594X.2020.1827221

Yang, C. (2021). Online teaching self-efficacy, social-emotional learning (SEL) competencies, and compassion fatigue among educators during the COVID-19 pandemic. *School Psychology Review*, 50(4), 505–518. DOI: 10.1080/2372966X.2021.1903815

Yilmaz, R. (2016). Knowledge sharing behaviors in e-learning community: Exploring the role of academic self-efficacy and sense of community. *Computers in Human Behavior*, 63, 373–382. DOI: 10.1016/j.chb.2016.05.055

Zhang, J., & Cui, Q. (2018). Collaborative learning in higher nursing education: A systematic review. *Journal of Professional Nursing*, 34(5), 378–388. DOI: 10.1016/j.profnurs.2018.07.007 PMID: 30243695

Zheng, F., Khan, N. A., & Hussain, S. (2020). The COVID-19 pandemic and digital higher education: Exploring the impact of proactive personality on social capital through internet self-efficacy and online interaction quality. *Children and Youth Services Review*, 119, 105694. DOI: 10.1016/j.childyouth.2020.105694

Zhu, M., Bonk, C. J., & Doo, M. Y. (2020). Self-directed learning in MOOCs: Exploring the relationships among motivation, self-monitoring, and self-management. *Educational Technology Research and Development*, 68(5), 2073–2093. DOI: 10.1007/s11423-020-09747-8

Zimmerman, B. J. (2012). Goal setting: A key proactive source of academic self-regulation. In *Motivation and self-regulated learning* (pp. 267–295). Routledge.

KEY TERMS AND DEFINITIONS

Collaboration: Working together with others towards a common goal or shared purpose, often involving communication, cooperation, and coordination among team members or stakeholders to achieve positive outcomes.

Communication: The process of exchanging information, ideas, thoughts, or messages through verbal, nonverbal, or written means between individuals or groups, to create a shared understanding and foster relationships.

Educational Psychology: The study of human behavior and mental processes in educational settings, focusing on understanding how individuals learn, develop, and interact with their environments to inform instructional practices, curriculum design, and student support services.

Educational Technology: The use of digital tools, resources, and technologies to enhance teaching, learning, and educational outcomes, facilitating access to information, promoting engagement, and enabling personalized and interactive learning experiences.

Higher Education: Post-secondary education beyond the high school level, including colleges, universities, and professional schools, offering academic and professional programs leading to degrees or certifications.

Online Learning: A form of education delivery that takes place primarily or entirely online, using digital technologies and the internet to facilitate teaching and learning, often providing flexibility, accessibility, and opportunities for interactive and self-paced learning experiences.

Online Instruction: The process of designing, delivering, and facilitating online courses or learning experiences using digital technologies and tools, including instructional design principles, multimedia resources, and communication platforms to engage learners and promote learning outcomes.

Online Instructors: Educators who design, deliver, and facilitate online courses or instructional materials, utilizing educational technologies and online platforms to engage learners, provide feedback, assess progress, and create interactive and effective learning experiences in virtual learning environments.

Self-Efficacy: is a person's belief in their ability to accomplish tasks, solve problems, or achieve goals based on their confidence, motivation, skills, and past experiences. It influences their behavior, efforts, and perseverance in overcoming challenges and achieving success.

Chapter 4
Creating and Maintaining Successful Online Learning Environments

Nurul Naimah Rose
https://orcid.org/0000-0003-3195-0685
Universiti Malaysia Perlis, Malaysia

Faten Khalida Khalid
Universiti Malaysia Perlis, Malaysia

Aida Shakila Ishak
https://orcid.org/0000-0002-8961-9154
Universiti Malaysia Perlis, Malaysia

Nazifah Hamidun
https://orcid.org/0009-0002-1635-3110
Universiti Malaysia Perlis, Malaysia

Nur Farhinaa Othman
Universiti Malaysia Perlis, Malaysia

ABSTRACT

This chapter is about creating and maintaining successful online learning environments emphasizing on the online learning in higher education especially in Malaysia. This chapter will have several segments which will begin with the overview of online learning in Malaysia. It will explore the scenarios of using online learning way back in the year 2000 until recently. Then, some explanations about the Online Collaborative Learning Theory (OCL) may benefit in some ways. The chapter continues with further discussion on the key points such as the access

DOI: 10.4018/979-8-3693-4407-1.ch004

and accessibility, the enhancement of online classroom engagement, building the online learning community and the personalization of learning experience to student tailored to their needs and pace. The future of online learning in Malaysia is highly promising, propelled by emerging trends and opportunities. As technology advances, online learning platforms in Malaysia are expected to integrate increasingly sophisticated tools and features, enhancing the educational experience and expanding opportunities for learners across the nation.

INTRODUCTION

An online learning environment is a dynamic space where learners can access resources, collaborate with peers, and interact with instructors from anywhere, anytime (Vanoostveen et al., 2019). Four key components of a successful online learning environment help educators achieve their online learning objectives. The four key components are accessibility (Seale & Cooper, 2010), engagement (Oncu & Cakir, 2011), community building (Misanchuk & Anderson, 2001) and personalisation (Ingkavara et al, 2022). The most significant challenge in online education is maintaining learner engagement over time (McKeithan et al, 2021). Effective online learning environments leverage interactive multimedia content, gamification elements, and collaborative activities to captivate learners' attention and foster active participation (Elmer & Dingli, 2024). Despite the physical distance between learners, a strong sense of community is essential to foster collaboration, peer support, and social interaction in online learning environments (Flaherty, 2022).

Online learning has been around in Malaysia since the late 20th century, the most notable expansion and advancement has taken place in the 21st century (Maria et al., 2018). With the beginning of distance education programs by universities like Universiti Sains Malaysia (USM) and Universiti Teknologi Malaysia (UTM) (Lateh & Raman, 2005). These programs mostly used printed materials for learning resources and communication. In the early 2000s, online learning platforms and initiatives became more prevalent in Malaysia due to the accessibility of the Internet. During the mid-2000s, Open University Malaysia (OUM) became the first remote-learning university with an extensive choice of online degree programs (Chiam et al., 2011; Lee, 2020). The mission of OUM is to increase access to high-quality education and possibilities for lifelong learning, especially for adult learners. Its goal is to become Malaysia's and the region's leading provider of flexible learning. Operating as a private institution, OUM is governed by the Ministry of Higher Education in Malaysia (Anuwar, 2009).

The relationship between online learning and the Malaysian context is important because of the country's mix of cultures, technology use, and strong government support for education. Malaysia's experience in online learning shows how it has tackled issues like accessibility and student engagement, especially in both cities and rural areas. By looking at how Malaysia has effectively used technology, developed teaching methods, and provided student support, educators and policymakers from other countries can learn valuable lessons. These insights can help them create better online learning experiences that are inclusive and effective, especially as education continues to change rapidly around the world. Recognizing that each learner has unique goals, preferences, and prior knowledge, a good online learning environment offers personalized learning experiences tailored to individual needs. In the context of online distance education in Malaysia, this chapter will highlight four key components that can help in creating and maintaining an online learning environment.

There isn't a single theory that summarizes all four components (engagement, accessibility, community building, and personalization). The Community of Inquiry (CoI) Framework comes closest to providing an integrated approach. The CoI framework emphasizes the importance of cognitive presence, which involves critical thinking and engagement with course materials. Active participation and interaction are key to fostering deep learning. The CoI framework implies the need for inclusive practices that ensure all learners can engage in the online learning community. Accessibility is a foundation for creating a supportive learning environment. The CoI framework is built on the idea of creating a learning community through social presence, teaching presence, and cognitive presence. It highlights how interactions among learners and instructors cultivate a supportive and collaborative atmosphere. The emphasis on teaching presence can involve tailored instructional strategies that consider individual learners' needs and preferences, thus promoting a more personalized learning experience.

THE COMMUNITY OF INQUIRY (CoI) FRAMEWORK

The Community of Inquiry (CoI) Framework was developed in the late 1990s by educational researchers, Garrison, Anderson, and Archer (Swan et al., 2009). The framework emerged from their work on distance education and online learning, aiming to understand and improve the educational experience in these contexts. The groundwork for the CoI framework was laid through research on the dynamics of online learning environments. Garrison and his colleagues sought to identify key elements that contributed to effective learning in a virtual space, leading to the development of the CoI model. Based on the CoI Framework, three elements constitute a meaningful online learning experience: social presence, cognitive presence, and teaching presence (Whiteside et al., 2023).

The Community of Inquiry (CoI) framework highlights important parts of effective online learning. Social Presence is essential because it creates a welcoming space where learners feel safe to share their ideas and connect with each other (Kreijns et al., 2022). This trust and open communication help foster teamwork. Cognitive Presence is about how learners build understanding through ongoing discussions and questioning (Akyol & Garrison, 2011). This includes steps like noticing something interesting, exploring it, making connections, and finding solutions, which all help deepen understanding and critical thinking. Teaching Presence is about how the learning experience is organized and how teachers guide discussions and provide support (Bangert, 2008). A strong teaching presence keeps learners engaged and helps them develop their knowledge. The CoI framework also emphasizes the need for active participation. Learners shouldn't just sit back and listen; they should actively engage with the material and their classmates to learn together.

The CoI framework is designed to be flexible, allowing educators to adapt it to various contexts and learner needs (Schwartz, D. L. et al, 2013). It can be applied to different formats and modalities of learning, making it relevant across diverse educational settings. The Community of Inquiry framework has significantly influenced the design and implementation of online learning environments by highlighting the importance of social, cognitive, and teaching presences. Its principles foster meaningful engagement, collaboration, and critical thinking, ultimately leading to enhanced learning experiences. As online education continues to evolve, the CoI framework remains a valuable tool for educators seeking to create effective and supportive learning communities. Understanding the CoI framework sets the stage for examining key components that enhance online learning. Engagement, accessibility, community building, and personalization are crucial for creating an effective online educational experience. Each of these elements contributes to a supportive learning environment where students can thrive and reach their full potential. In the Malaysian context, where diverse cultural backgrounds and varying levels of technological access exist, focusing on these components can help ensure that online education meets the needs of all learners and fosters inclusive participation.

Creating and maintaining a successful online learning environment in Malaysia comes with its own set of challenges, influenced by factors such as technological infrastructure (Yeap et al., 2021), cultural norms (Nordin & Norman, 2018), socioeconomic disparities (Yusoff et al., 2022) and educational policies (Jie & Ali, 2021). Malaysia is a multicultural and multilingual society (Su Kim, 2003) with Malay language as the official language along with other widely spoken languages such as English, Chinese and Tamil. Thus, providing online learning materials and instruction in multiple languages to cater to diverse linguistic backgrounds can be a logistical challenge for educators. Traditional cultural norms in Malaysia often prioritize face-to-face interaction and interpersonal relationships in education (Ni, 2022). Transitioning from traditional teaching methods to effective online pedagogy requires training and support for educators. Many instructors may lack experience with online teaching techniques, instructional design for online environments, and technologies such as learning management systems (LMS) (Ma et al, 2021). Providing professional development opportunities and resources for faculty is essential for maintaining the quality of online learning experiences.

ACCESS AND ACCESSIBILITY IN ONLINE LEARNING

Malaysian learners choose online learning for various reasons. Some of them live in rural areas where learning online is the only way for them to further their education. Some are working full-time and unable to attend classes on campus and scheduling online courses fits better with their work schedule. Second language learners might opt for online learning since they need additional time to overcome the language barrier. Online learning cost is cheaper, and it has become a preferred choice for its convenience, flexibility and accessibility (Henry et al., 2014). Online learning in Malaysia has surged in popularity, offering flexibility and convenience to learners worldwide. However, amidst this rapid growth, the importance of accessibility often gets overlooked. Accessibility in online learning refers to the design and implementation of digital educational materials, tools, and platforms that ensure all individuals, including those with disabilities, can access and engage with educational content effectively (Coleman & Berge, 2018). It encompasses various aspects aimed at removing barriers to learning and promoting equal participation for everyone, regardless of their abilities.

Making online learning accessible for all learners involves overcoming several challenges. In Malaysia, the issue of online learning has been discussed especially since it is a big challenge among middle-income parents who cannot afford to purchase a proper device for their children for online learning. Abdul Hamid & Khalidi (2020) highlighted that one of the main constraints to support online learning is the limited availability of devices. This is supported by a survey by the Ministry of Education (MOE), which showed that nearly 37% of 900,000 students do not have proper devices. This situation occurs when many households face financial problems. Another challenge when conducting teaching and learning online is the limited access to the internet. In Malaysia, states like Pahang, Kelantan, Sabah and Sarawak do not have adequate internet access (Siti Subaryani, et at., 2021) This situation occurs when many households are experiencing financial problems. For households that have personal computers, most would need to share with other household members for work or study (Abdul Hamid & Khalidi, 2020).

The challenges of online learning can also be classified into three (3) types of barriers, usage barrier, value barrier and risk barrier. The usage barrier occurs when people who have been accustomed to the traditional method struggle to adopt online learning since they are unfamiliar with the current practice. Besides, poor internet access and a lack of devices contribute towards the unfamiliarity of embracing a new approach. Meanwhile, value barriers occur when there is uncertainty about whether the value of technology is adequate with the value that can be obtained by the user. For example, when students are experiencing barriers to accessing the internet due to demographic factors. Despite the government's efforts to provide students with devices and data plan assistance, online learning does not only require internet access but also an internet connection at a high-speed level. Then, another barrier is known as risk barriers which refer to the uncertainty and unpredictability of the innovation that they have embraced. For example, parents fear that their children would misuse the internet and therefore, prefer traditional learning as it is less risky.

Online learning at the higher education level aims to provide accessible materials through textbooks, courseware and course materials. Nevertheless, not all publishers offer accessible digital formats of textbooks and courseware yet. Inaccessible materials will cause the institution to bear the burden of remediating them which will be time-consuming, and expensive and might cause public embarrassment if any legal action occurs. Therefore, institutions must abide by clear reliable processes to ensure the accessibility of the materials provided for the students (McAlvage & Rice, 2018). Another thing that needs to be considered is that, when deciding on any product for online learning, all teams should make informed decisions about the functionality of the tools as well as the cost and other considerations. Faculty members and staff need basic training in creating accessible content. Furthermore, making the courses accessible will not only benefit students with disabilities but also those without disabilities. For example, by making the lecture materials available in audio format, the student without any impairment can download and listen to them at their convenience.

Another issue is concerning students with disabilities in Malaysia. Distance or online education is seen as an appropriate channel to provide education for students with impairments. Universities' instructors and instructional designers are encouraged to accommodate students with impairments. Instructions designed must be made accessible to all types of students to allow them to pursue their learning goals. To help achieve this goal, education institutions in Malaysia are required to ensure reasonable accommodation and communicate with instructors on the specific needs of the student. Therefore, accessibility should be included in the analysis, design, development and implementation phases for all online courses to improve accessibility and provide equal access to all students.

Several attempts have been made to ensure equitable access in online learning environments such as providing captions for educational videos and screen reader compatibility to make sure the content of education can be accessed by students with disabilities. Moreover, the time of assessment should also be extended since students with impairments would require more time to complete the assessments and there should be alternative formats for course materials to support the diverse needs of the students. Smith & Johnson (2018) suggested reviewing the educational policy whether they promote accessibility and disability in the online learning environment or not. If necessary, the existing educational policies and systems need to be changed to promote equity in the digital learning environment. The authors added that inclusivity is something that requires collaboration among stakeholders, policymakers, educators and individuals with disabilities.

Most of the time, the accessibility of online learning is in terms of how it enables people who live at a distance to complete their education. On the other hand, online learning is the only realistic option for students with disabilities to complete or further their education. Accessibility in online learning is not merely a legal or ethical requirement; it is a cornerstone of inclusive education that enhances learning opportunities for students with disabilities and benefits all learners. By implementing best practices, raising awareness, and fostering collaboration, digital learning environments can be accessible to everyone, regardless of their abilities.

ENHANCEMENT OF ONLINE CLASSROOM ENGAGEMENT

In Malaysia, the Learning Management Systems (LMS) are the backbone for online learning environments. They provide a centralized platform where course materials, assignments, discussions, and assessments can be managed and accessed by both instructors and students. Platforms like Canvas, jam board and Moodle centralize course materials, assignments, and communications. By using this system, instructors can upload lecture videos, reading materials, and assignment instructions onto the LMS, the automated grading, creating an organized and easily navigable repository for students. The automated grading allows the instructors to easily grade the student's work and allow students to receive swift grades and feedback on their performance. The automated grading and integrated discussion boards enhance the overall learning experience by streamlining interactions and providing timely feedback (Coates et al., 2005).

Gamification and simulation elements are other ways to enhance online engagement among students. Instructors can incorporate gamified elements like points, badges, and leaderboards, incentivize participation as they can motivate students and make learning more engaging yet fun. One university in Malaysia namely Universiti Putra Malaysia (UPM) has introduced gamification in its courses through the use of educational games and competitions. For example, courses in agriculture may include simulation games that challenge students to manage resources and make decisions in a virtual environment. In addition, platforms like Kahoot! and Quizlet offer game-based learning experiences that make education interactive and entertaining. Simulations, on the other hand, provide hands-on learning experiences in a virtual environment, allowing students to apply their knowledge in practical, real-world contexts (Deterding et al., 2011). AR and VR Technologies: Augmented and virtual reality technologies also offer immersive learning experiences that bring abstract concepts to life and provide interactive opportunities for exploration and experimentation. For example, VR can simulate laboratory experiments or historical events, offering students a hands-on learning approach in a virtual setting (Merchant et al., 2014).

Engagement in the context of online learning is typically characterized by three primary dimensions namely cognitive, emotional, and behavioural (Fredricks et al., 2004). The first one, namely Cognitive engagement refers to students' investment in learning, their motivation, and the application of their skills to grasp and explore concepts deeply. Cognitive engagement involves students' investment in learning, their motivation, and the application of their skills (Chen et al., 2021). This dimension emphasizes critical thinking and the extent to which students go beyond the minimum requirements to understand the subject matter (Schaufeli et al., 2006). Malaysian university namely Universiti Malaya (UM) has designed active learning classrooms that facilitate group work and discussions. These spaces are equipped with movable furniture and technology, allowing students to collaborate easily on projects and engage more actively in their learning. Emotional engagement relates to students' feelings towards their learning experience, including their interest, boredom, or enjoyment. According to Rogers & Scott (2020), emotional engagement refers to the students' attitudes, feelings, and overall emotional responses to the learning process. The students must have a positive emotional engagement as it will have a great impact on learning. Positive emotional engagement fosters a deeper connection to the learning material and enhances students' motivation (Pekrun et al., 2002).

The third dimension which can contribute to the engagement in online learning is behavioural engagement. According to Davis (2028), behavioural engagement includes participation, interaction, and involvement in academic activities. Behavioural engagement encompasses the students' participation in academic activities, including attending classes, submitting assignments, and interacting with peers and instructors. High levels of behavioural engagement are often visible through active participation in discussions and consistent effort in coursework (Fredricks et al., 2004). To foster these aspects of engagement in an online setting, instructors must adopt strategies that address the unique needs of virtual learning environments. Enhancing engagement requires a strategic approach that integrates pedagogical techniques, and technological tools, and fosters a sense of community (Parker, 2022).

To attract the students to focus for a few hours in online learning requires extra work from instructors. The instructors have to think of interactive content elements and utilize them in class such as quizzes, polls, breakout rooms and discussion forums which can transform passive learning into an active process. Plus, they can be executed to foster active participation and group collaboration. Interactive content and active learning are pivotal in transforming passive students into active participants in their educational journey (Clark & Mayer, 2016). Quizzes embedded within course materials provide immediate feedback and reinforce knowledge retention (Brown et al., 2014). Meanwhile, polls can be used to gauge students' comprehension and make live sessions more dynamic and participatory. Polls can be used to gauge student opinions or check for understanding during live sessions, making classes more interactive and inclusive.

The discussion forum can enhance the students' engagement as they can participate in threaded discussions on the course actively allowing for synchronous but rich interactions with peers and instructors on the platform. Discussion forums provide the students to discuss topics, ask questions, and share insights (Hrastinski, 2009). For instance, instructors can provide discussion topics based on the lesson with thought-provoking questions and request students to participate and stimulate conversation. It is indeed encouraging the students to become active learners as they express their thoughts and share their experiences with the other students. For example, Monash University Malaysia has adopted the flipped classroom model in various courses. Students are assigned pre-class video lectures, and class time is used for discussions, problem-solving, and hands-on activities, enhancing engagement and interaction. This activity encourages active learning and allows them to apply theoretical knowledge to real-world scenarios. Moreover, this activity can enhance critical thinking, increase their understanding of particular topics and collaborate with their peers while completing this activity. Salmon, (2013) also stated that forums can promote deeper understanding through peer learning and help build a sense of community.

The interaction between instructors and students in an online learning environment is a critical component that significantly influences the effectiveness and quality of education. This interaction, often mediated through digital platforms, plays a pivotal role in fostering engagement, understanding, and satisfaction among students. Active interaction between instructors and students promotes higher levels of engagement in online learning. Students are more likely to participate in discussions, ask questions, and invest effort when they feel connected to their instructors. To maximize the effectiveness of online interactions, instructors can set clear expectations for the students such as the students must be present and accessible during the online class. At the beginning of the lesson, instructors provide an outline of communication protocols as well as provide a course schedule and detailed syllabus to help students manage their time and expectations.

A comprehensive syllabus and a detailed course schedule help student understand what to expect throughout the course. These documents should include information about course objectives, assessment methods, and deadlines, as well as guidance on how to succeed in the course (Boettcher & Conrad, 2016). Instructors can use announcements and regular updates to keep students informed and engaged. To function effectively in online learning, instructors must understand and know the students' needs. To fulfil those factors, providing feedback to the students is one of the effective ways to enhance the online learning environment. This engagement signals to students that their contributions are valued and encourages ongoing participation (Garrison et al., 2000). Timely feedback from instructors helps students understand their progress, identify areas for improvement, and stay motivated. Timely and constructive feedback is critical in online learning environments where face-to-face interactions are limited (Gikandi et al.,2011). Regular encouragement and feedback from instructors can significantly boost students' confidence and motivation (Bryson & Hand, 2007).

Providing virtual consultations via platforms like Zoom, Google Meet or Microsoft Teams allows students to seek personalized support and clarification outside regular class times. Tools like Zoom or Microsoft Teams can facilitate these interactions, allowing for face-to-face engagement even in a virtual environment. Teachers play important roles in facilitating interactions and discussions between students in the online learning environment. These sessions are crucial for providing targeted guidance and fostering instructor-student relationships. The scheduled virtual consultation provides students with opportunities to seek help and clarification outside of regular class times (Hew & Cheung, 2014). These sessions can be invaluable for personalized guidance and support for the students in the online learning environment. The instructors must also encourage peer interaction in online learning. Facilitating opportunities for peer interaction through group work, peer reviews, and collaborative projects can enhance learning and engagement. Students often learn effectively by explaining concepts to their peers and receiving diverse perspectives on the material (Hrastinski, 2009). Enhancing engagement in online classrooms for higher education is essential for fostering academic success, retention, and overall satisfaction. It contributes to the development of critical skills, supports the creation of a connected learning community, and prepares students for future digital and professional environments. By implementing these strategies, educators can create vibrant, interactive online learning environments that keep students engaged and motivated, leading to improved learning outcomes and overall satisfaction. As online education continues to grow, prioritizing strategies that enhance engagement will be vital for educational institutions aiming to provide high-quality, impactful learning experiences.

BUILDING AN ONLINE COMMUNITY FOR LEARNING

Building an online community for learning refers to creating a virtual environment where students, educators, and other stakeholders can connect, collaborate, and share knowledge. This community fosters relationships and support, enhancing the educational experience. These communities bring together individuals with the same interests and aspirations, using digital platforms to enable knowledge exchange, skill development, and meaningful relationships. Then, online learning is used interchangeably with various phrases such as web-based learning, e-learning, computer-assisted instruction, and Internet-based learning (Ruiz et al.,2006). It is now having a considerably larger use than remote learning had previously due to the use of modern technologies.

Online communities have completely changed the face of education and learning in the digital age. One of the major benefits of online learning is the opportunity to access diverse perspectives. Online communities enable students to engage with peers and professionals from all backgrounds and geographical regions, expanding their learning experience with new perspectives and insights. This engagement gives them unique insights into many cultures and lifestyles, preparing them to negotiate the global marketplace. The other benefits of online communities in learning have gained recognition as a method of facilitating deep learning and a fundamental tool in problem and experience-based learning. Active engagement in conversations, collaborative projects, and peer-to-peer feedback mechanisms allows members of online communities to enhance their grasp of subjects and learn new skills.

Creating a robust online community for learning in Malaysia is essential to enhancing educational experiences, particularly in an increasingly digital landscape. An effective online community fosters collaboration, support, and engagement among students, educators, and stakeholders. Given Malaysia's diverse population and educational context, building such a community can help bridge gaps, facilitate knowledge sharing, and promote inclusive learning environments. By focusing on key elements like communication, accessibility, and cultural relevance, Malaysian educational institutions can create online communities that empower all learners. Online communities, in contrast to traditional learning environments, offer flexibility regarding the availability of resources and the scheduling of engagement, making them appropriate for learners with different schedules and preferences.

A sense of belonging and support inside online communities can boost learners' motivation and persistence, allowing them to pursue their educational goals with more confidence. Motivation means different things to different people, and it is also context-dependent. Motivation is defined as the reason that moves us to do anything, a psychological construct, or an act, understanding, belief, or cause that drives a person to do and know something or satisfy their needs (Filgona et al., 2020).

In terms of learning, it is critical to establish what learning motivation is. Astuty (2019) echoes learning motivation as a motivator for a student to participate in learning activities with the goal of gaining something from the learning process. Building an online community for learning serves a crucial role in modern education, offering a dynamic platform where individuals can engage, collaborate, and grow collectively. Creating an online learning community is primarily intended to enhance knowledge sharing and skill development (Khoo et al., 2009). Whether it's a forum for academic courses, vocational training, or personal development, these communities offer learners access to a variety of information, resources, and knowledge. Members can obtain fresh insights and explore diverse viewpoints by participating in discussions, debates, and peer-to-peer exchanges. According to Amalia (2018), another important goal is to encourage student collaboration and teamwork. Online communities enable people from varied backgrounds and areas to work together on projects, assignments, or shared goals.

Furthermore, online learning communities strive to foster a helpful and inclusive environment in which learners can feel encouraged and inspired. These communities foster learners' confidence and resilience by giving opportunities for mentorship, peer support, and constructive criticism, assisting them in overcoming obstacles and achieving their learning goals (Baria & Gomez, 2022). Additionally, building an online learning community aims to foster lifelong learning habits and a culture of continual development (Deepshikha, 2023). These communities encourage members to keep updated on industry trends, broaden their knowledge base, and adapt to changing skill requirements by providing regular discussions, workshops, and training tools.

A successful and engaging online learning environment depends on selecting the appropriate learning platform. The selection process considers factors such as the platform's functionality, usability, and alignment with educational objectives (Alojaiman, 2021). It is critical to select a platform that supports a wide range of learning activities, encourages interaction between students and teachers, and includes powerful tools for content delivery, assessments, and collaboration. Furthermore, the platform should be dependable, secure, and expandable to handle a diverse range of users and instructional materials. By carefully evaluating these factors, educators and institutions can select a platform that enhances learning outcomes and meets the unique needs of their learners, (Piotrowski, 2010).

Developing clear and thorough community norms for online learning is critical for cultivating a healthy and effective virtual learning environment. These standards should explain expected conduct, communication norms, and rules of engagement among learners, instructors, and administrators. (Gray & DiLoreto, 2016). It is critical to emphasize respect, inclusivity, and professionalism across all encounters. Guidelines should also include plagiarism, proper technological use, and politeness during conversations and group activities. Establishing processes for resolving conflicts or dealing with unacceptable behaviour also helps to create a safe and supportive environment for all participants. Regular communication and reinforcement of these principles contribute to accountability and the integrity of the online learning community, fostering a favourable atmosphere for learning and collaboration.

Encouraging students to participate actively in online learning requires intentional strategies that foster dialogue and active participation. (Emma and Monique, 2024). First, educators should create an interactive and multimedia-rich curriculum that captures students' attention and improves understanding. Cultivating a feeling of community through social events, group projects, and peer support networks increases engagement by allowing for meaningful relationships and shared learning experiences. Overall, increasing engagement in online learning entails developing a vibrant and supportive atmosphere in which students are actively engaged, motivated, and inspired to succeed.

Providing great resources for online learning includes curating a varied range of content that enhance the educational experience and help learners achieve their goals. This includes providing comprehensive and current content such as textbooks, articles, videos, and interactive simulations that cater to a variety of learning styles and preferences. Organising resources in a systematic and accessible manner using a learning management system (LMS) or specialised online portal ensures easy navigation and retrieval. Regular updates and input from students help to improve resource selection, guaranteeing relevance and alignment with changing educational needs. Providing useful resources for online learning gives learners the tools and knowledge they need to effectively attain their learning objectives (Orr et al, 2015).

Facilitating networking and support in online learning entails providing opportunities for meaningful relationships and cultivating a friendly community atmosphere. Implementing discussion forums, virtual meetups, and joint projects promotes student involvement, peer support, and knowledge sharing (Lu & Smiles, 2022). Mentorship systems, where experienced persons can guide and advise newer learners, benefit both professional and personal development. Furthermore, organising networking events, webinars, and industry guest lectures allows students to meet with professionals and experts, broadening their professional networks and introducing them to new viewpoints. Zamiri and Esmaeili (2024) stated that regular communication and encouragement from teachers and facilitators help to reinforce a sense of belonging and motivation.

Building an online learning community has unique problems and considerations for educators and administrators to solve for successful implementation. In the Malaysian context of education, one key problem is encouraging active participation and engagement among learners. To solve this problem, establishing a community and connection requires meticulous preparation, which includes the use of interactive tools, engaging material, and scheduled activities that promote collaboration and conversation. By proactively addressing these issues and considerations, educators may foster a caring and enriching online learning environment that improves educational outcomes for all students. Building an online learning community is a dynamic process that requires thoughtful planning, active participation, and constant modification. Educators and students can improve educational performance and promote lifelong learning by utilizing digital platforms and creating a collaborative learning environment.

PERSONALIZE THE LEARNING EXPERIENCE

In simple words, personalized e-learning is a technique that modifies educational content and teaching methods to match the specific requirements and preferences of each learner. This approach focuses on the development of learner-centred teaching strategies that encourage self-directed and collaborative learning. It is different from standard online learning in that it enables students to learn and receive knowledge following their specific requirements. It can also be offered either asynchronously or synchronously, depending on the learners' requirements and course objectives. Taking these variables into account, educators and organizations may create interesting and successful online courses that cater to the specific requirements and interests of each learner.

Malaysian universities have been using platforms like Google Classroom, Moodle, Google Meet and Zoom to create virtual classrooms that offer numerous benefits for personalized e-learning. Particularly in the context of teaching English to university students in Malaysia, Google Classroom was particularly accessible to students, even though most of them relied on smartphones rather than laptops for their learning (A'yun et al., 2021). Educators can deliver live lectures where students can ask questions and participate in discussions, mirroring the dynamics of a traditional classroom. This real-time interaction fosters immediate feedback and clarification, enhancing the learning experience. Additionally, some of these platforms feature breakout rooms, allowing educators to divide students into smaller groups for discussions, peer reviews, or group projects. These features help in personalizing the learning experience to cater to students of different proficiency levels.

Other platforms used to personalize teachings are those with various activities such as Quizizz and JeopardyLabs. These two are often used to personalize learning by creating rooms tailored for students of different proficiency levels. This enables customized quizzes and activities that address specific learning needs and reinforce concepts at the appropriate difficulty level. The platforms' real-time feedback helps students identify areas for improvement, enhance their understanding, and engage more effectively with the lesson. Additionally, the competitive and interactive nature of these tools fosters a fun and motivating learning environment, encouraging active participation and continuous learning among students.

Online learning platforms enable students to learn at their own pace according to their individual proficiency levels and learning styles and help with good time management at the same time. A study by Sari & Oktaviani (2021) on undergraduate students' views on the use of online learning platforms shows that the respondents agreed that they can manage their study time effectively and complete assignments on time using an online learning platform. These platforms offer a wide range of resources, from video lectures and interactive quizzes to discussion forums and personalized feedback. Pre-recorded video lectures can be uploaded and shared with students to enhance their preparation and learning. Interactive quizzes and discussion forums promote active learning and facilitate easy participation, fostering collaboration and enhancing understanding through real-time feedback and peer interaction. By allowing students to progress at their speed, they can thoroughly understand each topic before moving on, reducing stress at the same time.

Personalisation of learning has become essential in the educational field at different levels such as social, government policy, school management, and lesson design (Verpoorten et. al, 2009). According to Anjali, B. (2024), online education is the process of delivering content through the Internet and various digital platforms using electronic devices such as laptops, desktops, tablets, and mobile devices. Meanwhile, traditional education is when the students or learners learn by attending their classes physically more which requires face-to-face interactions. This type of learning promotes more social interaction by allowing students to work or participate in activities in diverse groups. According to Amand (2023), traditional learning, often referred to as in-person or face-to-face learning, is the age-old method of education that has stood the test of time. In this model, students physically attend classrooms, engage directly with teachers, and interact with peers. The students attend the class for a fixed time duration and learn about specific topics and subjects, and they often get hands-on experience for a job (Neha, 2020).

Personalized learning is growing in popularity as a method of instruction. With personalized learning, students can receive instruction altered to their needs and interests rather than receiving the same courses from an instructor. According to Nahas (2022), personalized learning is an educational approach that alters instruction to each learner's unique learning needs, strengths, and interests. It is founded on the premise that everyone learns differently and that training should be personalized to the individual's needs rather than a one-size-fits-all approach. Providing students with a personalized learning path that lets them progress through the content at their own pace is more important than simply putting the materials online and enabling them to access it whenever they want. This approach is highly effective in maintaining student interest and engagement. Personalized learning is proven to be beneficial and appropriate for all ages, regardless of the subject or language being taught.

To develop individualized learning experiences for students, assessing their learning profiles is immensely helpful. This can be accomplished by measuring current and historical data from learners to discover the type and level of content they are most interested in, as well as how they learn best. Based on each learner's history and performance, the process offers the optimum methods while ensuring that they are learning, challenged but not bored, engaged in their work, and fully completing their objectives. The system also generates a personalized path for each learner based on their choices, allowing them to progress through the information at their own pace without becoming lost along the way.

Nahas (2022) stated that personalized learning helps learners move at their own pace, take initiative in their education, and learn from each other. It also increases engagement, knowledge retention, and the capacity to apply what they have learned. It is also crucial to understand how individualized learning might help learners in other ways. For example, it boosts engagement by allowing people to participate in discussions and activities related to their interests, which can improve information retention because they are more likely to remember what they learn. When students move at their own pace, this cuts down barriers between students of different skill levels (Sarah, 2022). Each learner is unique and has both skills and flaws. While some people pick up Math concepts quickly, others need a longer time to understand grammar rules. Even with a full classroom of pupils, no student learns at the same speed all the time. This gives learners the freedom to learn at their speed, enabling them to focus more on their areas of strength and take longer to master areas of weakness.

Focusing on the personalization of the e-learning environment, Hughey (2020) stated that the digital transformation of the educational landscape and the employment needs of the global society present the need for a revolutionary transformation in education. According to Oliver (2019), education must be "relevant to continue to shape our children's identity and integration into society". Frame (2013) discussed the revised role of the teacher in a constructivist and personalized approach encouraging educators to assume the role of facilitators, guides, and coaches rather than all-knowing providers of information. As a result, a personalized e-learning environment is crucial to meet the current educational requirements.

Personalized e-learning refers to an approach where educational content, resources, and assessments are customized to meet the individual learning needs of students (Farma, 2023). It considers each learner's specific background, such as past knowledge, learning style, pace, and interests. Personalized e-learning seeks to provide a modified learning experience that maximizes learner engagement while also encouraging deeper knowledge and mastery of ideas. According to Evanick (2023), personalized learning involves a shift in the traditional teaching paradigm from a teacher-centered approach to a learner-centered approach. Students are urged to actively participate in their education by establishing goals, monitoring their progress, and reflecting on what they have learned, as opposed to being passive consumers of knowledge while in the traditional learning setting.

Among the areas that could be the most affected by personalizing the e-learning environment are improving learner engagement and motivation, as well as improving learning outcomes and performances (Passi, 2023). Personalized e-learning content keeps learners engaged and motivated by taking into consideration their constraints and interests. This could lead to improved academic attainment and better learning outcomes. Furthermore, personalized e-learning can also aid learners in improving their academic performance and learning more effectively. This is because learners are more likely to understand and recall material that is suited to their specific needs and abilities. The best part is, they can have access to the materials wherever they are and whenever they wish to.

However, in implementing this method, several factors must be taken into consideration at the earlier stage. Passi (2023) further discussed one of the factors, which is the requirements or preferences of the learners. A detailed understanding of the requirements and preferences of the learners is necessary for the implementation of personalized e-learning for it to be effective. Surveys, interviews, and tests may be used in this evaluation to get data on the skills, interests, knowledge, and learning preferences of the participants. Educators should also bear in mind that individualization with social and collaborative learning must be balanced in implementing personalized e-learning. Sometimes, using personalized e-learning in collaborative work environments leads to stress on individual learning. Educators should work to strike a balance between customized learning and social and collaborative learning to ensure that learners can perform effectively.

CONCLUSION

In the Malaysian educational system, creating and maintaining successful online learning environments considers technological, pedagogical, and cultural factors. Building an online learning community, improving online classroom engagement, facilitating access and accessibility, and customizing the learning process for each student based on their unique needs and learning style are all essential components of online learning success. Malaysian students will benefit from an online learning environment that strikes a mix of the latest technology and careful pedagogical approaches, cultural inclusion, and robust support networks. Malaysia can establish a flexible and fair virtual learning environment that caters to the requirements of all students and equips them with the necessary skills for the future by tackling these elements.

Due to several developing opportunities and trends, online learning in Malaysia has a bright future. Malaysian online learning platforms will probably include increasingly advanced tools and capabilities as technology progresses. These include the application of advanced data analytics to monitor and enhance student performance, artificial intelligence to provide personalized learning experiences, and virtual and augmented reality to create immersive learning environments. There's an increased likelihood that the attempts to eradicate the technological gap will intensify, opening up online education to more students in underprivileged and isolated locations. Ensuring that all students may take advantage of online education, regardless of their location, will be made possible by government initiatives and private sector investments in digital infrastructure. Hopefully, this chapter can provide information and guidance to help instructors better understand the best practices and strategies to create and maintain a successful online learning environment.

REFERENCES

A'yun, K., Suharso, P., & Kantun, S. (2021, May). Google Classroom as The Online Learning Platform During the Covid-19 Pandemic for The Management Business Student at SMK Negeri 1 Lumajang. [). IOP Publishing.]. *IOP Conference Series. Earth and Environmental Science*, 747(1), 012025. DOI: 10.1088/1755-1315/747/1/012025

Abdul Hamid, H., & Khalidi, J. R. (2020). *Covid-19 and Unequal Learning*. Kuala Lumpur: Khazanah Research Institute. Licence: Creative Commons Attribution CC 3.0.

Akyol, Z., & Garrison, D. R. (2011). Understanding cognitive presence in an online and blended community of inquiry: Assessing outcomes and processes for deep approaches to learning. *British Journal of Educational Technology*, 42(2), 233–250. DOI: 10.1111/j.1467-8535.2009.01029.x

Ali, A. (2014) Quality Assurance in Open and Distance Learning: Strategies and Approaches from the Perspective of Open University Malaysia. In: *International Seminar on Quality Assurance and Sustainability of Higher Education Institutions*, 14-15 February 2014, Bali, Indonesia.

Alojaiman, B. 2021. Toward Selection of Trustworthy and Efficient E-Learning Platform. IEE Access, 9, 133889–133901. *(2) (PDF) Challenging the Status Quo: Open Journal Systems for Online Academic Writing Course*. DOI: 10.1109/ACCESS.2021.3114150

Amalia, E. R. (2018). Collaborative Learning: The concepts and practices in the classroom. International Journal of Research Studies in Education

Amand, S. (2023). *Blended Learning Vs. Traditional Learning: A Detailed Overview Of The Two Approaches*. https://elearningindustry.com/blended-learning-vs-traditional-learning-a-detailed-overview-of-the-two-approaches

Anjali, B. (2024). *Difference Between Traditional and Online Education*. GeeksforGeeks.https://www.geeksforgeeks.org/difference-between-traditional-and-online-education/

Bangert, A. (2008). The influence of social presence and teaching presence on the quality of online critical inquiry. *Journal of Computing in Higher Education*, 20(1), 34–61. DOI: 10.1007/BF03033431

Baria, K., & Gomez, D. (2022). Influence of social support to student learning and development

Boettcher, J. V., & Conrad, R. M. (2016). *The Online Teaching Survival Guide: Simple and Practical Pedagogical Tips* (2nd ed.). Jossey-Bass.

Bryson, C., & Hand, L. (2007). The role of engagement in inspiring teaching and learning. *Innovations in Education and Teaching International*, 44(4), 349–362. DOI: 10.1080/14703290701602748

Bryson, P. C., Roediger, H. L., & McDaniel, M. A. (2014). *Make It Stick: The Science of Successful Learning*. Harvard University Press.

Chiam, C. C., Lim, T. M., Halim, N. A., & Omar, N. A. (2011). Towards Excellence in Higher Education –The Experience of Open University Malaysia (OUM). In: *Symbiosis International Conference on Open & Distance Learning*, 21-23 Feb 2011, Pune, India.

Coates, H., James, R., & Baldwin, G. (2005). A critical examination of the effects of learning management systems on university teaching and learning. *Tertiary Education and Management*, 11(1), 19–36. DOI: 10.1080/13583883.2005.9967137

Coleman, M., & Berge, Z. L. (2018*) A Review of Accessibility in Online Higher Education.* https://ojdla.com/archive/spring211/coleman_berge211.pdf

Deepshikha, A. (2023). Advancement of Lifelong Learning ThroughOnline Communities. *Journal of Current Trends in Information TechnologyVolume*, 13(2).

Deterding, S., Dixon, D., Khaled, R., & Nacke, L. (2011). From game design elements to gamefulness: defining "gamification". In Proceedings of the *15th International Academic MindTrek Conference: Envisioning Future Media Environments* (pp. 9-15). DOI: 10.1145/2181037.2181040

Elmer, J., & Dingli, A. (2024). Enhancing Student Learning. In *INTED2024 Proceedings* (pp. 7771-7779). IATED. DOI: 10.21125/inted.2024.2076

Evanick, J. (2023). *From One-Size-Fits-All To Tailored Online Education: The Advantages Of Personalized Learning*. https://elearningindustry.com/from-one-size-fits-all-to-tailored-online-education-advantages-of-personalized-learning

Farma, A. (2023). 6 Expert Tips Personalized E-Learning Experiences: Enhancing Education in the Digital Age. Retrieved on 20th June 2024 from https://www.linkedin.com/pulse/personalized-e-learning-experiences-enhancing/

Filgona, J., Sakiyo, J., Gwany, D. M., & Okoronka, A. U. (2020). Motivation in learning. *Asian Journal of Education and Social Studies*, 16-37.DOI: 10.9734/ajess/2020/v10i430273

Flaherty, H. B. (2022). Using collaborative group learning principles to foster community in online classrooms. *Journal of Teaching in Social Work*, 42(1), 31–44. DOI: 10.1080/08841233.2021.2013390

Frame, K. (2013). *Pathways to Personalized Learning: Tapping the Potential, Realizing the Benefits*. Center for Digital Education.

Fredricks, J. A., Blumenfeld, P. C., & Paris, A. H. (2004). School engagement: Potential of the concept, state of the evidence. *Review of Educational Research*, 74(1), 59–109. DOI: 10.3102/00346543074001059

Garrison, D. R., Anderson, T., & Archer, W. (2000). Critical inquiry in a text-based environment: Computer conferencing in higher education. *The Internet and Higher Education*, 2(2-3), 87–105. DOI: 10.1016/S1096-7516(00)00016-6

Garrison, D. R., & Vaughan, N. D. (2008). *Blended Learning in Higher Education: Framework, Principles, and Guidelines*. Jossey-Bass.

Gikandi, J. W., Morrow, D., & Davis, N. E. (2011). Online formative assessment in higher education: A review of the literature. *Computers & Education*, 57(4), 2333–2351. https://doi.org/10.1016/j.compedu.2011.06.004. DOI: 10.1016/j.compedu.2011.06.004

Gray, J.A. & DiLoreto, M. (2016). The Effects of Student Engagement, Student Satisfaction, and Perceived Learning in Online Learning Environments. *NCPEA International Journal of Educational Leadership Preparation*, Vol. 11, No. 1– May 2016.

Henry, M. K., Pooley, J. A., & Omari, M. (2014). Student motivation for studying online: A qualitative study. https://ro.ecu.edu.au/ecuworkspost2013/869

Hew, K. F., & Cheung, W. S. (2014). *Using Blended Learning: Evidence-Based Practices*. Springer. DOI: 10.1007/978-981-287-089-6

Hrastinski, S. (2009). A theory of online learning as online participation. *Computers & Education*, 52(1), 78–82. DOI: 10.1016/j.compedu.2008.06.009

Hughey, J. (2020). Individual Personalized Learning. *Educational Considerations*, 46(2). Advance online publication. DOI: 10.4148/0146-9282.2237

, J., & Cooper, M. (2010). E-learning and accessibility: An exploration of the potential role of generic pedagogical tools. *Computers & Education, 54*(4), 1107-1116.

Jie, C. Y., & Ali, N. M. (2021). COVID-19: What are the challenges of online learning? A literature review. *International Journal of Advanced Research in Future Ready Learning and Education*, 23(1), 23–29. DOI: 10.37934/frle.23.1.2329

Kreijns, K., Xu, K., & Weidlich, J. (2022). Social presence: Conceptualization and measurement. *Educational Psychology Review*, 34(1), 139–170. DOI: 10.1007/s10648-021-09623-8 PMID: 34177204

Lateh, H., & Raman, A. (2005). Distance Learning and Educational Technology in Malaysia. In *Encyclopedia of Distance Learning* (pp. 641–653). IGI Global. DOI: 10.4018/978-1-59140-555-9.ch092

Lee, A. B. C. (2020) *Open University Malaysia (OUM): The Path Travelled (2000 – 2020) & The Way Forward (2021 – 2030) - Issues, Challenges, Opportunities.* Master's thesis, Open University Malaysia (OUM).

Lu, H., & Smiles, R. (2022). The Role of Collaborative Learning in the Online Education. *International Journal of Economics, Business and Management Research.* Vol. 6, No.06; 2022. ISSN: 2456-7760

Maria, M., Shahbodin, F., & Pee, N. C. (2018). Malaysian higher education system towards industry 4.0–current trends overview. In *AIP Conference Proceedings* (Vol. 2016, No. 1). AIP Publishing.

McAlvage, K., & Rice, M. (2018). Access and Accessibility in Online Learning: Issues in higher Education and K-12 Contexts. *OLC Research Centre for Digital Learning & Leadership.* https://eric.ed.gov/?id=ED593920

McKeithan, G. K., Rivera, M. O., Mann, L. E., & Mann, L. B. (2021). Strategies to promote meaningful student engagement in online settings. *Journal of Education and Training Studies*, 9(4), 1–11. DOI: 10.11114/jets.v9i4.5135

Merchant, Z., Goetz, E. T., Cifuentes, L., Keeney-Kennicutt, W., & Davis, T. J. (2014). Effectiveness of virtual reality-based instruction on students' learning outcomes in K-12 and higher education: A meta-analysis. *Computers & Education*, 70, 29–40. DOI: 10.1016/j.compedu.2013.07.033

Misanchuk, M., & Anderson, T. (2001). *Building Community in an Online Learning Environment: Communication.* Cooperation and Collaboration.

Nahas, E. (2022). *Impact Of Personalized Learning.* https://elearningindustry.com/impact-of-personalized-learning

Neha, J. (2020). *Online Learning Vs Traditional Learning.* https://www.evelynlearning.com/online-learning-vs-traditional-learning/

Nordin, N., & Norman, H. (2018). Cross-culture learning via massive open online courses for higher education. [Malaysian Journal of Education]. *Jurnal Pendidikan Malaysia*, 43(1), 35–39. DOI: 10.17576/JPEN-2018-43.01-05

Oliver, B. (2019). *Making micro-credentials work for learners, employers, and providers.*

Oncu, S., & Cakir, H. (2011). Research in online learning environments: Priorities and methodologies. *Computers & Education*, 57(1), 1098–1108. DOI: 10.1016/j.compedu.2010.12.009

Passi, D. (2023). *Why Personalized Learning is the Future of eLearning: Benefits and Impacts.* https://www.kytewayelearning.com/article/personalized-learning-in-elearning

Pekrun, R., Goetz, T., Titz, W., & Perry, R. P. (2002). Academic emotions in students' self-regulated learning and achievement: A program of qualitative and quantitative research. *Educational Psychologist*, 37(2), 91–105. DOI: 10.1207/S15326985EP3702_4

Piotrowski, M. (2010). *What is an E-Learning platform? In: Learning management system technologies and software solutions for online teach-ing: tools and applications,* pp. 20–36; 2010. DOI: 10.4018/978-1-61520-853-1.ch002

Ruiz, G., Mintzer, J., & Leipzig, M. (2006). The Impact of e-Learning in Medical Education. *Academic Medicine*, 31(3), 207–212. DOI: 10.1097/00001888-200603000-00002 PMID: 16501260

Sari, F. M., & Oktaviani, L. (2021). Undergraduate students' views on the use of online learning platform during COVID-19 pandemic. [Shute]. *Teknosastik*, 19(1), 41–47. DOI: 10.33365/ts.v19i1.896

Siti Subaryani Zainol, Suhaili Mohd. Hussin, Maisarah Syazwani Othman & Nur Hazrini Mohd Zahari. (2021). Challenges of Online Learning Faced by The B40 Income Parents In Malaysia. *International Journal of Education and Pedagogy.*, 3(2).

Su Kim, L. (2003). Multiple identities in a multicultural world: A Malaysian perspective. *Journal of Language, Identity, and Education*, 2(3), 137–158. DOI: 10.1207/S15327701JLIE0203_1

Swan, K., Garrison, D. R., & Richardson, J. C. (2009). A constructivist approach to online learning: The community of inquiry framework. In *Information technology and constructivism in higher education: Progressive learning frameworks* (pp. 43–57). IGI global. DOI: 10.4018/978-1-60566-654-9.ch004

Vanoostveen, R., Desjardins, F., & Bullock, S. (2019). Professional development learning environments (PDLEs) embedded in a collaborative online learning environment (COLE): Moving towards a new conception of online professional learning. *Education and Information Technologies*, 24(2), 1863–1900. DOI: 10.1007/s10639-018-9686-6

Vaughan, N. D., Cleveland-Innes, M., & Garrison, D. R. (2013). *Teaching in Blended Learning Environments: Creating and Sustaining Communities of Inquiry*. Athabasca University Press. DOI: 10.15215/aupress/9781927356470.01

Verpoorten, D., Glahn, C., Kravcik, M., Ternier, S., & Specht, M. (2009). Personalisation of Learning in Virtual Learning Environments. In Lecture notes in computer science (pp. 52–66). DOI: 10.1007/978-3-642-04636-0_7

Whiteside, A. L., Dikkers, A. G., & Swan, K. (Eds.). (2023). *Social presence in online learning: Multiple perspectives on practice and research*. Taylor & Francis.

Yeap, C. F., Suhaimi, N., & Nasir, M. K. M. (2021). Issues, challenges, and suggestions for empowering technical vocational education and training education during the COVID-19 Pandemic in Malaysia. *Creative Education*, 12(8), 1818–1839. DOI: 10.4236/ce.2021.128138

Yusoff, N. S., Rashid, M. F., & Halim, N. A. (2022). The Impact of Covid-19 Pandemic Towards Socioeconomic Wellbeing of Rural Community in Malaysia. [). IOP Publishing.]. *IOP Conference Series. Earth and Environmental Science*, 1064(1), 012054. DOI: 10.1088/1755-1315/1064/1/012054

Zamiri, M., & Esmaeili, A. (2024). Methods and Technologies for Supporting Knowledge Sharing within Learning Communities: A Systematic Literature Review. *Administrative Sciences*, 14(1), 17. DOI: 10.3390/admsci14010017

Chapter 5
Beyond Lectures:
The Flipped Learning Model

Elissar Gerges
https://orcid.org/0009-0005-4782-0246
Zayed University, UAE

ABSTRACT

Despite the robust evidence supporting active learning, it is quite surprising that students complete weeks of lectures before an assignment, the product of their learning, is due. In such classes, learning is assumed to occur as students complete the assigned readings and attend classes without demonstrating their understanding. Alternatively, courses designed based on an active learning approach require students to showcase their learning in various tasks in a collaborative environment. The literature provides a wealth of research studies with empirical evidence of the effectiveness of active learning strategies in enhancing student achievement shifting from didactic teaching to a student-centered environment. This chapter will introduce the Flipped Learning Model as an active learning pedagogy in an online classroom. The flipped learning model aligns with the social constructivist approach as a theoretical framework that underpins active learning. Two active learning strategies will be explored in the flipped classroom context: Jigsaw Groups and Active Reading.

BEYOND LECTURES: THE FLIPPED LEARNING MODEL

University-level teaching has historically relied on traditional lectures as the primary method for professors to convey knowledge to passive students. Over the past three decades, this approach has faced significant criticism for failing to engage students intellectually, maintain their attention, accommodate diverse learning paces, and teach higher-order skills such as application and analysis. Despite these

DOI: 10.4018/979-8-3693-4407-1.ch005

criticisms and innovations in teaching methods, traditional lectures remain dominant in higher education. Surprisingly, robust evidence supporting active learning has not significantly altered this trend, and students often complete weeks of lectures before any assignment is due, assuming learning occurs through attendance and reading without the need to demonstrate understanding.

In recent years, higher education has evolved significantly, facing increasing pressure to enhance student learning and demonstrate the effectiveness of its programs. Despite the dominance of traditional lectures, research consistently shows that students often fail to develop critical thinking, creativity, or advanced reasoning skills in unengaging classroom settings (O'Flaherty & Phillips, 2015). Policymakers, scholars, and advocacy groups collectively strive to elevate higher education by employing evidence-based strategies to improve student outcomes. These institutions seek cost-effective, student-centered methods and curricula that offer dynamic and innovative learning opportunities. However, despite the push for new teaching methods, the lecture format remains prevalent due to its economic efficiency, accommodating large numbers of students with a single professor.

Universities are expected to nurture graduates who are creative and critical thinkers capable of addressing complex social, ecological, technological, scientific, and political challenges. At the same time, they must innovate their teaching methods and support a diverse student population transitioning to higher education. These demands necessitate critical and reflective teaching and learning strategies. Instructors are no longer the primary source of information; instead, students are central to the learning experience. Modern teaching methods enhance students' creativity, collaboration, and skills. In the classroom, students engage in analysis, research, and activities prepared by the instructor, utilizing active learning strategies that encourage critical thinking and reflection.

These concerns have led to growing support for flipped learning in higher education (Akçayır & Akçayır, 2018; Althubaiti &Althubaiti, 2023; Baepler et al., 2014; Bhagat et al., 2016; Brewer & Movahedazarhouligh, 2018; Fisher et al., 2021; Lee & Wallace, 2018; Lundin et al., 2018; Steen-Utheim & Foldnes, 2018). The flipped classroom model, supported by theoretical foundations and empirical studies, effectively overcame traditional lecture challenges and promoted active learning strategies that engage students in higher-order thinking as outlined in Bloom's taxonomy, such as application, analysis, and synthesis. This approach reverses traditional teaching by having students complete classroom tasks at home and engage in interactive, meaningful activities in class. Higher education increasingly focuses on enhancing the learner experience, with technology-based pedagogies improving student satisfaction. Within the broader field of education, flipped learning has gained popularity as a contemporary teaching method. The appeal of flipped learning lies in its ability to reduce traditional lecturing and create more opportunities for active learning, motivating the focus of this chapter.

FLIPPED LEARNING: AN OVERVIEW

Over the last two decades, the flipped classroom has evolved from a vague idea to a dominant pedagogical approach across various academic fields and educational levels. This shift is driven by the recognition that lecture-based instruction is less effective than strategies that encourage active learning, prompting a move from 'transmissionist' instruction toward more flexible, active pedagogical approaches with greater emphasis on learner autonomy.

When effectively implemented, flipped learning engages students in their learning. Although the term "flipped classroom" is relatively recent, similar approaches, such as inverted classroom (Lage et al., 2000), just-in-time teaching (Novak, 2011), and inverted learning (Braun & Vasko, 2014), have been explored over the past decade, highlighting the importance of student preparation before class (Hung, 2017). A significant milestone for this constructivist approach was likely the publication of Flip Your Classroom: Reach Every Student in Every Class Every Day by Aaron Sams and Jonathan Bergmann (Bergmann & Sams, 2012; Talbert & Bergmann, 2017), which popularized the method. Nonetheless, the concept of "flipping the classroom" is now well-established in educational terminology.

This chapter aims to serve as a guide for educators seeking to adopt the flipped classroom model, aiding their decision-making process. The following sections explore the theoretical foundations and rationale for flipping the classroom. After demonstrating the model's effectiveness, we examine essential decisions instructors face during implementation, evaluate the advantages and disadvantages of prevalent active learning strategies, address challenges, and conclude with recommendations and future directions.

ACTIVE LEARNING IN HIGHER EDUCATION: AN OVERVIEW

For many years, lectures have been the primary teaching method in classrooms. However, lectures often lack the elements of active learning, including critical thinking, self-paced learning, and promoting dialogue and group discussions. The traditional "chalk and talk" teaching method is now often seen as a passive, transmission-based approach that offers limited opportunities for student involvement, results in low levels of student engagement, and promotes only superficial learning. This issue is even more pronounced in online courses, where lectures are less effective. A significant obstacle in online education is the insufficient active participation of students in online discussions (Morawo et al., 2020). This chapter introduces the Flipped Classroom Model as an active learning pedagogy in an online classroom. The Flipped Classroom Model aligns with the social constructivist theoretical framework that underpins active learning. This chapter will explore the implementation of two active learning strategies within the flipped classroom: Jigsaw Groups and Active Reading.

The academic literature provides a wealth of research studies with empirical evidence of the effectiveness of active learning strategies in enhancing student achievement. Innovative approaches to teaching and learning, such as seminars, problem-based learning, collaborative games, group podcasts, and debates, shift from didactic teaching to a student-centered environment that promotes engagement. Decades of research consistently show that students in active learning classrooms perform significantly better than those in traditional classes (Hao et al., 2021). However, what active learning entails in an online setting remains a pertinent question. Acknowledging the various definitions of active learning, this chapter adopts Chickering and Gamson's (1987; as cited in Jacob, 2023) early definition that in active learning classrooms, students "must talk about what they are learning, write about it, […] make what they learn part of themselves" (p. 4). In conjunction with more recent research, the active learning activities discussed in this chapter will align with Jacob's (2023) Active Cognitive Task (ACT) framework, which consists of three elements:

- Active: Students must have the agency to take responsibility for their learning rather than engage in passive tasks that depend on rote learning.
- Cognitive: The task must prompt cognitive engagement as students construct their learning meaningfully.
- Task: The significance of the task does not lie in the content per se but in how students apply it in different contexts.

ACTIVE LEARNING IN THE FLIPPED CLASSROOM

The concepts of 'active learning' and 'student-centered learning' gained significant attention from educators, researchers, psychologists, and instructional designers in the late 1970s and early 1980s. Bonwell and Eison (1991) offer one of the earliest definitions of active learning. They initially characterized active learning as instructional methods that require students to engage in meaningful learning activities and reflect on their learning process. Increasing evidence suggests active learning surpasses traditional lecture methods (Bishop & Verleger, 2013). This evidence prompted Freeman et al. (2014) to conduct a meta-analysis recommending that future research prioritize educational psychology and cognitive science advancements to explore optimal forms of active learning rather than using the traditional lecture as a standard control.

The literature on active learning has expanded significantly, introducing various innovative and effective methods to enhance students' critical thinking, discussion, debate, and overall achievement. The diversity of active learning strategies is extensive, serving various instructional objectives, often overlapping and drawing on similar pedagogical principles that emphasize student-centered instruction and course learning outcomes, such as walking seminars, problem-based collaborative games, and songwriting for second language learning, to mention a few. Despite the recognized benefits of active learning, educators face the challenge of integrating these strategies into their courses without compromising content coverage. This challenge, coupled with the rise of digital education, contributed to the development of 'inverted' or 'flipped' learning.

In the empirical literature, definitions of flipped learning vary considerably. Some emphasize the use of digital technology, while others focus on collaborative or group learning activities (Låg & Sæle, 2019). Flipped learning is described in various ways, such as a pedagogical approach, teaching technique, student-centered strategy, and active learning methodology. It prioritizes active engagement over traditional lectures, which are closely related to active learning, student-centered learning, and problem-based learning approaches. These are all rooted in constructivist educational theory, influential since Piaget (1957). Flipped learning aligns with constructivism by viewing learning as the learner's active engagement with content, instructors, and peers (Cheng et al., 2019). Despite lacking a universally accepted definition, active learning remains a consistent theme across flipped learning research definitions.

While the notion that learning requires active engagement is not novel, our current educational practices often do not fully reflect this understanding. Active learning is recognized for its ability to enhance student achievement (Freeman et al., 2014), yet many educators find it challenging to integrate it into their instructional plans. Recognizing the limitations of traditional lecture-based instruction, educators have sought more effective strategies to encourage students' active participation in their learning process. Creating an active learning environment and fostering student engagement in classroom discussions has proven challenging (Clinton & Kelly, 2020; Rezaei, 2020). However, it is important to note that educators should view direct instruction and active learning as complementary rather than opposing or mutually exclusive approaches. Skilled instructors will recognize the appropriate context for direct instruction, just as they would with active learning. Both strategies are valuable tools that can enhance one another to create a dynamic learning environment when used in the right context.

Advocates of flipped learning argue that its effectiveness stems from its basis in active learning principles (Adams & Lenton, 2017; Yang et al., 2019). Studies indicate that any performance gap between flipped and traditional classrooms diminishes when both use active learning strategies, affirming that active learning plays a crucial role in enhancing learning outcomes within the flipped classroom model (DeLozier & Rhodes, 2017; O'Flaherty & Phillips, 2015). Research suggests that the integration of active learning, rather than the flipped structure per se, correlates with improved student achievement (Jensen et al., 2015). The implementation and strategies of flipped learning can vary significantly across different courses. Still, at its core, it reorganizes the learning process by replacing passive classroom activities with active learning opportunities during what was traditionally lecture time. This working definition justifies using the term 'flipped,' emphasizing not only moving content delivery outside of class but also centering the classroom environment on engaging, meaningful educational activities rather than simple tasks for their own sake.

The flipped classroom model is a growing trend in active learning that has gained prominence in higher education. This pedagogical approach has accelerated the use of educational technology due to the integration of online, hybrid, and collaborative learning formats. It has shifted the responsibility of learning from instructors to students, promoting student autonomy and empowerment (Sohrabi & Iraj, 2016). This method encourages students to engage in active, problem-based learning, enhancing their skills in critical thinking, creative problem-solving, and teamwork. As a result, classroom time is utilized for collaborative projects, presentations, and discussions, allowing students to work together more effectively. Students engage in interactive tasks, exercises, and activities to apply their newly acquired knowledge, often solving problems in small groups with the instructor providing guidance and support.

Students' Perspectives and Challenges

Successful implementation of flipped learning requires careful planning and support from faculty. As institutions explore and implement this approach, understanding and responding to students' needs will be crucial for enhancing educational outcomes in flipped learning environments. Recent studies have explored higher education students' perspectives on flipped learning, revealing generally positive attitudes regarding its effectiveness compared to traditional teaching methods. Several studies highlight various aspects of this innovative pedagogical approach, including:

Increased Engagement: Students are generally open and positive towards the flipped classroom approach, expressing higher satisfaction and engagement than traditional lectures (Josifović-Elezović, 2022). They find that the interactive nature of flipped classrooms enhances their overall learning experience (Ha et al., 2019).

Active Learning: Students often appreciate the active learning environment that flipped classrooms foster. By engaging with the material beforehand, they can participate in discussions and problem-solving activities during class, which enhances their understanding and retention of the subject matter (Zain & Sailin, 2020). This shift from rote learning to active engagement is frequently cited as a key benefit, particularly in improved academic performance.

Self-Paced Learning: The flexibility of learning at their own pace is a significant advantage for many students. They can review recorded lectures or readings as needed, accommodating diverse learning speeds and styles. This autonomy encourages students to take responsibility for their learning, which many find empowering (Turan & Goktas, 2015).

Improved Collaboration: Flipped classrooms promote collaboration among peers. Students report that working together on assignments and projects during class time enhances their learning experience and builds teamwork skills. This collaborative atmosphere is often seen as more beneficial than traditional lecture formats (Ha et al., 2019; Turan & Goktas, 2015).

Development of Critical Skills: Flipped learning promotes the development of important skills such as critical thinking, problem-solving, and teamwork. Students engage in hands-on activities during class time, which helps them apply theoretical knowledge in practical contexts. For instance, a meta-analysis found that flipped learning positively impacts foundational knowledge and higher-order thinking skills. This approach is particularly beneficial for preparing students for real-world challenges (Bredow et al., 2021).

However, while students are open to the flipped approach, they express skepticism about completely replacing traditional lectures (Josifović-Elezović, 2022). Some students struggle to adapt and retain passive learning habits. Concerns are raised about technical and technological issues (Baig & Yadegaridehkordi, 2023; Singh et al., 2021), as well as language barriers for international students (Akçayır & Akçayır, 2018). Other challenges include:

Pre-Class Preparation Requirements: While many students appreciate the flexibility of flipped learning, some express concerns about the necessity for self-discipline to complete pre-classwork before class. This expectation can be challenging for those who are accustomed to traditional lecture formats where content is delivered in class.

Access to Resources: The effectiveness of flipped classrooms can be hindered by disparities in access to technology and reliable internet connections. Students without adequate resources may find it challenging to engage fully with pre-class materials, leading to frustration and disengagement (Baig & Yadegaridehkordi, 2023).

Adjustment to the Model: Transitioning to a flipped classroom model can be disorienting for some students. They may initially feel overwhelmed by the increased responsibility for their learning and the shift in classroom dynamics. Clear communication from instructors about expectations can help ease this transition (Khayat et al., 2021).

Overall, the flipped classroom method appears to fulfill students' basic cognitive needs and enhance their learning experiences in higher education, suggesting its potential for wider implementation in tertiary education contexts.

CONSTRUCTIVISM

Most research studies analyze the flipped classroom model through the lens of cognitive load theory. In a flipped classroom environment, students engage with the materials before attending class, allowing them to control the pace of their learning and select the strategies that best match their preferences. Consequently, they can identify intrinsic cognitive load ahead of time and minimize the extraneous cognitive load. From a cognitive load perspective, allowing students to engage in self-paced preparatory activities is more effective in managing working memory than traditional lectures.

This chapter will analyze flipped learning as a model rooted in the constructivist theory. Constructivist theory posits that knowledge is an evolving understanding shaped by ongoing interactions between individuals and their environment. Students enter the classroom with pre-existing experiences and perspectives. New information interacts with this prior knowledge, facilitating the development of a personalized understanding of the subject. Consequently, knowledge is continually constructed and reconstructed based on individuals' existing knowledge, personal experiences, and interactions with others.

The positive impacts of active learning are well-supported by the principles of constructivist theory. Constructivism emphasizes that students are actively engaged in learning, shifting from passive listening to active participation (King, 1993). In this approach, knowledge is constructed rather than received or discovered, necessitating restructuring existing cognitive frameworks rather than mere accumulation of information. Teaching under constructivism focuses on facilitating this cognitive restructuring rather than just transmitting facts. Furthermore, interactive and communicative learning activities where learners play active roles are seen as more effective for motivating learning than passive activities (Olusegun, 2015).

The flipped model fundamentally shifts from a teacher-focused, transmission-based method to a student-focused, constructivist method. A flipped classroom is a learning environment where direct instruction shifts from an individual to a group setting, transforming the group setting into an interactive and dynamic space. This approach reverses Bloom's taxonomy by having students complete lower-level cognitive tasks, such as understanding and comprehension, outside of class, while higher-order tasks like problem-solving, applying key concepts, and analysis are tackled during class through collaborative work and discussions.

Constructivist principles are evident in excerpts such as this one (as cited in Li et al., 2023):

The basis of flipped learning is active learning and builds on constructivism (...). It embraces problem-based learning, peer-assisted learning, cooperative learning, and collaborative learning under active learning (...). After all, flipped learning, which stresses the instructor's role as a coach, is a pedagogical option to provide opportunities for interactive and dynamic engagement in the learning process (Kwon & Woo, 2018, p. 3).

Adopting this student-centered, constructivist approach necessitates significant alterations in how students engage with the course, compelling faculty to redesign their curriculum. This often leads to more clearly defined learning objectives, the establishment of structured supports for student learning, the integration of engaging activities that encourage more profound understanding, and an increase in opportunities for both formative and summative assessments.

THE FLIPPED CLASSROOM: REVERSING BLOOM'S TAXONOMY

Why might instructors choose to flip their classes or courses? The most straightforward explanation is that educators recognize that the flipped approach maximizes the effectiveness of synchronous interactions with students, an instructional strategy emphasized in this chapter.

While Bergmann and Sams (2012) are often credited with the concept of Flipped Learning, it was first introduced by Lage et al. (2000) as Inverted Learning. Bergmann and Sams (2022) later popularized and extended the concept. Bergmann (2022) explained this clearly in three versions of Bloom's Taxonomy. Figure 1, widely recognized, depicts Bloom's pyramid, which represents class time before adopting flipped classrooms. In traditional settings, much time was devoted to transferring knowledge, with students expected to tackle more complex tasks such as applying, analyzing, and evaluating at home. However, with flipped classrooms, faculty found that little class time was needed for basic knowledge and comprehension, leading to a reimagined class structure, as shown in Figure 2.

Figure 1. Bloom's Taxonomy

Figure 2. Bloom's Taxonomy Inverted

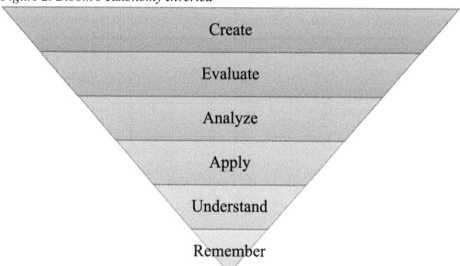

Furthermore, students do not spend most of their class time on evaluation and creation but rather focus on the intermediate levels of Bloom's Taxonomy (Figure 3). This more accurate representation aligns better with typical educational experiences (Bergmann, 2022).

Figure 3. Bloom's Taxonomy Diamond

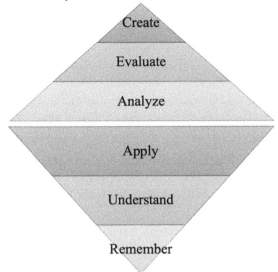

Generally, a flipped classroom involves moving activities traditionally done in class to outside the classroom and vice versa. According to a leading definition, "the flipped approach inverts the traditional classroom model by introducing course concepts before class, allowing educators to use class time to guide each student through active, practical, innovative applications of the course principles" (Academy of Active Learning Arts and Sciences, 2018). In another widely accepted interpretation, the flipped classroom encompasses pedagogical methods that involve moving information delivery outside of class, utilizing in-class time for active and collaborative learning activities, and requiring students to engage in pre- or post-class assignments to maximize their learning during class sessions (Abeysekera & Dawson, 2015).

According to Strayer (2012), the flipped classroom is a form of blended learning, with technology playing a significant role in its definition. While the flipped classroom model does not require blended learning, many implementations incorporate it to increase the accessibility of pre-class activities by offering them online. The model lacks a standardized approach, allowing various structures and a wide range of activities to be included outside and inside the classroom (O'Flaherty & Phillips, 2015). Most flipped learning literature emphasizes that the key to its success lies in designing online and face-to-face learning experiences in such a way that they complement and reinforce each other at both the overall course level and the individual lesson level. Essential components of a flipped classroom include (a) pre-class exposure to content, (b) incentives for students to prepare for class, (c) methods to assess understanding, and (d) in-class activities emphasizing higher-order cognitive tasks like peer learning and problem-solving (Abeysekera & Dawson, 2015).

Bishop and Verleger (2013) describe flipped classrooms as involving interactive, group-based learning activities in the classroom and individual, computer-based instruction outside the classroom. This creates two distinct learning environments: outside the classroom (before and after class) and inside the classroom (during class). In the first environment, students watch videos on various theoretical concepts. These video lessons are accessible anytime, allowing students to reinforce their learning by re-watching the material as needed. Although flipped learning is often associated with video content, other interactive technologies and materials, such as textbooks and handouts, can also be utilized. In the second environment, students engage in more interactive activities, reaching higher levels of Bloom's taxonomy, such as application, analysis, and synthesis, during class time. In-class interactive learning activities promote student autonomy and foster advanced cognitive skills. These activities enhance students' higher-order thinking and problem-solving abilities as well as their collaborative and time management skills. The flipped classroom model also allows for flexible implementation across disciplines, enabling instructors to select and combine diverse technical approaches and learning designs (Elmaadaway, 2018; Kim & Park, 2017; Long et al., 2017; Mohamed & Lamia, 2018).

Despite numerous definitions and examples of flipped or inverted classrooms in higher education, there is still no consensus on its definition. Since the development of the Flipped Learning methodology by Bergmann and Sams (2012), the approach has evolved significantly, and resolving these definitional issues is beyond the scope of this chapter. Today, the flipped classroom provides students greater opportunities to cultivate critical and independent thinking and enhance their learning processes through collaborative peer interactions. Initially, it is believed that the success of the Flipped Classroom approach is tied to the student's autonomy and responsibility, as they must independently prepare for the class. However, collaborative work within and outside the classroom is a fundamental component of the flipped model. This approach fosters social interaction and collaboration, allowing students to negotiate and refine their understanding with peers while continually monitoring their learning and addressing any misconceptions.

In traditional classrooms, the teaching strategy known as "I Do," "We Do," "You Do" has been long established. However, the flipped classroom reverses this approach to "You Do," "We Do," "I Do" (Schmidt & Ralph, 2016). Here, students engage in preparatory activities, allowing classroom time to focus on problem-solving, textual analysis, or solution exploration (Figure 4). In a flipped classroom, in-person sessions are used for exploring and exchanging ideas with individualized support, scaffolding, and motivation. This is enabled by shifting content delivery to online lectures, which are better at visual representation and allow for self-paced learning. Essentially, flipped learning optimizes the roles of both human instructors and technology, allowing each to perform to their strengths.

Figure 4. Aspects of Traditional and Flipped Learning Mapped against Bloom's Taxonomy

Adapted from *Flipped Learning: A Transformative Approach Designed to Meet the Needs of Today's Knowledge Economies and Societies* (p.16), by M. Şahin and C. F. Kurban, 2016, Emerald Group Publishing Limited. Copyright 2016 by Emerald Group Publishing Limited.

The growing popularity of flipped learning in higher education can be attributed to its emphasis on advancing students to higher cognitive levels, enhancing engagement, shifting from teacher-centered to student-centered learning, fostering lifelong learning skills, and cultivating abilities valued by employers such as critical thinking, collaboration, and self-direction.

First, allowing students to regulate the pace of flipped classroom activities (such as adjusting video or reading speeds and utilizing rewind/fast-forward options) decreases unnecessary cognitive load compared to traditional lecture formats. Cognitive load refers to the volume of information a learner handles simultaneously, constrained by the limits of working memory, which can impede comprehension and retention, as discussed in an earlier section of this chapter. Incorporating structured elements like quizzes or reflective exercises into pre-classwork likely enhances this reduction in cognitive load (Wilton et al., 2019). Moreover, empowering students with more autonomy enables them to tailor their engagement with pre-classwork materials according to their existing knowledge.

Second, the activities conducted in class allow students to apply the new knowledge gained beforehand, enhancing their comprehension. Chi and Wylie (2014) propose a framework for understanding different cognitive processes induced by various learning activities and their impact on learning outcomes. They categorize cognitive processes into passive (e.g., listening to a lecture), active (e.g., taking notes), constructive (e.g., explaining concepts), and interactive (e.g., collaborating with peers), with research indicating that transitions through these stages enhance learning quantity, quality, and retention. Applying this framework to the shift from traditional lectures to flipped classrooms, students progress from passive and active engagement to more constructive and interactive methods, which promises significant educational benefits. Moreover, ample evidence supports the idea that after acquiring foundational knowledge, students benefit most from retrieval and application activities (Dunlosky et al., 2013; Larsen et al., 2013).

Third, when students participate in learning activities both inside and outside the classroom, it creates ample opportunities for receiving feedback. These activities support learning and serve a formative role, potentially contributing to overall (summative) assessment. Feedback plays a crucial role in student learning by allowing them to monitor their understanding and receive specific guidance to address any gaps. Equally significant is the feedback received by instructors, which contrasts with traditional lecture methods by providing more opportunities to gauge student comprehension. This formative feedback helps instructors adjust their teaching, address misconceptions, and offer appropriate challenges to students. For instance, such feedback can be utilized to identify misunderstandings before class, which informs subsequent discussions and application exercises during class (Steinel et al., 2019). Additionally, in group learning environments like the flipped classroom, students can provide feedback to one another, enhancing collaborative learning experiences (Nokes-Malach et al., 2015).

Finally, the student-centered approach of the flipped classroom model enhances student motivation, persistence, and engagement. Promoting active, collaborative learning addresses essential student needs such as autonomy, competence, and relatedness. Encouraging active learning activities can also foster a growth mindset, leading students to develop positive beliefs about the benefits of effort and strategic practice, which correlates with increased resilience and academic achievement. Creating a collaborative rather than competitive environment through in-class group work and course culture encourages students to adopt mastery learning goals and engage in deeper learning processes.

The flipped classroom model acknowledges the value of repetition in improving memory retrieval during learning (Karpicke & Roediger, 2008). This helps them gauge their understanding and serves as a baseline for measuring progress towards summative assessments, which often occur after interactive in-class activities, either immediately or at the end of the course or unit. To achieve an effective macrostructure, it is essential to minimize traditional lecture time while maximizing opportunities for inquiry, discovery, and application in the learning process. Furthermore, the literature on the flipped learning approach emphasizes the importance of a well-defined course structure, including detailed syllabus descriptions and clear design principles, alongside an introductory orientation that addresses students' potential concerns or resistance to adopting new methods.

The Jigsaw Puzzle

Collaborative learning, a form of active learning, has demonstrated beneficial results across various disciplines. It operates on the premise that collaboration among students yields better educational outcomes than competition. Teaching models, such as flipped learning, incorporate more interactive methods, including collaborative activities, experience increased learning gains, and improve understanding of concepts. Additionally, collaboration fosters interpersonal relationships and teamwork, boosts self-esteem, and enhances motivation (Calkins & Rivnay, 2021; Tran, 2019).

Collaborative learning involves forming small, diverse groups where all members are expected to participate in collaborative tasks to enhance individual and group performance. However, effective collaboration in group work is not always guaranteed. To ensure the benefits of collaborative learning, certain conditions must be met: positive interdependence, promotion of interaction, personal and individual accountability, development of interpersonal and social skills, and regular group and self-evaluation (Pardo et al., 2023). Common issues such as the free-rider problem, excessive leadership, diffusion of responsibility, social loafing, and premature resignation must be avoided to achieve true collaboration.

The jigsaw learning method exemplifies the collaborative learning approach. Developed by Professor Elliot Aronson in 1971 (Calkins & Rivnay, 2021), this student-centered, active learning strategy involves collaborative efforts among students who depend on each other to meet their learning goals. During jigsaw activities, students are encouraged to share and discuss their perspectives, enhancing critical thinking skills and helping better assimilate the subject matter. Frequent reciprocal interactions among students foster detailed thinking and mutual knowledge exchange. This dynamic promotes higher-level discussions and cognitive growth by encouraging active learning through social interactions with peers and instructors. Students engage actively in the learning process, developing crucial skills such as participatory learning and team interaction.

The jigsaw method has been widely adopted and modified in various higher education fields, with examples found in engineering, chemistry, medical education, language learning, and psychology. Typically, it is a two-step process: (1) students initially collaborate in "expert groups" gaining mastery of a particular topic, and (2) these groups are then reformed into "jigsaw groups" where each new group includes an expert from each original topic group who will then teach their peers. The instructor may choose not to reveal the jigsaw groups until after the expert group phase of the activity is completed.

An innovative adaptation of the jigsaw method introduces a third stage that incorporates a real-world learning task (Calkins & Rivnay, 2021). After mastering content in "expert groups" and teaching their peers in "jigsaw groups," students proceed to a third stage within their jigsaw groups, where they tackle an authentic learning experience, where they tackle an authentic learning experience, providing a practical application of the course material. Such authentic learning experiences deepen students' understanding and facilitate the transfer of concepts to new situations. To prepare students for jigsaw activities, the instructor may need to make a deliberate effort to emphasize the significance of group interaction from the outset, foster students' comfort with teamwork, and set appropriate expectations.

In step one, students are organized into specialized groups to gain in-depth knowledge of a particular subject area as "experts" (Figure 5). As these experts, students are expected to thoroughly understand a specific topic or concept, which would inform their peer teaching in step two. Experts from each topic group convene to create a jigsaw group, where each member possesses expertise in a different but complementary area. In these groups, peer-teaching promotes knowledge exchange, allowing members to gain insights into the other topic areas (Figure 5). During jigsaw sessions, the instructor would act as a facilitator. At the end, the instructor discusses the topic as a whole with all the participants to clarify the concepts. At this stage, the overall understanding of both the group and individual members is then assessed. This approach ensures that students work individually and collaboratively in two different groups, promoting personal accountability while fostering positive interdependence and collaboration essential for effective group functioning.

Instead of concluding the collaborative team activities with the jigsaw group peer teaching and learning, students will have a subsequent session with their jigsaw group. They will be randomly assigned an activity or project related to the expert group topics, providing an authentic learning experience based on a shared foundation of the expert group topics.

Figure 5. Jigsaw Design Challenge

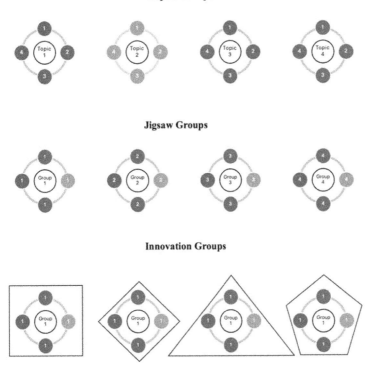

While the jigsaw puzzle technique values individual student differences, it employs a collaborative learning method that minimizes differences among students with varying learning styles. This approach is primarily utilized in secondary and higher education, requiring specific social skills for effective implementation. It aims to (a) enhance cooperative learning; (b) optimize individual and peer feedback; (c) promote a positive group dynamic; (d) boost academic achievement; (e) support meaningful, self-directed learning; (f) encourage sustained engagement with content, fostering deeper understanding rather than rote memorization; (g) build solidarity and civic responsibility; (h) develop social skills for group interaction and assertive communication; (i) promote learning autonomy; and (j) address the diverse interests, values, motivations, and abilities of students.

Traditional group work contrasts with the jigsaw puzzle approach in that it lacks structured group functions and planning, while the jigsaw puzzle method involves carefully organized and supervised group interactions. Several research studies have evaluated the jigsaw puzzle method against traditional lectures within a university setting, revealing that students using the jigsaw puzzle method achieved better grades, reported higher satisfaction with the teaching process, and demonstrated increased self-esteem. These improvements might stem from various factors, such as the novelty of new stimuli or a greater sense of involvement in learning. The jigsaw puzzle method fundamentally differs from lectures, with the former emphasizing group work and the latter focusing on individual work.

Active Reading

In a flipped classroom setting, student engagement with course readings is critical to their learning. Instructors often expect students to come to class prepared by completing assigned readings or related tasks, but this expectation is frequently unmet. Undergraduate students are expected to practice active reading to critically engage with assigned texts as part of their pre-class preparation. However, instructors predominantly focus on students' written work with minimal, if any, feedback provided on reading, making reading an invisible skill in the classroom. This creates a gap between how instructors expect students to prepare for class and how students actually do.

Some students might believe they can succeed in a course without doing the assigned readings, expecting the instructor to highlight all crucial points during class. Factors such as the difficulty and volume of reading material, lack of effective reading strategies, disinterest in the content, and external commitments (e.g., work, family, and other courses) can discourage students from engaging with the readings. Additionally, some students might not see the readings as essential for success. Instructors often and understandably express frustration when students fail to complete required reading assignments, which are selected for their importance and contribute to the creative potential of class discussions. Across disciplines, students are required to use critical and active reading skills involving continuous dialogue with the text, other texts, and their peers, leading to deeper and more nuanced understanding. Without these skills, even competent students may read passively or uncritically, accepting the text at face value.

Active reading might be a potential solution, emphasizing critical aspects of reading material and encouraging students to engage deeply by posing questions that prompt diverse ways of thinking. This approach involves critical thinking and often includes writing activities like annotating and note-taking. Rooted in constructivism, active reading is a student-centered method where learners actively interact with their existing knowledge structures, identify critical points in the text, and integrate new information with prior knowledge. According to Pulver (2020), active reading entails "the practice and skill of making meaning through deep engagement with a text or other composition, using the basic techniques of re-reading, annotating, responding, and sharing" (para. 1). This strategy involves students generating questions, reflecting on the reading material, and assessing their understanding to reinforce comprehension (Aziz, 2020; Biringkanae, 2018).

In the flipped classroom model, students engage with foundational materials through pre-class readings, while class sessions are dedicated to activities based on these readings. Reading assignments serve as a basis for intellectual discussions and analytical exercises. Effective student engagement with readings involves making connections among texts and responding to ideas in the readings. However, traditional reading can feel isolating, and without an immediate or genuine audience, students might lack motivation for in-depth engagement. A learning community provides an audience that offers diverse perspectives and mutual support, fostering active reading, deep engagement, and critical thinking. From a constructivist viewpoint, such a community enables information sharing and supports collaborative knowledge construction and problem-solving.

Social reading annotation tools allow students to engage with texts, peers, and instructors collaboratively. These tools enable students to annotate texts together, discuss content, highlight key points, and view each other's comments, fostering a collective learning experience (Kalir et al., 2020; Sun et al., 2023). Social annotation tools facilitate knowledge processing, argumentation, inquiry, literacy skills enhancement, and the integration of online learning spaces (Zhu et al., 2020). Social annotation helps students shift from individual text interpretations to collaborative inquiry, using diverse perspectives to build connections and associations (Kalir & Garcia, 2021). Kalir (2020) concludes that this group learning approach allows for negotiation and the shared construction of knowledge. For educators who adhere to constructivist principles, fostering a learning community is crucial, emphasizing the significance of social interactions in shaping values and identity. Additionally, focusing on community brings the advantage of connecting students from various locations, enabling them to share knowledge and learn collectively, thus applying theory to practice in innovative ways.

Perusall

One such tool is Perusall, an evidence-based social annotation tool designed to enhance student engagement. Developed by Harvard University and grounded in social constructivism, Perusall cultivates a learning community where students share their understanding of the readings, scaffold each other, and collaboratively construct new knowledge. Supported by extensive research, it employs active learning principles to visualize and deepen students' connection to the text. Perusall visualizes active reading to deepen students' engagement with the text by transforming independent reading into a collaborative experience as students engage with each other, the instructor, and the course readings. Social learning reduces students' intellectual dependency on instructors. Active learning occurs as the discussion occurs "during reading" on Perusall and "after reading" during class. However, it is important to note that an online reading tool is not inherently effective, nor does it automatically support active reading or the development of a learning community. Consistent implementation of expectations is necessary to support the social constructivist theory.

Perusall's annotation functions facilitate a detailed analysis of the reading and create a learning space for students to collectively annotate, highlight, add a question, and comment directly on the text while observing their peers' comments, thereby learning together and making their thought processes visible.

Using Perusall, students can:

- Highlight important text.
- Underline content they do not understand.
- Annotate sections that interest them.
- Comment in alignment with the text.
- Ask questions.
- Respond to peer and instructor comments for discussion.
- Add emojis.
- Tag individuals.
- Upvote ideas.
- Attach files or images to share additional resources.

Instructors can set expectations for thoughtful engagement, emphasizing the depth of comments and responses (e.g., not just "I agree" or "I disagree" but indicating why they agree or disagree, prompting connections to course content and real-world experiences) and provide examples of the annotations, sample sentence frames, and guiding questions. Instructors can give detailed feedback on Perusall engagement, establish expectations for subsequent annotations and peer responses in future reading assignments, follow up with students' annotations to further clarify class content, make connections between concepts, or prompt self-reflection from students within the context of the reading. Instructors can identify areas of confusion and interest to follow up on based on the statistics displayed by Perusall, such as the most frequently asked questions or annotations with the most upvotes.

Instructors can upload their texts or use e-textbooks, which can be open-access or purchased from the publisher. Recent updates now enable annotation of images and videos, broadening the scope of content students can engage with deeply, whether these videos are instructor-created for flipped classrooms or additional resources provided after class. Instructors can annotate texts, images, or videos to highlight key concepts or stimulate reflection on specific questions. Perusall integrates seamlessly with learning management systems such as Canvas, Blackboard, and Moodle, simplifying its incorporation into courses and student access. Through Perusall, instructors can set up assignments linked to specific readings and specify the number of comments each student must contribute. Students can read the assigned material and add comments and questions directly within the document. Perusall's system can automatically evaluate the quality and depth of student comments, providing instructors with detailed, comprehensive reports that include descriptive statistics and AI-driven assessments of contribution quality.

Perusall has become a significant tool in modern education, especially in blended and flipped learning settings. Perusall allows more time for higher-order thinking during in-person classes by fostering active interaction with course materials, as described in Bloom's Taxonomy. As an advanced social annotation tool, it is based on comprehensive educational data analytics and insights from behavioral research. Designed to engage and motivate students, Perusall enhances student-to-text and student-to-student interactions, particularly in online courses (Adams & Wilson, 2022; Morales et al., 2022). It is applicable in any higher education setting where active reading, critical thinking, and thoughtful discussion are desired.

BARRIERS TO ACTIVE LEARNING: THE CHALLENGES OF THE FLIPPED MODEL

Flipped learning has garnered significant positive recognition in academic circles, emphasizing the importance of delivering comprehensive subject content and fostering higher-order thinking skills. Research indicates that flipped instructional methods enhance student academic performance (Lee & Wallace, 2018; Wilson, 2023). Additionally, several studies highlight improvements in student learning attitudes even in the absence of improved academic performance (Baepler et al., 2014; Johnston & Dawn Martelli, 2017; Roach, 2014). The benefits of flipped learning are often reported in terms of learning achievement, self-efficacy, engagement, motivation, or course satisfaction.

While positive results have been reported, a growing body of literature indicates resistance to the flipped classroom approach (Cabı, 2018; Sammel et al., 2018; Tomas et al., 2019). Comber and Brady-Van den Bos (2018) noted the challenge of involving time-constrained undergraduate students in independent preparatory tasks, who perceived the change as a curriculum expansion rather than a flip. Sammel et al. (2018) found similar dissatisfaction among participants due to the extensive preparatory work, low motivation to complete it, and lack of perceived benefits from the active learning sessions. Additionally, other studies indicated a preference among participants for traditional face-to-face lectures followed by homework (Davenport, 2018). These studies do not theorize the reasons for resistance but present it as a phase in the flipped learning process or the isolated views of some participants, suggesting the pedagogy may not be suitable for all learners.

The flipped classroom model is becoming increasingly popular as an active learning strategy to engage students. However, not all courses are suited to a completely flipped format, and many instructors hesitate to adopt this approach due to the extra time and effort required. Two primary concerns temper the potential benefits of a flipped classroom: (1) the significant workload involved in creating and managing learning materials and activities, particularly high-quality videos, and (2) the possibility that students may resist completing the necessary homework, arriving unprepared for in-class activities. Additionally, there are concerns that posting videos online may not provide adequate support for some students, as they cannot ask questions in real-time, nor can instructors check for understanding as learning. Research indicates active learning improves students' knowledge, experience, and performance (Harris & Welch Bacon, 2019; Lin & Hwang, 2019). Nonetheless, one challenge with active learning is student resistance, especially for those unfamiliar with this new approach. Furthermore, a 2019 study by Deslauriers et al. found that students tend to favor low-effort learning strategies, like listening to lectures, even though they perform better with active learning.

Despite the intuitive appeal of the flipped learning model, its design and implementation are complex and vary across different contexts. Instructors often find creating activities for a flipped classroom challenging for several reasons. First, online classes must be of high instructional and technical quality to adequately prepare students for engaging classroom activities. However, even high-quality lessons might not be viewed or understood by students due to online distractions, lack of self-regulation, or insufficient live support from instructors. Second, face-to-face classes require extensive preparation and thoughtful design to provide interactive learning experiences that uphold the traditional values of higher education. More importantly, the design must ensure a strong connection between in-class and at-home activities, a link often missing in current models that separate the design processes for online lectures and classroom activities. Consequently, while flipped learning has many benefits, poor design and implementation can undermine its effectiveness, leading to minimal improvements in learning practices and outcomes.

Adopting this new approach presents another challenge: educators must shift from their conventional roles, minimizing direct instruction and, even more so, shifting from in-person to online teaching. Instructors who already use active learning in their classroom may also struggle to implement it in an online classroom and may resort to lectures or unstructured discussion boards. Moreover, activities not planned based on the ACT framework may cause disengagement or result in a shallow discussion of concepts. Instructors must enhance collaborative efforts by designing and organizing diverse activities such as role-playing, debates, and cooperative projects. Planning, executing, and assessing these activities requires significant time and dedication. Since it challenges traditional teaching methods, effective flipped classrooms necessitate enthusiastic and assured instructors, who need adequate time, resources, and support to establish a flipped model (Wang, 2017).

EMERGING TRENDS: AI IN THE FLIPPED CLASSROOM

Artificial Intelligence (AI) is revolutionizing higher education in online and hybrid learning environments. The literature on the application of AI, particularly in the context of flipped classrooms in higher education, highlights its transformative potential to enhance teaching and learning experiences. It is a cutting-edge topic that has garnered significant attention in recent research. As a rapidly expanding field, it has the potential to bring innovations and positive changes in teaching and learning practices in higher education institutions. Adopting these AI technologies can help address challenges associated with self-paced learning and facilitate cross-cultural and cross-linguistic communication.

AI Technologies: Opportunities and Challenges

AI technologies, such as intelligent tutoring systems (ITSs), AI-powered content delivery systems, and adaptive learning platforms, are being integrated to provide personalized learning experiences and improve student outcomes (Ray & Sikdar, 2023). For instance, implementing AI-driven adaptive content delivery systems in flipped classrooms has demonstrated the potential to enhance student engagement, motivation, and knowledge acquisition (Huang et al., 2023). Additionally, tools like chatbots, augmented reality, and virtual reality can create immersive learning experiences, enhancing collaboration and interactivity in hybrid education settings (Lo & Hew, 2023). For example, chatbots can improve student engagement by providing instant feedback and support and automating responses to common student questions. AI can provide immediate feedback on assessments and assignments, enabling students to quickly identify areas for improvement. This capability is particularly beneficial in a flipped classroom setting where students may have questions or need clarification on concepts before engaging in deeper discussions during class time.

AI-driven analytics tools in flipped classrooms allow instructors to track student progress through automated evaluations and customized instruction by providing personalized instruction and support. Such tools can address challenges in online education, including student self-regulation, curriculum planning, and personalized interaction (Yildirim et al., 2021). AI technologies can help instructors create and distribute learning materials in various formats (e.g., video, audio, text) to accommodate different learning needs, including those of students with disabilities. This flexibility ensures equitable access to educational resources.

Challenges

Challenges such as technology infrastructure, privacy concerns, and equity issues must be addressed to integrate AI in the flipped classroom successfully. Limited technical functionality of the chatbots, lack of authenticity in learning tasks, and lack of student motivation are reported in recent research studies.

Understanding these technologies raises concerns about accessibility and equity in education with the risk of exacerbating existing gaps in educational access, as not all students may have equal opportunities to engage with AI-powered resources. Furthermore, ethical implications regarding data privacy and the depersonalization of education are also important considerations that require ongoing attention.

Scope

An increasing volume of studies and articles are emerging, reflecting the growing recognition of AI's potential to enhance student engagement and improve educational outcomes. These publications span various thematic areas, including personalized learning experiences, adaptive assessment systems, and the use of AI-powered tools for content delivery and student feedback. This noticeable increase in the number of publications covering this emerging trend highlights the urgency and relevance of integrating AI into pedagogical practices.

The literature is not only growing in quantity but is also influencing subsequent studies and practical implementations. Moreover, interdisciplinary elements are at play, as scholars from fields such as computer science, education, and cognitive psychology are coming together to explore how AI can provide meaningful insights into learner behaviors, instructional design, and classroom dynamics (Lo & Hew, 2023). This collaboration enriches the literature and fosters innovative approaches to teaching and learning within flipped classrooms.

In summary, integrating AI applications in the context of online or hybrid learning in flipped classrooms is a substantial and growing area of inquiry. The increasing volume of research indicates a vibrant field that is likely to continue expanding as technology evolves and educational needs shift. By exploring the implications of this approach on student learning outcomes and motivation, researchers are paving the way for a more engaging and effective online learning environment.

CONCLUSION

Despite the challenges associated with transitioning to active learning in an online environment, this chapter aims to support instructors in thoughtfully planning effective pedagogical strategies to facilitate meaningful learning experiences for students in a dynamic and interactive online classroom. It explores the implementation of active learning strategies within the context of the Flipped Classroom Model in online education. Examining the theoretical underpinnings of constructivism and the practical application of active learning techniques demonstrates how this pedagogical approach can invert traditional tasks to prioritize active learning.

The flipped classroom model, rooted in constructivist theory, offers a promising shift from traditional teacher-centered instruction to a student-centered approach that promotes active learning. By engaging with course materials before class, students can come prepared to participate in higher-order thinking activities during face-to-face sessions, such as problem-solving, application, and analysis. This model aligns with the principles of cognitive load theory, which advocates for self-paced preparatory activities to manage working memory effectively and enhance students' engagement, motivation, and satisfaction. Numerous studies highlight the positive impacts of flipped learning on academic performance and learning attitudes, underscoring its potential to transform educational practices and foster deeper understanding and critical thinking skills among students.

Despite its benefits, the flipped classroom model presents significant challenges that must be addressed to ensure its successful implementation. Instructors face the demanding task of creating high-quality preparatory materials and designing interactive in-class activities that align with students' pre-class preparation. Resistance from students, who may prefer traditional lectures and feel overwhelmed by the additional preparatory workload and the intellectual demands of active learning, further complicates this shift. Educators need substantial support, including time, resources, and professional development, to overcome these barriers and adapt to their evolving roles in facilitating collaborative learning environments. By addressing these challenges and leveraging the strengths of flipped learning, educational institutions can better support student learning and achieve more meaningful educational outcomes.

REFERENCES

Abeysekera, L., & Dawson, P. (2015). Motivation and cognitive load in the flipped classroom: Definition, rationale and a call for research. *Higher Education Research & Development*, 34(1), 1–14. DOI: 10.1080/07294360.2014.934336

Academy of Active Learning Arts and Sciences. (2018). Updated definition of flipped learning. https://aalasinternational.org/updated-definition-of-flipped-learning/

Adams, B., & Wilson, N. S. (2022). Investigating students' during-reading practices through social annotation. *Literacy Research and Instruction*, 61(4), 339–360. DOI: 10.1080/19388071.2021.2008560

Adams, R., & Kevin, L. (2017). Engaging colleagues in active learning pedagogies through mentoring and co-design. *Proceedings of the 14th Conference on Education and Training in Optics and Photonics*. https://doi.org/DOI: 10.1117/12.2266663

Akçayır, G., & Akçayır, M. (2018). The flipped classroom: A review of its advantages and challenges. *Computers & Education*, 126(1), 334–345. DOI: 10.1016/j.compedu.2018.07.021

Althubaiti, A., & Althubaiti, S. M. (2024). Flipping the online classroom to teach statistical data analysis software: A quasi-experimental study. *SAGE Open*, 14(1), 21582440241235022. Advance online publication. DOI: 10.1177/21582440241235022

Aziz, I. N. (2020). Implementation of SQ3R method in improving the students' basic reading skills. *EDUCATIO: Journal of Education*, 1(2), 102–110.

Baepler, P., Walker, J., & Driessen, M. (2014). It's not about seat time: Blending, flipping, and efficiency in active learning classrooms. *Computers & Education*, 78, 227–236. DOI: 10.1016/j.compedu.2014.06.006

Baig, M. I., & Yadegaridehkordi, E. (2023). Flipped classroom in higher education: A systematic literature review and research challenges. *International Journal of Educational Technology in Higher Education*, 20(1), 61–26. DOI: 10.1186/s41239-023-00430-5

Bergmann, J. (2022). The mastery learning handbook: A competency-based approach to student achievement. In *ASCD* (1st ed.). ASCD.

Bergmann, J., & Sams, A. (2012). *Flip your classroom: Reach every student in every class every day* (1st ed.). International Society for Technology in Education.

Bhagat, K. K., Chang, C. N., & Chang, C. Y. (2016). The impact of the flipped classroom on mathematics concept learning in high school. *Journal of Educational Technology & Society*, 19(3), 134–142.

Biringkanae, A. (2018). The use of SQ3R technique in improving students' reading comprehension. *ELS Journal on Interdisciplinary Studies in Humanities*, 1(2), 218–225. DOI: 10.34050/els-jish.v1i2.4316

Bishop, J., & Verleger, M. A. (2013). The flipped classroom: A survey of the research. 120th American Society for Engineering Education Annual Conference and Exposition, 30, 1-18.

Bonwell, C. C., & Eison, J. A. (1991). *Active learning: Creating excitement in the classroom*. School of Education and Human Development, George Washington University.

Braun, I. S. R., & Vasko, M. (2014). Inverted classroom by topic - A study in mathematics for electrical engineering students. *International Journal of Engineering Pedagogy*, 4(3), 11–17. DOI: 10.3991/ijep.v4i3.3299

Bredow, C. A., Roehling, P. V., Knorp, A. J., & Sweet, A. M. (2021). To flip or not to flip? A meta-analysis of the efficacy of flipped learning in higher education. *Review of Educational Research*, 91(6), 878–918. DOI: 10.3102/00346543211019122

Brewer, R., & Movahedazarhouligh, S. (2018). Successful stories and conflicts: A literature review on the effectiveness of flipped learning in higher education. *Journal of Computer Assisted Learning*, 34(4), 409–416. DOI: 10.1111/jcal.12250

Cabı, E. (2018). The impact of the flipped classroom model on students' academic achievement. *International Review of Research in Open and Distance Learning*, 19(3), 202–222. DOI: 10.19173/irrodl.v19i3.3482

Calkins, S. C., & Rivnay, J. (2021). The jigsaw design challenge: An inclusive learning activity to promote cooperative problem-solving. *Journal of Effective Teaching in Higher Education*, 4(3), 19–35. DOI: 10.36021/jethe.v4i3.249

Cheng, L., Ritzhaupt, A. D., & Antonenko, P. (2019). Effects of the flipped classroom instructional strategy on students' learning outcomes: A meta-analysis. *Educational Technology Research and Development*, 67(4), 793–824. DOI: 10.1007/s11423-018-9633-7

Chi, M. T. H., & Wylie, R. (2014). The ICAP framework: Linking cognitive engagement to active learning outcomes. *Educational Psychologist*, 49(4), 219–243. DOI: 10.1080/00461520.2014.965823

Chickering, A. W., & Gamson, Z. F. (1987). *Seven principles for good practice in undergraduate education*. American Association for Higher Education.

Clinton, V., & Kelly, A. E. (2020). Student attitudes toward group discussions. *Active Learning in Higher Education*, 21(2), 154–164. DOI: 10.1177/1469787417740277

Comber, D. P. M., & Brady-Van den Bos, M. (2018). Too much, too soon? A critical investigation into factors that make Flipped Classrooms effective. *Higher Education Research & Development*, 37(4), 683–697. DOI: 10.1080/07294360.2018.1455642

Davenport, C. E. (2018). Evolution in student perceptions of a flipped classroom in a computer programming course. *Journal of College Science Teaching*, 47(4), 30–35. DOI: 10.2505/4/jcst18_047_04_30

DeLozier, S., & Rhodes, M. (2017). Flipped classrooms: A review of key ideas and recommendations for practice. *Educational Psychology Review*, 29(1), 141–151. DOI: 10.1007/s10648-015-9356-9

Deslauriers, L., McCarty, L. S., Miller, K., Callaghan, K., & Kestin, G. (2019). Measuring actual learning versus feeling of learning in response to being actively engaged in the classroom. *Proceedings of the National Academy of Sciences - PNAS, 116*(39), 19251-19257. https://doi.org/DOI: 10.1073/pnas.1821936116

Dunlosky, J., Rawson, K. A., Marsh, E. J., Nathan, M. J., & Willingham, D. T. (2013). Improving students' learning with effective learning techniques: Promising directions from cognitive and educational psychology. *Psychological Science in the Public Interest*, 14(1), 4–58. DOI: 10.1177/1529100612453266 PMID: 26173288

Elmaadaway, M. A. N. (2018). The effects of a flipped classroom approach on class engagement and skill performance in a Blackboard course. *British Journal of Educational Technology*, 49(3), 479–491. DOI: 10.1111/bjet.12553

Fisher, R., Perényi, Á., & Birdthistle, N. (2021). The positive relationship between flipped and blended learning and student engagement, performance and satisfaction. *Active Learning in Higher Education*, 22(2), 97–113. DOI: 10.1177/1469787418801702

Freeman, S., Eddy, S. L., McDonough, M., Smith, M. K., Okoroafor, N., Jordt, H., & Wenderoth, M. P. (2014). Active learning increases student performance in science, engineering, and mathematics. *Proceedings of the National Academy of Sciences of the United States of America*, 111(23), 8410–8415. DOI: 10.1073/pnas.1319030111 PMID: 24821756

Ha, A. S., O'Reilly, J., Ng, J. Y. Y., Zhang, J. H., & Serpa, S. (2019). Evaluating the flipped classroom approach in Asian higher education: Perspectives from students and teachers. *Cogent Education*, 6(1), 1638147. Advance online publication. DOI: 10.1080/2331186X.2019.1638147

Hao, Q., Barnes, B., & Jing, M. (2021). Quantifying the effects of active learning environments: Separating physical learning classrooms from ped- agogical approaches. *Learning Environments Research*, 24(1), 109–122. DOI: 10.1007/s10984-020-09320-3

Harris, N., & Bacon, C. E. W. (2019). Developing cognitive skills through active learning: A Systematic review of health care professions. *Athletic Training Education Journal*, 14(2), 135–148. DOI: 10.4085/1402135

Huang, A. Y. Q., Lu, O. H. T., & Yang, S. J. H. (2023). Effects of artificial Intelligence–Enabled personalized recommendations on learners' learning engagement, motivation, and outcomes in a flipped classroom. *Computers & Education*, 194, 104684. Advance online publication. DOI: 10.1016/j.compedu.2022.104684

Hung, H. T. (2017). Design-based research: Redesign of an English language course using a flipped classroom approach. *TESOL Quarterly*, 51(1), 180–192. DOI: 10.1002/tesq.328

Jacob, M. (2023). Active cognitive tasks- Synthesizing frameworks for active learning online. In Gowers, I., & Garnham, W. (Eds.), *Active learning in higher education: Theoretical considerations and perspectives* (1st ed., pp. 5–11). Routledge., https://www.taylorfrancis.com/chapters/edit/10.4324/9781003360032-6/active-cognitive-tasks-synthesising-frameworks-active-learning-online-mary-jacob DOI: 10.4324/9781003360032-6

Jensen, J. L., Kummer, T. A., & Godoy, P. D. D. M. (2015). Improvements from a flipped classroom may simply be the fruits of active learning. *CBE Life Sciences Education*, 14(1), 1–12. DOI: 10.1187/cbe.14-08-0129 PMID: 25699543

Johnston, V., & Martelli, C. D. (2017). Flipped learning: Student perceptions and achievement in teacher education. *Teacher Education and Practice*, 30(4).

Josifović-Elezović, S. (2022). Students' perceptions of the flipped classroom approach in tertiary EFL education: Aa case study from banja luka. *Folia Linguistica et Litteraria (Online)*, XIII(40), 351–373. DOI: 10.31902/fll.40.2022.18

Kalir, J. H., Morales, E., Fleerackers, A., & Alperin, J. P. (2020). When I saw my peers annotating student perceptions of social annotation for learning in multiple courses. *Information and Learning Science*, 121(4), 207–230. DOI: 10.1108/ILS-12-2019-0128

Kalir, R., & Garcia, A. (2021). Joining the 'great conversation'–the fundamental role of annotation in academic society. Impact of Social Sciences Blog. https://blogs.lse.ac.uk/impactofsocialsciences/

Karpicke, J. D., & Roediger, H. L.III. (2008). The critical importance of retrieval for learning. *Science*, 319(5865), 966–968. DOI: 10.1126/science.1152408 PMID: 18276894

Khayat, M., Hafezi, F., Asgari, P., & Talebzadeh Shoushtari, M. (2021). Comparison of the effectiveness of flipped classroom and traditional teaching method on the components of self-determination and class perception among University students. *Journal of Advances in Medical Education & Professionalism*, 9(4), 230–237. DOI: 10.30476/jamp.2021.89793.1385 PMID: 34692861

Kim, J., Park, H., Jang, M., & Nam, H. (2017). Exploring flipped classroom effects on second language learners' cognitive processing. *Foreign Language Annals*, 50(2), 260–284. DOI: 10.1111/flan.12260

King, A. (1993). From sage on the stage to guide on the side. *College Teaching*, 41(1), 30–35. DOI: 10.1080/87567555.1993.9926781

Kwon, J., & Woo, H. (2018). The Impact of Flipped Learning on Cooperative and Competitive Mindsets. *Sustainability (Basel)*, 10(1), 79. Advance online publication. DOI: 10.3390/su10010079

Låg, T., & Sæle, R. G. (2019). Does the flipped classroom improve student learning and satisfaction? A systematic review and meta-analysis. *AERA Open*, 5(3), 2332858419870489. Advance online publication. DOI: 10.1177/2332858419870489

Lage, M. J., Platt, G. J., & Treglia, M. (2000). Inverting the classroom: A gateway to creating an inclusive learning environment. *The Journal of Economic Education*, 31(1), 30–34. DOI: 10.1080/00220480009596759

Larsen, D. P., Butler, A. C., & Roediger, H. L.III. (2013). Comparative effects of test-enhanced learning and self-explanation on long-term retention. *Medical Education*, 47(7), 674–682. DOI: 10.1111/medu.12141 PMID: 23746156

Lee, G., & Wallace, A. (2018). Flipped Learning in the English as a Foreign Language Classroom: Outcomes and Perceptions. *TESOL Quarterly*, 52(1), 62–84. DOI: 10.1002/tesq.372

Li, R., Lund, A., & Nordsteien, A. (2023). The link between flipped and active learning: A scoping review. *Teaching in Higher Education*, 28(8), 1–35. DOI: 10.1080/13562517.2021.1943655

Lin, H.-C., & Hwang, G.-J. (2019). Research trends of flipped classroom studies for medical courses: A review of journal publications from 2008 to 2017 based on the technology-enhanced learning model. *Interactive Learning Environments*, 27(8), 1011–1027. DOI: 10.1080/10494820.2018.1467462

Lo, C. K., & Hew, K. F. (2023). A review of integrating AI-based chatbots into flipped learning: New possibilities and challenges. *Frontiers in Education*, 8, 1175715. DOI: 10.3389/feduc.2023.1175715

Long, T., Cummins, J., & Waugh, M. (2017). Use of the flipped classroom in higher education: Instructors' perspectives. *Journal of Computing in Higher Education*, 29(2), 179–200. DOI: 10.1007/s12528-016-9119-8

Lundin, M., Rensfeldt, A. B., Hillman, T., Lanzt-Andersson, A., & Peterson, L. (2018). Higher education dominance and siloed knowledge: A systematic review of flipped classroom research. *International Journal of Educational Technology in Higher Education*, 15(1), 20. DOI: 10.1186/s41239-018-0101-6

Marcos Pardo, P. J., González Gálvez, N., & Vaquero Cristobal, R. (2023). Jigsaw Puzzle technique vs. traditional group work: Academic performance and satisfaction of the university students. *Cultura, Ciencia y Deporte*, 18(58), 69–79. DOI: 10.12800/ccd.v18i58.2034

Mohamed, H., & Lamia, M. (2018). Implementing flipped classroom that used an intelligent tutoring system into learning process. *Computers & Education*, 124, 62–76. DOI: 10.1016/j.compedu.2018.05.011

Morales, E., Kalir, J. H., Fleerackers, A., & Alperin, J. P. (2022). Using social annotation to construct knowledge with others: A case study across undergraduate courses. *F1000 Research*, 11, 235. Advance online publication. DOI: 10.12688/f1000research.109525.1 PMID: 35388338

Morawo, A., Sun, C., & Lowden, M. (2020). Enhancing engagement during live virtual learning using interactive quizzes. *Medical Education*, 54(12), 1188. DOI: 10.1111/medu.14253 PMID: 32438462

Nokes-Malach, T. J., Richey, J. E., & Gadgil, S. (2015). When is it better to learn together? Insights from research on collaborative learning. *Educational Psychology Review*, 27(4), 645–656. DOI: 10.1007/s10648-015-9312-8

Novak, G. M. (2011). Just-in-time teaching. *New Directions for Teaching and Learning*, 2011(128), 63–73. DOI: 10.1002/tl.469

O'Flaherty, J., & Phillips, C. (2015). The use of flipped classrooms in higher education: A scoping review. *The Internet and Higher Education*, 25, 85–95. DOI: 10.1016/j.iheduc.2015.02.002

Olusegun, S. (2015). Constructivism learning theory: A paradigm for teaching and learning. *Journal of Research & Method in Education*, 5(6), 66–70. DOI: 10.9790/7388- 05616670

Pulver, C. J. (2020). Active reading to understand a problem. Introduction to professional and public writing. https://rwu.pressbooks.pub/wtng225/chapter/active-close-reading/

Ray, S., & Sikdar, D. (2023). Learning Motivation Scale (LMS): Development and validation with prospective-teachers in West Bengal, India. *Asian Journal of Education and Social Studies*.

Rezaei, A. R. (2020). Groupwork in active learning classrooms: Recommendations for users. *Journal of Learning Spaces*, 9(2), 1–21.

Roach, T. (2014). Student perceptions toward flipped learning: New methods to increase interaction and active learning in economics. *International Review of Economics Education*, 17, 74–84. DOI: 10.1016/j.iree.2014.08.003

Şahin, M., & Kurban, C. F. (2016). Flipped learning: A transformative approach designed to meet the needs of today's knowledge economies and societies. In *The Flipped Approach to Higher Education* (pp. 15–24). Emerald Group Publishing Limited., DOI: 10.1108/978-1-78635-744-120161006

Sammel, A., Townend, G., & Kanasa, H. (2018). Hidden Expectations Behind the Promise of the Flipped Classroom. *College Teaching*, 66(2), 49–59. DOI: 10.1080/87567555.2016.1189392

Schmidt, S. M. P., & Ralph, D. L. (2016). The flipped classroom: A twist on teaching. *Contemporary Issues in Education Research*, 9(1), 1–6. DOI: 10.19030/cier.v9i1.9544

Singh, J., Steele, K., & Singh, L. (2021). Combining the best of online and face-to-face learning: Hybrid and blended learning approach for COVID-19, post vaccine, & post-pandemic world. *Journal of Educational Technology Systems*, 50(2), 140–171. DOI: 10.1177/00472395211047865

Sohrabi, B., & Iraj, H. (2016). Implementing flipped classroom using digital media: A comparison of two demographically different groups perceptions. *Computers in Human Behavior*, 60, 514–524. DOI: 10.1016/j.chb.2016.02.056

Steen-Utheim, A. T., & Foldnes, N. (2018). A qualitative investigation of student engagement in a flipped classroom. *Teaching in Higher Education*, 23(3), 307–324. DOI: 10.1080/13562517.2017.1379481

Steinel, N., Palmer, G. C., Nowicki, E., Lee, E., Nelson, E., Whiteley, M., & Lee, M. W. (2019). Integration of microbiology, pharmacology, immunology, and infectious disease using active teaching and self-directed learning. *Medical Science Educator*, 29(1), 315–324. DOI: 10.1007/s40670-018-00689-8 PMID: 34457482

Strayer, J. F. (2012). How learning in an inverted classroom influences cooperation, innovation and task orientation. *Learning Environments Research*, 15(2), 171–193. DOI: 10.1007/s10984-012-9108-4

Sun, C., Hwang, G., Yin, Z., Wang, Z., & Wang, Z. (2023). Trends and issues of social annotation in education: A systematic review from 2000 to 2020. *Journal of Computer Assisted Learning*, 39(2), 329–350. DOI: 10.1111/jcal.12764

Talbert, R., & Bergmann, J. (2017). *Flipped learning : A guide for higher education faculty* (1st ed.). Stylus Publishing, LLC.

Tomas, L., Evans, N., Doyle, T., & Skamp, K. (2019). Are first year students ready for a flipped classroom? A case for a flipped learning continuum. *International Journal of Educational Technology in Higher Education*, 16(1), 1–22. DOI: 10.1186/s41239-019-0135-4

Tran, V. D. (2019). Does cooperative learning increase students' motivation in learning? *International Journal of Higher Education*, 8(5), 12–20. DOI: 10.5430/ijhe.v8n5p12

Turan, Z., & Goktas, Y. (2015). A new approach in higher education: The students' views on flipped classroom method. *Journal of Higher Education and Science*, 5(2), 156. DOI: 10.5961/jhes.2015.118

Wang, T. (2017). Overcoming barriers to 'flip': Building teacher's capacity for the adoption of flipped classroom in Hong Kong secondary schools. *Research and Practice in Technology Enhanced Learning*, 12(1), 6–17. DOI: 10.1186/s41039-017-0047-7 PMID: 30613255

Wilson, K. (2023). What does it mean to do teaching? A qualitative study of resistance to flipped learning in a higher education context. *Teaching in Higher Education*, 28(3), 473–486. DOI: 10.1080/13562517.2020.1822312

Wilton, M., Gonzalez-Nino, E., McPartlan, P., Terner, Z., Christoffersen, R. E., & Rothman, J. H. (2019). Improving academic performance, belonging, and retention through increasing structure of an introductory biology course. *CBE Life Sciences Education*, 18(4), ar53. Advance online publication. DOI: 10.1187/cbe.18-08-0155 PMID: 31675276

Yang, Q.-F., Lin, C.-J., & Hwang, G.-J. (2021). Research focuses and findings of flipping mathematics classes: A review of journal publications based on the technology-enhanced learning model. *Interactive Learning Environments*, 29(6), 905–938. DOI: 10.1080/10494820.2019.1637351

Yildirim, Y., Arslan, E. A., Yildirim, K., & Bisen, I. (2021). Reimagining education with artificial intelligence. *Eurasian. The Journal of Higher Education*, 4(4), 32–46. DOI: 10.31039/ejohe.2021.4.52

Zain, F. M., & Sailin, S. N. (2020). Students' experience with flipped learning approach in higher education. *Universal Journal of Educational Research*, 8(10), 4946–4958. DOI: 10.13189/ujer.2020.081067

Zhu, X., Chen, B., Avadhanam, R. M., Shui, H., & Zhang, R. Z. (2020). Reading and connecting: Using social annotation in online classes. *Information and Learning Science*, 121(5/6), 261–271. DOI: 10.1108/ILS-04-2020-0117

Chapter 6
Enhancing Adult Online Learners' Graduate Leadership Experiences Through the Lens of Care Theory

Carrie M. Grimes
https://orcid.org/0009-0007-5937-0048
Vanderbilt University, USA

ABSTRACT

This chapter aims to provide an in-depth analysis of how instructors can leverage Nel Noddings' care theory (1986, 2002, 2013, 2019) in order to design and deliver learning experiences which support the unique needs of adult online learners who are studying leadership in impactful ways. This chapter will also explore the ways in which online instructors may be seen as facilitators or coaches who use mental models of care theory to anticipate and positively guide relationships within the online learning environment through instructional and advising practices. This chapter will describe how online instructors may strategically use a care theory framework of modeling, dialogue, practice and confirmation to guide adult learners through different stages of the learning experience, in order to contribute to a caring and relational dynamic which drives students' learning outcomes and leadership capacity.

DOI: 10.4018/979-8-3693-4407-1.ch006

INTRODUCTION

The shift from traditional in-person classroom learning to legitimized programs of online learning for adult degree-seeking professionals has opened significant access and opportunity for institutions of higher education, as well as for the adult learners they serve. However, this ongoing dramatic increase in online graduate degree offerings has posed challenges to educators and students. One of the most significant challenges is building and maintaining strong connections, and a sense of authentic support, amidst the participants within the online learning environment. It is well documented that relationships and a sense of emotional connection within a learning environment play a crucial role in positively impacting student learning outcomes (Pekrun, et al., 2011; Scherer, 2009; Mega, et al., 2014). The absence of physical presence in online classrooms does not mitigate this need; in fact, it may amplify it.

This chapter aims to provide an in-depth analysis of how instructors can leverage Nel Noddings' care theory (Noddings, 1984, 2002, 2013, 2019) in order to design and deliver learning experiences which support the unique needs of adult online learners who are studying leadership in impactful ways. This chapter will also explore the ways in which online instructors may be seen as facilitators or coaches who use mental models of care theory to anticipate and positively guide relationships within the online learning environment through instructional and advising practices. This chapter will describe how online instructors may strategically use a care theory framework of modeling, dialogue, practice and confirmation to guide adult learners through different stages of the learning experience, in order to contribute to a caring and relational dynamic which drives students' learning outcomes and leadership capacity.

NODDINGS THEORY OF CARE: AN OVERVIEW

Nell Noddings' theory of care offers profound insights into the ethical and relational dimensions of education, particularly emphasizing the importance of caring relationships between educators and students. Rooted in feminist ethics, Noddings' work challenges traditional notions of moral education by positioning care at the center of ethical understanding and educational practice. In her seminal work "Caring: A Feminine Approach to Ethics and Moral Education," Noddings (1984) introduces care theory, which is built on the fundamental premise that human beings are relational and interdependent. Noddings (1984) theory identifies a trilogy of essential care components: engrossment in the other, displacement of one's own motives, and recognition. The carer must be deeply invested in the position and motivations of other people who are in the shared context (engrossment). The carer also directs his/her motivational energy toward the service of the cared-for's needs, goals and projects (motivational displacement). Care also requires that the one who is cared for accepts the care of the carer (recognition) (Fuglsang and Mattsson, 2009). This perspective contrasts with more conventional, justice-oriented pre-existing moral frameworks, which often emphasize autonomy and individual rights as opposed to interdependence. Noddings argues that care, characterized by attentiveness, responsiveness, and relational engagement, is essential for moral development and ethical behavior (1984, 1992).

Noddings proposes that relational dynamics between teachers and students are foundational to effective teaching and learning. Noddings (2012) articulates the significance of the teacher-student relationship, asserting that teaching is inherently a relational practice. According to Noddings, educators should strive to understand and respond to the needs of their students, fostering an environment where students feel valued and supported. This implies that teachers must always consider the expressed needs of their students—not necessarily fulfilling every request--but ensuring that students' needs play a key role in their decision-making processes (2019). Essential to Noddings' practical application of care theory in education are the concepts of choice, continuity, and connection. This approach advocates for actively listening to students and engaging in discussions to understand their interests, and guiding them in making informed decisions. Care theory also suggests that keeping students and teachers together over an extended period of time and encouraging interdisciplinary academic activities fosters positive learning experiences characterized by continuity and connection (2019). Care theory also highlights the necessity of fostering critical thinking and civility, with the goal of educating and not alienating those who offer up conflicting or negatively perceived moral views. Noddings' work underscores that care is not just an emotional attachment but a holistic pedagogical approach that enhances student outcomes; she outlines practical strategies for integrating care into the curriculum, suggesting that themes of care can be woven into various subjects to develop students' ethical and moral sensibilities. Noddings' care theory emphasizes that this approach not only enhances academic outcomes but also contributes to the overall well-being and moral growth of students as members of the broader society.

Noddings' care theory framework is scaffolded around four key components which drive moral decision making: modeling, dialogue, practice, and confirmation (Figure 1, Noddings, 2002). Modeling requires teachers to demonstrate caring behaviors, providing students with a tangible example of what it means to care. Dialogue involves open, respectful communication between teachers and students, where both parties actively listen and respond to each other in order to promote mutual understanding. Practice refers to opportunities for students to engage in caring activities, reinforcing the importance of care through action. Confirmation involves acknowledging and affirming others' efforts and identities, and encouraging their growth and development (Noddings, 2002). These four pillars uphold Noddings' approach to the teacher-student caring dynamic; she actively asserts the pivotal role the school and teacher have in building enduring value systems of caring for students. Whether it be modeling kindness and empathy for others, fostering respectful dialogic interactions, requiring engagement in community service, or reinforcing students' "best selves," Noddings depicts caring in schools as "the very bedrock of all successful education" (1992, p. 27). Her diagnosis of the ills of our culture emphasizes the power of caring in inoculating students from "a throwaway society…of carelessness" (1992, p. 20).

Figure 1. Model of Care Theory

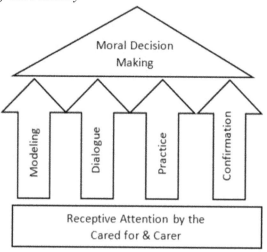

(Nodding Model of Care Theory, 2002)

Noddings' emphasis on relational ethics and care is not limited to the teacher-student relationship but extends to the broader educational environment. She highlights the role of school leaders in fostering a culture of care within educational institutions (2006). Effective leadership, according to Noddings, involves creating policies and practices that prioritize the well-being of all members of the school community, thereby promoting a supportive and inclusive educational environment. These assertions advance her earlier work (1999), which explores the interplay between care and professional competence. She argues that true competence in teaching is not merely a matter of technical skill or content knowledge but involves a deep commitment to the well-being of students. This holistic approach to competence underscores the idea that caring is integral to effective teaching and cannot be separated from the professional responsibilities of educators. Noddings also addresses the implications of care theory for curriculum design and instructional arrangements (1988); she critiques traditional, hierarchical structures in education that often marginalize the voices and needs of students. Instead, she advocates for more flexible, student-centered approaches that allow for greater responsiveness and adaptability to individual needs. In her later work, "The Language of Care Ethics" (2012), Noddings explores the linguistic dimensions of care, emphasizing how language can both reflect and shape caring relationships. She argues that educators need to be mindful of their language choices, as these can either foster or hinder the development of a caring classroom environment. Later in her career, Noddings revisited and expanded her original ideas on caring theory (2013) by reaffirming the importance of care in ethical theory and practice, highlighting new insights and applications in contemporary educational contexts. Noddings discusses the challenges and opportunities of implementing care ethics in increasingly diverse and digital learning environments.

Applications of Care Theory to Learning Contexts

Noddings' care theory has significantly influenced educational practices, particularly in fostering relational and ethical dimensions within teaching and learning contexts. Barrow (2015) delves into the intricate dynamics of care in teaching and argues that while care is fundamental to effective teaching, it can be challenging to balance care with other professional responsibilities. Barrow emphasizes that caring relationships in education require attentiveness to students' needs and an ethical commitment to their well-being, aligning closely with Noddings' assertion that care is a foundational aspect of moral education. Lussier (2020) examines the concepts of reciprocity, exchange, and indebtedness in Noddings' theory of care and how these elements create a framework for understanding caring teacher-student relationships as dynamic and mutually beneficial. Recognizing the reciprocal nature of care can enhance teacher-student relationships by fostering mutual respect and understanding, which are essential for effective teaching and learning (Lussier, 2020).

Interestingly, Glowacki-Dudka et al. (2018) discuss leveraging care theory in their framework for the design and implementation of educational programs which serve adult learners. The authors argue that integrating care ethics into program planning can significantly enhance adult learning experiences by fostering empathy, collaboration, and ethical responsibility among educators and learners. Their care-centric framework embraces a constructivist perspective in which learning is viewed as an active, social enterprise of ongoing, collective meaning-making (Bada & Olusegun, 2015). They highlight several key strategies for implementing care-based approaches for adult students, including creating supportive learning environments, promoting open communication, and addressing the diverse and unique needs of adult learners.

By prioritizing relational dynamics and attentiveness to learners' needs, designers of adult learning programs can develop more inclusive and responsive educational experiences which promote an atmosphere in which professional students feel safe, valued and respected (Glowacki-Dudka et al., 2018). This study underscores that care-based programmatic design in adult education involves being genuinely engaged with learners, understanding their unique challenges, and providing the necessary support to facilitate their growth and development.

Care Theory and Online Teaching and Learning

The four pillars of Noddings' care theory framework (2002)--modeling, dialogue, practice, and confirmation (Figure 1)--are resonant across the scholarship related to caring and online instruction. Additionally, scholars emphasize that the integration of technology in education must be guided by thoughtful pedagogical choices rooted in care, justice, and respect (Rose, 2017). This approach highlights the capacity for technology to be leveraged in shaping relationships and power dynamics in online classrooms (Bali & Zamora, 2022; Zakharova & Jarke, 2022). Studies have identified key practices that enhance care in online teaching, such as compassionate communication, strong instructor presence, and flexible course design (Burke & Larmar, 2020; Robinson et al., 2020). While dialogue can be challenging in virtual settings, intentional strategies like fostering open-ended discussions and responsive interactions can build a supportive learning community (Rabin, 2021; Kızılcık & Türüdü, 2022). Moreover, the use of personal, dialogic feedback and alternative assessment methods further cultivates a culture of care, reinforcing the ethical dimensions of online education (Burke & Larmar, 2020; Robinson et al., 2020).

Adams and Rose's (2014) research emphasizes the importance of creating a virtual environment where students feel seen and supported via instructional confirming care behaviors. They suggest that online instructors can also practice modeling and dialogue by being attentive to students' needs, offering personalized feedback, and maintaining open lines of communication. This approach helps bridge the gap between students and teachers, fostering a sense of community and belonging in online courses. Robinson et al. (2020) propose a comprehensive model for incorporating care theory into the design of online courses, outlining practical strategies for embedding care into online learning environments. Their recommended care-centered approach involves prioritizing relational interactions, providing meaningful and efficient feedback, and supporting the diverse needs of the learning community. Scholars concur that when online instructors design courses with care in mind, virtual spaces have the capacity to not only be academically rigorous, but also emotionally supportive. Al-Freih and Robinson's (2024) qualitative exploration of students' perceptions of care in online learning environments reveals that students highly prize instructors who engage in modeling by demonstrating empathy, responsiveness, and genuine concern for their well-being. Key behaviors that convey instructor care are recommended, such as personalized communication, and the creation of interactive and engaging learning experiences. The authors also propose "anticipating" as an additional caring practice for online instructors, which involves foreseeing and addressing students' needs proactively. The findings (Al-Freih and Robinson, 2024) illuminate the need for faculty professional development focused on fostering care in virtual classrooms, suggesting that such training can improve educators' ability to create supportive and inclusive online learning environments which benefit learners and institutions.

Care Theory and Leadership

Care theory has been applied to the domain of leadership in a relatively limited way, with a particular emphasis on relational and ethical dimensions that foster leaders' capacity to engage in behaviors which promote empathy, authenticity, and reciprocity. In "Educational Leaders as Caring Teachers," Noddings (2006) posits the importance of care in educational leadership, emphasizing that effective leaders are those who prioritize relationships and demonstrate genuine concern for their students and staff. Noddings argues that care-based leadership involves being attentive to the needs of others, fostering an environment of trust, and promoting a culture of support. This approach contrasts with more traditional hierarchical leadership models, suggesting that leadership rooted in care can lead to more inclusive, democratic and effective educational settings. Similarly, Smole (2001) and Smylie et al. (2016) propose multidisciplinary, cross-occupational models of caring leadership suggesting that effective school and nursing leaders are those who can balance power with caring by integrating care into their daily practices, from decision-making to interpersonal interactions.

Kropiewnicki and Shapiro (2001), Bass (2009), and Witherspoon and Arnold (2010) examine female leadership and the ethic of care through case studies. These studies illustrate the ways in which women leaders apply care ethics to their leadership practices, emphasizing that relational approaches that prioritize the well-being and development of employees have positive impacts. When leaders integrate care-based approaches that focus on nurturing relationships, building community, and providing support, more inclusive and effective organizational cultures result. Tomkins and Simpson (2015) and Turkel (2014) extend these ideas to provide a philosophical perspective on care in leadership, arguing that caring leadership involves being present and compassionate with those one leads, and fostering a sense of belonging, peace, shared purpose, and holistic well-being across work teams. Tuckwiller et al.'s (2024) study on educator resilience expands Noddings' ethics of care framework purporting that care-based leadership can help educators navigate the challenges of their profession, promoting their own resilience and well-being. It is important to note that the relatively limited scholarship related to care-based leadership was focused around female leadership and leadership in the fields of nursing and education.

Adult Online Learners

Recent studies highlight that adult online learners identify several key benefits of online education, such as access to a diverse community of learners, a wider selection of institutions and degree programs, increased agency and independence, the ability to work at their own pace, and the flexibility and convenience of online courses (Castro & Tumibay, 2021; Paudel, 2021; Tareen & Haand, 2020). Recognizing the unique characteristics and motivations of adult learners in professional graduate degree programs is crucial for designing effective online learning environments. Sagna and Vaccaro (2023) and Berry and Hughes (2020) note that adult learners often juggle significant personal and professional responsibilities, such as childcare and work, which impact their learning experiences. These learners typically enroll in graduate programs voluntarily and balance their studies around these responsibilities. Consequently, adult learners tend to be highly motivated and focused (Fenwick & Tennant, 2020). The learning process for adults involves self-discovery and transformation, affecting not just what they learn but also how they learn (Abedini et al., 2021). Understanding these distinctive features is essential for creating effective learning experiences for adults.

Research demonstrates that effective online instruction for adult learning communities necessitates particular attributes and methodologies to cater to the distinct needs and preferences of adult learners (Kaiser, et al. 2023; Bostwick, 2023). Proficient online instructors can best meet adult learners' needs by demonstrating an aptitude for communication and facilitation, both of which foster a sense of connection and ensure that instructions, expectations, and feedback are effectively conveyed to students (Bloomberg, 2022; Gaytan and McEwen, 2021). Effective online instruction for adults also provides chances for students to reflect upon their learning experiences and practice metacognition (Bloomberg, 2022). In synchronous learning environments, metacognition may be supported through facilitated reflective practice, small group discussions, and the utilization of multiple technical features of the virtual classroom during instruction such as digital polls, chat waterfalls, mind maps, and collaborative shared documents (Khudhair et al., 2023; Bloomberg, 2022).

The smooth integration of technology plays an important role in the delivery of effective online instruction for adult learners, who seek a low-friction virtual learning experience. Leveraging the expertise of instructional designers to build a learning management system (LMS) that is both user-friendly and intuitive has been shown to significantly reduce the cognitive load for online learners, and enhance the overall learning experience (Kalyuga, 2023). Offering easy access to educational materials, and delivering opportunities for learner interaction and collaboration have been emphasized by Dabbagh and Castaneda (2020) as elemental to the learner's positive perceptions of the online learning both asynchronously and synchronously. By integrating multimedia and interactive elements in online instruction, such as videos, graphics, and interactive simulations, the potential to enhance comprehension and retention of information among adult learners is also optimized (Palaming, 2022).

Graduate Programs in Leadership

Understanding the key attributes of high quality graduate leadership curricula and programs is integral to knowing how to effectively apply care theory to instructional strategies within these programs. Gigliotti and Spear (2022) emphasize that the integration of fundamental leadership theories into graduate programs best prepares students to navigate complex organizational dynamics effectively. Perkins (2021) explores the potential of unleashing leadership capabilities within the graduate classroom by fostering an engaging and supportive learning environment which encourages deep interaction with course material and peer collaboration, which are vital for developing practical leadership skills such as team building and project management. Delbert and Jacobs' (2021) case study on best practices in leadership curriculum design found that curricula that engages students in developing empathetic leadership skills contributes to their future capacity to build trust, foster collaboration, and lead inclusive environments.

Orr (2011) discusses the pipeline from preparation to advancement in leadership, emphasizing that graduates' experiences in, through, and beyond leadership preparation programs can be amplified by providing experiential learning opportunities that intentionally bridge theory and practice. Similarly, Simen and Meyer's research (2021) emphasizes the importance of embedding practical tools such as case studies into leadership curricula, which rigorously challenge program participants to actively engage with contemporary ethical and relational challenges of leadership, and increases their preparation to lead with integrity and social responsibility (Mullen and Eadens, 2018). These methods also encourage active learning and critical thinking, which are considered essential for effective leadership.

Joiner (2019) highlights training in agility as a core component for effective leadership development. He argues that leaders who exhibit high levels of agility can effectively balance short-term performance with long-term strategic goals. This dual capability allows leaders to pivot swiftly in response to market shifts, technological advancements, and unexpected challenges. Joiner's research emphasizes that leadership agility is not just a personal attribute but a strategic necessity that enables organizations to thrive in dynamic environments. Lawrence's research (2013) reinforces this discussion by situating leadership agility within the VUCA (volatility, uncertainty, complexity, and ambiguity) framework. He asserts that the unpredictability and complexity of today's business world demand leaders who are not only adaptable but also possess the cognitive and emotional flexibility to lead through change. Lawrence's work underscores the importance of training leaders who can anticipate and respond to emerging trends, inspire and mobilize their teams, and maintain resilience under pressure. He too advocates for leadership development programs that focus on enhancing these capabilities through experiential learning and real-world problem-solving scenarios.

Integrating emotional and social intelligence (ESI) competency building into leadership programs has shown promising results in enhancing teamwork and leadership skills. The works of Hobson et al. (2014) and Boyatzis & Cavanagh (2018) offer empirical insights into the transformative impact of ESI on students' personal and professional development as leaders.

Hobson et al.'s research (2014) demonstrates that ESI-focused training fosters better conflict resolution and collaborative problem-solving among students. These competencies are considered critical for leaders who often find themselves in dynamic and high-pressure environments where emotional and social skills are as crucial as technical knowledge. Similarly, Boyatzis & Cavanagh's (2018) work underscores a holistic approach to leadership development, which includes enhancing self-awareness, self-regulation, social awareness, and relationship management. Their study argues that ESI competencies are pivotal in cultivating leaders who are empathetic, resilient, and capable of navigating the complex interpersonal dynamics which characterize modern workplaces.

Along with emotional intelligence skills, scholars concur that it is imperative to cultivate strong communication skills in leadership programs. Gigliotti et al. (2020) argue that effective leadership hinges on the ability to articulate vision and values, suggesting that communication is not merely a skill but a core leadership competency. Similarly, Conrad and Newberry (2012) emphasize that business communication skills are critical for navigating complex organizational landscapes, particularly in high-stakes decision-making. They advocate for integrating communication training directly into leadership curricula, ensuring that graduates can lead with clarity and influence. Biggs, Johnston, and Russell (2024) reinforce this by demonstrating that communication is a key metric in assessing executive effectiveness, linking it directly to leadership success.

CARE THEORY STRATEGIES TO ENHANCE ADULT ONLINE LEARNERS'

Graduate Leadership Degree Experiences

As graduate leadership programs seek to provide comprehensive training that prepares leaders to be effective, empathetic, and socially responsible actors, the integration of care theory helps ensure that future leaders are well-equipped to navigate the complexities of their roles across various professional fields, ultimately contributing to more dynamic and inclusive organizational environments. The following evidence-based strategies seek to synthesize what is understood about care theory, adult online learning, and graduate leadership programs in order to empower instructors in their techniques and advance students' learning outcomes and leadership capacity.

Model Caring Behaviors

Instructors should demonstrate caring behaviors consistently. By embodying empathy, attentiveness, and responsiveness, teachers provide students with a tangible example of leadership rooted in care. In an online synchronous setting, non-verbals such as facial and upper body language, and using the chat feature and emoticons help to communicate expressions of care. This approach aligns with Noddings' (2002) emphasis on modeling as a foundational component of care theory. Regularly showing concern for students' well-being can foster a supportive and trustful learning environment, crucial for effective leadership development.

Examples

1. An instructor begins each online session by checking in with students about their well-being and any challenges they might be facing. One impactful method for modeling care as the instructor is by leading the learning community in a "two word check-in" warm-up exercise during which each participant has the opportunity to share how they are feeling, or share something personal about themselves with the larger group at the onset of class (Berry, 2019; Brackett, 2019). This valuable socio-emotional technique, which can be facilitated in a round-robin manner or through a chat waterfall (if time is limited), not only promotes care and interpersonal connection, but softens the sometimes abrupt transitions adult learners make from their personal and professional lives into the synchronous online environment.

2. During a synchronous session, the instructor shares a personal story about a leadership challenge they overcame with empathy and care, demonstrating vulnerability and encouraging students to discuss their own experiences.

Care Theory Pillars Used

- **Modeling:** The instructor exemplifies caring behaviors by sharing personal experiences and showing empathy.
- **Dialogue:** Encourages students to share their own experiences, fostering mutual understanding.

Facilitate Reflective Dialogue

Instructors should incorporate structured opportunities for reflective dialogue where students can discuss their experiences, challenges, and growth. This aligns with Noddings' (2002) principle of dialogue, promoting mutual understanding and respect. Such discussions can be integrated into synchronous online sessions or through reflective journals and discussion forums or vlogs in asynchronous formats, encouraging deeper self-awareness and emotional intelligence.

Examples

1. In a graduate leadership course, students are assigned to keep a weekly reflective journal where they write about or record their leadership experiences and how they applied course concepts to them. These reflections are shared in small breakout groups during synchronous online sessions, where peers provide feedback and support, fostering a deeper understanding of their leadership journey.
2. Instructors begin a lesson (asynchronous or synchronous) with an opening reflective prompt such as a brief video, a quote, or a poem. Dialogue is subsequently facilitated by the instructor or by an asynchronous tool such as Flip or VoiceThread in which students collectively share their thoughts about the prompt, and its connection to larger curricular themes of leadership.

Care Theory Pillars Used

- **Dialogue**: Facilitates open communication and sharing of experiences.
- **Confirmation**: Peers and instructors affirm students' reflections and growth.

Engage in Authentic Practice

Design authentic learning experiences that allow students to apply leadership theories to real-world contexts. Simulations, role-playing, and case studies provide practical applications, reinforcing the importance of care through action. This experiential learning approach, supported by Hobson et al. (2014) and Boyatzis & Cavanagh (2018), bridges the gap between theory and practice, enhancing students' leadership agility.

Examples

1. Students participate in a simulation exercise where they must lead a virtual team through a crisis scenario such as a significant drop in employee morale or a sudden market shift. Using an online platform, students can choose from various decision-making paths and see the potential outcomes of their choices. After completing the simulation, students participate in a live video discussion where they collectively reflect upon their decisions, share their thought processes, and receive feedback from peers and the instructor.
2. In breakout rooms, trios of students participate in role plays in which one student engages with another in a mock difficult conversation related to a challenging real-life work scenario, and the third student observes and subsequently provides formative feedback to both actors. Following feedback, the larger class reconvenes to share key insights.

Care Theory Pillars Used

- **Practice**: Provides a real-world application of leadership skills.
- **Dialogue**: Encourages reflection and discussion post-simulation/role-play.
- **Confirmation**: Feedback from peers and instructors acknowledges students' efforts and progress.

Provide Affirmation and Feedback

Implement feedback systems that acknowledge and affirm students' efforts and progress. Noddings (2002) highlights the importance of confirmation in care theory, which involves recognizing and encouraging the growth and development of others. Constructive feedback should be personalized, timely, and supportive, helping students to reflect and improve continuously.

Examples

1. The instructor sets up a system where students submit their assignments through the learning management system (LMS) and receive personalized video feedback. In these videos, the instructor highlights specific strengths and areas for improvement, affirming the student's progress and offering concrete suggestions for development.
2. The instructor utilizes tools like live polling and pulse surveys in synchronous sessions to collect immediate feedback on understanding of content and learner engagement. Data can help clarify concepts in real-time, adjusting the course flow relative to student responses.

Care Theory Pillars Used

- **Confirmation**: Personalized and in-the-moment feedback acknowledges and supports students' development and identifies students' needs.
- **Dialogue**: Provides avenues for ongoing communication between instructor and student.

Create Collaborative Peer Learning Communities

Foster a sense of community within online courses by encouraging collaboration and peer-to-peer learning. This strategy can include group projects, peer review sessions, and virtual discussion forums that promote interaction and shared learning experiences. Such an environment supports the social dimensions of learning, crucial for developing leadership skills in a VUCA world, as emphasized by Lawrence (2013).

Examples

1. The course includes a group project where students must collaboratively develop a strategic plan for a hypothetical organization. They use online collaboration tools like Google Docs and Slack to communicate and share ideas. Regular virtual meetings are scheduled to discuss progress, fostering a sense of teamwork and shared responsibility.
2. Each week, small teams of students present a 25-30 minute synthesis of the weekly course readings to the class in the synchronous session. Teams collaboratively design and share their presentation, and are encouraged to use dynamic technology tools to present. Peers subsequently complete a micro-survey about the presentation to offer peer-to-peer formative feedback.

Care Theory Pillars Used

- **Dialogue:** Facilitates communication and collaboration among students.
- **Practice:** Engages students in real-world team-based tasks and leadership presentation skills.
- **Modeling:** Instructors may participate in discussions, modeling effective collaboration.

Integrate Emotional and Social Intelligence (ESI) Training

Develop curricula that incorporate ESI competencies, such as self-awareness, self-regulation, social awareness, and relationship management. Hobson et al. (2014) and Boyatzis & Cavanagh (2018) stress the transformative impact of ESI on leadership development. Activities like mindfulness exercises, empathy mapping, and interpersonal communication workshops can be integrated into the program to enhance these skills.

Example

1. The curriculum includes a series of workshops focused on ESI skills such as active listening, conflict resolution, and empathy. In one workshop, students practice coaching another peer on a challenging professional dilemma. Coaching sessions are recorded or observed and then the instructor and/or peers provide guidance and feedback on students' emotional and social responses.

Care Theory Pillars Used

- **Practice**: Students apply ESI skills in coaching scenarios.
- **Dialogue**: Workshops encourage discussion and feedback.
- **Confirmation**: Instructors and peers provide affirmation through feedback.

Utilize Technology for Personalization

Leverage learning management systems and other digital tools to personalize the learning experience. Providing tailored resources, adaptive learning paths, and individualized support can help meet the diverse needs of adult learners, as suggested by Dabbagh and Castaneda (2020). Personalization fosters a sense of care and attention, crucial for adult learners who are often juggling multiple responsibilities.

Examples

1. The LMS is set up to offer adaptive learning paths based on individual student progress. If a student struggles with a particular concept, the system recommends additional resources such as videos, articles, and quizzes tailored to their needs.
2. The instructor schedules one-on-one virtual advising meetings with students to discuss their progress and provide personalized support.

Care Theory Pillars Used

- **Confirmation:** Personalized resources and support affirm students' learning needs.
- **Dialogue:** One-on-one meetings facilitate open communication and signal concern for individual student well-being..

Incorporate Service-Learning Projects

Design service-learning opportunities that require students to engage in community service as part of their leadership training. Such projects embody care ethics by fostering empathy and responsiveness among students, as demonstrated by Xia (2023). Service-learning not only enhances civic responsibility but also provides practical leadership experiences that are deeply rooted in care and social impact.

Example

1. As part of the course, students are required to participate in a service-learning project with a partner nonprofit organization. They must identify a leadership challenge within the organization and work in teams to develop and implement a solution to guide improvement. This project is documented through a series of reflective reports and presentations, allowing students to connect their academic learning with real-world leadership experiences.

Care Theory Pillars Used

- **Practice**: Provides real-world application through service-learning.
- **Dialogue**: Reflective reports and presentations encourage discussion and feedback.
- **Confirmation**: Recognition of students' contributions and reflections.

Peer Mentorship Program

Implement a peer mentorship program where more experienced students and/or alumni mentor new students in the leadership program. This strategy fosters a supportive learning environment and provides opportunities for students to develop leadership skills by guiding others.

Examples

1. In a graduate online leadership course, second-year students are paired with incoming first-year students to provide guidance on coursework, career advice, and personal development. The mentors and mentees meet bi-monthly in virtual sessions, where mentors share their experiences, offer advice on navigating the program, and help mentees set academic and professional goals.
2. Recent alumni host virtual networking events or informational webinars for students, providing access to valuable career development resources and capitalizing on the use of technology to bring geographically diverse networks together.

Care Theory Pillars Used

- **Modeling**: Mentors and alumni demonstrate caring behaviors and effective leadership practices.
- **Dialogue**: Ongoing communication between mentors and mentees fosters mutual understanding and support. Professional networks are cultivated through dialogic engagement.
- **Confirmation**: Mentors affirm mentees' progress and provide encouragement, helping them build confidence in their abilities.

These strategies, grounded in care theory and aligned with best practices in adult online learning and leadership education, provide a framework for enhancing students' leadership capacities and learning outcomes within a holistic and supportive learning environment.

CONCLUSION

This chapter has illuminated the vital role of Noddings' care theory in shaping the experiences of adult learners within online graduate leadership programs, recognizing that adult learners bring distinct needs and challenges to the educational environment. By integrating the core components of care—modeling, dialogue, practice, and confirmation—into online teaching, instructors can cultivate environments that not only enhance academic outcomes but also support the emotional and social development of future leaders. The strategies discussed are particularly attuned to the complexities of adult learners, who often juggle professional responsibilities and personal commitments alongside their studies. By fostering authentic relationships, responsive communication, and meaningful engagement, educators can nurture a sense of belonging and motivation that is crucial for adult learners, who thrive in supportive and flexible learning environments.

As the landscape of online education continues to evolve, it is imperative that we move beyond transactional models of learning and embrace instructional approaches that prioritize care, empathy, and relational integrity. In doing so, we prepare our students not just to succeed academically but to lead with compassion, resilience, and a deep commitment to the well-being of those they will serve. The application of care theory in online graduate education is not merely an add-on but a foundational approach that promotes the development of leaders who are equipped to navigate the complexities of modern organizational life with both competence and heart, all while addressing the unique needs of adult learners in a meaningful and impactful way.

REFERENCES

Abedini, A., Abedin, B., & Zowghi, D. (2021). Adult learning in online communities of practice: A systematic review. *British Journal of Educational Technology*, 52(4), 1663–1694. DOI: 10.1111/bjet.13120

Adams, C., & Rose, E. (2014). Will I ever connect with the students?" Online Teaching and the Pedagogy of Care. *Phenomenology & Practice*, 8(1), 5–16. DOI: 10.29173/pandpr20637

Al-Freih, M., & Robinson, H. (2024). A Qualitative Exploration of Students' Perception of Care When Learning Online: Implications for Online Teaching and Faculty Professional Development. [IJOPCD]. *International Journal of Online Pedagogy and Course Design*, 14(1), 1–15. DOI: 10.4018/IJOPCD.333715

Andenoro, A. C. (2007). Competencies of leadership professionals: A national study of premier leadership degree programs (Doctoral dissertation, Texas A&M University).

Bada, S. O., & Olusegun, S. (2015). Constructivism learning theory: A paradigm for teaching and learning. *Journal of Research & Method in Education*, 5(6), 66–70.

Bali, M., & Zamora, M. (2022). The equity–care matrix: Theory and practice. *Italian Journal of Educational Technology*, 30(1), 92–115. DOI: 10.17471/2499-4324/1241

Barrow, M. (2015). Caring in teaching: A complicated relationship. *The Journal of Effective Teaching*, 15(2), 45–59.

Bass, L. (2009). Fostering an ethic of care in leadership: A conversation with five African American women. *Advances in Developing Human Resources*, 11(5), 619–632. DOI: 10.1177/1523422309352075

Bennoun, S., Haeberli, P., & Schaub, M. (2018). Taking an ethics of care perspective on two university teacher training programmes. *South African Journal of Higher Education*, 32(6), 137–152. DOI: 10.20853/32-6-2651

Bergman, R. (2004). Caring for the ethical ideal: Nel Noddings on moral education. *Journal of Moral Education*, 33(2), 149–162. DOI: 10.1080/0305724042000215203

Berry, G. R., & Hughes, H. (2020). Integrating work–life balance with 24/7 information and communication technologies: The experience of adult students with online learning. *American Journal of Distance Education*, 34(2), 91–105. DOI: 10.1080/08923647.2020.1701301

Berry, S. (2019). Teaching to connect: Community-building strategies for the virtual classroom. *Online Learning : the Official Journal of the Online Learning Consortium*, 23(1), 164–183. DOI: 10.24059/olj.v23i1.1425

Biggs, A., Johnston, S., & Russell, D. (2024). Leadership and communication: How to assess executive skills. *The Journal of Business Strategy*, 45(3), 199–205. DOI: 10.1108/JBS-05-2023-0085

Bloomberg, L. D. (2023). Designing and delivering effective online instruction, how to engage the adult learner. *Adult Learning*, 34(1), 55–56. DOI: 10.1177/10451595211069079

Bostwick, D. (2023). Fostering community and engagement in online 'classrooms'. *Teaching Journalism Online*, 53.

Boyatzis, R. E., & Cavanagh, K. V. (2018). Leading change: Developing emotional, social, and cognitive competencies in managers during an MBA program. *Emotional intelligence in education: Integrating research with practice*, 403-426.

Boyd, B. L., Getz, C. A., & Guthrie, K. L. (2019). Preparing the leadership educator through graduate education. *New directions for student leadership*, 2019(164), 105-121.h Leadership Development. *New Directions for Student Leadership*, 2020(165).

Brackett, M. (2019). *Permission to feel: Unlocking the power of emotions to help our kids, ourselves, and our society thrive*. Celadon Books.

Breen, J. M., & Gleason, M. C. (2022). Setting the stage: An overview of articles in this issue. *New Directions for Student Leadership*, 2022(176), 5–8. DOI: 10.1002/yd.20525 PMID: 36565148

Burke, K., & Larmar, S. (2021). Acknowledging another face in the virtual crowd: Reimagining the online experience in higher education through an online pedagogy of care. *Journal of Further and Higher Education*, 45(5), 601–615. DOI: 10.1080/0309877X.2020.1804536

Castro, M. D. B., & Tumibay, G. M. (2021). A literature review: Efficacy of online learning courses for higher education institutions using meta-analysis. *Education and Information Technologies*, 26(2), 1367–1385. DOI: 10.1007/s10639-019-10027-z

Chatelier, S., & Rudolph, S. (2018). Teacher responsibility: Shifting care from student to (professional) self? *British Journal of Sociology of Education*, 39(1), 1–15. DOI: 10.1080/01425692.2017.1291328

Conklin, H. G. (2018). Caring and critical thinking in the teaching of young adolescents. *Theory into Practice*, 57(4), 289–297. DOI: 10.1080/00405841.2018.1518643

Conrad, D., & Newberry, R. (2012). Identification and instruction of important business communication skills for graduate business education. *Journal of Education for Business*, 87(2), 112–120. DOI: 10.1080/08832323.2011.576280

Covrig, D. M., & Baumgartner, E. (2010). Learning while leading: The Andrews University leadership program. *Journal of Applied Christian Leadership*, 4(1), 26–55.

Crigger, N. (2001). Antecedents to engrossment in Noddings' theory of care. *Journal of Advanced Nursing*, 35(4), 616–623. DOI: 10.1046/j.1365-2648.2001.01878.x PMID: 11529962

Crowley, M. A. (1994). The Relevance of Modelings' Ethics of Care to the Moral Education of Nurses. *The Journal of Nursing Education*, 33(2), 74–80. DOI: 10.3928/0148-4834-19940201-07 PMID: 8176501

Crumpton-Young, L., McCauley-Bush, P., Rabelo, L., Meza, K., Ferreras, A., Rodriguez, B., & Kelarestani, M. (2010). Engineering leadership development programs: A look at what is needed and what is being done. *Journal of STEM Education: Innovations and Research*, 11(3).

Dabbagh, N., & Castaneda, L. (2020). The PLE as a framework for developing agency in lifelong learning. *Educational Technology Research and Development*, 68(6), 3041–3055. DOI: 10.1007/s11423-020-09831-z

Dalton, J. E., & Hrenko, K. A. (2016). Caring as a Transformative Model for Arts Integration. *Curriculum & Teaching Dialogue*, 18.

De Meuse, K. P., Dai, G., & Hallenbeck, G. S. (2010). Learning agility: A construct whose time has come. *Consulting Psychology Journal*, 62(2), 119–130. DOI: 10.1037/a0019988

Delbert, T. M., & Jacobs, K. (2021). Best Practices in Leadership Curriculum Development: A Case Study of a Curriculum Designed to Foster Authentic Leadership Skills in Graduate Students. *Journal of Higher Education Theory and Practice*, 21(2).

Drago-Severson, E., Asghar, A., Blum-DeStefano, J., & Welch, J. R. (2011). Conceptual changes in aspiring school leaders: Lessons from a university classroom. *Journal of Research on Leadership Education*, 6(4), 83–132. DOI: 10.1177/194277511100600401

Eddy, L. L., Doutrich, D., Higgs, Z. R., Spuck, J., Olson, M., & Weinberg, S. (2009). Relevant nursing leadership: An evidence-based programmatic response. *International Journal of Nursing Education Scholarship*, 6(1). Advance online publication. DOI: 10.2202/1548-923X.1792 PMID: 19645690

Fenwick, T., & Tennant, M. (2020). Understanding adult learners. In *Dimensions of adult learning* (pp. 55–73). Routledge. DOI: 10.4324/9781003115366-6

Flint, A. S., Kurumada, K. S., Fisher, T., & Zisook, K. (2011). Creating the perfect storm in professional development: The experiences of two American teachers and a university research team. *Professional Development in Education*, 37(1), 95–109. DOI: 10.1080/19415250903425502

Fuglsang, L., & Mattsson, J. (2009). An integrative model of care ethics in public innovation. *Service Industries Journal*, 29(1), 21–34. DOI: 10.1080/02642060802116362

Gaytan, J., & McEwen, B. C. (2007). Effective online instructional and assessment strategies. *American Journal of Distance Education*, 21(3), 117–132. DOI: 10.1080/08923640701341653

Gigliotti, R. A., Dwyer, M., Brescia, S. A., Gergus, M., & Stefanelli, J. R. (2020). Learning leadership in higher education: Communicative implications for graduate education. *Atlantic Journal of Communication*, 28(4), 209–223. DOI: 10.1080/15456870.2020.1720990

Gigliotti, R. A., & Spear, S. E. (2022). Essential leadership concepts and models for graduate and professional school learners. *New Directions for Student Leadership*, 2022(176), 65–74. DOI: 10.1002/yd.20531 PMID: 36565144

Glowacki-Dudka, M., Mullett, C., Griswold, W., Baize-Ward, A., Vetor-Suits, C., & Londt, S. C. (2018). Framing care for planners of education programs. *Adult Learning*, 29(2), 62–71. DOI: 10.1177/1045159517750664

Heid, K. (2008). Care, sociocultural practice, and aesthetic experience in the art classroom. *Visual Arts Research*, 34(1), 87–98. DOI: 10.2307/20715464

Heid, K. A., & Kelehear, Z. (2007). *The challenge to care in schools: An alternative approach to education.*

Hobson, C. J., Strupeck, D., Griffin, A., Szostek, J., & Rominger, A. S. (2014). Teaching MBA Students Teamwork and Team Leadership Skills: An Empirical Evaluation of a Classroom Educational Program. *American Journal of Business Education*, 7(3), 191–212. DOI: 10.19030/ajbe.v7i3.8629

Hoggan, C., & Kloubert, T. (2020). Transformative Learning in Theory and Practice. *Adult Education Quarterly*, 70(3), 295–307. DOI: 10.1177/0741713620918510

Howard, P. (2019). Re-visioning teacher education for sustainability in Atlantic Canada. In *Environmental and sustainability education in teacher education: Canadian perspectives* (pp. 179–191). Springer International Publishing. DOI: 10.1007/978-3-030-25016-4_11

Joiner, B. (2019). Leadership Agility for organizational agility. *Journal of Creating Value*, 5(2), 139–149. DOI: 10.1177/2394964319868321

Kaiser, L., McKenna, K., Lopes, T., & Zarestky, J. (2023). Strategies for supporting adult working learners in the online learning environment. *New Directions for Adult and Continuing Education*, 2023(179), 53–65. DOI: 10.1002/ace.20502

Kalyuga, S. (2023). *Task Complexity, Learner Expertise, and Instructional Goals in Managing Instructional Guidance*. Copyright and Other Legal Notices, 122.

Khudhair, A. A., Khudhair, M. A., Jaber, M. M., Awreed, Y. J., Ali, M. H., AL-Hameed, M., Jassim, M., Malik, R., Alkhayyat, A., & Hameed, A. (2023). Impact on Higher Education and College Students in Dijlah University after COVID through E-learning. *Computer-Aided Design and Applications*, •••, 104–115. DOI: 10.14733/cadaps.2023.S12.104-115

Kızılcık, H. H., & Türüdü, A. S. D. (2022). Humanising online teaching through care-centred pedagogies. *Australasian Journal of Educational Technology*, 38(4), 143–159. DOI: 10.14742/ajet.7872

Knowles, M. (1975). *Self-directed learning: A guide for learners and teachers*. The Adult Education Company.

Knowles, M. Andragogy in Action, Malcolm S. Knowles and Associates. 1st ed. Jossey-Bass; 1984.

Komives, S. R., & Sowcik, M. (2020). How Academic Disciplines Approach Leadership Development. *New Directions for Student Leadership*, 2020(165). Advance online publication. DOI: 10.1002/yd.20365 PMID: 32187868

Kostenius, C., & Alerby, E. (2020). Room for interpersonal relationships in online educational spaces–a philosophical discussion. *International journal of qualitative studies on health and well-being*, 15(sup1), 1689603.

Kropiewnicki, M. I., & Shapiro, J. P. (2001). *Female Leadership and the Ethic of Care: Three Case Studies*.

Kumar, B., Swee, M. L., & Suneja, M. (2020). Leadership training programs in graduate medical education: A systematic review. *BMC Medical Education*, 20(1), 1–10. DOI: 10.1186/s12909-020-02089-2 PMID: 32487056

Lawrence, K. (2013). Developing leaders in a VUCA environment. *UNC Executive Development*, 2013, 1–15.

Leonard, J., Petta, K., & Porter, C. (2016). A fresh look at graduate programs in teacher leadership in the United States. In *Teacher Leadership and Professional Development* (pp. 29–44). Routledge.

Lu, Y., Hong, X., & Xiao, L. (2022). Toward high-quality adult online learning: A systematic review of empirical studies. *Sustainability (Basel)*, 14(4), 2257. DOI: 10.3390/su14042257

Lubker, J. R., & Petrusa, E. R. (2022). Utilizing co-curricular learning tools to foster leadership development in graduate and professional schools: Examples and lessons learned. *New Directions for Student Leadership*, 2022(176), 53–64. DOI: 10.1002/yd.20530 PMID: 36565143

Lussier, J. (2020). Reciprocity, Exchange, and Indebtedness in Noddings's Concept of Care. *Philosophy of Education*, (2020), 134-47.

Mccloskey, A. (2012). Caring in professional development projects for mathematics teachers: An example of stimulation and harmonizing. *For the Learning of Mathematics*, 32(3), 28–33.

McNamee, A., Mercurio, M., & Peloso, J. M. (2007). Who cares about caring in early childhood teacher education programs? *Journal of Early Childhood Teacher Education*, 28(3), 277–288. DOI: 10.1080/10901020701555580

Mega, C., Ronconi, L., & De Beni, R. (2014). What makes a good student? How emotions, self-regulated learning, and motivation contribute to academic achievement. *Journal of Educational Psychology*, 106(1), 121–131. DOI: 10.1037/a0033546

Merriam, S. B., & Baumgartner, L. M. (2020). *Learning in adulthood: A comprehensive guide*. John Wiley & Sons.

Mezirow, J. (1995). Transformation theory of adult learning. In Welton, M. (Ed.), *In defense of the lifeworld: Critical perspectives on adult learning* (pp. 37–90). State University of New York Press.

Mitchell, M. M., & Poutiatine, M. I. (2001). Finding an experiential approach in graduate leadership curricula. *Journal of Experiential Education*, 24(3), 179–185. DOI: 10.1177/105382590102400309

Mullen, C. A., & Eadens, D. W. (2018). "Quality leadership matters": A research-based survey of graduate programming. *Journal of Research on Leadership Education*, 13(2), 162–200. DOI: 10.1177/1942775117739415

Noddings, N. (1986). *Caring: A feminine approach to ethics and moral education.*

Noddings, N. (1988). An ethic of caring and its implications for instructional arrangements. *American Journal of Education*, 96(2), 215–230. DOI: 10.1086/443894

Noddings, N. (1992). *The challenge to care in schools: an alternative approach to education.*

Noddings, N. (1995). Teaching themes of care. *Phi Delta Kappan*, 76, 675–675.

Noddings, N. (1999). Caring and competence. *Teachers College Record*, 100(5), 205–220. DOI: 10.1177/016146819910000509

Noddings, N. (2002). Educating moral people: A caring alternative to character education. Teachers College Press, PO Box 20, Williston, VT 05495-0020

Noddings, N. (2006). Educational leaders as caring teachers. *School Leadership & Management*, 26(4), 339–345. DOI: 10.1080/13632430600886848

Noddings, N. (2007). Caring as relation and virtue in teaching. *Working virtue: Virtue ethics and contemporary moral problems*, 41-60.

Noddings, N. (2012). The caring relation in teaching. *Oxford Review of Education*, 38(6), 771–781. DOI: 10.1080/03054985.2012.745047

Noddings, N. (2012). The language of care ethics. *Knowledge Quest*, 40(5), 52.

Noddings, N. (2013). *Caring: A relational approach to ethics and moral education* (updated). Berkeley, CA and Los Angeles: University of California Press (Original work published 1984).

Noddings, N. (2019). Concepts of care in teacher education. In *Oxford Research Encyclopedia of Education*. DOI: 10.1093/acrefore/9780190264093.013.371

Normore, A. H., & Issa Lahera, A. (2019). The evolution of educational leadership preparation programmes. *Journal of Educational Administration and History*, 51(1), 27–42. DOI: 10.1080/00220620.2018.1513914

O'Brien, T. J. (2016). *Looking for development in leadership development: Impacts of experiential and constructivist methods on graduate students and graduate schools*. Harvard University.

Orr, M. T. (2011). Pipeline to preparation to advancement: Graduates' experiences in, through, and beyond leadership preparation. *Educational Administration Quarterly*, 47(1), 114–172. DOI: 10.1177/0011000010378612

Owens, L. M., & Ennis, C. D. (2005). The ethic of care in teaching: An overview of supportive literature. *Quest*, 57(4), 392–425. DOI: 10.1080/00336297.2005.10491864

Palaming, A. (2022). Online instructional strategies. *EPRA International Journal of Multidisciplinary Research* (IJMR).Published online 2022:176-179.

Paudel, P. (2021). Online education: Benefits, challenges and strategies during and after COVID-19 in higher education. *International Journal on Studies in Education*, 3(2), 70–85. DOI: 10.46328/ijonse.32

Pekrun, R., Goetz, T., Frenzel, A. C., Barchfeld, P., & Perry, R. P. (2011). Measuring emotions in students' learning and performance: The Achievement Emotions Questionnaire (AEQ). *Contemporary Educational Psychology*, 36(1), 36–48. DOI: 10.1016/j.cedpsych.2010.10.002

Perkins, M. Y. (2021). Beyond the building: Unleashing leadership potential in the graduate classroom. *Teaching Theology and Religion*, 24(2), 93–106. DOI: 10.1111/teth.12586

Quigley, C. F., & Hall, A. H. (2016). Taking care: Understanding the roles of caregiver and being cared for in a kindergarten classroom. *Journal of Early Childhood Research*, 14(2), 181–195. DOI: 10.1177/1476718X14548783

Rabin, C. (2021). Care ethics in online teaching. *Studying Teacher Education*, 17(1), 38–56. DOI: 10.1080/17425964.2021.1902801

Riegnell, J., & Bulthuis, S. (2022). *Successful Adult Learning Principles.*

Rikard, L. G. (2009). The significance of teacher caring in physical education. *Journal of Physical Education, Recreation & Dance*, 80(7), 4–5. DOI: 10.1080/07303084.2009.10598348

Robinson, H., Al-Freih, M., & Kilgore, W. (2020). Designing with care: Towards a care-centered model for online learning design. *The International Journal of Information and Learning Technology*, 37(3), 99–108. DOI: 10.1108/IJILT-10-2019-0098

Rose, E. (2017). Beyond social presence: Facelessness and the ethics of asynchronous online education. *McGill Journal of Education*, 52(1), 17–32. DOI: 10.7202/1040802ar

Sagna, S., & Vaccaro, A. (2023). "I Didn't Just Do It for Myself": Exploring the Roles of Family in Adult Learner Persistence. *The Journal of Continuing Higher Education*, 71(2), 168–182. DOI: 10.1080/07377363.2021.2023989

Scherer, K. R. (2009). The dynamic architecture of emotion: Evidence for the component process model. *Cognition and Emotion*, 23(7), 1307–1351. DOI: 10.1080/02699930902928969

Shevalier, R., & McKenzie, B. A. (2012). Culturally responsive teaching as an ethics- and care-based approach to urban education. *Urban Education*, 47(6), 1086–1105. DOI: 10.1177/0042085912441483

Simen, J. H., & Meyer, T. (2021). Leadership education in professional and graduate schools. *New Directions for Student Leadership*, 2021(171), 113–122. DOI: 10.1002/yd.20461 PMID: 34658177

Smole, V. (2001). School Leadership-Balancing Power With Caring. *American Secondary Education*, 29(4), 56.

Smylie, M. A., Murphy, J., & Louis, K. S. (2016). Caring school leadership: A multidisciplinary, cross-occupational model. *American Journal of Education*, 123(1), 1–35. DOI: 10.1086/688166

Tareen, H., & Haand, M. T. (2020). A case study of UiTM post-graduate students' perceptions on online learning: Benefits challenges. *International Journal of Advanced Research and Publications*, 4(6), 86–94.

Tomkins, L., & Simpson, P. (2015). Caring leadership: A Heideggerian perspective. *Organization Studies*, 36(8), 1013–1031. DOI: 10.1177/0170840615580008

Trout, M. (2008). The supervision dance: Learning to lead and follow a student teacher. *New Educator*, 4(3), 252–265. DOI: 10.1080/15476880802234649

Trout, M. (2010). Social skills in action: An ethic of care in social studies student teaching supervision. Advancing social studies education through self-study methodology: *The power, promise, and use of self-study in social studies education*, 119-137.

Tuckwiller, E., Fox, H., Ball, K., & St. Louis, J. (2024). More than just a "nod" to care: Expanding Nel Noddings' ethics of care framework to sustain educator resilience. *Leadership and Policy in Schools*, •••, 1–18. DOI: 10.1080/15700763.2024.2311249

Turkel, M. C. (2014). Leading from the heart: Caring, love, peace, and values guiding leadership. *Nursing Science Quarterly*, 27(2), 172–177. DOI: 10.1177/0894318414522663 PMID: 24740954

Witherspoon, N., & Arnold, B. M. (2010). Pastoral care: Notions of caring and the Black female principal. *The Journal of Negro Education*, 79(3), 220–232.

Xia, Y. (2023). Service-Learning Practices and Reflections in the Perspective of Nel Noddings' Theory of Caring Education: The "Care for the Elderly" Service-Learning Program as an Example. *Journal of Contemporary Educational Research*, 7(10), 25–32. DOI: 10.26689/jcer.v7i10.5479

Zakharova, I., & Jarke, J. (2022). Educational technologies as matters of care. *Learning, Media and Technology*, 47(1), 95–108. DOI: 10.1080/17439884.2021.2018605

Zhu, Y., Zhang, J. H., Au, W., & Yates, G. (2020). University students' online learning attitudes and continuous intention to undertake online courses: A self-regulated learning perspective. *Educational Technology Research and Development*, 68(3), 1485–1519. DOI: 10.1007/s11423-020-09753-w

Chapter 7
Implementing Online Project–Based Learning:
Opportunities for Social Capital Development

Youmei Liu
https://orcid.org/0009-0000-1973-1872
University of Houston, USA

ABSTRACT

This chapter examines the relationship between online Project-Based Learning (PBL) and social capital development, tracing the historical roots of PBL from learning by doing and experiential learning to modern implementations supported by digital platforms. It highlights how PBL, grounded in student-centered, real-world projects, fosters deep learning and critical thinking. As PBL has evolved, the integration of AI technology offers new tools to enhance learning but also introduces ethical challenges that must be carefully managed. The chapter emphasizes that building social capital – through trust, collaboration, and community engagement – is essential for the success of online PBL. It discusses strategies for overcoming the challenges of diverse student backgrounds and real-world complexities, focusing on the importance of ethical AI use and inclusive practices. Ultimately, this chapter underscores the potential of online PBL to not only enhance academic outcomes but also contribute to stronger, more resilient communities through the development of social capital.

DOI: 10.4018/979-8-3693-4407-1.ch007

INTRODUCTION

History of PBL

"Confucius and Aristotle were early proponents of learning by doing. Socrates modeled how to learn through questioning, inquiry, and critical thinking - all strategies that remain very relevant in today's PBL classrooms" (Boss, 2011, para. 3). In the 20th century, John Dewey has been credited for laying the groundwork for PBL. He has been recognized as one of the early promoters of project-based education or at least its principles through his idea of "learning by doing" (Bender, 2012). John Dewey advocated for experiential education, emphasizing the importance of learning through experience, reflection, and integrating real-world tasks into the curriculum for PBL. Following his suit, Kilpatrick further developed the idea of project-based learning. He built on Dewey's theory and introduced the project method as a component of Dewey's problem method of teaching (Beckett & Slater 2019). In his influential essay, *The Project Method*", Kilpatrick outlined an instructional method where students work on a purposeful project related to their interests (1918). He emphasized student autonomy and the value of projects in making learning more meaningful. Later research studies have further enriched the PBL with various components to make it more vibrant and effective by incorporating different focuses, such as Montessori's educational approach, which focused on student-centered, hands-on learning, also contributed to the development of PBL. The Italian physician, Maria Montessori launched an international movement during the 20th century with her approach to early-childhood learning (Boss, 2011). A Montessori classroom emphasizes hands-on learning and developing real-world skills (Jones, 2020). Vygotsky's sociocultural theory, particularly the concept of the Zone of Proximal Development (ZPD), has been influential in PBL. Vygotsky's sociocultural theory of cognitive development emphasizes the importance of the social and cultural context in which learning occurs (Leo, 2023). Vygotsky believed that learning is culturally dependent and that different cultures shape how people learn, and educators should consider the effects of culture on the learning environment.

In the modern era's implementation of PBL, the Buck Institute for Education (BIE) has been a leading advocate for PBL. The BIE defines PBL as "Project Based Learning (PBL) as a teaching method in which students learn by actively engaging in real-world and personally meaningful projects" (BIE, Homepage). New Tech Network defines PBL as "Project-based learning (PBL) is an inquiry-based and learner-centered instructional approach that immerses students in real-world projects that foster deep learning and critical thinking skills" (No date, para. 3). The definition varies in different research studies with enhanced focuses; however, the key points stay the same, which are student-centered learning and real-world projects. PBL has been recognized as a very effective approach to student learning. PBL gives students greater control and flexibility to prepare and engage more in their learning through integrating cooperation with industry or professional communities to build real-life issues to provide students with authentic learning experiences (Ma, 2022). "Authentic project-based learning (APBL) is a highly effective way for instructors to help students learn disciplinary skills, modes of thinking, and collaborative practices by creating solutions to real-world problems for real users and clients" (Rees Lewis, et al, 2019, abstract).

Internet Technology and Online PBL Platforms

Internet technology has immensely expanded the scope of the educational environment from classroom-based learning to boundless worldwide learning. Different online applications have been developed to facilitate online education delivery. The rise of online platforms of MOOCs (Massive Open Online Courses, https://onlinelearningconsortium.org/) since 2006 has provided free education to learners worldwide, and other establishments, such as MIT OCW (MIT OpenCourseWare, https://ocw.mit.edu/), Coursera (https://www.coursera.org/), edX (https://www.edx.org/), Udemy (https://www.udemy.com/), etc. follow suit and form an enormous global educational network. This inclusivity has empowered individuals to pursue their educational goals, irrespective of their circumstances. In addition to the popular CMS/LMS (Course Management Systems/Learning Management Systems), such as Blackboard (https://www.anthology.com/), Canvas (https://www.instructure.com/canvas), and Moodle-based LMS, specific PBL online learning platforms have been developed to enhance PBL learning, for instance, PBLWorks (Buck Institute for Education, https://www.pblworks.org/) developed by the Buck Institute for Education, is one of the most respected resources for PBL. It provides educators with comprehensive training, planning tools, and a library of project ideas aligned with standards. For example, High Tech High – San Diego, California, (https://www.hightechhigh.org/about/) a network of K-12 public charter schools that are well-known for their PBL approach. They also offer graduate school of education that motivates a global network of change leaders to disrupt the status quo through transformative learning experience (https://hthgse.edu/). Educators collaborate with PBLWorks to create a curriculum that focuses on real-world projects. Students engage in long-term, interdisciplinary projects that often culminate in presentations to the community.

Educurious (https://educurious.org/) is another platform that connects students with industry experts to work on real-world projects and emphasizes problem-solving and critical thinking, integrating real-world relevance into the learning process. Their inspiration is taking students on learning adventures and giving students voice and choice where students have agency in their learning – acquiring knowledge and engaging in projects fueled by their own interests through project-based learning environment. "Our project-based learning curriculum empowers youth to take charge of their learning. Technology is our friend. Real world experts are our allies" "Powering students to take on the world - We place youth at the center of their learning experience. Ready to open their minds. Ready for tomorrow." (https://educurious.org/).

"Trello (https://trello.com/), a project management tool, is often adapted for educational use in PBL helping students and educators organize tasks, set deadlines, and monitor progress visually. University of Texas at Austin (https://www.utexas.edu/) business students use Trello to manage large-scale marketing and business development projects. They developed a comprehensive business plan for a local Austin startup, organizing tasks and deadlines through Trello boards. Stanford University's design thinking courses use Trello as a project management tool for students working on interdisciplinary design challenges. Students use Trello to collaborate on projects that address complex social issues, such as affordable housing solutions for underserved communities. "Seeing the increasing popularity of PBL worldwide and the need to manage the learning process, the e-learning platforms specialized in supporting PBL emerged and have gained interest from teachers and educational institutes" (Meng, et al, para 5, 2023).

Theoretical Framework for Online PBL Learning

This chapter integrates multiple perspectives of theoretical frameworks that strongly impact online Project-Based Learning, providing a holistic view of how different pedagogical and social theories shape the learning environment. Through considering several theoretical foundations, educators and researchers can better understand how online PBL supports not only academic achievement but also the development of critical social skills, collaboration, and community engagement, all of which are essential for social capital development. The following theoretical frameworks are incorporated in addressing the challenges and implementation of online PBL learning.

1. **Social Capital Theory** – "a multifaceted concept in sociology, economics, and organizational behavior, examines the value and benefits derived from social networks and relationships" (TheoryHub, n.d. para. 1). Social capital theory contends that social relationships are resources that can lead to the development and accumulation of human capital (Machalek & Martin, 2015). In the traditional view of social capital, one of the network structural properties that can assume a pivotal role for the production of knowledge for network members is

cohesion (Coleman, 1988, Reagans and Zuckerman, 2001). Cohesion is helpful in promoting the creation of social norms and sanctions within networks, and to facilitate trust and effective coordination between network members (Coleman, 1988, Granovetter, 1985, Krackhardt, 1999, Reagans and McEvily, 2003). In online PBL learning, social capital helps students leverage relationships to enhance learning, build trust, and collaborate more effectively. This theory fits well with the chapter's emphasis on the role of PBL in fostering social capital, especially in online settings where building trust and cooperation can be challenging but is crucial for successful project outcomes.

2. **Sociocultural Theory** – Vygotsky's Sociocultural Theory emphasizes that learning is a socially mediated process, with social interaction playing an essential role in cognitive development. Vygotsky (1978) introduced the concept of mediation, where cultural tools, language, and interaction are key elements in facilitating the acquisition of higher mental functions. He argued that higher mental functions are first developed through interaction with others, particularly within a socio-cultural context, before they are internalized by the individual (Vygotsky, 1978). This framework is especially relevant to Project-Based Learning, where students work collaboratively, sharing knowledge, negotiating meanings, and relying on guidance from more knowledgeable others. In the virtual PBL environments, social capital – built through relationships, trust, and cooperation – becomes central to students' learning experiences. This process is central to PBL, where students often rely on collective problem-solving, peer feedback, and community involvement to construct knowledge. Research supports the notion that collaboration in learning environments enhances cognitive growth. According to Lave and Wenger (1991), learning is a situated process where knowledge is co-constructed through participation in social practices. Research by Johnson and Johnson (2009) on cooperative learning aligns with Vygotsky's theory, demonstrating that students working in collaborative environments achieve higher levels of learning, communication, and social skill development compared to those in competitive or individualistic settings. In the virtual PBL context, where students might not physically interact, this process of building social capital and trust takes place through structured interactions, peer reviews, and project-based tasks facilitated by online tools.

3. **Constructivist Theory**, rooted in the works of Jean Piaget and later expanded by scholars such as Lev Vygotsky and Jerome Bruner (1961), posits that learners construct knowledge through active engagement and interaction with their environment. Piaget's theory of cognitive development (1954) introduced the idea that learning is an active process, and students must construct new knowledge based on their existing cognitive structures, building their own understanding through drawing from personal experiences and previous knowledge. This

framework aligns strongly with Project-Based Learning, which centers on students actively engaging with real-world problems, thus constructing knowledge through exploration, collaboration, and problem-solving.

This principle is reflected in PBL as students are given open-ended, real-world problems that require them to connect prior knowledge to new experiences, ultimately fostering deeper cognitive development. In PBL, students are not passive recipients of information but rather active participants who engage in inquiry-based learning. This mirrors Piaget's assertion that learning occurs through assimilation (incorporating new experiences into existing knowledge) and accommodation (modifying existing knowledge structures to incorporate new information) (Piaget, 1954).

Vygotsky's work complements Piaget's in highlighting the social dimensions of constructivism. His theory introduced the concept of the Zone of Proximal Development (ZPD), which suggests that learners construct knowledge most effectively when working slightly beyond their current abilities, with the support of more knowledgeable peers or instructors (Vygotsky, 1978). This concept is central to PBL, as students frequently work in teams, allowing them to co-construct knowledge with peers and benefit from the diverse expertise within the group. Research shows that collaborative learning environments, such as those fostered in PBL, lead to higher levels of cognitive engagement and deeper understanding of subject matter (Johnson, Johnson, & Smith, 1998).

Contemporary research supports the constructivist underpinnings of PBL. For example, Thomas (2000) conducted a comprehensive review of PBL and found that it is highly effective in promoting active learning, critical thinking, and the application of knowledge to real-world scenarios. This active engagement in problem-solving aligns with constructivist principles, where learning is seen as a dynamic process of knowledge construction rather than the passive absorption of information. Similarly, Strobel and van Barneveld (2009) found that PBL promotes deeper learning and retention compared to traditional teaching methods, as students are actively involved in the learning process and must continuously construct and reconstruct their understanding.

4. **The Community of Inquiry (CoI)** framework is a widely recognized model for understanding the dynamics of online learning, emphasizing the interaction between cognitive, social, and teaching presence in creating a successful learning environment (Garrison, Anderson, & Archer, 2000). This framework is particularly relevant to online Project-Based Learning environments, as PBL relies on the integration of these three components to foster deep learning, engagement, and community-building – particularly in virtual settings where physical interaction is absent. In the context of online PBL, students form vir-

tual communities of practice that are bound by a shared goal and rely on one another's contributions, fostering social capital and facilitating deeper learning outcomes. Studies by Garrison and Anderson (2003) on the Community of Inquiry framework further emphasize the importance of social presence and interaction in online environments, noting that these interactions directly contribute to the creation of meaningful learning experiences, much like Vygotsky's sociocultural perspective.

The CoI framework is particularly suited to online PBL because it acknowledges the multifaceted nature of learning in virtual environments, where students must engage cognitively with the material, socially with peers, and under the guidance of an instructor. As Swan, Garrison, and Richardson (2009) highlight, the balance of these presences determines the overall success of the online learning experience, and their interplay is critical to fostering the deep learning and collaborative skills that are at the heart of PBL. In online PBL, where students are expected to collaborate on complex, real-world problems, the CoI framework offers a comprehensive model for understanding how to build a supportive, engaging, and effective learning community.

By weaving together these theoretical perspectives, this chapter illustrates how online PBL fosters a rich, multifaceted learning experience that goes beyond traditional academic outcomes to promote social capital and community development. This integration of frameworks enables a deeper exploration of both the educational and societal impacts of PBL in a digital age.

Challenges of PBL Implementation

Accompanied by the advancements of PBL are the challenges and complications. Authentic PBL provides tremendous learning experiences for students, the additional complexity caused by real-world problems could create additional challenges for instructors (Jonassen & Hung, 2015). The preparation and readiness of administrators, instructors, and resources are also possible barriers. A research study by Learning Ecosystems and Leadership found two categories of factors related to BPL implementation. "Some factors were knowledge-related, such as teachers' and administrators' understanding of PBL and ability to design and use projects in their teaching, along with their capacity to generate and manage meaningful, relevant, community-engaged projects. Some factors were organizational, most commonly the policy and administrative environment of the school and the system in which the school operated (for example, curricula, assessment, and standards requirements)" (para. 3, 2021). In a worldwide learning network, a diverse student body and multicultural communities will further contribute to the complications of online PBL implementation. Hence, in addition to the project-based learning activities, Vygotsky's sociocultural aspect becomes an important component of PBL. Creating an inclusive and trustworthy educational learning environment is crucial to the success of online PBL learning.

Industry 4.0 with the fast advancement of AI technology calls for an urgent educational reformation to redesign curriculum and update teaching approaches to close the gap between traditional education and modern societal needs. The mission of online PBL learning is beyond simply finding solutions to problems, more importantly; it is about the whole-person development of students, which equips students with the skills, values, and attitudes needed to contribute meaningfully to society. Effective engagement and interaction with people from extended communities promote cross-cultural understanding, mutual respect, and trust for meaningful engagement and collaboration. The whole-person development plays a crucial role in building strong, vibrant communities where social capital thrives. This, in turn, leads to more cohesive, supportive, and resilient societies. Hence, this chapter discusses the implementation of online PBL learning in extended communities to develop social capital and covers the following three topics.

1. Strategies to build an effective online PBL for social capital development
2. Create a student-centered inclusive online PBL learning environment
3. Effective integration of AI Technology in online PBL learning

MAIN FOCUS OF THE CHAPTER

Strategies to Build an Effective Online PBL for Social Capital Development

The rapid evolution of online education has opened new avenues for fostering collaborative learning and building meaningful connections within diverse communities. Project-based learning in an online environment presents a unique opportunity to engage students in a deep learning and to extend these interactions into broader community contexts. By implementing PBL in an extended online learning community, instructors can cultivate environments where students actively collaborate, share resources, and engage with a network of peers, mentors, and community members. Thus, online PBL not only enhances academic learning but also promotes the development of social capital – those networks of relationships contribute to collective well-being and success.

Social capital defined as the networks of relationships and trust that enable communities to function effectively (Putnam, 2000). It is a critical component of thriving communities, and it is built through trust, cooperation, and shared understanding. In an online learning community, PBL can serve as a powerful agent for creating and strengthening these connections. Students working together on real-world projects are encouraged to build relationships, both within their immediate groups and with external stakeholders, fostering a sense of belonging and mutual support. As they navigate these collaborative experiences, students develop essential social skills, such as communication, empathy, and teamwork, which are vital for both personal and professional growth. Moreover, by engaging with an extended community, students can apply their learning to address authentic challenges, further embedding themselves in networks that extend beyond the classroom and contribute to the collective social capital of the communities.

Impact of Social Capital and Sociocultural Effect on BPL Learning

"Social capital is the networks of relationships among people who live and work in a particular society, enabling that society to function effectively" (Oxford Dictionary, n. d.). Over the decades, researchers have extensively explored the core elements of social capital across various contexts and disciplines, including economics, sociology, politics, and psychology. These efforts have greatly broadened the research scope and deepened people's understanding of how social capital influences individuals, organizations, and societies as a whole. "Social capital revolves around three dimensions: interconnected networks of relationships between individuals and groups (social ties or social participation); levels of trust that characterize these ties, and resources or benefits that are both gained and transferred by virtue of social ties and social participation" (Britannica, n.d.).

No matter what area of social capital is investigated or researched, trust is the top important element in all types of social capital. Trust is the foundation for any type of relationship. "Trust is a fundamental component of interpersonal relationships" (Cialdini & Fincham, 1990, p. 1001). The research study by Learning Ecosystems and Leadership in 2021 stated that the "data seem to be beginning to suggest that social capital may be central to, and encompassing of, knowledge, motivation, and organizational factors to implementing PBL; and what is more, social capital may act to fill in the gaps created by challenges to PBL implementation" (para. 9, 2021). Online PBL learning provides students with the best opportunity to learn the knowledge that is socially constructed and practically situated as well as enacted, and involves examining the tacit assumptions and meaning that underpin processes of creating, sharing, and applying knowledge (Brown & Duguid, 1991, 2001; Wenger, 2000).

Project-based learning has long been celebrated for its ability to engage students in active problem-solving and the development of hard skills essential for academic and professional success. Traditionally, PBL research has emphasized the acquisition of technical knowledge and the application of critical thinking to tackle complex challenges. However, in online PBL learning environments, the importance of soft skills developed from social capital cannot be overstated. Trust becomes a cornerstone for any successful PBL project implementation and sustainability. Vygotsky's sociocultural theory emphasizes the crucial role of social interaction and cultural context in cognitive development (Vygotsky, 1978). Modern research studies further attest to the importance of social capital on student learning. A research project by Learning Ecosystems and Leadership reported that "Even though the knowledge, motivation, and organization were all supportive of PBL, this lack of trust made it unsustainable" (Learning Ecosystems and Leadership, para. 7, 2021). "As we are learning across the field, social capital – relationships, networks, and trust between and among different people in the education system – plays a big part in how successful education is for students. This is no different for PBL" (Learning Ecosystems and Leadership, para. 10, 2021).

Online PBL provides the best learning environment to enhance the true quality of education and to promote the development of social capital for the following reasons.

1. Online PBL provides a global community learning environment with limitless opportunities, which is impossible for traditional classroom teaching. Vygotsky strongly believed that community plays a central role in the process of "making meaning" (McLeod, 2024)
2. Online PBL brings in people from all over the world and provides opportunities to understand each other to reduce bias and stereotypes toward the different cultures that students are not familiar with, thus promoting mutual understanding, respect, and trust with a more comprehensive perspective rather than their own or superficial views, seeing things from a different cultural standpoint. Cognitive development is a socially mediated process in which students acquire cultural values, beliefs, and problem-solving strategies through collaborative dialogues with more knowledgeable members of society (McLeod, 2024).
3. Online PBL provides various learning opportunities for students with different methodologies and approaches to view and solve problems. Vygotsky believed that learning is culturally dependent and that different cultures shape how people learn. Through interaction with students from different cultures, students will enrich their skills of critical thinking and problem-solving with new tactics.

Effective Online PBL Learning Design via Community of Inquiry

In teaching practice, instructors should utilize existing available resources in consideration of possible collaboration partners in the extended learning community to create an effective online PBL learning environment. Incorporating social skills into PBL for online learners involves recognizing and addressing these diverse characteristics. It requires creating an inclusive environment where every student feels valued and empowered to contribute. Community of Inquiry (CoI) is widely used in online education research. It describes learning as the interplay of three elements: *cognitive presence* (deep learning and critical thinking), *social presence* (building relationships and a sense of belonging), and *teaching presence* (instructor guidance and organization). This framework aligns well with PBL in online settings, where building a strong community is essential for fostering trust and engagement, especially in virtual environments. Online PBL can be a powerful tool in this regard, as it encourages students to work together, often across time zones and cultural boundaries, to achieve common goals. Through structured group activities, peer feedback, and collaborative problem-solving, students develop the ability to navigate and appreciate diversity, build interpersonal relationships, and work effectively in teams. By focusing on social skills within online PBL projects, instructors can help students not only achieve academic success but also prepare them to engage meaningfully with diverse communities in their personal and professional lives. The following Table 1 provides ten ideas for setting up strategies and goals for building effective online project-based learning through CoI design.

Table 1. Strategies and Goals for Building Effective Online Project-Based Learning

Strategies	Goals
1. Foster Strong Virtual Collaboration (*Social Presence*) - Set clear expectations for group work, including roles, responsibilities, and deadlines to ensure accountability.	- Encourage meaningful collaboration among students and between students and the community to build social connections in an online environment. - Ensure that all students are actively engaged and contributing to the project, fostering a sense of shared responsibility.
2. Promote Inclusivity and Diversity (*Social Presence*) - Encourage diverse group compositions to bring various perspectives and skills to the project.	- Create an inclusive online environment where all students feel valued and able to contribute their unique perspectives. - Enhance the richness of project outcomes by integrating diverse viewpoints and fostering cultural sensitivity.
3. Foster Partnerships with External Organizations (*Social Presence*) - Collaborate with local NGOs, businesses, or virtual communities to offer students access to authentic challenges and mentorship.	- Establish strong connections with community organizations, businesses, and professionals to provide real-world context and resources for PBL projects. - Enhance the relevance of PBL projects by integrating community needs and expertise into the learning experience.

continued on following page

Table 1. Continued

Strategies	Goals
4. Leverage Community Resources Virtually (*Social Presence*) - Partner with local organizations, businesses, or community members who can provide virtual guest lectures or mentorship. - Utilize virtual field trips and online community forums to expose students to community concerns, issues, and solutions.	- Bridge the gap between the online classroom and the real world by incorporating community resources and experts into the learning process. - Connect students with real-world professionals and community members to make learning more relevant and applied. - Enhance students' understanding of community dynamics and encourage civic engagement through virtual experiences.
5. Facilitate Socially Relevant Project Themes (*Cognitive Presence*) - Choose project themes that are socially relevant, such as environmental sustainability, social justice, or community health.	- Engage students in projects that address real-world social issues, enhancing the relevance and impact of their work. - Equip students with the knowledge and skills to tackle complex social problems and contribute positively to society. Raise awareness of social issues and foster a sense of civic responsibility by encouraging students to share their work with the wider community.
6. Promote Cross-Disciplinary Collaboration (*Cognitive Presence*) - Design projects that require input from various disciplines, allowing students to work with peers and professionals from different backgrounds.	- Encourage collaboration across different fields of study to broaden students' perspectives and enhance problem-solving capabilities. - Develop well-rounded solutions that address complex, multifaceted problems by integrating knowledge and skills from multiple disciplines.
7. Provide Scaffolding and Support for Online Collaboration (*Teaching Presence*) - Create step-by-step guides, checklists, and tutorials to support students in managing virtual team dynamics and external collaborations.	- Offer structured guidance and resources to help students navigate the challenges of online collaboration with extended communities. - Ensure that students are equipped with the necessary skills and confidence to successfully engage with extended communities in their PBL projects.
8. Encourage Reflection and Social Learning (*Teaching Presence*) - Incorporate regular reflection sessions where students discuss their social and emotional experiences during the project. - Use peer review and feedback sessions to allow students to learn from each other's perspectives and experiences.	- Promote self-awareness and social responsibility by integrating reflection into the learning process. - Help students process and internalize their learning, fostering personal growth and a deeper understanding of social issues. - Build a supportive online community where students can exchange ideas and provide constructive feedback, enhancing their social learning experience.
9. Integrate Community Feedback into Project Development (*Teaching Presence*) - Schedule virtual feedback sessions where students present their project ideas to community members for input and suggestions.	- Involve community stakeholders in the feedback process to ensure that PBL projects are aligned with community needs and expectations. - Refine and improve project outcomes by incorporating diverse perspectives from extended community stakeholders.
10. Assess and Evaluate Community Impact (*Teaching Presence*) - Develop rubrics that include criteria for assessing community engagement, collaboration quality, and project sustainability.	- Implement assessment methods that evaluate both the learning outcomes for students and the impact of their projects on the extended community. - Measure the effectiveness of PBL projects in achieving educational objectives and contributing positively to extended community development.

These strategies start with establishing a strong internal learning community among students from diverse cultures, which lays a solid foundation before they interact with external communities. Recognizing and valuing each student's unique background can help students build trustworthy relationships among themselves so that they can collaborate and engage with each other professionally and respectfully on the PBL projects to promote social capital development. Instructors can reference the above strategies and goals to design their own online PBL learning based on the availability of the resources including the support from the school to decide on the scope of the project, not necessarily to cover every aspect, prioritizing the most important aspect first. Online PBL learning projects can be designed through sequential courses that can run across semesters, which will contribute to the sustainability of the collaboration efforts. The advantage is that students can have ample time to interact with the community and enrich the learning experience for in-depth understanding and building strong connections among students and with the external communities.

Creating a Learner-Centered Inclusive Online PBL Learning Environment

In today's rapidly changing educational setting, the pursuit of inclusive education has emerged as a fundamental goal to ensure equitable access and meaningful learning experiences for all students. Educational equity is not only "crucial to improving the learning and well-being outcomes of individuals within diverse populations but also to supporting all people to engage with others constructively in increasingly diverse and complex societies" (Santiago & Cerna, 2020, p. 2). Recognizing the unique strengths, needs, and diversities of learners, educational institutions and stakeholders are increasingly embracing the concept of a learner-centered inclusive learning environment. This approach prioritizes the creation of educational spaces that foster collaboration, respect, and empowerment, enabling each learner to thrive and reach their full potential.

Learner-centered inclusive education encourages active participation, collaboration, and mutual support among students, thereby strengthening social bonds and creating a sense of belonging. These interactions not only enhance academic learning but also contribute to the development of key social skills, such as empathy, communication, and teamwork. As students engage in collaborative learning experiences, they form networks of trust and reciprocity, which are essential components of social capital.

Creating a learner-centered inclusive learning environment aligns with the principles of equity, diversity, and human rights, and it fosters the holistic development of learners while preparing them for an interconnected and diverse world. By prioritizing inclusivity, educational institutions can empower students to reach their full potential, build a more inclusive society, and contribute to a brighter and more compassionate future. "Teachers should provide intellectually powerful, learner-centered, and technology-rich environments for students without undermining sound pedagogical practices" (Keengwe, Onchwari, & Onchwari, 2009, p. 11). Creating a learner-centered course is the fundamental step and preparation to engage diverse learners. However, no matter how good the course design is, without effective interaction and guidance from instructors, the course alone will have a limited impact on student learning. It is very important to establish a cross-cultural learning community and to develop student's sense of self-belonging, which is crucial for student success in inclusive education.

Involving Student Voices for Social Capital Evolvement

The creation and diffusion of knowledge within organizations rely on the development of social networks, shared systems of meaning, and the cultivation of shared values and norms (Spender, 1996). A more social or community-based approach to understanding knowledge creation, codification, and sharing within organizations thus becomes essential (Swan et al. 1999). However, one important missing aspect has been identified by Madda related to student learning in the process of social capital application. It fails "to incorporate student voice in the exploration of defining social capital", "some may incorporate qualitative interviews with students or student advisory groups, but these studies typically refrain from incorporating student perspectives into defining or quantifying social capital as students see it, in favor of fitting student perspectives into predefined descriptions or frameworks. This is a key miss" (Para. 15, 2023).

This critical element is essential to the success of online PBL learning. Students are the center of the entire PBL process, and their personal experiences offer valuable insights for ongoing improvements. These experiences include navigating complex social relationships, engaging with diverse communities, and interacting with peers from various cultural, social, political, and religious backgrounds. Instructors should integrate opportunities within the online PBL design for students to voice their concerns and propose solutions to challenges they encounter. Additionally, the traditional theoretical definition of social capital, which is largely static, requires updating to reflect the realities of our rapidly changing society. The fast-paced advancements in technology, along with the dynamic learning experiences of students and contributions from extended learning communities, are reshaping people's understanding of social capital. These changes necessitate a redefinition of social capital to remain relevant in today's context.

At the same time, it is important to increase student knowledge and awareness of the importance of social capital in their online PBL learning environment so that they can leverage different opportunities presented to them. For example, in 2022 ESG kicked off new work funded by the Siemens Foundation to build social capital development equitably into career pathways and related programs in five school districts across the country (Perez, para. 2, 2023). The Harvard Opportunity Insights organization created the "Social Capital Atlas" that analyzes Facebook relationships to explore "economic connectedness," a theoretical predictor of economic mobility. From the school's efforts, "education programs should place more emphasis on developing these relationships with institutional agents – not only because of the motivation factor but also because a single relationship can contribute multiple resources to a student's life" (Madda, Para. 8, 2023).

Student-Centered Constructive Online PBL Learning

Student's contribution to the educational process will greatly improve the quality of learning since students are the center and their concerns, opinions, and perspectives are very important to PBL implementation and improvement. "Education efforts to better support students on their path to prosperous futures should consider thoughts and suggestions from students themselves on the ways they can best be served" (Perez, para.1, 2023). This democratic process not only helps administrators and instructors to better understand students' needs and adjust policies and teachings to improve student learning outcomes, but more importantly, it can enhance the interaction, engagement, and trustworthy relationship between students and instructors as well as among students. Constructivist theory revolves around the idea that learners actively construct knowledge rather than passively receiving information. The key components are *active learning, prior knowledge and experiences, social interaction, problem-based learning, reflection, learner-centered environment, contextual learning, and constructive assessment* (Piaget, 1952, Vygotsky, 1978, Bruner, 1961 and Lave & Wenger, 1991). The following Table 2 provides some ideas on the course design strategies around the key components of constructivist theory for student-centered online PBL learning to promote social capital development.

Table 2. Course Design Strategies for Student-Centered Online PBL Learning

Strategy	Course Design Elements	Objectives
1. Empower Student Agency and Ownership (*Learner-centered environment*)	**Community-Focused Projects:** - Involve and allow students in the process to choose or design projects that address specific community needs. - After the project topic has been identified, encourage students to lead the planning and execution of the projects with guidance from instructors and community experts.	- By giving students the agency to select or create projects that resonate with them, they are more likely to feel invested and motivated, fostering a deeper connection to the community. - This approach builds leadership skills and a sense of responsibility, encouraging students to take ownership of both their learning and their impact on the community.
2. Facilitate Community Collaboration and Engagement (*Social interaction, prior knowledge and contextual learning*)	**Virtual Community Partnerships:** - Involve students in establishing partnerships with virtual communities for collaborative projects. - Integrate service-learning components that require students to engage with community members and address real-world challenges.	- Engaging with community partners helps students develop networks and relationships, fostering the growth of social capital through meaningful community connections. - Service-learning projects allow students to apply their skills in a real-world context, enhancing their understanding of community dynamics and the importance of social capital.
3. Scaffold Social Interaction and Communication (*active learning, prior knowledge and experiences, social interaction*)	**Structured Peer Collaboration:** - Design project activities that require students to work together in groups, with rotating roles to ensure diverse interactions. - Host online events where students can interact with community leaders, alumni, and other stakeholders.	- Encouraging collaboration in structured group settings helps students develop interpersonal skills, build trust, and create networks that contribute to social capital development. - Networking events provide students with opportunities to expand their social networks, learn from others' experiences, and establish valuable community connections.
4. Encourage Reflection on Social Impact (*reflection*)	**Reflective Journals on Community Engagement:** - Have students maintain journals reflecting on their interactions with the community and the impact of their work. - Facilitate online discussions where students share insights and challenges related to community engagement.	- Reflective practice encourages students to consider the broader social implications of their projects, deepening their understanding of social capital and its role in community development. - These discussions allow students to learn from each other's experiences, fostering a collaborative learning environment where social skills and community awareness are developed.

continued on following page

Table 2. Continued

Strategy	Course Design Elements	Objectives
5. Utilize Digital Tools to Foster Connection (*contextual learning*)	**Collaborative Online Platforms:** - Use online PBL platforms, such as Trello, Miro, or Zoom to facilitate ongoing communication and project management among students and community partners. - Encourage students to use social media platforms to share their projects and engage with broader community audiences.	- Digital tools enable seamless collaboration and communication, allowing students to build and maintain relationships across different geographical locations, thus strengthening social capital. - Leveraging social media helps students extend the reach of their work, connect with diverse audiences, and build a sense of community and shared purpose online.
6. Integrate Feedback of Social Capital Development (*constructive assessment*)	**Community Feedback as Part of Assessment:** - Include feedback from community members as a component of project evaluation. - Use self and peer assessments to evaluate students' growth in collaboration, communication, and community engagement skills.	- Incorporating community feedback into assessments ensures that students' work is aligned with community needs and highlights the value of social capital in achieving project success. - Self and peer assessments help students reflect on their social development and the effectiveness of their interactions, which are crucial elements of social capital development.
7. Promote Sustainability and Long-Term Impact (*social interaction*)	**Long-Term Community Partnerships:** - Create projects with sustainable outcomes that continue to benefit the community beyond the course. - Develop ongoing relationships with community organizations to allow students to see the impact of their work over time to sustain PBL learning and social capital development.	- Focusing on sustainability helps students understand the long-term value and importance of maintaining strong community relationships over time. - Establish connections with local NGOs, schools, or businesses for continuous collaboration. Students can work on multi-phase projects or continue projects initiated by previous classes.

Student-centered learning with strong support from the extended community will be the key contribution to the successful implementation and sustainability of online PBL learning and the development of social capital. In addition to the above-suggested ideas, some practical teaching approaches can also help students in the process of online PBL learning and provide students with opportunities to contribute to the success of the projects. For example, Perez's research study used a "Relationship Mapping" strategy to "signal to students (and the adults guiding them through the exercise) that they come into this social capital conversation with existing resources and supports through their various communities that can help them reach their postsecondary and career aspirations" (para. 4, 2023). In the pilot study, they also created a Student Advisory Group to give students from across the communities an opportunity to provide their perspectives on the social capital efforts in the project. The primary responsibilities of the Student Advisory Group include offering guidance for the continuous enhancement of projects, providing insights that help site teams better understand students' current knowledge and curiosity about social capital, and reflecting on their experiences as participants in the pilot to inform future sustainability and replication efforts (Perez, 2023). The contributions of students, drawn from their firsthand experiences in online PBL learning, play a vital role in driving these project improvements. The key components integrated in the course design strategies highlight the interactive, reflective, and collaborative nature of learning in constructivist theory focusing on student-centered learning.

Effective Integration of AI Technology in Online PBL Learning

Artificial Intelligence (AI) is rapidly transforming the way people live, work, and interact with the world. In the field of education, AI offers innovative opportunities to enhance learning experiences and prepare students for the future. Integrating AI technology into Project-Based Learning (PBL) in online course design not only provides students with hands-on experience with cutting-edge technology but also increases AI awareness in the community and benefits the community at large. AI technology provides students with powerful tools to facilitate their learning and manage their time in their PBL projects. One such powerful tool is ChatGPT, which has been increasingly used globally since its debut in November 2022. Despite the controversy in academics for using ChatGPT for plagiarism and misinformation, there are many success stories for using ChatGPT to improve teaching and learning efficiency and quality. ChatGPT uses natural language processing to generate human-like responses to user input. It has gained attention worldwide for its impressive performance in generating coherent, systematic, and informative responses (Zhai, 2022). As Zalaznick (2023) observes, view the advent of ChatGPT as a potential turning point. They argue that ChatGPT could lead to the demise of "mindless, irrelevant, inauthentic learning activities", suggesting that this technology might pave the way for more meaningful, engaging, and authentic educational experiences. This perspective introduces a constructive angle to the debate, indicating that the integration of AI in education, if approached thoughtfully and responsibly, could catalyze a shift towards more relevant and impactful learning methodologies. AI technology can be equally beneficial for online PBL learning.

Utilizing ChatGPT for Designing Online Project-Based Learning

ChatGPT, a powerful language model developed by OpenAI, offers a range of capabilities that can significantly enhance the PBL experience by supporting students in research, collaboration, and problem-solving. These AI-driven functionalities align closely with the core principles of PBL, where students actively engage in projects that require critical thinking, creativity, and collaboration to solve real-world problems. One of the primary benefits of using ChatGPT in online PBL is its ability to assist students in generating and refining ideas. During the brainstorming phase, students can interact with ChatGPT to explore a wide range of project topics, receive suggestions on narrowing their focus, or consider alternative approaches they might not have otherwise contemplated. In the research study by Divito et al, they used ChatGPT in problem-based learning and found out that in short of faculty resources, ChatGPT can assist in developing realistic case element, provide framework learning objectives that can be used to assist in meeting education core competences, as well as generating auxiliary Socratic lines of questioning that facilitator can use to lead the student to self-identify any potential gaps in understanding (2023). ChatGPT uses natural language processing to generate human-like responses to user input. It has gained attention worldwide for its impressive performance in generating coherent, systematic, and informative responses

Collaboration is another area where ChatGPT can make a significant impact. In online PBL, where students often work in distributed teams, ChatGPT can facilitate communication by providing real-time feedback, mediating discussions, and helping to resolve conflicts. "As a group, students can formulate potential solutions to case problems and ask ChatGPT to provide critical feedback that can elaborate on the student learning process, including revealing unidentified learning objectives or knowledge gaps" (Divito et al, 2023, para. 10). By acting as a neutral party that offers constructive suggestions, ChatGPT can enhance group dynamics and ensure that all team members contribute effectively. The following Table 3 outlines some ideas for designing an online PBL learning with ChatGPT.

Table 3. Incorporating ChatGPT in Designing an Online PBL Learning

Aspect	Course Design Strategies with ChatGPT	Student Learning Activities Using ChatGPT
1. Idea Generation and Brainstorming	- Incorporate ChatGPT as a tool for generating ideas and brainstorming project topics or problem statements. - Use ChatGPT to facilitate group brainstorming sessions by suggesting possible directions or perspectives.	- Students can engage ChatGPT in initial brainstorming sessions to generate a list of potential project ideas. - Use ChatGPT to refine and expand on brainstorming outputs, helping teams converge on a focused project idea.
2. Research and Resource Curation	- Integrate ChatGPT into research activities by having it suggest relevant articles, books, and other resources. - Use ChatGPT to guide students in structuring their research questions or hypotheses.	- Students use ChatGPT to search for and summarize key resources related to their project topic. - Engage ChatGPT in creating a preliminary literature review or summarizing findings from complex sources.
3. Collaborative Writing and Editing	- Use ChatGPT to assist students in drafting sections of their project reports or proposals, focusing on structure and clarity. - Implement ChatGPT as a peer-review tool to provide constructive feedback on written drafts.	- Students collaborate with ChatGPT to co-write project deliverables, ensuring clarity and coherence in their writing. - Utilize ChatGPT for editing and revising their reports, focusing on grammar, style, and readability.
4. Project Management and Planning	- Leverage ChatGPT to help students create project timelines, identify milestones, and allocate tasks within their teams. - Use ChatGPT to remind students of deadlines, upcoming tasks, and provide project management tips.	- Students can ask ChatGPT to help them outline a project plan, including setting key milestones and deadlines. - Use ChatGPT as a virtual assistant to track progress and suggest adjustments to the project timeline as needed.
5. Problem-Solving and Critical Thinking	- Encourage students to use ChatGPT to explore different solutions or approaches to the challenges they encounter in their projects. - Incorporate ChatGPT as a tool for scenario analysis, where students can ask "what if" questions and explore potential outcomes.	- Engage ChatGPT to discuss potential solutions and analyze the pros and cons of each approach. - Use ChatGPT to simulate different scenarios, helping students anticipate potential challenges and plan their responses.
6. Peer Collaboration and Feedback	- Design activities where ChatGPT is used as a mediator in peer collaboration, helping to facilitate discussions and resolve conflicts. - Use ChatGPT to provide neutral, constructive feedback on group dynamics and contributions.	- Students use ChatGPT to mediate discussions and generate ideas for how to improve teamwork and collaboration. - Engage ChatGPT to provide feedback on peer work, focusing on areas of improvement and highlighting strengths.

continued on following page

Table 3. Continued

Aspect	Course Design Strategies with ChatGPT	Student Learning Activities Using ChatGPT
7. Creative Problem Framing	- Integrate ChatGPT in activities that require students to frame or reframe the problems they are solving in innovative ways. - Use ChatGPT to challenge students with alternative perspectives or unexpected questions that stimulate creative thinking.	- Students interact with ChatGPT to reframe their project problem statement from different perspectives. - Use ChatGPT to challenge students to consider alternative approaches or solutions they hadn't previously thought of.
8. Reflection and Self-Assessment	- Use ChatGPT to guide reflective activities, prompting students to think critically about their learning processes and outcomes. - Incorporate ChatGPT in self-assessment tasks where students evaluate their own contributions and progress.	- Students engage with ChatGPT to reflect on what they've learned during the project, identifying strengths and areas for growth. - Use ChatGPT to assist in creating a personal learning journal, where students document their project journey and insights.

AI technology can significantly contribute to online PBL by providing adaptive learning environments that cater to the diverse needs of students. Through AI-powered tools, educators can offer personalized learning paths, real-time feedback, and intelligent tutoring systems that guide students through complex projects. This personalized approach not only addresses individual learning styles but also helps in identifying and supporting students who may need additional assistance, thereby promoting inclusivity in the learning environment.

However, the integration of AI in online PBL also presents challenges that educators must carefully navigate. Issues such as data privacy, the potential for algorithmic bias, and the ethical implications of AI usage in education need to be addressed to ensure that AI enhances rather than hinders the learning process. "Although ChatGPT has the potential to serve as an assistant for instructors (e.g., to generate course materials and provide suggestions) and a virtual tutor for students (e.g., to answer questions and facilitate collaboration), there were challenges associated with its use (e.g., generating incorrect or fake information and bypassing plagiarism detectors)" (Lo, 2023, abstract). Instructors must also be mindful of the digital divide, ensuring that all students have equitable access to the AI tools and resources necessary for their success in online PBL learning.

Ethical Considerations and Responsible AI Use in Community Projects

AI technology integrated into online Project-Based Learning within community projects presents both significant opportunities and challenges. The ethical use of AI in these contexts is crucial, not only for ensuring that technology serves the community's best interests but also for fostering the development of social capital. Technologies impact people in different ways. Some student populations may be at greater risk of harm than others (Gašević et al., 2023). When implemented thoughtfully, AI can enhance these networks by facilitating collaboration, improving communication, and providing innovative solutions to community challenges. However, without careful consideration of ethical principles such as fairness, transparency, and accountability, the use of AI can undermine these very foundations, leading to mistrust and social fragmentation. It is essential to critically evaluate the outputs generated by AI. "Human and systemic biases in generative AI algorithms and large language models' (LLMs) data impact the output of AI tools and consequently can perpetuate inequities when these biases are not removed or addressed" and "These models can provide inaccurate, misleading, and unethical information. (Center for Teaching Innovation, n. d, para. 5, 6). By addressing issues such as bias, privacy, inclusivity, and community involvement in AI decision-making, instructors and community leaders can harness the power of AI while safeguarding the values that underpin healthy social networks. The goal is to create learning experiences that not only advance students' knowledge and skills but also contribute positively to the communities they serve, ensuring that technology acts as a bridge rather than a barrier to social cohesion. The following Table 4 provides some ideas on the strategies for AI technology ethical implementation.

Table 4. Strategies for AI Technology Ethical Implementation

Strategy	Description	Implementation Examples
1. Educate on AI Ethics and Responsible Use	Provide foundational knowledge on AI ethics, focusing on fairness, transparency, and accountability.	- **Ethics Modules:** Integrate AI ethics modules into the PBL curriculum, covering topics like bias in AI, data privacy, and the societal impact of AI decisions. - **Case Study Analysis:** Have students analyze case studies of ethical dilemmas in AI, discussing the implications for communities and how responsible AI use can be ensured.
2. Implement Transparent AI Practices	Ensure that AI tools and processes used in community projects are transparent and understandable to all stakeholders.	- **Open AI Models:** Use open-source AI models and tools where possible, allowing community members to understand and review the technology being used in projects. - **Explainable AI:** Teach students how to use explainable AI techniques that make AI decisions interpretable, ensuring community members understand how outcomes are derived.
3. Engage the Community in Ethical AI Decisions	Involve community members in discussions and decisions about how AI will be used in projects that affect them.	- **Ethical AI Committees:** Form community-based ethical AI committees that include students, educators, and community members to oversee the ethical use of AI in projects. - **Town Hall Meetings:** Organize virtual town hall meetings where community members can voice concerns, ask questions, and provide input on AI-related decisions in PBL projects.
4. Address Bias and Fairness in AI	Teach students how to identify and mitigate bias in AI systems to ensure fairness in community-focused projects.	- **Bias Audits:** Implement AI bias audits in PBL projects where students evaluate AI models for potential biases and take corrective actions to ensure fairness. - **Diverse Data Sources:** Encourage the use of diverse and representative data sets in AI projects to minimize bias and ensure that AI solutions serve all community members equally.
5. Promote Privacy and Data Security	Ensure that all AI-driven community projects prioritize the privacy and security of individuals' data.	- **Data Anonymization:** Teach students techniques for anonymizing data to protect individuals' privacy when using community data in AI projects. - **Secure Data Practices:** Implement strict data security protocols in PBL projects, ensuring that all personal and sensitive data is handled responsibly and securely.
6. Foster Inclusivity in AI Design	Ensure that AI tools and solutions developed in PBL projects are inclusive and accessible to all community members.	- **Inclusive Design Workshops:** Conduct workshops on inclusive AI design, teaching students to consider diverse needs and perspectives in their AI projects. - **Community Co-Design Sessions:** Involve community members in the AI design process to ensure that the tools developed meet the needs of all users, particularly marginalized groups.

continued on following page

Table 4. Continued

Strategy	Description	Implementation Examples
7. Reflect on the Social Impact of AI Projects	Incorporate regular reflection activities to help students and community members consider the broader social implications of AI.	- **Impact Journals:** Have students maintain journals reflecting on the social impact of their AI projects, focusing on ethical considerations and community outcomes. - **Feedback Loops:** Establish feedback loops where community members can share their experiences and perspectives on the AI tools being developed, ensuring continuous ethical reflection and improvement.
8. Encourage Long-Term Ethical AI Engagement	Promote ongoing engagement with ethical AI practices in the community, even after the PBL project ends.	- **Ethical AI Fellowships:** Create fellowships for community members who have participated in PBL projects to continue exploring and advocating for ethical AI use. - **AI Ethics Resource Hub:** Develop an online resource hub that provides continuous education and updates on ethical AI practices, accessible to both students and community members.

AI technology is here to stay and will continue to develop and evolve at a fast pace. Understanding pros and cons of this technology will empower both instructors and students in full control of what they do instead of being manipulated and misled by the technology. These strategies aim to embed ethical considerations and responsible AI use into the process of online PBL community projects, ensuring that AI contributes positively to social capital development by fostering trust, inclusivity, and shared responsibility.

FUTURE RESEARCH STUDIES

As online learning continues to expand, particularly in the trend of global shifts towards digital education, understanding the implications for social capital development becomes increasingly important, especially with the impact of the current Fourth Industrial Revolution. In recent years, trust has been declining across various domains, including news media, government, and even in online personal interactions. A study conducted by the University of Oxford during virtual roundtable discussions with journalists and publishers in 2021 revealed widespread concern that digital platforms are partly responsible for the erosion of trust in news globally (Newman, 2022). Participants noted that these platforms often facilitate the spread of bad-faith criticism of journalism, contributing to a polluted information environment filled with low-quality substitutes for factual reporting (Mont'Alverne et al., 2022). Trust in the media has also notably declined in the United States, with only 23% of Americans in 2021 expressing confidence that the media reports the news "fairly and accurately" (Pew Research Center, 2022). Edelman, a global public relations and marketing firm, highlights that this trust crisis is a global phenomenon. In 2022, trust in institutions reached an all-time low in many countries, leading to negative societal impacts such as reduced civic engagement, increased extremism, and slowed economic growth (Edelman, 2022). These trends are alarming, especially in an era where social media is a primary platform for accessing resources. The level of trust individuals have significantly influences their attitudes toward using and sharing information online. Strengthening the development of social capital to build trust relationships is important for future society.

By examining the specific aspects in relation to online PBL learning and social capital development, the following suggested research topics aim to contribute valuable insights to the field of education, particularly as it adapts to new digital landscapes. They encourage a deeper exploration of how online PBL can be leveraged not only to enhance academic learning but also to build and strengthen the social fabric of communities. Understanding these dynamics is essential for educators, policymakers, and community leaders who seek to design effective online PBL experiences that promote social capital development in diverse and digitally connected societies.

1. The Role of Online Collaboration Tools in Enhancing Social Capital through Project-Based Learning: Challenges and Best Practices
    - This topic could explore how digital tools used in online PBL contribute to building social networks and trust among students and community members, and the challenges of effectively using these tools.
2. Fostering Social Capital in Diverse Communities through Online PBL: An Analysis of Barriers and Opportunities
    - This research could investigate how online PBL can be tailored to engage diverse community groups, the obstacles to building social capital in such settings, and the opportunities it presents for inclusive education.
3. Measuring the Impact of Online PBL on Social Capital Development in Virtual Learning Communities
    - A study focused on developing and applying metrics to assess how effectively online PBL initiatives build social capital among participants in virtual learning environments.
4. Ethical Considerations in Using AI-Driven Online PBL for Social Capital Development: Challenges and Strategies
    - This topic could explore the ethical challenges of using AI in online PBL, particularly how these technologies impact trust and cooperation in community-based projects.
5. The Influence of Student Agency in Online PBL on Social Capital Development: Opportunities and Constraints

- Research could focus on the relationship between student autonomy in online PBL projects and the growth of social capital within educational and community settings.
6. Challenges in Building Trust and Cooperation through Online PBL in Disadvantaged Communities
    - This study could investigate the specific challenges faced when implementing online PBL in under-resourced or disadvantaged communities and its implications for social capital development.
7. The Impact of Reflective Practices in Online PBL on Social Capital: An Examination of Student and Community Outcomes
    - This research could examine how structured reflection in online PBL projects contributes to building social capital among students and community participants.
8. Overcoming the Digital Divide in Online PBL to Enhance Social Capital Development
    - A study focused on the challenges posed by the digital divide in implementing online PBL and strategies to ensure equitable social capital development across different socio-economic groups.
9. Sustaining Social Capital in Post-Project Phases of Online PBL: Challenges and Long-Term Opportunities
    - This topic could explore the long-term sustainability of social capital developed during online PBL projects and how it can be maintained or grown after the project concludes.
10. The Role of Community Feedback in Shaping Social Capital Development through Online PBL
    - Research could focus on how incorporating continuous community feedback in online PBL projects affects the development of social capital and trust among participants.

The significance of these suggestions lies in their focus on the key challenges and opportunities that arise when implementing PBL in online settings. Each topic aims to explore different dimensions of how social capital can be developed, sustained, or even hindered within virtual environments. For example, the topics address the role of digital tools, the importance of inclusivity and diversity, the ethical implications of AI, and the sustainability of social capital post-project. These areas are crucial because they highlight both the potential of online PBL to foster strong community ties and the obstacles that must be overcome to achieve this goal. These topics aim to address various aspects of online PBL and its potential to foster social capital, considering both the challenges and opportunities presented by digital learning environments.

CONCLUSION

This chapter has outlined key strategies for building effective online PBL environments, emphasizing the importance of fostering social capital through trust, collaboration, and inclusivity. The implementation of online Project-Based Learning presents a powerful opportunity to enhance both educational outcomes and social capital development in a digitally connected world. By drawing on the rich history of PBL, rooted in experiential and student-centered learning, educators can create dynamic learning environments that engage students in meaningful, real-world projects. The integration of AI technology further expands the potential of PBL, offering innovative tools that can support collaboration, critical thinking, and personalized learning experiences. However, the ethical use of AI and the challenges of fostering trust and cooperation in diverse, virtual communities must be carefully navigated to ensure that PBL truly benefits all participants.

By addressing these elements, educators can create learning experiences that not only prepare students for academic and professional success but also strengthen the social fabric of their communities. The goal of Project-Based Learning (PBL) needs a fundamental shift in mindset from administration regarding the educational mission of the institution. This shift should lead to a curriculum redesign that prioritizes preparing students as a whole-person with marketable skills and fostering effective social interactions with extended communities. By emphasizing cross-cultural understanding and mutual respect, online PBL can significantly enhance the quality of education and promote social capital development.

REFERENCES

Beckett, G., & Slater, T. (2019). *Global perspectives on project-based language learning, teaching, and assessment: key approaches, technology tools, and frameworks*. Routledge. DOI: 10.4324/9780429435096

Bender, W. N. (2012). *Project-based learning: Differentiating instruction for the 21st century*. Corwin Press.

BIE – Buck Institute for Education. https://www.pblworks.org/

Boss, S. (2011). Project-Based Learning: A short history. https://www.edutopia.org/project-based-learning-history

Britannica. (n. d.). *Social capital*. https://www.britannica.com/topic/social-capital

Brown, J. S., & Duguid, P. (1991). Organizational learning and communities of practice: Towards a unified view of working, learning, and innovation. *Organization Science*, 2(1), 40–57. DOI: 10.1287/orsc.2.1.40

Brown, J. S., & Duguid, P. (2001). Knowledge and organization: A social practice perspective. *Organization Science*, 12(2), 198–213. DOI: 10.1287/orsc.12.2.198.10116

Bruner, J. S. (1961). The Act of Discovery. *Harvard Educational Review*.

Buck Institute for Education. (2016). PBLWorks. https://www.pblworks.org/what-is-pbl

Canvas. https://www.instructure.com/canvas

Center for Teaching Innovation. (n.d.). Ethical AI for teaching and learning. Cornell University. https://teaching.cornell.edu/generative-artificial-intelligence/ethical-ai-teaching-and-learning

Cialdini, R. B., & Fincham, R. L. (1990). Trust and the development of interpersonal relationships. *Psychological Bulletin*, •••, 1990.

Coleman, J. S. (1988). Social capital in the creation of human capital. *American Journal of Sociology*, 94, 95–120. DOI: 10.1086/228943

Coursera - https://www.coursera.org/

Oxford Dictionary. Lexicon.com

Divito, C. B., Katchikian, B. M., Gruenwald, J. E., & Burgoon, J. M. (2023). The tools of the future are the challenges of today: The use of ChatGPT in problem-based learning medical education. *Medical Teacher*, 46(3), 320–322. DOI: 10.1080/0142159X.2023.2290997 PMID: 38149617

Edelman. (2022). 2022 Edelman trust Barometer. https://www.edelman.com/trust/2022-trust-barometer

Educurious. https://educurious.org/

edX - https://www.edx.org/

Garrison, D. R., & Anderson, T. (2003). *E-Learning in the 21st Century: A Framework for Research and Practice*. Routledge.

Gašević, D., Siemens, G., & Sadiq, S. (2023). Empowering learners for the age of artificial intelligence. *Computers & Education: Artificial Intelligence*, 4, 100130. DOI: 10.1016/j.caeai.2023.100130

Granovetter, M. (1985). Economic action and social structure: The problem of embeddedness. *American Journal of Sociology*, 91(3), 481–510. DOI: 10.1086/228311

Johnson, D. W., & Johnson, R. T. (2009). *Cooperation and Competition: Theory and Research*. Interaction Book Company.

Johnson, D. W., Johnson, R. T., & Smith, K. A. (1998). Cooperative learning returns to college: What evidence is there that it works? *Change*, 30(4), 26–35. DOI: 10.1080/00091389809602629

Jonassen, D. H., & Hung, W. (2015). All problems are not equal: Implications for problem-based learning. In Walker, A., & Leary, H. (Eds.), *Essential readings in problem-based learning* (pp. 17–41). Purdue University Press. DOI: 10.2307/j.ctt6wq6fh.7

Jones, S. (2020). Computers and technology in Montessori Schools. *Montessori For Today*. https://montessorifortoday.com/computers-and-technology-in-montessori-schools/

Keengwe, J., Onchwari, G., & Onchwari, J. (2009). Thechnology and students learning: Towards a learner-centered teaching model. *AACE Review*, 17(1), 11–22.

Kilpatrick, W. H. (1918). The project method. The use of the purposeful act in the educative process. Teachers College, Columbia University. 525 West 120th Street. New York City DOI: 10.1177/016146811801900404

Krackhardt, D. (1999). The ties that torture: Simmelian tie analysis in organizations. *Research in the Sociology of Organizations*, 16, 183–210.

Lave, J., & Wenger, E. (1991). *Situated Learning: Legitimate Peripheral Participation*. Cambridge University Press. DOI: 10.1017/CBO9780511815355

Learning Ecosystems and Leadership. (2021). The hidden support from social capital to implementing PBL in diverse contexts globally. https://www.wise-qatar.org/hidden-support-social-capital-implementing-pbl-sarojani-mohammed/

Leo. (2023). Unlocking your child's potential: understanding the zone of proximal development. https://psychologily.com/zone-of-proximal-development/

Lo, C. K. (2023). What is the impact of ChatGPT on education? A rapid review of literature. *Education Sciences*, 13(4), 410. DOI: 10.3390/educsci13040410

Ma, W. W. K. (2022). Effective learning through project-based learning: collaboration, community, design, and technology. In: Tso, A.W.B., Chan, A.Ck., Chan, W.W.L., Sidorko, P.E., Ma, W.W.K. (eds) *Digital Communication and Learning. Educational Communications and Technology Yearbook*. Springer, Singapore. DOI: 10.1007/978-981-16-8329-9_17

Machalek, R., & Martin, M. W. (2015). Sociobiology and Sociology: A new synthesis. Editor(s): James D. Wright, *International Encyclopedia of the Social & Behavioral Sciences* (Second Edition), Elsevier, 2015, pp. 892-898. ISBN 9780080970875. DOI: 10.1016/B978-0-08-097086-8.32010-4

Madda, M. J. (2023). Why schools should focus on social capital development – not just skills. https://www.edsurge.com/news/2023-10-16-why-schools-should-focus-on-social-capital-development-not-just-skills

McLeod, S. (2024). Vygotsky's theory of cognitive development. https://www.simplypsychology.org/vygotsky.html

Meng, N., Dong, Y., Roehrs, D., & Luan, L. (2023). Tackle implementation challenges in project-based learning: a survey study of PBL e-learning platforms. https://link.springer.com/article/10.1007/s11423-023-10202-7

MIT OCW - MIT OpenCourseWare. https://ocw.mit.edu/

Mont'Alverne. C., Badrinathan, S., Ross Arguesdas, A., Toff, B., Fletcher, R., & Nielsen, R. (2022). The trust gas: how and why news on digital platforms is viewed more skeptically versus news in general. https://ora.ox.ac.uk/objects/uuid:42cc0bd8-f737-4a79-947f-e528e8116926

MOOCs - Massive Open Online Courses. https://onlinelearningconsortium.org/

Newman, N. (2022). Overview and key findings of the 2022 digital news report. https://reutersinstitute.politics.ox.ac.uk/digital-news-report/2022/dnr-executive-summary

PBLworks. https://www.pblworks.org/

Perez, S. (2023). Integrating student voice in social capital development. https://edstrategy.org/integrating-student-voice-in-social-capital-development/

Pew Research Center. (2022). *Public trust in government: 1958-2022*. https://www.pewresearch.org/politics/2022/06/06/public-trust-in-government-1958-2022/

Piaget, J. (1954). *The Construction of Reality in the Child*. Basic Books. DOI: 10.1037/11168-000

Putnam, R. D. (2000). *Bowling Alone: The Collapse and Revival of American Community*. Simon & Schuster.

Reagans, R., & McEvily, B. (2003). Network structure and knowledge transfer: The transfer problem revisited. *Administrative Science Quarterly*, 48, 240–267. DOI: 10.2307/3556658

Reagans, R., & Zuckerman, E. W. (2001). Networks, diversity and productivity: The social capital of corporate R&D teams. *Organization Science*, 12(4), 502–517. DOI: 10.1287/orsc.12.4.502.10637

Rees Lewis, D. G., Gerber, E. M., Carlson, S. E., & Easterday, M. W. (2019). Opportunities for educational innovations in authentic project-based learning: Understanding instructor perceived challenges to design for adoption. *Educational Technology Research and Development*, 67(4), 953–982. DOI: 10.1007/s11423-019-09673-4

Santiago, P., & Cerna, L. (2020). Strength through diversity: education for inclusive societies. *EDU/EDPC(2019)11/REV2*, Organization for Economic Co-operation and Development. https://www.oecd.org/education/strength-through-diversity/Design-and-Implementation-Plan.pdf

Spender, J. C. (1996). Organizational knowledge, learning, and memory: Three concepts in search of a theory. *Journal of Organizational Change Management*, 9(1), 63–78. DOI: 10.1108/09534819610156813

Strobel, J., & van Barneveld, A. (2009). When is PBL more effective? A meta-synthesis of meta-analyses comparing PBL to conventional classrooms. *The Interdisciplinary Journal of Problem-Based Learning*, 3(1), 44–58. DOI: 10.7771/1541-5015.1046

Swan, J. A., Newell, S., Scarbrough, H., & Hislop, D. (1999). Knowledge management and innovation: Networks and networking. *Journal of Knowledge Management*, 3(4), 262–275. DOI: 10.1108/13673279910304014

Swan, K., Garrison, D. R., & Richardson, J. C. (2009). A constructivist approach to online learning: The community of inquiry framework. In *Information technology and constructivism in higher education: Progressive learning frameworks* (pp. 43–57). IGI global.

TheoryHub. (n.d.). Social capital theory. https://open.ncl.ac.uk/academic-theories/45/social-capital-theory/#:~:text=Social%20Capital%20Theory%2C%20a%20multifaceted,James%20Coleman%2C%20and%20Robert%20Putnam

Thomas, J. W. (2000). *A Review of Research on Project-Based Learning*. The Autodesk Foundation.

Trello. https://trello.com/

Vygotsky, L. S. (1978). *Mind in Society: the Development of Higher Psychological Processes*. Harvard University Press.

Zalaznick, M. (2023). How ChatGPT can actually be a force for good rather than a boon for cheaters. https://districtadministration.com/chatgpt-impact-schools-teaching-cheating-writing/

Zhai, X. M. (2022). ChatGPT user experience: implications for education. *SSRN*: https://ssrn.com/abstract=4312418 or DOI: 10.2139/ssrn.4312418

ADDITIONAL READINGS

Carlson, S. E., Maliakal, L. V., Rees Lewis, D. G., Gorson, J., Gerber, E. M., & Easterday, M. W. (2018a). Defining and assessing risk analysis: The key to strategic iteration in real-world problem-solving. In Proceedings of the *International Conference of the Learning Sciences* (ICLS). London: ICLS.

Gold Standard, P. B. L. Essential Project Design Elements. https://www.pblworks.org/what-is-pbl/gold-standard-project-design

Ibrahi, D. S., & Rashid, A. M. (2022). Effect of project-based learning towards collaboration among students in the design and technology subject. *World Journal of Education*, 12(3), 2022. DOI: 10.5430/wje.v12n3p1

Iwamoto, D. H., Hargis, J., & Vuong, K. (2016). The effect of project-based learning on student performance: An action research study. *International Journal for the Scholarship of Technology Enhanced Learning*, 1(1), 24–42.

Matthew-DeNatale, G., Poklop, L., Plews, R., & English, M. (2024). Global challenges: Engaging undergraduates in project-based learning online. *Teaching & Learning Inquiry*, 12. Advance online publication. DOI: 10.20343/teachlearninqu.12.6

Moore, R., & Miller, C. (2022). Fostering Cognitive Presence in Online Courses: A Systematic Review (2008–2020). *Online Learning : the Official Journal of the Online Learning Consortium*, 26(1), 130–149. DOI: 10.24059/olj.v26i1.3071

Northeastern University. List of requirements and learning goals. https://core.northeastern.edu/requirements/

Prieto-Pastor, I., Martín-Pérez, V., & Martín-Cruz, N. (2018). Social capital, knowledge integration and learning in project-based organizations: A CEO-based study. *Journal of Knowledge Management*, 22(8), 1803–1825. DOI: 10.1108/JKM-05-2017-0210

Rey-Garcia, M., & Mato-Santiso, V. (2020). Enhancing the effects of university education for sustainable development on social sustainability: the role of social capital and real-world learning. https://www.emerald.com/insight/publication/issn/1467-6370

Terada, Y. (2021). New research makes a powerful case for PBL – two new gold-standard studies provide compelling evidence that project-based learning is an effective strategy for all students – including historically marginalized ones. https://www.edutopia.org/article/new-research-makes-powerful-case-pbl/

Yosso, T. J. (2005). Whose culture has capital? A critical race theory discussion of community cultural wealth. *Race, Ethnicity and Education*, 8(1), 69–91. DOI: 10.1080/1361332052000341006

Zhang, L., & Ma, Y. (2023). A study of the impact of project-based learning on student learning effects: a meta-analysis study. https://www.frontiersin.org/journals/psychology/articles/10.3389/fpsyg.2023.1202728/full

KEY TERMS AND DEFINITIONS

AI technology: Technology related to artificial intelligence that is the simulation of human intelligence.

Civic Responsibility: refers to the duties and obligations of citizens to participate actively in the governance and improvement of their community, society, and country.

Community Engagement: refers to the process by which individuals and organizations work collaboratively with community members to address issues, make decisions, and create positive change within the community.

Online Learning Community: refers to a group of learners, educators, and external project stakeholders who interact and collaborate through digital platforms to achieve shared educational goals.

Project-based Learning: is an instructional approach where students actively engage in real-world and meaningful projects to find solutions to problems in collaboration with community members.

Social Capital: refers to the networks of relationships, trust, and norms of reciprocity that exist within a community or group, which facilitate cooperation and collective action for mutual benefit.

Societal Impact: refers to the effect of actions, policies, projects, or innovations on society as a whole. In this chapter, it specifically refers to the effect of PBL learning on communities.

Student-Centered Learning: It refers to an educational method, such as teaching technique, learning and assessment activities, student support services, etc., that focuses on the needs, interests, and learning styles of students.

Student Voice: It refers to the perspectives, insights, and opinions of students regarding their educational experiences and environments. In this chapter, it refers to student feedback on their social interaction in their PBL learning experiences.

Chapter 8
A "Behind the Screens" Look at Humanizing Online Learning Spaces

Crystal Neumann
American College of Education, USA

Audra Pickett
American College of Education, USA

ABSTRACT

With recent advances in technology and education, it is important to explore programs, applications, and efforts which assist with interaction and humanizing online learning. Achieving student engagement goals for an online institution were evaluated through observations, document reviews, and narratives highlighting the best practices and achievements from American College of Education (ACE). Techniques ACE uses to promote faculty and student engagement within the online environment will be identified. Get a "behind the screens" look at how online communities can be built by promoting engagement techniques, such as implementing additional software applications, developing digital toolboxes for students, promoting the Diversity, Equity, Inclusion (DEI) Center, implementing a Virtual Student Wellness Center, and embracing the use of Artificial Intelligence (AI). The chapter explores the increasing availability of educational technology useful for engaging student interaction in the classroom.

DOI: 10.4018/979-8-3693-4407-1.ch008

INTRODUCTION

The chapter aims to articulate best practices the academics and curriculum departments implemented to impact the goals of increasing student and staff engagement in the online teaching and learning environment. The strategies, tools, and examples of building an online community could support other institutions that are in the nascent phases of developing an online learning platform or seek to improve opportunities to humanize online teaching and learning. Collaboration was necessary to build a future to preserve academic quality and exceptional student outcomes. Diversity within the student body creates a need for modifications within the higher education environment (Williams et al., 2018). With a need to support a diverse population of students and the online learning environment, collaboration emerged to create additional resources to make the learning experience feel more humanized. The student engagement goals, obstacles, and successes implemented by a for-profit, Benefit Corporation, an online higher education institution, American College of Education are explored.

According to the National Center for Education Statistics (2022), 60% of college students take at least one of their courses online, and 47% of college students complete all their courses online. Courses are synchronous, asynchronous, or a combination of the two. Synchronous courses present student engagement challenges for reasons like decreased interpersonal communication and instructor feedback (Gimpel, 2022; Landrum et al., 2021). Asynchronous course disengagement is even more pronounced. Factors such as a lack of teacher and peer presence can adversely affect asynchronous course engagement (Ozogul et al., 2022). Several strategies exist to increase online student engagement (Gimpel, 2022; Tsai et al., 2021). Gimpel (2022) noted that student engagement is high when instructors are quick to respond to discussion board posts or feedback on assignments, refer to the student by name, use interactive tools like whiteboards or Zoom, and are actively present in the classroom. Tsai et al (2021) found that interactive technological course activities help keep the student's attention and increases student learning. The purpose of this chapter is to demonstrate best practices on how the academic and curriculum departments at the American College of Education (ACE) impact student engagement goals. The best practices were reviewed via observations, document reviews, and narratives from the academic and curriculum departments.

BACKGROUND

The American College of Education (ACE) is a regionally accredited, online school specializing in education, business, healthcare, leadership, and nursing programs, with a stated mission, "to deliver high-quality, affordable, and accessible online programs grounded in evidence-based content and relevant application. We prepare graduates to serve, lead, and achieve personal and professional goals in diverse, evolving communities" (History and Mission, 2023, para. 1). ACE considers itself a leader in online education and finding innovative ways to reach and engage students in the online classroom. With a vision to be a significant presence in higher education by providing high value, and impactful programming, ACE prepares students to become leaders in their field. All of ACE's courses are designed to be asynchronous. There are no mandatory synchronous meeting times for instructors and students, though faculty are encouraged to engage with their students in a variety of ways. The flexibility related to when and how often students sign into their online courses appeals to several of ACE's online students. Most learners are working professionals who are balancing their careers, school, and personal lives. The academics and curriculum teams have noticed a correlation between engagement and student success. When faculty and students are actively engaged in the classroom, students perform more successfully on their assignments. On the other hand, when faculty are not engaged, students are not engaged. Lack of student engagement correlates to a negative impact on student completion and matriculation (Hollister et al., 2022).

It is crucial to keep in mind that learners possess learning styles that contribute to their ability to process and retain information (Nazempour & Darabi, 2023). As a result, ACE strives to accommodate all learning styles so each student may effectively understand a course's critical concepts. Certain students might find it useful to have transcripts to read or to follow along with slides from a PowerPoint presentation with visual aids. However, it would not be equitable to other students who have a different learning style if a curriculum is created to cater solely to those who have the reading and writing learning styles. For instance, auditory learners could prefer watching videos, listening to podcasts, or attending lectures. Information would need to be translated from written to spoken language for auditory learners. However, kinesthetic learners would rather use a hands-on drag-and-drop activity or participate in online simulations. ACE applies differentiated instruction through curriculum design and faculty training.

Collaboration from the academic and curriculum departments derived from the necessity to support both the online learning environment and the increasingly diverse student body. Collaboration between departments is crucial because it fosters the sharing of knowledge, resources, and diverse perspectives, leading to more innovative and effective solutions. It enhances the overall quality of education and research by integrating different expertise, and it promotes a cohesive institutional culture where departments work together toward common goals, improving outcomes for students and the institution as a whole. The departments developed and promoted extra resources to humanize the learning experience. Resources included Zoom, Faculty Commons, Mentor Commons, Kaltura, course simulations, the Writing Center, Digital Tool Center, DEI Center, Virtual Student Wellness Center, and the use of artificial intelligence.

Zoom in the Online Classroom

A challenge many online teachers and students experience in the online classroom is the lack of available face-to-face interaction and classroom engagement (Berges et al., 2021). Students sometimes have questions that go beyond what email has to offer. Students also want to know if there is a real person behind the screen. It is important to offer ways to increase digital literacy and provide opportunities for the college community to connect socially and emotionally (Dailey-Herbert, 2022). To mitigate the challenge of face-to-face interaction and humanize online teaching, American College of Education embeds Zoom into all the Canvas Learning Management System (LMS) courses. Zoom is an application that allows a person to schedule synchronous meetings with their intended audience. Instructors can schedule regular synchronous meetings with their class.

The Zoom meetings not only provide a more personalized experience for students, but they allow students to ask questions related to discussions, assignments, and assessments. Suresh et al. (as cited in Souheyla, 2021) noted the availability of Zoom can alleviate anxiety students might feel because they can ask their peers and instructor questions about the assignments. Additionally, Gimpel (2022) stated that a personalized experience can be offered through Zoom when instructors use their webcams for students to review nonverbal cues. Likewise, when students are encouraged to use their own webcams, instructors can better gauge the student interaction. In addition to allowing the use of microphones and chat features, students should also be urged to apply Zoom reaction emojis, such as the thumbs up, heart, clapping, or celebration (Gimpel, 2022). Directing a thumbs up or raised hand encourages student interaction. ACE instructors have asked students for a thumbs up in cases where they agree with a statement or asked for a raised hand in instances where a question needs to be asked.

Zoom promotes increased classroom engagement (Berges et al., 2021). Students at ACE appreciate the opportunity to ask instructors questions and interact with peers. The meetings also include screen sharing, a chat function, and recording capabilities. One of the benefits of asynchronous online learning is the flexibility to work during days and times that align best with students' schedules (Presley et al., 2023). When synchronous meetings are scheduled, it can present challenges to students who might not be able to attend the scheduled meeting time. However, Zoom also offers the opportunity for a host to record and save the meetings. For busy working adult learners, the recordings are valuable. Common questions about assignments are addressed. Instructors can post online meetings for students to view at a time that is convenient. Instructors can also schedule individual meetings with students who require or request additional support.

However, faculty members are also urged to apply additional methods of engagement to reach all students through differentiated instruction. Dailey-Herbert (2022) stated that particularly after the COVID-19 pandemic, students have experienced Zoom fatigue, which results in a lack of engagement within the classroom. Such fatigue can lead to a stressful learning experience (Gorghiu et al., 2021). Thus, ACE faculty have also been encouraged to host Zoom sessions which are both informative and informal to promote a stress-free learning environment.

During the Zoom sessions, some instructors have elected to use polls within the classrooms or applied Kahoot! games to make the learning experience more fun. For example, an instructor had participants play a Kahoot! game to prepare for the final exam, using previous or rewritten quiz questions for the students to refresh their memories from prior weeks. Gamification can be applied to Zoom by creating a points-based system where students earn points for participation, answering questions, or completing tasks during the lecture. For example, an instructor could introduce a "Zoom Leaderboard" where students are awarded points for correctly answering quiz questions, contributing to discussions, or solving problems in breakout rooms. These points could lead to small rewards, like virtual badges, extra credit (where policy allows), or the ability to choose the next topic for discussion. This approach turns the learning process into a fun, competitive experience, motivating students to engage more actively in the session. One faculty member stated that applying the Kahoot! game not only made the Zoom session fun, but they also reported successful final exam results. The exam results during that term were better than what they had seen in previous terms when they did not use games in their Zoom session.

Ultimately, incorporating multimedia, such as videos, animations, or virtual tours, can make the content more dynamic and visually appealing. Gamifying the course lecture with friendly competitions or challenges can add a sense of excitement. Additionally, fostering a relaxed and inclusive atmosphere by encouraging discussion, using humor, and acknowledging students' contributions helps make the session more enjoyable and memorable.

FACULTY COMMONS

For some brick-and-mortar schools, faculty often access information using links on the school's website. At ACE, this is called the Faculty Commons area. Faculty Commons is a digital repository where information is stored for reuse (Richardson et al., 2023). The American College of Education uses Canvas and creates a course for the Faculty Commons resources. Faculty resources, such as the faculty handbook, professional development opportunities, technology support, and dissertation committee support are included in this space. Faculty can submit requests for course revisions and general course feedback. Other support resources such as Faculty 180, writing support, grading, and plagiarism support are also included. Rather than emailing Human Resources or the department chair for helpful documents and links, Faculty Commons provides a one-stop-shop.

Instructors who serve on dissertation committees can access several helpful documents, too. Because a dissertation committee may be working with a doctoral student over various phases of the dissertation journey, the portal is divided into sections for the dissertation itself and the oral defense stage. Examples of dissertation resources include mini lessons over various methodologies (which are often used as a refresher for faculty), final dissertation submission forms, and sample announcements for the different chapters of the dissertation. For the oral defense, resources include protocol reminders and forms documenting next steps.

Every quarter, the academic team hosts a quarterly synchronous meeting to discuss updates, provide reminders, and share feedback and tips. For instructors who are not able to attend the quarterly meetings, the recordings can be retrieved within Faculty Commons in the archive section. Therefore, faculty are able to watch the recording at a time that is most convenient for them. Additionally, faculty can watch previous recordings should they want to review other meetings based on a different agenda.

Sometimes in the online environment, it may not always be clear who to go to with questions. Leadership over different departments is listed with their picture, job title, and email address. For example, if a faculty member wanted to inquire about how to further support a dissertation student, the faculty member is able to determine who they can contact and receive immediate attention.

MENTOR COMMONS

Like Faculty Commons, Mentor Commons is a designated online portal for faculty to have access to a different set of resources specifically designed for them. These mentor resources will allow faculty mentors to maximize their ability to mentor students required to have field experiences. Programs that require field experiences include student teaching, principal internship, principal practicum, superintendent, and nursing. Some examples of resources include handbooks, preferred timelines, training materials, orientation, remediation materials, evaluation instruments, and suggested activities. Many of the resources are offered in template form. However, video resources are also posted on the online portal.

Just as faculty can use discussions to humanize and personalize their online classroom, the mentor discussion boards are also provided to access as needed for guidance, support, and/or collegiality. Faculty members are encouraged to post questions, concerns, comments, suggestions, tips, tricks, or anything useful or helpful they feel would benefit the group. Many mentors use the discussion board space as a professional learning community. Professional learning communities promote discussion, reflection, and the sharing of best practices (Zhang et al., 2021). The academic department has found the interaction between faculty to prevent feeling isolated and or having a lack of collegial support.

Instead, the discussion boards have helped solidify the organizational culture and provide faculty with a humanized experience. ACE leadership believes that by leading the way and providing faculty with a humanized experience, faculty members will have direct knowledge of what a connected experience feels like. Therefore, faculty are better prepared to provide students with the same kind of connected learning experience.

KALTURA

Videos are highly effective for student engagement because they offer a dynamic and visually stimulating way to present information, making complex concepts easier to understand. They cater to different learning styles by combining visual, auditory, and sometimes even interactive elements, which can enhance comprehension and retention. Videos also allow for flexibility, as students can pause, rewind, and review the material at their own pace, promoting self-directed learning. By breaking down information into bite-sized, engaging segments, videos can maintain students' attention more effectively than traditional lectures, leading to a more immersive and enjoyable learning experience.

Instructional videos have the potential to increase student engagement and promote learning (You & Yang, 2021). Kaltura is a video recording platform embedded into each Canvas course. Instructors can use Kaltura to record welcome videos, weekly messages for announcements, or to increase student understanding of a complex topic. Students use Kaltura to create their audiovisual assignments. These assignments are saved to the students My Media page in Canvas where they can access their videos any time. If teachers want to provide audiovisual feedback on students' assignments, they can either use the media function in Canvas, or record feedback using Kaltura, which can then be uploaded to the comment section of a student's assignment. All of ACE's instructional videos use the Kaltura platform. Each video includes the closed captioning option and Annoto.

According to Zhang et al. (as cited in You & Yang, 2021, p. 2), instructional video interactivity increases learning effectiveness. Annoto allows students to take notes while they watch the video. Students can also leave comments for their peers or instructor at specific timestamps in the video. ACE students commented on the usefulness of the Annoto learning tool and the ability to leave notes while they watch videos. Students are also able to engage in conversation with their peers using the Annoto notes tool.

SIMULATIONS

Because they offer an immersive, hands-on learning experience that enables students to apply theoretical information in a practical, real-world setting, simulations are effective tools for increasing student engagement. Through the replication of workplace scenarios, simulations provide students the safe and risk-free environment to explore diverse methodologies, arrive at judgments, and observe the ramifications of their actions. This method of active learning improves comprehension, sharpens critical thinking, and develops problem-solving abilities. Furthermore, by giving abstract ideas a more concrete and relevant form, simulations can pique students' interest and motivate them to learn. Because simulations are interactive, they encourage debate and teamwork, which enhances the learning process and aids in students' retention and application of the material.

Critical thinking in an online classroom requires a well-designed curriculum that incorporates learning objectives, results, assessments, and problem-based activities (Gharib et al., 2016). The course needs to incorporate analytical assignments. There should be assignments that emphasize inventiveness. Memorization exercises should not be the primary focus of a lesson in the online classroom. There should be a purpose to the assignments and discussion boards. Knowledge and skills must be gained as a result. Not all assignments or discussion boards must be text-based. Instead, instructors can encourage creative and critical thinking by having students apply the content using simulation-based learning. Simulations provide students with the opportunity to apply their learning, think critically, and engage meaningfully with learning (Humpherys et al., 2022). To further engage students, simulations are used in discussion boards in which students investigate topics through challenging and realistic scenarios. Students are directed with prompts asking how they might handle a particular situation. With the discussion board being open for all students to see the initial responses, peers can respond to their classmates with alternative perspectives and higher-order thinking.

Students have reported being satisfied with the learning environment and found simulations to be easy to use, as long as the tasks are meaningful and not repetitive (Arie et al., 2022). Brigas (2019) stated that knowledge is built when the students think, act, and reflect on the simulation activity. At ACE, simulations have a person-centered approach and are situation based for the learner. For example, in a business communications course, there is a scenario involving a sales company which needs to adapt different strategies for intentional communication to various audiences. In this scenario, students discuss options and outcomes. As another example, within a business ethics course, a company has experienced embezzlement. In this discussion board, students identify different ways they can handle the situation.

Additionally, within the nursing program, simulations were created so that students can work through real-world clinic issues without running the risk of endangering patients. According to studies, when students take part in simulations, they learn more and feel more confident (O'Flaherty, 2020). According to O'Flaherty's (2020) research, using simulations allowed students to apply their knowledge in a real-life clinical scenario, which contributed to the development of critical thinking. Critical thinking via a simulation helped students gain confidence in their clinical assessments.

Another example of a simulation learning activity in online education could be a virtual lab for a biology course. In this simulation, students can conduct experiments such as dissecting a digital frog, mixing virtual chemicals to observe reactions, or simulating genetic crosses to understand inheritance patterns. The virtual lab replicates the experience of a physical lab, allowing students to make predictions, test hypotheses, and analyze results in real-time. This hands-on activity not only reinforces theoretical knowledge but also helps students develop practical skills, such as following scientific procedures, making observations, and interpreting data, all within a safe and controlled online environment.

Providing open-ended topics and simulations allow students to share multiple viewpoints. In every simulation, students are reminded that there is no right or wrong answer. The simulations are only a learning experience used to promote deep discussion.

ACE also applies the person-based approach within the simulations by ensuring inclusivity in the design. The simulations are designed for audio-visual learners. However, closed-captioning text is also provided to remain American Disabilities Act (ADA) compliant, though it can be helpful for the read-write learners, as well. The curriculum department also creates avatars of varying ages, genders, and cultures. The goal is for learners to be able to see people in the simulations who might look like them.

ACE WRITING CENTER

During the COVID pandemic of 2020, many colleges transitioned their writing centers online. However, ACE has always provided students with writing assistance from staff and self-guided resources found in the Writing Center. The Writing Center provides pages for frequently asked questions, APA resources, scholarly writing tips, and guidance on plagiarism. For students who are new or out of practice with academic writing, the ACE Writing Center includes support for writing journal articles and annotated bibliographies. Many of the ACE courses ask students to create presentations. The Writing Center includes a page for best practices when creating an audiovisual presentation. There are also templates and "how-to" guides for designing a presentation.

The ACE Writing Center differs from a traditional brick-and-mortar college writing center. When students have questions about writing academic papers, they complete a form and request support from one of the ACE Writing Center staff members. Faculty can also request support for a student using the Writing Center. These situations result from students who need more targeted support beyond what Tutor.com provides.

ACE students utilize resources from the Writing Center. For example, in the first two quarters of the 2023 calendar year, there were over 12,000 distinct user page requests. Table 1 demonstrates the student page requests for resources within the Writing Center for the first two quarters of the 2023 calendar year.

Table 1. Student Page Requests for Writing Center Resources

Writing Center Resource	Distinct User Page Requests	Total Page Requests
Main Page	3,593	64,455
APA Resources	3,040	280,380
Self-Plagiarism	1,795	55,625
Writing Center FAQs	1,306	36,793
Scholarly Writing Tips	1,077	31,714
Reading Resources	599	11,815
Best Practices for Presentations	545	7,864
Policies & Procedures	457	3,637
Writing Center-Contact Us	206	859
Total	12,618	493,142

DIGITAL TOOL CENTER

Digital tools have the potential to greatly improve student engagement because they offer personalized, interactive learning experiences that accommodate a variety of learning styles. Students can actively participate in the learning process. Deeper interest and understanding are fostered by features that make the content more visually appealing and pleasant, such as virtual reality, multimedia content, and gamified learning modules. Additionally, digital tools make it easier for teachers and students to collaborate and communicate with one another, fostering a more supportive and connected learning environment that promotes ongoing engagement and active participation.

The Digital Tools Center is an area in the LMS, where various technology tools are recommended for completing assignments. Some of the tools contribute to students' understanding of copyright or how to improve their productivity and organizational skills. To engage students and promote critical thinking, instructors can add a variety of digital activities into online classes. Tools and resources include:

- Copyright Resources: Tools for learning about copyright laws and regulations
- Digital Learning Connections: Resources and tips to assist with course assignments
- Gaming Resources: Tools for creating games to be used in educational settings
- Kaltura Resources: Guides for using Kaltura to create, manage, and embed videos in Canvas
- Presentation and Video Tools: These tools are a place to start when working on presentations or video assignments
- Productivity Tools: Tools for organizing information, streamlining processes, and increasing time on task
- Research Tools: Tools for organizing information, collecting data, and analyzing qualitative and quantitative research
- Social Media Tools: Resources meant to build a personal learning network with a list of educators to follow on X (formerly known as Twitter), social media influencers who discuss education, bloggers to follow, and hashtags to check out

An example of a non-text-based assignment would be developing information displays. Creating graphic organizers requires advanced critical thinking skills (Binoy & Raddi, 2022). Venn diagrams, for instance, encourage comparing and contrasting. Cause-and-effect diagrams illustrate causation. Students may be asked to design compare-and-contrast questions based on the course material and create a graphic organizer to present the data. Students can visit the Digital Tools Center for ideas on how to create the information displays.

Instructors can also engage students and promote critical thinking in the online classroom by implementing various digital activities from the Digital Tools Center. One idea that has been implemented by faculty is to assign students to make animated films or cartoons based on the lesson's goals. To illustrate opposing and comparing important parts of a lesson, the cartoon characters could engage in a dispute. The cartoon or movie can combine key terms that were covered in a class. When a cartoon has numerous frames, the learner can show how the events are sequenced. The cartoonist or filmmaker can use emotions, key concepts, or scene details to illustrate certain aspects of a tale or current event.

Instructors have also urged students to design avatars within videos, much like in cartoons, to show that they understand and are applying the material covered in a class or even to point out an issue that they may find perplexing. In a video, the avatar could clarify unclear points and solicit further information. Thereafter, peers could reply with more details in a video they make.

Students in a marketing class can be required to manage a social media campaign for a fictional brand or product as part of an assignment. Students would select a social media network, such as LinkedIn, X (formerly known as Twitter), or Instagram, and create posts, photographs, and hashtags that support their marketing plan. Students would have to interact with their target audience by leaving comments, publishing content frequently, and evaluating engagement data to determine how successful their campaign was. One possible component of the project may be a reflection section where students assess which techniques were successful, which weren't, and how they could improve on future campaigns. Through practical experience, students get an understanding of how social media is used in marketing and develop critical competencies in data analysis, audience interaction, and content development.

DIVERSITY, EQUITY, INCLUSION (DEI) CENTER

DEI is essential to an online institution since it fosters a learning atmosphere that is more encouraging, engaging, and inclusive for all students, irrespective of their origins. Students in an online environment come from a variety of backgrounds, cultures, and places, and DEI makes sure that these variations are acknowledged and respected. The institution makes higher education more inclusive by encouraging varied viewpoints, fostering a sense of belonging, and lowering barriers to learning through its promotion of DEI. This type of promotion improves education, while putting students in a position to succeed in the global workforce.

The use of the DEI Center is another way the institution humanizes the college experience. Hyunjin et al. (2023) found students to have positive attitudes through the adoption of inclusive teaching practices. ACE believes that encountering perspectives and experiences that are dissimilar from others is important because it creates an optimal learning environment for students, faculty, and staff. Fostering an inclusive environment with people from different backgrounds is essential. Although embracing diversity is a critical first step, continued work is required to achieve equity and greater inclusion. The college aims to provide programs and create a curriculum that supports equity and inclusion for everyone, through strategic planning and initiatives. Doing so ensures every member of the ACE community can realize their full potential.

The human experience is fundamentally shaped by interpersonal relationships. Human relationships are what encourage participation in and, eventually, enjoyment from teaching and learning activities. The college works to ensure that everyone is valued equally. In the DEI Center, ACE posts a Commitment to Freedom of Expression in order to build and maintain a learning community that is truly diverse, equitable, and inclusive.

Because the college is aware that the world is constantly evolving, reflecting a broader range of diversity, students are informed about diversity, equity, and inclusion (DEI) practices for different industries. For example, the Center includes various resources related to business, educational, and healthcare professionals. Some of the resources vary from the use of pronouns, to teaching diverse learners, to minority health. The purpose of the industry-related resources is to help prepare students for their intended workforce.

Additional trainings and recorded webinars are updated to cover topics, such as inclusive language or teaching in early childhood classrooms. The DEI Center also offers interactive games such as crossword puzzles and Jeopardy about different countries and continents. Self-assessments are offered on cultural competency, cultural awareness, and demonstrating inclusivity. The purpose of the self-assessments is to help make students more self-aware and conscientious about where they are in their DEI journey.

The Diversity, Equity, and Inclusion (DEI) manager hosts a bi-annual, synchronous panel discussion and provides opportunities for the ACE community to write an article for the bi-annual newsletter. The panel discussions consist of up to four panel members with the DEI manager to moderate. The panel members come from various backgrounds to provide alternative perspectives and consist of students, faculty, and staff to represent the entire college. Some examples of topics discussed included disabilities, gender, and polarized viewpoints.

Artwork submissions for the newsletter are also encouraged to convey additional ways for the community to express their thoughts and feelings. Students, faculty, and staff have all submitted original works for publication in the newsletter. All of the recorded panel discussions and newsletters are archived in the DEI Center for students to refer back to. Many of the resources from the DEI Center have also been highlighted in different courses, and faculty are offered professional development training to enhance inclusive teaching practices.

DEI in the Curriculum

DEI is a vital component of higher education curricula that broadens students' perspectives and equips them with the skills necessary to participate productively in a diverse society. By guaranteeing that many viewpoints, cultures, and experiences are represented and valued, a curriculum that embraces DEI principles promotes empathy and critical thinking. The various perspectives push students to consider prejudices and injustices in larger society situations, as well as in their areas of study. Institutions assist students in gaining the social awareness and cultural competency necessary to successfully navigate and make constructive contributions to a world that is becoming more diverse and interconnected by incorporating DEI into the curriculum.

Institutions must actively seek out new students in order to diversity their student bodies, but they need also update the curriculum to make sure DEI is emphasized (Jackson, Richardson, & Breen, 2022). When developing and integrating technology into the classroom, instructors and instructional designers should keep the learners' cultural backgrounds in mind (Abramenka-Lachheb & de Siqueira, 2022). To help ensure representation, a range of individuals and animations are included in many of the recorded video lectures and simulations. Students should be able to relate to the content more readily.

Additionally, by expanding staffing procedures and redesigning resources, the institution must reflect the diverse population (Cooper, 2024). As a result, the working environment and students both feel encouraged and have a better overall learning or work experience. The curriculum design does not intend for DEI to be a stand-alone learning module or unit. ACE, on the other hand, used the DEI lens as a framework to restructure previous content and activities to emphasize DEI concerns. A set of curriculum checklist questions was developed in order to assess courses and make sure that DEI was included in all courses. Some items on the checklist include, but are not limited to: diversity of authors, representation of global views, critical thinking, and different assignment types or discussion board submissions.

While offering accurate instruction and evaluations is crucial to a student's educational experience, equitable and inclusive learning requires giving students access to faculty experts and helpful feedback (Abramenka-Lachheb & de Siqueira, 2022). Offering students options for assessment also helps them to continue exploring concepts that are important to them. All students have access to the Digital Tools Center through the LMS, which provides them with a range of technological options for turning in assignments and tests. Infographics, maps, movies, slideshows, and games are a few examples. To maintain the content's relevance and utility, faculty members are invited to provide further ideas.

In order for students to feel comfortable using technology for learning, they also need to comprehend the goal of the assignment and how to finish it (Abramenka-Lachheb & de Siqueira, 2022). Cultural competency is one of the many qualities that professors must possess. The ability to help pupils understand and value their own culture while also learning about others' is known as cultural competence (Abramenka-Lachheb & de Siqueira, 2022). Building inclusive and equitable learning environments calls for a comprehensive and deliberate approach, not just considering one factor at a time.

VIRTUAL STUDENT WELLNESS CENTER

According to the American Psychiatric Association (2021), close to 40% of adults rely on telehealth services. These services include mental health and well-being. Stress, anxiety, and depression are common mental health issues, in which college leadership realizes that it can be easy for students to think they are alone in dealing with them. ACE urges students to know that they are not alone, and that it is okay to seek the help they may need. The Virtual Student Wellness Center allows students to discover mental health and mindfulness resources. The center also brings forward empathy and a humanized experience, provided by the college.

Synchronized meditation sessions were developed by staff who are passionate about mindfulness or have a certification in hypnotherapy. They developed the meditation sessions with the hopes of students being able to experience the following benefits: lower stress, improved memory and concentration, positive change within the brain, and better well-being (Bonney, 2020). Some of the different mindfulness meditations have included topics on stress reduction, kindness, body scans, relaxation, gratitude, and several others. Some of the students had never meditated before, so the college was able to offer these guided meditations free of charge. Students reported appreciation for learning how to meditate and having the ability to quiet the mind. Other students noted that having the meditations scheduled at a certain time allowed them to make space for mindfulness practice.

Within the Virtual Student Wellness Center, there also is a section called "Mindfulness Matters", in which different meditation apps are recommended for students to use on their own. However, the college makes it clear on the page that it is not affiliated with any of the companies. The apps are merely suggestions for students to check out. Some of the apps include:

- Calm.com – This app is designed for meditation and sleep with various guided meditations, sleep stories, breathing programs, and soothing music.
- Greater Good Science Center at UC Berkley – Their center includes a magazine and notes scientific information on how to socially bond with others and become compassionate people.
- Headspace – This is another app designed for meditation to de-stress and become more focused.
- Insight Timer – This resource includes various guided meditations and mindfulness discussions from subject matter experts. Relaxing music tracks are also included.
- Mindful – The company is a non-profit, which offers courses for those who want to explore more about mindfulness.

Another area of the Virtual Student Wellness Center includes the "Mental Health Resources" page. One of the resources includes a link to podcasts about daily wellness backed by scientific evidence and practical ways of including mindfulness into one's daily life. Other resources are linked to ways to practice self-care, such as mindful movement and methods for decreasing stress and anxiety. Another tool provided relates to maintaining healthy relationships with others.

Mental health can also relate to physical health. Exercise boosts a person's mood, regulates their hormones, stabilizes blood sugar, and reduces stress and anxiety (Caso et al., 2021). Food is often described as fuel for the brain. Tools for healthy eating for the body and mind are also provided. For example, students can locate guides, which recommend food good for the brain to increase productivity and improve memory. The self-care link offers several strategies students can use to improve their overall mental health.

Hotlines are tools people can use when they experience a variety of crises (Roth & Szlyk, 2022). For some students, having online resources readily available when they experience a crisis is a lifeline. The mental health resource page includes a crisis text line, a suicide prevention hotline, and a unique crisis hotline for veterans. The Disaster Distress hotline services those who are experiencing a natural or human-caused disaster.

LEARNING WITH ARTIFICIAL INTELLIGENCE

The use of Artificial Intelligence (AI) has increased with the rise of availability of tools like ChatGPT and several others. Rather than fear the power of AI, it is important to embrace technological advances (Singh & Hiran, 2022). The academic department is aware that the use of AI is not going anywhere. ACE views AI as something that can be advantageous to various stakeholders, such as faculty, staff, and learners. AI is also able to help colleges provide a richer learning experience, which faculty can personalize for students (Otto et al., 2023; Singh & Hiran, 2022).

Instead of resisting acceptance of its use, the academic integrity policy was updated to allow for AI with some restrictions. Through the policy, students are aware that using AI to create work presented as the student's own outside of any course guidelines is not permitted and will be treated as an academic integrity violation. Any AI-generated work must be appropriately cited. Students are urged to check with their instructor before using an AI tool in coursework and assignments.

Devi and Rroy (2023) noted that educators should discuss balancing the use of digital resources with the pitfalls of technology. The academic department developed guides to help students on appropriate AI usage. For instance, a "Do's and Don'ts" document was created. For all work, students are encouraged to use tools like Grammarly and SpellCheck to proofread. Reference-generating tools can also be used to help format the references section, though it is still the student's responsibility to check their work for appropriate APA format. Using plagiarism checking tools is also recommended for students.

Moreover, just as students are aware faculty have access to plagiarism checking tools, they are also aware that faculty have access to AI detection tools. Thus, creating original work is highly recommended. The guide on "Do's and Don'ts" promotes brainstorming ideas for assignments using AI. With appropriate training on the use of AI, creativity, critical thinking, and learning can be enriched (Xia & Li, 2022). ACE also views using AI as a part of learning how to deal with modern-day issues. However, students must still cite applicable AI tools where appropriate.

While AI tools can be cited to note where ideas are not original, students must still check credible sources for accuracy. This idea of checking sources is promoted by reminding students that as Wikipedia is not considered a scholarly source, ChatGPT or other content related to AI are not all considered to be reliable, scholarly sources. Ultimately, in various parts of each course, students are reminded of all the tools provided in the Writing Center, as well as the Digital Tools Center. ACE provides students with writing assistance and self-help resources found in the Writing Center. The Digital Tools Center is an area in the Learning Management System (LMS), where various technology tools are recommended for completing assignments.

Faculty have also applied the use of AI to make learning more engaging. For example, a faculty member used ChatGPT to enter information about Common Core Standards for education-based students. The instructor wanted the AI to return the results with the information in a rap format. From there, the instructor created a musical beat and recorded himself rapping the lyrics generated from ChatGPT. The faculty member received overwhelmingly positive feedback from the students for making a lesson about Common Core Standards fun. Students reported using the same idea to teach their own students about other topics in the K-12 setting. As the feedback continued to reach other leaders and departments at ACE, the faculty member was asked to share their process on using AI in the classroom with the entire college during a quarterly meeting. ACE wanted to share this successful outcome and positive feedback to share best practices. As a result of that staff and faculty-wide meeting, several faculty requested additional professional development courses on the use of AI.

FURTHER RESEARCH DIRECTIONS

ACE leverages online applications and technology to offer students, staff, and faculty tools to humanize the online experience. Technology is no longer only a tool for information delivery or a substitute for educators. Rather, technology and educators should work in tandem (Burbules et al., 2020). While some information is available on the ways the ACE community engages with the online materials, more research can be pursued. A qualitative case study could be used to provide insight into potentially beneficial process-related aspects of humanizing the online learning environment. Researchers might also find interest in pursuing a quantitative study, including a survey to report on the prevalence of students who use the online services the college provides. Additional quantitative research can be collected from faculty and their use of the online services. A mixed methodology study could report on the prevalence of using online tools, as well as the benefits and improvements that could be made.

CONCLUSION

When effectively implemented, personalizing and humanizing the online learning environment can benefit students and staff (Nazempour & Darabi, 2023). As a for-profit and online higher education institution, American College of Education is committed to offering equitable services to its students and staff. Tools like Zoom, Kaltura, and Annoto offer the chance for students to interact with other students and their instructors. Brick-and-mortar colleges and universities typically have a writing center, on-site tutoring service, and a location for health services. ACE provides each of these services online via Student Commons. The DEI resources housed in Student Commons support student and faculty understanding of the importance of DEI and hopefully demonstrate to the ACE community its commitment to serving all populations. Higher education institutions play a critical role in equipping the workforce with the skills required to compete in a world that is changing constantly. As colleges consider the pandemic's effects and the need to transfer learning online, they might consider ways to provide differentiated instruction to reach all learners. Higher education institutions can have a life-changing impact on students by continuing to develop their humanized learning experiences.

REFERENCES

Abramenka-Lachheb, V., & de Siqueira, A. (2022). Authentic assessments through the lenses of diversity, equity, inclusion, and justice in a fully online course. *Journal of Teaching and Learning with Technology*, 11(1), 18–36. DOI: 10.14434/jotlt.v11i1.34591

American College of Education. (2023). *History and Mission*. Retrieved from https://www.ace.edu/about/history-mission

American Psychiatric Association. (2021, May 27). *New nationwide poll shows an increased popularity for telehealth services*. https://www.psychiatry.org/news-room/news-releases/new-nationwide-poll-shows-an-increased-popularity#:~:text=Nearly%20four%20in%20ten%20Americans,of%20the%20pandemic%20(82%25)

Ari, F., Arslan-Ari, I., Abaci, S., & Inan, F. A. (2022). Online simulation for information technology skills training in higher education. *Journal of Computing in Higher Education*, 34(2), 371–395. DOI: 10.1007/s12528-021-09303-0 PMID: 35125847

Berges, S., Martino, S., Basko, L., & McCabe, C. (2021). "Zooming" into engagement: Increasing engagement in the online classroom. *Journal of Institutional Research*, 10, 5–11.

Binoy, S., & Raddi, S. A. (2022). Concept mapping to enhance critical thinking in nursing students. *International Journal of Nursing Education*, 14(2), 159–164. DOI: 10.37506/ijone.v14i2.18008

Bonney, L. (2020). Mindfulness for school leader well-being: Why mindfulness matters and how to make it work. *Leadership*, 50(1), 30–33.

Brigas, C. J. (2019). Modeling and simulation in an educational context: Teaching and learning sciences. *Research in Social Sciences and Technology,* 4(2), 1-12. Retrieved from https://ressat.org/index.php/ressat

Burbules, N. C., Fan, G., & Repp, P. (2020). Five trends of education and technology in a sustainable future. *Geography and Sustainability*, 1(2), 93–97. DOI: 10.1016/j.geosus.2020.05.001

Caso, D., Carfora, V., Capasso, M., Oliano, D., & Conner, M. (2021). Using messages targeting psychological versus physical health benefits to promote walking behaviour: A randomised controlled trial. *Applied Psychology. Health and Well-Being*, 13(1), 152–173. DOI: 10.1111/aphw.12224 PMID: 32945103

Cooper, M. D. (2024). Centring diversity, equity, inclusion and belonging in higher education marketing: Why it is essential and how to do it well. *Journal of Education Advancement & Marketing*, 8(4), 315–330. DOI: 10.69554/JLYM7102

Dailey-Hebert, A. (2022). Student perspectives on using virtual reality to create informal connection and engagement. InSight: *A Journal of Scholarly Teaching, 17,* 28–46. DOI: 10.46504/17202202da

Devi, D., & Rroy, A. D. (2023). Role of Artificial Intelligence (AI) in sustainable education of higher education institutions in Guwahati City: Teacher's perception. *International Management Review*, •••, 111–116. http://www.imrjournal.org/

Gharib, M., Zolfaghari, M., Mojtahedzadeh, R., Mohammadi, A., & Gharib, A. (2016). Promotion of critical thinking in e-learning: A qualitative study on the experiences of instructors and students. *Advances in Medical Education and Practice*, 7, 271–279. DOI: 10.2147/AMEP.S105226 PMID: 27217807

Gimpel, G. (2022). Bringing face-to-face engagement to online classes: Developing a high-presence online teaching method. *The Journal of Scholarship of Teaching and Learning*, 22(4), 32–49. DOI: 10.14434/josotl.v22i4.32702

Gorghiu, G., Lamanauskas, V., Makarskaite-Petkeviciene, R., Manea, V. I., & Pribeanu, C. (2021). Frustration and stress in the online education of university students from Lithuania and Romania. *ELearning & Software for Education*, 1, 162–169. DOI: 10.12753/2066-026X-21-021

Hollister, B., Nair, P., Hill-Lindsay, S., & Chukoskie, L. (2022). Engagement in online learning: Student attitudes and behavior during COVID-19. *Frontiers in Education*, 7(851019), 1–16. DOI: 10.3389/feduc.2022.851019

Humpherys, S. L., Bakir, N., & Babb, J. (2022). Experiential learning to foster tacit knowledge through a role play, business simulation. *Journal of Education for Business*, 97(2), 119–125. DOI: 10.1080/08832323.2021.1896461

Hyunjin, J. K., Yiren, K., & Tirotta-Esposito, R. (2023). Promoting diversity, equity, and inclusion: An examination of diversity-infused faculty professional development programs. *Journal of Higher Education Theory and Practice*, 23(11), 138–153. DOI: 10.33423/jhetp.v23i11.6224

Jackson, K. T., Richardson, S., & Breen, J. M. (2022). Enacting a diversity, equity, inclusion, and justice emphasis in graduate and professional leadership education. *New Directions for Student Leadership*, 2022(176), 75–87. DOI: 10.1002/yd.20532 PMID: 36565141

Landrum, B., Bannister, J., Garza, G., & Rhame, S. (2021). A class of one: Students' satisfaction with online learning. *Journal of Education for Business*, 96(2), 82–88. DOI: 10.1080/08832323.2020.1757592

National Center for Education Statistics. (2022). *Number and percentage of students enrolled in degree-granting postsecondary institutions, by distance education participation, location of student, level of enrollment, and control and level of institution: Fall 2020 and fall 2021.* https://nces.ed.gov/programs/digest/d22/tables/dt22_311.15.asp

Nazempour, R., & Darabi, H. (2023). Personalized learning in virtual learning environments using students' behavior analysis. *Education Sciences*, 13(5), 457. DOI: 10.3390/educsci13050457

O'Flaherty, J., & Costabile, M. (2020). Using a science simulation-based learning tool to develop students' active learning, self-confidence, and critical thinking in academic writing. *Nurse Education in Practice*, 47, 102839. Advance online publication. DOI: 10.1016/j.nepr.2020.102839 PMID: 32943173

Otto, F., Kling, N., Schumann, C.-A., & Tittmann, C. (2023). A conceptual approach to an AI-based adaptive study support system for individualized higher education. *International Journal of Advanced Corporate Learning*, 16(2), 69–80. DOI: 10.3991/ijac.v16i2.35699

Ozogul, G., Zhu, M., & Phillips, T. M. (2022). Perceived and actual cognitive presence: A case study of an intentionally-designed asynchronous online course. *Online Learning : the Official Journal of the Online Learning Consortium*, 26(1), 38–57. DOI: 10.24059/olj.v26i1.3051

Presley, R., Cumberland, D. M., & Rose, K. (2023). A comparison of cognitive and social presence in online graduate courses: Asynchronous vs. synchronous modalities. *Online Learning : the Official Journal of the Online Learning Consortium*, 27(2), 245–264. DOI: 10.24059/olj.v27i2.3046

Richardson, J. C., Castellanos Reyes, D., Janakiraman, S., & Duha, M. S. U. (2023). The process of developing a digital repository for online teaching using design-based research. *TechTrends*, 67(2), 217–230. DOI: 10.1007/s11528-022-00795-w PMID: 36258921

Roth, K. B., & Szlyk, H. S. (2022). Hotline use in the United States: Results from the collaborative psychiatric epidemiology surveys. *Administration and Policy in Mental Health*, 48(3), 564–578. DOI: 10.1007/s10488-020-01089-0 PMID: 33057932

Singh, S. V., & Hiran, K. K. (2022). The impact of AI on teaching and learning in higher education technology. *Journal of Higher Education Theory and Practice*, 12(13), 135–148. https://nabpress.com/higher-education-theory-and-practice

Souheyla, B. (2021). Zoom sessions in distant learning: Algerian EFL students' perceptions and attitudes. *Arab World English Journal*, 264–280.

Tsai, C.-L., Ku, H.-Y., & Campbell, A. (2021). Impacts of course activities on student perceptions of engagement and learning online. *Distance Education*, 42(1), 106–125. DOI: 10.1080/01587919.2020.1869525

Williams, S. A. S., Conyers, A., & Garcia, F. (2018). Practical applications of ecological consultation in higher education: Diversity and inclusion initiatives. *Public Administration Quarterly*, 42(2), 183–212. https://paq.spaef.org/. DOI: 10.1177/073491491804200204

Xia, X., & Li, X. (2022). Artificial Intelligence for higher education development and teaching skills. *Wireless Communications and Mobile Computing*, •••, 1–10. DOI: 10.1155/2022/7537764

You, J., & Yang, J. (2021). Engaging students with instructional videos: Perspectives from faculty and instructional designers. *Quarterly Review of Distance Education*, 22(3), 1–10.

Zhang, S., Gao, Q., Wen, Y., Li, M., & Wang, Q. (2021). Automatically detecting cognitive engagement beyond behavioral indicators: A case of online professional learning community. *Journal of Educational Technology & Society*, 24(2), 58–72.

Chapter 9
Online Teaching Readiness in the Era of Digital Transformation:
Challenges and Recommendations

Zhuqing Ding
https://orcid.org/0009-0004-8824-2609
Georgetown University, USA

Khalid Alharbi
Georgetown University, USA

ABSTRACT

Digital transformation requires faculty development professionals and decision-makers in higher education to equip faculty and institutions with the skills to enable teaching and learning with technologies in online spaces. This chapter reviews a range of studies on faculty online readiness conducted in the past ten years and proposes a new framework, the Interrelated model of online teaching readiness (IMOTR), providing a new perspective that accounts for the interrelated nature of technological, pedagogical, agentic, and contextual readiness categories and factors. The findings provide insights to help inform faculty development professionals and university decision-makers to design appropriate infrastructure and training needed to prepare faculty to teach online.

DOI: 10.4018/979-8-3693-4407-1.ch009

INTRODUCTION

Digital transformation requires faculty development professionals and decision-makers in higher education to equip faculty and institutions with the skills to enable teaching and learning with technologies in online spaces. Successful digital transformation is crucial for allowing institutions to build a quality and competitive education (Fernández et al., 2023). Online teaching readiness is especially important in higher education digital transformation in the wake of the COVID-19 pandemic, the rise of Artificial Intelligence (AI), and the overall increase in online education programs. This chapter outlines challenges and recommendations on faculty online teaching readiness in higher education, providing insights to help inform faculty development professionals and university decision-makers to design appropriate infrastructure and training needed to prepare faculty to teach online. The chapter focuses on identifying factors that contribute to and hinder online teaching readiness, particularly during a time of rapid digital transformation, before providing a range of recommendations on how to address potential faculty readiness challenges.

Research on factors that influence faculty online teaching readiness shows diverse findings and definitions (Scherer et al., 2022; Scherer et al., 2023; Singh & Thurman, 2019). The discussion of these factors in the literature focuses only on specific readiness categories in isolation from other potentially related considerations, further highlighting the need for a comprehensive account of online teaching readiness. In this chapter, we review a range of studies on faculty online readiness conducted in the past decade and propose a new framework, the Interrelated model of online teaching readiness (IMOTR). By doing so, we hope to provide a new perspective in which we account for the interrelated nature of technological, pedagogical, agentic, and contextual readiness categories and factors.

This chapter will start with a discussion of the definition of online education and readiness. The following section covers the main focus of this chapter, with two overarching themes: competency-based measurement in online teaching readiness, and teaching beliefs and attitudes. We conclude the chapter by discussing the IMOTR framework in relation to the overall findings of this review and present a set of recommendations for higher education administrators and policymakers to further improve readiness at all the relevant levels.

FACULTY ONLINE TEACHING READINESS

Online education is considered a critical part of long-term strategy for higher education institutions (Allen & Seaman, 2016). Faculty, as the main actors in delivering online education through course design and teaching, need to be both pedagogically and technologically ready with a well-supported institutional environment. Before defining online teaching readiness, it is important to engage with the broader definitions of online education. Online education has received varied definitions in the literature (Downing & Dyment, 2013). The debate around the definition of online education is discussed by many scholars, criticizing the lack of agreement on a general versus a narrow definition (Chigeza & Halbert, 2014), and the confusion around using the terms online education, elearning, and distance learning interchangeably (Lee, 2017), despite the potential meaning differences among these terms. Singh and Thurman (2019) conducted a literature review on online learning definitions and summarized five elements that have been used to define online education in the last decade, namely time, technology, physical distance, education context, and interactivity. Realizing the diverse definitions in the literature, they proposed a new detailed definition for online education as:

Education being delivered in an online environment through the use of the internet for teaching and learning. This includes online learning on the part of the students that is not dependent on their physical or virtual co-location. The teaching content is delivered online and the instructors develop teaching modules that enhance learning and interactivity in the synchronous or asynchronous environment. (p. 302)

For the purposes of this paper, we adopt this definition, especially considering it recognizes that quality online education cannot solely rely on content or technological expertise, but also a blend of skills and knowledge (Henry & Meadows, 2008). This further highlights the need for understanding what contributes to faculty readiness for online teaching. Faculty readiness to teach online is defined as a state of faculty preparation for online teaching (Martin, Budhrani, & Wang, 2019) as well as the mental and physical preparation of an organization for the delivery of online education (Borotis & Poulymenakou, 2004).

Since the COVID-19 pandemic, institutions across the world shifted immediately from traditional in-person teaching to online teaching, leading to questions about faculty online teaching readiness. While such a shift meets the definitions of online teaching above, some scholars further define the teaching mode as emergency online teaching (Lim, 2022), differentiating the nature of it from regular online teaching that entails heavy effort in modules development and preparation. What is yet to be explored is how faculty online teaching readiness is defined and examined during such modes of emergency online teaching.

RESEARCH QUESTIONS

Although there are an increasing number of studies related to online teaching readiness, particularly in the past decade, findings on factors that influence faculty online teaching readiness have been inconsistent and discussed in isolation from other potentially related factors. It is necessary to examine such inconsistency and provide a comprehensive account of the contributing and hindering factors to online teaching readiness, especially during a critical time with the recent rise of AI, and overall the acceleration of digital transformation after the COVID-19 pandemic. This chapter aims to build on previous research by providing a detailed account of challenges in faculty online teaching readiness, as well as recommendations to help faculty development professionals and higher education institutions address such challenges.

The research questions that guide this literature review are: *1) What factors contribute to and hinder faculty online teaching readiness? 2) What are the areas higher education institutions should focus on to improve their support for faculty online teaching readiness? 3) What are the areas that future research can further investigate in considering faculty online teaching readiness?*

We answer these questions by engaging with an extensive body of previous research. Based on the aforementioned definitions and context of online teaching, suitable sources are identified by using the search terms "online teaching readiness," "e-teaching readiness," "online education," "online course," "e-readiness," "faculty readiness," "instructor readiness," "teacher readiness." and "higher education." To capture the rapid trend and change in online education, the timeframe is set between 2011 and 2024. 2011 was the time when online education started to become more broadly accepted, and 65% of U.S. higher education institutions started incorporating online education as part of their critical long-term strategy (Allen & Seaman, 2016). The inclusion criteria for peer-reviewed journal articles are met if the study focuses on faculty or teachers' online teaching readiness as opposed to students' readiness, if it is within the context of higher education as opposed to secondary education, if it is a peer-reviewed journal as opposed to dissertations or book chapters, and if it is within the context of online education defined by this literature review.

With a screening review of fifty-two articles, of which 22 are included in the upcoming sections, this chapter covers research conducted in thirteen unique countries as well as in specific regions such as the Middle East and Africa and the Caribbean, or globally. The following sections of the paper present the two overarching themes that emerged in the literature: competency-based measurement in online teaching readiness, and teaching beliefs and attitudes.

COMPETENCY-BASED MEASUREMENT IN ONLINE TEACHING READINESS

Teaching evaluation based on competencies has not been traditionally done in higher education given the academic freedom faculty have. However, in online teaching readiness literature, it is common to measure the perception of faculty on their online teaching competencies. Perceptions are often measured using surveys or questionnaires (i.e. Badiozaman, 2021; Bolliger & Halupa, 2022; Elewa, 2022; Gay, 2016; Hosny et al., 2021; Junus et al., 2021). Studies usually recruit participants via social media (Junus et al., 2021; Paliwal & Singh, 2021), online newsletters of professional networks (Martin et al., 2019), institutional communication channels (Badiozaman, 2021) or a mixture of the abovementioned channels (Kim & Martin, 2023; Scherer et al., 2021; Scherer et al., 2022; Scherer et al., 2023). The design of the survey/questionnaire usually is based on an existing online teaching readiness assessment framework, such as the Technological and Pedagogical Content Knowledge (TPACK) framework, Faculty Readiness to Teach Online (FRTO) framework, and other adjusted versions to meet the need of the specific region and context (Elewa, 2022; Hosny et al., 2021; Gay, 2016; Lim, 2022; Paliwal & Singh, 2021; Tayyib et al., 2020). Common competencies researchers use to measure faculty online teaching readiness include technical readiness, pedagogical readiness, course design, attitude, resource readiness, communication skills, and time management skills, and these categories seem to be defined differently across contexts. In the next section, we will review and discuss each of these competencies. Although these readiness dimensions are discussed in independent sections, we hope to argue for their interrelated and interdependent nature, where each readiness dimension contributes to the success of the other ones in various contexts.

Technological Readiness

Technological readiness is one of the most frequently considered readiness dimensions in online teaching. Faculty technological readiness competency refers to their ability to demonstrate technical skills including utilizing features of Learning Management Systems (LMS), using technologies to present and organize content online, interacting and communicating with students via technologies (Gay, 2016; Martin, Budhrani, & Wang, 2019; Scherer et al., 2021; Scherer et al., 2022), and locating a variety of resources on the Internet (Lakshmi, 2021). Technological readiness appears in several frameworks derived from the Instructor Readiness Questionnaire developed by the University of Toledo (Martin, Budhrani, & Wang, 2019; Junus et al., 2021), and further defined by Martin, Budhrani, & Wang (2019) in their Faculty Readiness to Teach Online (FRTO) framework (Bolliger & Halupa,

2022; Matin, Wang, et al., 2019). However, some scholars have criticized that these frameworks were developed in European countries with stable Internet access and comparatively more abundant resources, and therefore, did not consider the aspect of technology accessibility as part of technological readiness (Junus et al., 2021). Being able to own well-functioning technological devices and access stable Internet for online teaching would be prerequisite necessary requirements for faculty's technical readiness. This is especially documented in the research done in the context of developing countries (Junus, et al., 2021; Roy et al., Zgheib et al., 2023). While technology accessibility is not related to faculty's competency in the dimension of technological readiness, the importance of device and Internet accessibility reflects that online teaching readiness does not only rely on personal readiness, but also contextual readiness with infrastructure support by higher education institutions.

In addition to the basic technical skills, some scholars suggest advanced levels of technological readiness involve faculty's ability to connect the application of technology to pedagogy, including representing teaching with technology, having knowledge about the instructional use of technology, and understanding the interplay between pedagogy, teaching content, and technology (Scherer et al., 2021; Scherer et al., 2022; Scherer et al., 2023). Educational technologies in online courses are supposed to support faculty to simulate a similar or even more engaging learning environment in an online space to an in-person class, while also achieving the learning outcomes (Wekerle et al., 2022). When well-designed and integrated, faculty believe educational technologies enhance their instructional practices effectively, make the learning process exciting and interactive, and keep learners motivated (Akram et al., 2022). However, such good integration of technology into teaching and courses requires an extensive amount of faculty development support, including comprehensive at-elbow work sessions in which faculty development professionals help design technology solutions to meet the specific pedagogical goals of faculty members (Cutri & Mena, 2020; Downing & Dyment, 2013; Scherer et al., 2021; Scherer et al., 2022).

Pedagogical Readiness

Pedagogical readiness directly influences faculty satisfaction with their online teaching experience (Downing & Dyment, 2013). Lack of confidence in pedagogical knowledge is one of the main reasons for faculty to avoid teaching online (Lim, 2022). Pedagogical readiness has been referred to in different terms and defined differently and is affected by an assortment of factors. Although rarely distinguished, the literature discusses pedagogical readiness in two phases: course preparation, and teaching.

Unlike traditional in-person teaching, online teaching requires a more intensive amount of time and effort during the preparation phase (Cavanaugh, 2005; Lim, 2022). Faculty often engage in course planning (Junus et al., 2021) and course design (Badiozaman, 2021; Hosni et al., 2021; Martin, Budhrani, & Wang, 2019; Martin et al., 2019; Paliwal & Singh, 2020; Zgheib et al., 2023) during the stage of preparation. A well-designed online course is expected to have aligned and explicitly laid out objectives, structure, content, activities, assessments, materials, and interactions (Kim & Martin, 2023). Course design skills refer to faculty's ability to write measurable learning objectives, design active and interactive learning activities (Junus et al., 2021; Gay, 2016), such as discussion boards and case studies (Paliwal & Singh, 2021), design accessible materials that accommodate students' needs, follow the fair use guidelines under the copyright law (Junus et al., 2021), design assignments with clear grading criteria (Paliwal & Singh, 2020), and create online course orientation (Martin et al., 2019). Organizing course materials in modules or units is also critical (Martin, Budhrani, & Wang, 2019, as it ensures needed clarity for online students in the absence of physical interactions with professors and peers (Badiozaman, 2021). A well-designed online course places learners at the center (Lakshmi, 2021; Zgheib et al., 2023) and takes into account students' context and level of engagement, offering clear and motivating guidance to students to progress through the course. Badiozaman (2021) found that some faculty expressed that designing a learner-centered course is challenging considering the various needs their students have. Preparing materials for various learners' needs and adopting a mixture forms of presentation and delivery such as video/audio lectures, simulations, or AR/VR (Badiozaman, 2021; Bolliger & Halupa, 2022) can be fruitful. This iterative design process for an inclusive online learning experience requires not only faculty's knowledge of instructional design (Zgheib et al., 2023) but also the support from faculty development professionals.

During the teaching stage, faculty teach synchronously and/or asynchronously using a variety of technologies. Pedagogical readiness during this stage of teaching is defined as the ability to have an active online teaching presence (Gay, 2016; Scherer et al., 2021; Scherer et al., 2022), interact and communicate with students (Bodiozaman, 2021; Scherer et al., 2022), and provide timely feedback to support students' learning process (Bolliger & Halupa, 2022; Gay, 2016). In fact, several studies seem to equate pedagogical readiness with time management and communication skills (Bolliger & Halupa, 2022; Junus et al., 2021; Paliwal & Singh, 2021), but these seem to be more aligned with agentic readiness discussed in the next subsection.

While pedagogical readiness is considered one of the most critical readiness to online teaching, only one study (Gay, 2016) defined pedagogical readiness by phases, and none have presented a clear and comprehensive framework that covers online pedagogical expectations by different stages (i.e., course preparation stage and teaching stage). What is rather problematic in the literature, particularly studies conducted during the COVID-19 pandemic, is that much of their focus was placed on the skills needed for the teaching stage (Lakshimi, 2021; Scherer et al., 2022), with little attention given to the skills needed for the course planning/design phase. Such focus is understandable given the lack of time for preparation and design at the beginning of the pandemic, which has been described as an emergency online teaching event (Lim, 2022). However, we should distinguish emergency online teaching from non-emergency online teaching, and the fundamental difference lies in the pre-course phase. Non-emergency online teaching contexts allow more effort and time for faculty to prepare for a learner-centered, interactive, and technology-enhanced online learning experience for their students. Provided sufficient planning time, faculty can benefit from relevant professional development programs to improve their instructional design knowledge (Zgheib et al., 2023) which is especially crucial in the course preparation stage, and contributes to better faculty online teaching readiness.

The findings above further highlight the importance of distinguishing emergency online teaching from non-emergency online teaching, as each context calls for a different set of pedagogical readiness strategies. Furthermore, they shed light on pedagogical readiness as an important element of online teaching, which has the ability to improve or hinder online overall readiness and success among faculty.

Agentic Readiness

Agentic readiness (Badiozaman, 2021) refers to the attitude and habits of faculty toward online teaching, which concerns agentic behaviors such as *"creating and/or taking advantage of opportunities, risk-taking behavior, in the pursuit of one's goals, persistence in goal pursuits, and willingness to change one's situation to achieve a better fit with interests, aspirations, and expectations"* (p. 52) (Sadri, 1996). Faculty's attitude to adopt or resist change (Gay, 2016; Zgheib et al., 2023), their self-efficacy beliefs regarding online teaching (Zgheib et al., 2023), and resilience and ability to be adaptive and interactive when encountering unexpected challenges when teaching online (Badiozaman, 2021) are all considered as contributing factors to agentic readiness. Transitioning from teaching traditional classes to online is significant considering the major shift in orientation from a teacher-centered approach to a learner-centered approach. Identity disruptions involving the shift in status from a classroom expert to a novice in the new environment can involve a wide range of emotions among faculty including vulnerability, fear, and excitement (Cutri et al., 2020; Cutri & Mena, 2020). A more detailed discussion of identity disruption factors will be discussed in the second theme of this chapter.

In addition to attitude readiness, behavior, habit, and lifestyle (Gay, 2016) such as time management and communication skills are also discussed under agentic readiness. Time management skills during teaching stages concern faculty's ability to set aside dedicated and uninterrupted time for their online courses (Gay, 2016), monitor student progress and support learners during the delivery of courses (Bolliger & Halupa, 2022), and communicate routinely with learners and technical support (Gay, 2016). Prior to the teaching stage, preparing, planning and designing online courses is also time-consuming (Cavanaugh, 2005; Lim, 2022). Being able to maintain a balance of time for mastering technologies, planning and designing courses, keeping a good amount of communication, and providing support to online students requires faculty to demonstrate excellent time management skills. This can be challenging when one takes into consideration that faculty have research and other teaching duties on top of their online teaching responsibilities. Such additional layers of workload often demotivate faculty from investing further in sharpening their online teaching skills (Cutri et al., 2020). Not surprisingly, lack of time is reported as one of the biggest obstacles for faculty to teach online (Mandernach et al., 2013; Phan & Dang, 2017). Institutions might consider several supportive policies to not only motivate faculty by providing incentives and rewards to teaching online but also provide flexibility of time and place to encourage faculty to excel their online teaching skills.

Communication skills, particularly the ability to provide timely and effective feedback and communication to online learners, are among the most critical factors that contribute to the success of online learners (Espasa & Meneses, 2010). Without the physical presence, faculty's timely feedback via course announcements, discussion boards, or emails is particularly critical in building an online teaching presence (Bodiozaman, 2021; Scherer et al., 2022). As part of their learning process, students are able to clarify misunderstandings and make progress toward learning goals (Martin et al., 2019) through communication messages with their teachers. Communication in online courses happens both synchronously and asynchronously (Lim, 2022), with asynchronous communications being critical in building an ongoing online teaching presence. Asynchronous communication is text-based, which requires thoughtful and time-consuming writing (Badiozaman, 2021), differing from the immediate and colloquial nature of verbal communication. Such a different nature of online communication skills may appear to be a challenge to faculty who shift from teaching face-to-face to online. However, there are technologies available in LMS that allow faculty to provide asynchronous audio and video comments to discussion boards, which can be explored further by faculty training professionals in faculty training and support. Faculty's good communication skills also help build connections with students (Martin et al., 2019). Some research considers being able to convey personality and emotion in writing and speaking as part of faculty's communication skills (Junus et al., 2021), considering that personality and emotions support relationship building between faculty and students. Research shows that there is a positive link between instructor-student rapport and students' learning outcomes (Downing & Dyment, 2013; Lammers & Gillaspy, 2013), further highlighting that satisfaction and likelihood for faculty to continue teaching online is high when there are positive interactions with their students (Shea et al., 2005). However, research also shares faculty's concern about constantly staying connected and how such time consuming communication tasks can lead to burnout (Badiozaman, 2021; Lim, 2022). Therefore, it is important to seek a good balance between communication and time management skills, and more recommendations to this effect will be discussed in the final part of this chapter.

Contextual Readiness

The technical, pedagogical and agentic competencies reviewed above all speak to personal-level readiness, which depends on individual faculty's knowledge, experience, and attitude, and which can vary from person to person. What is a prerequisite to all these personal types of readiness is contextual readiness, which refers to the institutional support and training that universities provide to faculty. To study faculty's profile and their online teaching readiness, Scherer et al. (2021) surveyed 739 higher education teachers from 58 countries and brought up the concepts of personal readiness and contextual readiness. They found that teachers in higher education are not a homogenous group, and identified three unique profiles: (1) teachers who had neither personal nor contextual readiness, (2) teachers who were contextually ready but personally unready, and (3) teachers who were ready personally and contextually. Faculty-perceived self-efficacy did not go hand in hand with perceived institutional support. The authors argued that teachers' readiness goes beyond simply their own personal readiness, and that institutional, cultural, and innovation contexts are also critical and closely connected to personal readiness. Leadership's support of online learning (Lim, 2022; Stickney et al., 2019) motivates faculty to implement online learning (Zgheib et al, 2023). Faculty colleagues' positive attitude and support (Tayyib et al., 2020) also contributes to stronger motivation to teach online. Badiozaman (2021) suggests that faculty readiness is susceptible and contingent on contextual readiness. Institutional support includes providing technological infrastructure, devices, internet access, as well as technical support (Badiozaman, 2021; Gay, 2016). In terms of the type of support faculty found most helpful, several studies report that faculty prefer individual at-elbow support (Cutri & Mena, 2020; Downing & Dyment, 2013; Scherer et al., 2021; Scherer et al.,

2022) and self-directed professional development instead of formal university and faculty-wide support (Downing & Dyment, 2013).

Contextual readiness doesn't only speak to institutional readiness, but also the cultural context (Scherer et al., 2021). Martin, Wang, et al. (2019) pointed out that cross-cultural differences may impact faculty perceived importance of online teaching competencies. Scherer et al. (2021) found that teachers in high readiness groups come from countries with a tendency toward uncertainty avoidance and long-term orientation, which broadly speaks to national strategies towards shifting to online education. However, further research is needed to confirm such a statement on the relationship between online teaching readiness and a country's cultural orientation.

Other Impacting Factors: Experience and Gender

Faculty online teaching experience is often assumed to be related to their online teaching readiness in a linear way. While some studies found that experience is positively related to online teaching readiness (Bolliger & Hulupa 2022; Downing & Dyment, 2017; Martin, Budhrani, & Wang, 2019; Martin, Wang, et al., 2019), Scherer et al. (2022) found that teachers' readiness for online teaching increased first and then decreased with more online teaching experience. Such a curvilinear experience-readiness relationship between faculty online teaching readiness and their years of online teaching experience implied that both novice and experienced instructors can benefit from professional training and tailored institutional support. While Scherer et al. (2022) were unable to explain the reasons, the curvilinear relationship might be due to teachers' beliefs, responsibilities for research, and the rewarding and ranking advancement structure in a university system (Cutri & Mena, 2020; Phan & Dang, 2017). More research is needed to better understand the curvilinear relationship between online teaching experience and online teaching readiness.

There is a body of research evidencing the digital gender divide in faculty's perceived level of online teaching readiness. For example, female faculty perceive certain aspects of online teaching as more important (Martin et al., 2019), and they are found to have a more active online teaching presence (Scherer et al., 2021). However, some scholars found no or little relationship between gender and online teaching readiness (Scherer et al., 2022). Lack of patterns in these potentially impacting factors demonstrates that faculty are not a homogenous group (Scherer et al., 2021), and that faculty experience and the specific institutional and cultural context they are in can exhibit great levels of variation, and therefore require more locally-oriented readiness considerations.

Theme Discussion

Competency-based measurement varies from context to context based on different samples conducted in different regions in each study. Such findings implied that faculty online teaching readiness is relevant to a variety of factors at both the personal and contextual levels. Competencies and skills required during course design and teaching stages also vary. Scholars emphasized the need for universities to provide tailored support such as experience-related support to both novice and experienced teachers, stage-related support such as before and during course preparation and teaching (Gay, 2016), and to meet faculty where they are and support their needs accordingly (Cutri & Mena, 2020; Downing & Dyment, 2013; Gay, 2016; Martin, Wang, et al., 2019; Phan & Dang, 2017; Scherer et al., 2022).

The review of the personal-level readiness as it relates to technological, pedagogical and agentic considerations and the contextual readiness in terms of institutional support and culture shows the interrelated nature of the readiness factors. The different dimensions of readiness contribute to the success of each other. By having both personal and contextual readiness, faculty's self-confidence and self-efficacy in online teaching can be greatly improved, further contributing to an overall more positive online teaching experience (Scherer et al., 2021).

Finally, it is important to note that there are two major problems in measuring faculty online teaching readiness based on competency. One is that given the academic freedom in higher education institutions, it is uncommon to measure faculty's *actual* ability to perform online teaching tasks. Researchers have been designing measurement frameworks based on faculty's perception of their readiness rather than their actual performance and abilities. Therefore, findings through perception-based competency measurement studies may not fully reflect the actual needs based on faculty abilities. The second issue is that, given their quantitative, mass-survey nature, competency-based measurement studies are not able to explore the underlying reasons for faculty's perceptions of their online teaching competencies. Therefore, it is critical to extend this discussion to insights from qualitative studies to gain a window into how teaching beliefs and attitudes affect online teaching readiness, as detailed in the next section.

TEACHING BELIEFS AND ATTITUDES IN ONLINE TEACHING READINESS

While competency is an important aspect of online teaching, when developing training programs for university faculty, teaching beliefs and attitudes are equally as important, considering the significant change in the format and environment of teaching. As detailed in the previous section, obtaining such qualitative insights from stakeholders can help explain the competency-based results, and potentially provide sufficient ground for a more accurate and thorough assessment of readiness needs. Often, these insightful reflections on teaching beliefs and attitudes are collected in mixed methods and qualitative studies (Cutri & Mena, 2020; Downing & Dyment, 2013). Among others, previous studies have obtained relevant attitudes via open-ended questions, structured interviews, and focus-group discussions. Previous work has explored faculty perception of their online teaching development (Downing & Dyment, 2013), highlighted the connection between attitudes and pedagogical practices (Phan & Dang, 2017), documented affective and identity disruption factors in the online teaching context (Cutri & Mena, 2020), and illustrated faculty perceptions under affective and academic cultural themes (Cutri et al., 2020). In what follows, we provide a detailed review of the findings of a selection of studies related to faculty attitudes and beliefs on online teaching readiness. In doing so, we follow Cutri and Mena's (2020) categorization and understanding of faculty readiness in terms of affective and academic cultural factors. While the overwhelming discussion of such factors has taken a quantitative approach in the literature, we believe that a similar categorization of attitudes and beliefs on faculty readiness would be especially fruitful in the case of qualitative findings.

Affective Factors

Affective factors in faculty online teaching readiness concern identity-related and emotional considerations resulting from the transition from in-person to online teaching. In this transition, teacher educators go through a journey in which their traditional roles in the classroom are altered due to the introduction of a range of technical and non-technical elements. The teacher identity of a knowledgeable individual who is in control and who is expected to address and resolve issues that emerge in the classroom does not necessarily transfer to the online environment. Previous studies have reported that in many cases, when technological issues arose in the new teaching environment, teachers deferred to their students for solutions. While this in itself does not constitute a negative change, one can make the argument that it is reflective of a broader shift in the traditional power dynamics (Cutri & Mena, 2020) in the classroom, further bringing to the forefront identity disruption issues that teacher educators could face as they go through their online teaching journeys.

In order to identify elements of a nuanced conceptualization of faculty readiness, Cutri and Mena (2020) conducted an integrated critical literature review to explore the variables and overarching themes which specifically focused on non-expert faculty transitioning, developing, and teaching online courses. Relevant to the affective domain, the study found that when faculty transition, develop, or implement online courses, the commonly associated emotions were related to fear and vulnerability. Such findings highlight the need for a better understanding of how such intense emotions and vulnerability may impact faculty's experience of online teaching, as a result hinder their readiness.

Cutri et al (2020) expand on the affective factors impacting faculty readiness for online teaching by interviewing six teacher educators with varying gender, ethnicities, professional rank and levels of online teaching experience. Their findings reveal that many faculty members tied their comfort with risk to their successful transition to online classes. Further, 'Willingness to try new things' emerged as relevant to participants in this focus group, as it provides new opportunities for educators to be creative and try new ways of teaching and creating materials in this new online space. Educators in the focus group recognized the role of embracing identity disruption and change in classroom dynamics and how it can result in enhanced faculty readiness. The new dynamic in which the role of the 'expert' isn't automatically assigned to the teacher educator but rather shared with students, whose knowledge of the technology in many cases surpasses that of teacher educators, can ultimately result in solving classroom technical challenges faster and overall contribute to a smoother online delivery. Such positive framings of what may get initially perceived as negative experiences could provide a helpful perspective for teacher educators preparing to go through an online teaching experience for the first time.

In focusing on the affective domain as it relates to readiness, one cannot ignore the more technological and pedagogical role contributing to these perceived emotions and attitudes. In a relatively early study exploring perceptions of online education and relevant lived experiences among academic staff in teacher education, Downing and Dyment (2013) found that instructors resisted teaching online because of their lack of pedagogical knowledge to teach well in the new space, their lack of technological skills to develop online learning materials, and their lack of confidence. It is clear that lack of confidence in online teaching abilities can be connected to the instructors' perceptions of lack of pedagogical knowledge and necessary technical skills. These perceptions of actual readiness needs, left unaddressed, can impact the status of the instructor in the online classroom, leading to an array of negative emotions which can hinder the learning journey. Among other recommendations to address this, instructors rank highly individual support provided by the e-learning support team, as having such support reduces and potentially addresses many of their concerns. Such findings emphasized the importance of individual attention in faculty development work. This study highlighted the emotions such as fear, concern, and joy that can be experienced by instructors in online teaching and which can be affected by their levels of readiness. Further, it identified areas for universities to reconsider its support models in building faculty online teaching readiness.

Recognizing the challenge of conveying both content expertise and teachers' passion and love for teaching through machines when planning for online education in Vietnam, Phan and Dang (2017) highlight further the extent to which both pedagogical considerations and attitudes are of crucial importance to any model attempting to account for online teaching readiness. They illustrate their conceptual framework, which incorporates insights from the literature and lists five influencing factors including attitudes, pedagogy & methodology, technology competence, training, and time constraints. Thus, recognizing faculty's emotions and attitudes towards online teaching as well as supporting their shift of paradigm to acquire the online pedagogical skills to design appropriate learning experiences are emphasized as the most important aspects that universities should focus on in faculty development. This work calls for more extensive and broader training that's not limited in focus to only technology skills.. Universities that intend to prepare faculty for online teaching should focus on addressing the pedagogical needs, providing tailored and effective technical training, as well as building an inclusive environment that is informed by attitudinal and emotional considerations.

Academic-Cultural Factors

Academic-Cultural factors refer to the impact of practices and requirements related to the culture of academia which teaching faculty are expected to observe. These include but are not limited to the teaching norms and expectations as well as the structural milestones for professional upward mobility within academia. As discussed earlier, teaching practices that are instructor-centered do not necessarily transfer well to the online environment (Lim, 2022), given the different classroom interaction dynamics. The same applies to practices related to summative and formative assessments, where teacher educators have to contend with new ways to ensure accountability and mastery of relevant content (Cutri et al, 2020). Online teaching readiness requires an evaluation of traditional practices and a pursuit of innovation-oriented initiatives to introduce new ones that are appropriately aligned with the new environment. However, innovation requires time-consuming efforts and introduces yet another challenge for faculty who are expected to meet certain teaching, research, and administrative milestones in order to advance their careers in the academic structure. This leaves very little time for innovative efforts to be dedicated to technological and pedagogical considerations, potentially hindering overall readiness for online teaching.

Focusing on perceptions of the various teaching readiness constructs, Cutri et al. (2020) focus group study revealed that a main theme of concern to faculty relates to cultural factors affecting readiness, including teaching norms, and equity and tenure norms. By highlighting the cultural factors related to the nature and norms of academia, the focus group results demonstrated the relevance of perceptions of 'correct' academic norms and practices and the extent to which these practices could be transferable to the online environment. For example, participants highlighted the challenge in attempting to replicate in-person teacher-centered pedagogical practices as well as other associated issues related to formative and summative assessments. Such a new teaching environment requires extensive efforts and time for teacher educators to provide a more meaningful learning journey for their students. While it is easy to expect such efforts, one needs to take into account other important commitments and aspects that faculty need to attend to in order to ensure their upward mobility within the academic ranks. As one participant in this focus group put it when reflecting on the effects of the transition on their own career aspirations: "I don't really know how it will affect me, but I know it is cutting into my writing time. I am spending a lot more time this summer in webinars and doing PD to learn the technology" (p. 538).

Cutri and Mena (2020) argue that the competitive structure of tenure reviews and trends in hiring contingent faculty does not create safe environments for faculty to acknowledge their fears and concerns, urging the need to interrogate how such structural vulnerability affects experiences of online teaching. Because the culture of academia rarely rewards or privileges teaching innovations, faculty are more incentivized to maintain the status quo without devoting a time-consuming effort to improve their online teaching skills at the expense of pursuing research and scholarship. The implications of this study call for researchers to move beyond competency-based assessment, and consider addressing the affective and identity disruption variables specific to the nature of academia involved and how they relate to faculty readiness to teach online.

Theme Discussion

By focusing on the underlying, perception-informed factors that influence faculty online teaching readiness, we hope to highlight the important role of faculty's attitudes and beliefs, particularly the emotions and vulnerabilities in the transition to online teaching. Due to the non-transferable teaching skills from in-person to online, lack of confidence in online pedagogical skills seems to cause identity disruption among faculty where their status seems to shift from being an expert to a novice (Cutri & Mena, 2020; Downing & Dyment, 2013; Phan & Dang, 2017). It is also found that fear and vulnerability are well-experienced emotions among faculty in the transition to online teaching online (Cutri & Mena, 2020; Phan & Dang, 2017). Finally, given the structural and cultural factors in academia, faculty are disincentivized to devote time to online teaching innovation.

Our review of the attitudes and beliefs emphasized the importance of paying attention to individual needs and tailoring pedagogical training and support accordingly. The help of online learning support systems and well-trained instructional designers can help make for a more productive environment for online teaching readiness. For university decision-makers, evidence from previous work shows that it is critical to acknowledge faculty's emotions and beliefs in the online teaching transition and provide appropriate structural support. This can be enhanced by taking a more flexible approach that rewards teaching innovation as well as addresses individual needs as they get identified (Cutri & Mena, 2020; Downing & Dyment, 2013; Phan & Dang, 2017).

DISCUSSIONS AND CONCLUSIONS

To explore factors that contribute to and hinder faculty online teaching readiness, this literature review explores themes of competency-based measurement and teaching beliefs and attitudes in online teaching readiness. It addresses the research questions on factors that contribute to and hinder faculty online teaching readiness and areas of support universities can focus on in improving faculty online teaching readiness. Although we attempt to pinpoint and address such issues with details, we must note that factors that contribute to faculty online teaching readiness vary from context to context at both personal and institutional levels. Fear and vulnerability towards a new teaching identity in online education, inadequate institutional support on technology and online teaching pedagogy, and the disconnect between online teaching excellence and faculty ranking advancement and reward are found to be factors hindering faculty online teaching readiness. Policy makers and administrators in higher education institutions may consider providing not only technology and pedagogy support to online teaching faculty but also fostering a supportive environment that motivates faculty to excel in online teaching by rewarding innovation in online teaching and addressing individual needs. Future research can further our understanding of online teaching readiness by pursuing a fine-grained exploration of the different categories of readiness. Further, future work could benefit from taking a qualitative approach to investigate the relationship between prior teaching experience and online teaching readiness, for which the quantitative results we reviewed above showed conflicting patterns.

RECOMMENDATIONS FOR A NEW FRAMEWORK

Based on the findings of this review chapter, and integrating the findings from a comprehensive set of studies conducting in the last decade, we present a new faculty readiness framework: Interrelated Model of Online Teaching Readiness (IMOTR).

Figure 1. Interrelated Model of Online Teaching Readiness (IMOTR)

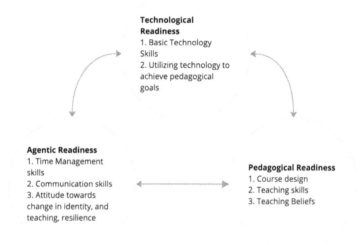

Interrelated Model of Online Teaching Readiness (IMOTR)

In this model, we address the importance of contextual readiness, which incubates the environment for faculty to excel their online teaching readiness. Contextual readiness at institutional-level speaks to whether institutions provide tailored at-elbow technological and pedagogical support. Since faculty are not a homogenous group, relevant training programs should be designed based on specific needs and focus on the skills faculty perceive as the least confident and skillful. To evaluate such specific needs, institutions should consider surveying the interrelated dimensions of online teaching readiness at the personal level.

As institutions in certain regions of the world move strategically to online education, access to technology devices and the internet should be ensured to provide faculty with the basic, prerequisite accessibility needs. Such access is fundamental and critical to the success of online teaching. In addition, a motivating structure within institutions that reward faculty who shift to online teaching and seek online teaching innovation will contribute to the success of online teaching more broadly. Given the time-consuming nature of online teaching, rewarding faculty's innovation in online teaching is a crucial step towards creative incentive and avoiding burnout. Higher education administrators and policy makers should reconsider expectations and milestones in ranking and career advancement, and the time and efforts dedicated to creating online versions of in-person courses should be recognized and taken into consideration. In addition to reimagining the academic culture in terms of career advancement, it must be noted that, based on previous work, leadership and colleagues' positive attitude toward online teaching has the power to create a culture that motivates more faculty to implement and innovate in online teaching.

At the personal level, technological, pedagogical, and agentic readiness are interrelated and contribute to the success of one another. Factors that contribute to technological readiness include not only the basic technology skills (e.g., using computer, downloading/uploading files, editing a page in Learning Management System, etc.), but also the advanced skills such as aligning the use of technology to enhance teaching and designing interactive web-based learning experiences to achieve predetermined pedagogical goals. When evaluating pedagogical readiness, two stages in the cycle of an online course should be considered: course design stage and teaching stage. Skills and relevant support expected during these two stages are somewhat different, with the teaching stage needing a heavier focus on communication skills and utilizing technologies that support faculty online teaching presence, giving timely feedback to students, and staying connected with their students. For course design stage, faculty are in need of training in comprehensive instructional design knowledge and support in shifting teaching approaches from teacher-centered to learner-centered (Zgheib et al., 2023). Specific training programs should focus on enhancing faculty ability to organize materials into modules or units, write measurable learning objectives, design active and interactive learning activities, design accessible materials that accommodate students' needs, follow the fair use guidelines under the copyright law, design assignments with clear grading criteria, and create online course orientation. Given the time-consuming nature of course design, institutions should also consider giving faculty flexible time and space to maintain a balance between their teaching and research. Teaching beliefs and the affective factors associated with change in teaching beliefs are also critical topics to be addressed in faculty development and training programs to support faculty with a successful and confident transition to online teaching.

Factors that contribute to agentic readiness include time management and communication skills, which are relevant to the success of pedagogical and technological readiness. Other than providing technical support in training faculty on how to utilize technology for communicating with students in a timely manner, technological and pedagogical support are needed to help faculty understand the evolving features of learning management systems and provide the forms of feedback in a way that is helpful to students. When shifting to online teaching, support for agentic readiness may focus on guidance in how to adapt and be resilient to such change in the context of significant identity disruption.

Excelling technological skills by mastering the features and purpose of technologies contributes to pedagogical readiness, further enhancing the teaching goals with the support of technologies. Being pedagogically ready to teach online allows faculty to teach in a learner-centered approach, and adjust and adapt their communication with students in a timely manner, the latter being an essential part of agentic readiness. Being resilient and ready to adapt to change—being agentic ready—motivates faculty to master their skills in technology and continue seeking ways to simulate an interactive learning experience online for their students.

What we hope to highlight by presenting this model is that the different categories of readiness cannot be examined in isolation; rather, they are interrelated and each category feeds into the others, with the success in one category enhancing success in the others, and the failure in one category contributing to failure in the others.

REFERENCES

Akram, H., Abdelrady, A. H., Al-Adwan, A. S., & Ramzan, M. (2022). Teachers' perceptions of technology integration in teaching-learning practices: A systematic review. *Frontiers in Psychology*, 13, 920317. DOI: 10.3389/fpsyg.2022.920317 PMID: 35734463

Allen, I. E., & Seaman, J. (2016). *Online report card: Tracking online education in the United States*. Babson Survey Research Group and Quahog Research Group., Retrieved from http://onlinelearningsurvey.com/reports/onlinereportcard.pdf

Badiozaman, I. F. A. (2021). Exploring online readiness in the context of the COVID 19 pandemic. *Teaching in Higher Education*, •••, 1–19. DOI: 10.1080/13562517.2021.1943654

Bolliger, D. U., & Halupa, C. (2022). An Investigation of Instructors' Online Teaching Readiness. *TechTrends*, 66(2), 185–195. DOI: 10.1007/s11528-021-00654-0 PMID: 34485992

Borotis, S., & Poulymenakou, A. (2004). E-Learning Readiness Components: Key Issues to Consider Before Adopting e-Learning Interventions. In J. Nall & R. Robson (Eds.), *Proceedings of E-Learn 2004--World Conference on E-Learning in Corporate, Government, Healthcare, and Higher Education*. 1622–1629. Washington, DC, USA: Association for the Advancement of Computing in Education (AACE). Retrieved September 3, 2023 from https://www.learntechlib.org/primary/p/11555/

Cavanaugh, J. (2005). Teaching online: A time comparison. *Online Journal of Distance Learning Administration*, 3(1), •••. http://www.westga.edu/~distance/oj

Chigeza, P., & Halbert, K. (2014). Navigating e-learning and blended learning for pre-service teachers: Redesigning for engagement, access and efficiency. *The Australian Journal of Teacher Education*, 39(11), 133–146. https://eric.ed.gov/?id=EJ1047088. DOI: 10.14221/ajte.2014v39n11.8

Cutri, R. M., & Mena, J. (2020). A critical reconceptualization of faculty readiness for online teaching. *Distance Education*, 41(3), 361–380. DOI: 10.1080/01587919.2020.1763167

Cutri, R. M., Mena, J., & Whiting, E. F. (2020). Faculty readiness for online crisis teaching: Transitioning to online teaching during the COVID-19 pandemic. *European Journal of Teacher Education*, 43(4), 523–541. DOI: 10.1080/02619768.2020.1815702

Downing, J. J., & Dyment, J. E. (2013). Teacher educators' readiness, preparation, and perceptions of preparing preservice teachers in a fully online environment: An exploratory study. *Teacher Educator*, 48(2), 96–109. DOI: 10.1080/08878730.2012.760023

Elewa, A. H., & mohamed, . (2022). Online teaching readiness, challenges and satisfaction as perceived by nursing faculty members during COVID-19 pandemics. *International Egyptian Journal of Nursing Sciences and Research*, 2(2), 568–579. DOI: 10.21608/ejnsr.2022.212573

Espasa, A., & Meneses, J. (2010). Analysing feedback processes in an online teaching and learning environment: An exploratory study. *Higher Education*, 59(3), 277–292. DOI: 10.1007/s10734-009-9247-4

Fernández, A., Gómez, B., Binjaku, K., & Meçe, E. K. (2023). Digital transformation initiatives in higher education institutions: A multivocal literature review. *Education and Information Technologies*, 28(10), 12351–12382. DOI: 10.1007/s10639-022-11544-0 PMID: 37361743

Gay, G. H. E. (2016). An assessment of online instructor e-learning readiness before, during, and after course delivery. *Journal of Computing in Higher Education*, 28(2), 199–220. DOI: 10.1007/s12528-016-9115-z

Henry, J., & Meadows, J. (2008). An absolutely riveting online course: Nine principles for excellence in web-based teaching. *Canadian Journal of Learning and Technology*, 34(1). Advance online publication. http://www.cjlt.ca/index.php/cjlt/index. DOI: 10.21432/T20C7F

Hosny, S., Ghaly, M., AlSheikh, M. H., Shehata, M. H., Salem, A. H., & Atwa, H. (2021). Developing, validating, and implementing a tool for measuring the readiness of medical teachers for online teaching post-COVID-19: A multicenter study. *Advances in Medical Education and Practice*, 12(755), 755–768. Advance online publication. DOI: 10.2147/AMEP.S317029 PMID: 34285628

Junus, K., Santoso, H. B., Putra, P. O. H., Gandhi, A., & Siswantining, T. (2021). Lecturer readiness for online classes during the pandemic: A survey research. *Education Sciences*, 11(3), 139. DOI: 10.3390/educsci11030139

Kim, S. Y., & Martin, F. (2023). Validation of the Faculty Readiness to Teaching Online (FRTO) scale. *Journal of Applied Research in Higher Education*, 23(3). Advance online publication. DOI: 10.1108/JARHE-03-2023-0108

Lakshmi, Y. V. (2021). eLearning Readiness of Higher Education Faculty Members. *Indian Journal of Educational Technology*, 3(2). https://ssrn.com/abstract=3970655

Lammers, W. J., & Gillaspy, J. A.Jr. (2013). Brief measure of student-instructor rapport predicts student success in online courses. *International Journal for the Scholarship of Teaching and Learning*, 7(2), 16. DOI: 10.20429/ijsotl.2013.070216

Lee, K. (2017). Rethinking the accessibility of online higher education: A historical review. *The Internet and Higher Education*, 33, 15–23. DOI: 10.1016/j.iheduc.2017.01.001

Lim, J. (2022). Impact of instructors' online teaching readiness on satisfaction in the emergency online teaching context. *Education and Information Technologies*, •••, 1–18. DOI: 10.1007/s10639-022-11241-y PMID: 36247026

Mandernach, B. J., Hudson, S., & Wise, S. (2013). Where has the time gone? Faculty activities and time commitments in the online classroom. *The Journal of Educators Online*, 10(2), 1–15. https://www.learn-techlib.org/p/114366/. DOI: 10.9743/JEO.2013.2.2

Martin, F., Budhrani, K., & Wang, C. (2019). Examining faculty perception of their readiness to teach online. *Online Learning : the Official Journal of the Online Learning Consortium*, 23(3), 97–119. DOI: 10.24059/olj.v23i3.1555

Martin, F., Wang, C., Jokiaho, A., May, B., & Grübmeyer, S. (2019). Examining Faculty Readiness to Teach Online: A Comparison of US and German Educators. *European Journal of Open. Distance and E-Learning*, 22(1), 53–69. DOI: 10.2478/eurodl-2019-0004

Paliwal, M., & Singh, A. (2021). Teacher readiness for online teaching-learning during COVID– 19 outbreak: A study of Indian institutions of higher education. *Interactive Technology and Smart Education*, 18(3), 403–421. Advance online publication. DOI: 10.1108/ITSE-07-2020-0118

Phan, T. T. N., & Dang, L. T. T. (2017). Teacher Readiness for Online Teaching: A Critical Review*. *International Journal on Open and Distance E-Learning*, 3(1). https://www.ijodel.com/index.php/ijodel/article/view/18

Roy, G., Babu, R., Abul Kalam, M., Yasmin, N., Zafar, T., & Nath, S. R. (2021). Response, readiness and challenges of online teaching amid COVID-19 pandemic: the case of higher education in Bangladesh. *Educational and Developmental Psychologist*, 1-11. https://doi.org/DOI: 10.1080/20590776.2021.1997066

Sadri, G. (1996). A Study of Agentic Self-Efficacy and Agentic Competence Across Britain and the USA. *Journal of Management Development*, 15(1), 51–61. DOI: 10.1108/02621719610107818

Scherer, R., Howard, S. K., Tondeur, J., & Siddiq, F. (2021). Profiling teachers' readiness for online teaching and learning in higher education: Who's ready? *Computers in Human Behavior*, 118, 1–16. DOI: 10.1016/j.chb.2020.106675

Scherer, R., Siddiq, F., Howard, S. K., & Tondeur, J. (2022). The more experienced, the better prepared? New evidence on the relation between teachers' experience and their readiness for online teaching and learning. *Computers in Human Behavior*, 139, 1–14. DOI: 10.1016/j.chb.2022.10753

Scherer, R., Siddiq, F., Howard, S. K., & Tondeur, J. (2023). Gender divides in teachers' readiness for online teaching and learning in higher education: Do women and men consider themselves equally prepared? *Computers & Education*, 199, 104774. DOI: 10.1016/j.compedu.2023.104774

Shea, P., Pickett, A., & Li, C. S. (2005). Increasing access to higher education: A study of the diffusion of online teaching among 913 college faculty. *International Review of Research in Open and Distance Learning*, 6(2), 1–27. DOI: 10.19173/irrodl.v6i2.238

Singh, V., & Thurman, A. (2019). How many ways can we define online learning? A systematic literature review of definitions of online learning (1988-2018). *American Journal of Distance Education*, 33(4), 289–306. DOI: 10.1080/08923647.2019.1663082

Stickney, L. T., Bento, R. F., Aggarwal, A., & Adlakha, V. (2019). Online higher education: Faculty satisfaction and its antecedents. *Journal of Management Education*, 43(5), 509–542. DOI: 10.1177/1052562919845022

Tayyib, N. A., Ramaiah, P., Alshmemri, M. S., Alsolami, F. J., Lind-say, G. M., Alsulami, S. A., & Asfour, H. I. (2020). Faculty members' readiness implementing e-learning in higher education Saudi Universities: A cross-sectional study. *Indian Journal of Science and Technology*, 13(25), 2558–2564. DOI: 10.17485/IJST/v13i25.828

Wekerle, C., Daumiller, M., & Kollar, I. (2022). Using digital technology to promote higher education learning: The importance of different learning activities and their relations to learning outcomes. *Journal of Research on Technology in Education*, 54(1), 1–17. DOI: 10.1080/15391523.2020.1799455

Zgheib, G., Al Daia, R., & Serhan, M. (2023). A contextual approach for exploring faculty readiness to teach online. *Heliyon*, 9(10), e20491. Advance online publication. DOI: 10.1016/j.heliyon.2023.e20491 PMID: 37867860

Chapter 10
Understanding the Cognitive Constituents of E-Learning

Swati Sharma
https://orcid.org/0000-0001-7727-1675
Indian Institute of Technology, Jodhpur, India

Deepak Kumar Saxena
https://orcid.org/0000-0002-9331-3799
Indian Institute of Technology, Jodhpur, India

ABSTRACT

With the rapid development of ICT, E-learning has experienced exponential growth and drastic transformation in past years (Yao et al, 2022). E-learning works on the model of virtual education. There are different formats, like fully online learning, hybrid learning model which uses the combination of in-person and online components, and Massive Open Online Courses (MOOCs) which enable course engagement across the globe. The domain explores innovative pedagogical approaches. This chapter discusses various formats such as fully online courses, blended learning models, and Massive Open Online Courses (MOOCs). It explores innovative pedagogical approaches, popular theories and adaptive technologies to cater to diverse learning styles, based on cognitive science principles. Chapter further highlights e-learning, its growth and transformation due to advancements in Information and Communication Technology (ICT) and important theoretical frameworks to understand the various components of e-learning. At the end of this chapter, challenges and future research directions are discussed.

DOI: 10.4018/979-8-3693-4407-1.ch010

INTRODUCTION

E-learning or online learning is a dynamic field that includes a diverse set of educational activities and resources delivery systems using digital platforms. It works on the idea of making learning accessible beyond the constraints of traditional classrooms which made it popular among educators during the time of pandemic. Online learning works in different formats based on the vision and requirement of the course. Online classes were extensively used by schools and universities during the time of COVID-19 pandemic when all education institutes were closed (Wlodarczyk et al., 2021). Consequently, it became the primary teaching and learning approach (Anderson et al., 2020). This mode of learning saved the students from their academic loss. Different names have been used in literature discussing online learning such as e-learning, blended learning, virtual learning, remote education, online education, web-based education, web-based instruction and online courses (Singh and Thurman, 2019). In fully online format, learning is dependent only on online platform content delivery. It can be a real-time class or a recorded lecture. Hybrid learning models use both in-person and online components for the delivery of content. Fully online learning involves synchronous or asynchronous classes conducted entirely over the internet, while hybrid online learning combines both online and onsite teaching, engaging students in both environments simultaneously (Mark et al, 2022). Research indicates that fully online courses can effectively maintain student performance, as seen in graduate microbiology coursework where students performed similarly across various online modalities(Davie, 2022). Massive Open Online Courses (MOOCs) is another popular format of e-learning. They have made their own mark in the domain of popular methods of online learning using both computer systems and mobile devices (Fidalgo-Blanco et al, 2016). These courses allow people from all over the world to participate, irrespective of their geological location and time. This mode of e-learning increases the feasibility of accessing the content of learning at learner's flexibility and offers ease of use to participants. MOOCs are not just for school or university students, they are open to everyone. The domain of e-learning is continuously evolving. With each passing year, new teaching methods are being developed. The flexibility of the online presence makes it easy to use for learners. Anyone from any age group can start learning at any moment from the comfort of their home. It uses engaging multimedia content and advanced technologies that serve different participants and their learning styles. It has also become a great online medium for different skill development and hobby classes. Online learning has removed the constraint of geographical boundaries (Yu, 2022). All you need is a laptop, tablet, or mobile phone with a stable internet connection. You can access quality lectures on any domain or topic, have advanced vocational training to enhance your career profile, and use it for your skill development anywhere in the world. Online learning is constantly evolving with improvements in learning management systems. It offers personalized instruction using digital media. It also utilizes state-of-the-art technologies like AR-VR (Petersen et al., 2023) and AI (Segundo et al., 2022) to provide a better user experience. In today's world, where digital tools are an essential part of our education systems, online learning is constantly evolving, challenging the ways we share, learn, and apply knowledge in our connected, tech-savvy society. E-learning has become a powerful tool for customized learning and training, which is readily accessible for education and professional development on-demand within organizations. Advancements in e-learning, like MOOCs, have gained attention for their potential to change traditional education. MOOCs provide widespread access to content created by well-known educators. If we talk about renowned institutions that came forward to support MOOCs in its initial days then MIT has its name on top. Now in 2023, almost 3,5 million learners registered on MIT MOOCs platform (Cagiltay et al., 2023). However, initial excitement surrounding the technology has been mild down by questions raised by research. The comparison with face-to-face classrooms has also affected the initial buzz. It has also been observed that fewer participants complete the course than the number of participants that register for the course. Attainment of learning outcomes is also a challenge in MOOCs and other modes of e-learning. Sustained attention is a cognitive skill essential for learners to maintain focus during the lecture. It is essential to control impulses and ignore distractions for better learning and performance of participants. Those learners who can sustain attention on learning tasks are more likely to process and encode information effectively. It leads to better memory retention and recall of events and information. It is important to customize the learning resources according to the cognitive inclinations of different students to improve the efficiency of the learning process. Many research studies revealed that e-learning can offer positive learning experiences for participants (Arbaugh, 2014; Eom et al., 2016). Also, some research suggests that learners express higher satisfaction with e-learning compared to traditional face-to-face instruction. However, contradicting findings exist, as certain studies propose that online learning falls short in terms of satisfaction and that learners exhibit lower engagement levels in comparison to face-to-face learning. The potential reasons for diminished engagement and satisfaction are attributed to inadequacies in course design and pedagogical approaches in the online learning environment. Due to the different opinions among researchers, there is a crucial need for a systematic and thorough understanding of the cognitive aspects of e-learning. Therefore, this chapter aims to explore the role of sustained attention and video lecture styles frequently used. It also sheds light on concepts like cognitive load and learning styles in E-learning setups.

The focus of this chapter is to illustrate the history of e-learning, how it grew to its current stage and developments in the field due to advancements in Information and Communication Technology (ICT). Chapter will also focus on popular theories to understand the cognitive components of e-learning. It will highlight multiple formats of e-learning, such as fully online courses, blended learning models, and Massive Open Online Courses (MOOCs). It will explore the research on different innovative pedagogical approaches, which are helpful for offering diverse learning styles based on cognitive science principles. Additionally, this chapter looks into the potential reasons for the said skepticism about e-learning which was on the boom for its potential to revolutionize education. It will look into different cognitive components that are important for effective learning in an online learning environment. It will also discuss the role of sustained attention in e-learning as a fundamental cognitive function that is the basis for learning and memory.

The chapter will also focus on methodologies for assessing the sustained attention in e-learning and discuss various approaches that can be applied to evaluate and understand it. Further, two theoretical frameworks are discussed that are important to understand the use of multimedia in e-learning setup. They are extensively used to offer design guidelines for creating educationally effective learning material. Toward the end, the chapter discusses the need for comprehensive research on how different cognitive components can impact student performance in online setups and can be used to enhance learning outcomes.

Background

The pandemic gave rise to the adoption and utilization of online learning formats across the globe due to the widespread closure of educational institutions to avoid the spread of the COVID-19 virus (Saleem et al., 2022). Educational institutions quickly turned toward digital platforms to ensure the continuity of education. This abrupt change led to a remarkable increase in the use of virtual classrooms, video conferencing, and e-learning management systems. The pandemic forced educators and learners to adapt to new modes of instruction and learning. Online learning became essential for schools, universities, professional development, vocational training, and skill enhancement. While the pandemic triggered this surge in online learning, the idea of online learning can trace its roots back to the 1960s. The concept of using digital platforms for learning and training emerged with the beginning of computer-based training (CBT). It involved using early computer systems to deliver instructional content. The actual growth of online learning platforms began in the 1990s when the internet became more accessible. The development of web-based technologies and platforms enabled the usage of virtual classrooms based on online format and allowed the dispersion of course materials using digital media.

The earliest online courses didn't involve video and audio components and mostly relied on text-based content delivery and primarily used for higher education and professional development. As internet connectivity improved and multimedia capabilities expanded, online learning became more interactive and engaging, paving the way for the diverse and dynamic online learning experiences we see today. The concept of Massive Open Online Courses (MOOCs) began to take shape in the early 2000s, but the first MOOC course, as it is understood today, was offered in 2008. The first online course was hosted on the University of Manitoba's learning management system and later on the newly created platform, "Ustream". George Siemens and Stephen Downes were two theorists who became the first ones to design and teach an online course. It was called "Connectivism and Connective Knowledge". The course explored the principles of Connectivism. It is a learning theory that emphasizes the role of networks and connections in the learning process in the digital age. The course was open to everyone who was interested in learning its content. It attracted a large number of participants from around the world and set the way for the MOOC movement that followed (Nguyen, 2022). This course is considered the first MOOC. However, the term "MOOC" was proposed in 2008 by Dave Cormier. He was part of the team that organized the course. The first successful MOOC course that gained widespread attention and helped popularize the MOOC movement was "Artificial Intelligence," offered by Stanford University in 2011. The course was taught by renowned professors Sebastian Thrun and Peter Norvig. The initial enrollment for the "Artificial Intelligence" course was around 160,000 students worldwide. It was a groundbreaking number at that time. The massive enrollment and global reach of the course attracted significant media coverage. It brought the concept of MOOCs to the forefront of discussions about the future of education. Learners who can sustain attention on learning tasks are more likely to process and encode information effectively, leading to better memory retention and recall (Mrazek et al. 2013). Numerous research studies indicate that online learning can offer a multitude of positive learning experiences for participants (Arbaugh, 2014). Additionally, there is evidence suggesting that learners express higher satisfaction with online learning compared to traditional face-to-face instruction. However, conflicting findings exist, as certain studies propose that online learning falls short in terms of satisfaction and that learners exhibit lower engagement levels in comparison to face-to-face learning. The potential reasons for diminished engagement and satisfaction are attributed to inadequacies in course design and pedagogical approaches in the online learning environment (Yu Q 2022). Therefore, it is of significant importance that we understand the effects of sustained attention, cognitive load, and cognitive styles in online learning scenarios.

E-Learning - Transformation, Theoretical Frameworks and Cognitive Aspects

E-learning has evolved significantly over the past few decades, driven by advancements in ICT. Initially, e-learning was a novel approach to delivering education, promising greater accessibility and flexibility. Online education can be implemented in two modes, namely. Synchronous and Asynchronous e-learning. Both modes have different effects and implications for the study and implementation of digital learning environments. Synchronous e-learning is based on utilizing a real-time platform to provide an interactive environment between teacher and students. This is implemented through live video based online sessions, with chat facility, where participants can engage simultaneously during the lecture. Key Features of synchronous e-learning includes real-time communication, learner and teacher can communicate in real-time, similar to a traditional classroom setting, Immediate Feedback: Learners can ask questions and receive immediate answers, Scheduled Sessions: Classes are held at specific times, requiring all participants to be online simultaneously. On the other hand, without interacting with peers or teachers in real time, asynchronous e-learning enables students to access course materials, take part in conversations, and finish activities and tests at their own leisure. It provides flexibility to learners. Learners can access content and complete tasks at any time, accommodating different schedules and time zones. Students have the freedom to learn as it suits their schedule offering Self-paced Learning. Many researchers have compared synchronous and asynchronous e-learning to understand which modes of e-learning are more effective under different circumstances. The main focus of research studies has been on determining differences in learning outcomes and comparing academic performance for two modes. Student satisfaction, engagement, and participation are also being studied. Various formats for Asynchronous e-learning have emerged over time. Both synchronous and asynchronous learning can work with different models of e-learning. In the following segment, we will discuss fully online learning model, a Hybrid learning model, and Massive Open Online Courses (MOOCs).

1. **Fully Online Learning Model:** In this model, lectures are dispersed in the form of videos and text through digital platforms. Online chat sessions or live discussions are offered for interaction between learner and instructor. This modality is characterized by 100% online delivery, utilizing asynchronous or synchronous formats (Gavassa et al., 2019). Virtual classes are conducted using video conferencing platforms. This model provides flexibility to attend the lecture and use learning content from any location with internet access. However, this format also demands a high degree of self-discipline and time management

from learners. Fully online learning model can work with live classes with the use of video conferencing as well as pre-recorded lectures share with learners through learning management system.

2. **Hybrid Learning Model:** This model offers the flexibility of mixing the online instructional model with traditional methods of face-to-face instruction and assessment. This model utilizes the capability of both online and in-person instruction. It offers a balanced approach that can enhance engagement and learning outcomes. Hybrid learning models often include synchronous and asynchronous elements. It provides opportunities for real-time interaction and self-paced study. The benefit of hybrid models is that it allows learners to have a regular in-person interaction with instructors which help them to feel connected. It also gives a sense of reliability and trust in learners. Hybrid learning integrates both online and in-person elements, facilitating synchronous participation from both remote and onsite students(Mark et al., 2022)(Raes et al., 2020). Studies show that hybrid formats can enhance engagement and flexibility, often leading to improved academic outcomes for underrepresented student groups compared to traditional face-to-face classes(Gavassa et al., 2019).

3. **Massive Open Online Courses (MOOCs):** MOOCs are online courses developed to deliver content across the globe. It allows learners to access learning and training from institutions far away while being at home. Many renowned universities are now offering MOOCs around the world. It is generally offered free and can be accessed by any learner who has a digital device and stable web connectivity. It has democratized education by making high-quality learning resources available globally. Many popular organizations and universities are developing their own MOOC platforms. Despite their potential, MOOCs face challenges such as low completion rates and the need for more personalized learning experiences. Many researchers have shown concerns regarding the design aspects of MOOCs which fail to keep learners engaged.

Theoretical Frameworks in E-Learning

Domain of e-learning has borrowed concepts and theories from psychology and cognitive science to see and understand the process of E-learning. It is important to look from the lens of cognitive science to have a clearer picture of various aspects of e-learning. Researchers have based their arguments on multiple theories to make assertions about the process of learning in an online environment. Two theoretical frameworks discussed below are particularly relevant to the use of multimedia in online learning setups. These frameworks offer design guidelines for creating educationally effective content.

1. **Cognitive Load Theory (CLT):** This theory was proposed by Chandler and Sweller in 1991 (Chandler & Sweller, 1991). CLT highlights the importance of reducing the cognitive load in order to maximize learning effectiveness and the limitations of working memory. Theory states that multimedia content should reduce cognitive burden and maximize working memory utilization. It is a concept within educational psychology that focuses on the mental effort involved in learning. It is an influential framework in instructional design and learning theory. The theory suggests that The ability of the human cognitive system to process information is finite and resources are limited. When individuals learn new material, their cognitive resources are allocated to various tasks, such as understanding new concepts, processing information, and storing it in memory. However, if the cognitive load becomes too high, learning can be impaired. CLT differentiates various cognitive load as follows:
   a. **Intrinsic Cognitive Load:** This conveys about the intrinsic complicated nature of the subject matter being studied. Because of their intrinsic complexity, certain concepts are more difficult to understand than others or are in abstract nature.
   b. **Extraneous Cognitive Load:** Refers to the load that's caused by how learning material is shown or the learning environment. Poorly designed instructional materials or unnecessary distractions can add to the additional cognitive load, making it harder to concentrate on the essential content.
   c. **Germane Cognitive Load:** This cognitive load is closely associated with the process of learning and comprehending the subject matter. It includes the mental effort required to arrange and incorporate fresh data into preexisting knowledge frameworks.

Research has established that different cognitive styles may influence how learners handle cognitive load at the time of attempting to learn. For example, students who focus more on visual information may find it easier to comprehend information presented through images or diagrams. It reduces extraneous cognitive load for them. CLT asserts that effective learning occurs when the total cognitive load (intrinsic, extraneous, and germane) is balanced. Educators can apply CLT principles while designing instructional material. It will optimize learning environments by reducing extraneous cognitive load. Also, it will provide support for managing intrinsic load. It can promote strategies that facilitate the transfer of information into long-term memory. The idea is to break up difficult tasks and concepts into smaller chunks of information which are easy to manage. It offers guidance during learning activities, and minimizes distractions in the learning environment. In this way, educators can help learners to maximize their cognitive resources and improve learning outcomes. A 2023 study, grounded within the cognitive learning paradigm, delineates the creation and evaluation of a linked list visualization software tool, grounded in the Split Attention effect of Cognitive Load Theory. The incorporation of spatial and temporal linked list node representations, along with the relevant example code for implementing basic operations, can assist students with learning deficiencies from prior beginning programming courses (Arevalo-Mercado et al, 2023). In a separate study, researchers evaluated the effect of utilizing preparatory online modules for weekly pre-briefing content on cognitive load and performance. The subjects were first-year postgraduate medical trainees, and their cognitive load (intrinsic, extraneous, and germane) was assessed using a modified cognitive load questionnaire (Gutierrez et al., 2023). Balamurugan et al. devised a brain-computer interface to collect data and assess a learner's cognitive state by monitoring MOOC videos and utilizing electroencephalogram (EEG) devices, grounded in John Sweller's Cognitive Load Theory. The framework was validated utilizing three machine learning algorithms (random forest with a non-Markovian model, support vector machine, and k-nearest neighbors) to construct a model with preprocessed training data and evaluate the classifiers to assess the effectiveness of their ensemble classifiers. Balamurugan et al., 2020. A study in China employed cognitive load theory as its theoretical framework to examine the expertise reversal effect on the simultaneous learning of English and Mathematics. The research aimed to determine whether an integrated approach—learning both subjects concurrently—could enhance the acquisition of mathematical skills and English as a foreign language more effectively and efficiently than a segregated learning approach, which involves studying each subject separately. The expertise reversal effect was confirmed: the integrated learning technique for English and Mathematics was more effective for learners with higher knowledge, but the separated learning condition was more advantageous for those with lower expertise (Jiang et al, 2023). Caskurlu and his team conducted a case study on instructional designers, concluding that these professionals regard CLT design methodologies as a factor enhancing online course quality (Caskurlu et al, 2020).

2. **Cognitive Theory of Multimedia Learning (CTML)**: The use of multimedia components is essential for e-learning to make it interactive. However, how they affect human cognition is also crucial to understand. Cognitive theory of multimedia learning is an important theory which is the basis of understanding the usage of multimedia for learning process in online setup. It was developed by Richard Mayer in 2001. This theory asserts that multimedia and graphics produce information in the form of verbal and visual data chunks in the brain that integrate with previous knowledge to build the basis for new knowledge (Mayer, 2001). This framework explains how people learn from multimedia presentations. It focuses on the cognitive processes involved when individuals engage with multimedia materials, such as text, images, audio, and video. It

provides guidelines for designing the learning content. It emphasizes the importance of designing multimedia presentations in a way that aligns with how the human cognitive system processes information. CTMLs focuses on how multimedia can enhance learning by leveraging dual-channel processing (visual and auditory). Key principles of CTML include:

a. Dual Coding: This principle suggests that presenting information using both visual and verbal channels can enhance learning. When information is presented in a multimedia format that combines text with relevant images or animations, learners can process the information using both the verbal and visual channels, leading to better comprehension and retention.

b. Multimedia Redundancy: Mayer suggests that presentation of the same chunk of information using more than one modalities (e.g., video, audio and graphical) can be redundant and may actually increase cognitive load without improving learning outcomes. According to this principle, designers should avoid unnecessary duplication of information across different modalities.

c. Spatial Contiguity: This principle emphasizes the importance of spatially integrating corresponding words and images. When relevant text and visuals are presented close to each other on the screen, learners can more easily integrate the information, leading to better understanding.

d. Temporal Contiguity: Similar to spatial contiguity, temporal contiguity suggests that corresponding words and images should be presented simultaneously rather than sequentially. When learners see and hear relevant information at the same time, they can better connect the verbal and visual representations, facilitating learning.

e. Coherence: Coherence refers to the organization and structure of multimedia presentations. According to Mayer, multimedia materials should be logically organized and coherent, with clear connections between different elements. Well-organized presentations help learners build mental models of the material, leading to better comprehension.

Above mentioned principles can be applied to learning material in order to make them more understandable and effective. Instructors can use them as guidelines for more effective learning. Mayer's theory has been influential in the field of educational technology and instructional design. It has been proved as an effective framework for the development of multimedia learning environments and materials. A meta-analysis study based on CTML has been conducted recentlyto examine the ideal design characteristics of computer-assisted instruction for children with reading challenges for their decoding/word reading and reading comprehension performance. A comprehensive study was conducted on 49 experimental papers utilizing Bayesian network meta-analysis. Their findings indicate that various combinations of design characteristics in CAI programs may produce distinct impacts. Reducing students' cognitive burdens by excluding extraneous content may be fundamental in creating successful computer instructions for kids with reading challenges (Yan et al, 2024).

The Cognitive Theory of Multimedia Learning (CTML) provides essential guidance for instructional material designers seeking to improve learning experiences. By implementing its principles, designers can produce more efficient multimedia resources that address varied student requirements. Effective instructional content must integrate multimedia, coherence, signaling, spatial and temporal contiguity, segmenting, pre-training, modality, customization, engaging voice, embodiment, and generative activity to optimize learning (Mayer, 2021).

Key Design Principles

1. **Manage Cognitive Load:** Instructional materials should minimize extraneous cognitive load by focusing on essential information and avoiding unnecessary complexity(Ge & Lai, 2021).
2. **Segment Content:** Break longer videos into manageable parts to facilitate understanding, especially for audiences like the elderly who may experience cognitive decline(Muñoz & Letouzé, 2022).
3. **Use Visuals Effectively:** Incorporate graphics and animations that complement verbal information, enhancing retention and understanding(Ge & Lai, 2021).
4. **Interactive Elements:** Integrate questions and prompts within multimedia lessons to promote active engagement and generative learning(Cavanagh & Kiersch, 2022).

While CTML provides a robust framework, it is essential to consider its limitations, particularly regarding accessibility for learners with disabilities. Alternative frameworks may be necessary to ensure inclusivity in multimedia learning environments.

Cognitive Load Theory (CLT) and the Cognitive Theory of Multimedia Learning (CTML) offer valuable insights for e-learning, yet they face significant limitations in the context of technology. These limitations primarily stem from the challenges of measuring cognitive load, the complexity of digital environments, and the evolving nature of learner interactions.

1. **Measurement Challenges:** Traditional methods for measuring cognitive load are often indirect and subjective, which can lead to inaccuracies in understanding how multimedia affects learning(Brünken et al., 2003). New approaches, such as dual-task methodologies, aim to provide direct measurements but are still in development(Brünken et al., 2003).

2. **Design Complexity:** Digital learning environments introduce extraneous cognitive load through interactive elements, which can sometimes enhance motivation but complicate the learning process(Skulmowski & Xu, 2021). The integration of multimedia can lead to cognitive overload if not designed carefully, as learners may struggle to manage competing information sources(Castro-Alonso et al., 2021).
3. **Evolving Learner Interactions:** The effectiveness of instructional strategies can vary based on learner expertise, with novice learners benefiting more from instructor-managed load, while experts may prefer self-managed approaches(Castro-Alonso et al., 2021). The rapid advancement of technology necessitates continuous adaptation of CLT and CTML principles, which may not always align with emerging digital learning trends(Sweller, 2020).

While CLT and CTML provide foundational frameworks for understanding cognitive processes in e-learning, their application must evolve to address the complexities introduced by technology and learner variability.

Cognitive Load and Cognitive/learning Style

Memory is an integral part of human cognition. It is the feature which allows retention of information According to Sweller et al. (1998), limited working memory is the most important feature of human cognitive architecture. It is the basis of all functions. Therefore, a cognitive load analysis for working memory should be performed on all instructional designs in order to find their suitability to the brain. According to educational research, it is more important to take into account each learner's unique learning style than to use the same teaching approach with every student (Dunn & Griggs, 2000). It is critical to acknowledge learners' unique learning methods while learners interact with video lectures. Robert J. Sternberg proposed the concept of "thinking styles" as part of his theory of mental self-government. It refers to individual differences in how people approach and engage in cognitive tasks. It includes their preferences for different approaches to handle problem-solving, decision-making, and information processing. According to Sternberg, thinking styles are shaped by cognitive processes, preferences, and strategies that learners utilize to manage and process chunks of information. These styles encompass various dimensions such as analytical thinking, practical thinking, creative thinking, and their combinations. Sternberg's theory suggests that understanding thinking styles can provide insights into how individuals approach different tasks, solve problems, and interact with their environment. The visualizer-verbalizer hypothesis is one of the important concepts to understand the cognitive styles related to multimedia learning that is especially crucial when considering individual differences in the use of video lectures for online learning. This is due to the fact that video lectures generally employ audio and video to concurrently provide slides, words, and pictures to students (Mayer & Massa, 2003). The process of making a video lecture is complex and requires careful organization and execution. Delivering the material of a video lecture requires an understanding of learning theories and their consequences for education (Ilioudi et al, 2013). Multimedia content should reduce cognitive burden and maximize working memory utilization. Working memory resources are limited, and complex visual and linguistic information must fight for them all. From a theoretical perspective, simultaneous presentation of information in visual and aural modalities might improve learning performance, especially in terms of retention and knowledge transfer. This is ascribed to learners who experience less cognitive strain and make the most use of their working memory. According to Mayer, when graphical animation and audio/video are integrated in learning content, students' performance on retention assessments typically improves more significantly than when material is provided just through text or simple narration. More research is necessary to determine how well these theories apply to multimedia presentations that take the form of lectures. Academic achievement can be predicted using thinking styles, and the theory of mental self-government (Sternberg, 1988) sheds light on people's preferred modes of thought in different contexts. Another study investigates how different evaluation techniques might favor distinct thinking styles and builds on research on thinking styles in the context of gifted education (Grigorenko et al, 1997). Lin et al. (2023) asserts that learning engagement levels and sustained attention were impacted by cognitive style, however had little effect from the type of video presentation. According to Zhang et al. (2002), thinking styles can influence students' academic performance. The importance of cognitive styles for individual learning, teacher-student relationships, and social behavior in educational settings is emphasized by Messick et al. (1984). A summary of the idea of cognitive styles, their historical significance, their effects on education and work performance, and the authors' own theory and research on the subject are given by Grigorenko & Sternberg (1997). It also covers how assessments of cognitive styles are developed and whether or not they are beneficial in learning environments. According to researchers, cognitive styles hold great potential for the future and can offer significant insights into the variations in performance among individuals.

Critical Factors for Learning Performance in E-Learning

Learning performance in e-learning refers to academic achievement of learners in an e-learning environment. There are many factors that influence learning performance including task-technology fit, student satisfaction, learning design, and course content support. Studies emphasize the importance of user-friendly interfaces, effective communication channels, collaboration, positive learning environments, and the impact of personalized feedback on reducing cognitive load and enhancing learning performance (Mohammed et al., 2024). Learning performance in e-learning setup is a multifaceted concept influenced by various factors and technologies that can be assessed and enhanced through data-driven approaches. It is evaluated to assess the effectiveness of the learning process. Some important factors from the cognitive front that affect learning are type of presentation and student's attention.

Types of Presentation style (Content delivery style)

Dispersion of knowledge is the core of learning. Video lectures are the most popular way of learning content distribution in an online learning environment. It is a complicated process. It can be impacted by a variety of factors, including complexity of content, user experience, learning preferences, and state of knowledge. Different video lecture formats include lecture capture, screencast with speech, voice-over presentation (Griffin et al., 2009), and picture-in-picture/slide which are frequently utilized in online learning environments.

1. Lecture Capture: In this technique, an on-going lecture is recorded for viewing online. Learners watch the video at their own convenience. Many MOOCs use recordings of lectures given in the past.
2. Voice-Over: In this type, specialized recording software such as Microsoft Producer or PowerCam are used. It synchronizes audio recordings of a lecture with accompanying PowerPoint slides. The instructor's image and lecture slides are displayed together with the instructor's voice, subtitles, and even flash animations.
3. Picture-in-Picture: In this method. In this technique, learners see an instructor's video on their screen. It uses PowerPoint slides, the instructor's voice, and a video/image of the instructor on the corner of the screen. It requires careful post-production work.
4. Voice-activated Screencasts: This technique mostly consists of handwritten lessons or code created and distributed via a tablet and digital pen, or screen sharing combined with a lecturer's audio narration. It is popularly used in courses that teach coding.

The empirical research on the effects of various video lecture formats on the effectiveness of online learning is very small. Ilioudi et al. (2013) examined the efficacy of lecture capture, voice lectures in Screencasts, and conventional paper book support for mathematics self-study in secondary education, among other limited studies. Their findings showed that for complicated subjects, lectures were more beneficial than books, and that lecture capture improved learning outcomes over alternative formats. Griffin et al. (2009) also evaluated the benefits of various video lecture formats, comparing asynchronous options utilized in pedagogy with synchronous PowerPoint slide presentations with a lecturer's voice. In terms of learning results, their research showed that the synchronous method performed better. Homer, Plass, and Blake (2008) looked into the effects of two different computer-based multimedia presentations: one included slides and a lecture video that was synced with the slides, and the other included just slides and an audio recording of the lecture. According to their research, adding video to PowerPoint slides caused a split-attention effect that increased cognitive load and might have a negative impact on learning outcomes.

Each video type offers unique advantages and challenges that influence learning outcomes. The differences between Lecture Capture, Voice-Over, Picture-in-Picture, and Voice-Activated Screencasts significantly impact student engagement, sustained attention, and instructional design in e-learning environments.

Lecture Capture (LC): Primarily consists of recordings of live lectures, which can enhance accessibility but may lead to passive viewing, reducing engagement(-Caglayan & Ustunluoglu, 2021).

Voice-Over: This format often lacks visual engagement, potentially diminishing sustained attention compared to more interactive formats(Kokoç et al., 2020).

Picture-in-Picture: Combines instructor presence with content, fostering higher engagement and learning performance, especially for students with varying attention levels(Kokoç et al., 2020).

Voice-Activated Screencasts: These can enhance interactivity and engagement by allowing students to control playback, promoting active learning(Kokoç et al., 2020).

While these formats vary in effectiveness, the integration of instructor presence, as seen in Picture-in-Picture, generally yields better engagement and learning outcomes, highlighting the importance of instructional design in e-learning. However, some students may prefer the flexibility of Lecture Capture, indicating a need for diverse approaches to cater to different learning preferences.

Additionally, researchers have the advantages of lecture capture for learners, including increased content comprehension, better understanding of difficult subjects, improved course note accuracy, and increased accessibility for individuals with physical disabilities and non-native English speakers. There was also a decrease in the number of clarification requests made by instructors. Chen and Wang (2011) investigated how different multimedia presentation techniques affected the feelings and academic performance of learners. They found out that video-based multimedia elements which have both audio and moving images produced better learning outcomes and made learners feel the most pleasant with respect to static text and image-based learning material. Furthermore, there was a decrease in the effectiveness of animated interaction-based multimedia resources that included interactive text and animated graphics to improve learning outcomes and emotional reaction.

In addition, Chen and Lin (2014) investigated the efficacy of distinct text display styles for mobile reading in a range of scenarios with the goal of improving reading comprehension, maintaining focus, and controlling cognitive load on small screens. It evaluated static, dynamic, and mixed-text types while participants walked, stood, and sat, using a two-factor experimental design. The findings showed that every text format had unique benefits and drawbacks, affecting reading comprehension, sustained attention, and cognitive load in various ways. Therefore, optimizing reading comprehension and attention or minimizing cognitive burden during mobile reading on small displays requires customizing text display forms to individual reading settings.

Although online instructional video lectures have advanced significantly in recent years, questions remain about their usefulness and learning potential (Ilioudi et al, 2013). Selecting the best sort of video lecture for individualized online learning would be substantially aided by assessing the effects of different formats on learning performance, mood, sustained attention, and cognitive load. The goal of this strategy is to maximize learning results in a self-directed learning environment.

E-Learning & Sustained Attention

Mackworth (1948) initially coined the study of sustained attention and tried to differentiate it from vigilance. Sustained attention serves as a fundamental cognitive function that forms the basis for other cognitive domains, including learning and memory (Fortenbaugh et al, 2017). It is responsible for how learners perceive, process, and retain information. Research in cognitive psychology and educational neuroscience has deeply explored the relationship between attention and learning. research has highlighted the significance of sustained attention for effective learning outcomes. Mrazek et al asserts the importance of attention control in learning. He suggests that learners who can sustain attention on learning tasks are more likely to process and encode information effectively. This leads to better memory retention and recall. The research also examines the phenomenon of "mind-wandering," which refers to the spontaneous shifts of attention away from the primary task. Research discusses how mind-wandering can interfere with learning and hinder optimal cognitive performance (Mrazek et al. 2013). Attention is a fundamental cognitive process that underlies successful learning and memory. The ability to direct and sustain attention on learning tasks is critical for consolidating the information into long-term memory. Whereas, mind-wandering can be defined as lapses of attention that can impede learning. It reduces the overall cognitive performance. Recent research has emphasized that sustained attention is dynamic rather than static. There can be variations in attention evident within the general population and throughout an individual's lifetime. Recent behavioral studies have aimed to describe the trends in sustained attention across the individual's lifespan. Fortenbaugh et al (2015) have done a web-based study which involved more than 10,000 participants. Subjects undertook the gradCPT task. Results of the study revealed that sustained attention skills undergo development from childhood through young adulthood and do not display age-related declines until around the mid-40s. In another study, Chen and Lin (2014) found that their brain activity related to attention during the reading process showed the highest level of sustained attention when participants were sitting in comparison to when they were standing or walking. As indicated by the earlier research, attention can be examined from various viewpoints, encompassing shifting attention (Wager et al., 2004), sustained attention (Chen & Lin, 2014), and selective attention (Driver, 2001). The capacity for sustained attention is a predictor of academic proficiency evaluated in group-based, realistic school environments, contrasting with previous studies utilizing individualized assessments (Gallen et. al., 2023). Sarter et al. (2001) outlined that sustained attention can be characterized as the individual's preparedness to detect rare and unpredictable signals over extended periods. Research shows that learners who can sustain attention on learning tasks are more likely to process information effectively. This leads to better memory retention and recall. It is crucial to design and personalize learning resources customized according to learners, considering their specific needs and cognitive variations to optimize the efficiency of learning.

Role of Attention in E-Learning

The effectiveness of students' learning is often impacted by their sustained attention during instruction. Liu et al. (2013) highlighted how sustained attention of learners affected their learning process. The success of e-learning based lectures hugely depends on a learner's capacity of paying attention. It may be that we lacked an accurate method of measuring attention in the past that the connection between attention and the effectiveness of e-learning has only lately come into focus. A lot of the studies on attention and information systems in general (or in e-learning specifically) have been based on behavioral or self-report. There is a connection between academic accomplishments and the heightened attention during the learning process, as indicated by Lin et al. (2022). Sumardani et al (2023) asserts that Reading activity has a higher attention level than VR learning due to cognitive overload caused by the many learning modalities in VR learning. The study of attention involves various forms, including visual attention, feature attention, and their role in guiding learning and memory. Attention plays a key role in directing learning to relevant components and relationships in the input (Lindsay, 2020).

Methodologies to Assess Role of Attention in E-learning

There is a dire need of assessing sustained attention, due to its impact on the learner's performance and learning outcomes. Various tools and techniques are used by researchers to evaluate sustained attention for different scientific studies. However, methodologies for assessing sustained attention in e-learning may not have been extensively documented in academic literature. Here are some general approaches and considerations for assessing sustained attention in the context of e-learning.

1. **Continuous Performance Tests (CPTs):** CPTs are commonly used in psychological assessments to evaluate sustained attention. In the context of e-learning, tasks can be designed to simulate real-world scenarios where learners need to maintain focus on a given online lecture or study material for an extended period. This could involve responding to stimuli or tasks presented at regular intervals.

    Limitations: Continuous Performance Tests (CPTs) are widely used to assess attention, but their limitations in the e-learning context are significant. These limitations stem from issues related to diagnostic utility, reliability, and specificity. While CPTs can differentiate between ADHD and non-ADHD groups, findings are inconsistent, suggesting they should not be used in isolation for diagnosis(Varela et al., 2024). Research indicates that while response time scores on CPTs may be reliable, performance accuracy and variability often lack stability, which is crucial for e-learning assessments. The presence of co-occurring disorders complicates the interpretation of CPT results, as multiple conditions can lead to similar performance impairments(Riccio & Reynolds, 2006). CPTs are sensitive to various central nervous system dysfunctions, which can lead to false positives in diagnosing ADHD, particularly in e-learning environments where attention may be affected by external factors(Riccio & Reynolds, 2006). In contrast, some argue that CPTs can still provide valuable insights when used as part of a comprehensive assessment strategy, particularly in identifying attention deficits in specific contexts, such as distinguishing ADHD from depressive symptoms(Mesquita et al., 2016).
2. **Eye-Tracking Technology:** Utilizing eye gaze to determine sustained attention is one of the most accurate methods. For this, eye-tracking devices can be employed to monitor learners' gaze patterns. It assesses their attention to specific elements on the screen. Analyzing eye movement can provide insights into the duration and frequency of attention to different regions of the e-learning interface.

Limitations: Eye-tracking technology offers valuable insights into sustained attention in e-learning contexts, but it also has notable limitations. These limitations can impact the effectiveness of assessments and the interpretation of data. Traditional eye-tracking methods often focus on static objects, which may not accurately reflect attention in dynamic e-learning environments where content frequently changes(Kim et al., 2020). Gaze Synchrony is also a challenge. While gaze synchrony can indicate attention levels, its correlation with learning outcomes is inconsistent. Studies show that while synchronized gaze may suggest attentiveness, it does not always predict academic performance(Bühler et al., 2024)(Sauter et al., 2023). Limited Contextual Analysis: Eye-tracking studies often analyze a narrow range of instructional materials, limiting the generalizability of findings. For instance, one study focused solely on a specific type of video learning, neglecting other instructional formats(Mu et al., 2019). Despite these challenges, eye-tracking remains a promising tool for understanding attention in e-learning, necessitating further research to enhance its applicability and reliability.

3. **Self-Report Measures:** Another way of assessing sustained attention is self-report. Surveys and questionnaires can be used to gather self-reported data on learners' perceived levels of attention during e-learning activities. These measures may include Likert-scale questions or open-ended prompts to capture subjective experiences.

    Limitations: Self-report instruments often suffer from biases, such as response styles and overconfidence, which can distort the accuracy of the data collected(Tempelaar et al., 2020). Studies indicate that self-reported attentional control does not consistently correlate with actual cognitive performance, raising concerns about their validity as proxies for cognitive abilities(Williams et al., 2017).

4. **Usage Analytics and Interaction Patterns:** Online learning management systems can provide data to find insights and patterns from learners' interaction. Analyzing the data collected by tracking learners' interactions with the e-learning platform can reveal patterns about sustained attention. Details such as time spent on tasks, completion rates, and navigation patterns, can offer indirect indicators of sustained attention. Analyzing usage data and interaction patterns can help identify when learners are most engaged and attentive.

    Limitations: Analytics derived from digital learning environments may lack compatibility with traditional constructs measured by self-reports, leading to potential misinterpretations of learning outcomes(Tempelaar et al., 2020). The reliance on trace data can overlook the subjective experiences of learners, which are crucial for understanding sustained attention in e-learning contexts(Hwu, 2023).

5. **Neurophysiological Measures:** EEG (electroencephalography) and other neurophysiological measures can be employed to assess brain activity associated with attention. These measures can provide objective data on cognitive processes and attention levels. This data is free of biases and can be very insightful.

   Limitations: While neurophysiological measures like pupillometry can provide objective data, they may not fully capture the complexities of sustained attention, particularly in diverse age groups where cognitive processing varies(Robison et al., 2022). The interpretation of neurophysiological data can be complicated by individual differences in cognitive strategies and emotional states, which are not always accounted for in analyses(Hwu, 2023).

In summary, while each method offers valuable insights, their limitations necessitate a cautious approach when interpreting results in the context of sustained attention in e-learning. Integrating multiple assessment methods may provide a more comprehensive understanding of attention dynamics.

Challenges

The COVID-19 pandemic accelerated interest in remote and hybrid learning models. In post-COVID world, researchers are keen about investigating the effectiveness of different delivery modes, as well as the challenges and opportunities associated with online and blended learning. Improving e-learning models is crucial to enhance the quality of online education and provide learners with effective, engaging, and personalized learning experiences. Improved e-learning models can lead to better learning outcomes by incorporating research-based instructional design, adaptive learning techniques, and effective assessment methods. Learners are more likely to grasp and retain information when presented in engaging and tailored ways. Well-designed e-learning models can increase learner engagement through interactive elements, gamification, multimedia, and other engaging techniques. When learners are actively involved in the learning process, their motivation and retention improve. Therefore, It is required to understand the factors affecting the expected outcome of MOOCs. One of the main factors influencing why live classroom instruction systems at universities perform more effectively than pre-recorded MOOCs is the integration of active learning techniques. As a result, students receive a live experience that can adjust to their shifting attention which MOOCs couldn't offer. Szpunar argued that MOOCs' incapacity to grab and hold students' attention, particularly in terms of their inability to avoid mind wandering, is also to blame (Szpunar et al, 2013). Assessing attention in E-learning setups for instructors is very difficult. It has various challenges due to the lack of immediate monitoring by instructors. Traditional methods used in physical classrooms, such as continuous engagement and monitoring, are not the same in online environments (Chen, 2012) and it is not easy to implement them just like face-to-face classroom. To address this, researchers are trying to develop student attentiveness and engagement detection systems. These systems utilize technologies like facial recognition and EEG signals to gauge students' attention levels accurately (Hossen & Uddin, 2023). These systems analyze facial expressions, brainwave patterns, and gaze synchrony to determine attentiveness during online classes (Chen et al., 2015). It provides valuable insights for personalized interventions and improved learning experiences (Bühler et al., 2024). The integration of face recognition and machine learning in student attention detection systems for e-learning raises significant ethical concerns. These issues primarily revolve around privacy, consent, and potential biases inherent in the technology. The collection of facial data for monitoring student engagement poses serious privacy risks. Students may not fully understand how their data is being used or stored, leading to potential misuse(Drachsler et al., 2015). The sensitive nature of biometric data necessitates stringent data protection measures to prevent unauthorized access and breaches(Raji et al., 2020). Many students may not provide informed consent for their facial data to be used, raising ethical questions about autonomy and the right to control personal information(Drachsler et al., 2015). The reliance on facial recognition technology can create a surveillance-like environment, which may deter students from participating freely in online learning settings(Raji et al., 2020). ML models can reinforce biases inherent in training data, leading to inaccurate assessments of student attentiveness for certain demographic groups(Raji et al., 2020). This bias can exacerbate existing inequalities in educational outcomes, as students from underrepresented backgrounds may be unfairly judged based on flawed algorithms(Elbawab & Henriques, 2023). While these concerns highlight the potential risks associated with using face recognition in e-learning, proponents argue that with proper ethical guidelines and transparency, such technologies can enhance educational experiences by providing valuable insights into student engagement. Despite swift research going on in the domain, there are still many challenges. The biggest challenge is accurately interpreting these signals as direct indicators of attention. Another challenge is to understand the complex interplay between attention, technology, and learning outcomes. This shows the crucial need for further research for effective implementation in E-learning environments.

SOLUTIONS AND RECOMMENDATIONS

It is noteworthy that cognitive aspects of e-learning can really help to understand the internal configuration and process of learning. To address challenges in E-learning setups, several recommendations can be considered. Firstly, leveraging machine learning techniques, such as facial expression analysis, can be used in detecting students' attention states effectively (Lim et al., 2024). Developing personalized learning content as per the needs of learners based on their learning style preferences can be beneficial. A system can be designed which detects the learner's thinking style and suggests to him/her the suitable learning content based on their preferences. Implementing personalized learning programs based on individual attention analysis, incorporating interactive teaching methods, and utilizing technology for real-time feedback to enhance student engagement and attention in classrooms (Ling et al, 2022). Additionally, for learners with visual impairments, ensuring access to adequate resources like digital recorders, Braille devices, and ICT facilities is crucial to enhance their E-learning experience. Moreover, implementing frameworks based on machine learning methods, like using Gabor wavelets, and support vector machine for automatic classification of students' eye states, can significantly contribute to measuring and improving attention levels in online learning environments (Deng & Wu, 2018). Lastly, adopting posture-based attentivity detection models, along with methods to measure drowsiness and emotions, can further enhance the monitoring of student attentiveness in virtual classrooms (Revadekar et al., 2020). By integrating these recommendations, E-learning platforms can better cater to diverse student needs and optimize attention detection for improved learning outcomes. In accessing student attention in an E-learning setup, it is crucial to implement specialized systems that can effectively monitor and enhance student engagement. Utilizing facial recognition technology for user authentication and attention detection (Hossen & Uddin, 2023), along with incorporating components like hand tracking, mobile phone detection, and pose estimation modules, can provide valuable insights into students' attentiveness during online classes. Additionally, promoting self-regulation skills among students in online learning environments, such as being interested, organized, responsible, engaged, and punctual, is essential for their success (Brammer & Punyanunt-Carter, 2022). By combining technological advancements with pedagogical strategies and intervention programs, educational institutions can create a more engaging and effective E-learning environment for students.

Practical Insights for Classroom Implementation

To enhance student attention and engagement in classrooms, several innovative strategies can be implemented. These approaches leverage technology, interactive activities, and data-driven insights to create a more engaging learning environment.

Gamification: Activities like "Classical Sticks" have been shown to improve engagement by making lectures more interactive and fun, allowing students to participate actively and check their understanding(Compeau et al., 2024). Incorporate game mechanics like quests, badges, and avatars to create a collaborative environment, enhancing student engagement and making classroom material more approachable and enjoyable.

Co-Designing Practices: Involving students in the design of learning activities can lead to tailored interventions that resonate with their experiences and needs, particularly in fields like computer science(Anderson et al., 2022).

Attention Engineering Techniques

Personalized Content and Multimedia: Employing attention engineering techniques, such as interactive multimedia and flipped learning, can significantly enhance student engagement and academic performance(Anannya et al., 2023).

Technology Integration

AI and Emotion Recognition: Utilizing AI frameworks for attention estimation can help teachers monitor student engagement in real-time, allowing for timely adjustments in teaching methods(Aruna et al., 2024).

Visualization Tools: Implementing real-time visualizations of student attention can help educators quickly identify engagement trends and modify their instructional strategies accordingly(Parambil et al., 2023).

While these strategies show promise, it is essential to consider that not all students may respond positively to technology-driven methods. Some may prefer traditional teaching styles, highlighting the need for a balanced approach that accommodates diverse learning preferences.

FUTURE RESEARCH DIRECTIONS

Comprehensive research into the cognitive components of e-learning can enhance learning outcomes and address existing challenges. Key areas for future research include:

1. **Understanding Cognitive Components:** It is important to have clarity of cognitive constituents of e-learning to develop a better e-learning environment. It is crucial to explore how different cognitive components, such as attention, memory, and cognitive load, impact student performance in online setups. Research on these topics can inform the design of more effective e-learning environments.
2. **Enhancing Course Design:** The design of the course plays an important role in its success. Improving course design and pedagogical approaches can reduce issues related to low course engagement and low learner's satisfaction. Research on design principles based on CLT and CTML can shed light to create more educationally effective content.
3. **Addressing Mind-Wandering:** Research work on developing strategies to reduce mind-wandering and enhance sustained attention can improve learning outcomes. Techniques such as mindfulness training and adaptive feedback can help learners maintain focus. More insightful research is required for developing robust methodologies for assessing sustained attention in e-learning. It can provide valuable insights into learner engagement and performance. Combining self-report measures, usage analytics, and neurophysiological data can offer a comprehensive understanding of attention dynamics.
4. **Personalizing Learning Experiences:** There is high potential for research in developing personalized learning environments based on learner's thinking style preferences. Upcoming researchers can focus on leveraging adaptive technologies to personalize learning experiences according to individual needs and cognitive differences. This approach can enhance engagement, satisfaction, and performance.

CONCLUSION

E-learning or virtual education has rapidly evolved in recent years. It has expanded beyond traditional classroom boundaries and embraced diverse formats. Popular formats in e-learning are fully online courses, blended learning models, and Massive Open Online Courses (MOOCs). This growth has been catalyzed by advancements in pedagogy, interactive multimedia content, and adaptive technologies. E-learning has made it feasible for global learners to have a high quality learning environment without any geological restrictions. The pandemic that hit the globe in 2020 created a dire need of instant switching of all educational activities to be conducted online to reduce the loss of learners, motivating educators and educational organizations to adopt e-learning environments and online platforms for continuity of education. Despite this surge, challenges persist in optimizing e-learning models to enhance learning outcomes. The pandemic forced both educators and learners to adapt to new modes of instruction and interaction, fostering digital literacy and remote collaboration skills. In post-COVID world, researchers are keen about investigating the effectiveness of different delivery modes, as well as the challenges and opportunities associated with online and blended learning. Attention is a fundamental cognitive process that underlies successful learning and memory. The ability to direct and sustain attention on learning tasks is critical for encoding and consolidating information into long-term memory. Gamification, co-designing practices, attention engineering techniques, and technology integration can enhance student engagement in classrooms. Interactive activities like "Classical Sticks" and personalized content can improve academic performance. AI and emotion recognition can help teachers monitor student engagement in real-time, allowing for timely adjustments in teaching methods. Real-time visualizations can help educators identify engagement trends and modify instructional strategies.Gamification, co-designing practices, attention engineering techniques, and technology integration can enhance student engagement in classrooms. Interactive activities like "Classical Sticks" and personalized content can improve academic performance. AI and emotion recognition can help teachers monitor student engagement in real-time, allowing for timely adjustments in teaching methods. Real-time visualizations can help educators identify engagement trends and modify instructional strategies. However, the effectiveness of e-learning technology greatly depends on a person's capacity of paying attention. It may be that we lacked an accurate method of measuring attention in the past that the connection between attention and the effectiveness of e-learning has only lately come into focus. A lot of the studies on attention and information systems in general (or in e-learning specifically) have been based on behavioral or self-report. However, there remains a research gap in understanding how various formats of video lecturing affect the sustained attention of learners and eventually affect their learning outcomes, highlighting the need for further empirical studies to inform effective instructional design strategies in online learning environments. Understanding cognitive components of e-learning is crucial for creating an effective environment. Research on attention, memory, and cognitive load can inform the design of more effective courses. Improving course design and pedagogical approaches can reduce low engagement and satisfaction. Strategies to reduce mind-wandering and enhance sustained attention can improve learning outcomes. Personalizing learning experiences based on individual needs and cognitive differences can enhance engagement, satisfaction, and performance.

ACKNOWLEDGMENT

This research received no specific grant from any funding agency in the public, commercial, or not-for-profit sectors.

REFERENCES

Abeysekera, I., Sunga, E., Gonzales, A., & David, R. (2024). The Effect of Cognitive Load on Learning Memory of Online Learning Accounting Students in the Philippines. *Sustainability (Basel)*, 16(4), 1686–1686. DOI: 10.3390/su16041686

Anderson, E., Vasiliou, C., & Crick, T. (2022). Co-Designing Classroom Practice to Improve Student Attention and Engagement in Computer Science Degree Programmes. *Proceedings of the 27th ACM Conference on Innovation and Technology in Computer Science Education*. DOI: 10.1145/3502717.3532149

Anderson, R. M., Heesterbeek, H., Klinkenberg, D., & Hollingsworth, T. D. (2020). How will country-based mitigation measures influence the course of the COVID-19 epidemic? *Lancet*, 395(10228), 931–934. DOI: 10.1016/S0140-6736(20)30567-5 PMID: 32164834

Arbaugh, J. B. (2014). System, scholar or students? Which most influences online MBA course effectiveness? *Journal of Computer Assisted Learning*, 30(4), 349–362. DOI: 10.1111/jcal.12048

Arévalo-Mercado, C. A., Muñoz-Andrade, E. L., Cardona-Reyes, H., & Romero-Juárez, M. G. (2023). Applying Cognitive Load Theory and the Split Attention Effect to Learning Data Structures. *IEEE Revista Iberoamericana de Technologias del Aprendizaje*, 18(1), 107–113. DOI: 10.1109/RITA.2023.3250580

S. Aruna, Maturi, S., Kotha, V., & K. Swarna. (2024). Leveraging AI for Student Attention Estimation. *CRC Press EBooks*, 15–21. DOI: 10.1201/9781003470939-3

Balamurugan, B., Mullai, M., Soundararajan, S., Selvakanmani, S., & Arun, D. (2020). Brain–computer interface for assessment of mental efforts in e-learning using the nonmarkovian queueing model. *Computer Applications in Engineering Education*, 29(2), 394–410. DOI: 10.1002/cae.22209

Brammer, S. E., & Punyanunt-Carter, N. M. (2022). Getting the attention of online learners. *Communication Education*, 71(2), 155–157. DOI: 10.1080/03634523.2021.2022732

Brunken, R., Plass, J. L., & Leutner, D. (2003). Direct Measurement of Cognitive Load in Multimedia Learning. *Educational Psychologist*, 38(1), 53–61. DOI: 10.1207/S15326985EP3801_7

Bühler, B., Bozkir, E., Deininger, H., Gerjets, P., & Trautwein, U., & Enkelejda Kasneci. (2024). On Task and in Sync: Examining the Relationship between Gaze Synchrony and Self-reported Attention During Video Lecture Learning. *Proceedings of the ACM on Human-Computer Interaction*, 8(ETRA), 1–18. DOI: 10.1145/3655604

Cagiltay, N. E., Toker, S., & Cagiltay, K. (2023). Exploring the Influence of Countries' Economic Conditions on Massive Open Online Course (MOOC) Participation: A Study of 3.5 Million MITx Learners. *International Review of Research in Open and Distance Learning*, 24(2), 1–17. DOI: 10.19173/irrodl.v24i2.7123

Caglayan, E., & Ustunluoglu, E. (2020). *A Study Exploring Students' Usage Patterns and Adoption of Lecture Capture*. Technology, Knowledge and Learning., DOI: 10.1007/s10758-020-09435-9

Caskurlu, S., Richardson, J. C., Alamri, H. A., Chartier, K., Farmer, T., Janakiraman, S., Strait, M., & Yang, M. (2020). Cognitive load and online course quality: Insights from instructional designers in a higher education context. *British Journal of Educational Technology*, 52(2), 584–605. DOI: 10.1111/bjet.13043

Castro-Alonso, J. C., de Koning, B. B., Fiorella, L., & Paas, F. (2021). Five Strategies for Optimizing Instructional Materials: Instructor- and Learner-Managed Cognitive Load. *Educational Psychology Review*, 33(4), 1379–1407. Advance online publication. DOI: 10.1007/s10648-021-09606-9 PMID: 33716467

Cavanagh, T. M., & Kiersch, C. (2022). Using commonly-available technologies to create online multimedia lessons through the application of the Cognitive Theory of Multimedia Learning. *Educational Technology Research and Development*, 71(3), 1033–1053. Advance online publication. DOI: 10.1007/s11423-022-10181-1 PMID: 36570341

Chandler, P., & Sweller, J. (1991). Cognitive Load Theory and the Format of Instruction. *Cognition and Instruction*, 8(4), 293–332. DOI: 10.1207/s1532690xci0804_2

Chen, C.-M., & Lin, Y.-J. (2014). Effects of different text display types on reading comprehension, sustained attention and cognitive load in mobile reading contexts. *Interactive Learning Environments*, 24(3), 553–571. DOI: 10.1080/10494820.2014.891526

Chen, C.-M., & Wang, H.-P. (2011). Using emotion recognition technology to assess the effects of different multimedia materials on learning emotion and performance. *Library & Information Science Research*, 33(3), 244–255. DOI: 10.1016/j.lisr.2010.09.010

Chen, C.-M., Wang, J.-Y., & Yu, C.-M. (2015). Assessing the attention levels of students by using a novel attention aware system based on brainwave signals. *British Journal of Educational Technology*, 48(2), 348–369. DOI: 10.1111/bjet.12359

Chen, H.-R. (2012). Assessment of Learners' Attention to E-Learning by Monitoring Facial Expressions for Computer Network Courses. *Journal of Educational Computing Research*, 47(4), 371–385. DOI: 10.2190/EC.47.4.b

Compeau, C., Talley, K., & Talley, A. (2024). Classicle Sticks: An Activity to Improve Student Engagement. *2024 ASEE Annual Conference & Exposition*. DOI: 10.18260/1-2--48462

Davie, J. (2022). Evaluation of the HyFlex, Hybrid, and Asynchronous Online Teaching Modalities on Student Learning in Graduate Microbiology Coursework. *The FASEB Journal*, 36(S1), fasebj.2022.36.S1.R6050. Advance online publication. DOI: 10.1096/fasebj.2022.36.S1.R6050

de Muñoz, J. H. O., & Letouze, P. (2022). Some considerations on the principles of the Cognitive Theory of Multimedia Learning for instructional video design for the elderly. *Research. Social Development*, 11(10), e499111032333. DOI: 10.33448/rsd-v11i10.32333

Deng, Q., & Wu, Z. (2018). Students' Attention Assessment in eLearning based on Machine Learning. *IOP Conference Series. Earth and Environmental Science*, 199, 032042. DOI: 10.1088/1755-1315/199/3/032042

Driver, J. (2001). A selective review of selective attention research from the past century. *British Journal of Psychology*, 92(1), 53–78. DOI: 10.1348/000712601162103

Dunn, R., & Griggs, S. A. (2000). *Practical Approaches to Using Learning Styles in Higher Education*. Bloomsbury Publishing USA. DOI: 10.5040/9798400699962

Eom, S., Ashill, N. J., & Arbaugh, J. B. (2016). Guest Editors' Introduction to the Special Issue. *Decision Sciences Journal of Innovative Education*, 14(2), 124–127. DOI: 10.1111/dsji.12099

Fidalgo-Blanco, Á., Sein-Echaluce, M. L., & García-Peñalvo, F. J. (2016). From massive access to cooperation: Lessons learned and proven results of a hybrid xMOOC/cMOOC pedagogical approach to MOOCs. *International Journal of Educational Technology in Higher Education*, 13(1), 24. Advance online publication. DOI: 10.1186/s41239-016-0024-z

Fortenbaugh, F. C., DeGutis, J., & Esterman, M. (2017). Recent theoretical, neural, and clinical advances in sustained attention research. *Annals of the New York Academy of Sciences*, 1396(1), 70–91. DOI: 10.1111/nyas.13318 PMID: 28260249

Fortenbaugh, F. C., DeGutis, J., Germine, L., Wilmer, J. B., Grosso, M., Russo, K., & Esterman, M. (2015). Sustained Attention Across the Life Span in a Sample of 10,000. *Psychological Science*, 26(9), 1497–1510. DOI: 10.1177/0956797615594896 PMID: 26253551

Gallen, C. L., Schaerlaeken, S., Younger, J. W., Anguera, J. A., & Gazzaley, A. (2023). Contribution of sustained attention abilities to real-world academic skills in children. *Scientific Reports*, 13(1), 2673. DOI: 10.1038/s41598-023-29427-w PMID: 36792755

Gavassa, S., Benabentos, R., Kravec, M., Collins, T., & Eddy, S. (2019). Closing the Achievement Gap in a Large Introductory Course by Balancing Reduced In-Person Contact with Increased Course Structure. *CBE Life Sciences Education*, 18(1), ar8. DOI: 10.1187/cbe.18-08-0153 PMID: 30807254

Ge, S., & Lai, X. (2021). Strategies for Information Design and Processing of Multimedia Instructional Software—Based on Richard E. Mayer's Multimedia Instructional Design Principles. *International Journal of Educational Technology and Learning*, 10(1), 40–46. DOI: 10.20448/2003.101.40.46

Griffin, D. K., Mitchell, D., & Thompson, S. J. (2009). Podcasting by synchronising PowerPoint and voice: What are the pedagogical benefits? *Computers & Education*, 53(2), 532–539. DOI: 10.1016/j.compedu.2009.03.011

Grigorenko, E. L., & Sternberg, R. J. (1997). Styles of Thinking, Abilities, and Academic Performance. *Exceptional Children*, 63(3), 295–312. DOI: 10.1177/001440299706300301

Gutiérrez, G., Lunsky, I., Heer, S. V., Szulewski, A., & Chaplin, T. (2023). Cognitive load theory in action: E-learning modules improve performance in simulation-based education. A pilot study. *Canadian Journal of Emergency Medical Care*, 25(11), 893–901. Advance online publication. DOI: 10.1007/s43678-023-00586-z PMID: 37751082

Homer, B. D., Plass, J. L., & Blake, L. (2008). The effects of video on cognitive load and social presence in multimedia-learning. *Computers in Human Behavior*, 24(3), 786–797. DOI: 10.1016/j.chb.2007.02.009

Hossen, M. K., & Uddin, M. S. (2023). Attention monitoring of students during online classes using XGBoost classifier. *Computers and Education: Artificial Intelligence*, 100191, 100191. Advance online publication. DOI: 10.1016/j.caeai.2023.100191

Hwu, S.-L. (2023). Developing SAMM: A Model for Measuring Sustained Attention in Asynchronous Online Learning. *Sustainability (Basel)*, 15(12), 9337. DOI: 10.3390/su15129337

Ilioudi, C., Giannakos, M. N., & Chorianopoulos, K. (2013). Investigating differences among the commonly used video lecture styles. In WAVe 2013 the Workshop on Analytics on video-based learning (pp. 21e26).

Jiang, D., Chen, O., Yong, H., & Kalyuga, S. (2023). Improving English language skills through learning Mathematic contents: From the expertise reversal effect perspective. *The British Journal of Educational Psychology*, 93(S2), 386–401. DOI: 10.1111/bjep.12596 PMID: 36990799

Kim, J., Singh, S., Thiessen, E. D., & Fisher, A. V. (2020). A hidden Markov model for analyzing eye-tracking of moving objects. *Behavior Research Methods*, 52(3), 1225–1243. DOI: 10.3758/s13428-019-01313-2 PMID: 31898297

Kokoç, M., IIgaz, H., & Altun, A. (2020). Effects of sustained attention and video lecture types on learning performances. *Educational Technology Research and Development*, 68(6), 3015–3039. DOI: 10.1007/s11423-020-09829-7

Lim, E. L., Murugesan, R. K., & Balakrishnan, S. (2024). Leveraging machine learning techniques for student's attention detection: A review. *IAES International Journal of Artificial Intelligence*, 13(2), 1195–1195. DOI: 10.11591/ijai.v13.i2.pp1195-1205

Lin, C.-H., Wu, W.-H., & Lee, T.-N. (2022). Using an Online Learning Platform to Show Students' Achievements and Attention in the Video Lecture and Online Practice Learning Environments. *Journal of Educational Technology & Society*, 25(1), 155–165. https://www.jstor.org/stable/48647037

Lin, X., Tang, W., Ma, W., Liu, Y., & Ding, F. (2023). The impact of media diversity and cognitive style on learning experience in programming video lecture: A brainwave analysis. *Education and Information Technologies*, 28(8), 10617–10637. DOI: 10.1007/s10639-023-11608-9

Lindsay, G. W. (2020). Attention in psychology, neuroscience, and machine learning. *Frontiers in Computational Neuroscience*, 14(29), 29. Advance online publication. DOI: 10.3389/fncom.2020.00029 PMID: 32372937

Ling, X., Yang, J., Liang, J., Zhu, H., & Sun, H. (2022). A Deep-Learning Based Method for Analysis of Students' Attention in Offline Class. *Electronics (Basel)*, 11(17), 2663–2663. DOI: 10.3390/electronics11172663

Liu, N.-H., Chiang, C.-Y., & Chu, H.-C. (2013). Recognizing the Degree of Human Attention Using EEG Signals from Mobile Sensors. *Sensors (Basel)*, 13(8), 10273–10286. DOI: 10.3390/s130810273 PMID: 23939584

Mackworth, N. H. (1948). The Breakdown of Vigilance during Prolonged Visual Search. *The Quarterly Journal of Experimental Psychology*, 1(1), 6–21. DOI: 10.1080/17470214808416738

Mayer, R. E. (2001). *Multimedia Learning*. DOI: 10.1017/CBO9781139164603

Mayer, R. E. (2021). Evidence-Based Principles for How to Design Effective Instructional Videos. *Journal of Applied Research in Memory and Cognition*, 10(2), 229–240. DOI: 10.1016/j.jarmac.2021.03.007

Mayer, R. E., & Massa, L. J. (2003). Three Facets of Visual and Verbal Learners: Cognitive Ability, Cognitive Style, and Learning Preference. *Journal of Educational Psychology*, 95(4), 833–846. DOI: 10.1037/0022-0663.95.4.833

Mesquita, C., Nazar, B. P., Pinna, C. M. S., Rabelo, B., Serra-Pinheiro, M. A., Sergeant, J., & Mattos, P. (2016). How can Continuous Performance Test help to assess inattention when mood and ADHD symptoms coexist? *Psychiatry Research*, 243, 326–330. DOI: 10.1016/j.psychres.2016.06.054 PMID: 27434202

Messick, S. (1984). The nature of cognitive styles: Problems and promise in educational practice. *Educational Psychologist*, 19(2), 59–74. DOI: 10.1080/00461528409529283

Mohammed, A. B., Maqableh, M., Qasim, D., & AlJawazneh, F. (2024). Exploring the Factors Influencing Academic Learning Performance Using Online Learning Systems. *Heliyon*, 10(11), e32584–e32584. DOI: 10.1016/j.heliyon.2024.e32584 PMID: 38912470

Mrazek, M. D., Phillips, D. T., Franklin, M. S., Broadway, J. M., & Schooler, J. W. (2013). Young and restless: Validation of the Mind-Wandering Questionnaire (MWQ) reveals disruptive impact of mind-wandering for youth. *Frontiers in Psychology*, 4(560). Advance online publication. DOI: 10.3389/fpsyg.2013.00560 PMID: 23986739

Mu, S., Cui, M., Wang, X. J., Qiao, J. X., & Tang, D. M. (2019). Learners' attention preferences of information in online learning. *Interactive Technology and Smart Education*, 16(3), 186–203. DOI: 10.1108/ITSE-10-2018-0090

Nguyen, L. Q. (2022). Learners' satisfaction of courses on Coursera as a massive open online course platform: A case study. *Frontiers in Education*, 7, 1086170. Advance online publication. DOI: 10.3389/feduc.2022.1086170

Parambil, M. M. A., Alhammadi, A. M. A., Alnajjar, F., Trabelsi, Z., Ali, L., & Swavaf, M. (2023). Visualizing Student Attention in Smart Classrooms: A Preliminary Study. *2023 15th International Conference on Innovations in Information Technology, IIT 2023*. IEEE. DOI: 10.1109/IIT59782.2023.10366478

Petersen, G. B., Stenberdt, V., Mayer, R. E., & Makransky, G. (2023). Collaborative generative learning activities in immersive virtual reality increase learning. *Computers & Education*, 207, 104931. DOI: 10.1016/j.compedu.2023.104931

Raes, A., Detienne, L., Windey, I., & Depaepe, F. (2019). A systematic literature review on synchronous hybrid learning: Gaps identified. *Learning Environments Research*, 23(23), 269–290. Advance online publication. DOI: 10.1007/s10984-019-09303-z

Revadekar, A., Oak, S., Gadekar, A., & Bide, P. (2020, December 1). *Gauging attention of students in an e-learning environment*. IEEE Xplore. DOI: 10.1109/CICT51604.2020.9312048

Riccio, C. A., & Reynolds, C. R. (2006). Continuous Performance Tests Are Sensitive to ADHD in Adults but Lack Specificity. *Annals of the New York Academy of Sciences*, 931(1), 113–139. DOI: 10.1111/j.1749-6632.2001.tb05776.x PMID: 11462737

Robison, M. K., Diede, N. T., Nicosia, J., Ball, B. H., & Bugg, J. M. (2022). A multimodal analysis of sustained attention in younger and older adults. *Psychology and Aging*, 37(3), 307–325. DOI: 10.1037/pag0000687 PMID: 35446084

Saleem, F., AlNasrallah, W., Malik, M. I., & Rehman, S. U. (2022). Factors Affecting the Quality of Online Learning During COVID-19: Evidence From a Developing Economy. *Frontiers in Education*, 7, 847571. Advance online publication. DOI: 10.3389/feduc.2022.847571

Sarter, M., Givens, B., & Bruno, J. P. (2001). The cognitive neuroscience of sustained attention: Where top-down meets bottom-up. *Brain Research. Brain Research Reviews*, 35(2), 146–160. DOI: 10.1016/S0165-0173(01)00044-3 PMID: 11336780

Sauter, M., Wagner, T., Hirzle, T., Rukzio, E., & Huckauf, A. (2023). Where are my students looking at? Using Gaze Synchronicity to Facilitate Online Learning. *Journal of Vision (Charlottesville, Va.)*, 23(9), 5538–5538. DOI: 10.1167/jov.23.9.5538

Segundo, S. M. T., Díaz, E. Z. G., Vizuete, O. M. Z., & Chávez, E. E. O. (2022). Analysis of Artificial Intelligence Applied in Virtual Learning Environments in Higher Education for Ecuador. *Frontiers in Artificial Intelligence and Applications*, 363. Advance online publication. DOI: 10.3233/FAIA220563

Sewandono, R. E., Thoyib, A., Hadiwidjojo, D., & Rofiq, A. (2022). Performance expectancy of E-learning on higher institutions of education under uncertain conditions: Indonesia context. *Education and Information Technologies*. Advance online publication. DOI: 10.1007/s10639-022-11074-9 PMID: 36247027

Singh, V., & Thurman, A. (2019). How Many Ways Can We Define Online Learning? A Systematic Literature Review of Definitions of Online Learning (1988-2018). *American Journal of Distance Education*, 33(4), 289–306. DOI: 10.1080/08923647.2019.1663082

Skulmowski, A., & Xu, K. M. (2021). Understanding cognitive load in digital and online learning: A new perspective on extraneous cognitive load. *Educational Psychology Review*, 34(1), 171–196. Advance online publication. DOI: 10.1007/s10648-021-09624-7

Sternberg, R. J. (1988). Mental Self-Government: A Theory of Intellectual Styles and Their Development. *Human Development*, 31(4), 197–224. DOI: 10.1159/000275810

Sumardani, D., & Lin, C.-H. (2023). Cognitive processes during virtual reality learning: A study of brain wave. *Education and Information Technologies*, 28(11), 14877–14896. DOI: 10.1007/s10639-023-11788-4

Sweller, J. (2020). Cognitive load theory and educational technology. *Educational Technology Research and Development*, 68(1), 1–16. Advance online publication. DOI: 10.1007/s11423-019-09701-3

Sweller, J., van Merrienboer, J. J. G., & Paas, F. G. W. C. (1998). Cognitive Architecture and Instructional Design. *Educational Psychology Review*, 10(3), 251–296. DOI: 10.1023/A:1022193728205

Szpunar, K. K., Moulton, S. T., & Schacter, D. L. (2013). Mind wandering and education: From the classroom to online learning. *Frontiers in Psychology*, 4. Advance online publication. DOI: 10.3389/fpsyg.2013.00495 PMID: 23914183

Tempelaar, D., Rienties, B., & Nguyen, Q. (2020). Subjective data, objective data and the role of bias in predictive modelling: Lessons from a dispositional learning analytics application. *PLoS One*, 15(6), e0233977. DOI: 10.1371/journal.pone.0233977 PMID: 32530954

Ulla, M. B., & Espique, F. P. (2022). Hybrid Teaching and the Hybridization of Education: Thai University Teachers' Perspectives, Practices, Challenges. *Journal of Interactive Media in Education*, 2022(1), 9. DOI: 10.5334/jime.758

Varela, J. L., Magnante, A. T., Miskey, H. M., Ord, A. S., Eldridge, A., & Shura, R. D. (2024). A systematic review of the utility of continuous performance tests among adults with ADHD. *The Clinical Neuropsychologist*, 38(7), 1–62. DOI: 10.1080/13854046.2024.2315740 PMID: 38424025

Wager, T. D., Jonides, J., & Reading, S. (2004). Neuroimaging studies of shifting attention: A meta-analysis. *NeuroImage*, 22(4), 1679–1693. DOI: 10.1016/j.neuroimage.2004.03.052 PMID: 15275924

Wang, X., Zhang, L., & He, T.-C. (2022). Learning Performance Prediction-Based Personalized Feedback in Online Learning via Machine Learning. *Sustainability (Basel)*, 14(13), 7654–7654. DOI: 10.3390/su14137654

Williams, P. G., Rau, H. K., Suchy, Y., Thorgusen, S. R., & Smith, T. W. (2017). On the validity of self-report assessment of cognitive abilities: Attentional control scale associations with cognitive performance, emotional adjustment, and personality. *Psychological Assessment*, 29(5), 519–530. DOI: 10.1037/pas0000361 PMID: 27504900

Wlodarczyk, J. R., Alicuben, E. T., Hawley, L., Sullivan, M., Ault, G. T., & Inaba, K. (2021). Development and emergency implementation of an online surgical education curriculum for a General Surgery program during a global pandemic: The University of Southern California experience. *the American Journal of Surgery*, 221(5), 962–972. DOI: 10.1016/j.amjsurg.2020.08.045

Yan, X., Peng, P., & Liu, Y. (2024). Optimal Design Feature of Computer-Assisted Reading Instruction for Students with Reading Difficulties? A Bayesian Network Meta-Analysis. *Computers in Human Behavior*, 152, 108062. Advance online publication. DOI: 10.1016/j.chb.2023.108062

Yao, Y., Wang, P., Jiang, Y., Li, Q., & Li, Y. (2022). Innovative Online learning strategies for the successful construction of student Self-awareness during the COVID-19 pandemic: Merging TAM with TPB. *Journal of Innovation & Knowledge*, 7(4), 100252. DOI: 10.1016/j.jik.2022.100252

Yu, Q. (2022). Factors Influencing Online Learning Satisfaction. *Frontiers in Psychology*, 13, 852360. Advance online publication. DOI: 10.3389/fpsyg.2022.852360 PMID: 35496260

Zhang, L.-F. (2002). Thinking Styles: Their relationships with modes of thinking and academic performance. *Educational Psychology*, 22(3), 331–348. DOI: 10.1080/01443410220138557

KEY TERMS AND DEFINITIONS

Cognition: It refers to the processing of events and information inside the brain through sensory experiences.

Cognitive Load: The amount of information the human brain can handle at any given moment.

E-Learning: A mode of learning where instructional material is in digital form and shared through electronic media using the internet beyond geographical boundaries.

Information and Communication Technology (ICT): It refers to the technological infrastructure, tools, and resources used to create, share and store the information.

Learning Style: It refers to the learner's preference of methods (visual, verbal etc) for understanding and interpreting a piece of information, a concept, or an idea.

Massive Open Online Courses (MOOCs): A model for online learning used to offer courses for large scale participation over the internet.

Mind-wandering: Refers to the random thoughts that are unrelated to task/learning at the moment which cause distraction from point of focus.

Online Content Distribution: Refers to the modes of sharing the information or content over the internet.

Sustained Attention: It refers to the ability to maintain the focus on a task of interest for a long time which is helpful in retention and recall of information later.

Working Memory: Cognitive part of the brain with limited capacity that handles the small amount of information for the processing of current cognitive task.

Chapter 11
Use of Scaffolding to Promote Engagement and Learning in Asynchronous Online Discussions

Linda Clark Ashar
https://orcid.org/0009-0009-1877-5916
American Public University System, USA

ABSTRACT

This chapter per the author proposes scaffolding as a best practice methodology for encouraging student learning and engagement in asynchronous discussions in the online higher education classroom. Grounded in Lev Semyonovich Vygotsky's Zone of Proximal Development and developmental theories that followed, scaffolding techniques harmonize with fundamental learning theories and practices, such as the tripartite Community of Inquiry framework of social, teaching, and cognitive presence. This chapter explains the value of scaffolding as supported by relevant research, and offers illustrative examples of the use of scaffolding to promote engagement and learning in online asynchronous discussions.

DOI: 10.4018/979-8-3693-4407-1.ch011

THE USE OF SCAFFOLDING TO PROMOTE ENGAGEMENT AND LEARNING IN ASYNCHRONOUS ONLINE DISCUSSIONS

Organized distance learning as it is conceived today can be traced back to at least 1728, when a pioneering entrepreneur named Caleb Phillips set up his successful shorthand-by-mail school out of Boston, Massachusetts Colony (Barrett & Ashar, 2024; Bozkurt, 2019). The growth of alternatives to live classrooms has not waned since. Entrepreneurial acumen and advancing technology have collaborated over the nearly 300 years since Caleb's day to bring the remote classroom paradigm into mainstream education worldwide. This trend was accelerated by the stay-in-place mandates of the COVID-19 pandemic, thrusting traditional brick-and-mortar institutions into an expanded virtual learning world (Nworie, 2021). Today, more than 180 million people are said to be engaged in online education ("The History of Distance Learning," 2024).

Beetham and Sharpe (2019) emphasized that a modern understanding of pedagogy is to recognize it is "an essential dialogue between teaching and learning: learning in the context of teaching, and teaching that has learning as its goal" (p. 2). With the growth of remote learning came the need to adapt pedagogy to overcome the nonsocial nature of the impersonal dynamic that is inherent in the lack of face-to-face interaction in real time between teacher and student, as well as among students in online peer discussions (Delahunty, 2018; Swan, 2017). The antidote for this problem is social presence (Swan, 2017), a key element of the Community of Inquiry (CoI) framework heralded in established research (Anderson, 2017; Avci & Ergulac, 2019; Garrison et al., 1999; Shea & Bidjerano, 2009; Swan & Richardson, 2017). According to the CoI theory, social, teaching, and cognitive presence combine to simulate the energy of a live classroom (The Community of Inquiry, 2024). These concepts refine a universal truth about learning: the intrinsic occurrence of communication in the learner's outward interaction with others and the environment (Andreev, 2024; Schunk, 2012).

CoI and related pedagogical theories are rooted in Russian psychologist Lev Semyonovich Vygotsky's concept of the zone of proximal development (ZPD), a cornerstone of his sociocultural theory of cognitive development (Vygotsky, 1978). Vygotsky built his theory on his profound insights into how learning and cognitive development are intertwined with experience and communication in social contexts and the observation that social interaction plays a fundamental role in the development of cognition. Levykh (2008) explained that educators can design learning activities in a "guided construction" to bridge Vygotsky's ZPD. Such "guided construction" of ZPD perfectly describes an educative process called scaffolding, by which a learner is provided assistance to "solve a problem, carry out a task or achieve a goal" (Bakker et al., 2015, p. 1048) that the learner cannot do independently (Wood et al., 1976). In the classroom, scaffolding is "any form of instructional support that enables students to complete tasks they would be unable to master without assistance" (Feng et al., 2017, p. 166). For scaffolding to be productive, learners must have at least a rudimentary idea about the subject matter (Schneider, 2016). The beauty of scaffolding is that it is a learner-centered philosophy that offers adaptability, creativity, and support for educators and learners in collaborative settings (Bakker et al., 2015; Rahma et al., 2020). Scaffolding techniques have proved to be versatile and effective in asynchronous online discussions to foster social, cognitive, and teaching presence (Kim, 2018; Koskey & Benson, 2017). In this chapter, the author presents the theory supporting these techniques and examples of specific scaffolding practices for asynchronous online discussions.

THE ZPD

Bridging the Knowledge Gap

The ZPD represents the gap in knowledge that exists between what a learner knows or can do independently and what is beyond the learner's knowledge or ability to do even with assistance. Within the ZPD, between these two poles of knowledge and no-knowledge, is the potential and opportunity to acquire knowledge and skill. Learners can acquire the skill or knowledge needed to advance through experience, guidance, and encouragement of others such as an instructor, mentor, coach or peers. Pedagogy provides a pathway through the ZPD. Learners' support is gradually reduced across the ZPD as they become more competent, allowing them to take on more responsibility for their learning until they can perform the task independently. This process of withdrawing assistance as it is less needed (moving the learner to independence) is often referred to as "fading" (Putnam et al., 2010).

Criticisms and Extensions of the ZPD

While the concept of ZPD is widely accepted and influential, it has encountered some criticism, such as a concern that the concept is too vague and difficult to apply consistently in practice, or that a learner's individual ZPD can be too easily overlooked, especially in online classroom settings (Smagorinsky, 2018). Despite such concerns, Vygotsky's (1978) ZPD theory has been extended and adapted in various ways. For example, the concept has been applied in digital learning environments, where technology serves as a learner's assistant in providing interactive and adaptive learning experiences (McLoughlin, 2002). Additionally, the ZPD has influenced other educational theories, such as the concept of "productive struggle," where learners are encouraged to engage with challenging tasks that are slightly beyond their current abilities (Roth, 2019).

The use of scaffolding teaching techniques in asynchronous online discussions resonates compatibly with theories of interactive engagement. As the classroom space for group dialogue, discussion forums highlight the role of social presence. Nevertheless, the asynchronous discussions in higher education online classrooms still pose the one-way impersonal barriers of time and distance between student and teacher. Online participants tend to be less interactive left on their own (Garrison et al., 1999). Scaffolding techniques offer a way to overcome these problems by providing a method of connecting course concepts to desired learning outcomes (Andreev, 2024), bridging the ZPD (Lim Abdullah et al., 2013) with clarity of question prompts and promoting deeper engagement with conversational prompting techniques. This approach enhances social presence in an exchange that incrementally reinforces learning in a collegial and supportive manner. According to studies, scaffolding techniques are significantly effective in online higher education learning environments (Doo et al., 2020; McNiff & Aicher, 2017). For effective use of scaffolding, it is important to understand not only why it is a useful technique and how it works, but also its symmetry with learning theories and recognized pedagogical practices intended to promote active student participation and engagement in remote classrooms.

SOCIAL LEARNING FOUNDATIONS OF ASYNCHRONOUS ONLINE DISCUSSIONS

As a vital component of online education, asynchronous online discussions provide flexibility of pedagogical design for meeting learning outcomes, and deeper engagement through a group learning paradigm. Research emphasizes that the discussion feature critically contributes to successful learning because it provides the dimension of social communication. One study beautifully captures the point by explaining the discussion paradigm enables students to "cross the threshold" from "feeling like outsiders to feeling like insiders" (Wegerif, 1998, p. 48). Two principal theories that illustrate how this can happen in the virtual classroom are constructivism and the related CoI framework. Both of these derive from collaborative learning theory (Nussbaum et al., 2004).

The Social Context of Learning

Vygotsky (1978) emphasized that cognitive development is fundamentally a social process. He explained that learning occurs first on a social level (interpsychological) and then on an individual level (intrapsychological). This process is known as internalization, where social interactions are transformed into internal processes (Liu, 2008). According to Vygotsky (1978), language plays a critical role in this process. Through dialogue and communication, learners can share knowledge, ask questions, and clarify their understanding. Over time, the external dialogue is internalized, becoming inner speech, which guides thinking and problem-solving. The ZPD emphasizes the dynamic nature of learning and the critical role of collaboration, scaffolding, and guided discovery in helping learners reach their full potential.

Collaborative Learning Theory

Collaboration combined with expert guidance ignites learning (Pham, 2023). Distilled to its essence, collaborative learning theory defines education as "conversation among people" (Yang, 2023, p. 719). The theory is that knowledge is constructed through dialogue and shared understanding among learners, rather than being passively received from an instructor. In the context of online asynchronous discussions in higher education, this theory grounds the framework for encouraging students to engage with one another and their instructor to enhance learning outcomes. The very nature of this interaction supports the use of scaffolding techniques to shape and direct the discussions without dictating or rotely supplying content.

Constructivism

Scaffolding's origin as a powerful and flexible teaching method is rooted in social constructivist theory (Roehler & Cantlon, 1997). The maxim of constructivism (also called constructivist learning theory) builds on collaborative learning theory. Through interaction with their environment and dialogue with the instructor and peers, learners uniquely derive (i.e., construct) knowledge (Hein, 1991). In other words, these social-based constructs recognize that learning does not occur in a vacuum. It is not effective to passively present information with the expectation students will somehow absorb it. "Self-expression and exchanges" are necessary to process and internalize the subject (Ackermann, 2001, p. 2).

Thus, verbalization and social exchange are central to the dynamic of asynchronous online discussions. Students are able to reflect on their instructor's and peers' contributions to the discussion, which contributes to their own understanding of the subject, adds new information and ideas, and integrates them with students' existing knowledge. Students' own active engagement in this discourse both tests and advances their understanding. This interactive process aligns the discussion with other learning activities, such as research and written assignments (Hawkey, 2003).

CoI Framework

Like constructivism, the CoI framework derives from the social element of online discussions. The CoI framework parses three key interlocking roles involved in the dynamics of a group learning situation. This is a triangle of communication-based "presences" interacting in the group's communications to create meaningful online experiences through the dynamic of social, cognitive, and teaching presence (Garrison, 2015; Garrison et al., 2003; The Community of Inquiry, 2024). These three elements of CoI interactively support each other. No one CoI presence exists in isolation from the dynamics of engagement that foster the other two. CoI is a combined synergy of communication and positive energy sparked by social interaction.

Cognitive Presence

Cognitive presence speaks to demonstrating critical thinking, exploring the subject matter, and integrating new ideas. This critical element of CoI involves the extent to which learners can construct meaning through sustained communication (Cleveland-Innes, 2020). Research shows that effective asynchronous discussions require careful planning and active attention to facilitate meaningful interaction and critical thinking (Cortázar et al., 2021; Sinha et al., 2022). Techniques such as peer moderation and structured prompts can significantly enhance cognitive engagement and knowledge construction. Discussions aligned with defined learning outcomes will facilitate teaching presence, as a platform for the instructor to utilize techniques such as scaffolding to promote learning progression (Cortázar et al., 2021). The ZPD aligns closely with cognitive presence in the CoI framework. Cognitive presence is about the construction of meaning through reflection and discourse. This occurs most effectively within the ZPD, where learners are engaged in tasks that challenge them, but are still within their reach with appropriate support. This aligns with the CoI framework process of inquiry that encourages learners to engage in critical thinking and problem-solving with the assistance of peers or instructors.

Social Presence

Social presence can be described as building a learning community in which learners express themselves and share experiences. A sense of community reduces stress and encourages cognitive presence (Whiteside et al., 2014). In the context of fostering community in the asynchronous online discussion, social presence is described as "the affective communication, open expression, and sense of group cohesion that learners experience as they interact with one another" (Rothstein et al, 2023, p. 192). This feature of CoI supports the rationale for a beginning discussion in a course designed as a "meet and greet" in which students introduce themselves and share interests relevant to the course subject. The purpose is to create a sense of community as a classroom and promote a level of comfort for topical discussions in the course. Indeed, research supports that "a strong sense of social presence is a prerequisite" for learning (Rothstein et al., 2023, p. 201).

Teaching Presence

Watson et al. (2023) categorized teaching presence as stylistic (e.g., introductory video) and substantive (e.g., assignment feedback and explaining content), finding that "students assign higher value to elements of teaching presence that provide meaningful substance," that is, "specifically designed to enhance student learning" (p. 297). Applying this premise in the context of online asynchronous discussions, teaching presence embraces the instructor helping students understand the focus of the discussion prompts, nudging them toward finding answers to their questions for themselves, and encouraging critical thinking with peer involvement in active conversation about the topic.

CoI Learning Theory and Scaffolding

The CoI concepts of cognitive, teaching, and social presence create a receptive atmosphere of learning fostered by interactive engagement among students and the instructor. Central to CoI theory, especially in the context of discussions, is that learning happens in the active discourse of addressing questions or problems with the assistance of pedagogical techniques (Cleveland-Innes, 2020). Scaffolding offers just such a technique as a structure to the process of assisting a learner through the ZPD (McLeod, 2024). Scaffolding is a means of providing temporary support to help learners achieve tasks that they would not be able to accomplish on their own. Using scaffolding the instructor can assess the learner's current abilities and provide a level of assistance geared to help the learner progress. The simplest form of scaffolding is traditional feedback on an assignment, to help the student gain knowledge in the subject matter. The process depends substantially on the learner's self-regulation and autonomy to understand and apply the feedback, or even care about it (Suwastini et al., 2021). This form of feedback remains hostage to the one-way aspect of online education. There is much more to best scaffolding techniques. The art of scaffolding is to provide enough assistance to steady the learner forward without spoon feeding answers in an interactive process that allows the learner to engage in active discovery of knowledge. This synergistic dynamic will not automatically ignite simply because a discussion group is formed. Thoughtful and focused course design must be nurtured by using constructivist techniques (Anderson, 2017). Scaffolding offers a tactile-type constructive mechanism to discover and apply learning.

Scaffolding and Its Importance as Derived From ZPD

While the pedagogical premise of a course is for students to grasp the subject matter and achieve the learning outcomes, the reality is that not all learners arrive at the beginning of the course with the same knowledge or experience base. In discussions, the instructor can assess a student's given response and provide a supportive, tailored reply that will help the student find the next step in the thought process. It might be a question, a reference, or a referral to another post, depending on the circumstance, to support learners as they familiarize themselves with the skills required to master the concept. Using scaffolding this way, the instructor breaks the desired story or analysis into manageable pieces (i.e., incremental steps) intended to lead the student toward an independent grasp of the material (Bloomberg, 2021). By continually assessing students' understanding as the discussion progresses, the instructor can then fade support by stepping back and allowing students more independence as they demonstrate responsibility in continuing the discussion (Puntambekar, 2022). New concepts are thus understood and assimilated into the "everyday domain of personal experience" (Moll, 2013, p. 35). In this way, "[r]esponsive, personalized scaffolding within each student's ZPD is effective for learning and is often recognized as a mark of excellent teaching" (Puntambekar, 2022, p. 458). Ideally, the use of scaffolding techniques will synchronize with a scaffolding approach that is also utilized in the course design. Specific to online courses, designing simple to complex instruction with basic elements early on, building to higher levels as the lessons progress, has been associated with learners' higher engagement (Cagiltay, 2006; Lange et al., 2023).

RELATING SCAFFOLDING TO THE CoI FRAMEWORK

Scaffolding techniques work within all three elements of CoI. The instructor carries a leading role, but peers in the discussion group also contribute to the process. In today's digital online environment, artificial intelligence "assistant" tools might be utilized with interactive prompts, hints, and suggestions, as well. Scaffolding both enhances and utilizes the components as an activity that integrates the CoI, as Figure 1 shows.

Figure 1. Scaffolding Integrates the Components of CoI

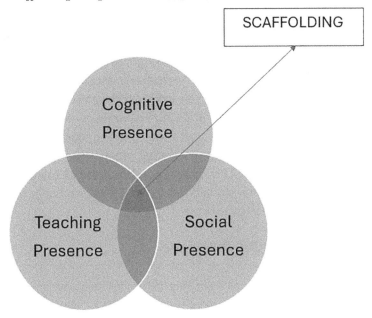

In harmony with CoI concepts, scaffolding techniques contribute to a supportive and effective learning environment.

Scaffolding and Cognitive Presence

Cognitive presence is about the construction of meaning through reflection and discourse (Sadaf et al., 2021). Within the ZPD, learners are engaged in tasks that challenge them but are still within their reach with appropriate support. This mirrors the process of inquiry in the CoI framework, where learners are encouraged to engage in critical thinking and problem-solving with the assistance of peers and teachers. Scaffolding offers a structure of instructional strategies to support learners as they move through various phases of inquiry, such as triggering events (recognizing a problem or issue), to exploration of concepts (researching resources and ideas), integration (connecting and synthesizing new information), and resolution (applying new knowledge) (Al Mamun & Lawrie, 2024). Effective scaffolding helps learners progress through these stages, which deepens cognitive presence.

Scaffolding and Social Presence

Social presence in the CoI framework is about building a sense of community and fostering open communication among learners. Scaffolding is crucial in creating this environment, especially in the early stages of group formation. By guiding how to communicate, collaborate, and interact effectively, instructors can scaffold the development of social presence, helping learners to feel comfortable and connected in the learning community. Vygotsky's (1978) emphasis on the social context of learning suggests that interaction with others is vital for cognitive development. Social presence facilitates this interaction, creating a supportive environment where learners can progress within their ZPD. Through collaboration with peers and guided discussions led by the instructor, learners can explore ideas, challenge each other's thinking, and build knowledge collectively.

Scaffolding and Teaching Presence

Teaching presence encompasses shaping both cognitive and social processes interactively in the learning environment (Garrison, 2015). This is essentially the process of scaffolding in action. Instructors scaffold learning by crafting activities that align with learners' needs to bridge the ZPD, by providing learners with just enough support to help them advance without overwhelming them. In discussions, this means providing feedback that adjusts the level of challenge as learners progress. The goal is to help learners move from dependence on external guidance to independent mastery, which is the essence of both effective scaffolding and teaching presence.

EXAMPLES OF SCAFFOLDING PRACTICES USED IN ASYNCHRONOUS ONLINE DISCUSSIONS

The following hypothetical examples illustrate the use of scaffolding techniques in asynchronous online discussions.

Scaffolding With Structured Discussion Prompts

A common scaffolding technique in a discussion is the use of question prompts (Xun & Land, 2004). This approach helps students address complex problems systematically, making it easier for them to articulate and defend their viewpoints. The scaffold structure can be included in the initial discussion prompt as well as through guiding questions in response to student posts. In the following hypothetical example, a discussion about Shakespeare's Sonnet 33 illustrates both.

Hypothetical: Dr. Smith's English Literature - Shakespeare's Sonnet 33

In Dr. Smith's English literature class, the main discussion prompt asks the students to analyze Shakespeare's Sonnet 33 (Shakespeare, n.d.). Dr. Smith provides an initial scaffolding structure for the discussion by listing the week's lesson elements for reviewing a sonnet:

Class, in your first discussion response, include these points of analysis, as we covered in this week's lesson: 1) Structure of the sonnet, 2) identification of theme, 3) analysis of imagery and language, and 4) comparison of the poem to other works read in the unit.

Adding structure to the discussion question, Dr. Smith provides students with a guide for structuring their response from the week's lesson. Student "Jane" posts the following initial response: "Hi Dr. Smith and everyone, OK, so I read Sonnet 33. It seems to be describing a dramatic change in the weather. Shakespeare is usually meaning this to mean something else, but I don't get this one. Help! Jane"

In this post, Jane has not expressed much insight about theme, structure or details of the poem's imagery, but she has related to other works where Shakespeare's pattern is to use poetry themes to "mean something else." Recognizing where she has expressed some insight and to encourage further reflection for deeper analysis, Dr. Smith provides a scaffolding response designed to redirect her:

Hi Jane, Thank you for opening the discussion about Sonnet 33! You are on the right track that Shakespeare's mind is surely on more than weather. As you saw in the Sonnets in this week's lesson, his imagery in the poem provides a structure for expressing a deeply felt sentiment or experience. In Sonnet 33, he sees in the clouds' masking of the sun a comparison to another fleeting bright moment in his life. In your analysis, think about the theme of the sun and how he uses the imagery of metaphor to convey the human experience. How does Shakespeare immortalize a love through the imagery of poetry? As you explore answering further, please feel free to ask more questions and share your thoughts as you continue your analysis of Sonnet 33. We would like to hear more of your ideas! Dr. Smith

In his reply, Dr. Smith relates the scaffold points of sonnet analysis to the student's reply and connects them to Sonnet 33 in a positive voice. Without fully laying out an answer, the teacher's response adds additional architecture to his original scaffold points for the student to navigate when reading the poem again. Table 1 illustrates how this scaffolding example aligns with the CoI framework.

Table 1. Dr. Smith's English Sonnet Discussion

Scaffolding structure	CoI framework
Dr. Smith's opening scaffold lists the points students should cover in the Sonnet analysis. This does not provide an answer for the Sonnet in question but provides structure. This reduces stress and provides focus for the group to discuss the poem.	Teaching presence: –Guidance provides direction from instructor. Cognitive presence: Guidance provides structure for thought. Social presence: Guidance reduces stress by providing topic focus for the group to address collectively.
Jane's initial response reveals her beginning level of understanding of the discussion question; this is her location in the ZPD.	Cognitive presence: Student's learning level is identified.
Dr. Smith's reply acknowledges the student's correct point, encourages further reflection with direction designed to channel the student's inquiry for the analysis, and invites further response. The instructor's follow-up builds on the scaffold structure set up with the initial discussion prompt.	Teaching presence: The teacher affirms student's insight, specifically answers student request for guidance, and provides direction. Social presence: Positive and encouraging tone invites further discourse.
Other students can read the exchange and benefit from the Dr. Smith's suggestions.	Cognitive presence: It advances an approach for addressing the analysis elements. Social presence: Group members can apply concepts discussed in their own analysis and have the opportunity to chime in.

Open-ended Questions Scaffolded to the Learning Materials

In a similar, but more open-ended approach, the instructor might launch a discussion with a broad open-ended question that encourages students to share their initial thoughts on a topic (e.g., "What are your first impressions of Vygotsky's concept of the ZPD?"). This is designed to get the discussion going based on the learning materials aligned with the discussion. After students have shared their responses, the instructor can assess the level of depth and critical thinking expressed, and post follow-up questions that require a higher level of critical thinking or application (e.g., "Can you relate the ZPD to your own learning experiences? How might you use this concept in a professional setting?"). With this technique, students are asked to simply engage with the topic at a basic level. Then, follow-up questions designed to focus and deepen understanding of the connection of theory to practice can be interposed in the discussion. How effective this approach might be in a given discussion will largely depend on the nature of the topic and the students' level of background experience and knowledge. Some studies have indicated a tendency for students to respond superficially, if at all, where they lack relevant prior knowledge (Xun & Land, 2004). This more loosely scaffolded approach could be used more successfully later in the course, when students have built a knowledge base and comfort level with the course subject matter.

Step-by-Step Guidance: Sequential Questioning

The various ways scaffolding can be designed all have the principal commonality of breaking a potentially incomprehensible whole into cognitively digestible parts. Sequential questioning in a discussion leads students through steps in thought, by taking them beyond what they know to the next revelation. In this regard, the process is analogous to Bloom's taxonomy–cognitively progressing from concrete concepts to increasingly abstract applications represented in six categories (Athanassiou et al., 2003). Typically depicted as a pyramid with the highest order of thinking at the top, these six categories are helpful for stating measurable learning objectives and formulating questions for research and analysis. Bloom's categories, from basic to highest order are: Remember (basic facts and concepts); understand (identify and simply explain facts, concepts); apply (use facts and concepts in a new situation); analyze (connect, compare, and differentiate ideas); evaluate (argue, defend, and draw a conclusion from information and ideas); create (formulate a new work or idea) (Persaud, 2024). As Venter (2005) explained,

a crucial and attractive feature of Bloom's taxonomy is that it identifies in a hierarchical manner the various developmental stages of cognitive development, and thus allows teachers to "scaffold" student's thinking by building on each level in an increasingly complex way.(p. 635)

Bloom's taxonomy is a useful reference tool in devising scaffolding material for online discussions (Mulcare & Schwedel, 2017). Consider the following hypothetical utilizing sequential questioning that reflects Bloom's hierarchical progression.

Hypothetical: Dr. Max's Stages of Project Management

In this discussion, the opening prompt asks students: "Discuss the stages of project management and their importance. Which stage do you consider most critical for ensuring project success? Justify your answer."

The following is a sequential exchange between student "Emory" and the instructor, "Dr. Max," in which Dr. Max uses sequential questioning as a scaffolding technique following Bloom's taxonomy.

Emory's first post is:

Hi Dr. Max and Classmates. In my view, the planning stage is the most critical in project management. During this stage, the project scope is defined, objectives are set, and a detailed plan is created to guide the project through its lifecycle. Without a clear plan, the project can easily go off track, leading to scope creep, budget overruns, and missed deadlines. I believe that a well-structured plan lays the foundation for the entire project, ensuring that all team members are aligned and that risks are identified early on. Thanks, Emory.

Initially, the student provides a relevant response, but stops at a brief summary and identifies only one planning stage. The concepts mentioned lack much analysis or definition. Emory has demonstrated understanding at Bloom's level 2. Dr. Max replies to Emory as follows:

Hi Emory. Great insights! You have correctly emphasized the importance of the planning stage to set a foundation for preventing problems. Now let's take your thoughts to the next step! You mentioned "scope creep" and "budget overruns" as possible risks. Are there strategies that could help mitigate these risks in the planning stage? How would you prioritize these strategies?

Thanks for your thoughts on these points! Dr. Max

The instructor has encouraged the student by validating the positive points of his response. Rather than prompt the student to expand his answer to all the stages, which might keep the discussion points at the recall/understanding level in terms of Bloom's taxonomy, she instead engages him in a deeper analysis of the planning stage that is the topic of his post. Emory is now challenged to analyze mitigating risk, apply strategies, and prioritize them. This sequential questioning approach provides a scaffold to help the student move cognitively from identification of concepts to analysis of how they work in action. Asking the student to prioritize challenges the student to level three of thinking on Bloom's taxonomy (i.e., analysis).

Emory replies:

Thank you, Dr. Max. To mitigate scope creep, one effective strategy is to establish a clear statement of the project scope and establish a change control process that requires formal approval for modifications. The purpose of this procedure is to make sure changes are reviewed before they are committed. A detailed budget that includes contingencies for unexpected costs would help monitor with an ongoing check against changes to prevent overruns. My priority in a change-prone environment would be keeping current in the change control process, with a clear definition of the project scope and schedule in hand. The process would include ongoing status checks, such as weekly progress reports. Emory

Emory's response demonstrates higher level cognitive analysis (i.e., analysis and application), but he can go higher. Dr. Max's next response scaffolds on Emory's own response and continues to prompt him to Bloom's highest level of evaluation and creative thinking. Emory's reply thereafter shows how he steps up:

Excellent, Emory! You have identified key strategies, like the scope and change control process. While I would agree that prioritizing scope management in resource-constrained environments is a worthy approach, I am interested in how you would adapt these strategies in a highly dynamic environment subject to sudden changes. Now, consider how these strategies could be adapted if you were managing a project in a highly dynamic environment where requirements might frequently change. How would you maintain both flexibility and control? Dr. Max

Emory replies:

Hi, Dr. Max. In a dynamic environment, I would implement an agile project management approach. In this way the project is broken down into smaller and manageable parts that can be adjusted when changes arise. I would want to have regular communication with stakeholders for their input help stay on track. I would ensure my team understands flexibility is needed to meet changes, but I want to keep the project objectives clearly in focus to maintain control. The plan also needs a contingency process in place that includes notification and response protocols to evaluate change consequence. Thanks for the help, Dr. Max. Emory.

This dialogue could continue with Dr. Max responding to Emory's ideas with further encouragement and questions. She might ask Emory to describe an example of a dynamic change that could affect project scope and the type of contingency to respond. As an alternative, she might ask him how he would kick off the project when the planning stage is complete, thus continuing to move the project plan forward. Or, she might be satisfied with Emory's progress at this point.

This hypothetical exchange demonstrates the instructor's use of sequential questioning to direct the student toward a deepening understanding of the topic. Using this scaffolding technique, Dr. Max has encouraged Emory to move from a general understanding of the discussion question to specific applications and then to adaptive strategies that require deeper thinking at a higher cognitive level. This sequential scaffolding approach helps students to progressively build their critical thinking skills systematically within the context of the discussion topic and illustrates how Bloom's taxonomy helps visualize the cognitive thread.

Social Scaffolding: Encouraging Peer-to-Peer Interaction

Vygotsky considered peer association an essential feature in advancing learning across the ZPD (Taber, 2018). Research supports that "interactive online discussions increase student cognitive levels" (Liu et al., 2023, p. 13). Peer involvement in teaching and assessment through group collaboration is a popular approach for learning "because it stimulates the learning of higher-order skills such as sharing responsibility, reflection, discussion, and collaboration" (Strijbos & Wichmann, 2018, p. 2). Social scaffolding focuses on leveraging social interactions and collaborative learning to support student understanding. It emphasizes the role of peers and group dynamics in the learning process. Activities include group assignments such as peer review exercises, debates, and group collective problem-solving. The choice of scaffolding strategies will depend on the learners' needs, the complexity of the content, and the desired learning outcomes (Duus & Cooray, 2022). The following hypothetical demonstrates the use of social scaffolding for group engagement in an asynchronous online discussion.

Hypothetical: Dr. Holmes' World War I Group Discussion Project

For this example, Dr. Holmes' higher education World History class has a typical discussion prompt about the causes of World War I (Thompson, 2023) for an asynchronous online discussion. She wants to change up the usual post/response format by using a scaffolded collaborative peer group structure, to encourage active discussion and deeper thinking. The discussion question is:

Examine the various causes of World War I, including social, political, and economic, factors stirring across Europe and worldwide. How did these factors interact to contribute to the outbreak of the war? In your response, consider the role of alliances, militarism, imperialism, and nationalism.

Dr. Holmes' asynchronous discussion project design for this question uses social scaffolding to encourage peer interaction and enhance social presence (Kraatz et al., 2020). Using classroom tools available in the classroom platform to facilitate groups, she has set up a discussion space in the classroom where each of the groups can meet. She will assign each group a specific aspect of the question to analyze and discuss within their group and then share the group's thoughts in a larger whole-class forum. The scaffolding demonstrated here is three-fold: 1) Structure of the two-tiered group discussion procedure; 2) break down of the causal factors of the war by assigning a specific focus to each group; 3) guidance for how students can approach peer review in the whole-group discussion phase of the project. The students are presented with the following project instructions for the week's work:

Causes of World War I Discussion Project

Class, this discussion about World War I is a collaborative learning project. For part of the project, you will work in small groups. This means it will be important for you to deeply engage in mutual dialogue. To help you organize your work, here are the steps to follow:

1. **Collaborative Group Formation (by Tuesday):** I have divided the class into small groups of four people each. Your group has an assigned group chat space in the classroom to collaborate. Please meet to get started. Your group will explore a specific factor of the causes of World War I (e.g., alliances, militarism, imperialism, and nationalism). I have posted each group's specific assignment. Within your group, discuss and share insights on how your assigned factor contributed to the war.

2. **Post Group Analysis (by Wednesday):** Reach a group consensus about your assigned factor and post your group's analysis in the class discussion for this project as a single group post. (Agree on a group representative to post for the group.) Explain your assigned factor, the causes you analyzed, and the group's conclusion.
3. **Individual Posts: Peer Review and Discussion Expansion (by Friday):** When your group's analysis is posted, then review the posts of at least two other groups and individually post a response to their analyses. When reading other groups' posts, look for connections between the causes your group explored and those presented by the other groups. Compare. For example, did they discuss how alliances interacted with militarism to escalate tensions? In your reply to two other group posts, offer your own new perspectives and ask questions that encourage further discussion. For example, if militarism is discussed, you might say, "Your analysis of alliances is compelling, especially about how they contributed to a sense of inevitability. Could we also consider how militarism might have influenced the decisions made within these alliances?" In addition, while you are posting your individual replies to two other group posts, also post at least one response to the peer replies in your own group's thread. In this way you will be engaging in discussion with two other groups and with your peers' commentary on your own group.
4. **Group Synthesis Post (by Sunday):** After engaging the individual discussion posts, meet again with your own group and collaborate on a synthesis post. This post should summarize the collective insights from your individual discussion posts and offer a more comprehensive analysis of how these factors combined to lead to World War I. Each group member should contribute to creating this final post. Post this group post in the class project discussion forum as a new thread.
5. **Individual Final Reflection Post About the Discussion (by Sunday):** While preparing your group's synthesis post, take a moment to reflect on how working with your peers as a group has broadened your understanding of the causes of World War I. Post a brief individual reflection on how the group dynamic helped you better see the connections between different historical factors. The total number of class discussion forum posts required for the project is: Group posts: 2, Individual: 4

> Please reach out to me with questions as you are working on this project. I will also be participating in the discussion conversations.

Dr. Holmes's project illustrates that social scaffolding creates a structured environment to encourage peer interaction. Rather than saying "here's your group, figure out what you think caused World War I and post your analysis," students are provided a group participation structure, guidance for approaching their analysis, and a structured format for reporting their findings and giving peer input. This scaffolding technique provides a platform for peer collaboration in groups synchronized with opportunity for individual expression as well. Scaffolded guidelines provide examples of the kinds of questions students can ask to advance their analysis and lead their peers to move the discussion forward (Nachowitz, 2018). The final group synthesis and individual reflection posts reinforce an understanding of the value of collaborative learning (Acquaro, 2020; Choi et al., 2005).

The rationale of a collaborative approach to social scaffolding is to help build a community of learners who support and contribute to each other's learning (Shaw, 2005). Guided interactions enrich and encourage a deeper and comprehensive understanding of complex issues (Sawyer, 2005). Significant in the scaffolding approach illustrated in Dr. Holmes's group project hypothetical is the point that she will engage in the class discussion as well. Although the focus of the project is peer-to-peer group engagement, teaching presence is not abdicated. The instructor's role here is to interpose encouragement, prompt questions or comments to assist in advancing the discussion and redirect incorrect or inappropriate digression. What Dr. Holmes will avoid is a shadowy sense of being persistently omnipresent as the discussion unfolds. Instead, Roehler and Cantlon (1997) characterized the instructor's involvement in scaffolding as "learner conversations" in which "all participants feel responsible for their own learning and the learning of others" (p. 11). To further foster student ownership of the discussion, a variation of Dr. Holmes's project would be a group video or brief audio-narrated PowerPoint, instead of a post.

Nudging Learner Response as Scaffolding in Asynchronous Discussions

Kraatz et al. (2020) emphasized the importance of the instructor keeping a balance in the cognitive and social dynamics in play in discussion dynamics. This burden is more complex for the online classroom, where students can more easily opt to be nonresponsive. Roehler and Cantlon (1997) characterized this as a "balance of challenge and support" afforded students (p. 37). The challenge is provided in the learning activities, which should be designed to create intellectual curiosity. The support comes from the instructor, who assists students in navigating the learning activities to achieve learning outcomes. A variety of scaffolding techniques will ideally be employed (Roehler & Cantlon, 1997).

Peer-to-peer communication becomes important to this process, as a critical part of the learning conversation (Maloch, 2002). However, keeping discussions alive and responsive to the scaffolding structure the instructor has provided remains the responsibility of the instructor. A concept helpful in advancing discussions is called "nudging." This time-old social construct has taken on new life as a millennial phenomenon (Fusaro et al., 2021), and it fits well into scaffolding technique. Nudging can be considered a subtle scaffolding technique in and of itself. Harvard professor, Cass Sunstein, explained a nudge is "an intervention that maintains freedom of choice but steers people in a particular direction" (Fusaro et al., 2021, para. 4). A nudge can be any type of positive assistance, such as an advance reminder that a bill payment is due soon. The point is, a nudge is positive, and not a mandatory directive.

Nudging is inherently part of teaching and can be put to good use in an asynchronous online discussion. For example, in the Shakespeare Sonnet 33 hypothetical, Dr. Smith utilized nudging with the question, "How does Shakespeare immortalize a love through the imagery of poetry?" This question created a scaffold between the lesson's element of "imagery" and the student's recognition that the poem is using weather to mean something else. Similarly, in the World War I hypothetical discussion, Dr. Holmes built nudges into the project instructions with sample questions students might use in their discussion. In this way, nudging artfully brings enhanced teaching presence to the discussion, and provides scaffolding material to build cognitive presence.

CONCLUSION

Scaffolding can be utilized in many ways to make asynchronous online discussions more inviting and engaging for students. Involving peer-to-peer activities in a discussion is a powerful tool to promote participation. Implementing technology tools will also aid student involvement, such as a student use of audio or video response, instead of written text. Studies demonstrate the importance of teacher facilitation skills in creating an inclusive and supportive discussion environment. Best practice scaffolding techniques can trigger ideas and nudge students along toward achieving the desired learning outcomes. Scaffolding in the asynchronous online discussion context also provides the instructor an opportunity to individualize teaching responses to students. Following the ZPD theory in a discussion, and with an eye on Bloom's taxonomy, an instructor has the opportunity to gauge a student's level of development on the topic and utilize scaffolding questions designed to lead to deeper understanding. Further, defining learning outcomes and discussion prompts with scaffolding design in mind gives active direction to both students and instructors by bringing focus to the steps needed to lead learners from what they do not know, yet, to desired level of new knowledge and skill they desire to learn. Thinking of a learning outcome as a destination, scaffolding provides the cognitive map to get there, while promoting social engagement and learning.

REFERENCES

Ackermann, E. (2001). *Piaget's constructivism, Papert's constructionism: What's the difference?* Semantic Scholar. https://learning.media.mit.edu/content/publications/EA.Piaget%20_%20Papert.pdf

Acquaro, P. (2020). Structuring and scaffolding the online course: A practical development framework. *Journal of Online Graduate Education.*, 3(1). https://ijoge.org/index.php/IJOGE/article/view/38

Al Mamun, M. A., & Lawrie, G. (2024). Cognitive presence in learner–content interaction process: The role of scaffolding in online self-regulated learning environments. *Journal of Computers in Education*, 11(3), 791–821. DOI: 10.1007/s40692-023-00279-7

Anderson, T. (2017). How communities of inquiry drive teaching and learning in the digital age. *North Contact, 1*, 1–6. https://teachonline.ca/fr/node/92055

Andreev, I. (2024, July 31). *Learning outcomes.*https://www.valamis.com/hub/learning-outcomes#5-types-of-learning-outcomes

Athanassiou, N., McNett, J., & Harvey, C. (2003). Critical thinking in the management classroom: Bloom's taxonomy as a learning tool. *Journal of Management Education*, 27(5), 533–555. DOI: 10.1177/1052562903252515

Avci, Z., & Ergulec, F. (2019, November). *The Community of Inquiry (CoI) framework for overcoming learning barriers in open and distance education* [Paper presentation]. International Open and Distance learning Conference Proceedings (pp. 137–153), Anadolu University, Turkey.

Bakker, A., Smit, J., & Wegerif, R. (2015). Scaffolding and dialogic teaching in mathematics education: Introduction and review. *ZDM Mathematics Education*, 47(7), 1047–1065. DOI: 10.1007/s11858-015-0738-8

Barrett, B., & Ashar, L. (2024). Creating artificial intelligence (AI) best practices in virtual learning environments: A primer approach for introducing the implementation of generative-AI as a teaching tool. In *Proceedings of the 16th International Conference on Education and New Learning Technologies (EDULEARN24)* (pp. 9197–9202). https://doi.org/DOI: 10.21125/edulearn.2024.2216

Beetham, H., & Sharpe, R. (Eds.). (2019). *Rethinking pedagogy for a digital age* (3rd ed.). Routledge., DOI: 10.4324/9781351252805

Bloomberg. L. D. (2021). *Designing and delivering effective online instruction: How to engage adult learners.* Teachers College Press.

Bozkurt, A. (2019). From distance education to open and distance learning: A holistic evaluation of history, definitions, and theories. In Sisman-Ugur, S., & Kurubacak, G. (Eds.), *Handbook of research on learning in the age of transhumanism* (pp. 252–273). IGI Global. DOI: 10.4018/978-1-5225-8431-5.ch016

Cagiltay, K. (2006). Scaffolding strategies in electronic performance support systems: Types and challenges. *Innovations in Education and Teaching International*, 43(1), 93–103. DOI: 10.1080/14703290500467673

Choi, I., Land, S. M., & Turgeon, A. J. (2005). Scaffolding peer-questioning strategies to facilitate metacognition during online small group discussion. *Instructional Science*, 33(5), 483–511. DOI: 10.1007/s11251-005-1277-4

Cleveland-Innes, M. (2020). The community of inquiry theoretical framework: Designing collaborative online and blended learning. In Beetham, H., & Sharpe, R. (Eds.), *Rethinking pedagogy for a digital age* (3rd ed., pp. 85–102). Routledge., DOI: 10.4324/9781351252805

Cortázar, C., Nussbaum, M., Harcha, J., Alvares, D., López, F., Goñi, J., & Cabezas, V. (2021). Promoting critical thinking in an online, project-based course. *Computers in Human Behavior*, 119, 106705. DOI: 10.1016/j.chb.2021.106705 PMID: 36571081

Delahunty, J. (2018). Connecting to learn, learning to connect: Thinking together in asynchronous forum discussion. *Linguistics and Education*, 46, 12–22. DOI: 10.1016/j.linged.2018.05.003

Doo, M. Y., Bonk, C. J., & Heo, H. (2020). A meta-analysis of scaffolding effects in online learning in higher education. *International Review of Research in Open and Distance Learning*, 23(3), 60–80. DOI: 10.19173/irrodl.v21i3.4638

Duus, R., & Cooray, M. (2022, August 17). *Empowering students to learn from each other: How digital tools can enhance peer learning across student teams.* https://www.hbsp.harvard.edu/inspiring-minds/empowering-students-to-learn-from-each-other

Feng, X., Xie, J., & Liu, Y. (2017). Using the community of inquiry framework to scaffold online tutoring. *International Review of Research in Open and Distance Learning*, 18(2), 162–188. DOI: 10.19173/irrodl.v18i2.2362

Fusaro, R., Sunstein, C., Thaler, R., & Sperling-Magro. (2021, October 15). *How does "nudging" work as an intervention technique?* https://www.weforum.org/agenda/2021/10/what-is-nudging-and-how-has-it-changed-over-time/

Garrison, D. R. (2015). *Thinking collaboratively: Learning in a community of inquiry*. Routledge. DOI: 10.4324/9781315740751

Garrison, D. R., Anderson, T., & Archer, W. (1999). Critical inquiry in a text-based environment: Computer conferencing in higher education. *The Internet and Higher Education*, 2(2-3), 87–105. DOI: 10.1016/S1096-7516(00)00016-6

Garrison, D. R., Anderson, T., & Archer, W. (2003). A theory of critical inquiry in online distance education. In M. Moore & W. Anderson (Eds.), *Handbook of distance education* (pp. 113–127). Lawrence Erlbaum Associates.

Hawkey, K. (2003). Social constructivism and asynchronous text-based discussion: A case study with trainee teachers. *Education and Information Technologies*, 8(2), 165–177. DOI: 10.1023/A:1024558414766

Hein, G. E. (1991, October 15-22). *Constructivist learning theory* [Paper presentation]. CECA (International Committee of Museum Educators) Conference, Jerusalem, Israel. https://www.exploratorium.edu/education/ifi/constructivist-learning

Kim, H. S., & Oh, E. G. (2018). Scaffolding argumentation in asynchronous online discussion: Using students' perceptions to refine a design framework. *International Journal of Online Pedagogy and Course Design*, 8(2), 29–43. DOI: 10.4018/IJOPCD.2018040103

Koskey, K. L., & Benson, S. N. (2017). A review of literature and a model for scaffolding asynchronous student-student interaction in online discussion forums. In Vu, P., Fredrickson, S., & Moore, C. (Eds.), *Handbook of research on innovative pedagogies and technologies for online learning in higher education* (pp. 263–280). IGI Global., DOI: 10.4018/978-1-5225-1851-8.ch012

Kraatz, E., Nagpal, M., Lin, T., Hsieh, M., Ha, S. Y., Kim, S., & Shin, S. (2020). Teacher scaffolding of social and intellectual collaboration in small groups: A comparative case study. *Frontiers in Psychology*, 11, 587058. Advance online publication. DOI: 10.3389/fpsyg.2020.587058 PMID: 33240179

Lange, C., Gorbunova, A., Shmeleva, E., & Costley, J. (2023). The relationship between instructional scaffolding strategies and maintained situational interest. *Interactive Learning Environments*, 31(10), 6640–6651. DOI: 10.1080/10494820.2022.2042314

Levykh, M. G. (2008). The affective establishment and maintenance of Vygotsky's zone of proximal development. *Educational Theory*, 58(1), 83–101. DOI: 10.1111/j.1741-5446.2007.00277.x

Lim Abdullah, M. R. T., Hussin, Z., & Zakaria, A. R. (2013). MLearning scaffolding model for undergraduate English language learning: Bridging formal and informal learning. *The Turkish Online Journal of Educational Technology*, 12(2), 217–233.

Liu, C. H. (2008). *A Vygotskyan educational psycho-semiotic perspective of interpsychology in classroom teaching and teacher socialization: Theories, instrument, and interpretive analyses* [Unpublished doctoral dissertation]. University of Adelaide., https://hekyll.services.adelaide.edu.au/dspace/bitstream/2440/69483/8/02whole.pdf

Liu, Z., Zhang, N., Peng, X., Liu, S., & Yang, Z. (2023). Students' social-cognitive engagement in online discussions. *Journal of Educational Technology & Society*, 26(1), 1–15. DOI: 10.30191/ETS.202301_26(1).0001

Maloch, B. (2002). Scaffolding student talk: One teacher's role in literature discussion groups. *Reading Research Quarterly*, 37(1), 94–112. DOI: 10.1598/RRQ.37.1.4

McLeod, S. (2024, February 1). *Constructivism learning theory & philosophy of education*. https://www.simplypsychology.org/constructivism.html

McLoughlin, C. (2002). Learner support in distance and networked learning environments: Ten dimensions for successful design. *Distance Education*, 23(2), 149–162. DOI: 10.1080/0158791022000009178

McNiff, J., & Aicher, T. (2017). Understanding the challenges and opportunities associated with online learning: A scaffolding theory approach. *Sport Management Education Journal*, 11(1), 13–23. DOI: 10.1123/smej.2016-0007

Moll, L. C. (2013). *L. S. Vygotsky and education*. Taylor and Francis Group. DOI: 10.4324/9780203156773

Mulcare, D., & Shwedel, A. (2017). Transforming Bloom's taxonomy into classroom practice: A practical yet comprehensive approach to promote critical reading and student participation. *Journal of Political Science Education*, 13(2), 121–137. DOI: 10.1080/15512169.2016.1211017

Nachowitz, M. (2018). Scaffolding progressive online discourse for literary knowledge building. *Online Learning : the Official Journal of the Online Learning Consortium*, 22(3), 133–156. DOI: 10.24059/olj.v22i3.1261

Nussbaum, E. M., Hartley, K., Sinatra, G. M., Reynolds, R. E., & Bendixen, L. D. (2004). Personality interactions and scaffolding in on-line discussions. *Journal of Educational Computing Research*, 30(1-2), 113–137. DOI: 10.2190/H8P4-QJUF-JXME-6JD8

Nworie, J. (2021, May 19). *Beyond COVID-19: What's next for online teaching and learning in higher education?* https://er.educause.edu/articles/2021/5/beyond-covid-19-whats-next-for-online-teaching-and-learning-in-higher-education

Persaud, C. (2024, May 15). *Bloom's taxonomy: The ultimate guide.* https://tophat.com/blog/blooms-taxonomy/

Pham, N. M. T. (2023). *The effects of question prompt-based scaffolding and social presence enhancement on students' argumentation and ill-structured problem-solving.* [Doctoral dissertation, University of Missouri-Columbia]. https://core.ac.uk/reader/578762458

Puntambekar, S. (2022). Distributed scaffolding: Scaffolding students in classroom environments. *Educational Psychology Review*, 34(1), 451–472. DOI: 10.1007/s10648-021-09636-3

Putnam, C., O'Donnell, J., & Bertozzi, N. (2010, June). *Scaffolding and fading within and across a six-semester CDIO design sequence* [Paper presentation]. The Proceedings of the 6th International CDIO Conference, Montreal, Canada.

Rahma, H., Leng, C. O., & Mashedi, R. (2020). Innovative educational practice for impactful teaching strategies through scaffolding method. *Asian Journal of University Education*, 16(4), 53–60. DOI: 10.24191/ajue.v16i4.11952

Roehler, L. R., & Cantlon, D. J. (1997). Scaffolding: A powerful tool in social constructivist classrooms. In K. Hogan & M. Pressley, M. (Eds.), *Scaffolding student learning: Instructional approaches & issues* (pp. 6–42). Brookline Books.

Roth, J. A. (2019). *Making the struggle productive: Conceptualizing the role and impact of the mathematics teacher in episodes of productive struggle* [Doctoral dissertation, Kennesaw State University]. https://digitalcommons.kennesaw.edu/seceddoc_etd/16/?utm_source=digitalcommons.kennesaw.edu%2Fseceddoc_etd%2F16&utm_medium=PDF&utm_campaign=PDFCoverPages

Rothstein, R., Lee, Y., Berger, E. J., Rhoads, J., & Deboer, J. (2023). Collaborative engagement and help-seeking behaviors in engineering asynchronous online discussions. *International Journal of Engineering Education*, 39(1), 189–207.

Sadaf, A., Wu, T., & Martin, F. (2021). Cognitive presence in online learning: A systematic review of empirical research from 2000 to 2019. *Computers and Education Open*, 2, 10050. DOI: 10.1016/j.caeo.2021.100050

Sawyer, R. K. (2005). Analyzing collaborative discourse. In Sawyer, R. K. (Ed.), *The Cambridge handbook of learning sciences* (pp. 187–204). Cambridge University Press. DOI: 10.1017/CBO9780511816833.013

Schneider, C. (2016). Using scaffolding techniques for legal research instruction. *Legal Info. Rev.*, 2, 61–80.

Schunk, D. H. (2012). *Learning theories: An educational perspective* (6th ed.). Pearson Education, Inc.

Shakespeare, W. (n.d.). *Sonnet 33: Full many a glorious morning have I seen.* https://www.poetryfoundation.org/poems/45093/sonnet-33-full-many-a-glorious-morning-have-i-seen

Shaw, E. (2005). Assessing and scaffolding collaborative learning in online discussions. In Looi, C. K., McCalla, G. I., Bredeweg, B., & Breuker, J. (Eds.), *AIED* (pp. 587–594). IOS Press., https://www.researchgate.net/publication/221297731_Assessing_and_Scaffolding_Collaborative_Learning_in_Online_Discussions

Shea, P., & Bidjerano, T. (2009). Community of inquiry as a theoretical framework to foster "epistemic engagement" and "cognitive presence" in online education. *Computers & Education*, 52(3), 543–553. DOI: 10.1016/j.compedu.2008.10.007

Sinha, B., Roberts, D. P., & Jane, C. (2022). Effective strategies for using asynchronous online discussion forums in educational curriculums. *American International Journal of Business Management*, 5(7), 87–98.

Smagorinsky, P. (2018). Deconflating the ZPD and instructional scaffolding: Retranslating and reconceiving the zone of proximal development as the zone of next development. *Learning, Culture and Social Interaction*, 16, 70–75. DOI: 10.1016/j.lcsi.2017.10.009

Strijbos, J. W., & Wichmann, A. (2018). Promoting learning by leveraging the collaborative nature of formative peer assessment with instructional scaffolds. *European Journal of Psychology of Education*, 33(1), 1–9. DOI: 10.1007/s10212-017-0353-x

Suwastini, N. K. A., Ersani, N. P. D., Padmadewi, N. N., & Artini, L. P. (2021). Schemes of scaffolding in online education. *Retorika: Jurnal Ilmu Bahasa*, 7(1), 10–18. DOI: 10.22225/jr.7.1.2941.10-18

Swan, K. (2017). Multiple perspectives on social presence in online learning. In Whiteside, A. L., Dikkers, A. G., & Swan, K. (Eds.), *Social presence in online learning: Multiple perspectives on practice and research* (pp. 22–29). Taylor & Francis.

Swan, K., & Richardson, J. (2017). Social presence and the Community of Inquiry framework. In Whiteside, A. L., Dikkers, A. G., & Swan, K. (Eds.), *Social presence in online learning: Multiple perspectives on practice and research* (pp. 83–95). Taylor & Francis.

Taber, K. S. (2018). Scaffolding learning: Principles for effective teaching and the design of classroom resources. In Abend, A. (Ed.), *Effective teaching and learning: Perspectives, strategies, and implementation* (pp. 1–43). Nova.

The Community of Inquiry. (2024). *The Community of Inquiry: About the framework.* The Community of Inquiry. https://www.thecommunityofinquiry.org/coi

The history of distance learning. (2024). Oxford Learning College. https://www.oxfordcollege.ac/news/history-of-distance-learning/

Thompson, G. (2023, December 21). *Understanding the causes of World War I.* https://www.worldhistory.org.uk/world-war-i-causes

Venter, C. M. (2005). Analyze this: Using taxonomies to scaffold students' legal thinking and writing skills. *Mercer Law Review*, 57(2), 621–644.

Vygotsky, L. S. (1978). *Mind in society: The development of higher psychological processes.* Harvard University Press.

Watson, S., Sullivan, D. P., & Watson, K. (2023). Teaching presence in asynchronous online classes: It's not just a façade. *Online Learning : the Official Journal of the Online Learning Consortium*, 27(2), 288–303. https://files.eric.ed.gov/fulltext/EJ1392861.pdf. DOI: 10.24059/olj.v27i2.3231

Wegerif, R. (1998). The social dimension of asynchronous learning networks. *Online Learning : the Official Journal of the Online Learning Consortium*, 2(1), 34–49. DOI: 10.24059/olj.v2i1.1928

Whiteside, A., Dikkers, A. L., & Lewis, S. (2014, May 19). *The power of social presence for learning.* https://er.educause.edu/articles/2014/5/the-power-of-social-presence-for-learning

Wood, D., Bruner, J. S., & Ross, G. (1976). The role of tutoring in problem solving. *Journal of Child Psychology and Psychiatry, and Allied Disciplines*, 17(2), 89–100. DOI: 10.1111/j.1469-7610.1976.tb00381.x PMID: 932126

Xun, G. E., & Land, S. M. (2004). A conceptual framework for scaffolding ill-structured problem-solving processes using question prompts and peer interactions. *Educational Technology Research and Development*, 52(2), 5–22. DOI: 10.1007/BF02504836

Yang, X. (2023). A historical review of collaborative learning and cooperative learning. *TechTrends*, 67(4), 718–728. DOI: 10.1007/s11528-022-00823-9 PMID: 36711122

ADDITIONAL READING

Ackermann, E. (2004). Constructing knowledge and transforming the world. In Tokoro, M., & Steels, L. (Eds.), *A learning zone of one's own: Sharing representations and flow in collaborative learning environments* (pp. 15–37). JOS Press.

Belland, B. R., Kim, C., & Hannafin, M. J. (2013). A framework for designing scaffolds that improve motivation and cognition. *Educational Psychologist*, 48(4), 243–270. DOI: 10.1080/00461520.2013.838920 PMID: 24273351

Darabi, A., Arrastia, M. C., Nelson, D. W., Cornille, T., & Liang, X. (2011). Cognitive presence in asynchronous online learning: A comparison of four discussion strategies. *Journal of Computer Assisted Learning*, 27(3), 216–227. DOI: 10.1111/j.1365-2729.2010.00392.x

Delahunty, J., Verenikina, I., & Jones, P. (2013). Socio-emotional connections: Identity, belonging and learning in online interactions. A literature review. *Technology, Pedagogy and Education*, 23(2), 243–265. DOI: 10.1080/1475939X.2013.813405

Ernawati, M. D. W., Rini, E. F. S., Aldila, F. T., Haryati, T., & Perdana, R. (2023). Do creative thinking skills in problem-based learning benefit from scaffolding? *Journal of Turkish Science Educucation*, 20(3), 399-417. https://files.eric.ed.gov/fulltext/EJ1408177.pdf

Hamadi, H., Tafili, A., Kates, F. R., Larson, S. A., Ellison, C., & Song, J. (2023). Exploring an innovative approach to enhance discussion board engagement. *TechTrends*, 67(4), 741–751. DOI: 10.1007/s11528-023-00850-0 PMID: 37362586

Hung, B. P., & Nguyen, L. T. (2022). Scaffolding language learning in the online classroom. In Sharma, R., & Sharma, D. (Eds.), *New trends and applications in Internet of things (IoT) and big data analytics* (pp. 109–122). Intelligent Systems Reference Library., DOI: 10.1007/978-3-030-99329-0_8

Nakayama, M., Kikuchi, S., & Yamamoto, H. (2023). Effectiveness of a "nudge" for online discussion participation about attitude toward essay writing. In Z. Kubincovi, F. Caruso, T. Kim, M., Ivanova, L. Lancia, L., & M.A. Pellegrino, (Eds.). *Methodologies and intelligent systems for technology enhanced learning,* Workshops - 13th International Conference. MIS4TEL 2023. Lecture Notes in Networks and Systems, vol 769. Springer, Cham. https://doi.org/DOI: 10.1007/978-3-031-42134-1_17

Verenkina, I., Jones, P., & Delahunty, J. (2017). *The guide to fostering asynchronous online discussions in higher education.* ResearchGate. DOI: DOI: 10.13140/RG.2.2.25787.26405

Zhao, H., Sullivan, K., & Mellenius, I. (2013). Participation, interaction, and social presence: An exploratory study of collaboration in online peer review groups. *British Journal of Educational Technology*, 45(5), 807–819. DOI: 10.1111/bjet.12094

KEY TERMS AND DEFINITIONS

Community of Inquiry Framework: Theory of three overlapping interactive human-engagement dynamics that contribute to learning in the classroom environment: Social Presence, Teaching Presence, and Cognitive Presence

Constructivism: Learning theory that people acquire knowledge through active engagement with their environment – building knowledge and higher levels of cognition through experience and application of information rather than by rote or passive exposure

Lev Semyonovich Vygotsky: Russian psychologist (1896-1934) who studied how humans learn and develop independent thought. He developed a framework called historical-cultural activity to explain the relationship between how people think and what they do. His theory of the Zone of Proximal Development (ZPD) formed the basis for the use of scaffolding techniques in teaching.

Social Presence: Part of the triangle of the Community of Inquiry Framework, social presence is the group dynamic of group both projecting themselves actively in the classroom and perceiving their peers as real people involved in the group discourse.

Teaching Presence: Part of the triangle of the Community of Inquiry Framework, teaching presence is the instructor's classroom role of facilitating and directing learning activities with students for their achievement of learning outcomes.

Zone of Proximal Development (ZPD): First introduced by Russian psychologist, Lev Semyonovich Vygotsky, the ZPD is the cognitive gap between what a person independently knows and can do without support and what they do not know and cannot do even with support.

Chapter 12
Effective Strategies for Teaching Mathematics in Virtual Higher Education Environments

Rocío Rodríguez-Padín
https://orcid.org/0000-0001-9731-7757
Universidade da Coruña, Spain

ABSTRACT

This chapter provides a comprehensive guide for higher education instructors on effective strategies for teaching mathematics in virtual environments. As the shift to online education accelerates, particularly after the COVID-19 pandemic, educators must adopt evidence-based methods to enhance student learning. The chapter explores key principles of instructional design tailored for online mathematics, focusing on creating interactive and personalized learning experiences. Strategies for fostering student engagement, leveraging educational technologies, and promoting self-regulation are discussed. Additionally, the chapter highlights the importance of formative assessment in virtual settings, emphasizing methods that provide constructive feedback and opportunities for self-assessment. By addressing the challenges and opportunities of online mathematics education, this chapter aims to equip educators with the tools needed to optimize teaching and learning in the digital age.

DOI: 10.4018/979-8-3693-4407-1.ch012

1. INTRODUCTİON

Purpose of the Chapter

The main objective of this chapter is to offer a comprehensive framework for mathematics instructors in higher education, focusing on the unique demands of teaching in virtual environments. As remote and online education continue to grow, particularly in the aftermath of the COVID-19 pandemic (Estrada-Araoz et al., 2020), it is essential for educators to apply strategies specifically designed to address the complexities of mathematics instruction. Unlike other subjects, mathematics requires specialized approaches to support students' understanding of abstract and often visually complex concepts (Artigue, 2007; Felmer, Perdomo-Díaz, & Reyes, 2019).

This chapter, therefore, seeks to explore best practices and innovative methods that enhance student engagement and promote active learning in virtual mathematics settings. To effectively support this process, the chapter will discuss the use of technological tools tailored to mathematics, such as augmented reality (Tout, 2020) and interactive platforms (García et al., 2020), as well as approaches to fostering mathematical competencies for interpreting data, which has become especially relevant in a global context marked by increased reliance on statistics (Aguilar & Castañeda, 2021; Gal & Geiger, 2022).

Moreover, the chapter will consider psychological factors impacting students' learning experiences, such as stereotype threat and self-efficacy. These elements significantly influence students' attitudes towards mathematics and their overall performance, particularly in an online context where self-perception and confidence play vital roles (Auzmendi, 1992; Huda, Wahyuni, & Fauziyah, 2021). Addressing these psychological dimensions, as well as practical instructional strategies, this chapter aims to equip math educators with insights and tools for creating effective, inclusive, and resilient virtual learning environments.

Importance of Teaching Mathematics in Virtual Environments

Teaching mathematics in virtual environments has become increasingly significant, driven by advancements in educational technology and a rapid shift to online learning models following the COVID-19 pandemic (Estrada-Araoz et al., 2020). Mathematics, as a discipline that demands both abstract reasoning and hands-on interaction with concepts, presents unique challenges in the online setting. Unlike other subjects, mathematics often requires specialized approaches to foster deep conceptual understanding and to mitigate issues such as math anxiety and stereotype threat, which can be intensified in virtual settings (Auzmendi, 1992; Huda, Wahyuni, & Fauziyah, 2021).

Virtual environments, however, provide several advantages for mathematics instruction that were previously less accessible. For one, online platforms allow the integration of dynamic mathematical tools, such as augmented reality and virtual simulations, which enable students to visualize and manipulate abstract concepts, thereby supporting a more interactive and immersive learning experience (Tout, 2020; Artigue, 2007). Tools like GeoGebra and Desmos, often used in online math classrooms, empower students to engage directly with mathematical ideas, facilitating critical thinking and problem-solving skills that are essential for their development (Felmer, Perdomo-Díaz, & Reyes, 2019).

Furthermore, virtual environments support the cultivation of essential competencies that extend beyond mere content knowledge. According to Aguilar and Castañeda (2021), fostering mathematical competencies in virtual classrooms is crucial in preparing students for real-world applications, particularly in interpreting data and statistics—a skill increasingly vital in today's data-driven society. Additionally, virtual instruction offers opportunities for personalized learning experiences, where educators can adapt content to meet diverse student needs and provide flexible learning paths that accommodate different paces and learning styles (Bringula et al., 2021; Galligan & Axelsen, 2022).

By addressing both the technical and psychological dimensions of mathematics learning, virtual education can offer an inclusive space for students who may have previously encountered barriers to success. For example, enhanced accessibility features and adaptive learning tools can make mathematics more approachable and equitable for students from varied backgrounds, including those who may have faced difficulties in traditional classroom settings (Evans et al., 2021; Coben & O'Donoghue, 2020). Therefore, teaching mathematics in virtual environments not only supports students' cognitive development but also fosters critical life skills and broadens access to quality education in mathematics.

Specific Challenges and Opportunities for Online Mathematics Education

Teaching mathematics online presents a distinctive set of challenges and opportunities that educators must address to ensure effective learning. One of the primary challenges lies in translating mathematical concepts, which often rely on spatial and visual representations, into an online format that maintains students' engagement and understanding. Research indicates that the transition to virtual mathematics instruction can intensify math anxiety and stereotype threat among students, potentially impacting their confidence and performance (Auzmendi, 1992; Bringula et al., 2021). Moreover, many students in virtual settings may lack the necessary self-regulation skills to independently manage their learning, which is critical for success in an online math course (Huda, Wahyuni, & Fauziyah, 2021).

However, virtual environments also offer unique opportunities for overcoming these challenges. The use of dynamic and interactive tools, such as augmented and virtual reality applications, can transform abstract mathematical concepts into tangible, visual experiences that support deep learning (Tout, 2020). Programs like GeoGebra and Desmos enable students to experiment with mathematical relationships in real-time, providing a platform for exploration and discovery that aligns with constructivist learning theories (Artigue, 2007; Felmer, Perdomo-Díaz, & Reyes, 2019). Such tools can also facilitate the "learning by doing" approach, which is crucial for developing problem-solving skills in mathematics (Diego-Mantecon et al., 2021).

Virtual mathematics education also opens the door for personalized and adaptive learning. With the flexibility of online platforms, instructors can create customized learning paths that cater to diverse student needs, making it possible to address individual learning gaps and support varied paces of understanding (Galligan & Axelsen, 2022; Aguilar & Castañeda, 2021). This level of personalization is particularly beneficial in mathematics, where students' prior knowledge and attitudes towards the subject can significantly impact their learning outcomes (Flores & Auzmendi, 2018).

Additionally, online mathematics education allows for a global, collaborative learning experience that can enhance students' understanding of mathematics as a socially and culturally relevant discipline. Through virtual classrooms, students can participate in group activities, collaborate across geographic boundaries, and engage with real-world mathematical applications, thus gaining a broader perspective on the importance of numeracy in daily life (Evans et al., 2021; Civil, Stoehr, & Salazar, 2020). These collaborative opportunities not only enrich students' learning experiences but also align with current educational goals to prepare students for a highly connected, globalized world.

In summary, while online mathematics education presents challenges related to engagement, self-regulation, and the unique cognitive demands of the subject, it also provides significant opportunities for enhancing interactivity, personalization, and global collaboration. By harnessing these opportunities, educators can create inclusive, effective virtual learning environments that support both mathematical understanding and essential life skills.

2. INSTRUCTİONAL DESİGN ADAPTED FOR VİRTUAL ENVİRONMENTS

Teaching mathematics in virtual environments requires a carefully adapted instructional design approach that considers the unique characteristics and needs of online students. As education shifts to digital platforms, traditional teaching methods must evolve to maintain the effectiveness and engagement of learning.

Instructional Design Principles for Teaching Mathematics Online

Effective instructional design for mathematics in virtual environments requires approaches that address the subject's unique cognitive demands and the specific needs of online learners. Key principles include fostering interactivity, adapting content to different learning styles, and creating supportive structures to mitigate challenges such as math anxiety and self-doubt, both of which can be more pronounced in virtual settings (Auzmendi, 1992; Bringula et al., 2021).

A central principle in designing online math instruction is *interactive learning*, which involves actively engaging students through tools that allow them to visualize and manipulate mathematical concepts. Dynamic software programs, such as GeoGebra and Desmos, support this goal by allowing students to experiment with variables and observe real-time changes in mathematical models. These tools align with constructivist learning theories, helping students develop a deeper understanding of mathematics through exploration and discovery (Artigue, 2007; Felmer, Perdomo-Díaz, & Reyes, 2019). Additionally, incorporating augmented and virtual reality can make abstract mathematical concepts more accessible, offering a tangible learning experience that traditional approaches may lack (Tout, 2020).

Personalization and adaptability are also crucial in virtual math instruction. Personalized pathways, which allow students to progress at their own pace, have proven particularly effective for mathematics, where learners often have diverse backgrounds and levels of confidence in their abilities. Online platforms that provide adaptive feedback and tailored content make it possible to address individual learning gaps and offer support that targets specific areas of improvement (Galligan & Axelsen, 2022; Aguilar & Castañeda, 2021). Moreover, by using tools that track progress and give immediate feedback, instructors can help students build self-regulation skills, a key factor in online learning success (Huda, Wahyuni, & Fauziyah, 2021).

In addition, instructional design in online mathematics should address *students' attitudes and beliefs*, which significantly influence their engagement and learning outcomes. Strategies to bolster self-efficacy and reduce stereotype threat are particularly relevant, as research shows that math anxiety and low self-confidence can hinder student performance (Flores & Auzmendi, 2018; Capote, Robaina, & Capote, 2022). Implementing support mechanisms, such as collaborative group work and peer interactions, can foster a positive learning community and reinforce students' confidence in their mathematical abilities (Civil, Stoehr, & Salazar, 2020).

Finally, *cultural and real-world relevance* should be woven into instructional design for mathematics, as this helps students see the practical applications of what they are learning. Research suggests that when students understand the societal implications of mathematics, their motivation and engagement increase (Evans, Wedege, & Yasukawa, 2013; Brantlinger, 2022). By incorporating authentic problems and data that relate to students' experiences, educators can create an inclusive and meaningful learning experience that aligns with modern educational goals.

In summary, instructional design for online mathematics should prioritize interactivity, personalization, support for self-efficacy, and real-world relevance. These principles not only enhance the virtual learning experience but also address the unique challenges associated with teaching mathematics in an online setting.

Unique Needs in Online Mathematics Instruction

Teaching mathematics in online environments requires special consideration of the unique cognitive and emotional needs associated with learning this subject. Unlike other disciplines, mathematics instruction often involves abstract concepts and problem-solving processes that benefit from visual and interactive learning approaches. Virtual settings can make it challenging to replicate the hands-on experiences and immediacy of feedback typically found in traditional classrooms, which are crucial for understanding complex mathematical ideas (Artigue, 2007; Tout, 2020).

One key need in online mathematics instruction is addressing *math anxiety* and *stereotype threat*, which can be intensified in remote learning environments where students may feel isolated and lack direct support from peers and instructors. Research shows that anxiety and negative self-perceptions can significantly impact performance and motivation in mathematics (Auzmendi, 1992; Flores & Auzmendi, 2018). Implementing targeted strategies, such as creating a supportive virtual community and using adaptive learning tools that adjust to each student's pace, can help mitigate these psychological barriers, thereby enhancing students' confidence and engagement (Capote, Robaina, & Capote, 2022; Bringula et al., 2021).

Another unique requirement in online math education is the need for *interactive and visual tools* that facilitate conceptual understanding. Software like GeoGebra and Desmos, as well as augmented reality applications, allow students to experiment with variables, visualize relationships, and explore mathematical concepts dynamically (Felmer, Perdomo-Díaz, & Reyes, 2019; Tout, 2020). Such tools are aligned with constructivist approaches to learning, which emphasize understanding through active participation and exploration, critical components in mathematics education (Artigue, 2007).

Personalized learning pathways are also particularly valuable in online mathematics instruction. Since students come to math courses with varying levels of prior knowledge and confidence, adaptive platforms that offer personalized feedback and customized content help meet students at their level, reinforcing strengths and addressing areas for improvement (Galligan & Axelsen, 2022; Aguilar & Castañeda, 2021). Personalized approaches not only improve comprehension but also support the development of self-regulation skills essential for success in online learning environments (Huda, Wahyuni, & Fauziyah, 2021).

Finally, a *focus on real-world relevance and cultural responsiveness* is critical for engaging students in online mathematics. By incorporating problems and applications that relate to students' lives and communities, educators can demonstrate the practical value of mathematical knowledge, thereby increasing student motivation and connection to the subject. Studies indicate that students are more engaged and perform better when they see the relevance of math to real-world contexts, such as interpreting public health data or financial literacy (Aguilar & Castañeda, 2021; Brantlinger, 2022; Evans, Wedege, & Yasukawa, 2013).

In summary, effective online mathematics instruction must account for students' emotional needs, utilize interactive and adaptive technologies, personalize learning experiences, and highlight the subject's real-world applications. These strategies are essential to addressing the distinctive challenges and opportunities presented by teaching mathematics in virtual environments.

Strategies for Creating a Student-Centered and Engaging Environment

Creating an engaging, student-centered environment in online mathematics instruction requires a blend of interactive tools, adaptive learning strategies, and supportive practices tailored to students' diverse needs. Given that virtual settings can sometimes lead to feelings of isolation and decreased motivation, it is essential to incorporate strategies that actively involve students in the learning process and foster a sense of community (Galligan & Axelsen, 2022; Bringula et al., 2021).

One effective strategy is the use of *interactive and collaborative tools* that enable students to engage directly with mathematical concepts and each other. Platforms like GeoGebra and Desmos allow students to visualize and manipulate mathematical problems, which supports a constructivist learning approach and promotes active problem-solving (Felmer, Perdomo-Díaz, & Reyes, 2019; Artigue, 2007). Additionally, implementing group activities and discussions in virtual settings helps create a sense of belonging, encouraging students to exchange ideas and perspectives, which is particularly valuable in challenging subjects like mathematics (Civil, Stoehr, & Salazar, 2020).

Personalized learning paths are also critical in online environments, where students benefit from content tailored to their specific skill levels and learning styles. Adaptive platforms that adjust to individual progress can help students build foundational knowledge and address gaps in understanding, supporting a positive and productive learning experience (Aguilar & Castañeda, 2021; Huda, Wahyuni, & Fauziyah, 2021). Research shows that personalized feedback not only boosts student confidence but also enhances their ability to engage in self-regulated learning, an important skill in online education (Galligan & Axelsen, 2022; Flores & Auzmendi, 2018).

Another strategy involves addressing *students' attitudes and psychological needs*, such as reducing math anxiety and stereotype threat, which are significant barriers in mathematics education. Creating a supportive environment where students feel encouraged to take risks and make mistakes can foster a growth mindset, helping them view challenges as opportunities to learn rather than as obstacles (Auzmendi, 1992; Capote, Robaina, & Capote, 2022). By promoting self-efficacy and resilience, instructors can positively influence students' attitudes towards mathematics and improve their overall engagement (Bringula et al., 2021).

Finally, a *focus on real-world applications* in mathematics instruction can increase student engagement by demonstrating the practical value of mathematical concepts. Incorporating examples that are relevant to students' lives, such as financial literacy or interpreting statistical data, not only makes mathematics more relatable but also helps students develop critical thinking skills essential for civic and professional contexts (Aguilar & Castañeda, 2021; Brantlinger, 2022). Studies suggest that when students understand how mathematics applies to real-world problems, their motivation and interest in the subject increase significantly (Evans, Wedege, & Yasukawa, 2013).

In summary, fostering a student-centered and engaging environment in online mathematics instruction involves utilizing interactive tools, providing personalized learning opportunities, supporting students' psychological needs, and connecting mathematics to real-world contexts. These strategies not only make online learning more effective but also help students build a positive and lasting relationship with mathematics.

3. PSYCHOLOGİCAL FACTORS İN ONLİNE MATHEMATİCS LEARNİNG

The psychological factors influencing online mathematics learning are critical to understanding and supporting students' engagement and success. Self-efficacy, stereotype threat, and student attitudes towards mathematics significantly impact how students approach learning in virtual environments. Addressing these factors is essential for creating an inclusive, supportive learning atmosphere that encourages students to persist and excel.

Self-Efficacy and Its Impact on Math Performance

Self-efficacy, or a student's belief in their ability to succeed in specific tasks, has a significant impact on performance in mathematics. Research shows that students with high self-efficacy are more likely to approach challenges with confidence, persist through difficulties, and perform better overall in mathematics (Capote, Robaina, & Capote, 2022; Flores & Auzmendi, 2018). In contrast, students with low self-efficacy may experience increased math anxiety, leading to avoidance behaviors and decreased engagement with the subject (Auzmendi, 1992).

In online mathematics education, where students often work independently, fostering self-efficacy is essential. Adaptive learning platforms that offer personalized feedback and support can play a critical role in building students' confidence. By providing tailored tasks that align with each student's skill level, these platforms enable students to experience success incrementally, reinforcing their belief in their own capabilities (Galligan & Axelsen, 2022; Bringula et al., 2021). This personalized approach helps students overcome initial challenges and gradually progress to more complex material, strengthening their self-efficacy as they advance (Aguilar & Castañeda, 2021).

Self-efficacy also promotes resilience and a growth mindset, encouraging students to view mistakes as learning opportunities rather than failures. Educators can foster this mindset by creating a supportive online environment that values effort and improvement. For example, collaborative projects and peer interactions can offer students additional support, helping them realize that challenges are a natural part of the learning process (Civil, Stoehr, & Salazar, 2020; Felmer, Perdomo-Díaz, & Reyes, 2019).

Furthermore, connecting mathematics to real-life applications enhances self-efficacy by demonstrating the relevance and practicality of math skills in everyday life. When students see how mathematical concepts apply to situations they encounter outside the classroom, such as financial literacy or interpreting data, they are more likely to believe in their ability to understand and use math meaningfully

(Brantlinger, 2022; Evans, Wedege, & Yasukawa, 2013). This real-world connection can motivate students to engage more deeply with mathematics and approach the subject with greater confidence.

In summary, building self-efficacy in online mathematics is critical to student success. By offering personalized support, fostering a growth mindset, and highlighting real-world applications, educators can empower students to approach mathematics with confidence, resilience, and a sense of purpose.

Stereotype Threat and Strategies for Mitigation

Stereotype threat—the fear of confirming negative stereotypes about one's social group—can significantly impact performance in mathematics, especially among students from underrepresented or marginalized backgrounds. Research shows that stereotype threat can lead to increased anxiety, reduced confidence, and a sense of alienation, all of which negatively affect a student's engagement and performance in mathematics (Auzmendi, 1992; Flores & Auzmendi, 2018). In online mathematics environments, where students may feel more isolated, addressing stereotype threat becomes especially important.

One effective strategy for mitigating stereotype threat is creating a supportive and inclusive online learning environment. By fostering a growth mindset and emphasizing effort over innate ability, educators can help students view challenges as opportunities to learn, reducing the fear of making mistakes (Capote, Robaina, & Capote, 2022). For example, instructors can design activities that celebrate problem-solving approaches and resilience rather than simply focusing on correct answers, which encourages students to engage more confidently with mathematics (Bringula et al., 2021).

Incorporating diverse role models and success stories is another way to counteract stereotype threat. When students see examples of individuals from similar backgrounds excelling in mathematics, it can challenge stereotypes and reinforce positive beliefs about their own capabilities (Aguilar & Castañeda, 2021). Educators can highlight mathematicians from diverse cultures, as well as use materials and examples that are culturally relevant and relatable to students' experiences, to further this goal (Civil, Stoehr, & Salazar, 2020).

Additionally, collaborative learning activities can provide a buffer against stereotype threat. When students work in groups and engage in peer learning, they often feel more connected and supported, which can reduce feelings of isolation and anxiety (Galligan & Axelsen, 2022). Peer interactions allow students to see a range of approaches to problem-solving, fostering a sense of community and shared purpose that helps mitigate the negative impacts of stereotype threat (Felmer, Perdomo-Díaz, & Reyes, 2019).

Addressing stereotype threat in online mathematics environments requires a combination of supportive teaching practices, positive role models, and collaborative learning opportunities. By implementing these strategies, educators can create an inclusive environment that empowers all students to participate confidently and succeed in mathematics.

Strategies to Empower Math Students and Improve Attitudes Towards the Subject

Improving students' attitudes toward mathematics and empowering them to engage with the subject confidently are central to successful online math instruction. By promoting a growth mindset, educators can help students view mathematical challenges as opportunities for learning and improvement rather than as fixed obstacles (Capote, Robaina, & Capote, 2022). Practical strategies include setting up collaborative activities that encourage peer interaction and support, which can enhance students' social connection and reduce feelings of isolation common in virtual learning (Galligan & Axelsen, 2022; Civil, Stoehr, & Salazar, 2020). Additionally, connecting mathematics to real-world applications, such as financial literacy or statistical reasoning, can make the subject more relevant and engaging, helping to improve students' attitudes by demonstrating the practical value of math skills (Aguilar & Castañeda, 2021; Brantlinger, 2022).

In sum, addressing psychological factors such as self-efficacy, stereotype threat, and student attitudes towards mathematics is crucial for fostering a positive and resilient online learning environment. By implementing strategies that support confidence, mitigate anxiety, and emphasize the value of mathematics, educators can empower students to engage more fully and successfully with the subject.

4. ADAPTİNG EDUCATİONAL MATERİALS FOR ONLİNE MATHEMATİCS INSTRUCTİON

To effectively teach mathematics in online environments, educators must adapt materials in ways that engage students, promote understanding, and foster independent learning skills. Math-specific technological tools, personalized learning approaches, and interactive resources are critical components for creating a supportive and effective virtual learning experience in mathematics.

Use of Math-Specific Technological Tools (GeoGebra, Desmos, etc.)

In online mathematics instruction, math-specific technological tools like GeoGebra and Desmos play a vital role in making abstract concepts accessible and engaging. These tools provide interactive, visual experiences that allow students to explore mathematical relationships, manipulate variables, and observe outcomes in real-time, which enhances their understanding of complex concepts (Felmer, Perdomo-Díaz, & Reyes, 2019; Tout, 2020). Through hands-on engagement, students are encouraged to take an active role in their learning, fostering a constructivist approach that supports deeper comprehension and retention of mathematical ideas (Artigue, 2007).

GeoGebra and Desmos, for instance, allow students to visualize equations, functions, and geometric constructions, making abstract mathematical content more concrete. This ability to experiment with and visualize mathematical properties helps students develop critical thinking and problem-solving skills by exploring "what-if" scenarios in a low-stakes environment (Galligan & Axelsen, 2022). By enabling students to experiment freely, these platforms not only build mathematical intuition but also reduce the math anxiety that can arise from more rigid problem-solving methods (Auzmendi, 1992).

These interactive tools also support collaborative learning. GeoGebra, for example, enables multiple students to work on the same mathematical construction simultaneously, allowing for real-time feedback and collaborative exploration (Felmer, Perdomo-Díaz, & Reyes, 2019; Civil, Stoehr, & Salazar, 2020). This fosters a sense of community and shared learning, which is particularly important in virtual environments where students may feel isolated.

Additionally, using these tools helps bridge the gap between theoretical knowledge and practical application, which is essential for students to understand the relevance of mathematics in real-world contexts (Brantlinger, 2022). Desmos, for example, is widely used in data analysis projects, allowing students to plot data points and analyze trends—skills that are increasingly relevant in today's data-driven world (Aguilar & Castañeda, 2021). By connecting mathematical concepts to real-life scenarios, educators can increase student motivation and engagement, helping students see the value of mathematics beyond the classroom (Evans, Wedege, & Yasukawa, 2013).

Math-specific technological tools like GeoGebra and Desmos are essential for online mathematics education, as they promote active, visual learning, support collaboration, and connect theoretical concepts with practical applications. These tools not only enhance students' understanding of mathematics but also empower them to explore and engage with mathematical ideas independently.

Personalizing Learning and Developing Self-Regulation Skills

Personalized learning is particularly valuable in online mathematics education, where students often come with varying levels of prior knowledge and confidence in their abilities. Adaptive learning platforms, which adjust content based on student performance, allow students to learn at their own pace and focus on areas where they need the most support. This approach not only addresses individual learning needs but also promotes self-regulation skills, as students take ownership of their learning progress (Galligan & Axelsen, 2022; Huda, Wahyuni, & Fauziyah, 2021). Self-regulation is essential for success in online environments, where students need to manage their time and learning independently. Through regular feedback and clear goals, adaptive platforms help students build these critical skills (Aguilar & Castañeda, 2021).

In online mathematics instruction, personalizing learning and fostering self-regulation skills are essential for supporting diverse student needs and promoting effective, independent learning. Personalized learning paths allow students to work at their own pace, focus on areas where they need additional support, and build confidence as they progress. This approach is particularly important in mathematics, where students often enter with varying levels of prior knowledge and confidence (Aguilar & Castañeda, 2021; Galligan & Axelsen, 2022).

Adaptive learning platforms play a central role in personalizing instruction by adjusting content in real time based on each student's progress. These tools provide targeted feedback and custom learning pathways, allowing students to reinforce foundational skills before advancing to more complex topics (Huda, Wahyuni, & Fauziyah, 2021). This form of adaptive feedback not only aids in comprehension but also helps reduce math anxiety, as students can tackle problems that match their current abilities, leading to a more positive learning experience (Auzmendi, 1992; Bringula et al., 2021).

Self-regulation, or the ability to manage one's own learning process, is critical for success in online environments. Through personalized learning, students are encouraged to set goals, monitor their progress, and reflect on their understanding—key components of self-regulated learning (Aparicio-Gómez & Ostos-Ortiz, 2020). Digital tools that track progress and provide immediate feedback, such as quizzes and interactive exercises, support these self-regulation skills by helping students identify strengths and areas for improvement (Galligan & Axelsen, 2022).

Moreover, personalizing learning with real-world applications helps students see the relevance of mathematics, increasing their motivation to engage with the material. For example, by applying mathematical concepts to projects related to financial literacy or statistical reasoning, students are able to connect their learning to practical, everyday situations (Brantlinger, 2022; Aguilar & Castañeda, 2021).

This relevance encourages self-directed learning, as students recognize the value of mathematics in their own lives (Evans, Wedege, & Yasukawa, 2013).

Personalized learning and self-regulation are fundamental to successful online mathematics education. By using adaptive tools and real-world applications, educators can support students' individual needs, foster independence, and help them develop the skills necessary for sustained success in mathematics and beyond.

Examples of Interactive Resources and Visual Materials for Mathematics

Interactive resources and visual materials are crucial for engaging students in mathematics online. Using virtual manipulatives, dynamic graphs, and visual aids, educators can provide students with hands-on experiences that closely replicate the benefits of traditional, in-person learning. For example, using digital graphing tools or geometry simulations allows students to experiment with mathematical concepts in an interactive format, enhancing both engagement and comprehension (Felmer, Perdomo-Díaz, & Reyes, 2019). Visual materials such as video tutorials and step-by-step guides also offer students additional learning resources, enabling them to review complex topics at their own pace (Galligan & Axelsen, 2022). By providing diverse types of resources, educators can accommodate different learning preferences, making mathematics instruction more inclusive and effective (Bringula et al., 2021; Aguilar & Castañeda, 2021).

Adapting educational materials for online mathematics instruction involves leveraging technology, personalizing learning experiences, and incorporating interactive resources. These strategies help create an engaging and supportive environment that empowers students to succeed in their mathematical studies.

5. FOSTERİNG ACTİVE PARTİCİPATİON AND ENGAGEMENT İN MATHEMATİCS

Active participation and engagement are essential for effective learning in mathematics, especially in online environments where students may feel isolated or disengaged. To overcome these challenges, educators can employ specific strategies that encourage students to actively participate, connect with their peers, and fully engage with mathematical content.

Specific Strategies for Promoting Participation in Math Classes

1. **Collaborative Learning and Peer Interaction.** Encouraging collaboration among students can significantly enhance participation and engagement in online math classes. Group activities and discussion forums allow students to share ideas, work through problems together, and learn from one another's perspectives, which helps build a community of learning (Civil, Stoehr, & Salazar, 2020). By promoting collaboration, educators create an environment where students feel more connected and supported, which is especially valuable in challenging subjects like mathematics (Galligan & Axelsen, 2022).
2. **Use of Interactive Math Tools.** Interactive tools like GeoGebra and Desmos provide students with hands-on opportunities to explore mathematical concepts, promoting engagement through active problem-solving. These tools allow students to manipulate variables, visualize functions, and experiment with real-time feedback, fostering a deeper understanding of mathematical relationships (Felmer, Perdomo-Díaz, & Reyes, 2019; Artigue, 2007). Additionally, interactive tools support a constructivist approach, helping students build knowledge through exploration and inquiry, which is essential for sustained engagement in mathematics (Tout, 2020).
3. **Personalized Feedback and Real-Time Support.** Providing timely and personalized feedback is crucial in online mathematics instruction. Adaptive platforms that deliver feedback tailored to each student's progress not only guide learning but also encourage students to participate actively by addressing areas of confusion and building confidence (Aguilar & Castañeda, 2021; Bringula et al., 2021). Regular, constructive feedback can motivate students to stay engaged, while real-time support, such as virtual office hours or live Q&A sessions, allows them to seek clarification and interact directly with their instructors (Galligan & Axelsen, 2022).
4. **Connecting Math to Real-World Contexts.** Making mathematics relevant to students' lives is an effective way to boost engagement and participation. When students see the real-world applications of mathematical concepts—such as in financial literacy, statistical analysis, or data interpretation—they are more likely to value the subject and participate actively (Aguilar & Castañeda, 2021; Brantlinger, 2022). By using authentic examples, educators help students connect mathematical concepts to their personal experiences, fostering a sense of purpose and curiosity in their studies (Evans, Wedege, & Yasukawa, 2013).
5. **Fostering a Growth Mindset and Reducing Math Anxiety.** Addressing math anxiety and promoting a growth mindset can significantly increase students' willingness to participate in online math classes. When students are encouraged to view challenges as opportunities for growth, they are more likely to engage

actively and persist in problem-solving tasks. Creating a supportive environment that celebrates effort and progress rather than solely focusing on accuracy can help reduce fear of failure and boost participation (Auzmendi, 1992; Capote, Robaina, & Capote, 2022).

Fostering active participation in online math classes requires a combination of collaborative opportunities, interactive tools, personalized feedback, real-world relevance, and a supportive learning environment. These strategies not only make mathematics more engaging but also empower students to take ownership of their learning and confidently tackle mathematical challenges.

Online Collaborative Activities for Mathematics Learning

Collaborative activities are crucial for fostering engagement and deepening understanding in online mathematics education. When students work together to explore mathematical concepts, they benefit from sharing diverse perspectives, developing problem-solving skills, and building a supportive learning community. In online settings, collaborative practices and interactive tools are instrumental in making mathematics more accessible and engaging.

Examples of Interactive Tools and Collaborative Practices

1. **Group Problem-Solving Sessions.** Virtual group problem-solving sessions encourage students to work together on mathematical challenges, share strategies, and discuss solutions. This approach not only strengthens their understanding of complex concepts but also fosters peer support, which can reduce math anxiety and enhance motivation (Civil, Stoehr, & Salazar, 2020). Instructors can facilitate these sessions using breakout rooms in video conferencing platforms, enabling students to collaborate in smaller groups and actively engage with the material (Galligan & Axelsen, 2022).
2. **Interactive Math Tools for Collaborative Exploration.** Interactive tools like GeoGebra and Desmos provide students with a hands-on, visual approach to mathematics, making abstract concepts more tangible and accessible. These platforms support collaborative exploration by allowing multiple users to work together on the same graph or function, manipulate variables in real time, and discuss changes as they observe the effects. Such tools align with constructivist principles, encouraging students to learn through inquiry and experimentation (Felmer, Perdomo-Díaz, & Reyes, 2019; Artigue, 2007). This collaborative use of interactive tools helps students develop a deeper understanding of mathematical relationships through shared discovery (Tout, 2020).

3. **Discussion Forums for Reflective Learning.** Online discussion forums are valuable for promoting reflective learning in mathematics. By posting and responding to questions, students engage in collaborative problem-solving and clarify their understanding of key concepts. These forums also create an asynchronous space where students can learn at their own pace, discuss various approaches, and support each other in overcoming challenges (Bringula et al., 2021). Such reflective practices help reinforce mathematical knowledge and build a sense of community among online learners (Aguilar & Castañeda, 2021).
4. **Collaborative Data Analysis Projects.** Collaborative data analysis projects are particularly effective for applying mathematics to real-world scenarios, such as interpreting statistical data or financial information. In these projects, students can work in teams to collect, analyze, and present data, using tools like spreadsheets or statistical software to support their findings. This practice not only develops critical thinking skills but also highlights the practical applications of mathematics, which increases student motivation and engagement (Aguilar & Castañeda, 2021; Brantlinger, 2022). By connecting math to real-world contexts, collaborative projects make the subject more relevant and meaningful (Evans, Wedege, & Yasukawa, 2013).
5. **Peer Review and Feedback Sessions.** Peer review activities allow students to assess each other's work, discuss different problem-solving approaches, and provide constructive feedback. This collaborative practice fosters a sense of accountability and encourages students to reflect on their learning. Through peer feedback, students also gain insights into various methods and perspectives, which enhances their mathematical reasoning skills (Galligan & Axelsen, 2022; Civil, Stoehr, & Salazar, 2020). Structured peer review sessions can be facilitated through online platforms that enable students to comment on and critique each other's submissions.

Collaborative activities, supported by interactive tools and structured online practices, play a vital role in online mathematics education. These strategies not only enhance student engagement but also foster a deeper understanding of mathematical concepts through collective learning experiences.

6. FORMATİVE AND MEANİNGFUL ASSESSMENT İN ONLİNE MATHEMATİCS ENVİRONMENTS

In online mathematics education, formative assessment plays a crucial role in guiding student learning, providing feedback, and enhancing understanding of mathematical concepts. Effective formative assessment methods must be adaptable, interactive, and directly aligned with learning objectives, helping students engage more deeply with the material and allowing educators to make timely adjustments to instruction.

Formative Assessment Methods Applied to Mathematics

1. **Adaptive Quizzes and Interactive Exercises.** Adaptive quizzes and interactive exercises are particularly effective in online math environments because they tailor the difficulty and content based on each student's progress. This method allows for real-time assessment, where students receive instant feedback on their work, enabling them to correct misconceptions immediately and build on their understanding of key concepts (Felmer, Perdomo-Díaz, & Reyes, 2019; Aguilar & Castañeda, 2021). Such adaptive platforms not only foster a personalized learning experience but also help students develop self-regulation skills, which are critical for success in online learning (Galligan & Axelsen, 2022).
2. **Real-Time Digital Feedback Tools.** Tools like Desmos and GeoGebra offer immediate, interactive feedback, which is essential for formative assessment in mathematics. These platforms allow students to manipulate variables, visualize equations, and experiment with mathematical models, making abstract concepts more tangible and easier to understand. By integrating real-time feedback, educators can help students actively engage with the material, facilitating a deeper comprehension of mathematical relationships (Artigue, 2007; Tout, 2020).
3. **Self-Assessment and Reflective Practices.** Self-assessment activities encourage students to evaluate their own understanding and identify areas for improvement. In online mathematics, self-assessment practices such as reflective journals or self-check quizzes help students develop metacognitive skills, fostering a sense of ownership over their learning (Aparicio-Gómez & Ostos-Ortiz, 2020; Huda, Wahyuni, & Fauziyah, 2021). Reflecting on their progress enables students to gain insight into their strengths and challenges, which can guide them in setting learning goals and seeking additional support when needed.
4. **Authentic Assessments with Real-World Applications.** Authentic assessments that connect mathematical concepts to real-world applications make learning more relevant and meaningful for students. Examples include data analysis projects, financial literacy tasks, or statistical interpretations based on real datasets. By applying mathematics to real-life scenarios, students gain practical skills and see the value of mathematics in everyday contexts (Brantlinger, 2022; Aguilar & Castañeda, 2021). These assessments also enhance critical thinking and problem-solving abilities, aligning with broader educational objectives that emphasize life skills (Evans, Wedege, & Yasukawa, 2013).

5. **Collaborative Peer Review and Group Problem-Solving.** Collaborative assessments, such as peer review and group problem-solving tasks, allow students to engage in mathematical discourse, share diverse approaches, and learn from one another. Through structured peer feedback, students develop a better understanding of mathematical concepts and build communication skills that are essential in both academic and professional settings (Civil, Stoehr, & Salazar, 2020). Group problem-solving tasks not only support collaborative learning but also help students feel more connected in online environments, which can reduce isolation and encourage active participation (Galligan & Axelsen, 2022).

Formative assessment methods in online mathematics should include adaptive quizzes, real-time feedback tools, self-assessment practices, authentic assessments, and collaborative activities. These methods enhance student engagement and understanding, creating a supportive learning environment that is both meaningful and effective.

Projects and Practical Tasks as Assessment in Mathematics

In online mathematics instruction, projects and practical tasks serve as valuable assessment tools, allowing students to apply their knowledge to real-world situations and deepen their conceptual understanding. These types of assessments go beyond rote memorization, encouraging students to engage in critical thinking and problem-solving. For example, data analysis projects or tasks that involve real-world scenarios, such as financial literacy or statistical reasoning, enable students to see the relevance of mathematics in everyday life (Aguilar & Castañeda, 2021; Brantlinger, 2022). Authentic assessments help bridge the gap between theoretical concepts and practical applications, making learning more meaningful and motivating for students (Evans, Wedege, & Yasukawa, 2013).

Moreover, practical tasks support the development of essential life skills by requiring students to work through complex problems, analyze information, and communicate their findings effectively. Such tasks foster a sense of accomplishment and provide students with a tangible understanding of how mathematics can be applied outside of the classroom (Civil, Ştoehr, & Salazar, 2020). This approach aligns with educational goals that prioritize skills over memorization, preparing students to navigate real-world challenges using mathematical knowledge (Felmer, Perdomo-Díaz, & Reyes, 2019).

Importance of Real-Time Feedback in Math Learning

Real-time feedback is crucial in online mathematics education, as it enables students to promptly correct misconceptions and reinforces their understanding of mathematical concepts. When students receive immediate feedback, whether through interactive exercises or digital platforms like Desmos and GeoGebra, they can adjust their approaches and solidify their comprehension as they progress (Artigue, 2007; Tout, 2020). This instant response mechanism is particularly valuable in mathematics, where small misunderstandings can quickly compound if left unaddressed (Felmer, Perdomo-Díaz, & Reyes, 2019).

Interactive digital tools that provide real-time feedback allow students to experiment with different solutions, explore mathematical relationships dynamically, and build confidence in their abilities. By integrating this type of feedback into online math instruction, educators help students become more self-aware learners who can independently evaluate their work and improve their problem-solving skills (Galligan & Axelsen, 2022; Bringula et al., 2021). Additionally, real-time feedback supports the development of self-regulation skills, which are essential for online learning, where students often work more autonomously (Aguilar & Castañeda, 2021).

Using projects and practical tasks as assessments and providing real-time feedback are essential strategies in online mathematics education. These methods promote meaningful learning, enhance engagement, and equip students with the skills needed to apply mathematics effectively in both academic and real-world contexts.

CONCLUSION

In online mathematics education, addressing the unique challenges and opportunities of virtual learning is essential for fostering student engagement, understanding, and confidence. This chapter has explored key strategies, including the use of adaptive and interactive tools, personalized and formative assessments, and the integration of real-world applications, all of which contribute to a more inclusive and effective learning environment (Felmer, Perdomo-Díaz, & Reyes, 2019; Aguilar & Castañeda, 2021). By emphasizing the psychological factors that affect student performance, such as self-efficacy and stereotype threat, educators can better support students in overcoming barriers to success in mathematics (Auzmendi, 1992; Capote, Robaina, & Capote, 2022).

One of the core recommendations of this chapter is the use of authentic assessments, such as data analysis projects and practical tasks, to make mathematics more meaningful and relevant. These tasks encourage students to apply mathematical concepts in real-world contexts, bridging the gap between theoretical knowledge and practical skills, thereby increasing both motivation and understanding (Evans, Wedege, & Yasukawa, 2013; Brantlinger, 2022). Additionally, formative assessments, supported by real-time feedback, empower students to reflect on their progress, enabling immediate adjustments that deepen comprehension and build self-regulation skills essential for online learning (Galligan & Axelsen, 2022; Artigue, 2007).

As the landscape of online education continues to evolve, mathematics instructors have a valuable opportunity to integrate innovative practices that enhance student learning and adapt to diverse needs. Tools like GeoGebra and Desmos, along with adaptive platforms, offer flexible, student-centered approaches that align with constructivist learning principles, allowing students to explore and engage with mathematics in an interactive and personalized way (Tout, 2020; Felmer, Perdomo-Díaz, & Reyes, 2019).

In conclusion, a student-centered approach that incorporates technological tools, adaptive assessments, and a focus on psychological and contextual factors can transform online mathematics education. These strategies not only improve students' understanding of mathematical concepts but also equip them with critical skills and a positive outlook that will serve them in academic and real-world settings. By leveraging these approaches, educators can create a supportive and dynamic online environment that empowers students to succeed in mathematics.

REFERENCES

Aguilar, M. I., & Castañeda, A. (2021). What mathematical competencies does a citizen need to interpret Mexico's official information about the COVID-19 pandemic? *Educational Studies in Mathematics*, 108(1–2), 227–248. DOI: 10.1007/s10649-021-10082-9 PMID: 34934238

Angermeier, K., & Ansen, H. (2020). Value and understanding of numeracy practices in German debt counselling from the perspective of professionals. *ZDM Mathematics Education*, 52(3), 461–472. DOI: 10.1007/s11858-019-01109-w

Aparicio-Gómez, O., & Ostos-Ortiz, O. (2020). Evaluación formativa. Universidad Santo Tomás, Working Paper No. 197523. https://doi.org/DOI: 10.13140/RG.2.2.31755.11049

Artigue, M. (2007). Learning Mathematics in a CAS Environment: The Genesis of a Reflection about Instrumentation and the Dialectics between Technical and Conceptual Work. *International Journal of Computers for Mathematical Learning*, 7(3), 245–274. DOI: 10.1023/A:1022103903080

Auzmendi, E. (1992). *Las Actitudes hacia la Matemática Estadística en las Enseñanzas Medias y Universitarias*. Mensajero.

Ball, S. J. (1994). *Education reform*. McGraw-Hill Education.

BIS. (Department of Business, Innovation and Skills). (2012). *The 2011 skills for life survey: A survey of literacy, numeracy and ICT levels in England* (BIS Paper 81). https://www.gov.uk/government/publications/2011-skills-for-life-survey

Boeren, E., & Whittaker, S. (2018). A typology of education and training provisions for low educated adults: Categories and definitions. *Studies in the Education of Adults*, 50(1), 4–18. DOI: 10.1080/02660830.2018.1520017

Brantlinger, A. (2022). Critical and vocational mathematics: Authentic problems for students from historically marginalized groups. *Journal for Research in Mathematics Education*, 53(2), 154–172. DOI: 10.5951/jresematheduc-2019-0025

Bringula, R., Reguyal, J. J., Tan, D. D., & Ulfa, S. (2021). Mathematics self-concept and challenges of learners in an online learning environment during COVID-19 pandemic. *Smart Learn. Environ.*, 8(1), 22. DOI: 10.1186/s40561-021-00168-5

Capote, M., Robaina, I., & Capote, M. (2022). Relaciones entre las actitudes hacia la Matemática y el rendimiento académico de los estudiantes. Mendive. *Review of Education*, 20, 1022–1035.

Carpentieri, J., Mallows, D., Amorim, J. P., & Freire, P. (2020). Credibility, relevance, and policy impact in the evaluation of adult basic skills programs: The case of the New Opportunities Initiative in Portugal. *Adult Literacy Education*, 2(1), 6–21. Advance online publication. DOI: 10.35847/JCarpentieri.JAmorim.DMallows.PFreire.2.1.6

Civil, M., Stoehr, K. J., & Salazar, F. (2020). Learning with and from immigrant mothers: Implications for adult numeracy. *ZDM Mathematics Education*, 52(3), 489–500. DOI: 10.1007/s11858-019-01076-2

Coben, D., & O'Donoghue, J. (2020). Adults learning mathematics. In Lerman, S. (Ed.), *Encyclopedia of mathematics education* (2nd ed., pp. 24–31). Springer., DOI: 10.1007/978-3-030-15789-0_5

Condelli, L., Safford-Ramus, K., Sherman, R., Coben, D., Gal, I., & Hector-Mason, A. (2006). *A review of the literature in adult numeracy: Research and conceptual issues*. American Institutes for Research. https://files.eric.ed.gov/fulltext/ED495456.pdf

Croce, K., & McCormick, M. K. (2020). Developing disciplinary literacy in mathematics: Learning from professionals who use mathematics in their jobs. *Journal of Adolescent & Adult Literacy*, 63(4), 415–423. DOI: 10.1002/jaal.1013

Dalby, D. (2021). Changing images of mathematics in the transition from school to vocational education. *Adults Learning Mathematics: An International Journal*, 15(1), 45–57.

Diego-Mantecon, J. M., Haro, E., Blanco, T. F., & Romo-Vazquez, A. (2021). The chimera of the competency-based approach to teaching mathematics: A study of carpentry purchases for home projects. *Educational Studies in Mathematics*, 107(2), 339–357. DOI: 10.1007/s10649-021-10032-5

Diez-Palomar, J. (2020). Dialogic mathematics gatherings: Encouraging the other women's critical thinking on numeracy. *ZDM Mathematics Education*, 52(3), 473–487. DOI: 10.1007/s11858-019-01092-2

Edwards, C. M. (2012). *Comparing middle school students' learning and attitudes in face-to-face and online mathematics lessons*. University of Northern Iowa.

Estrada-Araoz, E. G., Gallegos-Ramos, N., Mamani-Uchasara, H., & Huaypar-Loayza, K. (2020). Actitud de los estudiantes universitarios frente a la educación virtual en tiempos de la pandemia de COVID-19. *Rev. Brasil.Educ. Campo*, 5, e10237. DOI: 10.20873/uft.rbec.e10237

Evans, J., Wedege, T., & Yasukawa, K. (2013). Critical perspectives on adults' mathematics education. In A. Bishop, C. Keitel, J. Kilpatrick, & F. K. Leung (Eds.), *Third international handbook of mathematics education* (pp. 203–242). Springer.

Evans, J., Yasukawa, K., Mallows, D., & Kubascikova, J. (2021). Shifting the gaze: From the numerate individual to their numerate environment. *Adult Literacy Education*, 3(3), 4–18. DOI: 10.35847/JEvans.KYasukawa.DMallows.JKubascikova.3.3.4

Feinberg, I., Greenberg, D., Tighe, E. L., & Ogrodnick, M. M. (2019). Health insurance literacy and low wage earners: Why reading matters. *Adult Literacy Education*, 1(2), 4–18. DOI: 10.35847/IFeinberg.DGreenberg.ETighe.MOgrodnick.1.2.4

Felmer, P., Perdomo-Díaz, J., & Reyes, C. (2019). The ARPA experience in Chile: Problem Solving for teachers' professional development. In Liljedahl, P., & Santos-Trigo, M. (Eds.), *Mathematical Problem Solving, ICME-13 Monographs* (pp. 311–337). Springer. DOI: 10.1007/978-3-030-10472-6_14

FitzSimons, G. E. (2019). Adults learning mathematics: Transcending boundaries and barriers in an uncertain world. *Adults Learning Mathematics: An International Journal*, 14(1), 41–52.

Flores, W. O., & Auzmendi, E. (2018). Actitudes hacia las matemáticas en la enseñanza universitaria y su relación con las variables género y etnia. *Profes. Rev. Currículum Form.Profes.*, 22(3), 231–251. DOI: 10.30827/profesorado.v22i3.8000

Foley, G. D., Budhathoki, D., Thapa, A. B., & Aryal, H. P. (2023). Instructor perspectives on quantitative reasoning for critical citizenship. *ZDM Mathematics Education*, 55(5), 1009–1020. DOI: 10.1007/s11858-023-01520-4

Gal, I. (2000). The numeracy challenge. In Gal, I. (Ed.), *Adult numeracy development: Theory, research, practice* (pp. 9–31). Hampton Press.

Gal, I. (2022). Critical understanding of civic statistics: Engaging with important contexts, texts, and opinion questions. In Ridgway, J. (Ed.), *Statistics for empowerment and social engagement—Teaching Civic Statistics to develop informed citizens*. Springer., DOI: 10.1007/978-3-031-20748-8_13

Gal, I., & Geiger, V. (2022). Welcome to the era of vague news: A study of the demands of statistical and mathematical products in the COVID-19 pandemic media. *Educational Studies in Mathematics*, 111(1), 5–28. DOI: 10.1007/s10649-022-10151-7 PMID: 35496813

Galligan, L., & Axelsen, M. (2022). Online learning in adults learning mathematics: Literature review. *Adults Learning Mathematics: An International Journal*, 16(1), 6–19.

García, J., Cabanillas, L., Catarreira, S. M., & González, R. L. (2020). Contraste en la percepción sobre el uso de una plataforma virtual para la mejora de la enseñanza y aprendizaje de las matemáticas. *Rev. Ibérica d Sist.RISTI (Porto)*, 38(38), 33–47. DOI: 10.17013/risti.38.33-47

García, R. A., Chura, G., Llapa, M. P., & Arancibia, L. (2022). Validación de cuestionario de satisfacción de la enseñanza virtual para educación secundaria. *Rev. Fuentes*, 2(24), 162–173. DOI: 10.12795/revistafuentes.2022.19773

Geiger, V., Gal, I., & Graven, M. (2023). The connections between citizenship education and mathematics education. *ZDM Mathematics Education*, 55(3), 923–940. DOI: 10.1007/s11858-023-01521-3

Gray, C. M. K. (2019). Using profiles of human and social capital to understand adult immigrants' education needs: A latent class approach. *Adult Education Quarterly*, 69(1), 3–23. DOI: 10.1177/0741713618802271

Grotluschen, A., Buddeberg, K., Redmer, A., Ansen, H., & Dannath, J. (2019). Vulnerable subgroups and numeracy practices: How poverty, debt, and unemployment relate to everyday numeracy practices. *Adult Education Quarterly*, 69(4), 251–270. DOI: 10.1177/0741713619841132

Grotlüschen, A., Riekmann, W., Buddeberg, K., & Egloff, B. (2020). Scientific research on adults' competencies: Lessons from the German sample in the Programme for the International Assessment of Adult Competencies (PIAAC). *ZDM Mathematics Education*, 52(3), 401–412. DOI: 10.1007/s11858-019-01063-7

Gueudet, G. (2008). Investigating the secondary-tertiary transition. *Educational Studies in Mathematics*, 67(3), 237–254. DOI: 10.1007/s10649-007-9100-6

Hanushek, E. A., & Woessmann, L. (2008). The role of cognitive skills in economic development. *Journal of Economic Literature*, 46(3), 607–668. DOI: 10.1257/jel.46.3.607

Heilmann, L. (2020). Health and numeracy: The role of numeracy skills in health satisfaction and health-related behaviour. *ZDM Mathematics Education*, 52(3), 407–418. DOI: 10.1007/s11858-019-01106-z

Hernández, R., Fernández, C., & Baptista, P. (2014). Metodología de la investigación (6a. ed.). México D. F., México: McGraw-Hill

Heyd-Metzuyanim, E., Sharon, A. J., & Baram-Tsabari, A. (2021). Mathematical media literacy in the COVID-19 pandemic and its relation to school mathematics education. *Educational Studies in Mathematics*, 108(1-2), 201–225. DOI: 10.1007/s10649-021-10075-8 PMID: 34934235

Huda, N., Wahyuni, T. S., & Fauziyah, F. D. (2021). *Students' perceptions of online mathematics learning and its relationship towards their achievement*. Atlantis Press., DOI: 10.2991/assehr.k.210421.077

Jarvis, P. (2010). *Adult education and lifelong learning: Theory and practice* (4th ed.). Routledge.

Kelly, B. (2019). Motivating adults to learn mathematics in the workplace: A trade union approach. *International Journal of Lifelong Education*, 38(2), 132–147. DOI: 10.1080/02601370.2018.1555190

Kelly, B., Devlin, M., Giffin, T., & Smith, L. (2021). Family learning online during lockdown in the UK. *Adults Learning Mathematics: An International Journal*, 16(1), 20–35.

Larsen, J., & Liljedahl, P. (2022). Building thinking classrooms online: From practice to theory and back again. *Adults Learning Mathematics: An International Journal*, 16(1), 36–52.

Liu, J. (2020). Perceptions of student engagement with online mathematics learning: A systematic review of literature. *Journal of Online Learning Research*, 6(1), 1–22. DOI: 10.59495/jolr.2020.001

Lizzio, A., Wilson, K., & Simons, R. (2002). University students' perceptions of the learning environment and academic outcomes: Implications for theory and practice. *Studies in Higher Education*, 27(1), 27–52. DOI: 10.1080/03075070120099359

Londoño-Velasco, E., Montoya-Cobo, E., García, A., Bolaños-Martinez, I., Bolaños-Martinez, I., Osorio-Roa, D. M., & Isaza Gómez, G. D. (2021). Percepción de estudiantes frente a procesos de enseñanza-aprendizaje durante pandemia por la covid-19. *Educ. Educ.*, 24(2), 199–217. DOI: 10.5294/edu.2021.24.2.2

Mezirow, J. (1997). Transformative learning: Theory to practice. *New Directions for Adult and Continuing Education*, 1997(74), 5–12. DOI: 10.1002/ace.7401

OECD. (2023a). PISA 2022 results (volume I): The state of learning and equity in education. *OECD Publishing.* https://doi.org/DOI: 10.1787/53f23881-en

OECD. (2023b). *OECD skills outlook 2023: Learning for a more resilient future*. OECD Publishing., DOI: 10.1787/28a2ea09-

Patterson, M. B. (2020). PIAAC numeracy skills and home use among adult English learners. *Adult Literacy Education*, 2(1), 22–40. DOI: 10.35847/MPatterson.2.1.22

Pepin, B. (2014). Using the construct of the didactic contract to understand student transition into university mathematics education. *Policy Futures in Education*, 12(5), 646–658. DOI: 10.2304/pfie.2014.12.5.646

Redmer, A., & Dannath, J. (2020). The influence of number sense on financial literacy: Implications for numeracy education. *Journal of Financial Literacy and Education*, 12(1), 68–85.

Root, B., & Bhala, P. (2020). Tailoring online learning: How adaptive learning systems impact student achievement in mathematics. *Journal of Educational Technology Systems*, 49(2), 215–238. DOI: 10.1177/0047239518816260

Tout, K. (2020). Augmented and virtual reality in mathematics education: Current status and future trends. *Journal of Virtual Worlds Research*, 13(1), 1–25. DOI: 10.4101/jvwr.2020.13.1.1

Wedege, T. (2020). The role of adult numeracy in sustainable development goals. *ZDM Mathematics Education*, 52(3), 413–425. DOI: 10.1007/s11858-019-01083-1

Wikoff, N. (2022). Numeracy and financial wellbeing during the COVID-19 pandemic. *Numeracy*, 15(1), 4. Advance online publication. DOI: 10.5038/1936-4660.15.1.1399

Zhao, H., Liu, X., & Xu, Y. (2022). Innovative teaching methods and technology in mathematics education. *Educational Technology Research and Development*, 70(3), 659–678. DOI: 10.1007/s11423-022-10071-0

Chapter 13
Empowering Educators and Students Through Boundaries

Mary K. Lannon
https://orcid.org/0009-0003-5274-4028
Purdue University Global, USA

Holli Vah Seliskar
https://orcid.org/0009-0002-0411-0453
Purdue University Global, USA

David Alan White
http://orcid.org/0009-0000-6309-1331
Purdue University Global, USA

ABSTRACT

Setting and maintaining boundaries is critical to any healthy relationship; this is no less true of the relationship between faculty and students. Education aims to empower students by facilitating their development of independent decision-making, critical thinking, problem-solving, time management skills, accountability, and self-efficacy. This can be done by setting boundaries that balance being accessible to students and providing the space for them to learn, explore, and develop independence. Boundaries also empower faculty by helping to reduce stress, avoid burnout, and promote an appropriate work-life balance. The authors explore research on setting boundaries to promote student success, empower faculty, and promote a healthy learning environment. Recommendations are shared on how to set and maintain boundaries between faculty and students regarding classroom expectations, activities, communications, and grading.

DOI: 10.4018/979-8-3693-4407-1.ch013

EMPOWERING EDUCATORS AND STUDENTS THROUGH BOUNDARIES

There is a saying that good fences make good neighbors. By the same token, boundaries can make for good students and good educators. The idea of setting boundaries in our personal and professional lives is not new. Numerous sources from a wide variety of disciplines focus on the importance of setting and maintaining healthy boundaries (University of Massachusetts, 2023). Healthy boundaries are linked to self-care, mental health, and appropriate relationships – both personally and professionally (Tawwab, 2021). It is important to set boundaries and make expectations clear. The value of this is twofold; it helps to establish what behavior we will accept from others, and it helps to establish what behavior others can expect from us (Pattemore, 2021; Tawwab, 2021). In this chapter, we delve into the research concerning establishing boundaries to foster student success, empower faculty members, and cultivate an atmosphere conducive to learning. We will offer insights and suggestions on effectively establishing and upholding boundaries between faculty and students regarding classroom dynamics, activities, communication protocols, and grading procedures.

Throughout this chapter, we will share personal experiences and stories of interactions between ourselves (or our colleagues) and students within the online classroom environment. The purpose of this is not to be negative or to disparage anyone but to serve as cautionary tales to illustrate to the audience that many educators experience the same things and to demonstrate how setting boundaries can be a positive development for you and your students. We hope these examples will be useful to our readers in terms of identifying and setting appropriate boundaries for themselves (as educators) and their students.

The concept of establishing boundaries, both in our personal and professional lives, has been well-documented across diverse fields (Allen et al., 2021; Kariou et al., 2021; Pattemore, 2021). From self-help literature to academic studies, the emphasis on maintaining healthy boundaries remains consistent. These boundaries are crucial for promoting self-care, preserving mental well-being, avoiding burnout, and fostering positive interpersonal relationships (Kariou et al., 2021; Tawwab, 2021). Clearly defining and upholding boundaries serves a dual purpose: it delineates the standards of behavior we deem acceptable from others while also setting clear expectations for our students. Researchers have recognized that the ability to appropriately set and maintain boundaries, and therefore achieve an appropriate work-life balance, is a desirable but elusive objective (Allen et al., 2021). Particularly in the aftermath of the COVID-19 pandemic, research on effectively managing boundaries for remote workers continues to be important (Allen et al., 2021). There is a growing body of literature on boundaries in various occupations, including education. In addition, the components of working in online education can change in terms of what is considered flexible, thereby increasing the challenges associated with implementing boundaries and maintaining an appropriate work-life balance (Adisa et al., 2022).

Benefits of Boundaries

Boundaries allow educators to maintain an appropriate work-life balance, which is increasingly difficult to maintain in online education (Adisa et al., 2022; Hansen & Gray, 2018). Boundaries also help us to maintain fairness among all our students. Setting boundaries, clearly communicating them, and maintaining them ensures that all students have the same experience in terms of availability and accessibility. In addition, by ensuring that our boundaries are aligned with the policies of our institution, we know that we are upholding those expectations fairly for all students. This consistency advises students on exactly what they can expect from us, resulting in increased respect and professionalism from students. It is important to remember that *timely* does not mean *immediate*. By breaking ourselves of the feeling that we must immediately respond to students at all times of the day and week, we can promote a better work-life balance for ourselves and reduce stress and anxiety. Separating our personal and professional lives through the use of boundaries can empower us to confront individuals who attempt to breach boundaries that we have created for ourselves (Allen et al., 2021; Tawwab, 2021). Hopefully, this will also reduce stress on our students who know we will not respond immediately. No one can be at their best all the time. By maintaining these boundaries, our students will experience us at our best during appropriate work hours, which is beneficial to them as well.

Accountability as a Catalyst for Success

It is crucial to recognize that boundaries are not solely for the benefit of educators but also for the well-being of our students. When we establish and uphold boundaries with students, we aid in their development. As educators, we often feel that we are helping students by being lenient, meeting them where they are, and even lowering our expectations (whether for their coursework, adherence to policies, etc.). We can think of numerous arguments in favor of such an approach: We do not want to see students fail; we believe they are all doing their best; they do not deserve to be held accountable, etc. However, this is a disservice to students. Think of it on the flipside: We do not think they are capable, so we choose not to challenge them; we do not have confidence in their ability to rise to the occasion and be successful, etc. By setting boundaries, adhering to policy, and holding students accountable, we are providing them a great benefit – we are educating them, which is our primary purpose. If we set low expectations, we can expect low effort and performance. Rather, we should encourage and empower our students to break out of their comfort zone, learn, and develop. Ultimately, educators do not need to sacrifice their well-being, and their academic standards, or create more work for themselves to prove they want their students to succeed (Warner, 2024). Requiring students to increase their independence can encourage success, emotional intelligence, and a growth mindset to build confidence and resilience, both in and out of the classroom. By encouraging emotional intelligence and a growth mindset, we teach students valuable life skills, which foster important behaviors that include learning to express themselves; learning to be candid, which can be helpful in establishing boundaries; being flexible when needed; finding ways to interact informally; being intentional in their actions; learning to take risks and accept challenges, and learning to be supportive of others (Drigas & Papoutsi, 2018; Dweck & Yeager, 2021; Goleman, 2005; Goleman & Boyatzis, 2017; Mattingly & Kraiger, 2019; Miao et al., 2017).

Students should have the primary stake in their academic success, both now and in the future. While there is value in meeting students where they are, we also need to challenge them to be successful. Some argue that to motivate students we must be engaging, supportive, and even lower our expectations. Others argue that we must hold them accountable and ensure that real consequences are tied to their work. For example, "by giving students a greater and more immediate stake in their schoolwork and their learning, such student-accountability policies could bridge the gap between effort and reward" (Tyner & Petrilli, 2018, para. 8). We can be engaging and supportive while still linking outcomes to performance.

Moreover, each of us is unique, leading to varied boundaries and expectations, which must be conveyed to our students earlier rather than later. It may also be important to discuss boundaries with your supervisor if you are becoming overwhelmed with your current workload, as doing so encourages educators to retain the work-life balance they have created for themselves and will empower them to be clear about the boundaries they need to have in their lives (Tawwab, 2021). Some educators may be more inclined to share personal information or aspects about themselves with students, while others prefer distinct boundaries between their work and personal lives. There is nothing wrong with either approach; however, verbalizing the boundaries needed in our lives to our students can ultimately promote a healthier student-educator relationship. Helping students to understand and respect these differences is a vital life skill, essential not only in their academic journey but also in their future professional endeavors (Wyrick, 2022). By instilling this awareness, we are equipping students for success both inside and outside the classroom. According to Wyrick (2022):

As educators, we may worry that students will be offended if we establish what is and what is not OK in our relationship. But clear definitions of relationship norms actually decrease anxiety and assist students in knowing who plays what role in their lives. (para. 12)

Boundaries promote self-sufficiency in students, which is a critical skill both in and out of the classroom. If students do not receive an immediate response from us, they are encouraged to look for and find the answers themselves. This is empowering to students and over time, will give them the confidence to seek out the information and answers they are looking for before asking for help. Self-sufficiency is also a necessary skill in the workforce. By helping our students develop this skill and confidence in their ability, we are helping them to become responsible and accountable professionals. We must remember that we are not only educating them in the classroom but also preparing them to be professionals working in the field. As such, it is important that they assume responsibility for their own work and for earning their degree. Empowering our students in this way also increases their professionalism, civility, and respect for others – all important and admirable characteristics.

Each of Us is Different

It is important to keep in mind that boundaries are not just for us as educators or for our own personal benefit. When we set and maintain boundaries with our students, we are helping them as well. In addition, we know that we are different, and as a result, we will all set different boundaries and expectations. Articulating the boundaries in our lives to others, not just once but repeatedly, empowers us to be comfortable with the boundaries we have created and can improve our relationships and interactions because we learn when to say yes and when to say no (Tawwab, 2021). Some people are more open and sharing their personal lives than others. Some are willing to be more accessible during and after work hours. Understanding that different individuals will have different boundaries and expectations is an important life skill for students to learn (Wyrick, 2022). This will serve students not only in their educational careers but in the professional workforce as well. In this way, we are helping students prepare to be successful both in and out of the classroom.

On one end of the spectrum, some educators perceive their role as strictly confined to delivering the curriculum specified in their course outlines. With a narrower scope of responsibilities, they maintain high boundaries, as they do not see themselves accountable for addressing students' personal issues, guiding them through campus support resources, or advising them on significant life choices. Conversely, there are educators who embrace a broader perspective, and who view their role as encompassing advising, mentoring, modeling behavior, and being available around the clock. This broader array of duties leads to lower boundaries and more frequent informal interactions, ultimately leading to the greater possibility of burnout as well. Therefore, it is necessary to discern our responsibilities and roles as educators, recognizing that they may differ from person to person. From there, we can establish and refine appropriate boundaries (Rockquemore, 2015). Setting boundaries is not a one-size-fits-all endeavor. Each of us must determine what is optimal for ourselves and for our students. We should also remember that articulating boundaries not just once but consistently in our lives can improve the interactions we have with others (Tawwab, 2021). Simultaneously, students stand to gain valuable insights from understanding that boundaries and expectations can vary among educators and professionals. There are many differences in how educators can set and maintain boundaries, depending on how educators view themselves and their responsibilities toward students.

- Educators who have a short list of responsibilities tend to have high boundaries and formal interactions.
- Educators with a long list of responsibilities (such as believing that their role far exceeds delivering content in the classroom) tend to have lower boundaries and more frequent, informal interactions.
- Educators should determine our responsibilities first and, from there, determine what boundaries to set for ourselves and our students (Rockquemore, 2015)

Avoiding Burnout

Burnout among educators continues at increasing and somewhat alarming rates (Vyletel et al., 2023; Wyrick, 2022). This is often due in large part to feeling obligated to always be available. This is particularly true in online education. However, the more we immerse ourselves in the personal lives of students, the more energy and time we lose, increasing our risk of burnout (Wyrick, 2022). Researchers have found that blurring boundaries led to strain and exhaustion among online educators during the COVID-19 pandemic (Adisa et al., 2022). In addition, participants reported that work intensification led to increased pressure to demonstrate online presence and subsequent burnout. By contrast, individuals who engaged in boundary management tactics reported improved work-life balance, reduced pressure, and greater control over the separation between aspects of work and life (Adisa et al.,

2022). Vyletel et al. (2023) reported findings from the Healthy Minds Study (HMS) Faculty/Staff Survey:

Overall, 64% of faculty reported "feeling burned out because of work" either somewhat (30%), to a high degree (19%), or to a very high degree (15%). Burnout was higher among women (69%) and gender minority faculty (71%) relative to men (57%). A higher proportion of faculty at 4-year institutions (68%) felt burned out than at community colleges (54%). (para. 3)

Each of us probably knows at least one fellow educator – perhaps it is even ourselves – who has experienced or is experiencing burnout. The increasing demands on our time and focus as a result of technology can negatively impact our health and well-being. Many educators experience burnout because they have lost the ability or skill to set and maintain boundaries, to step away from their work and their students, and to maintain an appropriate work-life balance (Kariou et al., 2021). For example, how many of us have our institutional email on our phones? How many of us provide our personal telephone numbers to students for calls, texts, etc.? How many of us check our emails on nights and weekends even if we have put in a full day or week of work? How many of us feel guilty about not being constantly available and accessible to our students? These are all examples that contribute to a lack of appropriate boundaries and increased burnout among educators. At times, we must remind ourselves that we are our students' professor, not their friend, parent, or counselor. We must establish what it means to be the students' professor and then maintain those boundaries (Wyrick, 2022). When we say no to others, and essentially say yes to ourselves through the articulation of boundaries, we are promoting our own self-care and fostering the work-life balance we seek (Tawwab, 2021).

Learning to say no to others is an important boundary that can and should be set. This is particularly so when we are uncomfortable with a request that has been made, such as from a poor-performing student or a student who did not work well with others within a required team assignment for a course, who then asks their professor to write a recommendation letter. Additionally, faculty members are quite often asked to perform institutional service, and at times, these requests can become overwhelming and reduce productivity in other areas such as writing, publishing, and teaching, that would be required for promotion or for tenured positions at some institutions. A valuable resource on learning to say no to others, especially when it interferes with our professional goals overall is the National Center for Faculty Development and Diversity (https://www.ncfdd.org/), which provides educators with online communication on boundaries, finding a work-life balance, and creating healthy relationships (National Center for Faculty Development and Diversity, n.d.).

A Case for Consistency

As educators, we should also think of the example we set, not only for ourselves but for our colleagues and students. We know that in online education, many faculty are employed part-time. As of 2022, 44% of the 1.5 million faculty working in degree-granting postsecondary institutions were part-time (National Center for Education Statistics, 2024). Among online institutions, that number is often much higher. This can impact the consistency of availability and accessibility among faculty, as part-time educators often work nights and weekends due to their own availability. While this can be perfectly acceptable and even necessary, part-time faculty still can and should set and maintain boundaries. Simply because you may have to log into your course rooms and email on nights and weekends, it does not mean that you must be available or work every evening or each day of the weekend. Articulating the expectations and boundaries you wish to have should be something that you convey to your supervisor, as this can reduce the pressure (and guilt) some faculty members feel when they do have to work after a typical 9-5 shift (Perrigino et al., 2020). Students should experience and come to expect that different faculty members will have different availability. However, no faculty member should have constant or near-constant availability. We are not personal assistants to our students, nor should we act as though we are.

All faculty, whether they are part-time or full-time employees, should set specific days and times when they are available to students and maintain those boundaries throughout the term. These boundaries should not be stated only once but repeatedly throughout a term. This not only provides clear information for students in terms of what they can expect, but it also maintains consistency throughout the term for both students and educators. For example, faculty who are required to (or choose to) log into their courses on one day of the weekend should set one day at the start of the term, for example, on Saturdays, but not log in on Sundays. This way, students see faculty engaging at certain times and can expect and rely upon this. Certainly, there will be times that schedules must change, but this can also be communicated to students as needed.

For all faculty, we recommend not engaging with students on holidays observed by the institution or days the faculty member has taken personal time off. Be sure to review any existing employee and faculty handbooks to ensure you are following the guidelines set forth by your institution regarding personal time off. Students should never see faculty engaging on days the institution has indicated that it will be closed, or that no classes will be held, or that the faculty member has designated personal time off, etc. Faculty may see these days as a time to catch up on their workload, but is a disservice to the institution, other faculty, and the students to work when the institution has indicated otherwise. For those who do want to take an observed holiday to catch up on work, we recommend doing tasks that do not involve engagement with students or visibility within the online classroom. As an example, faculty might grade student assignments but wait to post those grades until the next business day. They might draft responses to discussion posts but wait to publish them until the next business day. Even emails can be drafted and saved or scheduled to be sent the next business day. When students consistently see faculty working on holidays, they come to expect that this is how all faculty should operate. The result is an increasing disregard for the observance of holidays (and healthy, necessary boundaries) across the institution.

When Students Develop Unreasonable and Unprofessional Expectations

Here, we share examples of students who have come to have both unreasonable and unprofessional expectations of faculty. While we cannot know how they came to develop these expectations, we can identify ways to correct them and help prevent them in the future, both for ourselves and our fellow educators.

Student A

This student was provided the personal cell phone number of the professor and made a habit of calling the professor in the middle of the night on weekends. The professor would see their phone ringing with an unknown number, and answer in fear that there was a family emergency. Instead, the professor was subjected to angry outbursts and profanities from a student in another country and time zone who was unhappy with their grade and found nothing wrong with calling the professor at this most inappropriate time and behaving in a most unprofessional manner. As a best practice, we suggest informing students that their professors will not respond to emails over the weekend, and establishing a time on Friday, such as 5 pm, to further inform students that emails after this time will be responded to on Monday or when the professor returns to the office on the next business day.

Student B

Since the start of the term, the student emailed the professor every single day, often emailing two or three times each day. The student would not only email but would call and text the professor in the late evening hours. This student had no specific issue that could not have been answered by entering the classroom and reviewing the guidelines within the assignment instructions or classroom resources, but considered their emergency as the professor's emergency, and would often email venting about personal issues or unrelated classroom matters. As a best practice, we suggest that only one email per day be responded to (per student), as this creates a clear boundary between the professor and the student, further establishing appropriate guidelines for online communication and netiquette.

Practice

Establishing boundaries can be challenging, with the initial hurdle being where to begin and which boundaries to define. Start by assessing your role and responsibilities as an educator, considering the boundaries and limitations you need to maintain a healthy work-life balance. Different schools may have varying policies and expectations for faculty, such as weekend availability and evening work commitments. Additionally, many educators juggle part-time or adjunct roles alongside full-time employment outside of academia. To recount, boundaries assist us in preventing overextension of ourselves, ensuring we establish appropriate parameters in our lives, and fostering clear expectations for the relationships we wish to have with our students.

It is crucial to prioritize your own well-being—mental, physical, and emotional—and identify areas where you can make improvements. If you are experiencing burnout or heading in that direction, assess what measures could alleviate it. Similarly, if the demands of students are overwhelming your time and energy, focus on setting boundaries for availability and communication. Remember, creating clear and articulated boundaries is a form of self-care and helps to communicate what is acceptable and not acceptable in relationships (Tawwab, 2021).

As educators, we should be consistent in applying and upholding the policies of our schools and programs. This is not to say that there may be times when we can and should allow for an exception. However, students should not automatically expect an exception or assume that the policies do not apply to them. When we provide an exception, it should be clearly communicated to the student that this is what we are doing for this specific (single) instance. We provide the following recommendations:

- Know and adhere to the set policies for your school and program.
- Review employee and faculty handbooks at your institution.
- Ensure students are aware of and understand policies related to the following: course due dates, institutional late policy, student code of conduct policies, academic integrity/plagiarism policy, offering remediation, writing, formatting and citation standards, and the acceptable and unacceptable uses of artificial intelligence tools, etc.
- Students should know that these policies exist and that they are expected to follow them.

- Utilizing institutional policies provides consistency among faculty and for students.
- Relaxing a policy should be the exception and not the norm (nor an expectation by students) and should be communicated as such.

Here, we provide an example of how an instructor would reply to a student regarding the institutional policy of a late policy, the authors make the following recommendation:

Example A

Hello [Student Name],

As per the Late Policy within the Course Syllabus, found under [the appropriate section of the classroom], as well as within the University's website, under the Student Code of Conduct, your paper will have a 10% deduction taken from the final score. If you have any questions or concerns, please reach out to me at [university email address].

Best Regards,

Professor [Your Name]

Example B

Here we provide an example of conveying institutional policy, surrounding remediation and/or plagiarism violations:

Hello [Student Name],

Unfortunately, your [include assignment name] has been returned from the Turnitin database with a [include Turnitin similarity report/percentage], which in alignment with the University's Student Code of Conduct, and the Plagiarism and Academic Integrity policy of the University requires remediation on the appropriate use of the APA Format and Citation Style. Therefore, I am offering remediation to you, in order for you to learn more about the proper use of the APA Format and Citation Style, 7th Edition. You will need to complete the remediation module and score 80% or better to move forward and rewrite the assignment. Please review the Academic Integrity-Student Guide (under the Help tab, Academic Integrity and at this link [include link to the University's Academic Integrity Policy] and follow the steps outlined there. You can find the Academic Integrity module under the Help tab of our course, then select Academic Integrity. Please take the assessment, scoring 80% or higher and submit a screenshot of your score to the Dropbox, and resubmit your revised paper **no later than [include a date for final submission]**.

Once the assessment and revised paper have been received within the grade book, I will review the revised paper and the zero score will be updated accordingly.

Please reach out with questions.

Best Regards, [Your name and contact information]

Practicing Boundaries with Our Students

Here, we share examples of practicing setting boundaries with our students and relying on institutional policies to support the decisions we make.

Student A

This student asked for a three-week extension at the beginning of the term, due to an injury. The institutional policy clearly states that the incomplete policy cannot be used to submit missing or late work, nor can it be used as a way to pass the course. The student assumed that a three-week extension would be granted to them, even though no accommodations were set in place and no physician note indicated an actual injury. In this case, the professor upheld the incomplete policy, and did not grant a three-week extension due to the request being unjustified and unnecessary.

Student B

The student was given the personal cell phone number of their professor and thought it appropriate to call the professor on Christmas Day to ask questions about an assignment. While we suggest not giving students our personal phone numbers, the primary issue here was that the student demonstrated no respect for the institutional holiday, and the fact that the professor was entitled to their private time with family. The professor did not respond to the student over the Winter Break and reinforced the institutional policy related to university closures, and complying with human resources when employees have designated personal time off from the university.

Setting boundaries requires experimentation, practice, and time (Tawwab, 2021). Starting with small, manageable steps is often the most effective approach. Initially, you may feel guilt or anxiety when enforcing boundaries, such as declining a weekend call or refraining from checking emails outside of work hours. However, these feelings are normal and temporary, akin to the challenges of forming new habits.

Remember, setting boundaries is a process that requires effort and willpower, but the benefits are worthwhile in the long run. It is important to keep in mind the following:

- Before working to set or adjust current boundaries, assessing your role and responsibilities as an educator is important.
- Assess your own physical, mental, and emotional well-being, current work-life balance, and goals.
- Setting boundaries takes some experimentation and a great deal of practice.
- Articulate the boundaries you want to have clearly and often, repeating them as needed (Tawwab, 2021).
- Prepare yourself for initial feelings of guilt and anxiety but remind yourself that these are normal parts of the process (Rockquemore, 2015).

There is – and should be - a power differential between you and your student, meaning that you create and set the boundaries of what happens in your interactions with students (Rockquemore, 2015). Students should be required to respect the position that we hold as faculty and educators. Moreover, students should be expected to always conduct themselves with professionalism and courtesy, which further aligns with institutional student codes of conduct and best practices for online netiquette

Setting Boundaries Through Institutional Policies

Here, we share examples of students who attempted to push multiple boundaries established by the professor in accordance with the policies of the institution.

Student A

The student asked for an extension in Week 9 to be applied to the assignment that had been due in Week 2 of the course. The student said that they had been sick during Week 2 and had forgotten to ask before Week 9. In this case, institutional policy clearly stated that assignments could not be accepted more than two weeks past the due date. The student failed to communicate with the professor in a timely manner and assumed that the late submission policy did not apply to them. The professor upheld the policy (and boundaries established at the start of the term) and did not grant the extension requested seven weeks late.

Student B

The student submitted their work from a previous unsuccessful attempt at a course, without following the institutional policy requiring that they first notify their professor and obtain permission to reuse the work from the previous course. This student resubmitted work with the assumption that the policy did not apply to them. The professor upheld the policy and did not accept the resubmission from the previous course attempt.

Student C

The student submitted numerous submissions for the same assignment. The institutional policy clearly states that students are limited to three submissions (to allow them to review plagiarism detection feedback). The student assumed that this policy did not apply to them. In this case, the professor upheld the policy and graded the third submission.

Student D

We have heard of several instances from colleagues in which students have waited until well after a course term has ended to ask their professors to accept additional assignments. In one instance, the student reached out to the professor a full ten days after the term had ended, claiming to be unaware that the course had ended. After the professor explained that the term had ended and no additional work could be submitted, the student called and texted the professor numerous times over the weekend, leaving multiple voicemails demanding that the professor (who the student repeatedly referred to by first name) call them back and accept their work. In a similar situation, a student emailed the professor several days after the term ended to ask why they had received a low grade despite having submitted the final assignment. The professor explained that the assignment had been submitted outside of the late policy and well after the course term had ended.

When Boundaries are Broken

Once you have set boundaries, be prepared to address instances where students overstep boundaries and stand firm, reiterating your expectations. It is common to hear claims that you are the first professor to introduce specific requirements or expectations, but verifying such statements is usually impractical and irrelevant. Ultimately, it is the student's responsibility to meet the expectations of the school, the course, and the educator. Here are some common examples of when students break boundaries:

- Making comparisons across faculty. Faculty would not compare students to one another and attempt to use this comparison when speaking to students, as this would be both inappropriate and disrespectful.
- Continuing to argue a point after you have communicated your position.

- Emailing you multiple times in the same day; seemingly sending you every thought they have after their first message has been sent. (As an example, one of the authors had a student who would email them every single day of the term and would typically receive 3-4 emails each day. The author would only respond to one email per day (as a best practice, and to establish an important boundary with this student).
- Becoming argumentative, rude, or disrespectful in their conduct. Students should be reminded of the institution's policy related to the code of conduct, and violations should be reported.
- Submitting/resubmitting an assignment after a deadline has passed. Be sure to check your institutional guidelines on late policies and on the number of resubmissions a student can make, as there is typically a limitation on how many times a student can resubmit their work for a single assignment.
- Making accusations against you to deflect from their behavior.
- Assuming and acting as though your expectations do not apply to them.
- Threatening to file an appeal or complaint if their request/demand is not met. The student has the right to appeal, and educators should not be threatened by this policy (if your institution has this type of policy in place). Educators should be empowered to report instances related to code of conduct, academic integrity violations, or other inappropriate behavior.
- Avoid engaging with students who are not behaving professionally or respectfully.

Continuing unproductive communication, especially if it turns hostile, serves no purpose. You can disengage and inform the student that the conversation or issue will be revisited later when emotions have settled. Similarly, there is no need to repeatedly explain yourself to a student who is arguing a moot point. While many educators feel obligated to respond to every student's email, being selective in your responses is acceptable when warranted. If an email is sent by a student that has a hostile or disrespectful tone, a helpful suggestion is to wait 24 hours to respond to the email to avoid an emotional or negative response to the student. Additionally, focus on only the main points or facts when responding to this type of email from a student, such as reiterating that the rubrics were followed, or that the late policy has been applied, etc. If the email violates the student code of conduct, another suggestion is to contact your supervisor regarding the communication from a student if additional steps are needed to address the student's inappropriate behavior. Remember, articulating clear and consistent boundaries informs students on how we expect to be treated, and reaffirms our needs to students by setting parameters for ourselves and for them (Tawwab, 2021).

Resist the urge to justify yourself or provide unnecessary explanations to students. Adhering to policy is the most effective approach in such situations. When your decision aligns with policy, you can simply direct the student to the policy and conclude the discussion. Additional information or explanations are not required once you have decided within your authority. Continuously engaging in a back-and-forth with a boundary-crossing student will unlikely lead to a successful resolution. Instead, it may reinforce inappropriate behavior and increase stress and anxiety for you.

Do not be deterred by students who threaten to file an appeal or complaint. When our boundaries align with the policies of our institutions, we are on solid ground. Moreover, we can be assured that we are providing consistency for all students. Once we have allowed our boundaries to become crossed or broken, that will become an expectation. We have experienced many instances in which students have threatened to file an appeal or have followed through with one. This is a part of the education system, and we should not be afraid of such an action. Students can and should advocate on their own behalf. Most importantly, we should not allow students to use that process to threaten or intimidate us into breaking our own boundaries or the policies of the institution.

The Student Who Checked Almost All the Boxes

In our efforts to encourage fellow educators to adopt boundaries with their students, we often share the example of a student who checked almost all the boxes in terms of pushing boundaries. While this type of student is certainly the exception rather than the norm, we are confident that at least several of these actions by our student will resonate with readers and help to illustrate the importance of setting and maintaining boundaries. This student:

Would Not Take "No" for an Answer

This student repeatedly asked the same questions multiple times during live lectures, via emails, and during phone calls held at their request. Despite being given the answers multiple times, the student persisted time after time, and course after course, to convince the professor to change their answer. The student repeatedly requested phone calls but refused to provide information about why the call was requested. The student repeatedly failed to provide the professor with an agenda in preparation for the call, and once on the call, would often ask only one simple question, such as what was meant by the requirement that papers have titles. Often, the question had already been asked and answered multiple times.

Asked for Information Easily Located in the Textbook and Reading Materials

The student would repeatedly ask that specific page numbers within the required textbook and reading materials be provided in order to avoid having to actually read the content themselves. Other times, the student would ask for definitions of words that were defined in the textbook as well as previous live lectures. The student later admitted to not having the textbook and not reading the required materials.

Asked for Review of Draft Assignments

The student would repeatedly ask the same professor to review drafts of their assignments before they were submitted for grading. Despite being repeatedly told that this was not the professor's practice (in accordance with institutional guidelines), the student would repeatedly ask. At times, the student would simply email the draft with a statement indicating their expectation of a review despite having been previously told this was not possible. In some cases, the drafts sent contained only a few sentences.

Tried to Negotiate Grades

The student consistently complained about the grades received and claimed not to understand their grades. However, the student never reviewed the feedback provided by the professor. The student often said: "I'm trying to work with you, Professor," and would threaten to appeal if the grades were not changed to their satisfaction. In several instances, the student did follow through by filing an unsubstantiated appeal.

Complained They Were Not Getting Help, Then Did Not Take it

The student filed a complaint that the professor would not assist him with his assignments. The professor then set up a one-hour Zoom meeting to discuss the next assignment. The student asked one question and had no additional questions or comments.

Recommendations for Setting Boundaries

Setting expectations for availability is important for you and for your students. With the increased accessibility that technology provides, students increasingly expect near-constant availability and accessibility from faculty. In turn, we as educators feel pressured to provide this near-constant availability. However, this is not only unrealistic, but also unnecessary and unhealthy. We like to joke that there are no emergencies in education – the fact is, this is true. Students and faculty may experience emergencies in their lives outside of the course room that might impact their activity in the course, but as educators, it is hard to think of an actual course-related emergency. As educators, we should work toward a reset to more realistic expectations. Students do not need immediate responses – even if they want them.

It is also important to remember our instruction is not limited to course content. As educators, we should also be encouraging and empowering students to develop as critical thinkers and independent learners. When students know (or expect) an immediate response from faculty, they will ask for the answers to their questions rather than look for them. However, if we do not respond immediately, they are encouraged (and empowered) to use and improve their skills to find the answer to their questions. In most cases, the information is provided in the course or the readings.

As we have discussed, it can be difficult to start setting boundaries and to know where to begin (Tawwab, 2021). We offer several recommendations that you may find helpful throughout this writing. Remember that we are all different, and what works well for some may not work for others. There is an element of trial and error here, and it can take time to figure out what works best for you and your students. We encourage you to try one or more of these recommendations, and to add more over time. Be sure to review your institution's communication policies as you consider each of these recommendations.

- Set and maintain weekly office hours. Using office hours each week allows students to understand the importance of time management and can create a healthy boundary, establishing clear parameters when you are available and when you are not.
- Do not give out your personal cell phone number to students (use Google Voice, Zoom, Hangouts, or similar options). Using Voice over Internet Protocol [VoIP] allows the professor to retain their privacy through the use of a designated phone number and to screen calls and text messages using a separate phone application.
- Check and respond to emails at certain times of the day and on certain days of the week. This allows educators to not feel obligated to immediately respond to emails.
- When students ask for a call, schedule it a day or two in advance and ask them to send you an agenda/questions so you are both prepared for the call. This will provide a set timeframe for the call and will create an organized schedule for all participants to follow.

- Do not engage in continuous emails with a student throughout the day – set the expectation that they communicate in one thoughtfully developed email. This reduces the chances of an ongoing argument with students.
- Ignore messages on the weekend.
- NOTE: While writing this chapter, two hurricanes made landfall in Florida that impacted our students, throughout the Southeastern United States. Emails over the weekends related to the hurricanes were not ignored, due to the gravity of the situation, thus the exception to the rule.
- Set and maintain expectations for communications.
- Prepare students to communicate professionally and respectfully in the workplace.
- Require students to refer to you by your title/preferred name/etc.
- Do not accept texting language in an email.
- Set boundaries through institutional policies (late policy, resubmission policy, maximum submissions, code of conduct, academic dishonesty, offering remediation, plagiarism, use of artificial intelligence tools, etc.).
- Remind yourself that there are no emergencies in education - a failure to plan on the part of a student does not constitute an emergency for you as the professor.

Remember that boundaries create healthy relationships. They help to foster positive communication and transparency between faculty and students. Boundaries help us to set and maintain realistic expectations for students. They empower students to become independent and to take ownership of their work. Finally, boundaries help educators to maintain a healthy and appropriate work-life balance, which in turn helps us to avoid burnout (Kariou et al., 2021, Tawwab, 2021).

SUMMARY

This chapter grew out of many conversations concerning boundaries being crossed in our professional lives as educators, and how to best prevent them from being crossed in the future. Through trial and error, and learning from boundaries being crossed at times, this sparked the necessity toward establishing clear boundaries and to facilitate a healthy work-life balance. We hope the recommendations provided will empower educators to create parameters in their personal and professional lives. Once boundaries have been articulated, realistic expectations and a growth mindset can be fostered in the relationships between educators and students (Dweck et al., 2021; Tawwab, 2021). This in turn can lead to increased independence, critical thinking, and confidence among students. Helping students to develop and strengthen these important skills sets them up for success in the classroom and beyond.

REFERENCES

Adisa, T. A., Antonacopoulou, E., Beauregard, T. A., Dickmann, M., & Adekoya, O. D. (2022). Exploring the impact of COVID-19 on employees' boundary management and work-life balance. *British Journal of Management*, 33(4), 1694–1709. DOI: 10.1111/1467-8551.12643

Allen, T. D., Merlo, K., Lawrence, R. C., Slutsky, J., & Gray, C. E. (2021). Boundary management and work-nonwork balance while working from home. *Applied Psychology*, 70(1), 60–84. DOI: 10.1111/apps.12300

Drigas, A. S., & Papoutsi, C. (2018). A new layered model on emotional intelligence. *Behavioral Sciences (Basel, Switzerland)*, 8(5), 45. https://www.mdpi.com/2076-328X/8/5/45/htm. DOI: 10.3390/bs8050045 PMID: 29724021

Dweck, C. S., & Yeager, D. (2021). *Global mindset initiative introduction: Envisioning the future of growth mindset research in education*.https://www.researchgate.net/profile/David-Yeager/publication/354168475_Global_Mindset_Initiative_Introduction_Envisioning_the_Future_of_Growth_Mindset_Research_in_Education/links/6128f9f00360302a0061103c/Global-Mindset-Initiative-Introduction-Envisioning-the-Future-of-Growth-Mindset-Research-in-Education.pdf

Goleman, D. (2005). *Emotional intelligence*. Bantam.

Goleman, D., & Boyatzis, R. (2017). Emotional intelligence has 12 elements. Which do you need to work on? *Harvard Business Review*, 84(2), 1–5. https://hbr.org/2017/02/emotional-intelligence-has-12-elements-which-do-you-need-to-work-on

Hansen, B. L., & Gray, E. (2018). Creating boundaries within the ubiquitous online classroom. *The Journal of Educators Online*, 15(3), n3. https://www.thejeo.com/. DOI: 10.9743/jeo.2018.15.3.2

Kariou, A., Koutsimani, P., Montgomery, A., & Lainidi, O. (2021). Emotional labor and burnout among teachers: A systematic review. *International Journal of Environmental Research and Public Health*, 18(23), 12760. DOI: 10.3390/ijerph182312760 PMID: 34886485

Mattingly, V., & Kraiger, K. (2019). Can emotional intelligence be trained? A meta-analytical investigation. *Human Resource Management Review*, 29(2), 140–155. https://www.sciencedirect.com/science/article/abs/pii/S1053482218301840. DOI: 10.1016/j.hrmr.2018.03.002

Miao, C., Humphrey, R. H., & Qian, S. (2017). A meta-analysis of emotional intelligence and work attitudes. *Journal of Occupational and Organizational Psychology*, 90(2), 177–202. https://bpspsychub.onlinelibrary.wiley.com/doi/abs/10.1111/joop.12167. DOI: 10.1111/joop.12167

National Center for Education Statistics. (2024). *Characteristics of postsecondary faculty. Condition of Education*. U.S. Department of Education, Institute of Education Sciences. https://nces.ed.gov/programs/coe/indicator/csc

National Center for Faculty Development and Diversity. (n.d.). https://www.ncfdd.org/home

Pattemore, C. (2021). Ten ways to build and preserve better boundaries. *PsychCentral,* https://psychcentral.com/lib/10-way-to-build-and-preserve-better-boundaries#types

Perrigino, M. B., & Raveendhran, R. (2020). Managing remote workers during quarantine: Insights from organizational research on boundary management. *Behavioral Science & Policy*, 6(2), 87–94. DOI: 10.1177/237946152000600211

Rockquemore, K. A. (2015). How to listen less. *Inside Higher Ed.* https://www.insidehighered.com/advice/2015/11/04/setting-boundaries-when-it-comes-students-emotional-disclosures-essay

Tawwab, N. G. (2021). *Set boundaries, find peace: A guide to reclaiming yourself.* Penguin.

Tyner, A., & Petrilli, M. J. (2018). The case for holding students accountable: How extrinsic motivation gets kids to work harder and learn more. *Education Next*, 18(3), 26–32. https://www.educationnext.org/wp-content/uploads/2022/01/ednext_xviii_3_tyner_petrilli.pdf

University of Massachusetts Amherst. (2023). *How to set boundaries.* https://www.umass.edu/studentsuccess/march-how-to-set-boundaries

Vyletel, B., Voichoski, E., Lipson, S., & Heinze, J. (2023). *Exploring faculty burnout through the 2022-23 HMS faculty/staff survey.* https://www.apa.org/ed/precollege/psychology-teacher-network/introductory-psychology/faculty-burnout-survey

Warner, J. (2024). In student-centered classrooms, the instructor must come first. *Inside Higher Ed.* https://www.insidehighered.com/opinion/blogs/just-visiting/2024/07/18/student-centered-teaching-should-consider-instructors-first?utm_source=Inside+Higher+Ed&utm_campaign=91db10faf5-DNU_2021_COPY_02&utm_medium=email&utm_term=0_1fcbc04421-91db10faf5-236162669&mc_cid=91db10faf5&mc_eid=a4ce5578c6

Wyrick, A. (2022). How to define boundaries with your students – and stick to them. *Harvard Business Publishing,* https://hbsp.harvard.edu/inspiring-minds/how-to-define-boundaries-with-your-students-and-stick-to-them

KEY TERMS AND DEFINITIONS

Boundaries: Establishing norms, guidelines, and time management strategies to foster a healthy work-life balance.

Burnout: Feelings of being stressed, mentally exhausted, overwhelmed, fatigued, and/or anxiety.

Code of Conduct: Institutional policies related to inappropriate, disrespectful, and/or unprofessional behavior, including communications.

Educator: Any faculty member of an educational institution providing instruction to students

Institutional Policy: An explicit set of operational processes and practices required throughout an organization.

Remediation: Additional training or education provided to students who have not met the required academic standards or expectations.

Work-Life Balance: Establishing boundaries between personal and professional obligations and responsibilities that promote an empowered and healthy lifestyle.

Chapter 14
Successful Teaching in Virtual Classrooms:
Strategies for Online Open Elective Educators

Vishnu Achutha Menon
https://orcid.org/0000-0003-4028-3685
Institute for Educational and Developmental Studies, India

ABSTRACT

The evolution of online education highlights its potential and challenges. It offers flexible, accessible learning opportunities but also underscores the need to address digital divides and provide robust support systems for students and educators. Future directions should focus on utilizing technological advancements, encouraging inclusive practices, and developing innovative pedagogical approaches. Key factors for effective online education include interactive platforms, multimedia content, personalized learning, engaging assessments, and strong support systems. Continuous professional development for educators and community building among students are essential to enhance the online learning experience.

INTRODUCTION

In today's dynamic educational landscape, the concept of open electives has emerged as a pivotal component in higher education curricula. Open electives provide students with the flexibility to choose courses outside their core disciplines, allowing them to explore diverse interests and tailor their academic journey to their individual passions and career aspirations. These courses often cover a wide range of topics, spanning various fields of study, and are typically offered as optional

DOI: 10.4018/979-8-3693-4407-1.ch014

supplements to the mandatory curriculum. Open electives refer to courses that are not mandatory for a student's degree program but are offered as optional subjects that students can choose to study based on their interests, academic goals, and career aspirations. Unlike core courses that are required for graduation, open electives provide students with the freedom to explore interdisciplinary topics, delve into niche subjects, or deepen their understanding of specific areas of interest.

Online open elective courses, available via the internet, enable students to explore subjects outside their primary fields of study. These courses offer flexibility and accessibility, allowing learners from diverse backgrounds to pursue interests and develop skills that complement their major coursework or professional goals. Typically, they allow access at any time and from any location, cover a wide range of topics, and accommodate different learning speeds and schedules. They also include interactive elements such as multimedia content, quizzes, discussion forums, and virtual group projects to enhance engagement. They are designed to be inclusive, often providing materials in multiple formats to support diverse learning needs and ensure accessibility for students with disabilities. The importance of online open elective courses in the educational landscape lies in their promotion of lifelong learning, offering opportunities for continued education beyond traditional settings and enhancing skill sets applicable to students' professional lives. Moreover, they support personal growth by enabling learners to explore new subjects and interests, contributing to personal development and intellectual curiosity. They increase educational access by breaking down barriers and making learning opportunities available to a broader audience regardless of geographic or financial constraints. These elements collectively enhance the educational experience, making online open elective courses a vital component of contemporary education systems. Karnataka, a state in southern India renowned for its rich cultural heritage and vibrant academic institutions, has been at the forefront of embracing online education initiatives. With a strong focus on utilizing technology to enhance learning outcomes and expand educational access, Karnataka has witnessed significant developments in the realm of online open elective courses. The objective of this book chapter is to provide comprehensive insights into effective teaching methodologies for online open elective courses, covering challenges, best practices, engagement strategies, technology integration, inclusivity, case studies, and actionable recommendations to improve instructional practices and student outcomes.

Best Practices for Online Instruction

Teaching in an online environment demands efficient time management and a focus on activities that maximize student learning and engagement (Cooper et al., 2023). The transition from traditional classroom settings to online courses presents unique challenges, as many pedagogical practices that are effective in face-to-face settings do not translate well to the virtual format (Jump & Schedlbauer, 2020). To overcome these challenges, teaching strategies should be both creative and innovative to ensure they effectively reach and engage all students (Pushpalatha et al., 2022).

One key approach is the use of diverse and flexible content delivery methods. Open educational resources (OERs) provide a wealth of materials that can be freely accessed and used to enhance learning. These include pre-recorded lectures, which allow students to learn at their own pace and revisit complex topics as needed, and podcasts, which can be particularly useful for auditory learners and for providing content in a more conversational and engaging format. Online-first textbooks, designed specifically for digital use, offer interactive features that traditional textbooks do not, such as embedded multimedia and hyperlinks to supplementary resources. These resources are not only appropriate for the online learning environment but are also cost-conscious options that can help reduce the financial burden on students (Mavo Navarro & McGrath, 2022). Online learning environments can also offer advantages for certain students, such as those who thrive with more flexible schedules or who prefer a self-paced learning approach (Psotka, 2022). To design effective online courses, educators can follow a structured four-step process: planning, development, implementation, and evaluation (P. Diep et al., 2021). This process helps ensure that the courses are well-organized, engaging, and capable of meeting the learning objectives. The role of facilitators in online education is crucial. Effective facilitators help guide students through the course material, encourage participation, and provide timely feedback, all of which are important for maintaining student engagement and performance (Lee, 2020). They must be adept at using the various technological tools available and be able to create an inclusive and supportive online learning community. It's important to acknowledge that many traditional pedagogical practices do not seamlessly adapt to online formats (Rodríguez-Hernández & Rincón-Flores, 2023). For example, in-class discussions and spontaneous interactions can be challenging to replicate online. Thus, instructors must find new ways to encourage interaction and collaboration, such as through the use of discussion boards, group projects, and virtual breakout rooms.

Online education can be an engaging and creative venue for teaching and learning when the right tools and supports are in place. Interactive learning platforms, such as Learning Management Systems like Moodle and Canvas, along with collaborative tools like Google Workspace, facilitate real-time collaboration and course management. Incorporating multimedia content, including videos, animations, interactive simulations, and podcasts, caters to different learning styles and makes lessons more engaging. Personalized learning experiences, supported by adaptive learning technologies and data analytics tools, allow students to learn at their own pace and receive targeted support. Engaging assessments, such as gamified quizzes, project-based evaluations, and peer assessments, add variety and dynamism to the learning process. Strong support systems, including technical, academic, and emotional support, are crucial for student success. Educators also need professional development in effective online teaching strategies, technical training, and continuous professional growth to deliver high-quality online education. Building a sense of community through virtual group projects, discussion boards, and regular events encourage a supportive and collaborative environment. With these elements effectively implemented, online education can provide a rich, engaging, and creative learning experience that meets diverse student needs.

Enhancing online teaching requires various tools and technologies to create a dynamic and effective learning environment. Learning Management Systems (LMS) like Moodle, Canvas, and Blackboard are essential for organizing and managing course content, assignments, quizzes, and tracking student progress. They streamline administrative tasks and provide a structured platform for students to access materials and engage with instructors and peers. Multimedia resources and interactive tools, including videos, podcasts, animations, and simulations, cater to different learning styles and simplify complex concepts. Interactive tools such as Kahoot! and Quizlet offer engaging quizzes and flashcards, while platforms like YouTube and Khan Academy provide a wealth of educational videos. Communication and collaboration are facilitated by platforms like Zoom, Microsoft Teams, and Google Meet, which enable live classes, webinars, and virtual office hours for real-time interaction. Tools like Google Workspace and Microsoft Office 365 support collaborative projects and real-time document sharing, promoting teamwork and peer learning. Discussion boards and social media groups offer spaces for ongoing discussions and community building among students, enhancing the overall online learning experience.

Effective communication is fundamental to the success of online teaching and learning, requiring a multifaceted approach to address the unique challenges of virtual education.

- Clear Communication of Expectations: Articulating course expectations is essential for setting the foundation of the learning process. This involves not only stating the course objectives, deadlines, and grading criteria but also explaining the rationale behind them. Detailed syllabi, rubrics, and instructional videos can help students understand what is expected and how they can meet those expectations. Providing examples of high-quality work can illustrate standards and reduce ambiguity. It's important to outline the policies for late submissions, academic integrity, and participation to preemptively address potential issues and nurtures a transparent and fair learning environment.

- Establishing Regular Contact with Students: Consistent and regular contact with students can significantly enhance their learning experience. Scheduled check-ins, whether through weekly announcements, virtual office hours, or personalized feedback, help build a connection and show that the instructor is engaged and invested in their success. Regular communication can also identify and address student difficulties early, providing opportunities for timely intervention. Personalized feedback on assignments is crucial, as it not only guides students on how to improve but also acknowledges their efforts, boosting motivation and engagement. Moreover, cultivating an open-door policy, where students feel comfortable reaching out with questions or concerns, can bridge the gap that often exists in online education.
- Utilizing Various Communication Channels: Utilizing multiple communication channels ensures inclusivity and accessibility, catering to different student preferences and needs. Email is effective for formal communication, providing a written record of important information. Discussion forums facilitate peer interaction and collaborative learning, allowing students to engage in meaningful discussions and share insights. Video calls through platforms like Zoom or Microsoft Teams enable real-time interaction, which is vital for complex discussions, immediate feedback, and building a sense of community. Instant messaging apps, such as Slack or Microsoft Teams, offer quick and informal communication, making it easier to address minor queries promptly. Social media groups can also create informal spaces for students to connect and support each other.

Critically, while utilizing various channels, it is important to establish boundaries and manage expectations about response times to prevent burnout and ensure that communication remains effective and sustainable. Understanding the diverse technological access and capabilities of students is crucial; providing multiple communication options can help accommodate those with limited resources or varying levels of digital literacy.

Assessment and Feedback Techniques

To enrich the assessment process, incorporating peer and self-assessment techniques can be highly beneficial. Peer assessment allows students to evaluate each other's work, creating a collaborative learning environment where they can learn from one another. This process helps students develop critical evaluation skills and exposes them to different perspectives and approaches, which can deepen their understanding of the subject matter. Self-assessment, on the other hand, encourages students to reflect on their learning and performance. It promotes self-regulation and metacognition, as students critically assess their strengths and weaknesses and set personal goals for improvement. Incorporating these varied assessment and feedback techniques creates a dynamic and supportive learning environment. It ensures that assessments are not just a measure of learning but a tool for continuous improvement and deeper understanding. By challenging students to think critically and creatively, providing actionable feedback, and encouraging reflective practices through peer and self-assessment, instructors can significantly enhance the educational experience and build a culture of lifelong learning.

Instructors face the important task of implementing effective assessment and feedback techniques to enhance student learning. Designing meaningful assessments is crucial, as they must align with learning objectives and evaluate a range of cognitive skills. Assessments should be varied and multifaceted, incorporating different types of questions and tasks such as essays, projects, presentations, and practical applications to cater to diverse learning styles and provide a well-rounded evaluation of student understanding. These assessments should challenge students to apply their knowledge critically and creatively, encouraging them to synthesize information, analyze complex problems, and draw connections between concepts. By doing so, assessments move beyond rote memorization and develop higher-order thinking skills essential for academic and professional success. Providing timely and constructive feedback is equally essential. Feedback should be specific, actionable, and oriented towards improvement, addressing both strengths and areas needing development. This feedback guides students' learning processes, helping them understand where they excel and what specific steps they can take to improve. Timeliness is key; prompt feedback ensures that students can immediately apply suggestions to their ongoing work, making the learning process more dynamic and iterative. Constructive feedback also plays a motivational role, helping students feel supported and engaged, reducing anxiety, and building confidence in their abilities.

Professors' departure from conventional feedback methods (Elsayed & Cakir, 2023) reflects a necessary evolution in pedagogy. Traditional feedback often operates on a one-size-fits-all model, lacking personalized guidance and failing to address individual student needs effectively. By shifting away from these approaches, educators can embrace more student-centered feedback methods that nurture active engagement and promote deeper learning. Active engagement with feedback is essential for students to derive maximum benefit from it (Chambers & Harkins Monaco, 2023). Simply receiving feedback is not enough; students must understand it, reflect on it, and use it to inform their future efforts. This active involvement in the feedback process empowers students to take ownership of their learning and facilitates continuous improvement. The call for varied and multifaceted assessments (Van der Kleij, 2022) recognizes the limitations of relying solely on traditional exams and essays to gauge student understanding. Such assessments often favor memorization over critical thinking and fail to capture the full range of students' abilities. By diversifying assessment methods to include projects, presentations, portfolios, and other forms of authentic assessment, educators can better assess students' holistic learning outcomes.

Feedback design in open-ended tasks plays a crucial role in stimulating a sense of connection between students and their instructors (Ajjawi et al., 2022). In online learning environments especially, where face-to-face interaction is limited, feedback becomes a vital means of establishing rapport and building a supportive learning community. By designing feedback that is constructive, personalized, and encouraging, educators can strengthen their relationships with students and create a more positive learning environment. Low-stakes quizzing offers several advantages in promoting student learning (Morris et al., 2021). It provides regular opportunities for retrieval practice, which enhances long-term retention of information. Low-stakes quizzes help reduce students' anxiety about assessment by removing the fear of failure associated with high-stakes exams. This allows students to approach learning with greater confidence and motivation. The importance of implementing effective assessment and feedback techniques cannot be overstated (Albinson et al., 2020). These techniques are essential for providing students with meaningful learning experiences and supporting their academic growth. By prioritizing quality feedback and employing diverse assessment strategies, educators can create a more inclusive and supportive learning environment that meets the needs of all students. The recognized potential of feedback to enhance student performance and learning (F. M. Van der Kleij & Lipnevich, 2021) underscores its significance in educational practice. Feedback serves not only to evaluate student progress but also to guide their development, cultivate critical thinking skills, and promote self-directed learning. As such, investing in effective feedback practices is essential for promoting student success in both academic and real-world contexts.

Feedback serves as a vital tool in guiding students towards learning objectives and facilitating their progress (Selvaraj & Azman, 2020). By providing students with clear and actionable feedback, educators can support them in understanding their strengths and areas for improvement, thereby helping them achieve the aims of the lesson. Furthermore, training students in feedback delivery using simple rubrics and offering opportunities to act on feedback can significantly enhance the quality of feedback they provide (Camarata & Slieman, 2020). This approach not only improves students' ability to provide constructive feedback but also promotes their own learning through reflection and implementation. The primary purpose of feedback is to drive improvement (Dawson et al., 2019). Effective feedback does not simply evaluate performance but rather provides specific guidance on how students can enhance their understanding, skills, and performance. By focusing on improvement-oriented feedback, educators can create a culture of continuous growth and development among students. To ensure that feedback remains impactful and sustainable, it is essential to redesign conventional assessment tasks in higher education contexts (Lam, 2017). By aligning assessment tasks with learning objectives and incorporating opportunities for feedback throughout the learning process, educators can create a feedback-rich environment that supports ongoing student learning and development. Implementing effective assessment and feedback techniques is a critical responsibility for instructors (Pedrosa-de-Jesus et al., 2018). By providing timely, specific, and actionable feedback, educators can maximize the impact of their instruction and promote student success. Effective feedback serves as a catalyst for development, offering guidance, opening doors to new opportunities, and empowering students to reach their full potential (Lichtenberger-Majzikné & Fischer, 2017). The timing of feedback is crucial to its effectiveness (McCarthy, 2017). Providing feedback in a timely manner allows students to make immediate connections between their actions and the outcomes, facilitating deeper understanding and reinforcement of learning concepts. By ensuring that feedback is delivered promptly and in context, educators can maximize its impact on student learning outcomes.

Individual written comments were found to be the most useful form of feedback The assertion that individual written comments represent the most advantageous form of feedback (Taylor & Burke da Silva, 2014) warrants a critical examination due to its significant implications for pedagogical practice. Several factors underpin the effectiveness of individual written comments, which deserve exploration. Individual written comments offer a level of personalization and specificity that other forms of feedback often lack. Unlike generic feedback, which may not address the unique needs and challenges of each student, individual written comments allow instructors to tailor their guidance to the individual learner. By directly addressing the student's work, instructors can provide targeted insights and suggestions for improvement. For example, instead of simply indicating that a student's essay lacks clarity, an instructor can provide specific feedback on areas where the argument could be strengthened or where additional evidence is needed.

Individual written comments provide a tangible record of feedback that students can reference and reflect upon. Unlike verbal feedback, which may be quickly forgotten, written comments offer a permanent reference point that students can revisit as they continue to develop their skills. This allows students to track their progress over time and identify recurring patterns or areas for growth. For instance, if a student consistently receives feedback on the organization of their writing, they can use written comments from previous assignments to identify specific strategies for improvement. It also promotes a sense of accountability and ownership over the feedback process. When students receive personalized comments on their work, they are more likely to take ownership of their learning and actively engage with the feedback provided. This can lead to greater motivation and self-regulation as students strive to implement the suggested changes. For example, if a student receives written feedback highlighting areas for improvement in their problem-solving approach, they may feel a sense of responsibility to address these shortcomings in future assignments. However, it's important to acknowledge that the effectiveness of individual written comments may vary depending on factors such as the clarity and specificity of the feedback provided, as well as the student's receptiveness to feedback. While individual written comments offer numerous benefits, they also require a significant investment of time and effort on the part of instructors. Therefore, it's essential for educators to strike a balance between providing thorough feedback and managing their workload effectively.

The study conducted by Randall and Zundel (2012) sheds light on the comparative effectiveness of oral and written formative feedback when students are given the opportunity to utilize it. This research underscores the importance of feedback as a pivotal aspect of the teaching and learning process (Fluckiger et al., 2010). The concept of "formative assessment" has gained prominence in educational discourse, emphasizing the integral role of feedback in facilitating student progress and learning outcomes (Wiliam, 2010). Indeed, effective feedback is instrumental in empowering adult learners to achieve their educational objectives and unlock their full potential (Sachdeva, 1996). By providing timely and constructive feedback, instructors can guide learners towards improvement, refine their skills, and bolster their understanding of course material. However, feedback alone may not suffice in driving meaningful learning outcomes. As highlighted by Brandt (2008), the incorporation of reflective conversations in post-teaching practice meetings can complement feedback processes by nurturing deeper engagement and critical thinking among learners. These reflective discussions provide students with opportunities to internalize feedback, evaluate their own performance, and identify areas for further development. By engaging in dialogue with peers and instructors, learners can gain valuable insights, perspectives, and strategies for improvement. Formative feedback that involves students as partners is a particularly effective strategy in enhancing the teaching and learning process (Fluckiger et al., 2010). When students are actively engaged in the feedback process, they become more invested in their own learning journey. By soliciting student input, instructors can gain valuable perspectives on the effectiveness of their feedback practices and tailor their approaches to better meet the needs of diverse learners. This collaborative feedback model promotes a culture of mutual respect, trust, and shared responsibility for learning outcomes.

Professional Development and Support for Instructors

Professional development programs play a pivotal role in enhancing the effectiveness of faculty members in online teaching contexts by exposing them to evidence-based instructional strategies. As highlighted by Wynants and Dennis (2018), such programs provide faculty with valuable insights into effective pedagogical techniques tailored specifically for the online environment, thereby empowering them to refine their teaching practices. These programs are designed to address the unique needs of online teachers in higher education, recognizing the distinct challenges and opportunities associated with virtual instruction (Baran & Correia, 2014). Institutions typically offer structured professional development opportunities through their teaching or learning centers, providing faculty members with access to workshops, seminars, and training sessions focused on online pedagogy (Zhao et al., 2022). Through sustained engagement with these programs, instructors can initiate instructional change and cultivate a deeper understanding of effective teaching methods in the online realm (Hinson & LaPrairie, 2005).

Technology serves as a powerful tool for meeting the diverse learning needs of students in online settings, offering innovative ways to engage learners and facilitate meaningful interactions (Hicks et al., 2001). However, to fully harness the potential of technology in education, teachers must engage in ongoing professional development that encompasses three essential elements: investigation, reflection, and constructive dialogue (Prestridge & Tondeur, 2015). By critically examining their instructional practices, reflecting on their experiences, and engaging in dialogue with peers, instructors can continuously refine their approach to online teaching. It is crucial that professional development programs for online instructors are designed to align with the types of online courses that the institution aims to offer (Borup & Evmenova, 2019). By modeling effective online course design and facilitation, these programs provide faculty members with practical insights and strategies that they can directly apply in their own teaching contexts. Moreover, it is recommended that faculty members undergo professional development before they begin teaching online, ensuring that they are adequately prepared to navigate the unique challenges of virtual instruction (Leary et al., 2020).

Ensuring that instructors are well-prepared and continuously supported is crucial for the success of online education. Professional development and support systems empower educators to effectively utilize technology, engage students, and adapt to the evolving landscape of online teaching. Comprehensive training and workshops are essential components of professional development for online instructors. These programs should cover a range of topics, including:

1. Effective online teaching strategies: Instructors should learn best practices for virtual instruction, including how to design engaging courses, facilitate interactive discussions, and assess student performance.
2. Technology integration: Training should focus on the use of various digital tools and platforms, from Learning Management Systems (LMS) like Moodle and Canvas to multimedia creation tools and collaborative software.
3. Pedagogical approaches: Workshops should explore different pedagogical models suitable for online education, such as flipped classrooms, blended learning, and gamification techniques.

Creating communities of practice and peer learning networks can significantly enhance professional development by facilitating collaboration and knowledge sharing among instructors. These networks can:

- Facilitate peer mentoring: Experienced online educators can mentor newcomers, providing guidance and sharing best practices.
- Promote collaborative problem-solving: Instructors can collectively address challenges, share solutions, and develop innovative teaching strategies.
- Encourage continuous learning: Regular interactions within these communities help instructors stay updated on the latest trends and advancements in online education.

Instructors need access to a variety of resources and ongoing support to continually improve their online teaching practices. Essential resources and supports include:

- Technical support: Immediate assistance with technical issues related to online teaching platforms and tools.
- Academic resources: Access to digital libraries, research databases, and instructional design materials.
- Professional development courses: Opportunities to enroll in advanced courses and certifications focused on online education.
- Emotional and psychological support: Services that address the mental health and well-being of educators, helping them manage the stresses associated with online teaching.

Learning from real-world examples and best practices can provide valuable insights and inspiration for online instructors. Case studies of successful online teaching initiatives can highlight effective strategies and innovative approaches. Exemplary practices might include:

- Innovative course designs: Showcasing courses that have successfully integrated multimedia, interactive elements, and adaptive learning technologies.
- Engagement techniques: Highlighting methods that have proven effective in maintaining student interest and participation, such as gamified assessments and project-based learning.
- Support systems: Examples of robust support systems that provide comprehensive assistance to both students and instructors.

Effective professional development and robust support systems for instructors are essential to the success of online education. By learning from successful implementation stories, understanding lessons from experienced instructors, and exploring innovative teaching approaches, educators can enhance their online teaching skills and strategies. Successful implementation stories provide valuable insights into how online teaching can be effectively executed. These stories often highlight:

1. Case Study: University A: University A transitioned to online education by integrating a comprehensive Learning Management System (LMS) and offering extensive training for faculty. They saw a significant increase in student engagement and satisfaction by incorporating interactive elements such as live polls, discussion forums, and virtual breakout rooms.
2. Case Study: School District B: In School District B, the introduction of blended learning models, combining online and in-person instruction, resulted in improved student outcomes. Teachers used adaptive learning technologies to tailor instruction to individual student needs, leading to higher achievement levels.

Experienced instructors can offer practical advice and share lessons learned from their time teaching online. Key lessons include:

- Flexibility and Adaptability: Instructors need to be flexible and ready to adapt their teaching methods to meet the diverse needs of online learners. This includes being open to using new technologies and pedagogical approaches.
- Engagement Techniques: Experienced instructors emphasize the importance of keeping students engaged through interactive activities, regular feedback, and promoting a sense of community. Techniques such as synchronous video sessions, interactive discussions, and group projects are commonly highlighted.
- Continuous Improvement: Continuous professional development is crucial. Instructors should seek out opportunities for learning and improvement, whether through formal training programs, peer collaborations, or self-directed learning.

Innovative teaching approaches can transform the online learning experience and make it more effective and engaging. Examples include:

- Flipped Classroom Model: In this model, instructors provide lecture materials and readings online for students to review before class. During synchronous sessions, the focus is on interactive activities, problem-solving, and discussions. This approach encourages active learning and allows students to apply concepts in real time.
- Gamification: Incorporating game elements into the learning process can increase motivation and engagement. This can include using leaderboards, badges, and interactive quizzes that reward students for their progress and achievements.
- Project-Based Learning: This approach involves students working on projects over an extended period, which helps them develop deep understanding and practical skills. Projects can be collaborative and interdisciplinary, integrating various subjects and real-world applications.
- Adaptive Learning Technologies: These technologies use algorithms to personalize the learning experience for each student. By analyzing data on student performance, adaptive learning systems can adjust the content and pace to suit individual learning needs, ensuring that all students stay engaged and challenged.

Challenges Faced by Instructors

Instructors grapple with a myriad of challenges in their teaching endeavors, with technology integration, engagement and participation, assessment and evaluation, and diversity of learners' backgrounds and learning styles being prominent areas of concern. The rapid evolution of technology necessitates instructors to adeptly incorporate it into their teaching methodologies, selecting suitable tools while ensuring equitable access for all students. Maintaining student engagement and encouraging active participation, particularly in larger classes or when dealing with complex concepts, requires a diverse array of strategies such as interactive lectures and multimedia content. Crafting fair and effective assessments that align with learning objectives and provide valuable feedback poses an ongoing challenge, alongside managing grading consistency and addressing instances of academic dishonesty. The diverse backgrounds and learning styles present in modern classrooms demand inclusive teaching practices and a supportive learning environment to accommodate varying needs while upholding academic rigor. To navigate these challenges successfully, instructors can utilize professional development opportunities, collaborate with peers, utilize educational technology wisely, and remain responsive to student feedback.

The integration of technology into classrooms has significantly transformed the traditional role of teachers, reshaping their responsibilities and methodologies in profound ways. In the past, teachers primarily served as disseminators of information, delivering content through lectures, textbooks, and other conventional teaching materials. However, with the advent of technology, teachers have evolved into facilitators of learning, guiding students in navigating vast digital resources and engaging with interactive learning platforms. Technology integration has empowered teachers to adopt a more student-centered approach to instruction, focusing on personalized learning experiences tailored to individual needs and preferences. Instead of being the sole source of knowledge, teachers now curate digital content, design multimedia presentations, and facilitate collaborative online discussions to stimulate critical thinking and creativity among students.

Technology has expanded the scope of teaching beyond the physical confines of the classroom, enabling educators to connect with students remotely through online platforms and virtual learning environments. This shift towards online instruction has necessitated teachers to develop new skills in digital communication, time management, and online pedagogy to effectively engage students in virtual settings. Moreover, technology integration has heightened the importance of digital literacy and information fluency among teachers, requiring them to stay abreast of emerging technologies and trends in educational technology. Teachers must not only be proficient in using educational software and digital tools but also be able to critically evaluate the quality and relevance of online resources for instructional purposes.

Teachers in Pakistan exhibit positive perceptions regarding technology integration in their teaching-learning practices across all educational levels (Akram et al., 2022). They may integrate activities designed to keep students engaged throughout the lesson, enhancing the overall learning experience (Clarin & Baluyos, 2022). However, the specific challenges that students and teachers face with technological use in blended learning environments remain underexplored (Rasheed et al., 2020). It is important to note that being an experienced faculty member with advanced technology skills does not automatically make an instructor an effective e-instructor (Gülbahar & Adnan, 2020). Advanced technology has certainly opened up new opportunities for its application in education, allowing for innovative teaching methods and interactive learning experiences (Chew et al., 2018). Despite these opportunities, barriers to the integration of instructional technology exist both within teachers themselves and within their external environments (DiGregorio & Liston, 2018). The availability of school resources and the overall environment significantly impact the practices of beginning teachers, underscoring the importance of institutional support in technology integration (Ottenbreit-Leftwich et al., 2018). Instructors face issues related to learners' expectations, readiness, identity, and participation in online courses, which can complicate the effective use of technology in education (Kebritchi et al., 2017).

The realization that "regurgitating the textbook" is no longer an effective instructional delivery method can become a barrier if educators do not adapt their teaching strategies accordingly. This shift necessitates a fundamental change from traditional rote memorization techniques to more dynamic, interactive, and student-centered learning experiences. Several barriers may arise in this context. Some educators may resist changing their long-established teaching methods, feeling comfortable with the traditional approach and skeptical about the effectiveness of new strategies. A lack of professional development and training can hinder educators' ability to implement active learning, critical thinking exercises, and technology-enhanced teaching. Resource constraints, such as limited access to technology and instructional materials, also pose significant challenges, particularly in schools with tight budgets. Standardized testing and traditional assessment methods, which focus heavily on factual recall, can pressure educators to continue relying on textbook-based instruction. Students accustomed to traditional methods might initially resist more interactive forms of learning, creating additional hurdles. Lastly, without strong administrative support, efforts to move away from traditional methods may lack the necessary backing, making it difficult for educators to implement innovative teaching approaches. Overcoming these barriers requires comprehensive support, resources, and a willingness to embrace change in the educational landscape.

Educators should carefully use, evaluate, and adopt changes to utilize technologies effectively and track their impacts (Akbar, 2016). Teachers often identify several obstacles to technology integration in the classroom, including the time needed to prepare materials for quality technology-rich lessons, policies and security restrictions, access to resources, and their level of comfort with using technology (Alenezi, 2017). Teachers and instructors need a theoretical and knowledge base to provide a solid foundation for their teaching practices (Tony, 2016). To navigate these barriers, teachers could actively participate in and engage with school communities of practice. These communities offer a platform for educators to share experiences, exchange best practices, and collaboratively develop new instructional strategies. Through ongoing professional development and peer support, teachers can gain the skills and confidence needed to move away from traditional textbook-based methods. Collaborative problem-solving within these communities can help educators address resource constraints, find innovative solutions to engage students, and align teaching practices with modern educational standards. Engaging in these communities also helps teachers stay updated with the latest educational technologies and pedagogical advancements, creating an environment of continuous learning and adaptation. By drawing on the collective knowledge and support of their peers, educators can more effectively integrate technology into their teaching, ultimately enhancing the learning experience for their students.

The Cognitive Apprenticeship Model can help teachers confront the challenges of technology integration (Boling & Beatty, 2013). This model emphasizes the importance of teachers changing their mindsets to understand that teaching is not effective without the appropriate use of information and communication technology (ICT) resources to facilitate student learning (Ertmer & Ottenbreit-Leftwich, 2010). Research has shown that technology can positively influence teaching and learning (Brill & Galloway, 2007). Advances such as more intuitive software, CD-ROM media, and networks offer powerful new tools that can enhance educational practices and outcomes. Teachers must be open to adopting these new technologies and integrating them effectively into their instructional strategies to maximize their benefits for student learning.

CONCLUSION

The evolution of online education has demonstrated both its potential and its challenges. As we move forward, it is essential to reflect on the lessons learned and consider the future directions that will shape this dynamic field. Online education has shown its capability to provide flexible, accessible learning opportunities, especially during times when traditional in-person instruction is disrupted. However, it has also highlighted the importance of addressing digital divides, ensuring equitable access to technology, and providing robust support systems for both students and educators. Future directions should focus on utilizing technological advancements, and developing innovative pedagogical approaches that enhance the online learning experience. Key insights from the current state of online education reveal several critical factors that contribute to its effectiveness. Interactive learning platforms and multimedia content significantly enhance student engagement by catering to diverse learning styles. Personalized learning experiences, facilitated by adaptive technologies, allow for tailored educational journeys that meet individual needs. Engaging assessments and strong support systems are crucial for maintaining student motivation and success. Professional development for educators ensures they are equipped with the necessary skills and knowledge to deliver high-quality online instruction. Community building promotes a sense of belonging and collaboration among students, which is vital for a supportive learning environment.

To maximize the effectiveness of online teaching, several recommendations can be made. Firstly, educators should utilize interactive learning platforms that offer a range of tools for real-time collaboration and feedback. Incorporating a variety of multimedia content can make lessons more engaging and accessible to all students.

Personalized learning should be prioritized, with adaptive technologies used to tailor the educational experience to individual needs. Assessments should be varied and interactive, incorporating elements of gamification, project-based learning, and peer evaluation. Strong support systems must be established, including technical, academic, and emotional support services. Continuous professional development for educators is essential to keep them updated on the latest technologies and teaching strategies.

Future Research

Several areas within online education warrant further research and exploration. One key area is the impact of online learning on student outcomes compared to traditional in-person instruction. Research should investigate the long-term effects of online education on knowledge retention, critical thinking skills, and career readiness. Another area of interest is the role of artificial intelligence and machine learning in personalizing the learning experience and providing real-time feedback. The effectiveness of various multimedia tools and interactive simulations in enhancing student engagement and understanding also deserves further study. The social and emotional aspects of online learning, such as building community and providing emotional support, should be explored to ensure comprehensive student well-being. Finally, research into best practices for professional development in online teaching can help educators continually improve their skills and adapt to new technologies and methodologies.

REFERENCES

Adarkwah, M. A. (2021). The power of assessment feedback in teaching and learning: A narrative review and synthesis of the literature. *SN Social Sciences*, 1(3), 75. Advance online publication. DOI: 10.1007/s43545-021-00086-w

Ajjawi, R., Kent, F., Broadbent, J., Tai, J. H.-M., Bearman, M., & Boud, D. (2022). Feedback that works: A realist review of feedback interventions for written tasks. *Studies in Higher Education*, 47(7), 1343–1356. DOI: 10.1080/03075079.2021.1894115

Akbar, M. (2016). Digital technology shaping teaching practices in higher education. *Frontiers in ICT (Lausanne, Switzerland)*, 3. Advance online publication. DOI: 10.3389/fict.2016.00001

Akram, H., Abdelrady, A. H., Al-Adwan, A. S., & Ramzan, M. (2022). Teachers' perceptions of technology integration in teaching-learning practices: A systematic review. *Frontiers in Psychology*, 13, 920317. Advance online publication. DOI: 10.3389/fpsyg.2022.920317 PMID: 35734463

Albinson, P., Cetinkaya, D., & Orman, T. (2020). Using technology to enhance assessment and feedback: A framework for evaluating tools and applications. *Proceedings of the 2020 9th International Conference on Educational and Information Technology*. DOI: 10.1145/3383923.3383940

Alenezi, A. (2017). Obstacles for teachers to integrate technology with instruction. *Education and Information Technologies*, 22(4), 1797–1816. DOI: 10.1007/s10639-016-9518-5

Baran, E., & Correia, A.-P. (2014). A professional development framework for online teaching. *TechTrends*, 58(5), 95–101. DOI: 10.1007/s11528-014-0791-0

Boling, E. C., & Beatty, J. (2013). Overcoming the tensions and challenges of technology integration: How can we best support our teachers? In *K-12 Education* (pp. 1504–1524). IGI Global.

Borup, J., & Evmenova, A. (2019). The effectiveness of professional development in overcoming obstacles to effective online instruction in a college of education. *Online Learning : the Official Journal of the Online Learning Consortium*, 23(2). Advance online publication. DOI: 10.24059/olj.v23i2.1468

Brandt, C. (2008). Integrating feedback and reflection in teacher preparation. *ELT Journal*, 62(1), 37–46. DOI: 10.1093/elt/ccm076

Brill, J. M., & Galloway, C. (2007). Perils and promises: University instructors' integration of technology in classroom-based practices. *British Journal of Educational Technology*, 38(1), 95–105. DOI: 10.1111/j.1467-8535.2006.00601.x

Camarata, T., & Slieman, T. A. (2020). Improving student feedback quality: A simple model using peer review and feedback rubrics. *Journal of Medical Education and Curricular Development*, 7, 238212052093660. DOI: 10.1177/2382120520936604 PMID: 33029557

Chambers, A. W., & Harkins Monaco, E. (2023). Increasing Student Engagement with Instructor Feedback using Criteria-Based Rubrics as a tool for Self-Assessment. *The Journal of Scholarship of Teaching and Learning*, 23(2). Advance online publication. DOI: 10.14434/josotl.v23i2.33715

Chew, S. W., Cheng, I.-L., Kinshuk, , & Chen, N.-S. (2018). Exploring challenges faced by different stakeholders while implementing educational technology in classrooms through expert interviews. *Journal of Computers in Education*, 5(2), 175–197. DOI: 10.1007/s40692-018-0102-4

Clarin, A. S., & Baluyos, E. L. (2022). Challenges encountered in the implementation of online distance learning. *EduLine: Journal of Education and Learning Innovation*, 2(1), 33–46. DOI: 10.35877/454RI.eduline591

Cooper, L., Loster-Loftus, A., & Mandernach, J. (2023). Seven strategies for more efficient, effective online instruction: Effective eLearning (special series). *ELearn, 2023*(10). DOI: 10.1145/3626767.3595382

Dawson, P., Henderson, M., Mahoney, P., Phillips, M., Ryan, T., Boud, D., & Molloy, E. (2019). What makes for effective feedback: Staff and student perspectives. *Assessment & Evaluation in Higher Education*, 44(1), 25–36. DOI: 10.1080/02602938.2018.1467877

Diep, P., C., T.L. Nguyen, G., & T. Vo, N. (. (2021). Structure and procedure for developing an online course. *Journal of Technical Education Science*, 62, 83–98. DOI: 10.54644/jte.62.2021.83

DiGregorio, N., & Liston, D. D. (2018). Experiencing technical difficulties: Teacher self-efficacy and instructional technology. In *Self-Efficacy in Instructional Technology Contexts* (pp. 103–117). Springer International Publishing. DOI: 10.1007/978-3-319-99858-9_7

Elsayed, S., & Cakir, D. (2023). Implementation of assessment and feedback in higher education. *Acta Pedagogia Asiana*, 2(1), 34–42. DOI: 10.53623/apga.v2i1.170

Ertmer, P. A., & Ottenbreit-Leftwich, A. T. (2010). Teacher technology change: How knowledge, confidence, beliefs, and culture intersect. *Journal of Research on Technology in Education*, 42(3), 255–284. DOI: 10.1080/15391523.2010.10782551

Fluckiger, J., Vigil, Y. T., Pasco, R., & Danielson, K. (2010). Formative feedback: Involving students as partners in assessment to enhance learning. *College Teaching*, 58(4), 136–140. DOI: 10.1080/87567555.2010.484031

Gülbahar, Y., & Adnan, M. (2020). Faculty professional development in creating significant teaching and learning experiences online. In *Handbook of Research on Creating Meaningful Experiences in Online Courses* (pp. 37–58). IGI Global. DOI: 10.4018/978-1-7998-0115-3.ch004

Hicks, M., Reid, I., & George, R. (2001). Enhancing on-line teaching: Designing responsive learning environments. *The International Journal for Academic Development*, 6(2), 143–151. DOI: 10.1080/713769258

Hinson, J. M., & LaPrairie, K. N. (2005). Learning to teach online: Promoting success through professional development. *Community College Journal of Research and Practice*, 29(6), 483–493. DOI: 10.1080/10668920590934198

Jump, M., & Schedlbauer, M. (2020). Effective practices for online teaching. *Proceedings of the 51st ACM Technical Symposium on Computer Science Education*. DOI: 10.1145/3328778.3372534

Kebritchi, M., Lipschuetz, A., & Santiague, L. (2017). Issues and challenges for teaching successful online courses in higher education: A literature review. *Journal of Educational Technology Systems*, 46(1), 4–29. DOI: 10.1177/0047239516661713

Lam, R. (2017). Enacting feedback utilization from a task-specific perspective. *Curriculum Journal*, 28(2), 266–282. DOI: 10.1080/09585176.2016.1187185

Leary, H., Dopp, C., Turley, C., Cheney, M., Simmons, Z., Graham, C. R., & Hatch, R. (2020). Professional development for online teaching: A literature review. *Online Learning : the Official Journal of the Online Learning Consortium*, 24(4). Advance online publication. DOI: 10.24059/olj.v24i4.2198

Lee, J. W. (2020). The roles of online instructional facilitators and student performance of online class activity. *Journal of Asian Finance Economics and Business*, 7(8), 723–733. DOI: 10.13106/jafeb.2020.vol7.no8.723

Lichtenberger-Majzikné, K., & Fischer, A. (2017). The role of feedback in developing reflective competence. *Practice and Theory in Systems of Education*, 12(3), 119–127. DOI: 10.1515/ptse-2017-0012

Mavo Navarro, J. C., & McGrath, B. M. (2022). Strategies for effective online teaching and learning: Practices and techniques with a proven track of success in online education. In *Handbook of Research on Future of Work and Education* (pp. 495–510). IGI Global.

McCarthy, J. (2017). Enhancing feedback in higher education: Students' attitudes towards online and in-class formative assessment feedback models. *Active Learning in Higher Education*, 18(2), 127–141. DOI: 10.1177/1469787417707615

Morris, R., Perry, T., & Wardle, L. (2021). Formative assessment and feedback for learning in higher education: A systematic review. *Review of Education*, 9(3), e3292. Advance online publication. DOI: 10.1002/rev3.3292

Ottenbreit-Leftwich, A., Liao, J. Y.-C., Sadik, O., & Ertmer, P. (2018). Evolution of teachers' technology integration knowledge, beliefs, and practices: How can we support beginning teachers use of technology? *Journal of Research on Technology in Education*, 50(4), 282–304. DOI: 10.1080/15391523.2018.1487350

Pedrosa-de-Jesus, H., Moreira, A. C., da Silva Lopes, B., Guerra, C., & Watts, M. (2018). Assessment and Feedback. In *Academic Growth in Higher Education* (pp. 200–216). BRILL. DOI: 10.1163/9789004389342_016

Prestridge, S., & Tondeur, J. (2015). Exploring elements that support teachers engagement in online professional development. *Education Sciences*, 5(3), 199–219. DOI: 10.3390/educsci5030199

Psotka, J. (2022). Exemplary online education: For whom online learning can work better. *Interactive Learning Environments*, 30(2), 199–201. DOI: 10.1080/10494820.2022.2031065

Pushpalatha, K., Sheela, A. J., Kumar, S. D., & Gokila, S. (2022). Effective methodology to improve teaching-learning process and teacher education in online classes. [IJHS]. *International Journal of Health Sciences*, •••, 8289–8295. DOI: 10.53730/ijhs.v6nS3.7840

Randall, L., & Zundel, P. (2012). Students' perceptions of the effectiveness of assessment feedback as a learning tool in an introductory problem-solving course. *The Canadian Journal for the Scholarship of Teaching and Learning*, 3(1). Advance online publication. DOI: 10.5206/cjsotl-rcacea.2012.1.3

Rasheed, R. A., Kamsin, A., & Abdullah, N. A. (2020). Students and teachers' challenges of using technology in blended learning environments. *Proceedings of the 2020 the 3rd International Conference on Computers in Management and Business*. DOI: 10.1145/3383845.3383875

Rodríguez-Hernández, C. F., & Rincon-Flores, E. G. (2023). Comparative study between delivery modalities in higher education during emergency remote teaching due to COVID-19. *Frontiers in Education*, 8, 1179330. Advance online publication. DOI: 10.3389/feduc.2023.1179330

Sachdeva, A. K. (1996). Use of effective feedback to facilitate adult learning. *Journal of Cancer Education: The Official Journal of the American Association for Cancer Education*, 11(2). Advance online publication. DOI: 10.1080/08858199609528405 PMID: 8793652

Selvaraj, A. M., & Azman, H. (2020). Reframing the effectiveness of feedback in improving teaching and learning achievement. [IJERE]. *International Journal of Evaluation and Research in Education*, 9(4), 1055. DOI: 10.11591/ijere.v9i4.20654

Taylor, C., & Burke da Silva, K. (2014). An analysis of the effectiveness of feedback to students on assessed work. *Higher Education Research & Development*, 33(4), 794–806. DOI: 10.1080/07294360.2013.863840

Tony, B. (2016). *Teaching in a Digital Age*. BC campus. DOI: 10.14288/1.0224023

Van der Kleij, F. (2022). Reimagining classroom assessment and feedback to meet learner needs. *Research Conference 2022: Reimagining Assessment: Proceedings and Program*. DOI: 10.37517/978-1-74286-685-7-5

Van der Kleij, F. M., & Lipnevich, A. A. (2021). Student perceptions of assessment feedback: A critical scoping review and call for research. *Educational Assessment, Evaluation and Accountability*, 33(2), 345–373. DOI: 10.1007/s11092-020-09331-x

Wiliam, D. (2010). The role of formative assessment in effective learning environments. In *Educational Research and Innovation* (pp. 135–159). OECD.

Wynants, S., & Dennis, J. (2018). Professional development in an online context: Opportunities and challenges from the voices of college faculty. *The Journal of Educators Online*, 15(1). Advance online publication. DOI: 10.9743/JEO2018.15.1.2

Zhao, L., Dixon, R., Dousay, T., & Carr-Chellman, A. (2022). Outsourced Professional Development for Online Instructors: Recommendations from research. *ELearn, 2022*(4). DOI: 10.1145/3532688.3529094

Chapter 15
The Role of Virtual Classrooms in Realizing Effective Online Learning

Servet Kılıç
https://orcid.org/0000-0002-1687-3231
Ordu University, Turkey

Seyfullah Gökoğlu
https://orcid.org/0000-0003-0074-7692
Bartın University, Turkey

ABSTRACT

As of 2020, with the pandemic occurring worldwide, face-to-face learning activities at all levels, from preschool to higher education, have been moved to online environments. The importance of virtual classes has become more evident when these courses are conducted synchronously or asynchronously. This chapter mentions the roles of virtual classrooms in effectively executing online learning activities. The features of virtual classrooms in the context of teacher, student, and content are included. In this context, we examined widely used virtual classroom platforms such as Adobe Connect, BigBlueButton, Moodle, Zoom, Microsoft Teams, OpenMeetings, Google Meet, Electa, ClassDojo, WizIQ, and Kahoot. These platforms have many standard features, such as video conferencing, screen sharing, image sharing, presentation features, voice and text chat, document sharing, classroom management, lesson planning, and alternative measurement and evaluation tools.

DOI: 10.4018/979-8-3693-4407-1.ch015

VIRTUAL CLASSROOMS

In their simplest definition, virtual classrooms are learning environments where students and teachers come together in online learning environments. Participants can come together in these environments regardless of place. With a more comprehensive definition, virtual classrooms are a learning environment where participating individuals come together synchronously or asynchronously, teachers play more of a guiding role, different activities are carried out through information technologies, and certain principles and rules are applied like real classroom environments (Can, 2020; Kaya, 2011). Virtual classrooms are preferred as an alternative to traditional classrooms, with features such as providing interaction between students, improving social awareness, and bringing learners together in different places (Martin & Parker, 2014). Adobe Connect, Big Blue Button, Moodle, Zoom, and Open Meetings applications are examples of widely used virtual classroom applications.

Virtual classrooms have been extensively researched in the literature. Relevant studies focus on the academic success of virtual classes, learning attitudes, course participation, the impact of communication and interaction, and material development. Dikmenli and Ünaldı Eser (2013) stated that virtual classes are more effective in academic success than blended classes. Çetin and Günay (2011) stated that interactive virtual classes positively affect students' attitudes toward the course. It has also been demonstrated that virtual classroom environments provide permanent information (Yılmaz & Sarı, 2010) and increase class participation (Blaine, 2019). In addition to applied research on virtual classrooms, studies on the theoretical framework have also been conducted (Can, 2020; Ceylan, 2020).

ADVANTAGES AND DISADVANTAGES OF VIRTUAL CLASSROOMS

Virtual classrooms have emerged as an alternative to real classroom environments. Due to the impact of the COVID-19 pandemic that affected the world in 2020, virtual environments were necessarily preferred. Around the world, training at all education levels, from primary to higher education, is given synchronously or asynchronously in virtual classroom environments. In this process, the advantages and disadvantages of virtual classroom environments have been observed more clearly.

Advantages of Virtual Classrooms

The advantages of virtual classroom environments may vary depending on the features of the application used, teacher and student characteristics, and the technological infrastructure adequacy of the affiliated institution. The advantages of commonly used virtual classrooms can be listed as follows:

- Courses can be conducted synchronously or asynchronously, regardless of time and place (Erten, 2019),
- Live courses can be recorded and accessed after the course (Akkuş & Acar, 2017),
- The system is easy to access and has features that will increase collaboration and interaction (Gedera, 2014),
- It provides significant advantages to learners in terms of time and economy (Kaya, 2011),
- In a real classroom environment, shy and introverted individuals feel more comfortable participating in class (Mills, 1996),
- It eliminates transportation and accommodation costs for learners and provides flexibility in terms of time and place for those dealing with different jobs (Willmann et al., 2020),
- It provides learners with access to rich resources by allowing the uploading of different types of documents,
- Depending on the characteristics of virtual classroom environments, education can be provided in much more crowded classes compared to real classroom environments,
- It has features such as screen sharing, image sharing, presentation features, voice, and text chat, document management, creation and planning of classes,
- It allows the use of alternative measurement and evaluation approaches,
- It enables parents to control and monitor students' learning processes.

Disadvantages of Virtual Classrooms

Some disadvantages may arise in virtual classrooms due to insufficient infrastructure, application-based deficiencies, and teacher and student behaviors. These disadvantages can be listed as follows:

- In synchronous courses, courses may not be conducted due to technical problems related to electricity, computers, and the Internet (Kalelioğlu et al., 2016),

- Depending on internet speed, sound and image quality may be reduced (Akkuş & Acar, 2017),
- Communication, interaction, and attention concentration problems may be experienced compared to face-to-face learning environments (Dumont & Raggo, 2018; Kalelioğlu et al., 2016),
- Students engaging in behaviors such as messaging each other, sharing images, or voice chatting with each other during the course may cause distraction,
- It may be challenging to check whether learners follow the course during the live course,
- Measurement activities conducted through virtual classrooms may be unreliable (King et al., 2009),
- Various difficulties may be encountered during the execution of application-oriented, experiment-based, or technical-oriented courses (mechanical, electrical, construction, handicrafts, etc.),
- There may be a lack of discipline and seriousness in students (Erten, 2019),
- There may be difficulties in meeting the guidance needs of students in need of special education (Pokhrel & Chhetri, 2021).

VIRTUAL CLASS VARIABLES

Variables affecting teaching activities in virtual classrooms show characteristics similar to those of traditional learning environments. Variables affecting traditional classroom environments can be listed as teacher, student, parent, school, participation, organization, content, social environment, physical environment, communication tools, resources, educational programs, teaching methods, and communication tools (Aydın, 2017; Balyer, 2018; Ceylan, 2020). Due to virtual classrooms' unique structure and conditions, some differences exist in the abovementioned variables. These differences can be listed as variables such as technological infrastructure, features related to virtual classroom software, and synchronous, asynchronous, or blended teaching.

The technological infrastructure in virtual classrooms generally refers to the features of information technologies (computers, tablets) and the Internet used to access the virtual classroom. Hardware features of information technologies (processor, graphics card, microphone, speakers, etc.) and internet speed are critical in using virtual classroom applications and carrying out courses smoothly. There are features within the applications that enable text, audio, and display sharing. Thanks to the application, Teachers can share their screens, present the documents they have prepared, give lectures via the whiteboard, provide voice communication through microphones and speakers, and share their images via the camera. Teachers and students can communicate more effectively with the features specified in synchronous teaching activities. In asynchronous environments, students can participate in virtual classes independently of time. They can follow their learning activities through documents (text-based notes, videos, images, etc.) uploaded to the system. Students can communicate with their teachers and other friends via forums or email.

Responsibilities of Teachers in Virtual Classrooms

Teachers have specific duties and responsibilities to carry out teaching activities effectively, achieve the targeted learning outcomes, and increase the quality of teaching. These can be listed as effective design, organization, planning, presentation of virtual classes, use of technological tools, student behavior management, measurement, and evaluation of student achievements. Factors such as teacher, learner, content, strategy, method and technique, resources, tools, and evaluation of success, which are valid in traditional classrooms, are also crucial for virtual classrooms.

Pedagogical knowledge, content knowledge, pedagogical content knowledge, and technological pedagogical content knowledge are the essential competencies that teachers are expected to have in order to carry out teaching activities in traditional classrooms (Koehler & Mishra, 2008). Teachers' content knowledge is their expertise on the subject taught. Pedagogical knowledge is the strategies, methods, and techniques necessary to conduct courses. Pedagogical content knowledge is handling subjects with appropriate strategies, methods, and techniques. This information comes to the fore in attracting students' attention and ensuring their active participation in the course. Technology pedagogical content knowledge is teachers' knowledge of information and communication technologies and their effective use in classroom practices (Koehler & Mishra, 2008). Gündüz and Can (2013) stated that teachers must have professional knowledge, general culture, content knowledge, and classroom management skills to carry out classroom activities. These stated competencies are also valid in virtual classes. Among teachers' technology knowledge, their computer skills and experience using online virtual classroom applications come to the fore (Mishra et al., 2020). Virtual classes have several tools to convey the topics, provide support from different sources, increase communication and interaction, carry out measurement activities, and ensure classroom management. We can say that it is teachers' primary responsibility to know about these tools and use them appropriately in courses.

Chickering and Gamson (1987) mentioned the necessity of seven principles to increase the quality of teaching. These principles include student-teacher interaction, collaboration among students, and providing rapid feedback. It is stated that these principles expressed for traditional classroom environments are also crucial in virtual classrooms (Çakıroğlu, 2014). Bigatel et al. (2012) stated that teachers should consider creating a social learning environment, student movement within the learning community, and active participation in virtual classes to increase academic success. There are appropriate tools in virtual classroom applications to ensure teacher-student, student-student, and student-content interactions. Teachers can chat with students via text, voice, or video. In addition, teachers can provide feedback on both subject-related questions and students' technical problems within and outside the course. Students can also communicate with each other in the specified ways. Students can access course content and additional resources through the system. Especially in synchronous courses, using the abovementioned features significantly affects classroom management. During the course, students can occupy the chat area with unnecessary topics, create discussion environments, send private messages, project some background sounds to the class, or chat with each other out loud. Virtual classroom applications provide teachers with the authority to control these situations.

Teachers' responsibilities in virtual classrooms include grading, sending homework, monitoring student groups, and measuring and evaluating (Rufai et al., 2015). Teachers may choose process- or outcome-oriented assessment in virtual classrooms. The exam add-on for virtual classroom applications allows the preparation of multiple-choice tests and open-ended, fill-in-the-blank, or matching-style assessment questions. In process-oriented measurement processes, teachers may prefer features such as preparing surveys, conducting questions and answers, creating discussion groups, and giving the right to speak. Teachers are also responsible for uploading students' course documents to the system, assigning and receiving assignments, making announcements, and creating forums for discussion groups outside of class. Teachers must also have the necessary technical knowledge and experience to carry out and control all in-class and extra-curricular practices mentioned above.

Responsibilities of Students in Virtual Classrooms

Students, who are one of the most important variables of virtual classroom management, also have important roles and responsibilities in the virtual environment. Students need to fulfill some of the responsibilities in face-to-face learning environments, such as following courses, actively participating in courses, interacting with teachers and peers, providing feedback on questions, participating in discussions, and completing homework and projects, in virtual classrooms (Akman, 2021; Martin et al., 2011; Rufai et al., 2015). Among the principles put forward to increase learning success; activities such as student-teacher communication, collaboration among students, monitoring the active learning process, providing rapid feedback, paying attention to task duration, and respecting various abilities and learning methods are included (Chickering & Gamson, 1987). It is expected that these activities will also be carried out in virtual classroom environments. In addition to these responsibilities in virtual classrooms, pre-qualifications such as having technological tools and the internet to access courses and effective use of technological tools are required. The effective use of virtual classroom applications that provide an online learning environment is important for students to be able to conduct courses smoothly, actively participate in courses, and interact with their peers. In addition, students' responsibilities such as being able to present their own work to the class by sharing the screen, using features such as camera and microphone for written, voice or video chat, sharing documents through the system, participating in the course by asking to speak during the course, and participating in discussion environments using forums come to the fore.

Although there are no studies in the literature that directly address students' responsibilities in virtual classroom environments, there are some studies that emphasize students' responsibilities. Bigatel et al (2012) emphasized the importance of three conditions for the success of courses in a virtual environment: having a social learning environment, students forming a learning community, and actively participating in learning activities. In addition, interaction, communication, and active participation of students were seen as important for student-centered teaching in a virtual environment. Akdeniz and Uzun (2022) addressed the opinions of teachers regarding the problems they encountered in classroom management during the distance education process. In this study, it was emphasized that technical problems experienced at home, students not giving feedback during courses, and their cameras being off were among the important problems. In addition, insufficient technological literacy of students and parents and lack of interest of parents were also shown among the problems. In the study examining student opinions on classroom management in a virtual classroom environment, it was stated that students' communication with the instructor and classmates increased learning success (Yılmazsoy et al., 2018). Martin et al. (2011) stated that in virtual classrooms, students' interactions with each other and with teachers are important, so students feel like social beings and are also motivated by receiving feedback from their friends and teachers.

Virtual Classroom Tools

Teaching activities can be carried out synchronously or asynchronously in virtual classrooms. Several tools are used in both environments to carry out these teaching activities. The tools included in most virtual classroom applications are briefly summarized below:

Screen sharing: Teachers or students share the current screenshot of their computers in the classroom. In this way, teachers can make presentations and transfer topics through software. Additionally, students' homework or course presentations can be monitored using this method.

Display sharing: Teachers and students can share their images with the class via camera.

Text chat: Students can ask the teacher questions in writing during the lesson. Teachers can provide information or answer students' questions.

Forum: It is used to create discussion environments outside of class. Teachers may ask students to discuss a topic, or students may create discussion topics among themselves.

Voice chat: Teachers can create chat environments with students or among students with the help of a microphone.

Video conferencing: It is a form of communication that allows many users in different locations to synchronize video or audio conversations. In this way, hundreds of users can synchronize in the same environment.

Whiteboard application: It is an application that functions the same as whiteboards used in traditional classrooms but is used in a virtual environment. With this application, the teacher can make drawings using the pen or ready-made text writing feature. Formatting can be made using texts and visual materials.

Document sharing: Teachers can upload written, audio, and video documents to the system and share them with students. Students can download these documents to their computers.

Classroom management: Teachers can turn on or off microphones, cameras, and chat environments within the scope of lesson control. Students can use the raise hand feature to get the right to speak.

Measurement tools: Teachers can use the measurement plugin to perform remote measurement and evaluation. This tool allows the preparation of multiple-choice tests, open-ended, fill-in-the-blank, or matching-type questions. It also offers several options for evaluating and announcing measurement results to students.

Survey: Teachers can use the survey to vote on any issue within or outside the classroom. Survey results can be formatted visually.

VIRTUAL CLASSROOM APPLICATIONS

Commonly used applications for creating and managing virtual classrooms are Adobe Connect, BigBlueButton, Moodle, Zoom, Microsoft Teams, OpenMeetings, Google Meet, WizIQ, ClassDojo, Perculus, Electa, and Kahoot. This section introduces the well-known ones among these applications according to the classification made by İzmirli and Akyüz (2017) for comparing virtual classroom applications.

Adobe Connect

Figure 1. Adobe Connect interface

Adobe Connect is a web-based meeting and teaching platform developed by Adobe. It was first launched in 2002. It was specifically developed to organize online meetings, web-based seminars, and teaching sessions and to create interactive virtual classrooms. It has features that facilitate distance learning, collaboration, and communication. Various user groups use Adobe Connect for different purposes. Universities, colleges, and other educational institutions use Adobe Connect to organize online classroom sessions and provide distance learning for their students. Businesses use Adobe Connect for business meetings, collaboration projects, and training programs. With the proliferation of the remote working model, businesses need this platform to connect and collaborate with their employees. Government organizations use Adobe Connect to interact with citizens, provide training, and organize meetings.

Adobe Connect offers several licensing options for different needs and budgets: free, basic, professional, and enterprise. The free license enables Adobe Connect's core features, such as audio and video meetings, file sharing, interactive whiteboards, and surveys. The Basic license includes all the features of the free license plus features such as private rooms, meeting recording and playback, remote control, and language support. The professional license includes all the basic license features plus larger meetings, more storage space, and enhanced security features. The enterprise license includes all the features of the professional license plus a customized interface, email integration, learning management system integration, and mobile device support.

Adobe Connect allows users to share files, documents, presentations, and other content in meetings. Users can use webcams, screen sharing, and file sharing for sharing. Adobe Connect's high-quality video playback feature enables seamless playback of live videos and video recordings in meetings. Adobe Connect provides options for users to control other participants' computers remotely. This feature can be used for technical support or training. With Adobe Connect, users can take notes during the meeting. These notes can be accessed online after the meeting. Supporting more than 20 languages, Adobe Connect makes it easy for participants speaking different languages to come together. Adobe Connect offers a break room for users when leaving meetings or relaxing. Users can share files, exchange messages, or interact with other participants in the break room. Users can message each other during the session via Adobe Connect. This feature helps participants to ask questions or share ideas during the meeting. Adobe Connect has an email integration feature. This feature allows users to share meeting invitations and recordings via email. Users can record meetings and then access these recordings online or download them in video format. Adobe Connect is available on iOS and Android devices. Users can join meetings via their mobile devices. Adobe Connect supports various file formats such as PowerPoint, PDF, Word, and Excel. Users can customize the Adobe Connect interface according to their needs. This feature helps users make meetings more efficient and valuable. Adobe Connect can work integrated with learning management systems (LMS). Users can participate in Adobe Connect meetings through learning management systems. Various browsers, including Chrome, Firefox, Edge, and Safari support Adobe Connect. Users can conduct surveys and tests during the meeting via Adobe Connect. Thus, participants' knowledge can be measured, or feedback can be received. With Adobe Connect, reports about users' participation in meetings and organized events can be received. These reports help to monitor the efficiency and effectiveness of the meetings. Adobe Connect is an easy-to-use application. Exceptional technical knowledge or skills are optional to organize and participate in meetings. The number of active users of Adobe Connect has exceeded 20 million as of 2023. Thanks to the features listed above, Adobe Connect has become a widely used platform for meeting online communication and collaboration needs in education, business, and the public sector. More detailed information about the application is available at https://www.adobe.com/products/adobeconnect.html.

BigBlueButton

Figure 2. BigBlueButton interface

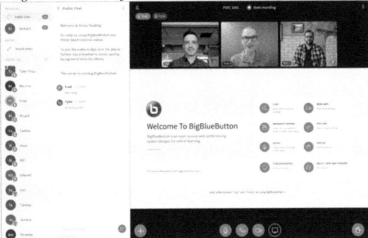

Unlike Adobe Connect, BigBlueButton is an open-source web-based online meeting and virtual classroom platform. This platform was developed specifically for educational purposes. Designed to organize interactive virtual classroom sessions with students and participants, educational institutions and teachers mostly use BigBlueButton. Businesses and other organizations also use it to organize meetings, seminars, and collaboration sessions.

BigBlueButton is a free and open-source application that users can use without licensing fees. The number of active users of BigBlueButton has exceeded 10 million as of 2023. When analyzing the virtual classroom features it offers, BigBlueButton has features similar to those of Adobe Connect. Since it is offered free of charge as an open-source platform, it has the advantage of providing a virtual classroom and meeting experience at a low cost. More detailed information about the application is available at https://www.bigbluebutton.org.

Moodle

Figure 3. Moodle interface

Moodle is an open-source learning management system. It is also a virtual learning platform. Moodle was developed to support educational material creation, student management, student-teacher interaction, and online learning processes. It is an open-source software that users can use without paying any fees. Moodle was developed in 2002 by Martin Dougiamas, an Australian educational scientist and software developer. Dougiamas created Moodle to emphasize the importance of student-centered educational systems suitable for online learning.

Moodle, which has a broad user group, is used by various educational institutions for corporate, open, and distance education. Universities, colleges, high schools, and primary schools use Moodle to provide an interactive learning environment between students and teachers. Moodle also manages educational processes such as sharing course materials, administering exams and quizzes, and entering grades. In addition to educational institutions, Moodle is also used in business to train and develop employees. Moodle also benefits new employee training, skill management, business processes, and corporate training programs. Distance education organizations and open universities mostly use Moodle to provide online education and access to student resources.

Unlike Adobe Connect and BigBlueButton, Moodle has features for asynchronous applications. Users can create, edit, and track courses on Moodle. Instructors can upload content to Moodle courses and assign students tasks and exams. Students and teachers can share course materials and documents via Moodle. Moodle offers a variety of quizzes and assessment tools for teachers. Teachers can create quizzes, exams, and assignments on Moodle. Also, exam results can be automatically evaluated and stored for as long as desired. Teachers can follow students' progress and evaluate their performance with Moodle. They can also view student grades and reports generated by Moodle. Moodle provides chat, forums, surveys, and live chat tools to support student-teacher and student-student interaction. Moodle can be customized according to users' needs and institutional requirements by editing themes, plugins, and language files. Moodle is available in more than 100 languages. The number of active users of Moodle is over 200 million as of 2023. Moodle has a large and active developer community. This community provides technical support, training, and guidance to users. In addition to these features, Moodle can be time-consuming to learn and use, especially for users who want to create large and complex courses. Extensive courses or high-traffic environments may experience performance issues. More detailed information about Moodle is available at https://www.moodle.com.

Zoom

Figure 4. Zoom interface

Zoom is an application that offers various communication tools, such as video conferencing, webinars, and online meetings. This platform allows users to collaborate regardless of location to make live video calls, share screens, conduct surveys, and organize online training. Zoom Video Communications, a company founded by Eric Yuan in 2011, developed Zoom. Zoom gained popularity after the COVID-19 pandemic caused people to switch to remote working and learning. Mainly designed to create a more user-friendly and effective video conferencing platform, Zoom's active users exceeded 500 million by 2023.

Zoom is often used for business, education, and personal communication. Businesses use Zoom for internal meetings, customer meetings, collaboration projects, and to meet remote working needs. Educational institutions and organizations use Zoom to communicate with students, organize classes, provide distance learning, and encourage student participation. Zoom is also widely used by individuals to meet with family and friends, organize events, and maintain social connections.

Zoom offers four licensing options: free, basic, professional, and enterprise. The free version is limited to meetings of up to 40 minutes and 100 participants. The basic version is limited to meetings lasting up to 40 minutes and 100 participants. The Professional version allows meetings with up to 300 participants and offers 24/7 support. The Enterprise edition offers customizable features and more participant options. Zoom allows users to share files, documents, presentations, and other content in meetings. Sharing options are webcam, screen sharing, and file sharing. Zoom allows users to play high-quality videos. Thus, live videos and video recordings can be shown seamlessly in meetings. The application is available in more than 100 languages. Zoom authorizes the user with administrator authority to create central meeting and sub-meeting sessions. Other users can be directed to these sub-meeting rooms by the administrator and can be called back to the main meeting room. Through Zoom, users can send messages to all users or a specific user. Zoom allows meetings to be recorded. The mobile-compatible application can be used on iOS and Android devices. Various browsers, including Chrome, Firefox, Edge, and Safari, support Zoom. It can also be used as a desktop application. Zoom supports typical file formats such as PowerPoint, PDF, Word, and Excel. Users can organize surveys and ask questions to participants during presentations or trainings conducted through Zoom. Zoom ensures the security of meetings and seminars by offering security measures such as encryption and participant authentication. Zoom users can customize the application interface according to their needs. Zoom can report messages exchanged by participants during meetings. Users can use Zoom to organize and participate in meetings without the need for any special technical knowledge. More detailed information about the application is available at https://zoom.us.

Microsoft Teams

Figure 5. Microsoft Teams interface

Microsoft Teams is a collaboration platform developed by Microsoft. This platform facilitates team communication, shares files, organizes meetings, and more. It was launched in 2017 to provide Microsoft Office users with an integrated communication and collaboration solution. Microsoft Teams is widely used by office workers, educational institutions, and other groups for collaboration, communication, and project management, especially in remote working and learning processes. As of 2023, Teams has more than 250 million active users.

Microsoft Teams offers a variety of features to its users. Users can make individual or group chats, share files and media content, and send instant messages to each other by using Microsoft Teams. It allows users to create channels for various user groups. These channels can represent projects, topics, or departments, allowing user groups to work through the relevant channels. Files can be shared directly from Microsoft Teams and edited online using Microsoft Office applications. Teams make it possible to organize meetings and invite participants to these meetings. Microsoft Teams also allows video conferencing, audio conferencing, and screen sharing during meetings. Microsoft Teams can be integrated with other Microsoft products (e.g., SharePoint, OneNote, Planner) and third-party applications (e.g., Trello, GitHub). Within Microsoft Teams, tasks can be created, assigned to specific users, and followed to coordinate project management and workflows. Microsoft Teams offers special educational features for educational institutions, students, and teachers, such as classroom chats, file sharing, and student performance monitoring. Microsoft

Teams uses Microsoft's security infrastructure for data security and authentication. This feature ensures a high level of protection of Microsoft Teams user data.

Microsoft Teams offers four licensing options: free, basic, professional, and enterprise. The free version is limited to meetings lasting up to 30 hours and 100 participants. The basic version is limited to meetings lasting up to 60 minutes and 100 participants. The Professional edition offers 24/7 round-the-clock support and meetings for up to 300 participants. The enterprise edition offers customizable features and support for more participants. Microsoft Teams is available in more than 60 languages. Microsoft Teams features email integration. Users can share meeting invitations and meeting recordings via email. Microsoft Teams can be integrated with learning management systems (LMS). Microsoft Teams is an easy-to-use application that allows users to organize and participate in meetings without special technical knowledge. More detailed information about the application is available at https://www.microsoft.com/en-us/microsoft-teams/group-chat-software.

OpenMeetings

Figure 6. OpenMeetings interface

OpenMeetings is an open-source online meeting and collaboration platform. Apache Software Foundation developed OpenMeetings in 2007. Users can customize and distribute the platform to suit their needs. OpenMeetings offers a variety of features, such as live video conferences, webinars, training sessions, and business meetings for businesses, educational institutions, open communities, and other organizations.

OpenMeetings allows users to organize live video conferences for business, customer, and training sessions. Users can share their computer screens or documents with other participants to make presentations, provide technical support, or edit documents. OpenMeetings allows participants to draw and take notes on a shared digital whiteboard to enhance their session interaction. Participants can exchange messages with each other during the meeting. OpenMeetings allows users to upload, edit, and share documents with other participants to work on collaborative projects. Meetings and training sessions organized on OpenMeetings can be recorded and archived for later retrieval. Users can create meeting tasks to coordinate workflows and assign these tasks to specific users with OpenMeetings. OpenMeetings can be integrated with authentication systems such as LDAP, CAS, and Shibboleth. It can also integrate with learning management systems such as Moodle. Open Meetings is available in more than 20 languages. OpenMeetings is popular for organizations seeking a low-cost, user-friendly online meeting and collaboration solution. More detailed information about the application is available at https://openmeetings.apache.org.

Google Meet

Figure 7. Google Meet interface

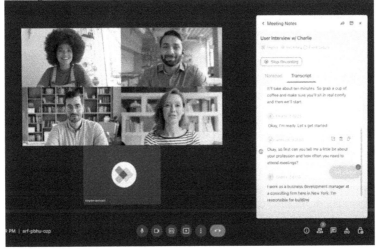

Google Meet is a video-conferencing application that Google developed. This application is used for online meetings, job interviews, training sessions, and other communication needs. It has been widely preferred, especially during remote working and learning periods. Meet (formerly Hangouts Meet) was launched by Google in 2017. Although it was developed as an integrated solution, especially for Google Workspace (formerly G Suite) users, anyone with a Google account can use Meet.

Google Meet allows participants to hold live video conferences among themselves. On Meet, multiple participants can be viewed on the same screen, and their conversations can be followed. Screen or document sharing is available during Meet meetings to make presentations or edit a document. Live voice chat is available to increase interaction and discuss meeting content. Users can also send text messages through Google Chat integration. Google Meet is integrated with Google Calendar, allowing users to schedule meetings in the calendar application and to send invitations directly. Meet meetings can be automatically saved and uploaded to Google Drive for later access. Hosts can manage participants, turn microphones off and on, disable cameras, and control the meeting.

Google Meet is offered under the Google Workspace subscription. It is costless for all users with a Google account, but a paid version for Google Workspace users has more features. Google Meet does not offer remote control to participants. The host cannot remotely intervene on participants' computers. Google Meet does not have a feature that allows participants to take notes during the meeting. Google Meet does not have a specific collaboration or private meeting room feature. However, participants can turn off their microphones and disable their cameras anytime. Google Meet is available on mobile devices such as iOS and Android. Users can join and organize meetings through mobile apps. Google Meet works well with Google Drive integration to share documents and presentations. Google Meet's interface is generally presented in a standard format for Google Workspace users. However, users can make basic customizations. Google Meet is not directly integrated with learning management systems. Only Google Workspace users can create specific integrations to make it compatible with such systems. Google Meet works seamlessly with most modern browsers (Google Chrome, Firefox, Safari, etc.). Google Meet cannot conduct surveys or tests directly. Google Meet provides basic user reports, including meeting attendance data and meeting durations. It has an easy-to-use interface. More detailed information about the application is available at https://meet.google.com.

ClassDojo

Figure 8. ClassDojo interface

ClassDojo is a learning management application that enables teachers to communicate and share classroom interactions with students and their parents. ClassDojo is widely used in educational institutions, mainly primary and secondary schools. Developed by Sam Chaudhary and Liam Don in 2011, ClassDojo follows student behavior, provides feedback, rewards student achievements, and strengthens communication with parents. Students and parents can access updates in the classroom using the ClassDojo mobile app or website. ClassDojo has over 10 million active users worldwide.

ClassDojo helps teachers manage student behavior in the classroom. With ClassDojo, teachers can monitor student behavior in the classroom, reward positive behavior, and give feedback to correct negative behavior. ClassDojo can give teachers custom badges and feedback to reward and encourage student achievement. Teachers can send updates to parents via ClassDojo about students' behavior, achievements, and homework. Parents can also monitor students' classroom performance and communicate with their teachers. Teachers and parents can also send private messages to each other to discuss special student situations or schedule appointments. ClassDojo offers a class gallery feature where photos and videos shared by teachers can be viewed to create a visual record of classroom activities. The most crucial feature of ClassDojo is the ability to create student portfolios. Teachers can create a custom portfolio to show student progress and share it with parents. Teachers can also create separate profile pages for each student on ClassDojo and provide student-specific feedback and rewards through these pages.

ClassDojo offers two different licensing options, free and paid. The free version is limited to a limited number of features and users. Paid versions offer more features and user support. ClassDojo allows teachers to share files, documents, presentations, and other content with their classes. ClassDojo offers a note-taking system to help teachers keep track of students' behavior and progress. ClassDojo is available in more than 100 languages. ClassDojo does not allow users to customize the interface to suit their needs. ClassDojo allows teachers to create surveys and tests to measure student understanding and progress. ClassDojo is an easy-to-use application. Teachers can create and manage their classrooms without special technical knowledge. More information about the application is available at https://www.classdojo.com.

Electa

Figure 9. Electa interface

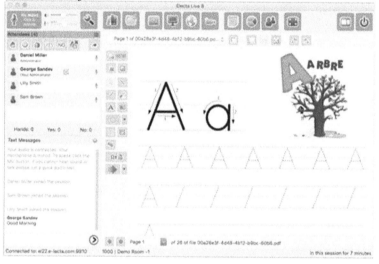

Electa LMS is a virtual classroom and online teaching software developed by Electa Virtual Classroom in 2005. It allows users to organize live online, group, and one-to-one lessons. Electa LMS is designed to meet different educational needs. It is used by educational institutions, private educators, companies, and non-profit organizations to deliver various training programs. Trainers and schools deliver educational courses or training programs to students with Electa LMS. A rich set of LMS elements allows administration, documentation, tracking, evaluation, and reporting. Instructors can administer tests and other assignments, track student progress, and manage record-keeping. Schools can deliver all forms of learning - online, blended, synchronous, and asynchronous with Electa LMS. Some users of Electa

LMS are K-12 schools and high schools, universities and colleges, private tutoring and study centers, in-house training departments, and non-profit organizations.

Electa LMS offers its users a comprehensive online teaching platform. Users can deliver real-time interactive lessons with audio and video chat, screen sharing, and whiteboard tools. They can organize lessons for small groups and interact with participants. They can deliver private lessons and work one-on-one with students. They can create and share course content in various formats, including text, images, video, and audio. They can track student progress using assessment tools such as quizzes, assignments, and surveys. They can generate comprehensive reports that include data such as attendance, performance, and completion rates. Mobile learning is natural with Electa Virtual Classroom, as we support all popular mobile devices. Teachers can have students attend live classes and online courses using tablets and phones, along with students and teachers using computers and laptops simultaneously.

Electa LMS is a powerful, easy-to-use virtual classroom and online teaching software that meets various educational needs. Different educational institutions and individuals can use it to deliver various educational programs. More information about the application is available at https://www.e-lecta.com.

WizIQ

Figure 10. WizIQ interface

WizIQ is a learning management and virtual classroom platform that offers distance learning and live online classroom experiences. The platform enables teachers, trainers, and institutions to organize online classes, interact with students, and share various learning materials. Harman International founded WizIQ in 2007. The main objective is to meet teachers' and educational institutions' online education needs and provide interactive learning experiences.

WizIQ has features similar to those of other virtual classroom applications. Teachers can create live virtual classrooms and interact with students. This can be used for real-time lectures, presentations, discussions, and demonstrations. Recordings of live lectures can be taken and archived for later access by students. This feature allows students who cannot attend to watch and repeat the lectures. Teachers can share lecture notes, presentations, documents, and other materials with students. This gives students more access to the course content. Teachers and students can discuss and interact with each other in live lessons. These discussions help students gain a deeper understanding of the topics. Teachers can create online quizzes and monitor students' performance. This can be used to assess student progress. Teachers can track students' course progress and provide support when needed. WizIQ can be integrated with other learning management systems and platforms. This integration allows users to synchronize their existing systems with WizIQ. WizIQ can also be used on mobile devices. This compatibility gives students and teachers access to online education anytime and anywhere. WizIQ stands out as a comprehensive platform used to meet the distance learning needs of teachers and educational institutions and provide interactive learning experiences. More information about the application is available at https://www.wiziq.com.

Kahoot

Figure 11. Kahoot interface

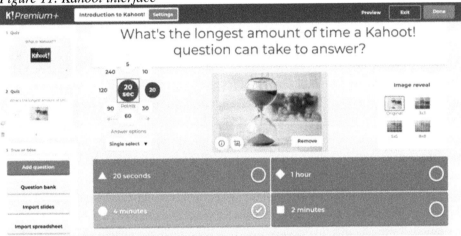

Kahoot was developed by Johan Brand, Jamie Brooker, and Morten Versvik in 2013. The platform is designed to increase student engagement, make learning fun, and teach learning material more effectively. It is an interactive game-based platform combining education, learning, and entertainment. Students and participants can ask questions to compete and create interactive quizzes through this platform. Teachers and trainers widely use the app for in-class assessments, quizzes, educational games, meetings, and interactive presentations. Kahoot has more than 70 million active users worldwide.

Users can create interactive quizzes and determine the answers and duration of the quiz questions using Kahoot. Participants in quizzes earn points by answering the questions within the specified time. Thus, a competitive environment can be created among the participants. In addition to creating quizzes, Kahoot can also be used to organize interactive presentations and meetings. Participants can answer the questions posed during the presentation using their mobile devices. Kahoot is designed to support students to learn by playing games. Since the questions are in a game format, students can participate more in learning. Users can customize quizzes and presentations in Kahoot according to their needs. Features such as visual theme, time limit, and correct answer options can be changed. Available in more than 20 languages, Kahoot offers two different licensing options: free and paid. Kahoot is a very easy-to-use application. Users can create and use surveys and tests without the need for any special technical knowledge. More detailed information about the application is available at https://kahoot.it.

CONCLUSION

Virtual classrooms are an online teaching and learning environment where teachers and students can synchronously conduct lessons, present course materials, interact with other students, and work in groups. Virtual classrooms offer online opportunities when teachers and students cannot come together in face-to-face learning environments. Virtual classes are advantageous because they are held synchronously, many students can attend classes regardless of time and place, and they eliminate costs such as transportation and accommodation. In virtual classrooms, in addition to the variables affecting the learning activities carried out in regular classrooms, variables such as technological infrastructure, internet access, and software features of the virtual classroom come to the fore. Access to virtual classes remains very limited in rural areas where access to the Internet is limited. Students who need more technological equipment also have limited participation in classes. In addition to the content knowledge of the courses, teachers must also be competent to use virtual classrooms. Teachers must use virtual classroom tools effectively to carry out learning activities. Therefore, we can say that teachers' duties and responsibilities in virtual classrooms are more significant than in regular classrooms. There are widely used virtual classroom applications, both free and paid, worldwide. The most preferred applications are Adobe Connect, BigBlueButton, Moodle, Zoom, Microsoft Teams, OpenMeetings, Google Meet, ClassDojo, and Kahoot. These platforms are structured to maximize student, teacher, and content interactions. These platforms have tools such as screen sharing, text and voice chat, document sharing, authorization, measurement and evaluation tools, surveys, and forums. Recording live classes in the system provides significant advantages and convenience to students. These classes can be held simultaneously with much larger groups of students than in traditional classes.

REFERENCES

Akdeniz, İ., & Uzun, M. (2022). Teachers' views on the problems they have experienced in classroom management during the distance education process. *Kahramanmaras Sutcu Imam University Journal of Education*, 4(1), 45–75.

Akkuş, İ., & Acar, S. (2017). A research on determining the effect of technical problems in simultaneous learning environments on teachers and learners. *Inonu University Journal of the Faculty of Education*, 18(3), 363–376.

Akman, Y. (2021). Investigation of the relationship between digital literacy, online learning, and academic aspiration. *The Journal of Turkish Educational Sciences*, 19(2), 1012–1036. DOI: 10.37217/tebd.982846

Aydın, A. (2017). *Classroom management*. Pegem Academy.

Balyer, A. (2018). *Classroom management*. Efe Academy Publications.

Bigatel, P. M., Ragan, L. C., Kennan, S., May, J., & Redmond, B. F. (2012). The identification of competencies for online teaching success. *Online Learning : the Official Journal of the Online Learning Consortium*, 16(1), 59–77. https://eric.ed.gov/?id=EJ971040. DOI: 10.24059/olj.v16i1.215

Blaine, A. M. (2019). Interaction and presence in the virtual classroom: An Analysis of the perceptions of students and teacher in online and blended advanced placement courses. *Computers & Education*, 132, 31–43. DOI: 10.1016/j.compedu.2019.01.004

Çakıroğlu, Ü. (2014). Evaluating students' perspectives about virtual classrooms with regard to seven principles of good practice. *South African Journal of Education*, 34(2), 1–19. DOI: 10.15700/201412071201

Can, E. (2020). Sanal sınıf yönetimi: İlkeler, uygulamalar ve öneriler. [Virtual classroom management: Principles, practices and recommendations]. *Açıköğretim Uygulamaları ve Araştırmaları Dergisi*, 6(4), 251–295.

Çetin, O., & Günay, Y. (2011). Preparation of a web-based teaching material designed for science education and evaluation of this material according to teachers' and students' views. *Ahi Evran University Journal of Kırşehir Education Faculty*, 12(2), 175–202.

Ceylan, M. (2020). Sanal sınıfların yönetimi [Management of virtual classrooms]. Dilruba Kürüm Yapıcıoğlu (Ed.) *Pandemi Döneminde Eğitim içinde [In Education During the Pandemic]* (pp. 295-352). Ankara: Anı publishing.

Chickering, A. W., & Gamson, Z. F. (1987). Seven principles for good practice in undergraduate education. *AAHE Bulletin*, 39, 3–7.

Dikmenli, Y., & Ünaldı Eser, Ü. (2013). Students' views on blended learning and virtual classroom. *Amasya Education Journal*, 2(2), 326–347.

Dumont, G., & Raggo, P. (2018). Faculty perspectives about distance teaching in the virtual classroom. *Journal of Nonprofit Education and Leadership*, 8(1), 41–61. DOI: 10.18666/JNEL-2018-V8-I1-8372

Erten, P. (2019). Opinions of preservice ınformation technologies teachers on virtual classroom and ımplementations. *Batman University Journal of Life Sciences*, 9(2), 236–252.

Gedera, D. S. P. (2014). Students' experiences of learning in a virtual classroom. [IJEDICT]. *International Journal of Education and Development Using Information and Communication Technology*, 10(4), 93–101.

Gündüz, Y., & Can, E. (2013). The compliance level of primary and high school teachers to classroom management principles according to student's views. *Educational Administration-Theory and Practice*, 19(3), 419–446.

İzmirli, S., & Akyüz, H. İ. (2017). Examining synchronous virtual classroom software. *Journal of Theory and Practice in Education*, 13(4). Advance online publication. DOI: 10.17244/eku.347815

Kalelioğlu, F., Atan, A., & Çetin, Ç. (2016). Experiences of instructors and learners in a virtual classroom environment. *Mersin University Journal of the Faculty of Education*, 12(2), 555–568.

Kaya, S. (2011). *Sanal sınıf yönetiminde görev alacak öğretim elemanlarının eğitim gereksinimlerinin belirlenmesi* [Identifying the educational needs of instructors commissioned in the virtual classroom management] [Doctoral dissertation]. Anadolu University, Eskişehir. Available from the Council of Higher Education, National Dissertation Center, Dissertation ID: 286819.

King, C. G., Guyette, R. W. Jr, & Piotrowski, C. (2009). Online exams and cheating: An empirical analysis of business students' views. *The Journal of Educators Online*, 6(1), n1. https://files.eric.ed.gov/fulltext/EJ904058.pdf. DOI: 10.9743/JEO.2009.1.5

Koehler, M. J., & Mishra, P. (2008). Introducing TPCK. In AACTE Committee on Innovation and Technology. (Ed.), Handbook of technological pedagogical content knowledge (TPCK). New York: Routledge

Martin, F., & Parker, M. A. (2014). Use of synchronous virtual classrooms: Why, Who, and How? *Journal of Online Learning and Teaching*, 10(2), 192–210.

Martin, F., Parker, M. A., & Ndoye, A. (2011). *Measuring success in a synchronous virtual classroom.* Student satisfaction and learning outcomes in E-Learning: An introduction to empirical research. Edt (Sean B. Eom., & J.B. Arbaugh), USA: IGI Global. DOI: 10.4018/978-1-60960-615-2.ch011

Mills, J. (1996). Virtual classroom management and communicative writing pedagogy. *Paper presented at theEuropean Writing Conferences, pp:1-19.* Barcelona, Spain, October 23-25.

Mishra, L., Gupta, T., & Shreee, A. (2020). Online teaching-learning in higher education during lockdown period of COVID-19 pandemic. *International Journal of Educational Research Open*, 1, 100012. DOI: 10.1016/j.ijedro.2020.100012 PMID: 35059663

Pokhrel, S., & Chhetri, R. (2021). A literature review on impact of COVID-19 Pandemic on teaching and learning. *Higher Education for the Future*, 8(1), 133–141. DOI: 10.1177/2347631120983481

Rufai, M. M., Alebiosu, S. O., & Adeakin, O. A. S. (2015). Conceptual model for virtual classroom management. *International Journal of Computer Science* [IJCSEIT]. *Engineering and Information Technology*, 5(1), 27–32. PMID: 26029735

Willmann, R., Zebedin, G., & Miksche, D. (2020). Technical setup of an inverted virtual classroom. *2020 IEEE Global Engineering Education Conference (EDUCON)*, pp. 931-936. 27–30 April, 2020, Porto, Portugal

Yılmaz, Ş., & Sarı, İ. (2010). Php Gd Kütüphanesi Kullanılarak Etkileşimli Uygulama Geliştirme [Interactive Application Development Using Php GD Library]. G. T. Yamamoto, U. Demiray, & M. Kesim (Ed), Türkiye'de e-Öğrenme: Gelişmeler ve Uygulamalar içinde [e-Learning in Turkey: Developments and Applications] (185-200). Denizli.

Yılmazsoy, B., Özdinç, F., & Kahraman, M. (2018). Investigating student opinions about classroom management in a virtual classroom. *Trakya Üniversitesi Eğitim Fakültesi Dergisi*, 8(3), 513–525.

Key Terms in this Chapter

Asynchronous: It refers to situations where participants interact at different times and their own pace. For example, tools such as email communication or online course content that can be accessed offline provide asynchronous interaction because participants communicate or access content at different times rather than at the same time.

LMS: It is a software or online platform used to support digital education and training processes.

Pedagogy: Pedagogy covers educational methods, learning processes, teaching strategies, and student development. Its main aim is to develop methods and approaches to create effective learning environments and maximize students' potential. Pedagogy helps educators prepare course plans and improve educational processes based on students' needs and learning styles.

Synchronous: It refers to activities where participants interact simultaneously and in real-time. For example, communication tools such as live video conferences or instant messaging applications enable synchronous interaction because participants exchange information simultaneously.

Virtual classroom: It is an online learning environment where students interact with an instructor or teacher over the Internet. These environments are often supported by tools such as live video conferences, interactive whiteboards, messaging, and file sharing. Through remote access, students can attend classes, share course content, and communicate with their teachers. In this way, they can study even from geographically far distances without having to come together physically.

Chapter 16
Using Video Feedback to Create Faculty Presence in the Virtual Classroom

Mary Streit
https://orcid.org/0009-0005-5420-7132
National University, USA

Madia Levin
National University, USA

Alycia Harris
https://orcid.org/0000-0003-0955-2840
National University, USA

ABSTRACT

The inherent transactional distance in online learning often leads to student feelings of disengagement, disconnection, and anxiety. The increasing reliance on technology exacerbates this issue by eliminating key elements of human communication such as facial expressions and tone of voice. To mitigate these issues, faculty are increasingly turning to video feedback which can enhance the sense of faculty presence. This approach aims to replicate aspects of in-person communication vital to fostering a connected, engaging, and supportive learning environment. This chapter explores the efficacy of video feedback in establishing social, teaching, and cognitive presence as described by the Community of Inquiry Model. Through an examination of recent research on faculty perceptions, the chapter underscores the potential of video feedback to foster a more interactive, engaging, and humanized online learning environment, while also highlighting the need for further faculty training and best practices.

DOI: 10.4018/979-8-3693-4407-1.ch016

USING VIDEO FEEDBACK TO CREATE FACULTY PRESENCE IN THE VIRTUAL CLASSROOM

Given the transactional distance inherent in online learning (Moore, 2013), students often report feeling disengaged, disconnected, anxious, and alone. To add to this, increasing trends toward the use of technology without human interaction are rampant. Examples of this in everyday life include self-checkouts, self-driving cars, online travel arrangements, and using artificial intelligence applications like ChatGPT. As a result, the shift towards more technology and less human interaction has eliminated many of the more unique elements of human communication, such as facial expressions, eye contact, pauses, tone of voice, gestures, and other non-verbal cues that cannot be replicated by technology – even emojis fail here (Hehir et al., 2021; Waytz, 2019). To address student concerns about feeling disengaged, disconnected, anxious, and alone in the online classroom, many faculty have explored video feedback to bridge the virtual distance. The hope is that, at the same time, this will also help to provide a stronger sense of faculty presence (Bialowas & Steimel, 2019; Collins et al., 2019). Using video feedback or asynchronous video exchanges assists with humanizing the fully online classroom. It is believed to be a pivotal factor when establishing faculty presence in the fully online classroom. This presence is essential to work towards creating, as most research suggests that faculty presence facilitates learning and engagement in the fully online classroom (Seckman, 2018). Lazarevic et al. (2023) agree and emphasize the potential of using video technology to create teaching, social, and cognitive presence in the online classroom.

Faculty presence was first alluded to within the *Community of Inquiry Model* proposed by Garrison et al. (2003). In this model, Garrison describes how learning occurs within a community through three different routes, namely:

1. *Social presence*, where learning occurs by engaging and interacting with other individuals.
2. *Teaching presence*, where learning occurs through the direct instruction of faculty.
3. *Cognitive presence*, where learning occurs by creating a sense of puzzlement and interest in a subject.

As discussed above, creating this learning community with different types of presence is particularly important in the fully online classroom. By creating social, teaching, and cognitive presence, students can feel part of a larger community where they are no longer disconnected, isolated, and alone. As a result, student learning and engagement are enhanced.

The focus of this chapter is twofold. First, to examine the research on optimal ways to provide video feedback to establish the three types of presence that Garrison described. Second, this chapter will examine faculty perceptions of using video feedback in the online classroom. Most research focuses solely on student perceptions, leaving out the other half of the equation, the faculty member providing the feedback. Let us focus now on the research on the three types of presence and what the research suggests about how to provide video feedback to establish a presence in mind. The use of asynchronous video exchanges in a fully online classroom has frequently been examined from the perspective of the student taking the course. For this chapter, the authors explored faculty perceptions of using asynchronous video exchanges and how they viewed the role of these exchanges in incorporating teaching, cognitive presence, and social presence in a fully online PhD course. This emphasis recognizes the importance of faculty perceptions, training, and knowledge of evidence-based best practices. If well implemented, asynchronous video exchanges may help promote student engagement, motivation, learning, and retention.

A purposive sample of online either full-time or part-time employed faculty members from the social and behavioral sciences responded to the survey. Participants taught fully asynchronous 8- or 12-week long non-clinical psychology and marriage and family therapy coursework at the master's and doctoral levels. Some taught a foundational course in which both faculty and students must provide a video nearly every week. Other participants used video feedback voluntarily in other early courses, more advanced courses, and dissertation feedback. No demographic data was collected. Using the Banerjee et al. (2020) list of behaviors associated with social, teaching, and cognitive presence from the Community of Inquiry (CoI) model, the 8-item open-ended survey asked:

1. Tell us about your use of video exchanges in the online classroom.
2. How do you communicate important course topics and goals, as well as specific directions about course learning activities in your video feedback?
3. How does video feedback help to keep students engaged and actively participating in a productive dialogue?
4. How does using video feedback impact on your ability to get to know your students?
5. How does the use of video feedback impact students' ability to get to know you as an instructor? How might this be impactful?
6. How do you use video feedback to help students connect ideas in new and meaningful ways?
7. How do you use video feedback to help students apply their learning to solve real-world problems?
8. Is there anything else that you want to share?

The data were analyzed using thematic analysis based on Braun and Clarke (2006) to identify recurring themes and patterns in the faculty's descriptions. This approach allowed for an in-depth understanding of faculty perspectives on the effectiveness and challenges of video feedback in fostering a collaborative and meaningful learning environment. The results and recommendations will be discussed by type of presence. However, it is critical to note that it became clear that social, teaching, and cognitive presence appear to be interrelated. Emerging themes overlapped, indicating that all three types of presence are vital when providing video feedback. Learning from the review of the literature (Streit et al., 2023) and the research conducted (Streit et al., 2024) helped develop best practices in how to optimize the use of asynchronous video exchanges in a fully online classroom and, hopefully, educate faculty about the different types of presence to establish when using asynchronous video exchanges in the online classroom.

Teaching Presence

Teaching presence is established early by designing and structuring course materials, assessments, and activities to create a meaningful learning experience (Turk et al., 2022). Teaching presence positively influences students' affective learning outcomes (Lim & Richardson, 2021). Teaching presence plays a crucial role in improving students' online learning satisfaction (Cui et al., 2024), and the mediating effects of teaching presence can increase online learning engagement (Kangwa et al., 2024). Teaching presence, including instructional design and organization, facilitating interaction, and direct instruction, is the first mechanism for developing online learning communities. Li and Wang (2024) found that facilitating interaction had the most significant and influencing impact on the online learning experience. To enhance online teaching, it is essential to support educators in comprehensively improving their teaching presence. This includes adopting diverse teaching strategies and improvement measures tailored to various student groups, as well as prioritizing the collection and analysis of student behavioral data to facilitate reflective practices and enhance instructional effectiveness (Li & Wang, 2024). Teaching presence serves as a significant and positive mediator in the relationships between self-regulation and learning engagement, as well as between online interactions and learning engagement. It is a critical factor in understanding how these variables influence learning engagement within online educational contexts (Kangwa et al., 2024).

According to Garrison et al. (2003), when creating this type of presence, faculty need to connect feedback to course and program outcomes. Specifically, online teaching presence influences student success through a thoughtful instructional design structure that promotes active interaction with the instructor, facilitation of discourse such as virtual meetings and discussion feedback, and direct instruction where substantive explanatory feedback is provided (Sanders, 2022). Banerjee et al. (2020) recommend that faculty focus on clearly communicating the design and organization of the class through introductory videos explaining the structure and layout of the course, what is covered, and how it will be taught. Providing direct discussion about how different assignments connect to the more extensive course and program learning outcomes is encouraged. This type of authoritative discussion style helps the student understand why they are being asked to do a specific activity or assignment, facilitating a greater understanding of the bigger picture (Ahn et al., 2023). This is similar in principle to Baumrind's findings on the authoritative parenting style (Pellerin, 2005), where providing a clear rationale to the student helps them to understand 'why' they are engaging in an activity. As such, students are believed to be more motivated and vested in their coursework.

Students have indicated that opportunities to engage with faculty in facilitation and instruction greatly impacted their success (Sanders, 2022). In fact, students rated discourse as more important than direct instruction, while teachers rated direct instruction as more important. Facilitating discourse by sharing personal stories and creating meaning when working collaboratively with students through videos and synchronous Zoom meetings seems key. These findings suggest that video feedback facilitates discourse through instruction and creates an online teaching presence. This understanding of the impact of video feedback on teaching presence is important for faculty to promote student success.

In an online environment, asynchronous video applications are often favored to maintain connection and engagement since opportunities for live synchronous meetings may be limited. The nature of asynchronous video communication supports the building of teacher presence as it encourages active learning and provides more opportunities for reflection, equitable participation, and fewer technological issues (Lowenthal et al., 2020). According to Banerjee et al. (2020), behaviors aligned with teaching presence and video feedback in the fully online classroom include weekly summary videos, zoom office hours, welcome videos, and module/assignment videos.

There is a pressing need for more direct instruction and faculty training on providing video feedback to establish a teaching presence effectively. Taking the time to thoroughly explain why a student needs to perform an activity, facilitating discourse, sharing stories, and establishing clear connections between assignments and course outcomes are vital to facilitating teaching presence.

Best Practices and Strategies for Teaching Presence through Video Feedback

Our research showed that video feedback played a crucial role in teaching presence in the community of inquiry. One significant difference emerged in terms of how video was used. Some participants used synchronous video uploads only for feedback, while others used an asynchronous video exchange integrated into a few course designs. Overall, several themes emerged related to teaching presence. First, design and structure play a crucial role in teaching presence (Turk et al., 2022), and both video feedback and asynchronous exchange are key here. Next, the faculty emphasized the value of facilitation, discussing both the ability to connect feedback to course elements and outcomes as well as facets of the course with practice and research. Third, faculty appreciated the ability to integrate personal experiences. Finally, faculty indicated that video feedback became a teaching tool facilitating clarity by showing and not just writing about something.

Design and Structure

Some of the participants taught a course that required not just video feedback from faculty, but also video submissions from students where they commented on and discussed previous feedback. Participants expressed some mixed feelings about this approach. While some students and faculty appeared to enjoy the process, others struggled. One faculty member indicated they had students "worried that all courses would be designed in this manner." Some faculty expressed concern about the technology. Despite some less-than-positive feelings, many expressed tremendous value. For example, one participant wrote, "the video exchanges are an excellent avenue for building trust, communicating effectively, and honoring individual time." Asynchronous video exchange provided an opportunity to have a dialogue that allows the student to think through and prepare for questions:

They had to prepare and then present themselves each week. They were able to discuss previous feedback. They were able to ask questions that I could answer in my feedback. One example is I recall one girl had a list of my feedback at the beginning of each assignment [and how] she addressed it.

Video exchanges also helped faculty better understand if and how students might be using feedback:

Sometimes it is difficult to tell if they are watching the videos. I try to ask questions so we can keep a "conversation" going. I also make it a point to address any questions they asked so they know I carefully watch their videos. For some students, this method works, and we have a nice dialogue and it's clear that the students are using the feedback they receive. On the other hand, I also have students who very quickly try to address some of the prompts but don't really try to engage in meaningful conversation.

Video exchanges provide a tremendous opportunity, but they have their challenges. Faculty need to feel comfortable with the technology with providing feedback in this manner. In turn, as faculty gain comfort, they can support students in developing comfort.

Video exchanges also facilitate learning of technical skills:

Video feedback is a powerful tool in assisting students solve their own issues, by talking them out, and building a solution focused approach to help them resolve issues throughout the program. Graduate studies are a series of hoops to navigate, with video feedback, students may feel more secure in experimenting with podcasts and presentations that may be used in the real world. Feedback on their presentations helps them in their continuous improvement process.

By building video exchanges into the design of the course, students work with technology, developing skills while also receiving feedback to scaffold their learning in a supportive way.

Facilitation

Video feedback and video exchanges allow the instructor to go beyond direct instruction, which is critical to creating teaching presence (Turk et al., 2022). Both video feedback and video exchange allowed the instructor to make important connections with course outcomes, which Garrison et al. (2003) and Turk et al. (2022) both emphasized, as well as connecting ideas with practice and research. Faculty liked using video to connect ideas to the intended learning outcomes, "I make a point of discussing the course outcomes - and how the assignment connects with the different outcomes." Another participant explained that they use video to "review the syllabus and course expectations, along with tips for how to be successful." Faculty described connecting coursework and real-world applications, such as professional practice and research, as a significant benefit of video feedback. This ability to bridge theoretical concepts with practical examples and current research findings provided several key advantages. According to several faculty members, video feedback allowed them to contextualize course material within the framework of professional practice: "I often use video feedback to help students grasp some important concepts for the course, and then connect it directly to how it may be beneficial to them as an MFT." Furthermore, video feedback was a venue for connecting students to resources. One participant wrote, "I provide additional resources or tips to help students find pertinent research" and another participant shared, "I give feedback as well as information about resources they aren't using."

Integrating Personal Experiences

Faculty enjoyed being able to convey their own experience in their video feedback to facilitate understanding. This personalization makes the faculty member more relatable, normalizing student experiences and giving students ideas for managing challenges. For example, one participant talked about "telling stories about when I made a similar mistake and about the professor who helped me back in the day." By drawing on their own experiences and industry examples, faculty can also illustrate how concepts are applied in real-world scenarios. For example, in exploring the role of diversity in an industrial and organizational psychology course, another participant indicated they use video to "describe what Diversity, Equity and Inclusion (DEI) in Industrial Organization Psychology means to me."

Useful Teaching Tool

Participants described video feedback as a means of facilitating teaching. Video feedback provided a way of sharing other forms of feedback that could not be easily conveyed in written form. They emphasized the ability to show ideas and concepts visually, to discuss rather than tell: "I may do a screencast to walk them through ways to enhance their CV" (pertaining to an assignment where students create a curriculum vitae), and another participant said, "I use it fairly regularly with my students, especially in courses where it may be helpful to show something (such as in quantitative analysis courses)."

In summary, video exchanges can be an invaluable component of a course. Interestingly, several participants note that teaching presence should be established first. To establish teaching presence, faculty relate spending time modeling how to create videos, allowing for imperfection, directly talking about how they want to be addressed (e.g. – professor) and how the video exchange process will work. Direct instruction of key concepts, theories, and ideas must also be evident, along with making sure students answer all parts of the prompts and strategies for how to do so when using video exchanges. Of interest is the importance of communicating how the assignment connects with the larger goals of the course and the program. This type of information is not often provided when giving only written feedback. With the use of videos, the feedback is more likely to be focused on communicating big picture types of goals and ideas.

Social Presence

Social presence is defined as the ability to create an environment that allows for risk-free expression and a comfortable exchange of thoughts, ideas, and emotions (Mosher et al., 2023). For the intent and purpose of this chapter, the focus of this exchange is between the student and the faculty member (Garrison et al., 2003). This exchange can occur during a live synchronous meeting such as via Zoom, through recorded asynchronous video feedback from the faculty member to the student, or asynchronously via the use of video exchanges where the student shares their thoughts and ideas through a recorded video to the faculty member, and the faculty member responds with a video in exchange. It is important to note that video feedback includes the face and the voice of the faculty member. This provides a unique opportunity for faculty to give non-verbal social cues and spoken audio feedback in real-time. This type of 'humanized' communication is much richer than the more typically encountered basic written feedback and, if done correctly, can lead to a greater likelihood of establishing faculty social presence.

A distinct feature of social presence is perceived as real and present interaction and results in an interpersonal relationship (Oh et al., 2018). Establishing such relationships results in trust, goodwill being built; and higher predicted performance (Grant & Shandell, 2022). Positive correlations have been found between social presence and increased student cognitive load as well as perceived learning. It is also associated with enhanced student satisfaction – to the student, instructor presence is motivational (Alemdag, 2022). As noted earlier, social presence can enhance a student's educational experience by creating a learning community that builds trust and promotes learning (Garrison, 2009). Creating a sense of psychological safety through social presence is paramount, as this leads to greater student sharing behaviors in online learning environments (Catyanadika & Rajasekera, 2022). With this goal in mind, faculty need to find ways to establish a sense of trust and a safe space where students can express their thoughts and ideas without fear of retribution or ridicule.

According to Banerjee et al. (2020), to establish social presence, faculty must facilitate an atmosphere where open communication and effective expression of ideas are prevalent. Asynchronous video exchanges are one way to do so. Asynchronous video exchanges where students can express their thoughts, feelings, and ideas and pose questions directly to faculty through videos, and faculty can respond to student questions in response, appear to lead to a more interactive and individualized dialogue. It is essential to note that when a student shares a video with faculty on a topic, a new and different opportunity to assess student learning is provided. Usually focused solely on student learning, topics not typically addressed in the classroom, such as students' feelings, attitudes, and self-efficacy beliefs, can be discussed in these videos. In other words, students can communicate their social and emotional needs directly to faculty. Given these multifaceted needs, it is not enough for educators to only focus on students' learning, but rather a response should engage the whole person (Kim et al., 2021). This 'whole human' education is key to creating a safe space with trust and open communication (Uzondu, 2021).

Active listening skills are paramount in facilitating an atmosphere of trust and open communication (McKay et al., 2009). This skill set may need to be assessed and developed further by faculty who are teaching in the fully online classroom. Listening is a skill that takes considerable time and effort to do well. This is particularly relevant in the fully online classroom, where students often may not have opportunities to express their thoughts and feelings fully. Written forms of expression are more commonly encountered within these more formal content-focused topic assignments. Discussions can be disjointed, and comment threads are not always fully closed loops. As such, the social and emotional needs of the student may be overlooked. Also, the cultural competency of the faculty member is an important consideration in an increasingly diverse world. This is a key ingredient to successfully establishing a social presence and a safe space. Cultural competency is another important consideration when using asynchronous video exchanges to create social presence in the online classroom (Chu et al., 2024).

Interestingly, in studies looking at the use of technology, participants viewed video feedback as more important to creating faculty social presence than written feedback (Borup et al., 2014; Thomas et al., 2017). Along the same lines, video feedback was said to create a more relaxed conversational tone and greater closeness with the faculty member than purely written feedback (Borup et al., 2014). A possible explanation for this phenomenon can be drawn from social psychology. The effort heuristic is a mental shortcut that humans use to equate visible human effort with importance or significance. In other words, because you are seeing your faculty's face and hearing their voice in a video, it signifies importance because the faculty member took the time to do it (Kruger et al., 2004). Written feedback doesn't convey this importance because a human being is not visible. Similarly, research by Wood et al. (2021) claims that faculty-generated video content substantially impacts student perceptions of presence more than generic pre-existing or canned video content. The research suggests that faculty who provide personalized video feedback add a much-needed human touch to the online learning process, and as such, faculty social presence is more likely to be established (Andel et al., 2020; Kyungbin et al., 2010; Ryan, 2021; Seckman, 2018).

Faculty members who can accurately utilize both body language and tone of voice during synchronous and asynchronous video interactions with students will likely be more successful in establishing a social presence. Further, being able to monitor and self-regulate emotional responses and reactions during live synchronous sessions is an important piece of the puzzle. Faculty may need additional training and practice to effectively manage their emotions and present themselves positively and encouragingly when interacting synchronously through Zoom and providing video feedback asynchronously to students. Some faculty may need to be more aware of how they come across on camera. For example, the facial expressions that they are providing and tone of voice. Modeling positive non-verbal behaviors by using encouraging facial expressions such as smiling, maintaining eye contact and looking directly into the webcam, leaning forward with interest, and holding a relaxed and upright posture are all examples of specific behaviors faculty can engage in to create a positive social presence (Faucett et al., 2017). Further, speaking clearly with an appropriate pace, avoiding the use of slang words or phrases, using the student's first name to personalize the feedback, providing a positive future-focused emphasis, and encouraging tone of voice are beneficial behaviors to engage in (Leibold & Schwarz, 2015; Martin, 2020). Proper lighting, a quiet setting, and a professional background are essential to creating warm and inviting videos. While many of these behaviors may seem obvious, faculty may not be fully aware of the research findings on the specific behaviors they can engage in and the environmental conditions they should try to create within their videos to help promote social presence. Using video feedback in a fully online classroom is a skill set that takes both time and practice. More direct faculty instruction and supervised practice are needed to do this well.

Best Practices and Strategies for Social Presence through Video Feedback

Two themes emerged in the research around social presence and faculty's ability to foster an environment of meaningful interaction: personal connection and relationship building and the ability to communicate tone and facial expressions.

Personal Connection and Relationship Building

Faculty reported having a greater ability to foster an environment of meaningful human interaction and connection when using video exchanges because students could see them as real people. One subject shared: "For some reason, I think it's the presence of another human being that seems to open them up and get them more engaged. Perhaps they feel as if they are being given more of our attention when we do these videos? I'm not sure why it works - but it helps to make me seem more 'human'.' As such, students seemed less anxious and were more likely to reach out for help." Stewart (2023) emphasizes the importance of creating more humanizing learning online environments through the addition of weekly introductory instructor videos, and detailed feedback videos) and found that as a result, students felt a strong connection to the instructor, other students and coursework.

The theme of personal connection and relationship building emerged as the most common and recurring concept in the data, highlighted by nearly every participant. Participants frequently mentioned that video feedback "increases the personal touch." One participant explained, "There is a personal connection made that is not made with audio or simply text communication". At the same time, another highlighted that "I've been using video feedback for a few years now - and I think it is a great way to establish a connection with my students." Participants felt that connection was fostered because students could see them as real people:

"For some reason, I think it's the presence of another human being in person - that seems to open them up and get them more engaged. This aligns with findings of Miao et al. (2022), that learning engagement and attitudes about learning are deeply influenced by the teacher-student interaction. Perhaps they feel as if they are being given more of our attention when creating these videos? I'm not sure why it works - but the videos help to make me seem more 'human'. They get to see me in my living room - I think that this humanizes the experience a bit more for them". Another participant stated that "video feedback allows me to share a bit of myself in an authentic way". Participants also stated that students express positive reactions to that connection, "video feedback seems to help them to feel more connected to me as their faculty," and another suggested that "Students say they feel more connected to me (the professor)". These positive findings around teacher-student interactions mirror findings by Ong and Quek (2023) regarding the value students have for building connections with their faculty. A diversity of interactions available to students may enhance the likelihood of individuals experiencing a sense of connection, which, in turn, contributes to an improved learning process (Hehir et al., 2021).

Ability to Communicate Tone and Facial Expressions

Another theme emerged relating to tone and expression. Video provided participants with a way to communicate better by incorporating tone and facial expressions, essential elements of effective communication. These non-verbal cues significantly enhance the clarity and emotional impact of the feedback given. One participant described student feedback emphasizing the value of video for conveying tone, "They say they also can sense the tone of the feedback from the things I say, so it's easier to realize that the professor is not intending to be cruel." In online learning, warm facial expressions and tone of voice, along with the stance of the instructor improves the student's perception of the instructor, and motivation to engage in deep cognitive processing (Lawson et al., 2021).

In summary, faculty note that social presence is important to create an open, comfortable and relaxed learning environment. Viewing their professor as a live human being through video feedback significantly reduces student stress and anxiety levels. Students cannot hide when they are on camera, and you get a clearer picture of the 'whole' student when they do so. Through video feedback, students are more likely to share where they live, hobbies, interests, and any fears or concerns they might have about the program, including questions about their topic and where to go next. Faculty note that these types of questions often would not come up in written exchanges. Students appear to be more comfortable asking questions in their course after the asynchronous video exchanges took place.

Cognitive Presence

The final type of presence is what is referred to as cognitive presence. Of the three, cognitive presence is the most challenging type of presence to create within an online classroom. Streit et al. (2023) hypothesize that this type of presence typically occurs after both social and teaching presence is well-established. However, it is key to note that cognitive presence alone is insufficient in promoting student learning. Research has shown that creating an environment where students experience interactive learning and feel a sense of belonging will increase student engagement and affects students' cognitive and critical thinking development (Roddy, 2017; Wai-Cook, 2021).

According to Garrison et al. (2003), cognitive presence helps students develop their critical thinking skills, including problem-solving and exploring various opinions and perspectives on a subject. Critical thinking skills are recognized as one of the most important indicators of student learning quality (Alsaleh, 2020). An online learning environment promotes independence, giving students unique opportunities to develop critical thinking skills. To cultivate cognitive presence instructors should create a vibrant learning community incorporating instructional materials such as videos and interactive multimedia, while ensuring that tasks are aligned with assessments. Research shows that students can develop their oral and written communication skills online when the materials are relevant and valuable. For example, students improved their public speaking and presentation abilities after engaging with model videos (McBain et al., 2015; Wai-Cook, 2021). Instructors who provide feedback through live chats or recorded videos outside of class help students refine their skills in conveying information clearly, despite the inherent challenges of related technology. Students become more curious, confident in articulating their ideas, and adept at constructing arguments, and as such online courses can be more effective, when students find the content relevant and engaging, thus fostering greater cognitive engagement (Wai-Cook, 2021).

According to Banerjee et al. (2020), cognitive presence develops through four stages. First, a triggering event, next, exploring ideas, thirdly, integration of those ideas (often the hardest phase as moving from exploration usually requires support from instructors or more experienced peers), and, lastly, the resolution of the problem or issue. To enhance cognitive presence, research emphasizes the value of designing online course elements such as video feedback that foster a favorable social space to share resources and experiences while building supportive networks. Using video feedback in a scaffolding strategy, such as where instructors ask questions to guide discussions toward a solution or using case-based discussions that immerse students in real-life scenarios and authentic problem-solving, can significantly strengthen cognitive presence (Guo et al. 2021; Lee et al., 2022; Sadaf et al; 2021).

Banerjee et al. (2020) suggest that cognitive presence can be facilitated by using videos in the online classroom in three possible ways: first, by providing a triggering event that creates a sense of curiosity, uncertainty, or wonder within the student, which helps to get them thinking. For example, students can be given open-ended questions or plausible scenarios and case studies to reflect on and respond to – without a clear resolution provided. Experiential learning is an effective means to improve students' critical thinking skills (Rodzalan et al., 2020). Next, providing a summary video at the end of a module or assignment can direct students to think more about a topic and how the various concepts and ideas connect. For example, faculty might ask students to integrate, synthesize, and apply various concepts and theories to new settings. These exchanges help establish a greater sense of faculty cognitive presence in the fully online classroom. Finally, providing possible answers and clear resolutions to the questions posed at the start of a course, with thorough explanations included within the video feedback is recommended. The belief is that this may further enhance the cognitive presence of a faculty member in the fully online classroom. It is important to note that video feedback is believed to be more detailed, with clearer and more enhanced explanations of feedback and key concepts provided by faculty. As such, cognitive presence is more likely to lead to enhanced learning (Cheng & Li, 2020; Kleinknecht & Gröschner, 2016).

It is important to note that exposure to a faculty member's inner dialogue and thought processes is rare in the fully online classroom. Instead, the bulk of the feedback is corrective and provided in written form (Leibold & Schwarz, 2015). Along the same lines, there is some evidence that multi-modal (e.g., audio/video as well as written feedback) is more likely to lead to more detailed and elaborate feedback for the student, including prompts that question the student to think more deeply and critically about a topic (Martin, 2020). As such, the use of video feedback within the online classroom, along with written feedback, is an indispensable tool for faculty to use when developing students' critical thinking skills. For example, faculty can share their thoughts aloud and describe how they go about problem-solving and critically evaluate the research evidence supporting or against a theory or idea. Through modeling, students can observe and eventually begin to 'think like' their teacher. As noted above, this type of 'thinking out loud' is not typically encountered in the fully online classroom, so teaching faculty how to do this more often via video feedback is key to facilitating cognitive presence and helping students to think more critically. The emphasis here is on providing more direct instruction to faculty about 'how' to give effective video feedback to establish a cognitive presence. These are just a few examples of how video feedback can be used to create faculty cognitive presence in the online classroom.

Best Practices and Strategies for Online Cognitive Presence through Video Feedback

Two main themes emerged related to cognitive presence and faculty's ability to communicate and promote engagement with the content: communicating complex ideas and connecting different aspects of the course. Encouraging deeper level processing and engagement with course content is key to establishing cognitive presence. Overall, participants felt that videos allowed them to provide "more details or clarification or elaboration on the issue at hand." Faculty were better able to break down complex topics into more manageable segments, using tone and emphasis to clarify points. Again, utilizing visual aids such as diagrams or slides to enhance understanding was reported to be helpful. A multi-modal approach appears to facilitate deeper-level cognitive processing. One participant felt that students "better understood the feedback given," suggesting that video exchanges may allow alternative ways to assess student learning. Faculty reported that using video feedback enabled them to emphasize the interrelatedness of various topics within the curriculum, thereby enhancing students' depth of understanding and long-term retention. The dynamic nature of video exchanges and feedback facilitated active learning, with more profound discussions about the intersection of course concepts, practice, and research.

Communicate Complex Ideas

Participants highlighted the ability to communicate complex ideas as a significant advantage of using video feedback. Faculty reported that video allowed them to elaborate on intricate concepts more effectively than written feedback alone, such as "where it may be helpful to show something (such as in quantitative analysis courses)." Participants felt that video feedback allowed them to provide "details or clarification or elaboration on the issue at hand." Through visual and auditory explanations, participants could break down complex topics into more manageable segments, use tone and emphasis to clarify points, and utilize visual aids such as diagrams or slides to enhance understanding. This multi-modal approach helped students grasp challenging material more thoroughly and facilitated deeper cognitive processing. One participant verbalized a sentiment shared by others i.e., that with videos, the students "better understand the feedback given."

Connect Course Ideas

Participants reported that video exchanges enabled them to emphasize the interrelatedness of various topics within the curriculum, thereby enhancing students' understanding and retention of the material. This method also provided a more personalized and engaging approach to feedback, which they believed contributed to a deeper and more integrated learning experience for students. Video enabled faculty to make key connections between course elements. Participants expressed value in being able to connect ideas between different aspects of the course and the intended outcomes, "I make a point of discussing the course outcomes - and how the assignment connects with the different outcomes," and connecting what the courses are intended to convey with the work the student is or will do, "I often use video feedback to help students grasp some important concepts for the course, and then connect it directly to how it may be beneficial to them."

In summary, this type of presence is most likely to occur last, after both teaching and social presence were established. Faculty agree that cognitive presence is the 'fruit of their labor.' Challenging a student's way of thinking about their topic without creating a sense of defensiveness or frustration or a reduced level of motivation is the key to the growth and learning of the student. A positive, nurturing learning experience is more likely to occur for the student when video feedback is provided.

Overlapping Presence

For effective student learning, all three elements—cognitive, social, and teaching presence—must be present. For example, relying solely on teaching is not enough to foster learning. Research highlights the crucial role instructors play in a community of inquiry, as they can cultivate an environment that encourages interactive learning and fosters a sense of belonging among students. This supportive atmosphere can enhance engagement and lower dropout rates. Additionally, social presence significantly influences students' cognitive and critical thinking development. Therefore, these three 'presences' are fundamentally interconnected (Wai-Cook, 2021).

The empirical data also demonstrated that the three types of presence—cognitive, social, and teaching—are interrelated. Emerging themes overlap in many cases, indicating that all three types of presence can play a role in video feedback. Participant comments demonstrate this interconnectedness. For example, one participant highlighted aspects of both social and cognitive presence, stating, "Students say they feel more connected to me (the professor) and better understand the feedback given." Another participant noted, "Students really seemed to enjoy seeing me each week and responded positively to my feedback." Overall, many participants echoed the sentiment that "the personal connection is helpful to keep the student confident and willing to improve," underscoring the vital role of social presence in enhancing the effectiveness of video feedback.

As shown above, the dynamic and personal nature of video feedback facilitated deeper discussions about the intersection of coursework, practice, and research. Faculty could pose thought-provoking questions, encourage students to reflect on how theoretical concepts relate to their own experiences or future careers, and provide tailored advice on how to apply what they have learned in professional settings. This interactive engagement helped to cultivate a more integrated and holistic understanding of the subject matter (Kim et al., 2021).

Most participants had a favorable view of video feedback and encouraged more of its use. However, challenges in providing video feedback emerged related to the limitations of its use, and the lack of awareness about what video feedback might provide. Video feedback does require time and skills which can present a challenge. Participants indicated, "It takes some technical abilities and more time, so I have not been doing it as much during a busier time in my life." When asked survey questions related to their experiences using video feedback to communicate, promote engagement, and connect ideas, a couple of participants had not thought to consider video feedback in this way. For example, one participant stated, "I provided feedback on the assignment just completed. I didn't know that I should provide any directions for future assignments or topics. I did not. I could. But I did not." In another case, the participant was honest that they did not know how to use video to connect ideas in a new and meaningful way. In another case, a participant honestly reported that they "have not used video feedback in this capacity."

A strong teaching presence in an online environment will facilitate student participation and interaction, foster students developing higher order thinking skills, and can be the link to social and cognitive presences (Morrison & Jacobsen, 2023). Effective online teaching presence can improve social and cognitive presence which in turn can lead to better educational outcomes and relationships. The faculty-student relationship is important to the students' success, and the psychological remoteness created by relational distance between faculty and students can negatively impact a learning environment (Singh et al., 2022).

Teaching presence is crucial for meaningful learning, shaped by well-designed course materials and active student engagement (Turk et al., 2022). It enhances undergraduate students' affective outcomes (Lim & Richardson, 2021). Faculty should connect feedback to course outcomes and facilitate discourse through tools like video and Zoom meetings (Sanders, 2022). Clear communication about course structure and the rationale behind assignments increases student motivation, similar to authoritative parenting principles (Pellerin, 2005). Students value interaction with faculty and rated discourse more important than direct instruction. Asynchronous video applications can strengthen teaching presence, highlighting the need for faculty training in video feedback strategies (Lowenthal et al., 2020). Video feedback is essential for establishing teaching presence within a community of inquiry. While video exchanges present challenges, they foster dialogue, build trust, and help students develop technical skills, ultimately enhancing engagement and learning outcomes.

Social presence can occur through synchronous meetings or asynchronous video exchanges, which allow for richer, non-verbal communication. Establishing social presence fosters trust and enhances student satisfaction and perceived learning, and faculty must facilitate open communication and actively listen to address students' emotional needs (Grant & Shandell, 2022). Video feedback is more effective than written feedback in establishing presence, as it conveys effort and personal engagement (Borup et al., 2014). Video allows for better communication of tone and non-verbal cues, enhancing feedback clarity and emotional impact. Overall, video feedback creates a comfortable atmosphere, encouraging students to share more openly than traditional written communication.

Cognitive presence is the most challenging type of presence to establish in online classrooms and is typically built upon strong social and teaching presences. It enhances critical thinking and problem-solving skills by creating an interactive learning environment (Roddy, 2017; Streit et al., 2023). Cognitive presence develops through four stages: triggering events, exploring ideas, integrating concepts, and resolving issues. Faculty can foster this presence through effective video feedback that includes open-ended questions, summary videos, and detailed explanations. Utilizing video enhances communication, encourages deep thinking, and models critical thought processes, making it a vital tool for promoting cognitive engagement in online learning (Cheng & Li, 2020). Ultimately, cognitive presence develops after establishing teaching and social presence, with effective video feedback creating a supportive environment that challenges students while maintaining motivation (Streit et al., 2023).

Effective student learning hinges on the interconnection of cognitive, social, and teaching presence. Video feedback exemplifies this interconnectedness, as faculty noted that it strengthens personal connections, boosts confidence, and deepens understanding of course material. Relying solely on teaching is inadequate; instructors must foster an interactive learning community to enhance engagement and reduce dropout rates. The findings indicate that educators, instructors, and instructional designers should prioritize the enhancement of presence in online education courses and similar pedagogical approaches. This can be achieved through the implementation of various strategies, including the establishment of clear course structures and consistent objectives, the facilitation and moderation of online discussions, the provision of timely and constructive feedback (written and video), the sharing of expertise and resources, and the cultivation of a sense of community and belonging among learners (Kangwa et al., 2024).

In conclusion, although our understanding of the optimal use of video feedback for fostering faculty presence in fully online classrooms remains incomplete, we have made considerable advancements in knowledge over the past decade. Using video feedback appears to be overwhelmingly supported by the research evidence to create the three types of presence that Garrison et al. (2003) describe. Faculty should be encouraged to make use of several different types of feedback (written, audio, video) throughout the online course (where appropriate). The use of video feedback in the fully online classroom is key to optimizing faculty presence, leading to greater levels of student engagement and learning. Finally, and perhaps most importantly, it is evident that more formal training and practice in providing video feedback to students is needed to help faculty create the three different types of presence. By doing so, faculty help students to feel a stronger sense of belonging to a learning community. This in turn helps students learn, grow and develop their knowledge, skills and abilities.

REFERENCES

Ahn, L. H., Hill, C. E., Gerstenblith, J. A., Hillman, J. W., Mui, V. W., Yetter, C., Anderson, T., & Kivlighan, D. M.Jr. (2023). Helping Skills Training: Outcomes and Trainer Effects. *Journal of Counseling Psychology*, 70(4), 396–402. DOI: 10.1037/cou0000667 PMID: 37199956

Alemdag, E. (2022). Effects of instructor-present videos on learning, cognitive load, motivation, and social presence: A meta-analysis. *Education and Information Technologies*, 27(9), 12713–12742. DOI: 10.1007/s10639-022-11154-w

Alsaleh, N. J. (2020). Teaching critical thinking skills: Literature review. *Turkish Online Journal of Educational Technology-TOJET*, 19(1), 21–39.

Amir, D., Hanim Rahmat, N., & Shazri, S. S. (2021).*Is there cognitive presence during online learning?* In *International Virtual Symposium: Research, Industry & Community Engagement (RICE)* (pp. 99-103).

Andel, S. A., de Vreede, T., Spector, P. E., Padmanabhan, B., Singh, V. K., & de Vreede, G. J. (2020). Do social features help in video-centric online learning platforms? A social presence perspective. *Computers in Human Behavior*, 113, 106505. Advance online publication. DOI: 10.1016/j.chb.2020.106505

Banerjee, M., Wolf, J., Chalasani, S., Dhumal, P., & Gee, M. (2020). Creating teaching presence in online courses through videos. *Business Education Innovation Journal*, 12(1), 190–198.

Bialowas, A., & Steimel, S. (2019). Less is more: Use of video to address the problem of teacher immediacy and presence in online courses. *International Journal on Teaching and Learning in Higher Education*, 31(2), 354–364.

Borup, J., West, R., Thomas, R., & Graham, C. (2014). Examining the impact of video feedback on instructor social presence in blended courses. *The International Review of Research in Open and Distributed Learning,* 15(3). https://doi.org/.v15i3.1821DOI: 10.19173/irrodl

Borup, J., West, R. E., & Graham, C. R. (2012). Improving online social presence through asynchronous video. *The Internet and Higher Education*, 15(3), 195–203. DOI: 10.1016/j.iheduc.2011.11.001

Catyanadika, P. E., & Rajasekera, J. (2022). Influence of psychological safety and social presence on knowledge sharing behavior in higher education online learning environment. *VINE Journal of Information and Knowledge Management Systems*, 52(3), 335–353. DOI: 10.1108/VJIKMS-06-2021-0094

Cheng, D., & Li, M. (2020). Screencast video feedback in online TESOL classes. *Computers and Composition*, 58, 102612. Advance online publication. DOI: 10.1016/j.compcom.2020.102612

Chu, C., Hooper, T., Takahashi, M., & Herke, M. (2024). The effect of asynchronous virtual exchange on intercultural competence among undergraduate students. *Journal of Comparative & International Higher Education*, 16(2), 213–226. DOI: 10.32674/jcihe.v16i2.5229

Collins, K., Grof, S., Mathena, C., & Kupczynski, L. (2019). Asynchronous video and the development of instructor social presence and student engagement. *Turkish Online Journal of Distance Education*, 20(1), 53–70. DOI: 10.17718/tojde.522378

Cui, T., Bin, J., Lu, X., & Wang, W. (2024, June). The influence of offline teaching presence on students' online learning satisfaction: A case study of online design workshops. In *Proceedings of the 2024 9th International Conference on Distance Education and Learning* (pp. 334-339). DOI: 10.1145/3675812.3675828

Faucett, H., Lee, M., & Carter, S. (2017). I should listen more: Real-time sensing and feedback of non-verbal communication in video telehealth. *Proceedings of the ACM on Human-Computer Interaction Volume 1 (issue CSCW)*, Article No.: 44pp 1–19. https://doi.org/DOI: 10.1145/3134679

Garrison, D. R. (2009). Communities of inquiry in online learning: Social, teaching and cognitive presence. In Howard, C. (Eds.), *Encyclopedia of Distance and Online Learning* (2nd ed., pp. 352–355). IGI Global.

Garrison, D. R., Anderson, T., & Archer, W. (2003). Critical inquiry in a text-based environment: Computer conferencing in higher education. *The Internet and Higher Education*, 2(2-3), 87–105. DOI: 10.1016/S1096-7516(00)00016-6

Grant, A. M., & Shandell, M. S. (2022). Social motivation at work: The organizational psychology of effort for, against, and with others. *Annual Review of Psychology*, 73(1), 301–326. DOI: 10.1146/annurev-psych-060321-033406 PMID: 34280327

Guo, P., Saab, N., Wu, L., & Admiraal, W. (2021). The Community of Inquiry perspective on students' social presence, cognitive presence, and academic performance in online project-based learning. *Journal of Computer Assisted Learning*, 37(5), 1479–1493. DOI: 10.1111/jcal.12586

Hehir, E., Zeller, M., Luckhurst, J., & Chandler, T. (2021). Developing student connectedness under remote learning using digital resources: A systematic review. *Education and Information Technologies*, 26(5), 6531–6548. DOI: 10.1007/s10639-021-10577-1 PMID: 34220282

Kangwa, D., Xiulan, W., Msambwa Msafiri, M., & Fute, A. (2024). Enhanced learning engagement through teaching presence in online distance education. *Distance Education*, •••, 1–18. DOI: 10.1080/01587919.2024.2347998

Kim, D., Wortham, S., Borowiec, K., Yatsu, D. K., Ha, S., Carroll, S., Wang, L., & Kim, J. (2021). Formative education online: Teaching the whole person during the global COVID-19 pandemic. *AERA Open*, 7, 23328584211015229. DOI: 10.1177/23328584211015229

Kleinknecht, M., & Gröschner, A. (2016). Fostering preservice teachers' noticing with structured video feedback: Results of an online and video-based intervention study. *Teaching and Teacher Education*, 59, 45–56. DOI: 10.1016/j.tate.2016.05.020

Kohli, H., Wampole, D., & Kohli, A. (2021). Impact of online education on student learning during the pandemic. *Studies in Learning and Teaching*, 2(2), 1–11. DOI: 10.46627/silet.v2i2.65

Kruger, J., Wirtz, D., Van Boven, L., & Altermatt, T. W. (2004). The effort heuristic. *Journal of Experimental Social Psychology*, 40(1), 91–98. DOI: 10.1016/S0022-1031(03)00065-9

Kyungbin, K., Daehoon, H., Eun-Jun, B., & Armstrong, S. (2010). Feelings of isolation and coping mechanism in online learning environments: A case study of Asian international students. *International Journal of Learning*, 17(2), 343–355.

Lawson, A. P., Mayer, R. E., Adamo-Villani, N., Benes, B., Lei, X., & Cheng, J. (2021). Recognizing the emotional state of human and virtual instructors. *Computers in Human Behavior*, 114, 106554. DOI: 10.1016/j.chb.2020.106554

Lazarevic, B., Fuller, J., & Cain, J. (2023). Facilitating community of inquiry through video-enhanced online instruction: What are learners' impressions? *TechTrends*, 67(4), 611–625. DOI: 10.1007/s11528-023-00864-8

Lee, J., Soleimani, F., Irish, I., Hosmer, J., Soylu, M. Y., Finkelberg, R., & Chatterjee, S. (2022). Predicting cognitive presence in at-scale online learning: MOOC and for-credit online course environments. *Online Learning : the Official Journal of the Online Learning Consortium*, 26(1), 58–79. DOI: 10.24059/olj.v26i1.3060

Leibold, N., & Schwarz, L. (2015). The art of giving online feedback. *The Journal of Effective Teaching*, 15(1), 34–46.

Li, W., & Wang, W. (2024). The impact of teaching presence on students' online learning experience: Evidence from 334 Chinese universities during the pandemic. *Frontiers in Psychology*, 15, 1291341. DOI: 10.3389/fpsyg.2024.1291341 PMID: 38947911

Lim, J., & Richardson, J. C. (2021). Predictive effects of undergraduate students' perceptions of social, cognitive, and teaching presence on affective learning outcomes according to disciplines. *Computers & Education*, 161, 104063. Advance online publication. DOI: 10.1016/j.compedu.2020.104063

Lowenthal, P., Borup, J., West, R., & Archambault, L. (2020). Thinking beyond zoom: Using asynchronous video to maintain connection and engagement during the COVID-19 pandemic. *Journal of Technology and Teacher Education*, 28(2), 383–391.

Martin, D. (2020) Providing students with multimodal feedback experiences. *Journal of Curriculum, Teaching, Learning and Leadership in Education, 5*(7). https://digitalcommons.unomaha.edu/ctlle/vol5/iss1/2

Mc Kay, M., Davis, M., & Fanning, P. (2009). *Messages: The communication skills workbook* (3rd ed.). New Harbinger Publications, Inc.

McBain, B., Drew, A., James, C., Phelan, L., Harris, K. M., & Archer, J. (2016). Student experience of oral communication assessment tasks online from a multidisciplinary trial. *Education + Training*, 58(2), 134–149. www.emeraldinsight.com/0040-0912.htm. DOI: 10.1108/ET-10-2014-0124

Miao, J., Chang, J., & Ma, L. (2022). Teacher-student interaction, student-student interaction and social presence: Their impacts on learning engagement in online learning environments. *The Journal of Genetic Psychology*, 183(6), 514–526. DOI: 10.1080/00221325.2022.2094211 PMID: 35815529

Moore, M. G. (2013). The theory of transactional distance. In *Handbook of distance education* (pp. 84–103). Routledge. DOI: 10.4324/9780203803738.ch5

Morrison, L., & Jacobsen, M. (2023). The role of feedback in building teaching presence and student self-regulation in online learning. *Social Sciences & Humanities Open*, 7(1), 100503. DOI: 10.1016/j.ssaho.2023.100503

Mosher, C. J., Morton, A., Tarbet, A., & Palaganas, J. C. (2023). Factors of engagement in synchronous online learning conversations and distance debriefing: A realist synthesis review. *Simulation in Healthcare*, 18(2), 126–134. DOI: 10.1097/SIH.0000000000000650 PMID: 35470345

Oh, C. S., Bailenson, J. N., & Welch, G. F. (2018). A systematic review of social presence: Definition, antecedents, and implications. *Frontiers in Robotics and AI*, 5, 409295. DOI: 10.3389/frobt.2018.00114 PMID: 33500993

Ong, S. G. T., & Quek, G. C. L. (2023). Enhancing teacher-student interactions and student online engagement in an online learning environment. *Learning Environments Research*, 26(3), 681–707. DOI: 10.1007/s10984-022-09447-5 PMID: 36685638

Pellerin, L. A. (2005). Applying Baumrind's parenting typology to high schools: Toward a middle-range theory of authoritative socialization. *Social Science Research*, 34(2), 283–303. DOI: 10.1016/j.ssresearch.2004.02.003

Prodgers, L., Travis, E., & Pownall, M. (2023). "It's hard to feel a part of something when you've never met people": Defining "learning community" in an online era. *Higher Education*, 85(6), 1219–1234. DOI: 10.1007/s10734-022-00886-w PMID: 35919398

Roddy, C., Amiet, D. L., Chung, J., Holt, C., Shaw, L., McKenzie, S., Garivaldis, F., Lodge, J. M., & Mundy, M. E. (2017, November). Applying best practice online learning, teaching, and support to intensive online environments: An integrative review. *Frontiers in Education*, 2, 59. DOI: 10.3389/feduc.2017.00059

Rodzalan, S. A., Noor, N. N. M., Arif, L. S. M., & Saat, M. M. (2020). Factors influencing the improvement of students' critical thinking and problem-solving skill: An industrial training intervention. *International Journal of Emerging Technologies in Learning*, 15(22), 134–145. DOI: 10.3991/ijet.v15i22.16303

Ryan, T. (2021). Designing video feedback to support the socioemotional aspects of online learning. *Educational Technology Research and Development*, 69(1), 137–140. DOI: 10.1007/s11423-020-09918-7 PMID: 33456286

Sadaf, A., Kim, S. Y., & Wang, Y. (2021). A comparison of cognitive presence, learning, satisfaction, and academic performance in case-based and non-case-based online discussions. *American Journal of Distance Education*, 35(3), 214–227. DOI: 10.1080/08923647.2021.1888667

Sanders, M. (2022). *Creating inclusive and engaging online courses: A teaching guide*. Edward Elgar Publishing. DOI: 10.4337/9781800888883

Seckman, C. (2018). Impact of interactive video communication versus text-based feedback on teaching, social, and cognitive presence in online learning communities. *Nurse Educator*, 43(1), 18–22. DOI: 10.1097/NNE.0000000000000448 PMID: 28858951

Singh, J., Singh, L., & Matthees, B. (2022). Establishing social, cognitive, and teaching presence in online learning: A panacea in COVID-19 pandemic, post vaccine and post pandemic times. *Journal of Educational Technology Systems*, 51(1), 28–45. DOI: 10.1177/00472395221095169

Stewart, O. G. (2023). Understanding what works in humanizing higher education online courses: Connecting through videos, feedback, multimodal assignments, and social media. *Issues and Trends in Learning Technologies*, 11(2), 2–26.

Streit, M., Levin, M., & Harris, A. (2024, August 8–10). *A qualitative analysis of faculty perceptions: Using asynchronous video exchanges and video feedback in A fully online classroom.* [Conference presentation]. APA 2024 Convention, Seattle, WA, United States.

Streit, M., Levin, M., Harris, A., & Watters, Y. (2023, August 4–6). *Using asynchronous video exchanges to promote faculty presence in the online classroom.* [Conference presentation]. APA 2023 Convention, Washington, D.C., United States.

Thomas, R. A., West, R. E., & Borup, J. (2017). An analysis of instructor social presence in online text and asynchronous video feedback comments. *The Internet and Higher Education*, 33, 61–73. DOI: 10.1016/j.iheduc.2017.01.003

Turk, M., Heddy, B. C., & Danielson, R. W. (2022). Teaching and social presences supporting basic needs satisfaction in online learning environments: How can presences and basic needs happily meet online? *Computers & Education*, 180, 104432. DOI: 10.1016/j.compedu.2022.104432

Uzondu, I. C. (2021). Innovative trends and advances in education and communication in Africa. *AMAMIHE Journal of Applied Philosophy*, 19(3), 120–134.

Uzondu, I. C. (2021). Innovative trends and advances in education and communication in Africa. *AMAMIHE Journal of Applied Philosophy,* 19(3).

Wai-Cook, M. S. S. (2021). Students' perceptions of interactions from instructor presence, cognitive presence, and social presence in online lessons. *International Journal of TESOL Studies*, 3(1), 134–161.

Wang, Y., Stein, D., & Shen, S. (2021). Students' and teachers' perceived teaching presence in online courses. *Distance Education*, 42(3), 373–390. DOI: 10.1080/01587919.2021.1956304

Waytz, A. (2019). *The power of human.* W.W. Norton & Co.

Wood, A., Symons, K., Falisse, J. B., Gray, H., & Mkony, A. (2021). Can lecture capture contribute to the development of a Community of Inquiry in online learning? *Distance Education*, 42(1), 126–144. DOI: 10.1080/01587919.2020.1869521

KEY TERMS AND DEFINITIONS

Active Listening: The skill of fully concentrating, understanding, and responding to what the student is saying, crucial for establishing a supportive and communicative learning environment (McKay et al., 2009).

Asynchronous Video Exchanges: A method where students and faculty communicate through recorded video messages, allowing for a more personal and interactive exchange of ideas and feedback (Streit et al., 2022).

Cognitive Presence: The engagement of students in deep thinking and problem-solving, facilitated by instructors through activities that provoke curiosity and critical reflection (Garrison et al., 2003).

Cultural Competency: The ability of faculty to interact effectively with students from diverse cultural backgrounds is essential for creating an inclusive and supportive online learning environment (Chu et al., 2024).

Effort Heuristic: A psychological principle where visible effort is perceived as more significant or valuable, which can affect students' perceptions of feedback (Kruger et al., 2004).

Emotional Responses: Faculty's ability to manage and convey their emotions effectively during synchronous and asynchronous interactions, impacting the quality of communication and presence (Faucett et al., 2017).

Facilitated Discourse: The act of promoting meaningful discussions and interactions between students and faculty, which is vital for establishing teaching presence and enhancing learning (Wang et al., 2021).

Faculty Presence: The sense of an instructor's engagement and involvement in an online course, which is crucial for creating a supportive learning environment (Bialowas & Steimel, 2019; Collins et al., 2019).

Humanized Communication: Interaction methods that incorporate personal elements, such as facial expressions and tone of voice, to enhance the richness and relatability of communication (Waytz, 2019).

Integration of Feedback: The process of connecting feedback to course objectives and real-world applications, which helps students understand the relevance and improve their learning (Banerjee et al., 2020).

Multimodal Feedback: The use of different types of feedback, such as video and written comments, to provide a more comprehensive and detailed response to students (Martin, 2020).

Personal Connection: The establishment of a rapport between faculty and students through personalized communication, which enhances engagement and reduces anxiety (Borup et al., 2014).

Social Presence: The ability to create an environment where students feel safe to express themselves and engage in open communication, which helps build trust and a sense of community (Garrison et al., 2003).

Student Self-Beliefs: The attitudes and perceptions students hold about their own abilities and learning (Streit et al., 2022).

Teaching Presence: The role of the instructor in guiding and facilitating learning through clear communication of course content, structure, and feedback, which impacts students' learning outcomes (Garrison et al., 2003).

Transactional Distance: The psychological and communication gap between students and instructors in an online learning environment, which can lead to feelings of disengagement and isolation (Moore, 2013).

Triggering Event: An activity or prompt used to stimulate students' thinking and curiosity about a topic, which is an essential part of fostering cognitive presence (Banerjee et al., 2020).

Chapter 17
Strategies and Practices for Instructors in Online Open Elective Courses:
Teacher Lessons

Patcha Bhujanga Rao
https://orcid.org/0000-0003-4736-8497
Jain University, India

B. G. Guruprasad
https://orcid.org/0000-0002-6533-1068
Surana Evening College, India

V. S. Vainik
https://orcid.org/0000-0001-6203-1513
Jain University, India

D. Deepak
Jain University, India

Usha Prabhu
https://orcid.org/0000-0001-6219-5358
Jain University, India

ABSTRACT

The importance of online open elective courses (OOECs) in contemporary education is examined in this study, along with the difficulties teachers have when instructing them. Despite the advantages of OOECs—accessibility, flexibility, range of subjects, and individualized learning—teachers still have challenges in maintaining student

DOI: 10.4018/979-8-3693-4407-1.ch017

engagement, supervising big classes, guaranteeing high-quality assessment systems, overcoming technological problems, and encouraging diversity. This study's primary focus is on the tactics and best practices that educators can use to overcome these obstacles and increase OOEC effectiveness. This work is important because it has the potential to improve the caliber of online education. It responds to the growing need for online education, provides teachers with the resources and information they require to improve student learning outcomes, trains them in research-based techniques, and works in tandem with

INTRODUCTION

In contemporary times, online open elective courses have become a game changer in our ever changing educational landscape by driving the way students learn and grow academically. These courses, which give room for students to delve into topics outside their main area of study, are very important in ensuring customized education is embraced and lifelong learning is promoted. In addition to expanding educational opportunities, online open elective courses have also been instrumental in democratising education globally by offering a variety of theme options and eliminating geographical limitations as well as time table constraints.

The importance of these programs lies in the fact that they can cater for different learner preferences and needs. Flexible and accessible online study spaces are increasingly becoming more evident with advances in educational technology. Recent research shows that the need for individualized educational experiences that suit their busy lifestyles perfectly aligns with modern learners' desire to learn anytime from anywhere (Hollis et al., 2022; Kim & Lee, 2023).

Additionally, the diverse range of open elective courses offered through online platforms provides a variety of learning opportunities to meet different interests and academic objectives. This variety serves as a source of enhancement for education perspectives of students and also promotes a culture that is exploratory and intellectually curious. In light of recent studies, allowing students freedom to choose electives based on their personal interests can lead to increased involvement and contentment with their learning (Bawa, 2023; Parker et al., 2021).

However, there are some difficulties experienced by instructors in providing good online open elective courses. There are several obstacles educators must overcome when it comes to sustaining high levels of student engagement across diverse populations while dealing with large scale cohorts as well as quality assessment and feedback. Solving these problems require out-of-box strategies and best practices that are responsive to specific demands posed by online teaching (Cruz et al., 2023; Zhou et al., 2023).

This chapter will show why it is important for instructors to understand and tackle these challenges so as to maximize the efficiency of their online open elective courses. Using recent studies' findings plus evidence from empirical researches, this paper intends to provide practical suggestions and ideas which would help teachers improve on their e-learning techniques. The goal is to empower instructors with the tools and strategies needed to create impactful and meaningful learning experiences in the digital age.

OVERVIEW OF THE IMPORTANCE OF ONLINE OPEN ELECTIVE COURSES IN MODERN EDUCATION

Online open elective courses have become an integral part of modern education, bringing numerous advantages that resonate with the changing needs of students and academic institutions. The current studies have stressed their importance in different aspects:

Accessibility and Flexibility: Online open elective courses eliminate conventional obstacles like geographical location or scheduling conflicts. This makes it possible for students to manage other commitments while pursuing their education and learn from anywhere. Recent investigations show that online learning has contributed greatly to increasing accessibility to education, especially for nontraditional students and those from underserved areas (Hollis et al., 2022; Hachey et al., 2021).

Diversity of Learning Opportunities: Through various subjects provided by online open elective courses, one can investigate interests outside the core curriculum. It is more individualized thus helps one gain knowledge in areas complementary to his/her major field of study. There is evidence suggesting that such variety enhances student academic engagement and satisfaction (Bawa, 2023; Thompson et al., 2022).

Transforming the personal learning experience: With adaptive technologies, self-paced modules, and customized feedback, online platforms make learning personalized. This individualization enables students to become the managers of their own learning process, hence attaining their academic objectives. According to Zhou et al., (2023) and Liao & Chang (2022), recent studies have shown that personalized learning strategies can be very helpful in improving student outcomes and engagement.

Enhancing Engagement and Collaboration: Interactive educational tools as well as multimedia resources can encourage dynamic or interesting lessons. These methods allow students to work together on projects thereby creating a better understanding of course materials in new ways. These interactive elements foster motivation among learners; hence they are critical for maintaining student involvement with education according to the recent studies by Cruz et al., (2023) and Parker et al., (2021).

Global Connections and Knowledge Sharing: Online open elective courses offer global educational opportunities for cross-cultural exchange and wider horizons for students. Moreover, this mode of study prepares individuals for a world that is more diverse than ever before. This paper will discuss global accessibility via online courses along with intercultural understanding as depicted by Kim & Lee, 2023; Martin et al., 2022.

LITERATURE REVIEW

A notable surge in the number of digital learning environments has occurred within the realm of online education leading to its rapid growth and transformation. As educational institutions grow, more online elective courses are offered. Therefore, it is imperative to know how best practices and strategies that guarantee effective instruction in these environments. This literature review examines recent studies on best practices in online education with a focus on elective courses. It also considers how different teaching strategies have influenced the development of online pedagogies.

Evolution of Online Instructional techniques

Technology advancements and better understanding of e-learning have greatly influenced how online teaching is done. At first, internet education relied on traditional methods that were very similar to face-to-face classrooms, such as video lectures and simple quizzes. These methods were effective but frequently did not make the best use of the different features provided by the online platforms (Bozkurt et al., 2020).

In recent years, there has been a trend towards using interactive and student-centered instructional strategies grounded in constructivist learning theory. This strategy emphasizes the importance of students actively engaging with information, peers, and instructors in the process of knowledge creation (Kang & Im, 2020). An illustration to this trend is employment of adaptive learning technologies that tailor educational content according to individual student's needs. These technologies serve dual purpose; they facilitate student engagement while at the same time addressing specific difficulties faced by learners in an online context (Siemens & Baker, 2022).

Revolutionizing online teaching methods including implementing adaptive learning platforms characterize collaborative learning. Students can use these platforms to communicate with each other, partner in projects and create a sense of community among themselves as a way of enhancing belongingness and active participation in the online environment (Hrastinski, 2021). The use of game design elements to enhance learning known as gamification has grown increasingly popular providing an immersive and engaging learning experience (Deterding et al., 2021).

Optimal Strategies for Online Education

Considerable research has been devoted towards identifying effective techniques that can be employed for online education especially in elective courses where students' levels of motivation or interest may vary considerably. One of the most important recommendations was fostering camaraderie amongst students. Studies have shown that facilitating interaction and collaboration through discussion forums, group activities and synchronous virtual meetings are necessary for sustaining student engagement and creating deeper understanding of course materials (Hrastinski, 2019).

Moreover, it is impossible to overstate the importance of formative assessments. These evaluations are a set of assessments that include quizzes, peer reviews as well as self-assessment tools which continuously provide learners with feedback that helps them sustain their progress and gradually improve their performance (Gikandi et al., 2022). Additionally, research has found out that by employing formative assessment techniques in online courses, such as elective courses for any major open to students from various backgrounds and interests, the grades of students and satisfaction can be increased (Nicol & Macfarlane-Dick, 2020).

Making sure accessibility is implemented while practicing the best strategies in e-learning is important. To make course materials and activities accessible to all students including disabled ones goes beyond fulfilling legal obligations; it also promotes inclusivity and fairness within the institution (Burgstahler, 2020). Other strategies involve using captions on videos, providing alternative text for images; ensuring compatibility of digital content with screen readers or other assistive technology. Incorporating universal design principles into course content helps foster an inclusive learning environment accommodating diverse learning needs (Meyer et al., 2014).

Successful Approaches to Teaching Online Elective Classes

The teaching of online elective courses presents distinct challenges and opportunities for instructors. An efficient method involves the use of integrative approaches that connect elective course content with wider themes and issues. When a course connects subject matter to current events or societal concerns, it can be more applicable and interesting for students (Chen et al., 2023). Apart from boosting learning experiences, this method also allows students to see practical applications in what they are being taught, thereby increasing their motivation levels.

Online elective courses have demonstrated profound success when using Project Based Learning (PBL). Problem based learning (PBL) is one way through which students should utilize their knowledge in solving problems that affects them in real life situations thus enhancing their conceptualization on the topic area as well as developing critical thinking skills and problem solving abilities (Capraro et al., 2020). On the internet, this can be facilitated through PBL with collaborative tools where by students are able to collaborate even if they are physically apart.

Besides, instructors are encouraged to use flexible instructional strategies that can adapt to different learning preferences and schedules of online elective course students (Johnson et al., 2020). Some of the things that could be done include; provision of asynchronous material that allows students to take the lessons at their own pace together with various ways of delivering content like movies, texts and interactive simulations which addresses each student's needs hence improving their overall experience in learning.

Problems with Enforcing Best Practices

Though these well-known approaches have several benefits, there are problems in applying them appropriately to internet elective courses. One of the biggest obstacles is called digital divide, which refers to inequality between individuals who have access to computers and reliable Internet services, and those who don't (Reich et al., 2021). This disparity has a huge effect on the involvement and academic success rates in online instruction, thus necessitating instructors as well as institutions alike to tackle it head-on. Among possible solutions would be promoting access by providing essential technologies needed for participation when offline or preparing curriculum that accommodates learners with varying levels of network connectivity.

Another barrier is the need for continuous professional development among teachers. For instructors to effectively teach online courses, they must be conversant with the newest best practices and tools in line with progression of online teaching techniques and technologies (Veletsianos & Houlden 2020). Institutions should offer comprehensive training and ample resources that can help tutors acquire relevant capabilities required to ensure successful implementation of the practices. Additionally, cultivating a culture of continuous improvement so that teachers continuously consider and enhance their pedagogical approaches may address issues associated with online instruction (Palloff & Pratt, 2011).

It can be difficult to achieve student engagement in elective courses offered online especially when students have no strong inherent interest in the subject area. By considering such tactics as integration of practical applications, giving choices in tasks, and employing interactive materials among others will most likely sustain students' motivation throughout the course life span (Muir et al., 2021).

RESEARCH GAP

The literature underscores the significance of student engagement and formative assessments. However, there is limited research regarding the effectiveness of personalized learning experiences especially highly personalised ones in a case of online elective courses that use adaptive learning technologies where content and assessments are personalized to suit each student's uniqueness.

Although more studies have been done on effective approaches for online learning in elective courses, particularly, there are areas that have not been explored. The literature provides evidence for the effectiveness of integrative approaches that link course content to broader themes. Nonetheless, there are not many longitudinal studies available that assess the lasting effects of such methods on learners' outcomes and retention in elective courses. Despite the well-documented importance of accessibility in online education, a lack of research exists on the challenges instructors face when using universal design principles in diverse online elective courses. Moreover, more empirical research is needed to test out different mechanisms for making content accessible to all learners including those with impairments. The digital divide still poses a huge impediment to online education; however, little has been done by institutions in order to address this challenge effectively through elective course units especially in regions having limited technological infrastructure. While there is need for continuous professional development, further studies are necessary to look into the specific professional development models and their efficacy towards equipping instructors with required skills that will enable them successfully implement best practices in elective online courses.

PROBLEM STATEMENT

Online education has its benefits especially in elective courses but still, there are significant challenges to engaging students, promoting diversity and ensuring personalized learning. Our research identifies the best strategies and techniques that can be employed by online educators in their teaching methods. However, more needs to be done in terms of understanding the long-term effects of integrative pedagogical techniques and the effectiveness of universal design for learning principles as well as addressing the digital divide among heterogeneous student populations. In addition, persistent need for specialized professional development for teachers raises concerns about scaling up and maintaining quality online education in elective courses. To close these gaps, this paper examines innovative ways to bolster learner engagement, encourage accessibility as well as improve instructional delivery mechanisms within elective online courses.

METHODOLOGICAL INQUIRY

This study employs a variety of mixed-methods research techniques. It is a combination of quantitative and qualitative methods that are used to fully understand the strategies and practices that tutors employ in elective online courses. For an all-round view, the study was divided into two sections: The first phase involved gathering data qualitatively through interviews, document analysis, and thematic exploration of instructor experiences whereas the second phase prioritized collection of quantitative data through surveys and learning analytics. This is a two-step approach which helps examine teacher experiences as well as how different teaching techniques affect course effectiveness. It involves a close-knit personal perspective along with verifiable factual information.

CHOICE OF SAMPLES

The study targets educators who teach online elective courses at different higher learning institutions. To get a wide range of representation, the sampling technique will be purposefully used to select about 125 lecturers with substantial knowledge in this area. As such, this method ensures that the sample is knowledgeable and experienced in teaching in an online environment and the difficulties faced. For the purposes of carrying out the quantitative phase, a well-structured questionnaire will be given to these instructors that would allow for collecting various views on teaching approaches. Therefore, the study is meant to explore how teachers teach without regarding thoughts from students thus focusing entirely on those trainers.

Collecting Data

Gathering data is divided into two steps. The first step involves collecting qualitative data such as semi-structured interviews from a specific group of teachers, which will explore their teaching experiences, strategies and challenges faced by them. These interviews will be woven into the context of course syllabi, effective practices identified through document analysis of teaching materials and recurring trends. Second phase will involve obtaining quantifiable data by using structured questionnaires on the same instructors being interviewed. This study will employ Likert-scale questions for measuring impressions concerning instructional efficacy in general, accessibility as well as the influence of different tactics on the process of learning in some respect or another. Moreover, while looking at learning analytics drawn from Learning Management Systems (LMS), unbiased metrics about teaching outcomes and instructor performance may be obtained.

Analysis of Data

The analysis of data will be done in two stages, qualitative part and quantitative part. For the first stage, thematic analysis will be used to classify and interpret qualitative data from interviews and document reviews. In doing so, the study will identify significant themes related to teaching strategies, barriers as well as possible ways forward. Consequently, content analysis will systematically categorize educational resources so as to measure their effectiveness. After that, descriptive statistics would be conducted on the survey data; thereby providing a succinct overview of key findings. Moreover, inferential statistics would be applied for investigating interrelationship between various variables. Thus, learning analytics can identify patterns or relationships in methods of instruction and outcomes that provide an entire picture of how successful this training is.

Methodological Constraints

Several limitations are recognized by this research's methodology. There may be biases that are created by purposively sampling instructors as the selected sample may not be a true representation of all online elective course instructors. In addition, there is the problem of self-reporting bias when participants tend to produce socially desirable results in surveys and interviews. Technological limitations may hinder participation, especially in regions with restricted internet connectivity. Also, time limits can significantly hamper r Data analysis

Ethical Considerations

To ensure the safety of participants and the accuracy of data, this study will fully comply with stringent ethical standards. All teachers involved will be required to give informed consent which implies their complete understanding of why this research is being conducted and the role each one has in it. In order not to disclose any information, all data will be anonymized so that no single person knows whose data was used for analysis. By encrypting digital information and storing hard copies securely, we guarantee the inviolability of our records. It should be noted that participation will be voluntary thus offering students an opportunity to withdraw without penalty at any particular time. These precautions protect the privacy of respondents and secure an ethically sound investigation.

OBJECTIVES

1. The aim of this study is to investigate the online elective instructors' efficient teaching methods.
2. This research aims to identify the challenges that face educators while they are teaching in online elective courses and also know what strategies they use to overcome them.
3. The objective of this research is to assess how different teaching techniques affect the perceived effectiveness of online elective classes.
4. The purpose is examining technology's impact on helping teachers strategize their approach towards online electives.
5. The main aim of this paper is therefore, to come up with recommendations for improving teaching methodologies used in online electives based on input from instructors.

HYPOTHESIS

1. H1: Instructors that employ diverse teaching tactics have more efficacy in online elective courses.
2. H2: Educators face significant challenges in terms of technology and accessibility which influence their ability to teach effectively.
3. H3: Creative teaching methods are positively associated with instructors' perception of student engagement in online elective courses.
4. H4: Teachers who frequently alter their instructional approaches based on feedback experience increased course effectiveness.
5. H5: For teachers, the effective integration of technology into electronic education is closely related with teacher's own evaluation of their classroom performance and the entire success of a class.

EMPIRICAL ANALYSIS

Demographic Characteristics of the Study Respondents

The table below presents a comprehensive overview of the demographic characteristics of the study respondents. The data includes information on age group, gender, years of experience, academic discipline, and institution type. This demographic analysis provides valuable insights into the diversity of the sample, which consists of 125 participants. The distribution of respondents across various categories offers a foundational understanding of the sample's composition, which is essential for interpreting the study's findings.

Table 1. Demographic Characteristics of the Study Respondents

Demographic Factor	Category	Frequency	Percent
Age Group	18-24	40	32.00%
	25-34	35	28.00%
	35-44	25	20.00%
	45-54	15	12.00%
	55 and above	10	8.00%
Gender	Male	61	48.80%
	Female	64	51.20%
Experience (Years)	Less than 1 year	3	2.40%
	2-3 years	3	2.40%
	4-6 years	6	4.80%
	7-10 years	26	20.80%
	More than 10 years	87	69.60%
Academic Discipline	Humanities	30	24.00%
	Business	35	28.00%
	Sciences	20	16.00%
	Engineering/Tech	25	20.00%
	Social Sciences	15	12.00%
Institution Type	Public University	60	48.00%
	Private University	65	52.00%
Total		125	100.00%

Demographics Analysis

The demographic data presents insights into the attributes of the 125 teachers involved in the study. The bulk of instructors, comprising 80%, are aged between 18 and 44, reflecting a combination of youthful and seasoned educators. The gender distribution is quite equitable, with a little higher proportion of female professors (51.20%). A substantial percentage of educators possess over ten years of experience (69.60%), indicating a considerable depth of teaching competence. The represented academic disciplines are varied, with humanities and business being the most prevalent. The research encompasses educators from public (48%) and private universities (52%), offering a thorough insight into online teaching methodologies across varied institutional settings. This demographic information is essential for comprehending the distinct viewpoints and experiences of the instructors participating in the research and for contextualising the findings within their varied backgrounds.

INTERPRETATION OF HYPOTHESIS

Hypothesis H1: Instructors that employ diverse teaching tactics have more efficacy in online elective courses.

Table 2. Model Summary

Model	R	R Square	Adjusted R Square	Std. Error of the Estimate
1	.609[a]	0.371	0.351	1.98307

a. **Predictors:** (Constant), DTT, SE, TI, FA

The correlation coefficient of 0.609 suggests a moderate positive correlation between the independent variables, Diverse Teaching Tactics (DTT), Technology Integration (TE), Feedback Adaptation (FA), Student Engagement(SE) and the dependent variable (Teaching Effectiveness). The R^2 value of 0.371 indicates that around 37.1% of the variance in Teaching Effectiveness (TE) can be attributed to the independent variables. The adjusted R^2 value is 0.351, which takes into account the number of predictors in the model. This suggests a more conservative estimate, with 35.1% of the variance explained. The standard error of the estimate, which is 1.98307, gives us an idea of the standard deviation of the residuals.

Table 3. ANOVA[a]

Model		Sum of Squares	df	Mean Square	F	Sig.
1	Regression	278.894	4	69.724	17.730	.000[b]
	Residual	471.906	120	3.933		
	Total	750.800	124			

a. **Dependent Variable:** TE
b. **Predictors:** (Constant), DTT, SE, TI, FA

The F-statistic of 17.730, with a significance level of 0.000, demonstrates that the regression model is highly significant. This suggests that the independent variables effectively predict Teaching Effectiveness (TE). The p-value of less than 0.05 confirms the overall significance of the model.

Table 4. Coefficients[a]

Model		Unstandardized Coefficients		Standardized Coefficients	t	Sig.
		B	Std. Error	Beta		
1	(Constant)	9.503	6.461		1.471	0.144
	SE	0.201	0.025	0.888	8.026	0.000
	TI	0.223	0.101	0.222	2.206	0.029
	FA	-0.302	0.044	-0.926	-6.872	0.000
	DTT	0.320	0.234	0.107	1.369	0.173

a. **Dependent Variable:** TE

The coefficient for Diverse Teaching Tactics (DTT) is 0.320, and the p-value is 0.173. At the 0.05 level, it can be concluded that DTT does not have a significant impact on Teaching Effectiveness (TE).

The coefficient for technology integration is 0.223, with a p-value of 0.029. It is evident that Technology Integration (TI) plays a crucial role in predicting Teaching Effectiveness (TE) and has a positive influence on it. The coefficient for feedback adaptation is -0.302, with a p-value of 0.000. There is a clear and important negative correlation with Teaching Effectiveness (TE). The coefficient for student engagement is 0.201, with a p-value of 0.000. This demonstrates a robust and noteworthy correlation with Teaching Effectiveness (TE).

In summary the ANOVA results indicate the significance of the overall model.

Technology integration and student engagement have been found to have a positive impact on teaching effectiveness, while feedback adaptation has been found to have a negative impact.

Thus, the hypothesis H1 is only partially supported, as the analysis did not find statistically significant evidence for the effectiveness of diverse teaching tactics (DTT). Additionally, teaching effectiveness is influenced by various factors such as technology integration and student engagement.

Hypothesis H2: Educators face significant challenges in terms of technology and accessibility, which influence their ability to teach effectively.

Table 5. Model Summary

Model	R	R Square	Adjusted R Square	Std. Error of the Estimate
1	.711[a]	0.505	0.489	1.75276

a. Predictors: (Constant), TE, DTT, FA, SE

The correlation coefficient of 0.711 suggests a strong positive relationship between the predictor variables Student Engagement (SE), Diverse Teaching Tactics (DTT), Teaching Effectiveness (TE), Feedback Adaptation (FA) and the dependent variable Technology Integration (TI). The R Square value of 0.505 indicates that approximately 50.5% of the variance in Technology Integration (TI) can be attributed to the predictors used in the model. This indicates that the model possesses a moderate level of explanatory capability. The adjusted R Square value 0.489 takes into account the number of predictors and offers a more precise measure of the model's explanatory power, suggesting that the model is quite good but has room for improvement. The standard error of the estimate is 1.75276. It indicates the average difference between the observed values and the values predicted by the model. A higher value indicates a poorer fit of the model to the data.

Table 6. ANOVA[a]

Model		Sum of Squares	df	Mean Square	F	Sig.
1	Regression	376.139	4	94.035	30.609	.000[b]
	Residual	368.661	120	3.072		
	Total	744.800	124			

a. Dependent Variable: TI
b. Predictors: (Constant), TE, DTT, FA, SE

The F-value of 30.609 is used to determine the overall significance of the regression model. If the F-value is high and the p-value is less than 0.05, it indicates that the model is a strong match for the data. The p-value of 0.000 suggests that the regression model is highly statistically significant, as it is lower than the commonly accepted threshold of 0.05. The predictors have a significant impact on Technology Integration (TI).

Table 7. Coefficients[a]

Model		Unstandardized Coefficients		Standardized Coefficients	t	Sig.
		B	Std. Error	Beta		
1	(Constant)	27.044	5.206		5.195	0.000
	SE	-0.073	0.027	-0.326	-2.759	0.007
	FA	0.284	0.038	0.872	7.487	0.000
	DTT	-0.594	0.201	-0.199	-2.950	0.004
	TE	0.175	0.079	0.175	2.206	0.029

a. Dependent Variable: TI

The value remains constant at 27.044 degrees. This value represents the intercept of the regression equation. This value represents the predicted outcome of Technology Integration (TI) when all other variables are held constant at zero. -0.594 There is a negative coefficient that suggests a correlation between a decrease in Technology Integration (TI) and an increase in Diverse Teaching Tactics (DTT). The standardised beta coefficient demonstrates the strength of the inverse relationship. The significance level of 0.004 suggests that Diverse Teaching Tactics (DTT) has a significant impact on Technology Integration (TI). A coefficient of 0.175 suggests that an improvement in Teaching Effectiveness is linked to an increase in Technology Integration. The standardised Beta coefficient illustrates the strength of the positive correlation. The significance level (Sig.) is 0.029. The p-value is less than 0.05, suggesting that Teaching Effectiveness (TE) significantly impacts Technology Integration (TI). FA 0.284 shows a positive correlation between an increase in Feedback Adaptation (FA) and an increase in Technology Integration (TI).

The standardised Beta coefficient suggests a significant positive correlation. The p-value of 0.000 suggests that Feedback Adaptation (FA) strongly impacts Technology Integration (TI). Decreased technology integration has been found to be associated with increased student engagement, as suggested by the negative coefficient. The standardised Beta coefficient illustrates the strength of the negative correlation. The significance level is 0.007. The p-value is less than 0.05, which suggests a significant impact of Student Engagement on Technology Integration.

Hypothesis H3: Educators face significant challenges in terms of technology and accessibility which influence their ability to teach effectively.

Table 8. Model Summary

Model	R	R Square	Adjusted R Square	Std. Error of the Estimate
1	.890a	0.793	0.786	3.48678

a. Predictors: (Constant), TI, TE, DTT, SE

The correlation coefficient of 0.890 suggests a robust positive association between the predictors, Technology Integration (TI), Teaching Effectiveness (TE), Diverse Teaching Tactics (DTT), SE) and the dependent variable Feedback Adaptation (FA). The R Square value of 0.793 indicates that a significant portion, specifically 79.3%, of the variance in Feedback Adaptation (FA) can be attributed to the predictors included in the model. The adjusted R Square value of 0.786 takes into account the number of predictors and sample size, indicating a slightly lower but still significant level of explanatory power. The standard error of the estimate, 3.48678, represents the average difference between the observed values and the predicted values of Feedback Adaptation (FA).

Table 9. ANOVA^a

Model		Sum of Squares	df	Mean Square	F	Sig.
1	Regression	5581.536	4	1395.384	114.775	.000^b
	Residual	1458.912	120	12.158		
	Total	7040.448	124			

a. Dependent Variable: FA
b. Predictors: (Constant), TI, TE, DTT, SE

The model's F-value of 114.775 with a significance value of 0.000 demonstrates its statistical significance, indicating that the predictors collectively have a substantial impact on Feedback Adaptation (FA).

Table 10. Coefficients^a

Model		Unstandardized Coefficients		Standardized Coefficients	t	Sig.
		B	Std. Error	Beta		
1	(Constant)	1.695	11.461		0.148	0.883
	SE	0.472	0.033	0.682	14.115	0.000
	DTT	0.086	0.414	0.009	0.207	0.837
	TE	-0.934	0.136	-0.305	-6.872	0.000
	TI	1.123	0.150	0.365	7.487	0.000

a. Dependent Variable: FA

The intercept does not have a statistically significant impact on Feedback Adaptation (FA) when all predictors are at zero (p = 0.883). The coefficient of 0.086 is not statistically significant (p = 0.837), indicating that diverse teaching tactics have no significant impact on Feedback Adaptation (FA). The coefficient of -0.934 is statistically significant (p = 0.000) and negative, suggesting that there is a correlation between higher teaching effectiveness and lower feedback adaptation. The coefficient of 0.472 is statistically significant (p = 0.000) and indicates a positive relationship between student engagement and feedback adaptation. The coefficient of 1.123 is statistically significant (p = 0.000) and shows a positive relationship, suggesting that improved technology integration is linked to increased feedback adaptation.

Hypothesis H4: Teaching Influence significantly impacts the effectiveness of educators, as measured by DTT (Dependent Variable).

Table 11. Model Summary

Model	R	R Square	Adjusted R Square	Std. Error of the Estimate
1	.392[a]	0.154	0.126	0.76801

a. Predictors: (Constant), FA, TE, TI, SE

The regression model shows a moderate level of predictive power, with an R-square value of 0.154. According to the analysis, around 15.4% of the variation in the dependent variable, DTT, can be attributed to the combined impact of the predictors: Teaching Experience, Student Engagement, Teaching Influence, and Faculty Attitude. The Adjusted R Square value of 0.126 reflects the influence of the predictors in the model, indicating a comparable level of explained variance after accounting for the number of predictors.

Table 12. ANOVA[a]

Model		Sum of Squares	df	Mean Square	F	Sig.
1	Regression	12.868	4	3.217	5.454	.000[b]
	Residual	70.780	120	0.590		
	Total	83.648	124			

a. Dependent Variable: DTT
b. Predictors: (Constant), FA, TE, TI, SE

The ANOVA results indicate that the overall regression model shows statistical significance (F = 5.454, p < 0.001). It can be inferred that the predictors as a whole have a strong correlation with DTT. Nevertheless, it is crucial to analyse the unique contributions of each predictor in order to comprehend their specific effects.

Table 13. Coefficients[a]

Model		Unstandardized Coefficients		Standardized Coefficients	t	Sig.
		B	Std. Error	Beta		
1	(Constant)	25.925	0.879		29.480	0.000
	TE	0.048	0.035	0.144	1.369	0.173
	SE	-0.008	0.012	-0.111	-0.700	0.485
	TI	-0.114	0.039	-0.340	-2.950	0.004
	FA	0.004	0.020	0.038	0.207	0.837

a. Dependent Variable: DTT

The coefficient for Teaching Influence (TI) is -0.114 (p = 0.004), indicating statistical significance. There is an inverse relationship between Teaching Influence and DTT, meaning that as Teaching Influence increases, DTT tends to decrease. This finding emphasises the significance of Teaching Influence in shaping DTT and indicates that interventions focused on this factor could successfully alter DTT outcomes. The coefficient for teaching experience is 0.048 (p = 0.173), indicating that it is not statistically significant. Teaching experience does not seem to have a significant influence on DTT in this model, and its impact may vary or be inconsistent in different situations. The coefficient for student engagement is -0.008 (p = 0.485), which is also not statistically significant. Based on the findings, it appears that Student Engagement does not play a significant role in explaining variations in DTT. Its impact in the model is minimal. The coefficient for faculty attitude (FA) is 0.004 (p = 0.837), indicating that it is not statistically significant. It appears that the attitude of faculty members does not play a major role in determining DTT. This implies that there may be other factors that have a greater influence on DTT.

Hypothesis H5: There is a significant positive relationship between Teaching Experience (TE) and Student Engagement (SE).

Table 14. Model Summary

Model	R	R Square	Adjusted R Square	Std. Error of the Estimate
1	.850[a]	0.722	0.712	5.83399

a. Predictors: (Constant), FA, TE, DTT, TI

The regression model demonstrates a strong level of explanatory power, as evidenced by the R-square value of 0.722. This suggests that around 72.2% of the variation in the dependent variable, Student Engagement (SE), can be attributed to the collective impact of the independent variables: Faculty Attitude (FA), Teaching Experience (TE), DTT, and Teaching Influence (TI). The Adjusted R Square value of 0.712 indicates that the model remains strong even after accounting for the number of predictors. This confirms that the predictors play a significant role in explaining the variance in SE.

Table 15. ANOVA[a]

Model		Sum of Squares	df	Mean Square	F	Sig.
1	Regression	10590.263	4	2647.566	77.789	.000[b]
	Residual	4084.249	120	34.035		
	Total	14674.512	124			

a. **Dependent Variable:** SE
b. **Predictors:** (Constant), FA, TE, DTT, TI

The ANOVA results reveal that the overall regression model demonstrates a significant statistical impact (F = 77.789, p < 0.001). The significance level of this analysis indicates that the combination of independent variables has a significant influence on Student Engagement (SE). The model's high F-value reinforces the robust predictive capability of the chosen predictors.

Table 16. Coefficients[a]

Model		Unstandardized Coefficients		Standardized Coefficients	t	Sig.
		B	Std. Error	Beta		
1	(Constant)	-12.606	19.144		-0.659	0.511
	DTT	-0.484	0.692	-0.037	-0.700	0.485
	TE	1.739	0.217	0.393	8.026	0.000
	TI	-0.813	0.295	-0.183	-2.759	0.007
	FA	1.322	0.094	0.916	14.115	0.000

a. **Dependent Variable:** SE

The constant in this model does not have statistical significance (B = -12.606, p = 0.511). This suggests that the baseline level of SE is not meaningful or interpretable in this context when all independent variables are set to zero. The coefficient for DTT is -0.484 (p = 0.485), indicating that it is not statistically significant. Based on the model, it appears that DTT does not have a substantial impact on Student Engagement (SE). The coefficient with a negative value, although not statistically significant, suggests a possible inverse relationship. However, this relationship does not have a meaningful impact on the prediction of SE. The coefficient for teaching experience is 1.739 (p < 0.001), indicating its statistical significance. There is a clear correlation between Teaching Experience and Student Engagement, suggesting that as teachers gain more experience, student engagement tends to improve. The beta coefficient of 0.393 indicates a significant impact, indicating that Teaching Experience plays a crucial role in determining Student Engagement in this model. The coefficient for Teaching Influence (TI) is -0.813 (p = 0.007), indicating statistical significance. There is a clear indication that when Teaching Influence levels are higher, Student Engagement scores tend to be lower. It is important to address certain aspects of Teaching Influence that may have a negative impact on Student Engagement, as this is a crucial area that requires intervention. The coefficient for faculty attitude is 1.322 (p < 0.001), indicating a statistically significant and highly positive relationship. Based on the standardised beta of 0.916, it is evident that Faculty Attitude holds the greatest sway over Student Engagement compared to other factors. This discovery highlights the importance of positive faculty attitudes in boosting student engagement implementing strategies to enhance faculty attitudes can greatly benefit overall student engagement.

FINDINGS

The study findings highlight the importance of technology integration and student engagement in enhancing teaching effectiveness. While feedback adaptation is found to have a negative impact on teaching effectiveness, it is influenced by the use of diverse teaching tactics and the level of student engagement. Although teaching experience significantly influences student engagement, the impact of various teaching strategies and technology integration on student engagement is less pronounced. These findings suggest that a balance between authority and flexibility in teaching methods is crucial, and effective feedback processes require active student participation and seamless technology use. Overall, the study provides valuable insights into the dynamics of teaching effectiveness and the factors that contribute to it.

IMPEDIMENTS OF THE STUDY

The study identifies several impediments to teaching effectiveness, including the disconnect between feedback mechanisms and teaching goals, the limited impact of diverse teaching tactics, challenges in integrating technology into diverse teaching environments, the negative influence of teacher control on the use of varied teaching approaches, and the impact of technology and accessibility on feedback adaptation. Additionally, the study highlights the potential drawbacks of student engagement on technology integration, emphasizing the need for careful alignment between student engagement strategies and the use of technology. These findings suggest that addressing these challenges is crucial for improving teaching effectiveness and optimizing the use of technology in educational settings.

CONCLUSION

This study offers valuable insights into the impact of different factors on teaching effectiveness, technology integration, and student engagement. It is evident that incorporating technology and promoting student engagement greatly improves teaching effectiveness. However, it seems that adjusting feedback, although necessary, may have a negative impact on teaching outcomes. Various teaching methods did not demonstrate a substantial influence on teaching efficacy, indicating that other factors may hold greater importance. The study emphasises the challenges in technology and accessibility, showcasing how feedback adaptation and teaching effectiveness positively influence technology integration. However, diverse teaching tactics and student engagement have a negative impact on technology integration. In addition, it was discovered that the influence of teaching had a negative impact on the utilisation of various teaching strategies, suggesting a possible requirement for greater adaptability in instructional methods. The significant impact of teaching experience on student engagement highlights the importance of experienced educators in promoting engagement. However, the influence of various teaching strategies and technology integration on engagement was found to be less pronounced. The findings highlight the importance of enhancing feedback mechanisms, maximising technology utilisation, and adopting a more well-rounded approach to teaching methods. Future research should focus on addressing these challenges in order to develop strategies that can significantly improve teaching and learning outcomes.

FUTURE RESEARCH

Future research should focus on various aspects to further improve our comprehension of online teaching and learning. Long-term evaluations are crucial for understanding the impact of different teaching methods on student learning outcomes and engagement. These studies offer valuable insights into the sustainability and effectiveness of various instructional practices. In addition, it is essential to prioritise the exploration of adaptive feedback solutions for large online classes. This involves examining automated feedback tools, peer review systems, and hybrid approaches that combine human and technological support. By examining various disciplines, we can gain valuable insights into how they approach and incorporate best practices in online elective courses. This allows us to better grasp the unique challenges and successful strategies specific to each field. Ultimately, it is crucial to prioritise the viewpoints of students when conducting research on engagement and learning preferences in online courses. Developing a comprehensive understanding of student experiences can be instrumental in customising instructional methods to effectively meet their needs and improve the overall effectiveness of the course.

REFERENCES

Anderson, T., & Shattuck, J. (2012). Design-based research: A decade of progress in education research? *Educational Researcher*, 41(1), 16–25. DOI: 10.3102/0013189X11428813

Baker, R. S., & Siemens, G. (2014). Educational data mining and learning analytics. *Learning Analytics and Knowledge Conference (LAK '14)*, Indianapolis, IN, 4-8 March 2014, ACM.

Baran, E., & Correia, A.-P. (2014). A pedagogical model for online learning: Educators' perspectives on course design. *British Journal of Educational Technology*, 45(5), 792–806.

Bawa, P. (2023). Student engagement and satisfaction in online learning environments: The role of elective courses. *Educational Technology Research and Development*, 71(2), 224–239.

Biggs, J., & Tang, C. (2011). *Teaching for quality learning at university: What the student does* (4th ed.). Open University Press.

Bozkurt, A., Akgün-Özbek, E., & Zawacki-Richter, O. (2020). Trends and patterns in distance education research: A content analysis of journals 2009–2013. *The International Review of Research in Open and Distributed Learning*, 16(1), 330–362.

Burgstahler, S. (2020). *Universal design in higher education: Promising practices*. Harvard Education Press.

Capraro, R. M., Capraro, M. M., & Morgan, J. R. (2020). *STEM project-based learning: An integrated science, technology, engineering, and mathematics (STEM) approach*. Springer.

Chen, B., deNoyelles, A., & Thompson, K. (2023). Fostering relevance in online courses: Connecting content to current events and societal issues. *Journal of Educational Technology & Society*, 26(1), 134–147.

Cruz, J. M., Parker, K. R., & Vyas, D. (2023). Challenges in teaching large-scale online elective courses: Strategies for enhancing student engagement. *International Journal of Educational Technology in Higher Education*, 20(1), 1–20.

Deterding, S., Khaled, R., Nacke, L. E., & Dixon, D. (2021). Gamification: Toward a definition. CHI 2011 Gamification Workshop Proceedings, 12-15.

Garrison, D. R., & Vaughan, N. D. (2008). *Blended learning in higher education: Framework, principles, and guidelines*. Jossey-Bass.

Gikandi, J. W., Morrow, D., & Davis, N. E. (2022). Online formative assessment in higher education: A review of the literature. *Computers & Education*, 57(4), 2333–2351. DOI: 10.1016/j.compedu.2011.06.004

Hachey, A. C., Wladis, C. W., & Conway, K. M. (2021). Do prior online course outcomes provide more information than GPA alone in predicting online course grades? An investigation of students in online undergraduate mathematics courses. *Educational Technology Research and Development*, 59(1), 59–82. PMID: 33469254

Hattie, J. (2009). *Visible learning: A synthesis of over 800 meta-analyses relating to achievement*. Routledge.

Hodges, C., Moore, S., Lockee, B., Trust, T., & Bond, A. (2020, March). The difference between emergency remote teaching and online learning. *EDUCAUSE Review*, 27, https://er.educause.edu/articles/2020/3/the-difference-between-emergency-remote-teaching-and-online-learning

Hollis, A., Kim, S., & Lee, Y. (2022). The impact of online learning environments on student satisfaction and academic performance. *Journal of Computer Assisted Learning*, 38(3), 527–542.

Hrastinski, S. (2019). What do we mean by blended learning? *TechTrends*, 63(5), 564–569. DOI: 10.1007/s11528-019-00375-5

Hrastinski, S. (2021). Student-student online collaboration: A critical review of theoretical approaches. *International Review of Research in Open and Distributed Learning*, 22(2), 19–37.

Jaggars, S. S., & Bailey, T. (2010). *Effectiveness of fully online courses for college students: Response to a Department of Education meta-analysis*. Community College Research Center, Teachers College, Columbia University.

Johnson, L., Adams Becker, S., Cummins, M., Estrada, V., Freeman, A., & Hall, C. (2020). *NMC horizon report: 2020 higher education edition*. The New Media Consortium.

Kang, M., & Im, T. (2020). Blended learning in Korea: Issues and challenges. *The Asia-Pacific Education Researcher*, 19(1), 1–11.

Kim, S., & Lee, Y. (2023). Global access to education through online open elective courses: A review. *The Journal of Educational Research*, 10(4), 345–359.

Liao, Y., & Chang, C. C. (2022). Personalized learning environments and their impact on student engagement. *Journal of Educational Technology Systems*, 50(3), 273–294.

Martin, F., Polly, D., & Ritzhaupt, A. D. (2022). Global trends in online education: Pedagogical strategies for the digital classroom. *The International Review of Research in Open and Distributed Learning*, 23(3), 1–26.

Means, B., Bakia, M., & Murphy, R. (2014). *Learning online: What research tells us about whether, when and how*. Routledge. DOI: 10.4324/9780203095959

Merrill, M. D. (2002). First principles of instruction. *Educational Technology Research and Development*, 50(3), 43–59. DOI: 10.1007/BF02505024

Meyer, A., Rose, D. H., & Gordon, D. (2014). *Universal design for learning: Theory and practice*. CAST Professional Publishing.

Muir, T., Milthorpe, N., Stone, C., Dyment, J., Freeman, E., & Hopwood, B. (2021). Challenging and supporting pre-service teachers in a fully online mathematics education course. Journal of Open. *Flexible and Distance Learning*, 24(1), 4–16.

Nicol, D. J., & Macfarlane-Dick, D. (2020). Formative assessment and self-regulated learning: A model and seven principles of good feedback practice. *Studies in Higher Education*, 31(2), 199–218. DOI: 10.1080/03075070600572090

Palloff, R. M., & Pratt, K. (2011). *The excellent online instructor: Strategies for professional development*. Jossey-Bass.

Parker, K. R., Lenhart, A., & Moore, M. (2021). How students' choice of online elective courses influences engagement and learning outcomes. *Distance Education*, 42(2), 153–170.

Reich, J., Buttimer, C. J., & Murray, J. (2021). The digital divide and the challenges of online learning during the COVID-19 pandemic. *Education Policy Analysis Archives*, 29(110), 1–28.

Salmon, G. (2021). *E-tivities: The key to active online learning* (2nd ed.). Routledge.

Sharma, P., & Hannafin, M. J. (2022). Scaffolding in technology-enhanced learning environments. *Interactive Learning Environments*, 15(1), 27–46. DOI: 10.1080/10494820600996972

Siemens, G. (2005). Connectivism: A learning theory for the digital age. *International Journal of Instructional Technology and Distance Learning*, 2(1), 3–10.

Smith, S. M., & Cardaciotto, L. A. (2011). Is active learning like broccoli? Student perceptions of active learning in large lecture classes. *The Journal of Scholarship of Teaching and Learning*, 11(1), 53–61.

Stone, C., & Springer, M. (2019). Interactivity and collaboration: How professional development changes the way faculty teach. *Journal of Interactive Online Learning*, 17(3), 233–249.

Taber, K. S. (2018). Scaffolding students' learning: Strategies to promote active engagement. *Learning and Instruction*, 54(1), 39–47.

Veletsianos, G., & Kimmons, R. (2020). What is online learning? The past, present, and future of online education. *Learning and Instruction*, 2(4), 7–16.

Wiliam, D., & Thompson, M. (2017). Integrating assessment with instruction: What will it take to make it work? *The Future of Assessment*, 2(3), 53–83. DOI: 10.4324/9781315086545-3

Zawacki-Richter, O., Baecker, E., & Vogt, S. (2009). Review of distance education research (2000 to 2008): Analysis of research areas, methods, and authorship patterns. *International Review of Research in Open and Distance Learning*, 10(6), 21–50. DOI: 10.19173/irrodl.v10i6.741

Chapter 18
Curriculum Design in the Crossroads at Higher Education Institutions (HEIs) Boosting Quality Assurance:
Satelliting Intellectual Property, Innovation – Legal Landscape

Bhupinder Singh
 https://orcid.org/0009-0006-4779-2553
Sharda University, India

Christian Kaunert
 https://orcid.org/0000-0002-4493-2235
Dublin City University, Ireland

ABSTRACT

Innovation is the key factor boosting economics and international competitiveness, but it takes a long time for a nation to get to the point where innovation becomes the main force. The concept of innovation has to be seen somewhat differently when applied to latecomer nations than it is when applied to leaders. The technology combines textual feedback and machine learning and this approach examines the remarks, viewpoints and assessments of instructors made by students. Also, textual criticism enhances teaching style and provides valuable insights on the effectiveness of instruction. The inputs are recorded by the technology and stored in an authorized database. To assist the teacher see the input, ratings and graphs are provided. This

DOI: 10.4018/979-8-3693-4407-1.ch018

chapter evaluates current econometric research on how changes in IPR policy affect educational growth and comes to research points to the acceleration of education and innovation development with stronger IPR regimes.

INTRODUCTION AND BACKGROUND

The technologically advanced sectors indicate that protracted periods of education and innovation growth with inadequate IPR regimes may lead to issues that manifest over time with regard to quality education with curriculum advancement in HEIs. The leading nations are eager in keeping their advantage via "world-first" advances in goods, services or generally abstract knowledge. Innovation refers to "new-to-the-country" innovation for latecomer nations whose main strategic objective is to catch up, which entails the management of rapid diffusion of technology from advanced to catch-up countries (Zint et al., 2024). The idea offers a method for improving the quality of academic instruction via the study of student feedback systems. This method improves student learning by providing teachers with insightful feedback (Singh & Kaunert, 2024). The economic leaders in developing nations have resisted calls to make their intellectual property rights (IPR) regimes stronger for decades. Many of them have cited the development of high-tech industries in Asia as evidence for the idea that weakening IPR regimes at certain periods of economic development might serve as an infant industry strategy, promoting the expansion of locally based enterprises with cutting-edge technology (Singh et al., 2024).

Higher education institutions (HEIs) face a transformation in the design of their curricula by demands regarding quality assurance, innovation and integrating academic property (IP), all placed within legal parameters. With the stakes of global competition getting higher HEIs are required to create curricula that not only comply with academic guidelines but also train students so they can thrive in a fast-changing world (Singh & Kaunert, 2024). This change calls for a systemic understanding of curriculum development governed not only by quality assurance mechanisms, but also innovative pedagogy and deep knowledge on intellectual property aspects (Raaj, 2024).

Historically, curriculum design has focused on what content should be delivered to students based on academic or industry standards. Nonetheless, with the higher education landscape transforming it has started becoming important to build curricula that nurture creativity, critical thinking and entrepreneurial mindset (Singh, 2024). Technological changes, globalisation and a knowledge economy that places increasing emphasis on innovation rather than physical products are among the reasons behind this shift. In turn, the curricular framework of HEIs is being reevaluated to encompass these must-have aspects so that graduating students can navigate their way and make a difference in this new age (Singh et al., 2024).

Figure 1. The Landscape of Introduction Section (Source- Self created the models or graphs)

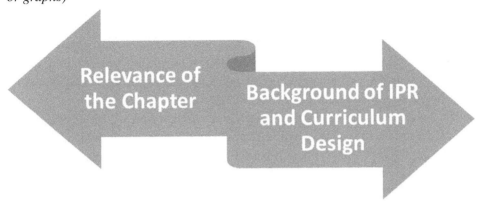

Relevance of the Chapter

The relevance and implications of intellectual property (IP) in course designs are even more pertinent. Students and faculty participate in research using intellectual property; knowledge of IP rights is essential to protect their input and develop creativity in the cycle. If IP education was integrated into the curriculum, this would help students create responsibly and start to engage with their intellectual creations at university in a beneficial way. This integration creates a culture of innovation and support, providing the students with techniques to become leaders in their fields (Singh et al., 2024). The revamping of curriculum not only concerns the content but also revolves around delving into innovative delivery methods and learning spaces. The integration of digitization and online learning platforms provides an incredible scope to strengthen the overall impact. With blended and hybrid models of education traditional classroom instruction combined with online experiences that can expand to include virtual, augmented or mixed reality technology in the full term from K–12 as well to college (Singh et al., 2024). Because these are mainly asynchronous learning models, this type of model provides more flexibility and greater access to the courses allowing students to learn at their own pace in a way that may better fit their personal needs. HEIs must also ensure that any new approaches take their place in changing quality assurance standards and do not compromise educational integrity or effectiveness (Singh & Kaunert, 2024).

At the center of curriculum design, quality assurance succeeded as a means to review and improve educational offers in HEIs. This includes recommending that there are clear standards, expectations and measures in place to ensure academic programs meet the intended program goals as well as needs of students and stakeholders. QA processes are working as catalysts for improvement in building a culture of Quality and accountability. QA is all about continuous process improvement. Through additional integration of QA with innovation and IP consideration, HEIs can develop curricula which remain academically robust while also being contemporary challenges aware (Garg & Singh, 2022).

The law of the land in higher education is yet another bedrock series of considerations that drive curriculum creation. Compliance with academic-related policies, laws and quality standards is not only essential for upholding the integrity of educational institutions but also indispensable in establishing trust among students (Singh & Kaunert, 2024). For example, legal constraints extend to matters of copyright and licensing a pressing topic in the digital age where creative output as well as its distribution are ubiquitous. HEIs must grapple with these legal frameworks when developing curricula that, on the one hand comply and abide by a host of standards in local law for example whilst also respecting this aspect yet only to an extent given academic freedom requires innovation (Singh, 2024).

The quality assurance frame and innovation, IPR & legal imperatives are determining direction of curriculum design in HEIs. The curriculum is how we prepare students to understand and navigate their place in the world knowledge that they may use to innovate or harness / protect as intellectual property (or both) and information about legal systems throughout our evolving, interconnected universe. As HEIs in this time of revolution, they now have the freedom to reimagine education and provide an environment for innovation, quality learning outcomes and lifelong learners (Singh, 2023).

Background of IPR and Curriculum Design

With innovation, creativity and associated rights at their core IPR have rapidly evolved to feature prominently within the curriculum design of higher education institutions (HEIs). Since the evolution of education systems, these have been synonymous with knowledge transfer and skill development. But intellectual property has come to take on increased importance in modern economies such as the knowledge economy, making it needful for students everywhere to learn about it (Singh & Kaunert, 2024).

It is an IPR which covers legal protection like patents, copyrights, trademarks and some trade secrets that are meant to grant exclusive rights for the creations of innovations from individuals or companies. The IPR As a result becomes vital for HEIs in the context of protecting institutional research and inventions, but also more importantly to develop a culture on innovation among students as well faculty-held convictions. HEIs can better equip students to understand the value of their creative work, legally make use of it and take advantage for an entrepreneurial venture just by incorporating IPR education into curriculum esthetically (Wang & Chao, 2022).

As such, it aligns with wider educational aims in developing critical thinking compliant applied research that combines creativity and ethics for knowledge production. In addition, it helps students to be equipped for the challenges of today´s workplace environment in which knowledge management and IPR are more strongly related than ever before with business success as well as helping their individuals advances. For this reason, IPR is necessary within a modern curriculum that not only aids students increase their knowledge but also complements to all round development of a student (Czerkawski, & Lyman, 2015).

Curriculum Design in Higher Education

The curriculum design in higher education significantly determines both student learning experiences and outcomes. This includes designing a well-organized learning system, integrating instructional strategies with educational aims and ensuring that the students attain what is absolutely essential. Curriculum design, done well, includes basic principles and elements which meet the needs of diverse learners while responding to current challenges in a global workplace landscape (Romero et al., 2017). The pillars of effective course design in higher education There are a number of core principles including alignment: making sure that learning objectives match instructional methods which in turn align with assessment. This alignment ensures a logical learning pathway for students, enabling them to process desired outcomes. Moreover, the curricula must be designed according to learner characteristics in terms of background (experience and education), learning style, preference for modalities as well. This allows active participation and improves their grasp on the topic (Agbo et al., 2019).

On the 7th point, flexibility is another great principle that allows curricula to keep up with the latest in their field and embrace novel teaching strategies. Use of tech and online resources in the curriculum can make learning experiences interesting while giving students a chance to learn future-ready digital skills. One of the pillars is interdisciplinarity which promotes knowledge integration across disciplines and encourages critical thinking, problem-solving with a comprehensive approach (Apiola & Sutinen, 2021). The teaching of a curriculum at universities is also encumbered by keeping up with fast-paced technological and workforce churn. New fields and disciplines are always being born, thus there is a constant need for updating curricula to remain relevant and applicable. This means that needs of the workforce and industry is changing, necessitating institutional investment in continuous RnD together with partnership from Industry to find out what are the emerging skills and know how (Pollock et al., 2019).

A big one is it trying to find a balance between rigor and practical applications. However, this does not mean that there is no need to better integrate more experiential learning experiences into the curriculum such as paid internships, research and scholarship opportunities, industry collaboration projects or community engagement initiatives (Lee et al., 2020). In addition, the recent growth of e-learning and blended learning models offers both challenges and opportunities. Although these models lead to greater accessibility and flexibility, they demand thoughtful choices in terms of instructional design and student support reaches for better learning outcomes (Psycharis et al., 2018).

Stakeholders in Curriculum Design

Understanding curriculum development in higher education as curriculum design is the linchpin of effective educational programs, and all stakeholders have a role to play Faculty absolutely play a central role in this process, lending expertise and insight to the course content as well as delivery. They are tasked with creating/updating curriculum, implementing new teaching methods and evaluations of student learning. Faculty involvement has given the curriculum both dynamism and responsiveness to current field changes (Pulimood et al., 2016). The other stakeholders that were at scaffold during this program, the students who are not enough participatory in activities about curriculum because they actually have become primary beneficiaries of it. This information can be very important for the newly onboard and help in improving the curriculum by giving feedback of their teaching stuff. Involving students in designing the curriculum increases their ownership and motivation, which ultimately enhances learning outcomes (Weintrop et al., 2016).

In fields where workforce demands change rapidly, industry partners are incredibly important stakeholders in curriculum design. Colleges can also work with experts in industries to match their curriculum effectively with the job needs of today and tomorrow, building graduate skill sets upon which employers instead count (Montiel et al., 2021). Collaborations with industry can create platforms for internships, mentorship and cooperative learning opportunities which would add value to student experience. So, curriculum design in higher education is a complicated and intricate process that must take into account major principles, challenges and importantly engagement of all those interested parties. In developing curricula that effectively prepares students for lifelong learning and success in their careers, institutions can align learning objectives with instructional methods through innovation and greater engagement of the various stakeholders. Tens of thousands were required to immediately return home and all face-to-face instruction ceased the standard higher-education curriculum suddenly faced an existential threat (Qin, 2019).

Online Instructor Practices and Strategies in Curriculum Design in HEIs

With more higher education institutions (HEIs) shifting to online learning, creating a curriculum that effectively caters for digital learners is now heavily dependent on lecturers designing and delivering said content (Barcelos et al., 2012). Teaching online is also happening in ways that effectively leverage technology and innovative practices to create interactive, high-impact learning experiences. Educators need to rethink the way they teach and include new applications or approaches that support better engagement, cooperation, critical thinking of students. Creating great, interactive content that holds students attention is a key strategy of online curriculum design. It does so by incorporating multimedia including videos, podcasts, infographics or interactive simulations that offer information in a dynamic and engaging manner. With different content formats exposed to, instructors can thereby accommodate the learning styles of a variety meaning that you could better relate and in love with complex ideas. Interactive content (quizzes, polls and discussion forums) will also be used to engage students actively so they can better remember the materials (Gross et al., 2024).

Creating online learning communities is also good practice for any online instructor. Nurturing an online learning community is vital in ensuring that our students do not feel isolated, and instead work together. Teachers can do this via creating a community of students; communicating with them on regular basis, holding virtual office hours and having group projects that make the whole class work together. Instructors are able to promote peer interaction, which facilitates social learning and aids in the development of skills including but not limited to team building, communication, problem solving. Assessment is also strategic in effective online instruction (García-Peñalvo & Mendes, 2018). Most traditional exams and quizzes do not provide a comprehensive picture of the understanding or skills that students have, especially in an online context. This recommend for instructors to also use different means of assessments like reflective journals, projects based assignments and peer evaluations alongside traditional assessment methods in order to get a complete picture of students learning capabilities. Given assessments should be aligned to what students are expected to learn and provide formative feedback pathways that facilitate student learning (Psycharis, 2018).

The other important part of this online curriculum development is technology integration. They need to manage the course content in a digital system and be competent at educating with these tools. Blackboard, Canvas or Moodle which are the learning management systems (LMS) that provide a centralized space for material organization, student tracking and communications (Bati et al., 2018). In addition, instructors can use different online collaboration tools like Google Workspace and Microsoft Teams to aid in group projects or live interaction. The online teachers need to maintain flexibility and be available for their students. It has to be willing to take any constructive criticism and adjust the way you teach or what's in your curriculum. Regular experience check-ins and surveys are the best way to understand learners, zero in on their issues so you can basal them better. Through flexibility and student-centered design, educators can ensure the relevancy of this new online learning experience (Papadakis, 2020).

Event Online education trends and best practices evolve over time, so professional development is key for instructors to keep up with the latest. Involving in workshops, webinars, and online courses can boost the educators' talents and knowledge to use several teaching techniques while sharpening their curriculum designs. Relating to peers and engaging in professional communities are great ways of sharing day-to-day experiences with other individuals (Yadav et al., 2024). Online instructor practices in terms of curriculum design are imperative in ensuring that high-quality education is provided to establish better learning outcomes within higher education institutions. In a Digital Age, by using technology to build community and deliver diverse assessments with flexibility modern educators can offer students vlauable online learning experiences -guided digital natives know all about. As long as instructors invest time in developing and creativity, online learning will become increasingly dynamic model of delivering education for modern higher education (Pollak & Ebner, 2019).

Quality Assurance in Curriculum Design

Curriculum design quality assurance is an indispensable component of the delivery of a high-quality curriculum that meets both student and stakeholder needs one assumes, in all higher education institutions (HEIs). Standards and benchmarks for gauging the effectiveness and quality of academic programs These standards may include learning goals, teaching methods and assessment strategies, as well as overall student results. National and international bodies like Bologna in Europe or the Council for Higher Education Accreditation (CHEA) in the U.S. have come up with frameworks to help institutions tailor their curricula that comply with recognized standards. Benchmarks provide concrete standards that HEIs can determine how well they are performing, compare themselves with other institutions and learn where shortcomings exists (Saritepeci, 2020). In the long run, abiding by standards and benchmarks established can bring about a degree of consistency, transparency as well accountability to how HEIs design their curriculum which will ultimately improve education quality available for students. These standards also encourage international recognition and mobility, thus enabling students to receive attend a different International School elsewhere or further their education world-wide (Buitrago-Florez, 2021).

Methods of Identifying Curriculum Quality

Curriculum quality assessment is a systematic examination of the components and elements of academic programs to determine their ability to meet institutional objectives as well as standards. Institutional Perspectives: Colleges and universities use surveys, focus groups, peer reviews (academics at one institution review the curriculum in another), to data analytics. They gain feedback on the experiences of students and faculty through surveys discussed in this blog, which allows them to capitalize on strengths as well identify areas for improvement (Gokçe & Yenmez, 2023). Peer reviews of course content, teaching approaches and student learning experiences conducted by faculty or external reviewers offer impartial assessments. How are established institutions using data analytics to track outcomes and diagnose trends based on that vast pool of student performance information? Similarly, self-review reports and internal audits are frequently employed to appraise curriculum quality as well as shape decision-making. These evaluations regularly occur, engage several audiences, faculty members to students to administrative personnel and provide an all-encompassing evaluation. The use of a variety of tools means that the HE sector can achieve highly granular levels understanding in to what constitutes curriculum quality and enables tailored interventions to be put into place support improvements in education (Lodi & Martini, 2021).

Contribution of Accreditation Bodies Towards Quality Assurance

The organization educates independent, non-profit agencies that play an essential part in the provision of quality educational programs across a wide range of curricular level and specialization--and it does this by accrediting postsecondary institutions according to standards for college admission. The most commonly recognized by academic organizations work at the national or regional level and are also responsible for thorough evaluations of university programs, institutional governance and operations to ensure they meet established standards. Accreditation is a comprehensive evaluation of the educational program (includes learning and performance objectives, content covered in course work, instructional methods utilized/assessment strategies employed) together with institutional support services and resources. Accreditation bodies act as external validators of the quality and rigor at an institution, thereby increasing both their credibility in context to other institutions but also its own reputation. For students, accreditation ensures that an education meets the standards of quality established by a sector and guarantees their abilities have been tested in due course professionally accepted manner. The reinforcement of some level of continuous improvement is further instilled through the accreditation processes, which require institutions to review and adapt their curricula and practices at regular intervals in light of dynamic needs from educational demand side (like students or employers). Accreditation essentially forces institutions to operate at a high level, and encourages innovation and change by signifying that an institution has the flexibility to respond quickly for programs which have become stale or obsolete (Tsortanidou et al., 2019).

Iterative Processes and Feedback Loops

In higher education, continuous improvement processes and feedback loops are crucial for sustaining and improving curriculum quality. It is a cycle involving the systematic gathering, review and analysis of data to make decisions about curriculum creation. Feedback loops through which to check with students, faculty and other stakeholders can collect their input in order for it to be included into decision-making. It starts by reviewing programs on a regular basis, as well as auditing course content and curriculum design to evaluate the effectiveness of teaching based upon learning outcomes; enabling institutions to pinpoint areas for improvement where they can target their interventions. Such processes help instil a culture of reflection and innovation that encourages faculty and staff to explore new approaches for teaching learning (Yilmaz Ince & Koc, 2021). It also helps the institutions stay current to ongoing changes and feedback in education system maki curricula more relevant for students (providing industry demand needs). By focusing on improvement and implementation of loops for feedback, HEIs will have academic programs that are both elastic and responsive to student success while serving the overall mission and vision. An iterative process for building curriculum promotes a cycle of learning, growing and excelling that result in better education to the student (Sırakaya et al., 2020).

Figure 2. Points on Quality Assurance in Curriculum Design (Source- Self created the models or graphs)

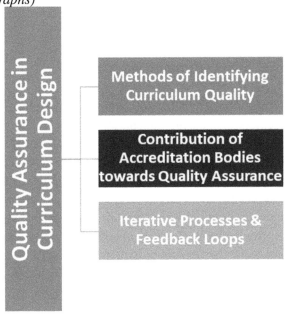

Intellectual Property in Higher Education: Understanding Intellectual Property Rights and their Relevance to HEIs

In other words intellectual property rights or IPR refers to those legal protections provide for by the patent, trademark and copyright laws applicable in commerce. Intellectual property rights including patents, copyrights, trademarks and trade secrets are vitally important to advance innovation and creativity by enabling inventors/innovators (or creators) the exclusive right over their creations. The importance of IPR for higher education institutions (HEIs) is paramount because they play a major role in research and development & dissemination of knowledge. Higher education institutions are bastions of innovation, places where new technologies, procedures and artistic works are constantly being devised. Recognizing IPR allows the institutions to secure its innovations and in return provide recognition, appreciation & some possible monetary advantage for same to their faculty members as well as student (Hutchins et al., 2020).

IPR also has a major role in fostering academia-industry collaboration. It allows HEIs to engage in research and development partnerships, thereby helping all entities involved; At the same time it protects their rights by setting IPR policies clearly. But it is also important for students who are potentially entering an intellectually creative workforce to understand concepts of intellectual property rights. HEIs prepare students to face this complication in their careers, and they use IPR education as a tool to promote responsible innovation and entrepreneurship among the youth (Valovicova et al., 2020).

Approaches to IP Education across Curricula

The curriculum cannot be complete without including intellectual property education, which is necessary to make the students aware of this complicated maze into which they need to tread on their professional lives. There are various methods that can be utilized to effectively assimilate IP education into higher educational training programs (Lockwood & Mooney, 2017). An avenue could be, that schools offer separate papers including but not limited to intellectual property and law along with courses related to economic studies which give them a broad level of understanding on types of the nature for example copyright or trademarks what are their respective legal frameworks and how they can fit in various sectors. These courses can also be discipline-specific, i.e. for engineering and business (vocation-oriented), or arts etc.) making it more relevant to their future career choices of students.

The other approach is to integrate IP education into regular courses such as by building modules or units centered on intellectual property concepts. A non-legal approach enables students to discuss the practical functions of IPR in their areas of study, nurturing realisation on how IP affects innovation, research and entrepreneurship. The guest lectures, workshops and seminars conducted by the industry experts and IP professionals help the students to gather practical insights. Furthermore, the department provides hands-on control of intellectual property; co-authoring with industrialists etc in some experiential learning opportunities like internships and capstone projects. IP education can be improved by cross-collaborations among students from various disciplines to collaborate on IP projects. Such collaborative initiatives challenge students to think openly and apply their conceptual understanding towards addressing complex problems, all the while raising awareness of intellectual property as a tool for innovation (Denning & Tedre, 2021).

Defending the Innovations of Faculty and Students

In intellectual property management in higher education institutions, protecting faculty and student innovations is key. HEIs should have clear guidelines in place to identify and declare created intellectual property at the institutional level. Dragging this and putting infrastructure that is foster based at both the government level, innovating in such a way wherever we have our patents commercializations that will able them to do so. Faculty may find they must first investigate their rights and responsibilities where intellectual property is concerned. Guidelines from the institution for this process would remind faculty of new products, inventions and creations were to be reported. These offices or departments within institutions, which may be called Technology Transfer Offices (TTO) in the U.S., are responsible for helping faculty through patent applications, copyright registrations, and licensing agreements. They also enable collaborations with industry partners in order to transition new innovations for commercialization and impact (Hsu & Liang, 2021).

Students should receive education and resources as part of the university experience to help them understand their intellectual property rights, as well as processes for protecting what they create. These can also include workshops, seminars and mentorship programmes helping students recognize their innovative solutions as well in securing them. It is also could be good exposure for students to an experience of learning intellectual property management through collaboration work with faculty member as well as the members from the industry. For the protection of faculty and student innovations, establishing a supportive innovation culture that acknowledges and rewards creativity is critical. Recognition programs, awards and incentives for intellectual property achievements can be established by institutions to cultivate a culture of creativity and entrepreneurship.

Case Studies: Global Perspectives on Curriculum Design

Case Study 1: Stanford University

Stanford University has for many years been at the vanguard of incorporating intellectual property education into its entrepreneurship programs. Yet at the same time, courses offered by another department in many colleges and universities like this one course taught each spring quarter to its MBA students point out how crucial IP is for technology commercialization and entrepreneurship. They get hands-on experience in IP management through access to the Silicon Valley's entrepreneurial ecosystem and by working with industry leaders. It teaches the students how to address IP headwinds and also how they can harness intellectual property in startup companies (Tedre & Denning, 2024).

Case Study 2: Massachusetts Institute of Technology (MIT) - Technology Licensing Office

The Technology Licensing Office (TLO) at MIT is focused on helping create a culture of innovation and an awareness of how assets in intellectual property can be used to make that happen. The TLO conducts workshops and provide resources throughout the year to educate faculty members about IP rights, as well commercialization opportunities available from UA-invented technologies. IP education is embedded into the engineering and business curricula at MIT, giving students a well-rounded perspective of how intellectual property contributes to innovation. Collaborative project works as well industry partnerships provide more opportunity to students apply the IP in real world context (Agbo et al., 2021).

Case Study 3: University of California

The UC, Berkeley Law school offer strong IP in the form of a Jordan Helfenstien curriculum via its well-established and prominent BCLT. The center offers a variety of classes, workshops and research opportunities in the field of IP law and policy. In a similar vein, the interdisciplinary approach at Berkeley encourages law students to collaborate with their engineering and business counterparts in order understand all of the facets that come into play when dealing with IP problems. Interaction with industry professionals and legal experts through BCLT's programs enhances the student experience, preparing them to tackle complex IP problems.

The common thread in all of these case studies is the necessity for IP education to become an established component across North American higher-education curricula through a combination of dedicated coursework, interdisciplinary relationships with other fields and training opportunities alike. By teaching students about the intricacies of intellectual property, these institutions are arming the next generation to be able step forward as leaders and innovators in their own sectors (Ulger, 2018).

Figure 3. Case Studies (Source- Self created the models or graphs)

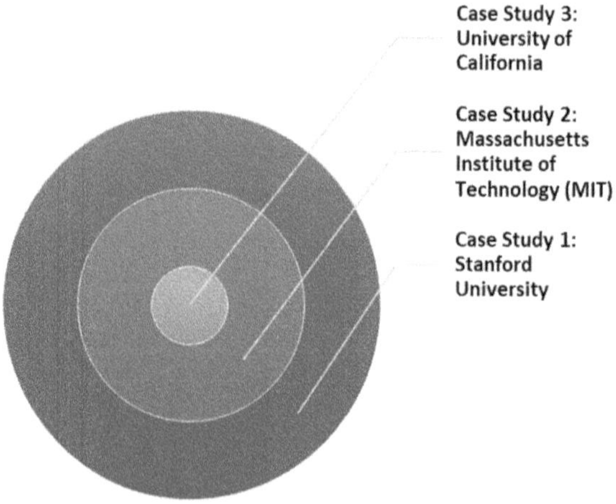

Fostering Innovation in Curriculum Design

To embed innovation with the academic programs, by incorporating creative thinking, problem solving & experiential learning exercises in the curriculum. The use of project-based learning, where students participate in a variety of working scenarios which directly mimic real-life situations. The real-world application of theoretical know-how of learners enhances their thinking, creativity and innovation. Incorporating courses that cross traditional boundaries of fields and think about things in new ways not only provides a complete picture to students, but also solutions for the complexities faced. Digital learning needs to move towards creating an environment using simulations, virtual labs and collaboration tools so that we combine the elements together just like a lab culture. Bringing design thinking processes to the classroom also introduces students to a method of user-centered problem solving that emphasizes empathy, practices prototype ideas and iterates solutions (Li et al., 2020).

The continual feedback loops can also serve as drivers of curriculum innovation with inputs from students, faculty members and industry experts. Iterative curriculum updates like it based on new trends and technology along with feedback makes sure programs are relevant to the modern workforce. Incorporating innovation into academic programs ensures that students are taught how to create new value and develop an innovation-oriented mindset, skills critical for success in a fast-changing future.

Nurturing the Nature of Enterprise and Innovation

Fostering an entrepreneurial mindset and promoting creativity in academic programs will help students become successful innovators, leaders and change-makers. A good start is to introduce entrepreneurship classes, and methods right into the school curriculum allowing students grow with a minimum body of knowledge about business development, marketing approaches or innovation management. They typically have real-world components such as business plan development, pitch competitions and case studies where students apply entrepreneurial concepts to actual situations.

The creativity can also be instilled by creating other environments that allow students to experiment and take risks. For example, maker spaces, innovation labs and incubators are increasingly offered by institutions as co-creation spaces, where students can come together to discus, collaborate, prototype ideas, receive mentorship from experienced entrepreneurs and industry professionals. Such environments help build risk-taking culture and creative mindset, as they challenge students to push the boundaries of what is known and possible, explore new technologies and approaches to solve problems. Multidisciplinary collaboration is essential to spark students' creativity (Leonard et al., 2024). Academic institutions bring students from diverse experiences and educational backgrounds to teach and learn together learning that can be supplemented by shared research and designs sharing activities, co-remoting or travelling intensive sessions of group work with practical implementation. This exposure enables students to learn about and understand issues holistically and inspires creative processes by pushing them to look at problems from different angles. Moreover, the components can be integrated with students' role as innovators, reflecting on the use of new technologies or innovative teaching methods, encouraging student to apply what they learned in their daily basis. Expanding entrepreneurship and innovation to curriculum can be accomplished with the involvement of internships, co-motion programs, and working in close collaboration with industries.

The second is industry advisory boards where professionals from the multiple industries provide some pointers towards curriculum development. They serve as sounding boards on where industry is headed, point us in the direction of curriculum updates and provides options for student interfacing with latest projects among industries. Research collaborations can of course lead to innovation, by bringing the latest research into academic programs. These partnerships with research institutions will give faculty and students the opportunity to work on joint collaborative projects, access high-end facilities or expand into new areas of inquiry. This collaboration enhances the curriculum, enabling students to observe new scientific findings and technological advances (Hava & Koyunlu Unlu, 2021).

Internships, co-op programs and industry-sponsored projects allow students to experience hands on components of their education in the real world. These are collaborations that further enrich our students learning experience and enable them to acquire skills they will actually need within their careers. Local industry- and research-driven collaborations can also help in the creation of curricula around new industries or disruptive technologies. Higher education institutions can enable students for an ever more specialized global landscape by promoting collaboration to create a dynamic learning environment (Gonzalez-Perez & Ramírez-Montoya, 2022).

Legal Considerations in Curriculum Design

Legal considerations in teaching, learning and assessment involve equitable access to education or training; student privacy related protection of Personal Learning Data (PLD) Shared by students; Entitlements: rights-oriented measures for ensuring that diverse perspectives are included. Institutions must be complete in ensuring that their curricula is compliant with anti-discrimination laws so all students, no matter the colour of your skin or if you are a woman/man/same entry/gay person/disabled/wealthy background have equal opportunities. In addition, legal frameworks might require specific content areas like civic education, ethics or cultural diversity to be included in order for learning to become more comprehensive. They need to be aware of any legislative changes and educational reforms in practice education so that the content delivered in their curriculum matches what is required legally. Legal frameworks may also dictate the use of technology and digital resources in education, calling for institutions to adopt policies protecting student data and privacy. Compliance with legal frameworks should enable higher education institutions to provide curricula that are not only compliant but also indicative of social norms, thus adding value and inclusiveness into their educational programs (Iversen et al., 2018).

In order to ensure the quality and credibility of programs, higher education institutions positively meet their competency through adherence with educational policies regulations in which offering a credit-bearing course is one. Not even the policies that are supposed to guide curriculum design, delivery and assessment in educational institutions set by government agencies as well accrediting bodies. Policies are in place so that institutions of higher learning can provide high-quality education to the community, universities must abide by these policies. Regulations will often contain rules about curriculum design in general, such as type of degree programs e.g., 3 year vs. 4-year degrees, number and size of credits required for completion, assessment methods etc. It is also the responsibility of institutions to ensure that their curricula meet these standards and structure processes for regular program review and update. In addition, compliance includes that faculty will meet certain qualifications, instructional materials adhere to various standards and applies to different types of student support services (Miller et al., 2023).

There are the policy dimensions of international students that include visa regulations and language requirements which pose barriers to a more open learning space for these institutions. Non-compliance with educational policies and regulations can lead to legal ramifications, de-accreditation, or harm the university's brand. In particular, by managing compliance more effectively from a centralized point of view and at the same time dealing with protecting staff jobs so as not to make them redundant during these times schools can continue their tradition for academic brilliance whilst maintaining their place in the general educational community.

Copyright and Licensing Concerns

Copyright and licensing considerations are important in curriculum design, especially since more and more educational resources appear online. Copyright laws support the rights of creators to have control over the way their works are used and distributed. To conclude the above information, students must also consider whether they have permission to include another content (like articles and/or multimedia) within a module or platform that is made available with certain terms based on copyright laws and licensing agreements when it comes to curriculum design.

Educators and curriculum developers should understand what they are allowed to do with copyrighted works, get the appropriate permissions or licenses for use of them in their classes. This could mean negotiating licenses with publishers, or it might involve finding open-access resources that provide free, low-cost educational content. Another area of focus is ensuring that faculty and staff are informed about copyright compliance, including how to cite properly or create original content with proper consideration for intellectual property rights. The provenance of open educational resources (OER) provides an alternative, in that materials are freely available for use as often modification and redistribution too. In the process, institutions are able to elevate their curricula while lessening financial and legal risks related to copyright infringement. Proactive steps taken to address copyright and licensing issues can help ensure that institutions respect intellectual property rights, while also encouraging responsible educational practices (Bocconi et al., 2022).

Legal Injunctions and Curriculum Design

There are many reasons for curriculum design to become a legal challenge, such as discrimination accusations, copyright infringement claims and problems with the standards of education. The challenges have far-reaching consequences for institutions, from risking their reputation and accreditation status to court action. Acknowledging these challenges and distilling lessons learned from case studies, institutions will be able to manage legal risks more effectively as well refine their curricular design processes. The key legal issue relates to curricular diversity and representation. If their programs are seen as discriminatory, or they do not provide the same opportunities to students from different backgrounds, institutions could be sued. In many situations, this may mean that institutions are compelled to rethink their curricula in terms of cultural sensitivity and inclusivity if educational material has been called out for stereotyping or alienating any particular group (Singh, 2023).

Where going after institutions that allow unauthorized use of copyrighted materials or face being caught for copyright infringement. After looking at a university that adopted some proprietary software without licensing it correctly we can see just how important copyright law and the terms of any agreement are with educational materials. Reviewing these legal challenges and case studies then allows institutions to determine ways that they may be exposed or at-risk, and thus can prepare for preventative measures. At minimum, this can involve setting clear guidelines for how curriculum is developed and providing education/promotion on legal compliance as well as creating a culture of inclusivity and respect re: IP. It helps institutions to successfully negotiate legal challenges while continuing a strong commitment to offering quality and equitable education.

Role of Technology in Curriculum Design

Curriculum development has been revolutionized by digital tools and platforms that give educators more methods to help prices experiences in enhancing learning. Incorporating digital technologies into the course design helps in the development of needful and engaging learning experiences that accommodate a range of learner personalities. These tools may include platforms like Learning Management Systems (LMS) such as Moodle, Blackboard or Canvas which are spaces to centralize course material for assignments and evaluations making organization of content seamless both from educators' perspective but also students' (Singh, 2024).

These types of objects can include videos, simulations and interactive exercises through the use digital tools that enable educators to make their courses quite engaging. These tools also enable students and teachers to share information back-and-forth if desired in instances such as instant feedback, discussions and peer interaction. This change from traditional and fixed curricula to interactive mode of learning supported by technology enhances critical thinking, creativity and problem solving skills. In addition, such platforms allow for more targeted learning as they can be customized according to each students strengths and weaknesses. Data analytics in adaptive learning technologies, helps us understand where students needs lie and accordingly design personalized learning paths to help them improve their areas of interest. Thus, the digital tools & platforms are significantly helping in transforming curriculum development to bring accessible, engaging and better education.

Online vs Blended Learning Modes

In blended learning, it merge the traditional face to face instruction and some online elements together with a hybrid methodology that offers best of both capabilities. This structure allows students to learn the material at their own speed but retain access to face-to-face interaction and help from instructors. In contrast, online learning provides education entirely over the Internet so that students can take courses and access resources from virtually anywhere in the world. It is flexible, as it caters to the needs of students with varying schedules and commitments. Online learning can also accommodate different instructional styles with video lectures, discussion forums and interactive assessments.

Blended and online learning both stress student-centered personalized approaches, leveraging active participation and collaboration. Such models also support lifelong learning by opening pathways for upskilling and reskilling. Yet they also raise questions about the importance of intentional curriculum and pedagogy as a principle for achieving learning outcomes essential to providing students with high-quality education through effective use of technology. Students must also have access to appropriate technology and support services, which is difficult for institutions given the issues of digital divide. Blended and online learning models have the potential to increase access in higher education, promote innovative approaches to teaching and learning that can improve educational outcomes for students in areas such as improving critical thinking skills among others (Singh, 2024).

Curriculum Improvement through AI and Data Analytics

With utilizing artificial intelligence (AI) and data analytics, it is allowing educational institutions to liberate the potential within curriculums by enabling them with crucial insights on student learning patterns and outcomes. Using AI tools that can process innumerable data, trends are spotted and student performance is predicted to suggest personalized learning interventions. Approaching literacy instruction from a data-driven perspective helps teachers know what aspects of their curriculum are working, and which can be improved upon it permits the educator to make educated decisions regarding his or her curriculum design/delivery so as to provide quality education (Singh, 2024). A simple educational application, this is an example that demonstrates how A.I can be used in curriculum enrichment, it also serves as a booster for learning abilities of students. These systems monitor student progress on an ongoing basis and adapt learning materials to offer both like personalized support and greater challenges. Such an approach is not only boosts student engagement but also improves learning outcomes by filling in knowledge gaps and reinforcing strengths.

The sharing of data analytics have a more significant contribution to curriculum evaluation and improvement. There now exists rich data related to student performance, engagement and feedback that can help schools understand the need for curriculum adjustment or augmentation. For instance, data analytics can illuminate which concepts students are struggling with the most and help educators tailor instruction and resources to better meet learning needs. Predictive modeling can be ensured with the help of AI and data analytics that allow universities to detect students who are at-risk so that early interventions could be implemented in promoting student outcomes for retention & success (Singh, 2023). This holistic approach helps ensure that students are getting the tailored support to help them be successful, leading to a more efficient and responsive system of education. AI and data analytics can optimise curriculum design, increase personalisation in learning experience and improve education outcome continuously for higher ed institutes (Sharma & Singh, 2022). These technologies help educators generate data-driven curricula that can better identify the needs of students and align them with those required by an ever-changing workforce (Díaz, 2024).

CONCLUSION AND FUTURE SCOPE

The design of curriculum for higher education institutions (HEIs) sits at a convergence among quality assurance, intellectual property (IP), innovation and legal issues. Evolving a rapidly changing educational landscape is more difficult than before as HEIs are walking the fine line between academic excellence and new demands (Norman & Zoncita, 2024). So an effective curriculum design has to account for those divergent needs of students while still being objectively good and compliant with state and federal laws. This emphasis on testing for quality is unlikely to end, especially when institutions are being tasked with creating the sorts of programs which not only fill state and federal metrics but also answer demands from a global economy (Albuquerque et al., 2024). Embedding IP in the curriculum increases knowledge about intellectual property rights and innovation for students in addition to providing much-needed skills that are necessary for thriving within a knowledge-based economy (Zahra et al., 2024). Through integrating IP education in the curriculum, HEIs promote a mindset of creativity and appreciation for intellectual works essential to spur innovation and economic development. So, taking into account legislative considerations in designing curricula also helps to comply with educational policies and regulations that ultimately protect the institutions from possible legal actions. The changing Legal landscape and considerable issues behind as regards to copyright, licensing and regulatory compliance drives the HEIs has more importance in Innovative Curriculum coupled with also having legality (Nicolaides et al., 2024).

In future, curriculum design in HEIs is likely to involve increased use of technology and data analytics as well for better educational outcomes. To stay viable and impactful, institutions will have to adopt adaptive learning technologies and advance pedagogical practices. Publication and research with industry/academia will help in course curricula to be in-line with recent trend/approach of real world application. While HEIs will refine their curricula in innovative and future-oriented ways, the opportunity to do more can be found in integrating IP strategies into existing structures, promoting innovation culture further within all disciplines and addressing the real world legal challenges. With focusing on these elements, for example, institutions can establish strong curricular processes that are capable of equipping students with the skills required to navigate an increasingly complex world while meeting robust benchmarks for educational quality and compliance.

REFERENCES

Agbo, F. J., Oyelere, S. S., Suhonen, J., & Adewumi, S. (2019, November). A systematic review of computational thinking approach for programming education in higher education institutions. In *Proceedings of the 19th Koli Calling International Conference on Computing Education Research* (pp. 1-10). DOI: 10.1145/3364510.3364521

Agbo, F. J., Yigzaw, S. T., Sanusi, I. T., Oyelere, S. S., & Mare, A. H. (2021, October). Examining theoretical and pedagogical foundations of computational thinking in the context of higher education. In *2021 IEEE Frontiers in Education Conference (FIE)* (pp. 1-8). IEEE. DOI: 10.1109/FIE49875.2021.9637405

Albuquerque, U. P., Maroyi, A., Ladio, A. H., Pieroni, A., Abbasi, A. M., Toledo, B. A., Dahdouh-Guebas, F., Hallwass, G., Soldati, G. T., Odonne, G., Vandebroek, I., Vallès, J., Hurrell, J. A., Pardo de Santayana, M., La Torre-Cuadros, M. Á., Silva, M. T. P., Jacob, M. C. M., da Fonseca-Kruel, V. S., & Ferreira Júnior, W. S. (2024). Advancing ethnobiology for the ecological transition and a more inclusive and just world: A comprehensive framework for the next 20 years. *Journal of Ethnobiology and Ethnomedicine*, 20(1), 18. DOI: 10.1186/s13002-024-00661-4 PMID: 38360640

Apiola, M., & Sutinen, E. (2021). Design science research for learning software engineering and computational thinking: Four cases. *Computer Applications in Engineering Education*, 29(1), 83–101. DOI: 10.1002/cae.22291

Barcelos, T. S., & Silveira, I. F. (2022, October). Teaching computational thinking in initial series an analysis of the confluence among mathematics and computer sciences in elementary education and its implications for higher education. In *2012 XXXVIII Conferencia Latinoamericana En Informatica (CLEI)* (pp. 1-8). IEEE.

Bati, K., Yetişir, M. I., Çalışkan, I., Güneş, G., & Gül Saçan, E. (2018). Teaching the concept of time: A steam-based program on computational thinking in science education. *Cogent Education*, 5(1), 1507306. DOI: 10.1080/2331186X.2018.1507306

Bocconi, S., Chioccariello, A., Kampylis, P., Dagienė, V., Wastiau, P., Engelhardt, K., ... & Stupurienė, G. (2022). Reviewing computational thinking in compulsory education: State of play and practices from computing education.

Buitrago-Flórez, F., Danies, G., Restrepo, S., & Hernández, C. (2021). Fostering 21st Century Competences through Computational Thinking and Active Learning: A Mixed Method Study. *International Journal of Instruction*, 14(3), 737–754. DOI: 10.29333/iji.2021.14343a

Czerkawski, B. C., & Lyman, E. W.III. (2015). Exploring issues about computational thinking in higher education. *TechTrends*, 59(2), 57–65. DOI: 10.1007/s11528-015-0840-3

Denning, P. J., & Tedre, M. (2021). Computational thinking: A disciplinary perspective. *Informatics in Education*, 20(3), 361.

Díaz, C. A. (2024). *From transdisciplinary concepts to undisciplined futures*. The Routledge International Handbook of Transdisciplinary Feminist Research and Methodological Praxis.

García-Peñalvo, F. J., & Mendes, A. J. (2018). Exploring the computational thinking effects in pre-university education. *Computers in Human Behavior*, 80, 407–411. DOI: 10.1016/j.chb.2017.12.005

Garg, N., & Singh, B. (2022). Sustainable Development-Adopting a Balanced Approach between Development and Development Induced Changes. *ECS Transactions*, 107(1), 15–31. DOI: 10.1149/10701.0015ecst

Gökçe, S., & Yenmez, A. A. (2023). Ingenuity of scratch programming on reflective thinking towards problem solving and computational thinking. *Education and Information Technologies*, 28(5), 5493–5517. DOI: 10.1007/s10639-022-11385-x

González-Pérez, L. I., & Ramírez-Montoya, M. S. (2022). Components of Education 4.0 in 21st century skills frameworks: Systematic review. *Sustainability (Basel)*, 14(3), 1493. DOI: 10.3390/su14031493

Gross, S., Kim, M., Schlosser, J., Mohtadi, C., Lluch, D., & Schneider, D. (2024l). Fostering computational thinking in engineering education: Challenges, examples, and best practices. In *2014 IEEE Global Engineering Education Conference (EDUCON)* (pp. 450-459). IEEE.

Hava, K., & Koyunlu Ünlü, Z. (2021). Investigation of the relationship between middle school students' computational thinking skills and their STEM career interest and attitudes toward inquiry. *Journal of Science Education and Technology*, 30(4), 484–495. DOI: 10.1007/s10956-020-09892-y

Hsu, T. C., & Liang, Y. S. (2021). Simultaneously improving computational thinking and foreign language learning: Interdisciplinary media with plugged and unplugged approaches. *Journal of Educational Computing Research*, 59(6), 1184–1207. DOI: 10.1177/0735633121992480

Hutchins, N. M., Biswas, G., Maróti, M., Lédeczi, Á., Grover, S., Wolf, R., Blair, K. P., Chin, D., Conlin, L., Basu, S., & McElhaney, K. (2020). C2STEM: A system for synergistic learning of physics and computational thinking. *Journal of Science Education and Technology*, 29(1), 83–100. DOI: 10.1007/s10956-019-09804-9

Iversen, O. S., Smith, R. C., & Dindler, C. (2018, August). From computational thinking to computational empowerment: a 21st century PD agenda. In *Proceedings of the 15th participatory design conference: Full papers-Volume 1* (pp. 1-11).

Lee, I., Grover, S., Martin, F., Pillai, S., & Malyn-Smith, J. (2020). Computational thinking from a disciplinary perspective: Integrating computational thinking in K-12 science, technology, engineering, and mathematics education. *Journal of Science Education and Technology*, 29(1), 1–8. DOI: 10.1007/s10956-019-09803-w

Leonard, J., Buss, A., Gamboa, R., Mitchell, M., Fashola, O. S., Hubert, T., & Almughyirah, S. (2016). Using robotics and game design to enhance children's self-efficacy, STEM attitudes, and computational thinking skills. *Journal of Science Education and Technology*, 25(6), 860–876. DOI: 10.1007/s10956-016-9628-2

Li, Y., Schoenfeld, A. H., diSessa, A. A., Graesser, A. C., Benson, L. C., English, L. D., & Duschl, R. A. (2020). Computational thinking is more about thinking than computing. *Journal for STEM Education Research*, 3(1), 1–18. DOI: 10.1007/s41979-020-00030-2 PMID: 32838129

Liu, H. P., Perera, S. M., & Klein, J. W. (2017). Using model-based learning to promote computational thinking education. *Emerging research, practice, and policy on computational thinking*, 153-172.

Lockwood, J., & Mooney, A. (2017). Computational Thinking in Education: Where does it fit? A systematic literary review. *arXiv preprint arXiv:1703.07659*.

Lodi, M., & Martini, S. (2021). Computational thinking, between Papert and Wing. *Science & Education*, 30(4), 883–908. DOI: 10.1007/s11191-021-00202-5

Miller, L. D., Soh, L. K., Chiriacescu, V., Ingraham, E., Shell, D. F., Ramsay, S., & Hazley, M. P. (2013, October). *Improving learning of computational thinking using creative thinking exercises in CS-1 computer science courses. In 2013 ieee frontiers in education conference (fie)*. IEEE.

Montiel, H., & Gomez-Zermeño, M. G. (2021). Educational challenges for computational thinking in k–12 education: A systematic literature review of "scratch" as an innovative programming tool. *Computers*, 10(6), 69. DOI: 10.3390/computers10060069

Nicolaides, A., Lim, A., Herr, N., & Barefield, T. (Eds.). (2024). *Reimagining Adult Education as World Building: Creating Learning Ecologies for Transformation*. Taylor & Francis. DOI: 10.4324/9781003371359

Norman, P. D., & Zoncita, D. (2024). Elaborating the Efficacy of Outdoor Arts-based Cooperative Learning Experiences on the Latino Immigrant Students' Engagement, and Academic & Social Success in ESL-STEAM Education. *Available atSSRN* 4757518.

Papadakis, S. (2020). Evaluating a teaching intervention for teaching STEM and programming concepts through the creation of a weather-forecast app for smart mobile devices. In *Handbook of research on tools for teaching computational thinking in P-12 education* (pp. 31–53). IGI Global. DOI: 10.4018/978-1-7998-4576-8.ch002

Pollak, M., & Ebner, M. (2019). The missing link to computational thinking. *Future Internet*, 11(12), 263. DOI: 10.3390/fi11120263

Pollock, L., Mouza, C., Guidry, K. R., & Pusecker, K. (2019, February). Infusing computational thinking across disciplines: Reflections & lessons learned. In *Proceedings of the 50th ACM Technical Symposium on Computer Science Education* (pp. 435-441). DOI: 10.1145/3287324.3287469

Psycharis, S. (2018). STEAM in education: A literature review on the role of computational thinking, engineering epistemology and computational science. computational steam pedagogy (CSP). *Scientific Culture*, 4(2), 51–72.

Psycharis, S., Kalovrektis, K., Sakellaridi, E., Korres, K., & Mastorodimos, D. (2018). Unfolding the curriculum: physical computing, computational thinking and computational experiment in STEM's transdisciplinary approach. *European Journal of Engineering and Technology Research*, 19-24.

Pulimood, S. M., Pearson, K., & Bates, D. C. (2016, February). A study on the impact of multidisciplinary collaboration on computational thinking. In *Proceedings of the 47th ACM technical symposium on computing science education* (pp. 30-35). DOI: 10.1145/2839509.2844636

Qin, H. (2019). Teaching computational thinking through bioinformatics to biology students. In *Proceedings of the 40th ACM technical symposium on Computer science education* (pp. 188-191).

Raaj, S. (2024). EDUCATION, RESEARCH AND INNOVATION IN INDIA: THE SHIFTING PARADIGMS. *Journal of Higher Education Theory and Practice*, 24(1), 75.

Romero, M., Lepage, A., & Lille, B. (2017). Computational thinking development through creative programming in higher education. *International Journal of Educational Technology in Higher Education*, 14(1), 1–15. DOI: 10.1186/s41239-017-0080-z

Saritepeci, M. (2020). Developing computational thinking skills of high school students: Design-based learning activities and programming tasks. *The Asia-Pacific Education Researcher*, 29(1), 35–54. DOI: 10.1007/s40299-019-00480-2

Sharma, A., & Singh, B. (2022). Measuring Impact of E-commerce on Small Scale Business: A Systematic Review. *Journal of Corporate Governance and International Business Law*, 5(1).

Singh, B. (2023). Blockchain Technology in Renovating Healthcare: Legal and Future Perspectives. In *Revolutionizing Healthcare Through Artificial Intelligence and Internet of Things Applications* (pp. 177-186). IGI Global.

Singh, B. (2023). Blockchain Technology in Renovating Healthcare: Legal and Future Perspectives. In *Revolutionizing Healthcare Through Artificial Intelligence and Internet of Things Applications* (pp. 177-186). IGI Global.

Singh, B. (2023). Federated Learning for Envision Future Trajectory Smart Transport System for Climate Preservation and Smart Green Planet: Insights into Global Governance and SDG-9 (Industry, Innovation and Infrastructure). *National Journal of Environmental Law*, 6(2), 6–17.

Singh, B. (2023). Tele-Health Monitoring Lensing Deep Neural Learning Structure: Ambient Patient Wellness via Wearable Devices for Real-Time Alerts and Interventions. *Indian Journal of Health and Medical Law*, 6(2), 12–16.

Singh, B. (2023). Unleashing Alternative Dispute Resolution (ADR) in Resolving Complex Legal-Technical Issues Arising in Cyberspace Lensing E-Commerce and Intellectual Property: Proliferation of E-Commerce Digital Economy. *Revista Brasileira de Alternative Dispute Resolution-Brazilian Journal of Alternative Dispute Resolution-RBADR*, 5(10), 81–105. DOI: 10.52028/rbadr.v5i10.ART04.Ind

Singh, B. (2024). Cherish Growth, Advancement and Tax Structure: Addressing Social and Economic Prospects. *Journal of Taxation and Regulatory Framework*, 7(1), 7–10.

Singh, B. (2024). Evolutionary Global Neuroscience for Cognition and Brain Health: Strengthening Innovation in Brain Science. In *Biomedical Research Developments for Improved Healthcare* (pp. 246-272). IGI Global.

Singh, B. (2024). Evolutionary Global Neuroscience for Cognition and Brain Health: Strengthening Innovation in Brain Science. In Prabhakar, P. (Ed.), *Biomedical Research Developments for Improved Healthcare* (pp. 246–272). IGI Global., DOI: 10.4018/979-8-3693-1922-2.ch012

Singh, B. (2024). Green Infrastructure in Real Estate Landscapes: Pillars of Sustainable Development and Vision for Tomorrow. *National Journal of Real Estate Law*, 7(1), 4–8.

Singh, B. (2024). Legal Dynamics Lensing Metaverse Crafted for Videogame Industry and E-Sports: Phenomenological Exploration Catalyst Complexity and Future. *Journal of Intellectual Property Rights Law*, 7(1), 8–14.

Singh, B. (2024). Social Cognition of Incarcerated Women and Children: Addressing Exposure to Infectious Diseases and Legal Outcomes. In Reddy, K. (Ed.), *Principles and Clinical Interventions in Social Cognition* (pp. 236–251). IGI Global., DOI: 10.4018/979-8-3693-1265-0.ch014

Singh, B., Jain, V., Kaunert, C., Dutta, P. K., & Singh, G. (2024). Privacy Matters: Espousing Blockchain and Artificial Intelligence (AI) for Consumer Data Protection on E-Commerce Platforms in Ethical Marketing. In Saluja, S., Nayyar, V., Rojhe, K., & Sharma, S. (Eds.), *Ethical Marketing Through Data Governance Standards and Effective Technology* (pp. 167–184). IGI Global., DOI: 10.4018/979-8-3693-2215-4.ch015

Singh, B., & Kaunert, C. (2024). Computational Thinking for Innovative Solutions and Problem-Solving Techniques: Transforming Conventional Education to Futuristic Interdisciplinary Higher Education. In Fonkam, M., & Vajjhala, N. (Eds.), *Revolutionizing Curricula Through Computational Thinking, Logic, and Problem Solving* (pp. 60–82). IGI Global., DOI: 10.4018/979-8-3693-1974-1.ch004

Singh, B., & Kaunert, C. (2024). Harnessing Sustainable Agriculture Through Climate-Smart Technologies: Artificial Intelligence for Climate Preservation and Futuristic Trends. In Kannan, H., Rodriguez, R., Paprika, Z., & Ade-Ibijola, A. (Eds.), *Exploring Ethical Dimensions of Environmental Sustainability and Use of AI* (pp. 214–239). IGI Global., DOI: 10.4018/979-8-3693-0892-9.ch011

Singh, B., & Kaunert, C. (2024). Revealing Green Finance Mobilization: Harnessing FinTech and Blockchain Innovations to Surmount Barriers and Foster New Investment Avenues. In Jafar, S., Rodriguez, R., Kannan, H., Akhtar, S., & Plugmann, P. (Eds.), *Harnessing Blockchain-Digital Twin Fusion for Sustainable Investments* (pp. 265–286). IGI Global., DOI: 10.4018/979-8-3693-1878-2.ch011

Singh, B., & Kaunert, C. (2024). Salvaging Responsible Consumption and Production of Food in the Hospitality Industry: Harnessing Machine Learning and Deep Learning for Zero Food Waste. In Singh, A., Tyagi, P., & Garg, A. (Eds.), *Sustainable Disposal Methods of Food Wastes in Hospitality Operations* (pp. 176–192). IGI Global., DOI: 10.4018/979-8-3693-2181-2.ch012

Singh, B., & Kaunert, C. (2024). Salvaging Responsible Consumption and Production of Food in the Hospitality Industry: Harnessing Machine Learning and Deep Learning for Zero Food Waste. In Singh, A., Tyagi, P., & Garg, A. (Eds.), *Sustainable Disposal Methods of Food Wastes in Hospitality Operations* (pp. 176–192). IGI Global., DOI: 10.4018/979-8-3693-2181-2.ch012

Singh, B., & Kaunert, C. (2024). Integration of Cutting-Edge Technologies such as Internet of Things (IoT) and 5G in Health Monitoring Systems: A Comprehensive Legal Analysis and Futuristic Outcomes. *GLS Law Journal*, 6(1), 13–20. DOI: 10.69974/glslawjournal.v6i1.123

Singh, B., Kaunert, C., & Vig, K. (2024). Reinventing Influence of Artificial Intelligence (AI) on Digital Consumer Lensing Transforming Consumer Recommendation Model: Exploring Stimulus Artificial Intelligence on Consumer Shopping Decisions. In *AI Impacts in Digital Consumer Behavior* (pp. 141-169). IGI Global.

Sırakaya, M., Alsancak Sırakaya, D., & Korkmaz, Ö. (2020). The impact of STEM attitude and thinking style on computational thinking determined via structural equation modeling. *Journal of Science Education and Technology*, 29(4), 561–572. DOI: 10.1007/s10956-020-09836-6

Tedre, M., & Denning, P. J. (2016, November). The long quest for computational thinking. In *Proceedings of the 16th Koli Calling international conference on computing education research* (pp. 120-129).

Tsortanidou, X., Daradoumis, T., & Barberá, E. (2019). Connecting moments of creativity, computational thinking, collaboration and new media literacy skills. *Information and Learning Science*, 120(11/12), 704–722. DOI: 10.1108/ILS-05-2019-0042

Ulger, K. (2018). The effect of problem-based learning on the creative thinking and critical thinking disposition of students in visual arts education. *The Interdisciplinary Journal of Problem-Based Learning*, 12(1). Advance online publication. DOI: 10.7771/1541-5015.1649

Valovičová, Ľ., Ondruška, J., Zelenický, Ľ., Chytrý, V., & Medová, J. (2020). Enhancing computational thinking through interdisciplinary STEAM activities using tablets. *Mathematics*, 8(12), 2128. DOI: 10.3390/math8122128

Wang, C., Shen, J., & Chao, J. (2022). Integrating computational thinking in STEM education: A literature review. *International Journal of Science and Mathematics Education*, 20(8), 1949–1972. DOI: 10.1007/s10763-021-10227-5

Weintrop, D., Beheshti, E., Horn, M., Orton, K., Jona, K., Trouille, L., & Wilensky, U. (2016). Defining computational thinking for mathematics and science classrooms. *Journal of Science Education and Technology*, 25(1), 127–147. DOI: 10.1007/s10956-015-9581-5

Yadav, A., Mayfield, C., Zhou, N., Hambrusch, S., & Korb, J. T. (2024). Computational thinking in elementary and secondary teacher education. [TOCE]. *ACM Transactions on Computing Education*, 14(1), 1–16. DOI: 10.1145/2576872

Yilmaz Ince, E., & Koc, M. (2021). The consequences of robotics programming education on computational thinking skills: An intervention of the Young Engineer's Workshop (YEW). *Computer Applications in Engineering Education*, 29(1), 191–208. DOI: 10.1002/cae.22321

Zahra, A., Waheed, Z., Fatima, T., & Khong, K. W. (2024). Leveraging Technology for Environmental Awareness: Insights from Experimental Research with Middle School Students in Malaysia. *RMLE Online: Research in Middle Level Education*, 47(4), 1–17. DOI: 10.1080/19404476.2024.2322046

Zint, M., Michel, J. O., Valentine, T., & Collins, S. (2024). *Collaborating with Students to Advance Climate Change Education at the University of Michigan*. Insights and Recommendations.

Compilation of References

A'yun, K., Suharso, P., & Kantun, S. (2021, May). Google Classroom as The Online Learning Platform During the Covid-19 Pandemic for The Management Business Student at SMK Negeri 1 Lumajang. []. IOP Publishing.]. *IOP Conference Series. Earth and Environmental Science*, 747(1), 012025. DOI: 10.1088/1755-1315/747/1/012025

Abdul Hamid, H., & Khalidi, J. R. (2020). *Covid-19 and Unequal Learning*. Kuala Lumpur: Khazanah Research Institute. Licence: Creative Commons Attribution CC 3.0.

Abedini, A., Abedin, B., & Zowghi, D. (2021). Adult learning in online communities of practice: A systematic review. *British Journal of Educational Technology*, 52(4), 1663–1694. DOI: 10.1111/bjet.13120

Abeysekera, I., Sunga, E., Gonzales, A., & David, R. (2024). The Effect of Cognitive Load on Learning Memory of Online Learning Accounting Students in the Philippines. *Sustainability (Basel)*, 16(4), 1686–1686. DOI: 10.3390/su16041686

Abeysekera, L., & Dawson, P. (2015). Motivation and cognitive load in the flipped classroom: Definition, rationale and a call for research. *Higher Education Research & Development*, 34(1), 1–14. DOI: 10.1080/07294360.2014.934336

Aboagye, E., Yawson, J. A., & Appiah, K. (2020). COVID-19 and e-learning: The challenges of Students in tertiary institutions. *Social Education Research*, 2(1), 1–8. DOI: 10.37256/ser.212021422

Abramenka-Lachheb, V., & de Siqueira, A. (2022). Authentic assessments through the lenses of diversity, equity, inclusion, and justice in a fully online course. *Journal of Teaching and Learning with Technology*, 11(1), 18–36. DOI: 10.14434/jotlt.v11i1.34591

Academy of Active Learning Arts and Sciences. (2018). Updated definition of flipped learning. https://aalasinternational.org/updated-definition-of-flipped-learning/

Ackermann, E. (2001). *Piaget's constructivism, Papert's constructionism: What's the difference?* Semantic Scholar. https://learning.media.mit.edu/content/publications/EA.Piaget%20_%20Papert.pdf

Acquaro, P. (2020). Structuring and scaffolding the online course: A practical development framework. *Journal of Online Graduate Education.*, 3(1). https://ijoge.org/index.php/IJOGE/article/view/38

Adala, A. A. (2016). The current state of advancement of Open Educational Resources in Kenya. *UNESCO Institute for Information Technologies in Education. Retrieved from* http://iite.unesco.org/pics/publications/en/files/3214744.pdf

Adams, B., & Wilson, N. S. (2022). Investigating students' during-reading practices through social annotation. *Literacy Research and Instruction*, 61(4), 339–360. DOI: 10.1080/19388071.2021.2008560

Adams, C. M. (2012). Calling and career counseling with college students: Finding meaning in work and life. *Journal of College Counseling*, 15(1), 65–80. DOI: 10.1002/j.2161-1882.2012.00006.x

Adams, C., & Rose, E. (2014). Will I ever connect with the students?" Online Teaching and the Pedagogy of Care. *Phenomenology & Practice*, 8(1), 5–16. DOI: 10.29173/pandpr20637

Adams, R., & Kevin, L. (2017). Engaging colleagues in active learning pedagogies through mentoring and co-design. *Proceedings of the 14th Conference on Education and Training in Optics and Photonics.* https://doi.org/DOI: 10.1117/12.2266663

Adarkwah, M. A. (2021). The power of assessment feedback in teaching and learning: A narrative review and synthesis of the literature. *SN Social Sciences*, 1(3), 75. Advance online publication. DOI: 10.1007/s43545-021-00086-w

Adedoyin, O. B., & Soykan, E. (2023). Covid-19 pandemic and online learning: The challenges and opportunities. *Interactive Learning Environments*, 31(2), 863–875. DOI: 10.1080/10494820.2020.1813180

Adisa, T. A., Antonacopoulou, E., Beauregard, T. A., Dickmann, M., & Adekoya, O. D. (2022). Exploring the impact of COVID-19 on employees' boundary management and work-life balance. *British Journal of Management*, 33(4), 1694–1709. DOI: 10.1111/1467-8551.12643

Aduba, D. E., & Mayowa-Adebara, O. (2022). Online platforms used for teaching and learning during the COVID-19 era: The case of LIS students in Delta State University, Abraka. *The International Information & Library Review*, 54(1), 17–31. DOI: 10.1080/10572317.2020.1869903

Agbo, F. J., Yigzaw, S. T., Sanusi, I. T., Oyelere, S. S., & Mare, A. H. (2021, October). Examining theoretical and pedagogical foundations of computational thinking in the context of higher education. In *2021 IEEE Frontiers in Education Conference (FIE)* (pp. 1-8). IEEE. DOI: 10.1109/FIE49875.2021.9637405

Agbo, F. J., Oyelere, S. S., Suhonen, J., & Adewumi, S. (2019, November). A systematic review of computational thinking approach for programming education in higher education institutions. In *Proceedings of the 19th Koli Calling International Conference on Computing Education Research* (pp. 1-10). DOI: 10.1145/3364510.3364521

Aguilar, M. I., & Castañeda, A. (2021). What mathematical competencies does a citizen need to interpret Mexico's official information about the COVID-19 pandemic? *Educational Studies in Mathematics*, 108(1–2), 227–248. DOI: 10.1007/s10649-021-10082-9 PMID: 34934238

Ahmadi, M. M. (2024). E-Learning for College Students with Disabilities in the UAE: Challenges and Solutions. *The Palgrave Encyclopedia of Disability*, 1-11.

Ahmad, T. (2020). A scenario-based approach to re-imagining the future of higher education which prepares students for the future of work. Higher Education. *Skills and Work-Based Learning*, 10(1), 217–238. DOI: 10.1108/HESWBL-12-2018-0136

Ahmad, T., Zhang, D., Huang, C., Zhang, H., Dai, N., Song, Y., & Chen, H. (2021). Artificial intelligence in the sustainable energy industry: Status Quo, challenges and opportunities. *Journal of Cleaner Production*, 289, 125834. DOI: 10.1016/j.jclepro.2021.125834

Ahmed, V., & Opoku, A. (2022). Technology supported learning and pedagogy in times of crisis: The case of COVID-19 pandemic. *Education and Information Technologies*, 27(1), 365–405. DOI: 10.1007/s10639-021-10706-w PMID: 34462626

Ahn, J., Weng, C., & Butler, B. S. (2013, January). The dynamics of open, peer-to-peer learning: what factors influence participation in the P2P University? In *2013 46th Hawaii International Conference on System Sciences* (pp. 3098-3107). IEEE. DOI: 10.1109/HICSS.2013.515

Ahn, L. H., Hill, C. E., Gerstenblith, J. A., Hillman, J. W., Mui, V. W., Yetter, C., Anderson, T., & Kivlighan, D. M.Jr. (2023). Helping Skills Training: Outcomes and Trainer Effects. *Journal of Counseling Psychology*, 70(4), 396–402. DOI: 10.1037/cou0000667 PMID: 37199956

Ajayi, F. A., & Udeh, C. A.Funmilayo Aribidesi AjayiChioma Ann Udeh. (2024). Review of workforce upskilling initiatives for emerging technologies in IT. *International Journal of Management & Entrepreneurship Research*, 6(4), 1119–1137. DOI: 10.51594/ijmer.v6i4.1003

Ajjawi, R., Kent, F., Broadbent, J., Tai, J. H.-M., Bearman, M., & Boud, D. (2022). Feedback that works: A realist review of feedback interventions for written tasks. *Studies in Higher Education*, 47(7), 1343–1356. DOI: 10.1080/03075079.2021.1894115

Akbar, M. (2016). Digital technology shaping teaching practices in higher education. *Frontiers in ICT (Lausanne, Switzerland)*, 3. Advance online publication. DOI: 10.3389/fict.2016.00001

Akçayır, G., & Akçayır, M. (2018). The flipped classroom: A review of its advantages and challenges. *Computers & Education*, 126(1), 334–345. DOI: 10.1016/j.compedu.2018.07.021

Akdeniz, İ., & Uzun, M. (2022). Teachers' views on the problems they have experienced in classroom management during the distance education process. *Kahramanmaras Sutcu Imam University Journal of Education*, 4(1), 45–75.

Akkuş, İ., & Acar, S. (2017). A research on determining the effect of technical problems in simultaneous learning environments on teachers and learners. *Inonu University Journal of the Faculty of Education*, 18(3), 363–376.

Akman, Y. (2021). Investigation of the relationship between digital literacy, online learning, and academic aspiration. *The Journal of Turkish Educational Sciences*, 19(2), 1012–1036. DOI: 10.37217/tebd.982846

Akram, H., Abdelrady, A. H., Al-Adwan, A. S., & Ramzan, M. (2022). Teachers' perceptions of technology integration in teaching-learning practices: A systematic review. *Frontiers in Psychology*, 13, 920317. DOI: 10.3389/fpsyg.2022.920317 PMID: 35734463

Akyol, Z., & Garrison, D. R. (2011). Understanding cognitive presence in an online and blended community of inquiry: Assessing outcomes and processes for deep approaches to learning. *British Journal of Educational Technology*, 42(2), 233–250. DOI: 10.1111/j.1467-8535.2009.01029.x

Al Mamun, M. A., & Lawrie, G. (2024). Cognitive presence in learner–content interaction process: The role of scaffolding in online self-regulated learning environments. *Journal of Computers in Education*, 11(3), 791–821. DOI: 10.1007/s40692-023-00279-7

Al-Adwan, A., & Smedley, J. (2012). Implementing e-learning in the Jordanian Higher Education System: Factors affecting impact. *International Journal of Education and Development using ICT*, 8(1).

Alam, A. (2022). Platform utilizi blockchain technology for eLearning and online education for open sharing of academic proficiency and progress records. In Smart data intelligence [Singapore: Springer Nature Singapore.]. *Proceedings of ICSMDI*, 2022, 307–320.

Alamri, H., Lowell, V., Watson, W., & Watson, S. L. (2020). Using personalized learning as an instructional approach to motivate learners in online higher education: Learner self-determination and intrinsic motivation. *Journal of Research on Technology in Education*, 52(3), 322–352. DOI: 10.1080/15391523.2020.1728449

Albinson, P., Cetinkaya, D., & Orman, T. (2020). Using technology to enhance assessment and feedback: A framework for evaluating tools and applications. *Proceedings of the 2020 9th International Conference on Educational and Information Technology*. DOI: 10.1145/3383923.3383940

Albuquerque, U. P., Maroyi, A., Ladio, A. H., Pieroni, A., Abbasi, A. M., Toledo, B. A., Dahdouh-Guebas, F., Hallwass, G., Soldati, G. T., Odonne, G., Vandebroek, I., Vallès, J., Hurrell, J. A., Pardo de Santayana, M., La Torre-Cuadros, M. Á., Silva, M. T. P., Jacob, M. C. M., da Fonseca-Kruel, V. S., & Ferreira Júnior, W. S. (2024). Advancing ethnobiology for the ecological transition and a more inclusive and just world: A comprehensive framework for the next 20 years. *Journal of Ethnobiology and Ethnomedicine*, 20(1), 18. DOI: 10.1186/s13002-024-00661-4 PMID: 38360640

Alemdag, E. (2022). Effects of instructor-present videos on learning, cognitive load, motivation, and social presence: A meta-analysis. *Education and Information Technologies*, 27(9), 12713–12742. DOI: 10.1007/s10639-022-11154-w

Alenezi, A. (2017). Obstacles for teachers to integrate technology with instruction. *Education and Information Technologies*, 22(4), 1797–1816. DOI: 10.1007/s10639-016-9518-5

Al-Freih, M., & Robinson, H. (2024). A Qualitative Exploration of Students' Perception of Care When Learning Online: Implications for Online Teaching and Faculty Professional Development. [IJOPCD]. *International Journal of Online Pedagogy and Course Design*, 14(1), 1–15. DOI: 10.4018/IJOPCD.333715

Ali, A. (2014) Quality Assurance in Open and Distance Learning: Strategies and Approaches from the Perspective of Open University Malaysia. In: *International Seminar on Quality Assurance and Sustainability of Higher Education Institutions*, 14-15 February 2014, Bali, Indonesia.

Ali, I., Narayan, A. K., & Sharma, U. (2021). Adapting to COVID-19 disruptions: Student engagement in online learning of accounting. *Accounting Research Journal*, 34(3), 261–269. DOI: 10.1108/ARJ-09-2020-0293

Allen, I. E., & Seaman, J. (2016). *Online report card: Tracking online education in the United States*. Babson Survey Research Group and Quahog Research Group., Retrieved from http://onlinelearningsurvey.com/reports/onlinereportcard.pdf

Allen, T. D., Merlo, K., Lawrence, R. C., Slutsky, J., & Gray, C. E. (2021). Boundary management and work-nonwork balance while working from home. *Applied Psychology*, 70(1), 60–84. DOI: 10.1111/apps.12300

Alojaiman, B. 2021. Toward Selection of Trustworthy and Efficient E-Learning Platform. IEE Access, 9, 133889–133901. *(2) (PDF) Challenging the Status Quo: Open Journal Systems for Online Academic Writing Course.*DOI: 10.1109/ACCESS.2021.3114150

Alsaleh, N. J. (2020). Teaching critical thinking skills: Literature review. *Turkish Online Journal of Educational Technology-TOJET*, 19(1), 21–39.

Alsulami, S. A., & Sherwood, G. D. (2020). The experience of culturally diverse faculty in academic environments: A multi-country scoping review. *Nurse Education in Practice*, 44, 102777. Advance online publication. DOI: 10.1016/j.nepr.2020.102777 PMID: 32252017

Alsuwaida, N. (2022). Online courses in art and design during the Coronavirus (COVID-19) pandemic: Teaching reflections from a first-time online instructor. *SAGE Open*, 12(1), 1–9. DOI: 10.1177/21582440221079827

Alt, D., & Naamati-Schneider, L. (2021). Health management students' self-regulation and digital concept mapping in online learning environments. *BMC Medical Education*, 21(1), 1–15. DOI: 10.1186/s12909-021-02542-w PMID: 33596899

Althubaiti, A., & Althubaiti, S. M. (2024). Flipping the online classroom to teach statistical data analysis software: A quasi-experimental study. *SAGE Open*, 14(1), 21582440241235022. Advance online publication. DOI: 10.1177/21582440241235022

Amalia, E. R. (2018). Collaborative Learning: The concepts and practices in the classroom. International Journal of Research Studies in Education

Amand, S. (2023). *Blended Learning Vs. Traditional Learning: A Detailed Overview Of The Two Approaches.* https://elearningindustry.com/blended-learning-vs-traditional-learning-a-detailed-overview-of-the-two-approaches

Amato, C. (2021). *Community college faculty and competency-based education: a grounded theory study* (Doctoral dissertation, Franklin University).

American College Health Association. (2023). *National college health assessment.* https://www.acha.org/ncha/data-results/survey-results/

American College of Education. (2023). *History and Mission.* Retrieved from https://www.ace.edu/about/history-mission

American Psychiatric Association. (2021, May 27). *New nationwide poll shows an increased popularity for telehealth services.* https://www.psychiatry.org/news-room/news-releases/new-nationwide-poll-shows-an-increased-popularity#:~:text=Nearly%20four%20in%20ten%20Americans,of%20the%20pandemic%20(82%25)

American Psychological Association. (2020). *Stress in America 2020: A national mental health crisis.* https://www.apa.org/news/press/releases/stress/2020/sia-mental-health-crisis.pdf

American Psychology Association. (2012). *Resilience.* https://www.apa.org/topics/resilience

Amir, D., Hanim Rahmat, N., & Shazri, S. S. (2021*).Is there cognitive presence during online learning?* In *International Virtual Symposium: Research, Industry & Community Engagement (RICE)* (pp. 99-103).

Andel, S. A., de Vreede, T., Spector, P. E., Padmanabhan, B., Singh, V. K., & de Vreede, G. J. (2020). Do social features help in video-centric online learning platforms? A social presence perspective. *Computers in Human Behavior*, 113, 106505. Advance online publication. DOI: 10.1016/j.chb.2020.106505

Andenoro, A. C. (2007). Competencies of leadership professionals: A national study of premier leadership degree programs (Doctoral dissertation, Texas A&M University).

Anderson, T. (2017). How communities of inquiry drive teaching and learning in the digital age. *North Contact, 1*, 1–6. https://teachonline.ca/fr/node/92055

Anderson, E., Vasiliou, C., & Crick, T. (2022). Co-Designing Classroom Practice to Improve Student Attention and Engagement in Computer Science Degree Programmes. *Proceedings of the 27th ACM Conference on Innovation and Technology in Computer Science Education.* DOI: 10.1145/3502717.3532149

Anderson, R. M., Heesterbeek, H., Klinkenberg, D., & Hollingsworth, T. D. (2020). How will country-based mitigation measures influence the course of the COVID-19 epidemic? *Lancet*, 395(10228), 931–934. DOI: 10.1016/S0140-6736(20)30567-5 PMID: 32164834

Anderson, T., & Shattuck, J. (2012). Design-based research: A decade of progress in education research? *Educational Researcher*, 41(1), 16–25. DOI: 10.3102/0013189X11428813

Andrade, M. S., & Bunker, E. L. (2009). A model for self-regulated distance language learning. *Distance Education*, 30(1), 47–61. DOI: 10.1080/01587910902845956

Andreev, I. (2024, July 31). *Learning outcomes.* https://www.valamis.com/hub/learning-outcomes#5-types-of-learning-outcomes

Angermeier, K., & Ansen, H. (2020). Value and understanding of numeracy practices in German debt counselling from the perspective of professionals. *ZDM Mathematics Education*, 52(3), 461–472. DOI: 10.1007/s11858-019-01109-w

Anjali, B. (2024). *Difference Between Traditional and Online Education.* GeeksforGeeks. https://www.geeksforgeeks.org/difference-between-traditional-and-online-education/

Ansell, C., & Gash, A. (2018). Collaborative platforms as a governance strategy. *Journal of Public Administration: Research and Theory*, 28(1), 16–32. DOI: 10.1093/jopart/mux030

Aparicio-Gómez, O., & Ostos-Ortiz, O. (2020). Evaluación formativa. Universidad Santo Tomás, Working Paper No. 197523. https://doi.org/DOI: 10.13140/RG.2.2.31755.11049

Apiola, M., & Sutinen, E. (2021). Design science research for learning software engineering and computational thinking: Four cases. *Computer Applications in Engineering Education*, 29(1), 83–101. DOI: 10.1002/cae.22291

Arbaugh, J. B. (2014). System, scholar or students? Which most influences online MBA course effectiveness? *Journal of Computer Assisted Learning*, 30(4), 349–362. DOI: 10.1111/jcal.12048

Archambault, L., Leary, H., & Rice, K. (2022). Pillars of online pedagogy: A framework for teaching in online learning environments. *Educational Psychologist*, 57(3), 178–191. DOI: 10.1080/00461520.2022.2051513

Arévalo-Mercado, C. A., Muñoz-Andrade, E. L., Cardona-Reyes, H., & Romero-Juárez, M. G. (2023). Applying Cognitive Load Theory and the Split Attention Effect to Learning Data Structures. *IEEE Revista Iberoamericana de Technologias del Aprendizaje*, 18(1), 107–113. DOI: 10.1109/RITA.2023.3250580

Ari, F., Arslan-Ari, I., Abaci, S., & Inan, F. A. (2022). Online simulation for information technology skills training in higher education. *Journal of Computing in Higher Education*, 34(2), 371–395. DOI: 10.1007/s12528-021-09303-0 PMID: 35125847

Arrieta, G. S., Calabio, R. C., & Rogel, E. M. (2021). Accompanying students in online learning: Challenges and interventions. *Jurnal Inovatif Ilmu Pendidikan*, 2(2), 106–119. DOI: 10.23960/jiip.v2i2.21787

Artal-Sevil, J. S., Romero, E., & Artacho, J. M. (2018). Using new multimedia learning technologies: presentation design tools, dynamic animations, interactive maps, visual content and multimedia resources. In *EDULEARN18 Proceedings* (pp. 9617-9627). IATED. DOI: 10.21125/edulearn.2018.2307

Artigue, M. (2007). Learning Mathematics in a CAS Environment: The Genesis of a Reflection about Instrumentation and the Dialectics between Technical and Conceptual Work. *International Journal of Computers for Mathematical Learning*, 7(3), 245–274. DOI: 10.1023/A:1022103903080

Asad, M. M., Naz, A., Churi, P., & Tahanzadeh, M. M. (2021). Virtual reality as a pedagogical tool to enhance experiential learning: A systematic literature review. *Education Research International*, 2021(1), 7061623. DOI: 10.1155/2021/7061623

Athanassiou, N., McNett, J., & Harvey, C. (2003). Critical thinking in the management classroom: Bloom's taxonomy as a learning tool. *Journal of Management Education*, 27(5), 533–555. DOI: 10.1177/1052562903252515

Auzmendi, E. (1992). *Las Actitudes hacia la Matemática Estadística en las Enseñanzas Medias y Universitarias*. Mensajero.

Avci, Z., & Ergulec, F. (2019, November). *The Community of Inquiry (CoI) framework for overcoming learning barriers in open and distance education* [Paper presentation]. International Open and Distance learning Conference Proceedings (pp. 137–153), Anadolu University, Turkey.

Aydın, A. (2017). *Classroom management*. Pegem Academy.

Ayeni, O. O., Al Hamad, N. M., Chisom, O. N., Osawaru, B., & Adewusi, O. E. (2024). AI in education: A review of personalized learning and educational technology. *GSC Advanced Research and Reviews*, 18(2), 261–271. DOI: 10.30574/gscarr.2024.18.2.0062

Azizan, M. T. (2023). Promoting cognitive engagement using technology enhanced book-end method in online active learning strategies. *ASEAN Journal of Engineering Education*, 7(2), 8–16. DOI: 10.11113/ajee2023.7n2.129

Aziz, I. N. (2020). Implementation of SQ3R method in improving the students' basic reading skills. *EDUCATIO: Journal of Education*, 1(2), 102–110.

Bachik, M. A. K., Carey, G., & Craighead, W. E. (2020). VIA character strengths among U.S. college students and their associations with happiness, well-being, resiliency, academic success and psychopathology. *The Journal of Positive Psychology*, 16(4), 512–525. DOI: 10.1080/17439760.2020.1752785

Badiozaman, I. F. A. (2021). Exploring online readiness in the context of the COVID 19 pandemic. *Teaching in Higher Education*, •••, 1–19. DOI: 10.1080/13562517.2021.1943654

Baepler, P., Walker, J., & Driessen, M. (2014). It's not about seat time: Blending, flipping, and efficiency in active learning classrooms. *Computers & Education*, 78, 227–236. DOI: 10.1016/j.compedu.2014.06.006

Baig, M. I., & Yadegaridehkordi, E. (2023). Flipped classroom in higher education: A systematic literature review and research challenges. *International Journal of Educational Technology in Higher Education*, 20(1), 61–26. DOI: 10.1186/s41239-023-00430-5

Baker, R. S., & Siemens, G. (2014). Educational data mining and learning analytics. *Learning Analytics and Knowledge Conference (LAK '14)*, Indianapolis, IN, 4-8 March 2014, ACM.

Bakker, A., Smit, J., & Wegerif, R. (2015). Scaffolding and dialogic teaching in mathematics education: Introduction and review. *ZDM Mathematics Education*, 47(7), 1047–1065. DOI: 10.1007/s11858-015-0738-8

Balamurugan, B., Mullai, M., Soundararajan, S., Selvakanmani, S., & Arun, D. (2020). Brain–computer interface for assessment of mental efforts in e-learning using the nonmarkovian queueing model. *Computer Applications in Engineering Education*, 29(2), 394–410. DOI: 10.1002/cae.22209

Bali, M., & Zamora, M. (2022). The equity–care matrix: Theory and practice. *Italian Journal of Educational Technology*, 30(1), 92–115. DOI: 10.17471/2499-4324/1241

Ball, S. J. (1994). *Education reform*. McGraw-Hill Education.

Bandura, A. (1977). Self-efficacy: Toward a unifying theory of behavioral change. *Psychological Review*, 84(2), 191–215. DOI: 10.1037/0033-295X.84.2.191 PMID: 847061

Bandura, A. (1986). *Social foundations of thought and action: A social cognitive theory*. Prentice Hall.

Bandura, A., & Wessels, S. (1997). *Self-efficacy*. Cambridge University Press.

Banerjee, M., Wolf, J., Chalasani, S., Dhumal, P., & Gee, M. (2020). Creating teaching presence in online courses through videos. *Business Education Innovation Journal*, 12(1), 190–198.

Bangert, A. (2008). The influence of social presence and teaching presence on the quality of online critical inquiry. *Journal of Computing in Higher Education*, 20(1), 34–61. DOI: 10.1007/BF03033431

Barakabitze, A. A., William-Andey Lazaro, A., Ainea, N., Mkwizu, M. H., Maziku, H., Matofali, A. X., Iddi, A., & Sanga, C. (2019). Transforming African education systems in science, technology, engineering, and mathematics (STEM) using ICTs: Challenges and opportunities. *Education Research International*, 2019(1), 6946809. DOI: 10.1155/2019/6946809

Baran, E., & Correia, A.-P. (2014). A pedagogical model for online learning: Educators' perspectives on course design. *British Journal of Educational Technology*, 45(5), 792–806.

Baran, E., & Correia, A.-P. (2014). A professional development framework for online teaching. *TechTrends*, 58(5), 95–101. DOI: 10.1007/s11528-014-0791-0

Barcelos, T. S., & Silveira, I. F. (2022, October). Teaching computational thinking in initial series an analysis of the confluence among mathematics and computer sciences in elementary education and its implications for higher education. In *2012 XXXVIII Conferencia Latinoamericana En Informatica (CLEI)* (pp. 1-8). IEEE.

Baria, K., & Gomez, D. (2022). Influence of social support to student learning and development

Barrett, B., & Ashar, L. (2024). Creating artificial intelligence (AI) best practices in virtual learning environments: A primer approach for introducing the implementation of generative-AI as a teaching tool. In *Proceedings of the 16th International Conference on Education and New Learning Technologies (EDULEARN24)* (pp. 9197–9202). https://doi.org/DOI: 10.21125/edulearn.2024.2216

Barrow, M. (2015). Caring in teaching: A complicated relationship. *The Journal of Effective Teaching*, 15(2), 45–59.

Bass, L. (2009). Fostering an ethic of care in leadership: A conversation with five African American women. *Advances in Developing Human Resources*, 11(5), 619–632. DOI: 10.1177/1523422309352075

Bati, K., Yetişir, M. I., Çalişkan, I., Güneş, G., & Gül Saçan, E. (2018). Teaching the concept of time: A steam-based program on computational thinking in science education. *Cogent Education*, 5(1), 1507306. DOI: 10.1080/2331186X.2018.1507306

Bawa, P. (2023). Student engagement and satisfaction in online learning environments: The role of elective courses. *Educational Technology Research and Development*, 71(2), 224–239.

Beauchemin, J. D. (2018). Solution-focused wellness: A randomized controlled trial of college students. *Health & Social Work*, 43(2), 94–100. DOI: 10.1093/hsw/hly007 PMID: 29490041

Beckett, G., & Slater, T. (2019). *Global perspectives on project-based language learning, teaching, and assessment: key approaches, technology tools, and frameworks*. Routledge. DOI: 10.4324/9780429435096

Beetham, H., & Sharpe, R. (Eds.). (2019). *Rethinking pedagogy for a digital age* (3rd ed.). Routledge., DOI: 10.4324/9781351252805

Ben Hassen, T. (2021). The state of the knowledge-based economy in the Arab world: cases of Qatar and Lebanon. *EuroMed Journal of Business, 16*(2), 129-153.

Bender, W. N. (2012). *Project-based learning: Differentiating instruction for the 21st century*. Corwin Press.

Bennani, S., Maalel, A., & Ben Ghezala, H. (2022). Adaptive gamification in E-learning: A literature review and future challenges. *Computer Applications in Engineering Education*, 30(2), 628–642. DOI: 10.1002/cae.22477

Bennoun, S., Haeberli, P., & Schaub, M. (2018). Taking an ethics of care perspective on two university teacher training programmes. *South African Journal of Higher Education*, 32(6), 137–152. DOI: 10.20853/32-6-2651

Berge, Z. L., & Muilenburg, L. Y. (Eds.). (2013). *Handbook of mobile learning* (pp. 133-146). Routledge. DOI: 10.1108/EMJB-03-2020-0026

Berges, S., Martino, S., Basko, L., & McCabe, C. (2021). "Zooming" into engagement: Increasing engagement in the online classroom. *Journal of Institutional Research*, 10, 5–11.

Bergmann, J. (2022). The mastery learning handbook: A competency-based approach to student achievement. In *ASCD* (1st ed.). ASCD.

Bergmann, J., & Sams, A. (2012). *Flip your classroom: Reach every student in every class every day* (1st ed.). International Society for Technology in Education.

Bergman, R. (2004). Caring for the ethical ideal: Nel Noddings on moral education. *Journal of Moral Education*, 33(2), 149–162. DOI: 10.1080/0305724042000215203

Berry, G. R., & Hughes, H. (2020). Integrating work–life balance with 24/7 information and communication technologies: The experience of adult students with online learning. *American Journal of Distance Education*, 34(2), 91–105. DOI: 10.1080/08923647.2020.1701301

Berry, S. (2019). Teaching to connect: Community-building strategies for the virtual classroom. *Online Learning : the Official Journal of the Online Learning Consortium*, 23(1), 164–183. DOI: 10.24059/olj.v23i1.1425

Bhagat, K. K., Chang, C. N., & Chang, C. Y. (2016). The impact of the flipped classroom on mathematics concept learning in high school. *Journal of Educational Technology & Society*, 19(3), 134–142.

Bhutoria, A. (2022). Personalized education and artificial intelligence in the United States, China, and India: A systematic review using a human-in-the-loop model. *Computers and Education: Artificial Intelligence*, 3, 100068. DOI: 10.1016/j.caeai.2022.100068

Bialowas, A., & Steimel, S. (2019). Less is more: Use of video to address the problem of teacher immediacy and presence in online courses. *International Journal on Teaching and Learning in Higher Education*, 31(2), 354–364.

BIE – Buck Institute for Education. https://www.pblworks.org/

Bigatel, P. M., Ragan, L. C., Kennan, S., May, J., & Redmond, B. F. (2012). The identification of competencies for online teaching success. *Online Learning : the Official Journal of the Online Learning Consortium*, 16(1), 59–77. https://eric.ed.gov/?id=EJ971040. DOI: 10.24059/olj.v16i1.215

Biggs, A., Johnston, S., & Russell, D. (2024). Leadership and communication: How to assess executive skills. *The Journal of Business Strategy*, 45(3), 199–205. DOI: 10.1108/JBS-05-2023-0085

Biggs, J., & Tang, C. (2011). *Teaching for quality learning at university: What the student does* (4th ed.). Open University Press.

Binoy, S., & Raddi, S. A. (2022). Concept mapping to enhance critical thinking in nursing students. *International Journal of Nursing Education*, 14(2), 159–164. DOI: 10.37506/ijone.v14i2.18008

Biringkanae, A. (2018). The use of SQ3R technique in improving students' reading comprehension. *ELS Journal on Interdisciplinary Studies in Humanities*, 1(2), 218–225. DOI: 10.34050/els-jish.v1i2.4316

BIS. (Department of Business, Innovation and Skills). (2012). *The 2011 skills for life survey: A survey of literacy, numeracy and ICT levels in England* (BIS Paper 81). https://www.gov.uk/government/publications/2011-skills-for-life-survey

Bishop, J., & Verleger, M. A. (2013). The flipped classroom: A survey of the research. 120th American Society for Engineering Education Annual Conference and Exposition, 30, 1-18.

Bizami, N. A., Tasir, Z., & Kew, S. N. (2023). Innovative pedagogical principles and technological tools capabilities for immersive blended learning: A systematic literature review. *Education and Information Technologies*, 28(2), 1373–1425. DOI: 10.1007/s10639-022-11243-w PMID: 35919874

Blaine, A. M. (2019). Interaction and presence in the virtual classroom: An analysis of the perceptions of students and teachers in online and blended Advanced Placement courses. *Computers & Education*, 132, 31–43. DOI: 10.1016/j.compedu.2019.01.004

Bloomberg. L. D. (2021). *Designing and delivering effective online instruction: How to engage adult learners.* Teachers College Press.

Bloomberg, L. D. (2023). Designing and delivering effective online instruction, how to engage the adult learner. *Adult Learning*, 34(1), 55–56. DOI: 10.1177/10451595211069079

Bocconi, S., Chioccariello, A., Kampylis, P., Dagienė, V., Wastiau, P., Engelhardt, K., ... & Stupurienė, G. (2022). Reviewing computational thinking in compulsory education: State of play and practices from computing education.

Boeren, E., & Whittaker, S. (2018). A typology of education and training provisions for low educated adults: Categories and definitions. *Studies in the Education of Adults*, 50(1), 4–18. DOI: 10.1080/02660830.2018.1520017

Boettcher, J. V., & Conrad, R. M. (2016). *The Online Teaching Survival Guide: Simple and Practical Pedagogical Tips* (2nd ed.). Jossey-Bass.

Boling, E. C., & Beatty, J. (2013). Overcoming the tensions and challenges of technology integration: How can we best support our teachers? In *K-12 Education* (pp. 1504–1524). IGI Global.

Bolliger, D. U., & Halupa, C. (2022). An Investigation of Instructors' Online Teaching Readiness. *TechTrends*, 66(2), 185–195. DOI: 10.1007/s11528-021-00654-0 PMID: 34485992

Bonde, S., Briant, C., Firenze, P., Hanavan, J., Huang, A., Li, M., Narayanan, N. C., Parthasarathy, D., & Zhao, H. (2016). Making choices: Ethical decisions in a global context. *Science and Engineering Ethics*, 22(2), 343–366. DOI: 10.1007/s11948-015-9641-5 PMID: 25962719

Bonney, L. (2020). Mindfulness for school leader well-being: Why mindfulness matters and how to make it work. *Leadership*, 50(1), 30–33.

Bonwell, C. C., & Eison, J. A. (1991). *Active learning: Creating excitement in the classroom*. School of Education and Human Development, George Washington University.

Boothe, K. A., Lohmann, M. J., Donnell, K. A., & Hall, D. D. (2018). Applying the principles of universal design for learning (UDL) in the college classroom. *The Journal of Special Education Apprenticeship*, 7(3), n3. DOI: 10.58729/2167-3454.1076

Borotis, S., & Poulymenakou, A. (2004). E-Learning Readiness Components: Key Issues to Consider Before Adopting e-Learning Interventions. In J. Nall & R. Robson (Eds.), *Proceedings of E-Learn 2004--World Conference on E-Learning in Corporate, Government, Healthcare, and Higher Education*. 1622–1629. Washington, DC, USA: Association for the Advancement of Computing in Education (AACE). Retrieved September 3, 2023 from https://www.learntechlib.org/primary/p/11555/

Borrego, M., & Henderson, C. (2014). Increasing the use of evidence-based teaching in STEM higher education: A comparison of eight change strategies. *Journal of Engineering Education*, 103(2), 220–252. DOI: 10.1002/jee.20040

Borup, J., West, R., Thomas, R., & Graham, C. (2014). Examining the impact of video feedback on instructor social presence in blended courses. *The International Review of Research in Open and Distributed Learning*, 15(3). https://doi.org/.v15i3.1821 DOI: 10.19173/irrodl

Borup, J., & Evmenova, A. (2019). The effectiveness of professional development in overcoming obstacles to effective online instruction in a college of education. *Online Learning : the Official Journal of the Online Learning Consortium*, 23(2). Advance online publication. DOI: 10.24059/olj.v23i2.1468

Borup, J., West, R. E., & Graham, C. R. (2012). Improving online social presence through asynchronous video. *The Internet and Higher Education*, 15(3), 195–203. DOI: 10.1016/j.iheduc.2011.11.001

Boss, S. (2011). Project-Based Learning: A short history. https://www.edutopia.org/project-based-learning-history

Bostwick, D. (2023). Fostering community and engagement in online 'classrooms'. *Teaching Journalism Online*, 53.

Boud, D., & Molloy, E. (2013). Rethinking models of feedback for learning: The challenge of design. *Assessment & Evaluation in Higher Education*, 38(6), 698–712. DOI: 10.1080/02602938.2012.691462

Bower, M., Dalgarno, B., Kennedy, G. E., Lee, M. J., & Kenney, J. (2015). Design and implementation factors in blended synchronous learning environments: Outcomes from a cross-case analysis. *Computers & Education*, 86, 1–17. DOI: 10.1016/j.compedu.2015.03.006

Boyatzis, R. E., & Cavanagh, K. V. (2018). Leading change: Developing emotional, social, and cognitive competencies in managers during an MBA program. *Emotional intelligence in education: Integrating research with practice*, 403-426.

Boyd, B. L., Getz, C. A., & Guthrie, K. L. (2019). Preparing the leadership educator through graduate education. *New directions for student leadership*, 2019(164), 105-121.h Leadership Development. *New Directions for Student Leadership*, 2020(165).

Bozkurt, A. (2019). From distance education to open and distance learning: A holistic evaluation of history, definitions, and theories. In Sisman-Ugur, S., & Kurubacak, G. (Eds.), *Handbook of research on learning in the age of transhumanism* (pp. 252–273). IGI Global. DOI: 10.4018/978-1-5225-8431-5.ch016

Bozkurt, A., Akgün-Özbek, E., & Zawacki-Richter, O. (2020). Trends and patterns in distance education research: A content analysis of journals 2009–2013. *The International Review of Research in Open and Distributed Learning*, 16(1), 330–362.

Bozkurt, A., Jung, I., Xiao, J., Vladimirschi, V., Schuwer, R., Egorov, G., Lambert, S., Al-Freih, M., Pete, J., Olcott, D.Jr, & Rodes, V. (2020). A global outlook to the interruption of education due to COVID-19 pandemic: Navigating in a time of uncertainty and crisis. *Asian Journal of Distance Education*, 15(1), 1–126.

Brackett, M. (2019). *Permission to feel: Unlocking the power of emotions to help our kids, ourselves, and our society thrive*. Celadon Books.

Brammer, S. E., & Punyanunt-Carter, N. M. (2022). Getting the attention of online learners. *Communication Education*, 71(2), 155–157. DOI: 10.1080/03634523.2021.2022732

Brandt, C. (2008). Integrating feedback and reflection in teacher preparation. *ELT Journal*, 62(1), 37–46. DOI: 10.1093/elt/ccm076

Brantlinger, A. (2022). Critical and vocational mathematics: Authentic problems for students from historically marginalized groups. *Journal for Research in Mathematics Education*, 53(2), 154–172. DOI: 10.5951/jresematheduc-2019-0025

Braun, I. S. R., & Vasko, M. (2014). Inverted classroom by topic - A study in mathematics for electrical engineering students. *International Journal of Engineering Pedagogy*, 4(3), 11–17. DOI: 10.3991/ijep.v4i3.3299

Bredow, C. A., Roehling, P. V., Knorp, A. J., & Sweet, A. M. (2021). To flip or not to flip? A meta-analysis of the efficacy of flipped learning in higher education. *Review of Educational Research*, 91(6), 878–918. DOI: 10.3102/00346543211019122

Breen, J. M., & Gleason, M. C. (2022). Setting the stage: An overview of articles in this issue. *New Directions for Student Leadership*, 2022(176), 5–8. DOI: 10.1002/yd.20525 PMID: 36565148

Brewer, R., & Movahedazarhouligh, S. (2018). Successful stories and conflicts: A literature review on the effectiveness of flipped learning in higher education. *Journal of Computer Assisted Learning*, 34(4), 409–416. DOI: 10.1111/jcal.12250

Brigas, C. J. (2019). Modeling and simulation in an educational context: Teaching and learning sciences. *Research in Social Sciences and Technology, 4*(2), 1-12. Retrieved from https://ressat.org/index.php/ressat

Brill, J. M., & Galloway, C. (2007). Perils and promises: University instructors' integration of technology in classroom-based practices. *British Journal of Educational Technology*, 38(1), 95–105. DOI: 10.1111/j.1467-8535.2006.00601.x

Bringula, R., Reguyal, J. J., Tan, D. D., & Ulfa, S. (2021). Mathematics self-concept and challenges of learners in an online learning environment during COVID-19 pandemic. *Smart Learn. Environ.*, 8(1), 22. DOI: 10.1186/s40561-021-00168-5

Britannica. (n. d.). *Social capital.* https://www.britannica.com/topic/social-capital

Brown, C., Hartnett, M., Ratima, M. T., Forbes, D., Datt, A., & Gedera, D. (2022). Putting whanaungatanga at the heart of students' online learning experiences. In S. Wilson, N. Arthars, D. Wardak, P. Yeoman, E. Kalman, & D.Y.T. Liu (Eds.), *Reconnecting relationships through technology. Proceedings of the 39th International Conference on Innovation, Practice and Research in the Use of Educational Technologies in Tertiary Education, ASCILITE 2022*. Article e22146. DOI: 10.14742/apubs.2022.146

Browning, B. R., Mcdermott, R. C., Scaffa, M. E., Booth, N. R., & Carr, N. T. (2018). Character strengths and first-year college students' academic persistence attitudes: An integrative model. *The Counseling Psychologist*, 46(5), 608–631. DOI: 10.1177/0011000018786950

Brown, J. S., & Duguid, P. (1991). Organizational learning and communities of practice: Towards a unified view of working, learning, and innovation. *Organization Science*, 2(1), 40–57. DOI: 10.1287/orsc.2.1.40

Brown, J. S., & Duguid, P. (2001). Knowledge and organization: A social practice perspective. *Organization Science*, 12(2), 198–213. DOI: 10.1287/orsc.12.2.198.10116

Brown, T. H., & Mbati, L. S. (2015). Mobile learning: Moving past the myths and embracing the opportunities. *International Review of Research in Open and Distance Learning*, 16(2), 115–135. DOI: 10.19173/irrodl.v16i2.2071

Bruner, J. S. (1961). The Act of Discovery. *Harvard Educational Review*.

Brunken, R., Plass, J. L., & Leutner, D. (2003). Direct Measurement of Cognitive Load in Multimedia Learning. *Educational Psychologist*, 38(1), 53–61. DOI: 10.1207/S15326985EP3801_7

Bryson, C., & Hand, L. (2007). The role of engagement in inspiring teaching and learning. *Innovations in Education and Teaching International*, 44(4), 349–362. DOI: 10.1080/14703290701602748

Bryson, P. C., Roediger, H. L., & McDaniel, M. A. (2014). *Make It Stick: The Science of Successful Learning*. Harvard University Press.

Buck Institute for Education. (2016). PBLWorks. https://www.pblworks.org/what-is-pbl

Bühler, B., Bozkir, E., Deininger, H., Gerjets, P., & Trautwein, U., & Enkelejda Kasneci. (2024). On Task and in Sync: Examining the Relationship between Gaze Synchrony and Self-reported Attention During Video Lecture Learning. *Proceedings of the ACM on Human-Computer Interaction*, 8(ETRA), 1–18. DOI: 10.1145/3655604

Buitrago-Flórez, F., Danies, G., Restrepo, S., & Hernández, C. (2021). Fostering 21st Century Competences through Computational Thinking and Active Learning: A Mixed Method Study. *International Journal of Instruction*, 14(3), 737–754. DOI: 10.29333/iji.2021.14343a

Buraga, R. (2019). Students' perspectives on the integration of online collaboration tools for learning. *International Journal of Innovative Technology and Exploring Engineering*, 8(5), 951–955.

Burbules, N. C., Fan, G., & Repp, P. (2020). Five trends of education and technology in a sustainable future. *Geography and Sustainability*, 1(2), 93–97. DOI: 10.1016/j.geosus.2020.05.001

Burcin, M. M., Armstrong, S. N., Early, J. O., & Godwin, H. (2019). Optimizing college health promotion in the digital age: Comparing perceived well-being, health behaviors, health education needs and preferences between college students enrolled in fully online versus campus-based programs. *Health Promotion Perspectives*, 9(4), 270–278. DOI: 10.15171/hpp.2019.37 PMID: 31777706

Burgstahler, S. (2020). *Universal design in higher education: Promising practices*. Harvard Education Press.

Burke, K., & Larmar, S. (2021). Acknowledging another face in the virtual crowd: Reimagining the online experience in higher education through an online pedagogy of care. *Journal of Further and Higher Education*, 45(5), 601–615. DOI: 10.1080/0309877X.2020.1804536

Cabı, E. (2018). The impact of the flipped classroom model on students' academic achievement. *International Review of Research in Open and Distance Learning*, 19(3), 202–222. DOI: 10.19173/irrodl.v19i3.3482

Cabrera, V., & Donaldson, S. I. (2023). PERMA to PERMA+4 building blocks of well-being: A systematic review of the empirical literature. *The Journal of Positive Psychology*, 19(3), 510–529. DOI: 10.1080/17439760.2023.2208099

Cagiltay, K. (2006). Scaffolding strategies in electronic performance support systems: Types and challenges. *Innovations in Education and Teaching International*, 43(1), 93–103. DOI: 10.1080/14703290500467673

Cagiltay, N. E., Toker, S., & Cagiltay, K. (2023). Exploring the Influence of Countries' Economic Conditions on Massive Open Online Course (MOOC) Participation: A Study of 3.5 Million MITx Learners. *International Review of Research in Open and Distance Learning*, 24(2), 1–17. DOI: 10.19173/irrodl.v24i2.7123

Caglayan, E., & Ustunluoglu, E. (2020). *A Study Exploring Students' Usage Patterns and Adoption of Lecture Capture*. Technology, Knowledge and Learning., DOI: 10.1007/s10758-020-09435-9

Çakıroğlu, Ü. (2014). Evaluating students' perspectives about virtual classrooms with regard to seven principles of good practice. *South African Journal of Education*, 34(2), 1–19. DOI: 10.15700/201412071201

Calia, C., Guerra, C., Reid, C., Marley, C., Barrera, P., Oshodi, A. G. T., & Boden, L. (2022). Developing an evidence-base to guide ethical action in global challenges research in complex and fragile contexts: A scoping review of the literature. *Ethics & Social Welfare*, 16(1), 54–72. DOI: 10.1080/17496535.2021.1916830

Calkins, S. C., & Rivnay, J. (2021). The jigsaw design challenge: An inclusive learning activity to promote cooperative problem-solving. *Journal of Effective Teaching in Higher Education*, 4(3), 19–35. DOI: 10.36021/jethe.v4i3.249

Camarata, T., & Slieman, T. A. (2020). Improving student feedback quality: A simple model using peer review and feedback rubrics. *Journal of Medical Education and Curricular Development*, 7, 238212052093660. DOI: 10.1177/2382120520936604 PMID: 33029557

Can, E. (2020). Sanal sınıf yönetimi: İlkeler, uygulamalar ve öneriler. [Virtual classroom management: Principles, practices and recommendations]. *Açıköğretim Uygulamaları ve Araştırmaları Dergisi*, 6(4), 251–295.

Canvas. https://www.instructure.com/canvas

Capote, M., Robaina, I., & Capote, M. (2022). Relaciones entre las actitudes hacia la Matemática y el rendimiento académico de los estudiantes. Mendive. *Review of Education*, 20, 1022–1035.

Capraro, R. M., Capraro, M. M., & Morgan, J. R. (2020). *STEM project-based learning: An integrated science, technology, engineering, and mathematics (STEM) approach*. Springer.

Carnahan, C. R., & Lowrey, K. A. (2018). Facilitating Evidence-Based Practice for Students with ASD. *A Paul H Brookes Publishing Co*.

Carpentieri, J., Mallows, D., Amorim, J. P., & Freire, P. (2020). Credibility, relevance, and policy impact in the evaluation of adult basic skills programs: The case of the New Opportunities Initiative in Portugal. *Adult Literacy Education*, 2(1), 6–21. Advance online publication. DOI: 10.35847/JCarpentieri.JAmorim.DMallows.PFreire.2.1.6

Carta, F. (2021). Covid pandemic-2019: Upskilling and reskilling pathways to respond to new professional needs imposed by digitalization. In *Edulearn21 Proceedings* (pp. 5641–5650). IATED. DOI: 10.21125/edulearn.2021.1145

Casey, K. (2018). Moving toward Mastery: Growing, Developing and Sustaining Educators for Competency-Based Education. Competency Works Report. *iNACOL)*.

Caskurlu, S., Richardson, J. C., Alamri, H. A., Chartier, K., Farmer, T., Janakiraman, S., Strait, M., & Yang, M. (2020). Cognitive load and online course quality: Insights from instructional designers in a higher education context. *British Journal of Educational Technology*, 52(2), 584–605. DOI: 10.1111/bjet.13043

Caso, D., Carfora, V., Capasso, M., Oliano, D., & Conner, M. (2021). Using messages targeting psychological versus physical health benefits to promote walking behaviour: A randomised controlled trial. *Applied Psychology. Health and Well-Being*, 13(1), 152–173. DOI: 10.1111/aphw.12224 PMID: 32945103

Cassidy, S. (2004). Learning styles: An overview of theories, models, and measures. *Educational Psychology*, 24(4), 419–444. DOI: 10.1080/0144341042000228834

Castro-Alonso, J. C., de Koning, B. B., Fiorella, L., & Paas, F. (2021). Five Strategies for Optimizing Instructional Materials: Instructor- and Learner-Managed Cognitive Load. *Educational Psychology Review*, 33(4), 1379–1407. Advance online publication. DOI: 10.1007/s10648-021-09606-9 PMID: 33716467

Castro, M. D. B., & Tumibay, G. M. (2021). A literature review: Efficacy of online learning courses for higher education institutions using meta-analysis. *Education and Information Technologies*, 26(2), 1367–1385. DOI: 10.1007/s10639-019-10027-z

Catyanadika, P. E., & Rajasekera, J. (2022). Influence of psychological safety and social presence on knowledge sharing behavior in higher education online learning environment. *VINE Journal of Information and Knowledge Management Systems*, 52(3), 335–353. DOI: 10.1108/VJIKMS-06-2021-0094

Cavanagh, T. M., & Kiersch, C. (2022). Using commonly-available technologies to create online multimedia lessons through the application of the Cognitive Theory of Multimedia Learning. *Educational Technology Research and Development*, 71(3), 1033–1053. Advance online publication. DOI: 10.1007/s11423-022-10181-1 PMID: 36570341

Cavanaugh, J. (2005). Teaching online: A time comparison. *Online Journal of Distance Learning Administration*, 3(1), •••. http://www.westga.edu/~distance/oj

Center for Teaching Innovation. (n.d.). Ethical AI for teaching and learning. Cornell University. https://teaching.cornell.edu/generative-artificial-intelligence/ethical-ai-teaching-and-learning

Çetin, O., & Günay, Y. (2011). Preparation of a web-based teaching material designed for science education and evaluation of this material according to teachers' and students' views. *Ahi Evran University Journal of Kirkşehir Education Faculty*, 12(2), 175–202.

Ceylan, M. (2020). Sanal sınıfların yönetimi [Management of virtual classrooms]. Dilruba Kürüm Yapıcıoğlu (Ed.) *Pandemi Döneminde Eğitim içinde [In Education During the Pandemic]* (pp. 295-352). Ankara: Anı publishing.

Chakraborty, M., & Nafukho, F. M. (2015). Strategies for virtual learning environments: Focusing on teaching presence and teaching immediacy. Internet learning, 4(1).

Chambers, A. W., & Harkins Monaco, E. (2023). Increasing Student Engagement with Instructor Feedback using Criteria-Based Rubrics as a tool for Self-Assessment. *The Journal of Scholarship of Teaching and Learning*, 23(2). Advance online publication. DOI: 10.14434/josotl.v23i2.33715

Chandler, P., & Sweller, J. (1991). Cognitive Load Theory and the Format of Instruction. *Cognition and Instruction*, 8(4), 293–332. DOI: 10.1207/s1532690xci0804_2

Chang, G. C., Huong, L. T., Moumne, R., ... (2020) COVID-19: a glance at national coping strategies on high-stakes examinations and assessments. *Working Document*. Available at. chrome-extension://efaidnbmnnnibpcajpcglclefindmkaj/ https://en.unesco.org/sites/default/files/unesco_review_of_high-stakes_exams_and_assessments_during_covid-19_en.pdf

Chang, B. (2019). Reflection in learning. *Online Learning : the Official Journal of the Online Learning Consortium*, 23(1), 95–110. DOI: 10.24059/olj.v23i1.1447

Chasokela, D. & Mpofu, S. (2024). Towards Addressing 21st-Century Digital Transformation Skills: The Zimbabwean Higher Education Context. In M. Kayyali (Ed.), *Building Resiliency in Higher Education: Globalization, Digital Skills, and Student Wellness* (pp. 424-442). IGI Global. https://doi.org/10.4018/979-8-3693-5483-4.ch022

Chasokela, D. & Ncube, C. M. (2024). Leveraging Technology for Organizational Efficiency and Effectiveness in Higher Education. In M. Kayyali (Ed.), *Building Organizational Capacity and Strategic Management in Academia* (pp. 381-410). IGI Global. https://doi.org/10.4018/979-8-3693-6967-8.ch014

Chasokela, D. (2024). Exploring the Virtual Frontier: AR and VR for Engineering Skills Development. In R. Siva Subramanian, M. Nalini, & J. Aswini (Eds.), *Navigating the Augmented and Virtual Frontiers in Engineering* (pp. 62-81). IGI Global. https://doi.org/10.4018/979-8-3693-5613-5.ch004

Chasokela, D., Shava, G. N., & Mpofu, S. (2024). Challenges and Opportunities of Learning Management System Integration from a Zimbabwean University Perspective. In M. Kayyali (Ed.), *Building Resiliency in Higher Education: Globalization, Digital Skills, and Student Wellness* (pp. 73-98). IGI Global. https://doi.org/10.4018/979-8-3693-5483-4.ch005

Chatelier, S., & Rudolph, S. (2018). Teacher responsibility: Shifting care from student to (professional) self? *British Journal of Sociology of Education*, 39(1), 1–15. DOI: 10.1080/01425692.2017.1291328

Chau, P. (2010). Online higher education commodity. *Journal of Computing in Higher Education*, 22(3), 177–191. DOI: 10.1007/s12528-010-9039-y

Chen, B., deNoyelles, A., & Thompson, K. (2023). Fostering relevance in online courses: Connecting content to current events and societal issues. *Journal of Educational Technology & Society*, 26(1), 134–147.

Chen, C.-M., & Lin, Y.-J. (2014). Effects of different text display types on reading comprehension, sustained attention and cognitive load in mobile reading contexts. *Interactive Learning Environments*, 24(3), 553–571. DOI: 10.1080/10494820.2014.891526

Chen, C.-M., & Wang, H.-P. (2011). Using emotion recognition technology to assess the effects of different multimedia materials on learning emotion and performance. *Library & Information Science Research*, 33(3), 244–255. DOI: 10.1016/j.lisr.2010.09.010

Chen, C.-M., Wang, J.-Y., & Yu, C.-M. (2015). Assessing the attention levels of students by using a novel attention aware system based on brainwave signals. *British Journal of Educational Technology*, 48(2), 348–369. DOI: 10.1111/bjet.12359

Cheng, D., & Li, M. (2020). Screencast video feedback in online TESOL classes. *Computers and Composition*, 58, 102612. Advance online publication. DOI: 10.1016/j.compcom.2020.102612

Cheng, L., Ritzhaupt, A. D., & Antonenko, P. (2019). Effects of the flipped classroom instructional strategy on students' learning outcomes: A meta-analysis. *Educational Technology Research and Development*, 67(4), 793–824. DOI: 10.1007/s11423-018-9633-7

Cheng, M. Y., & Chen, P. (2021). Applying PERMA to develop college students' English listening and speaking proficiency in China. *International Journal of English Language and Literature Studies*, 10(4), 333–350. DOI: 10.18488/journal.23.2021.104.333.350

Cheng, S., Huang, J. C., & Hebert, W. (2022). Profiles of vocational college students' achievement emotions in online learning environments: Antecedents and outcomes. *Computers in Human Behavior*, 138, 107452. Advance online publication. DOI: 10.1016/j.chb.2022.107452

Chen, H.-R. (2012). Assessment of Learners' Attention to E-Learning by Monitoring Facial Expressions for Computer Network Courses. *Journal of Educational Computing Research*, 47(4), 371–385. DOI: 10.2190/EC.47.4.b

Chessa, M., & Solari, F. (2021). The sense of being there during online classes: Analysis of usability and presence in web-conferencing systems and virtual reality social platforms. *Behaviour & Information Technology*, 40(12), 1237–1249. DOI: 10.1080/0144929X.2021.1957017

Chew, S. W., Cheng, I.-L., Kinshuk, , & Chen, N.-S. (2018). Exploring challenges faced by different stakeholders while implementing educational technology in classrooms through expert interviews. *Journal of Computers in Education*, 5(2), 175–197. DOI: 10.1007/s40692-018-0102-4

Chhatlani, C. K. (2023). Review the Role of Holistic Learning in Cultivating Global Citizenship Skills. EIKI Journal of Effective Teaching Methods, 1(2).

Chiam, C. C., Lim, T. M., Halim, N. A., & Omar, N. A. (2011). Towards Excellence in Higher Education –The Experience of Open University Malaysia (OUM). In: *Symbiosis International Conference on Open & Distance Learning*, 21-23 Feb 2011, Pune, India.

Chickering, A. W., & Gamson, Z. F. (1987). Seven principles for good practice in undergraduate education. *AAHE Bulletin*, 39, 3–7.

Chickering, A. W., & Gamson, Z. F. (1987). *Seven principles for good practice in undergraduate education*. American Association for Higher Education.

Chigbu, B. I., Ngwevu, V., & Jojo, A. (2023). The effectiveness of innovative pedagogy in the industry 4.0: Educational ecosystem perspective. *Social Sciences & Humanities Open*, 7(1), 100419. DOI: 10.1016/j.ssaho.2023.100419

Chigeza, P., & Halbert, K. (2014). Navigating e-learning and blended learning for pre-service teachers: Redesigning for engagement, access and efficiency. *The Australian Journal of Teacher Education*, 39(11), 133–146. https://eric.ed.gov/?id=EJ1047088. DOI: 10.14221/ajte.2014v39n11.8

Chi, M. T. H., & Wylie, R. (2014). The ICAP framework: Linking cognitive engagement to active learning outcomes. *Educational Psychologist*, 49(4), 219–243. DOI: 10.1080/00461520.2014.965823

Choi, I., Land, S. M., & Turgeon, A. J. (2005). Scaffolding peer-questioning strategies to facilitate metacognition during online small group discussion. *Instructional Science*, 33(5), 483–511. DOI: 10.1007/s11251-005-1277-4

Choukaier, D. (2024). Enhancing English as A Foreign Language (EFL) Instruction Through Digital Teaching Platforms: Analyzing The Impact of Microsoft Teams, Zoom, And Google Meet On Communication and Participation. *Educational Administration: Theory and Practice*, 30(6), 2404–2418.

Chuang, H. H., Shih, C. L., & Cheng, M. M. (2020). Teachers' perceptions of culturally responsive teaching in technology-supported learning environments. *British Journal of Educational Technology*, 51(6), 2442–2460. DOI: 10.1111/bjet.12921

Chu, C., Hooper, T., Takahashi, M., & Herke, M. (2024). The effect of asynchronous virtual exchange on intercultural competence among undergraduate students. *Journal of Comparative & International Higher Education*, 16(2), 213–226. DOI: 10.32674/jcihe.v16i2.5229

Cialdini, R. B., & Fincham, R. L. (1990). Trust and the development of interpersonal relationships. *Psychological Bulletin*, ●●●, 1990.

Civil, M., Stoehr, K. J., & Salazar, F. (2020). Learning with and from immigrant mothers: Implications for adult numeracy. *ZDM Mathematics Education*, 52(3), 489–500. DOI: 10.1007/s11858-019-01076-2

Clarin, A. S., & Baluyos, E. L. (2022). Challenges encountered in the implementation of online distance learning. *EduLine: Journal of Education and Learning Innovation*, 2(1), 33–46. DOI: 10.35877/454RI.eduline591

Clark, C., & Gorski, P. (2002). Multicultural education and the digital divide: Focus on socioeconomic class background. *Multicultural Perspectives*, 4(3), 25–36. DOI: 10.1207/S15327892MCP0403_6

Clark, I. (2012). Formative assessment: Assessment is for self-regulated learning. *Educational Psychology Review*, 24(2), 205–249. DOI: 10.1007/s10648-011-9191-6

Cleary, M., Visentin, D., West, S., Lopez, V., & Kornhaber, R. (2018). Promoting emotional intelligence and resilience in undergraduate nursing students: An integrative review. *Nurse Education Today*, 68, 112–120. DOI: 10.1016/j.nedt.2018.05.018 PMID: 29902740

Clinton, V., & Kelly, A. E. (2020). Student attitudes toward group discussions. *Active Learning in Higher Education*, 21(2), 154–164. DOI: 10.1177/1469787417740277

Coates, H., James, R., & Baldwin, G. (2005). A critical examination of the effects of learning management systems on university teaching and learning. *Tertiary Education and Management*, 11(1), 19–36. DOI: 10.1080/13583883.2005.9967137

Coben, D., & O'Donoghue, J. (2020). Adults learning mathematics. In Lerman, S. (Ed.), *Encyclopedia of mathematics education* (2nd ed., pp. 24–31). Springer., DOI: 10.1007/978-3-030-15789-0_5

Coleman, M., & Berge, Z. L. (2018) *A Review of Accessibility in Online Higher Education*. https://ojdla.com/archive/spring211/coleman_berge211.pdf

Coleman, J. S. (1988). Social capital in the creation of human capital. *American Journal of Sociology*, 94, 95–120. DOI: 10.1086/228943

Collins, K., Grof, S., Mathena, C., & Kupczynski, L. (2019). Asynchronous video and the development of instructor social presence and student engagement. *Turkish Online Journal of Distance Education*, 20(1), 53–70. DOI: 10.17718/tojde.522378

Comber, D. P. M., & Brady-Van den Bos, M. (2018). Too much, too soon? A critical investigation into factors that make Flipped Classrooms effective. *Higher Education Research & Development*, 37(4), 683–697. DOI: 10.1080/07294360.2018.1455642

Compeau, C., Talley, K., & Talley, A. (2024). Classicle Sticks: An Activity to Improve Student Engagement. *2024 ASEE Annual Conference & Exposition*. DOI: 10.18260/1-2--48462

Condelli, L., Safford-Ramus, K., Sherman, R., Coben, D., Gal, I., & Hector-Mason, A. (2006). *A review of the literature in adult numeracy: Research and conceptual issues*. American Institutes for Research. https://files.eric.ed.gov/fulltext/ED495456.pdf

Conklin, H. G. (2018). Caring and critical thinking in the teaching of young adolescents. *Theory into Practice*, 57(4), 289–297. DOI: 10.1080/00405841.2018.1518643

Conrad, D., & Newberry, R. (2012). Identification and instruction of important business communication skills for graduate business education. *Journal of Education for Business*, 87(2), 112–120. DOI: 10.1080/08832323.2011.576280

Coombs, N. (2022). Embedding Components of the Write on Race Intervention in a Cultural Diversity Course for Pre-Service Teachers, to Increase Cultural Humility, and the Likelihood for Future Implementation of Instructional Strategies Designed to Improve School Climate, Sense of Belonging, and Teacher-Student Relationships for Diverse Students (Doctoral dissertation, University of Missouri-Columbia).

Cooper, L., Loster-Loftus, A., & Mandernach, J. (2023). Seven strategies for more efficient, effective online instruction: Effective eLearning (special series). *ELearn, 2023*(10). DOI: 10.1145/3626767.3595382

Cooper, M. D. (2024). Centring diversity, equity, inclusion and belonging in higher education marketing: Why it is essential and how to do it well. *Journal of Education Advancement & Marketing*, 8(4), 315–330. DOI: 10.69554/JLYM7102

Cortazar, C., Nussbaum, M., Harcha, J., Alvares, D., Lopez, F., Goni, J., & Cabezas, V. (2021). Promoting critical thinking in an online, project-based course. *Computers in Human Behavior*, 119, 106705. DOI: 10.1016/j.chb.2021.106705 PMID: 36571081

Coursera - https://www.coursera.org/

Courtad, C. A. (2019). *Making your classroom smart: Universal design for learning and technology. In Smart education and e-learning* (pp. 501-510). Springer Singapore.

Covrig, D. M., & Baumgartner, E. (2010). Learning while leading: The Andrews University leadership program. *Journal of Applied Christian Leadership*, 4(1), 26–55.

Crigger, N. (2001). Antecedents to engrossment in Noddings' theory of care. *Journal of Advanced Nursing*, 35(4), 616–623. DOI: 10.1046/j.1365-2648.2001.01878.x PMID: 11529962

Croce, K., & McCormick, M. K. (2020). Developing disciplinary literacy in mathematics: Learning from professionals who use mathematics in their jobs. *Journal of Adolescent & Adult Literacy*, 63(4), 415–423. DOI: 10.1002/jaal.1013

Crowley, M. A. (1994). The Relevance of Modelings' Ethics of Care to the Moral Education of Nurses. *The Journal of Nursing Education*, 33(2), 74–80. DOI: 10.3928/0148-4834-19940201-07 PMID: 8176501

Crumpton-Young, L., McCauley-Bush, P., Rabelo, L., Meza, K., Ferreras, A., Rodriguez, B., & Kelarestani, M. (2010). Engineering leadership development programs: A look at what is needed and what is being done. *Journal of STEM Education: Innovations and Research*, 11(3).

Cruz, J. M., Parker, K. R., & Vyas, D. (2023). Challenges in teaching large-scale online elective courses: Strategies for enhancing student engagement. *International Journal of Educational Technology in Higher Education*, 20(1), 1–20.

Csikszentmihalyi, M. (1988). The flow experience and its significance for human psychology. In Csikszentmihalyi, M., & Csikszentmihalyi, I. S. (Eds.), *Optimal experience: Psychological studies of flow in consciousness* (pp. 15–35). Cambridge University Press. DOI: 10.1017/CBO9780511621956.002

Cui, T., Bin, J., Lu, X., & Wang, W. (2024, June). The influence of offline teaching presence on students' online learning satisfaction: A case study of online design workshops. In *Proceedings of the 2024 9th International Conference on Distance Education and Learning* (pp. 334-339). DOI: 10.1145/3675812.3675828

Curtin, A. L., & Sarju, J. P. (2021). Students as partners: Co-creation of online learning to deliver high-quality, personalized content. In *Advances in Online Chemistry Education* (pp. 135-163).

Curtis, V. (2018). *Online citizen science and the widening of academia*. Palgrave Macmillan. DOI: 10.1007/978-3-319-77664-4

Cutri, R. M., & Mena, J. (2020). A critical reconceptualization of faculty readiness for online teaching. *Distance Education*, 41(3), 361–380. DOI: 10.1080/01587919.2020.1763167

Cutri, R. M., Mena, J., & Whiting, E. F. (2020). Faculty readiness for online crisis teaching: Transitioning to online teaching during the COVID-19 pandemic. *European Journal of Teacher Education*, 43(4), 523–541. DOI: 10.1080/02619768.2020.1815702

Czerkawski, B. C., & Lyman, E. W. III. (2015). Exploring issues about computational thinking in higher education. *TechTrends*, 59(2), 57–65. DOI: 10.1007/s11528-015-0840-3

Dabbagh, N., & Castaneda, L. (2020). The PLE as a framework for developing agency in lifelong learning. *Educational Technology Research and Development*, 68(6), 3041–3055. DOI: 10.1007/s11423-020-09831-z

Dailey-Hebert, A. (2022). Student perspectives on using virtual reality to create informal connection and engagement. InSight: *A Journal of Scholarly Teaching, 17*, 28–46. DOI: 10.46504/17202202da

Dailey-Hebert, A. (2018). Maximizing interactivity in online learning: Moving beyond discussion boards. *The Journal of Educators Online*, 15(3), n3. DOI: 10.9743/jeo.2018.15.3.8

Dalby, D. (2021). Changing images of mathematics in the transition from school to vocational education. *Adults Learning Mathematics: An International Journal*, 15(1), 45–57.

Dalton, J. E., & Hrenko, K. A. (2016). Caring as a Transformative Model for Arts Integration. *Curriculum & Teaching Dialogue*, 18.

Darnell, J. D. (2020). *Next evolution of workforce experiential learning for 21st century global access learners*. Pepperdine University.

Daumiller, M., Rinas, R., Hein, J., Janke, S., Dickhäuser, O., & Dresel, M. (2021). Shifting from face-to-face to online teaching during COVID-19: The role of university faculty achievement goals for attitudes towards this sudden change, and their relevance for burnout/engagement and student evaluations of teaching quality. *Computers in Human Behavior*, 118, 106677. DOI: 10.1016/j.chb.2020.106677 PMID: 36570330

Davenport, C. E. (2018). Evolution in student perceptions of a flipped classroom in a computer programming course. *Journal of College Science Teaching*, 47(4), 30–35. DOI: 10.2505/4/jcst18_047_04_30

Davie, J. (2022). Evaluation of the HyFlex, Hybrid, and Asynchronous Online Teaching Modalities on Student Learning in Graduate Microbiology Coursework. *The FASEB Journal*, 36(S1), fasebj.2022.36.S1.R6050. Advance online publication. DOI: 10.1096/fasebj.2022.36.S1.R6050

Dawson, P., Henderson, M., Mahoney, P., Phillips, M., Ryan, T., Boud, D., & Molloy, E. (2019). What makes for effective feedback: Staff and student perspectives. *Assessment & Evaluation in Higher Education*, 44(1), 25–36. DOI: 10.1080/02602938.2018.1467877

de Andres Martinez, C. (2012). Developing metacognition at a distance: Sharing students' learning strategies on a reflective blog. *Computer Assisted Language Learning*, 25(2), 199–212. DOI: 10.1080/09588221.2011.636056

De Meuse, K. P., Dai, G., & Hallenbeck, G. S. (2010). Learning agility: A construct whose time has come. *Consulting Psychology Journal*, 62(2), 119–130. DOI: 10.1037/a0019988

de Muñoz, J. H. O., & Letouze, P. (2022). Some considerations on the principles of the Cognitive Theory of Multimedia Learning for instructional video design for the elderly. *Research. Social Development*, 11(10), e499111032333. DOI: 10.33448/rsd-v11i10.32333

DeCoito, I., & Estaiteyeh, M. (2022). Transitioning to online teaching during the COVID-19 pandemic: An exploration of STEM teachers' views, successes, and challenges. *Journal of Science Education and Technology*, 31(3), 340–356. DOI: 10.1007/s10956-022-09958-z PMID: 35369535

Deepshikha, A. (2023). Advancement of Lifelong Learning ThroughOnline Communities. *Journal of Current Trends in Information TechnologyVolume*, 13(2).

Delahunty, J. (2018). Connecting to learn, learning to connect: Thinking together in asynchronous forum discussion. *Linguistics and Education*, 46, 12–22. DOI: 10.1016/j.linged.2018.05.003

Delbert, T. M., & Jacobs, K. (2021). Best Practices in Leadership Curriculum Development: A Case Study of a Curriculum Designed to Foster Authentic Leadership Skills in Graduate Students. *Journal of Higher Education Theory and Practice*, 21(2).

DeLozier, S., & Rhodes, M. (2017). Flipped classrooms: A review of key ideas and recommendations for practice. *Educational Psychology Review*, 29(1), 141–151. DOI: 10.1007/s10648-015-9356-9

Dembo, M. H., Gubler, J. L., & Lynch, R. (2013). Becoming a self-regulated learner: Implications for web-based education. In *Web-Based Learning* (pp. 185–202). Routledge.

DeMink-Carthew, J., Netcoh, S., & Farber, K. (2020). Exploring the potential for students to develop self-awareness through personalized learning. *The Journal of Educational Research*, 113(3), 165–176. DOI: 10.1080/00220671.2020.1764467

Deng, Q., & Wu, Z. (2018). Students' Attention Assessment in eLearning based on Machine Learning. *IOP Conference Series. Earth and Environmental Science*, 199, 032042. DOI: 10.1088/1755-1315/199/3/032042

Dennen, V. P., & Bong, J.Dennen and Bong. (2018). Cross-cultural dialogues in an open online course: Navigating national and organizational cultural differences. *TechTrends*, 62(4), 383–392. DOI: 10.1007/s11528-018-0276-7

Denning, P. J., & Tedre, M. (2021). Computational thinking: A disciplinary perspective. *Informatics in Education*, 20(3), 361.

Deslauriers, L., McCarty, L. S., Miller, K., Callaghan, K., & Kestin, G. (2019). Measuring actual learning versus feeling of learning in response to being actively engaged in the classroom. *Proceedings of the National Academy of Sciences - PNAS*, 116(39), 19251-19257. https://doi.org/DOI: 10.1073/pnas.1821936116

Deterding, S., Dixon, D., Khaled, R., & Nacke, L. (2011). From game design elements to gamefulness: defining "gamification". In Proceedings of the *15th International Academic MindTrek Conference: Envisioning Future Media Environments* (pp. 9-15). DOI: 10.1145/2181037.2181040

Deterding, S., Khaled, R., Nacke, L. E., & Dixon, D. (2021). Gamification: Toward a definition. CHI 2011 Gamification Workshop Proceedings, 12-15.

Detweiler, , K. LDetweiler, , S. L. (2020). Evaluating mental illness among college students: Implications for online students. *Journal of Online Higher Education: Volume*, 4(1).

Devi, D., & Rroy, A. D. (2023). Role of Artificial Intelligence (AI) in sustainable education of higher education institutions in Guwahati City: Teacher's perception. *International Management Review*, •••, 111–116. http://www.imrjournal.org/

Devkota, K. R. (2021). Inequalities reinforced through online and distance education in the age of COVID-19: The case of higher education in Nepal. *International Review of Education*, 67(1), 145–165. DOI: 10.1007/s11159-021-09886-x PMID: 33678863

Dhawan, S. (2020). Online learning: A panacea in the time of COVID-19 crisis. *Journal of Educational Technology Systems*, 49(1), 5–22. DOI: 10.1177/0047239520934018

Díaz, C. A. (2024). *From transdisciplinary concepts to undisciplined futures*. The Routledge International Handbook of Transdisciplinary Feminist Research and Methodological Praxis.

Diego-Mantecon, J. M., Haro, E., Blanco, T. F., & Romo-Vazquez, A. (2021). The chimera of the competency-based approach to teaching mathematics: A study of carpentry purchases for home projects. *Educational Studies in Mathematics*, 107(2), 339–357. DOI: 10.1007/s10649-021-10032-5

Diep, P., C., T.L. Nguyen, G., & T. Vo, N. (. (2021). Structure and procedure for developing an online course. *Journal of Technical Education Science*, 62, 83–98. DOI: 10.54644/jte.62.2021.83

Diez-Palomar, J. (2020). Dialogic mathematics gatherings: Encouraging the other women's critical thinking on numeracy. *ZDM Mathematics Education*, 52(3), 473–487. DOI: 10.1007/s11858-019-01092-2

DiGregorio, N., & Liston, D. D. (2018). Experiencing technical difficulties: Teacher self-efficacy and instructional technology. In *Self-Efficacy in Instructional Technology Contexts* (pp. 103–117). Springer International Publishing. DOI: 10.1007/978-3-319-99858-9_7

Dikmenli, Y., & Ünaldı Eser, Ü. (2013). Students' views on blended learning and virtual classroom. *Amasya Education Journal*, 2(2), 326–347.

Divito, C. B., Katchikian, B. M., Gruenwald, J. E., & Burgoon, J. M. (2023). The tools of the future are the challenges of today: The use of ChatGPT in problem-based learning medical education. *Medical Teacher*, 46(3), 320–322. DOI: 10.1080/0142159X.2023.2290997 PMID: 38149617

Donaldson, S. I., van Zyl, L. E., & Donaldson, S. I. (2022). PERMA+4: A framework for work-related wellbeing, performance and positive organizational psychology 2.0. *Frontiers in Psychology*, 12, 817244. Advance online publication. DOI: 10.3389/fpsyg.2021.817244 PMID: 35140667

Doo, M. Y., Bonk, C. J., & Heo, H. (2020). A meta-analysis of scaffolding effects in online learning in higher education. *International Review of Research in Open and Distance Learning*, 23(3), 60–80. DOI: 10.19173/irrodl.v21i3.4638

Downing, J. J., & Dyment, J. E. (2013). Teacher educators' readiness, preparation, and perceptions of preparing preservice teachers in a fully online environment: An exploratory study. *Teacher Educator*, 48(2), 96–109. DOI: 10.1080/08878730.2012.760023

Drago-Severson, E., Asghar, A., Blum-DeStefano, J., & Welch, J. R. (2011). Conceptual changes in aspiring school leaders: Lessons from a university classroom. *Journal of Research on Leadership Education*, 6(4), 83–132. DOI: 10.1177/194277511100600401

Drigas, A. S., & Papoutsi, C. (2018). A new layered model on emotional intelligence. *Behavioral Sciences (Basel, Switzerland)*, 8(5), 45. https://www.mdpi.com/2076-328X/8/5/45/htm. DOI: 10.3390/bs8050045 PMID: 29724021

Driver, J. (2001). A selective review of selective attention research from the past century. *British Journal of Psychology*, 92(1), 53–78. DOI: 10.1348/000712601162103

Dumont, G., & Raggo, P. (2018). Faculty perspectives about distance teaching in the virtual classroom. *Journal of Nonprofit Education and Leadership*, 8(1), 41–61. DOI: 10.18666/JNEL-2018-V8-I1-8372

Dunlosky, J., Rawson, K. A., Marsh, E. J., Nathan, M. J., & Willingham, D. T. (2013). Improving students' learning with effective learning techniques: Promising directions from cognitive and educational psychology. *Psychological Science in the Public Interest*, 14(1), 4–58. DOI: 10.1177/1529100612453266 PMID: 26173288

Dunn, R., & Griggs, S. A. (2000). *Practical Approaches to Using Learning Styles in Higher Education*. Bloomsbury Publishing USA. DOI: 10.5040/9798400699962

Durlak, J. A., Weissberg, R. P., Dymnicki, A. B., Taylor, R. D., & Schellinger, K. B. (2011). The impact of enhancing students' social and emotional learning: A meta-analysis of school-based universal interventions. *Child Development*, 82(1), 405–432. DOI: 10.1111/j.1467-8624.2010.01564.x PMID: 21291449

Dutta, S., Ranjan, S., Mishra, S., Sharma, V., Hewage, P., & Iwendi, C. (2024, February). Enhancing Educational Adaptability: A Review and Analysis of AI-Driven Adaptive Learning Platforms. In *2024 4th International Conference on Innovative Practices in Technology and Management (ICIPTM)* (pp. 1-5). IEEE. DOI: 10.1109/ICIPTM59628.2024.10563448

Duus, R., & Cooray, M. (2022, August 17). *Empowering students to learn from each other: How digital tools can enhance peer learning across student teams.* https://www.hbsp.harvard.edu/inspiring-minds/empowering-students-to-learn-from-each-other

Dweck, C. S., & Yeager, D. (2021). *Global mindset initiative introduction: Envisioning the future of growth mindset research in education.* https://www.researchgate.net/profile/David-Yeager/publication/354168475_Global_Mindset_Initiative_Introduction_Envisioning_the_Future_of_Growth_Mindset_Research_in_Education/links/6128f9f00360302a0061103c/Global-Mindset-Initiative-Introduction-Envisioning-the-Future-of-Growth-Mindset-Research-in-Education.pdf

Ealangov, S., Kadir, I. F., Zakaria, N. A., Soppy, A. H., & Mahamod, Z. (2022). Challenges, impacts, and strategies of online learning on mental health of community college students and lecturers. *Online Journal for TVET Practitioners, 7*(2), 53–65. https://penerbit.uthm.edu.my/ojs/index.php/oj-tp/article/view/11207

Eddy, L. L., Doutrich, D., Higgs, Z. R., Spuck, J., Olson, M., & Weinberg, S. (2009). Relevant nursing leadership: An evidence-based programmatic response. *International Journal of Nursing Education Scholarship*, 6(1). Advance online publication. DOI: 10.2202/1548-923X.1792 PMID: 19645690

Edelman. (2022). 2022 Edelman trust Barometer. https://www.edelman.com/trust/2022-trust-barometer

Educurious. https://educurious.org/

Edwards, C. M. (2012). *Comparing middle school students' learning and attitudes in face-to-face and online mathematics lessons.* University of Northern Iowa.

edX - https://www.edx.org/

El-Amin, A. (2020). Andragogy: A theory in practice in higher education. *Journal of Research in Higher Education*, 4(2), 54–69. DOI: 10.24193/JRHE.2020.2.4

Elewa, A. H., & mohamed, . (2022). Online teaching readiness, challenges and satisfaction as perceived by nursing faculty members during COVID-19 pandemics. *International Egyptian Journal of Nursing Sciences and Research*, 2(2), 568–579. DOI: 10.21608/ejnsr.2022.212573

Eliyas, S., & Ranjana, P. (2022). Gamification: Is e-next learning's big thing? *Journal of Internet Services and Information Security*, 12(4), 238–245. DOI: 10.58346/JISIS.2022.I4.017

Elmaadaway, M. A. N. (2018). The effects of a flipped classroom approach on class engagement and skill performance in a Blackboard course. *British Journal of Educational Technology*, 49(3), 479–491. DOI: 10.1111/bjet.12553

Elmer, J., & Dingli, A. (2024). Enhancing Student Learning. In *INTED2024 Proceedings* (pp. 7771-7779). IATED. DOI: 10.21125/inted.2024.2076

Elsayed, S., & Cakir, D. (2023). Implementation of assessment and feedback in higher education. *Acta Pedagogia Asiana*, 2(1), 34–42. DOI: 10.53623/apga.v2i1.170

Emde, R. J., Doherty, E. K., Ellis, B., & Flynt, D. (2020). Relationships in online learning experiences. In Kyei-Blankson, L., Ntuli, E., & Blankson, J. (Eds.), *Handbook of research on creating meaningful experiences in online courses* (pp. 140–152). IGI Global., DOI: 10.4018/978-1-7998-0115-3.ch010

Endres, T., Weyreter, S., Renkl, A., & Eitel, A. (2020). When and why does emotional design foster learning? Evidence for situational interest as a mediator of increased persistence. *Journal of Computer Assisted Learning*, 36(4), 514–525. DOI: 10.1111/jcal.12418

Eom, S., Ashill, N. J., & Arbaugh, J. B. (2016). Guest Editors' Introduction to the Special Issue. *Decision Sciences Journal of Innovative Education*, 14(2), 124–127. DOI: 10.1111/dsji.12099

Erten, P. (2019). Opinions of preservice information technologies teachers on virtual classroom and implementations. *Batman University Journal of Life Sciences*, 9(2), 236–252.

Ertmer, P. A., & Ottenbreit-Leftwich, A. T. (2010). Teacher technology change: How knowledge, confidence, beliefs, and culture intersect. *Journal of Research on Technology in Education*, 42(3), 255–284. DOI: 10.1080/15391523.2010.10782551

Espasa, A., & Meneses, J. (2010). Analysing feedback processes in an online teaching and learning environment: An exploratory study. *Higher Education*, 59(3), 277–292. DOI: 10.1007/s10734-009-9247-4

Espinoza, D., & Reed, D. (2018). Wireless technologies and policies for connecting rural areas in emerging countries: A case study in rural Peru. *Digital Policy. Regulation & Governance*, 20(5), 479–511. DOI: 10.1108/DPRG-03-2018-0009

Estrada-Araoz, E. G., Gallegos-Ramos, N., Mamani-Uchasara, H., & Huaypar-Loayza, K. (2020). Actitud de los estudiantes universitarios frente a la educación virtual en tiempos de la pandemia de COVID-19. *Rev. Brasil.Educ. Campo*, 5, e10237. DOI: 10.20873/uft.rbec.e10237

Evanick, J. (2023). *From One-Size-Fits-All To Tailored Online Education: The Advantages Of Personalized Learning*. https://elearningindustry.com/from-one-size-fits-all-to-tailored-online-education-advantages-of-personalized-learning

Evans, J., Wedege, T., & Yasukawa, K. (2013). Critical perspectives on adults' mathematics education. In A. Bishop, C. Keitel, J. Kilpatrick, & F. K. Leung (Eds.), *Third international handbook of mathematics education* (pp. 203–242). Springer.

Evans, J., Yasukawa, K., Mallows, D., & Kubascikova, J. (2021). Shifting the gaze: From the numerate individual to their numerate environment. *Adult Literacy Education*, 3(3), 4–18. DOI: 10.35847/JEvans.KYasukawa.DMallows.JKubascikova.3.3.4

Evolve Project Team. (2020). The impact of virtual exchange on student learning in higher education: EVOLVE project report.

Farley, A., Kennedy-Behr, A., & Brown, T. (2020). An investigation into the relationship between playfulness and well-being in Australian adults: An exploratory study. *OTJR (Thorofare, N.J.)*, 41(1), 56–64. DOI: 10.1177/1539449220945311 PMID: 32723209

Farley, I. A., & Burbules, N. C. (2022). Online education viewed through an equity lens: Promoting engagement and success for all learners. *Review of Education*, 10(3), e3367. DOI: 10.1002/rev3.3367

Farma, A. (2023). 6 Expert Tips Personalized E-Learning Experiences: Enhancing Education in the Digital Age. Retrieved on 20th June 2024 from https://www.linkedin.com/pulse/personalized-e-learning-experiences-enhancing/

Faturoti, B. (2022). Online learning during COVID-19 and beyond A human right based approach to internet access in Africa. *International Review of Law Computers & Technology*, 36(1), 68–90. DOI: 10.1080/13600869.2022.2030027

Faucett, H., Lee, M., & Carter, S. (2017). I should listen more: Real-time sensing and feedback of non-verbal communication in video telehealth. *Proceedings of the ACM on Human-Computer Interaction Volume 1 (issue CSCW)*, Article No.: 44pp 1–19. https://doi.org/DOI: 10.1145/3134679

Feiler, K. E. (2018). Brain breaks go to college. *Pedagogy in Health Promotion*, 5(4), 299–301. DOI: 10.1177/2373379918799770

Feinberg, I., Greenberg, D., Tighe, E. L., & Ogrodnick, M. M. (2019). Health insurance literacy and low wage earners: Why reading matters. *Adult Literacy Education*, 1(2), 4–18. DOI: 10.35847/IFeinberg.DGreenberg.ETighe.MOgrodnick.1.2.4

Felmer, P., Perdomo-Díaz, J., & Reyes, C. (2019). The ARPA experience in Chile: Problem Solving for teachers' professional development. In Liljedahl, P., & Santos-Trigo, M. (Eds.), *Mathematical Problem Solving, ICME-13 Monographs* (pp. 311–337). Springer. DOI: 10.1007/978-3-030-10472-6_14

Fendler, R. (2021). Improving the "other side" to faculty presence in online education. *Online Journal of Distance Learning Administration*, 24(1). https://www.westga.edu/~distance/ojdla/spring241/fendler241.pdf

Feng, X., Xie, J., & Liu, Y. (2017). Using the community of inquiry framework to scaffold online tutoring. *International Review of Research in Open and Distance Learning*, 18(2), 162–188. DOI: 10.19173/irrodl.v18i2.2362

Fenwick, T., & Tennant, M. (2020). Understanding adult learners. In *Dimensions of adult learning* (pp. 55–73). Routledge. DOI: 10.4324/9781003115366-6

Fernández, A., Gómez, B., Binjaku, K., & Meçe, E. K. (2023). Digital transformation initiatives in higher education institutions: A multivocal literature review. *Education and Information Technologies*, 28(10), 12351–12382. DOI: 10.1007/s10639-022-11544-0 PMID: 37361743

Fidalgo-Blanco, Á., Sein-Echaluce, M. L., & García-Peñalvo, F. J. (2016). From massive access to cooperation: Lessons learned and proven results of a hybrid xMOOC/cMOOC pedagogical approach to MOOCs. *International Journal of Educational Technology in Higher Education*, 13(1), 24. Advance online publication. DOI: 10.1186/s41239-016-0024-z

Filgona, J., Sakiyo, J., Gwany, D. M., & Okoronka, A. U. (2020). Motivation in learning. *Asian Journal of Education and Social Studies*, 16-37. DOI: 10.9734/ajess/2020/v10i430273

Fisher, K., & Newton, C. (2014). Transforming the twenty-first-century campus to enhance the net-generation student learning experience: Using evidence-based design to determine what works and why in virtual/physical teaching spaces. *Higher Education Research & Development*, 33(5), 903–920. DOI: 10.1080/07294360.2014.890566

Fisher, R., Perényi, Á., & Birdthistle, N. (2021). The positive relationship between flipped and blended learning and student engagement, performance and satisfaction. *Active Learning in Higher Education*, 22(2), 97–113. DOI: 10.1177/1469787418801702

FitzSimons, G. E. (2019). Adults learning mathematics: Transcending boundaries and barriers in an uncertain world. *Adults Learning Mathematics: An International Journal*, 14(1), 41–52.

Flaherty, H. B. (2022). Using collaborative group learning principles to foster community in online classrooms. *Journal of Teaching in Social Work*, 42(1), 31–44. DOI: 10.1080/08841233.2021.2013390

Flanigan, A. E., Akcaoglu, M., & Ray, E. (2021). Initiating and maintaining student-instructor rapport in online classes. *The Internet and Higher Education*, 53, 100844. Advance online publication. DOI: 10.1016/j.iheduc.2021.100844

Flint, A. S., Kurumada, K. S., Fisher, T., & Zisook, K. (2011). Creating the perfect storm in professional development: The experiences of two American teachers and a university research team. *Professional Development in Education*, 37(1), 95–109. DOI: 10.1080/19415250903425502

Flores, W. O., & Auzmendi, E. (2018). Actitudes hacia las matemáticas en la enseñanza universitaria y su relación con las variables género y etnia. *Profes. Rev. Currículum Form.Profes.*, 22(3), 231–251. DOI: 10.30827/profesorado.v22i3.8000

Fluckiger, J., Vigil, Y. T., Pasco, R., & Danielson, K. (2010). Formative feedback: Involving students as partners in assessment to enhance learning. *College Teaching*, 58(4), 136–140. DOI: 10.1080/87567555.2010.484031

Foley, G. D., Budhathoki, D., Thapa, A. B., & Aryal, H. P. (2023). Instructor perspectives on quantitative reasoning for critical citizenship. *ZDM Mathematics Education*, 55(5), 1009–1020. DOI: 10.1007/s11858-023-01520-4

Fong, C. J., Dillard, J. B., & Hatcher, M. (2019). Teaching self-efficacy of graduate student instructors: Exploring faculty motivation, perceptions of autonomy support, and undergraduate student engagement. *International Journal of Educational Research*, 98, 91–105. DOI: 10.1016/j.ijer.2019.08.018

Forbes, L. (2021). The process of playful learning in higher education: A phenomenological study. *Journal of Teaching and Learning*, 15(1), 57–73. DOI: 10.22329/jtl.v15i1.6515

Forbes, L., & Thomas, D. (2023). *Professors at play playbook*. Carnegie Mellon Press., DOI: 10.57862/appf-kp25

Fortenbaugh, F. C., DeGutis, J., & Esterman, M. (2017). Recent theoretical, neural, and clinical advances in sustained attention research. *Annals of the New York Academy of Sciences*, 1396(1), 70–91. DOI: 10.1111/nyas.13318 PMID: 28260249

Fortenbaugh, F. C., DeGutis, J., Germine, L., Wilmer, J. B., Grosso, M., Russo, K., & Esterman, M. (2015). Sustained Attention Across the Life Span in a Sample of 10,000. *Psychological Science*, 26(9), 1497–1510. DOI: 10.1177/0956797615594896 PMID: 26253551

Frame, K. (2013). *Pathways to Personalized Learning: Tapping the Potential, Realizing the Benefits*. Center for Digital Education.

Fredricks, J. A., Blumenfeld, P. C., & Paris, A. H. (2004). School engagement: Potential of the concept, state of the evidence. *Review of Educational Research*, 74(1), 59–109. DOI: 10.3102/00346543074001059

Freeman, S., Eddy, S. L., McDonough, M., Smith, M. K., Okoroafor, N., Jordt, H., & Wenderoth, M. P. (2014). Active learning increases student performance in science, engineering, and mathematics. *Proceedings of the National Academy of Sciences of the United States of America*, 111(23), 8410–8415. DOI: 10.1073/pnas.1319030111 PMID: 24821756

Freire, C., Ferradas, M. D. M., Regueiro, B., Rodríguez, S., Valle, A., & Nunez, J. C. (2020). Coping strategies and self-efficacy in university students: A person-centered approach. *Frontiers in Psychology*, 11, 530329. DOI: 10.3389/fpsyg.2020.00841 PMID: 32508707

Freire, C., Ferradás, M. D., Valle, A., Núñez, J. C., & Vallejo, G. (2016). Profiles of psychological well-being and coping strategies among university students. *Frontiers in Psychology*, 7, 1554. Advance online publication. DOI: 10.3389/fpsyg.2016.01554 PMID: 27790168

Froehlich, A., Siebrits, A., Kotze, C., Froehlich, A., Siebrits, A., & Kotze, C. (2021). Towards the Sustainable Development Goals in Africa: Space Supporting African Higher Education. *Space Supporting Africa: Volume 2. Education and Healthcare as Priority Areas in Achieving the United Nations Sustainable Development Goals*, 2030, 1–90.

Fuglsang, L., & Mattsson, J. (2009). An integrative model of care ethics in public innovation. *Service Industries Journal*, 29(1), 21–34. DOI: 10.1080/02642060802116362

Fusaro, R., Sunstein, C., Thaler, R., & Sperling-Magro. (2021, October 15). How does "nudging" work as an intervention technique? https://www.weforum.org/agenda/2021/10/what-is-nudging-and-how-has-it-changed-over-time/

Gaebel, M., Zhang, T., Bunescu, L., & Stoeber, H. (2018). Learning and teaching in the European higher education area. European University Association asbl.

Gal, I. (2000). The numeracy challenge. In Gal, I. (Ed.), *Adult numeracy development: Theory, research, practice* (pp. 9–31). Hampton Press.

Gal, I. (2022). Critical understanding of civic statistics: Engaging with important contexts, texts, and opinion questions. In Ridgway, J. (Ed.), *Statistics for empowerment and social engagement—Teaching Civic Statistics to develop informed citizens*. Springer., DOI: 10.1007/978-3-031-20748-8_13

Gal, I., & Geiger, V. (2022). Welcome to the era of vague news: A study of the demands of statistical and mathematical products in the COVID-19 pandemic media. *Educational Studies in Mathematics*, 111(1), 5–28. DOI: 10.1007/s10649-022-10151-7 PMID: 35496813

Gallen, C. L., Schaerlaeken, S., Younger, J. W., Anguera, J. A., & Gazzaley, A. (2023). Contribution of sustained attention abilities to real-world academic skills in children. *Scientific Reports*, 13(1), 2673. DOI: 10.1038/s41598-023-29427-w PMID: 36792755

Galligan, L., & Axelsen, M. (2022). Online learning in adults learning mathematics: Literature review. *Adults Learning Mathematics: An International Journal*, 16(1), 6–19.

Gallup & Lumina Foundation. *State of higher education2024report*. https://www.gallup.com/analytics/644939/state-of-higher-education.aspx

Gallup, A. (2024). What We Know About Registered Apprenticeship: A Systematic Review and Synthesis of 30 Years of Empirical Research. *Economic Development Quarterly*, 38(1), 25–39. DOI: 10.1177/08912424231196792

Galvin, R. (2012). Peer support: Enhancing the online learning experience. *International Journal of Innovation and Learning*, 12(1), 41–53. DOI: 10.1504/IJIL.2012.047309

Gambs, S. (2019). Privacy and Ethical Challenges in Big Data. In Zincir-Heywood, N., Bonfante, G., Debbabi, M., & Garcia-Alfaro, J. (Eds.), Lecture Notes in Computer Science: Vol. 11358. *Foundations and Practice of Security. FPS 2018*. Springer., DOI: 10.1007/978-3-030-18419-3_2

García, J., Cabanillas, L., Catarreira, S. M., & González, R. L. (2020). Contraste en la percepción sobre el uso de una plataforma virtual para la mejora de la enseñanza y aprendizaje de las matemáticas. *Rev. Ibérica d Sist.RISTI (Porto)*, 38(38), 33–47. DOI: 10.17013/risti.38.33-47

Garcia-Morales, V. J., Garrido-Moreno, A., & Martín-Rojas, R. (2021). The transformation of higher education after the COVID disruption: Emerging challenges in an online learning scenario. *Frontiers in Psychology*, 12, 616059. DOI: 10.3389/fpsyg.2021.616059 PMID: 33643144

García-Peñalvo, F. J., & Mendes, A. J. (2018). Exploring the computational thinking effects in pre-university education. *Computers in Human Behavior*, 80, 407–411. DOI: 10.1016/j.chb.2017.12.005

García, R. A., Chura, G., Llapa, M. P., & Arancibia, L. (2022). Validación de cuestionario de satisfacción de la enseñanza virtual para educación secundaria. *Rev. Fuentes*, 2(24), 162–173. DOI: 10.12795/revistafuentes.2022.19773

Garg, N., & Singh, B. (2022). Sustainable Development-Adopting a Balanced Approach between Development and Development Induced Changes. *ECS Transactions*, 107(1), 15–31. DOI: 10.1149/10701.0015ecst

Garrison, D. R., & Anderson, T. (2003). *E-Learning in the 21st Century: A Framework for Research and Practice*. Routledge.

Garrison, D. R., Anderson, T., & Archer, W. (2003). A theory of critical inquiry in online distance education. In M. Moore & W. Anderson (Eds.), *Handbook of distance education* (pp. 113–127). Lawrence Erlbaum Associates.

Garrison, D. R. (2009). Communities of inquiry in online learning: Social, teaching and cognitive presence. In Howard, C. (Eds.), *Encyclopedia of Distance and Online Learning* (2nd ed., pp. 352–355). IGI Global.

Garrison, D. R. (2015). *Thinking collaboratively: Learning in a community of inquiry*. Routledge. DOI: 10.4324/9781315740751

Garrison, D. R., Anderson, T., & Archer, W. (2000). Critical inquiry in a text-based environment: Computer conferencing in higher education. *The Internet and Higher Education*, 2(2-3), 87–105. DOI: 10.1016/S1096-7516(00)00016-6

Garrison, D. R., & Vaughan, N. D. (2008). *Blended learning in higher education: Framework, principles, and guidelines*. Jossey-Bass.

Garrison, D. R., & Vaughan, N. D. (2008). *Blended Learning in Higher Education: Framework, Principles, and Guidelines*. Jossey-Bass.

Gašević, D., Siemens, G., & Sadiq, S. (2023). Empowering learners for the age of artificial intelligence. *Computers & Education: Artificial Intelligence*, 4, 100130. DOI: 10.1016/j.caeai.2023.100130

Gasparro, K. E. (2019). *Crowdfunding Our Cities: Three Perspectives on Stakeholder Dynamics During Innovative Infrastructure Delivery*. Stanford University.

Gavassa, S., Benabentos, R., Kravec, M., Collins, T., & Eddy, S. (2019). Closing the Achievement Gap in a Large Introductory Course by Balancing Reduced In-Person Contact with Increased Course Structure. *CBE Life Sciences Education*, 18(1), ar8. DOI: 10.1187/cbe.18-08-0153 PMID: 30807254

Gay, G. H. E. (2016). An assessment of online instructor e-learning readiness before, during, and after course delivery. *Journal of Computing in Higher Education*, 28(2), 199–220. DOI: 10.1007/s12528-016-9115-z

Gaytan, J., & McEwen, B. C. (2007). Effective online instructional and assessment strategies. *American Journal of Distance Education*, 21(3), 117–132. DOI: 10.1080/08923640701341653

Gedera, D. S. P. (2014). Students' experiences of learning in a virtual classroom. [IJEDICT]. *International Journal of Education and Development Using Information and Communication Technology*, 10(4), 93–101.

Geiger, V., Gal, I., & Graven, M. (2023). The connections between citizenship education and mathematics education. *ZDM Mathematics Education*, 55(3), 923–940. DOI: 10.1007/s11858-023-01521-3

Ge, S., & Lai, X. (2021). Strategies for Information Design and Processing of Multimedia Instructional Software—Based on Richard E. Mayer's Multimedia Instructional Design Principles. *International Journal of Educational Technology and Learning*, 10(1), 40–46. DOI: 10.20448/2003.101.40.46

Gharib, M., Zolfaghari, M., Mojtahedzadeh, R., Mohammadi, A., & Gharib, A. (2016). Promotion of critical thinking in e-learning: A qualitative study on the experiences of instructors and students. *Advances in Medical Education and Practice*, 7, 271–279. DOI: 10.2147/AMEP.S105226 PMID: 27217807

Gibson, K. L., Rimmington, G. M., & Landwehr-Brown, M. (2008). Developing global awareness and responsible world citizenship with global learning. *Roeper Review*, 30(1), 11–23. DOI: 10.1080/02783190701836270

Gigliotti, R. A., Dwyer, M., Brescia, S. A., Gergus, M., & Stefanelli, J. R. (2020). Learning leadership in higher education: Communicative implications for graduate education. *Atlantic Journal of Communication*, 28(4), 209–223. DOI: 10.1080/15456870.2020.1720990

Gigliotti, R. A., & Spear, S. E. (2022). Essential leadership concepts and models for graduate and professional school learners. *New Directions for Student Leadership*, 2022(176), 65–74. DOI: 10.1002/yd.20531 PMID: 36565144

Gikandi, J. W., Morrow, D., & Davis, N. E. (2011). Online formative assessment in higher education: A review of the literature. *Computers & Education*, 57(4), 2333–2351. https://doi.org/10.1016/j.compedu.2011.06.004. DOI: 10.1016/j.compedu.2011.06.004

Gilboy, M. B., Heinerichs, S., & Pazzaglia, G. (2015). Enhancing student engagement using the flipped classroom. *Journal of Nutrition Education and Behavior*, 47(1), 109–114. DOI: 10.1016/j.jneb.2014.08.008 PMID: 25262529

Gimpel, G. (2022). Bringing face-to-face engagement to online classes: Developing a high-presence online teaching method. *The Journal of Scholarship of Teaching and Learning*, 22(4), 32–49. DOI: 10.14434/josotl.v22i4.32702

Gloria, C. T., & Steinhardt, M. A. (2016). Relationships among positive emotions, coping, resilience and mental health. *Stress and Health*, 32(2), 145–156. DOI: 10.1002/smi.2589 PMID: 24962138

Glowacki-Dudka, M., Mullett, C., Griswold, W., Baize-Ward, A., Vetor-Suits, C., & Londt, S. C. (2018). Framing care for planners of education programs. *Adult Learning*, 29(2), 62–71. DOI: 10.1177/1045159517750664

Goh, M. (2012). Teaching with cultural intelligence: Developing multiculturally educated and globally engaged citizens. *Asia Pacific Journal of Education*, 32(4), 395–415. DOI: 10.1080/02188791.2012.738679

Gökçe, S., & Yenmez, A. A. (2023). Ingenuity of scratch programming on reflective thinking towards problem solving and computational thinking. *Education and Information Technologies*, 28(5), 5493–5517. DOI: 10.1007/s10639-022-11385-x

Goleman, D. (2005). *Emotional intelligence*. Bantam.

Goleman, D., & Boyatzis, R. (2017). Emotional intelligence has 12 elements. Which do you need to work on? *Harvard Business Review*, 84(2), 1–5. https://hbr.org/2017/02/emotional-intelligence-has-12-elements-which-do-you-need-to-work-on

González-Pérez, L. I., & Ramírez-Montoya, M. S. (2022). Components of Education 4.0 in 21st century skills frameworks: Systematic review. *Sustainability (Basel)*, 14(3), 1493. DOI: 10.3390/su14031493

Gorghiu, G., Lamanauskas, V., Makarskaite-Petkeviciene, R., Manea, V. I., & Pribeanu, C. (2021). Frustration and stress in the online education of university students from Lithuania and Romania. *ELearning & Software for Education*, 1, 162–169. DOI: 10.12753/2066-026X-21-021

Gouedard, P., Pont, B., & Viennet, R. (2020). Education responses to COVID-19: Implementing a way forward.

Granovetter, M. (1985). Economic action and social structure: The problem of embeddedness. *American Journal of Sociology*, 91(3), 481–510. DOI: 10.1086/228311

Grant, A. M., & Shandell, M. S. (2022). Social motivation at work: The organizational psychology of effort for, against, and with others. *Annual Review of Psychology*, 73(1), 301–326. DOI: 10.1146/annurev-psych-060321-033406 PMID: 34280327

Gray, J.A. & DiLoreto, M. (2016). The Effects of Student Engagement, Student Satisfaction, and Perceived Learning in Online Learning Environments. *NCPEA International Journal of Educational Leadership Preparation*, Vol. 11, No. 1– May 2016.

Gray, C. M. K. (2019). Using profiles of human and social capital to understand adult immigrants' education needs: A latent class approach. *Adult Education Quarterly*, 69(1), 3–23. DOI: 10.1177/0741713618802271

Gray, L. E., & Dunn, S. D. (Eds.). (2024). *Humanizing Online Teaching and Learning in Higher Education*. IGI Global. DOI: 10.4018/979-8-3693-0762-5

Green, Z. A., Faizi, F., Jalal, R., & Zadran, Z. (2021). Emotional support moderated academic stress and mental well-being in a sample of Afghan university students amid COVID-19. *The International Journal of Social Psychiatry*, 68(8), 1748–1755. DOI: 10.1177/00207640211057729 PMID: 34903066

Griffin, D. K., Mitchell, D., & Thompson, S. J. (2009). Podcasting by synchronising PowerPoint and voice: What are the pedagogical benefits? *Computers & Education*, 53(2), 532–539. DOI: 10.1016/j.compedu.2009.03.011

Grigorenko, E. L., & Sternberg, R. J. (1997). Styles of Thinking, Abilities, and Academic Performance. *Exceptional Children*, 63(3), 295–312. DOI: 10.1177/001440299706300301

Gross, S., Kim, M., Schlosser, J., Mohtadi, C., Lluch, D., & Schneider, D. (2024l). Fostering computational thinking in engineering education: Challenges, examples, and best practices. In *2014 IEEE Global Engineering Education Conference (EDUCON)* (pp. 450-459). IEEE.

Grotluschen, A., Buddeberg, K., Redmer, A., Ansen, H., & Dannath, J. (2019). Vulnerable subgroups and numeracy practices: How poverty, debt, and unemployment relate to everyday numeracy practices. *Adult Education Quarterly*, 69(4), 251–270. DOI: 10.1177/0741713619841132

Grotlüschen, A., Riekmann, W., Buddeberg, K., & Egloff, B. (2020). Scientific research on adults' competencies: Lessons from the German sample in the Programme for the International Assessment of Adult Competencies (PIAAC). *ZDM Mathematics Education*, 52(3), 401–412. DOI: 10.1007/s11858-019-01063-7

Guardia, L., Clougher, D., Anderson, T., & Maina, M. (2021). IDEAS for transforming higher education: An overview of ongoing trends and challenges. *International Review of Research in Open and Distance Learning*, 22(2), 166–184. DOI: 10.19173/irrodl.v22i2.5206

Gudino Paredes, S., Jasso Pena, F. D. J., & de La Fuente Alcazar, J. M. (2021). Remotely proctored exams: Integrity assurance in online education? *Distance Education*, 42(2), 200–218. DOI: 10.1080/01587919.2021.1910495

Gueudet, G. (2008). Investigating the secondary-tertiary transition. *Educational Studies in Mathematics*, 67(3), 237–254. DOI: 10.1007/s10649-007-9100-6

Gülbahar, Y., & Adnan, M. (2020). Faculty professional development in creating significant teaching and learning experiences online. In *Handbook of Research on Creating Meaningful Experiences in Online Courses* (pp. 37–58). IGI Global. DOI: 10.4018/978-1-7998-0115-3.ch004

Gündüz, Y., & Can, E. (2013). The compliance level of primary and high school teachers to classroom management principles according to student's views. *Educational Administration-Theory and Practice*, 19(3), 419–446.

Guo, P., Saab, N., Wu, L., & Admiraal, W. (2021). The Community of Inquiry perspective on students' social presence, cognitive presence, and academic performance in online project-based learning. *Journal of Computer Assisted Learning*, 37(5), 1479–1493. DOI: 10.1111/jcal.12586

Gutiérrez, G., Lunsky, I., Heer, S. V., Szulewski, A., & Chaplin, T. (2023). Cognitive load theory in action: E-learning modules improve performance in simulation-based education. A pilot study. *Canadian Journal of Emergency Medical Care*, 25(11), 893–901. Advance online publication. DOI: 10.1007/s43678-023-00586-z PMID: 37751082

Ha, A. S., O'Reilly, J., Ng, J. Y. Y., Zhang, J. H., & Serpa, S. (2019). Evaluating the flipped classroom approach in Asian higher education: Perspectives from students and teachers. *Cogent Education*, 6(1), 1638147. Advance online publication. DOI: 10.1080/2331186X.2019.1638147

Hachey, A. C., Wladis, C. W., & Conway, K. M. (2021). Do prior online course outcomes provide more information than GPA alone in predicting online course grades? An investigation of students in online undergraduate mathematics courses. *Educational Technology Research and Development*, 59(1), 59–82. PMID: 33469254

Hadri, O. E. (2022). African Languages Development in Education-Bilingualism and African Languages. *International Journal of Language and Literary Studies*, 4(2), 223–241. DOI: 10.36892/ijlls.v4i2.893

Haleem, A., Javaid, M., Qadri, M. A., & Suman, R. (2022). Understanding the role of digital technologies in education: A review. *Sustainable operations and computers, 3*, 275-285.

Hall, J. A., Widdall, C., & Lei, J. (2021). Preparing for virtual student teaching: A presence experience design case. *TechTrends*, 65(6), 963–976. DOI: 10.1007/s11528-021-00660-2 PMID: 34485993

Hampton, D., Culp-Roche, A., Hensley, A., Wilson, J., Otts, J. A., Thaxton-Wiggins, A., Fruh, S., & Moser, D. K. (2020). Self-efficacy and satisfaction with teaching in online courses. *Nurse Educator*, 45(6), 302–306. DOI: 10.1097/NNE.0000000000000805 PMID: 31972846

Han, J., & Geng, X. (2023). University students' approaches to online learning technologies: The roles of perceived support, affect/emotion, and self-efficacy in technology-enhanced learning. *Computers & Education*, 194, 104695. DOI: 10.1016/j.compedu.2022.104695

Hansen, B. L., & Gray, E. (2018). Creating boundaries within the ubiquitous online classroom. *The Journal of Educators Online*, 15(3), n3. https://www.thejeo.com/. DOI: 10.9743/jeo.2018.15.3.2

Hanushek, E. A., & Woessmann, L. (2008). The role of cognitive skills in economic development. *Journal of Economic Literature*, 46(3), 607–668. DOI: 10.1257/jel.46.3.607

Hao, Q., Barnes, B., & Jing, M. (2021). Quantifying the effects of active learning environments: Separating physical learning classrooms from ped- agogical approaches. *Learning Environments Research*, 24(1), 109–122. DOI: 10.1007/s10984-020-09320-3

Harris, N., & Bacon, C. E. W. (2019). Developing cognitive skills through active learning: A Systematic review of health care professions. *Athletic Training Education Journal*, 14(2), 135–148. DOI: 10.4085/1402135

Hattie, J. (2009). *Visible learning: A synthesis of over 800 meta-analyses relating to achievement*. Routledge.

Hava, K., & Koyunlu Ünlü, Z. (2021). Investigation of the relationship between middle school students' computational thinking skills and their STEM career interest and attitudes toward inquiry. *Journal of Science Education and Technology*, 30(4), 484–495. DOI: 10.1007/s10956-020-09892-y

Hawkey, K. (2003). Social constructivism and asynchronous text-based discussion: A case study with trainee teachers. *Education and Information Technologies*, 8(2), 165–177. DOI: 10.1023/A:1024558414766

Hehir, E., Zeller, M., Luckhurst, J., & Chandler, T. (2021). Developing student connectedness under remote learning using digital resources: A systematic review. *Education and Information Technologies*, 26(5), 6531–6548. DOI: 10.1007/s10639-021-10577-1 PMID: 34220282

Heid, K. A., & Kelehear, Z. (2007). *The challenge to care in schools: An alternative approach to education.*

Heid, K. (2008). Care, sociocultural practice, and aesthetic experience in the art classroom. *Visual Arts Research*, 34(1), 87–98. DOI: 10.2307/20715464

Heilmann, L. (2020). Health and numeracy: The role of numeracy skills in health satisfaction and health-related behaviour. *ZDM Mathematics Education*, 52(3), 407–418. DOI: 10.1007/s11858-019-01106-z

Hein, G. E. (1991, October 15-22). *Constructivist learning theory* [Paper presentation]. CECA (International Committee of Museum Educators) Conference, Jerusalem, Israel. https://www.exploratorium.edu/education/ifi/constructivist-learning

Henry, M. K., Pooley, J. A., & Omari, M. (2014). Student motivation for studying online: A qualitative study. https://ro.ecu.edu.au/ecuworkspost2013/869

Henry, J., & Meadows, J. (2008). An absolutely riveting online course: Nine principles for excellence in web-based teaching. *Canadian Journal of Learning and Technology*, 34(1). Advance online publication. http://www.cjlt.ca/index.php/cjlt/index. DOI: 10.21432/T20C7F

Herminingsih, A., & Rizki, M. (2021). Quality culture to improve knowledge sharing and the positive effect on engagement of academic staff. *Archives of Business Research*, 9(1), 65–74. DOI: 10.14738/abr.91.9578

Hernández, R., Fernández, C., & Baptista, P. (2014). Metodología de la investigación (6a. ed.). México D. F., México: McGraw-Hill

Hernandez-de-Menendez, M., Vallejo Guevara, A., Tudon Martinez, J. C., Hernandez Alcantara, D., & Morales-Menendez, R. (2019). Active learning in engineering education. A review of fundamentals, best practices and experiences. [IJIDeM]. *International Journal on Interactive Design and Manufacturing*, 13(3), 909–922. DOI: 10.1007/s12008-019-00557-8

Hew, K. F., & Cheung, W. S. (2014). *Using Blended Learning: Evidence-Based Practices*. Springer. DOI: 10.1007/978-981-287-089-6

Heyd-Metzuyanim, E., Sharon, A. J., & Baram-Tsabari, A. (2021). Mathematical media literacy in the COVID-19 pandemic and its relation to school mathematics education. *Educational Studies in Mathematics*, 108(1-2), 201–225. DOI: 10.1007/s10649-021-10075-8 PMID: 34934235

Hicks, M., Reid, I., & George, R. (2001). Enhancing on-line teaching: Designing responsive learning environments. *The International Journal for Academic Development*, 6(2), 143–151. DOI: 10.1080/713769258

Hinson, J. M., & LaPrairie, K. N. (2005). Learning to teach online: Promoting success through professional development. *Community College Journal of Research and Practice*, 29(6), 483–493. DOI: 10.1080/10668920590934198

Hobson, C. J., Strupeck, D., Griffin, A., Szostek, J., & Rominger, A. S. (2014). Teaching MBA Students Teamwork and Team Leadership Skills: An Empirical Evaluation of a Classroom Educational Program. *American Journal of Business Education*, 7(3), 191–212. DOI: 10.19030/ajbe.v7i3.8629

Hodges, C., Moore, S., Lockee, B., Trust, T., & Bond, A. (2020, March). The difference between emergency remote teaching and online learning. *EDUCAUSE Review*, 27, https://er.educause.edu/articles/2020/3/the-difference-between-emergency-remote-teaching-and-online-learning

Hoggan, C., & Kloubert, T. (2020). Transformative Learning in Theory and Practice. *Adult Education Quarterly*, 70(3), 295–307. DOI: 10.1177/0741713620918510

Holflod, K. (2022). Playful learning and boundary-crossing collaboration in higher education: A narrative and synthesising review. *Journal of Further and Higher Education*, 47(4), 465–480. DOI: 10.1080/0309877X.2022.2142101

Hollis, A., Kim, S., & Lee, Y. (2022). The impact of online learning environments on student satisfaction and academic performance. *Journal of Computer Assisted Learning*, 38(3), 527–542.

Hollister, B., Nair, P., Hill-Lindsay, S., & Chukoskie, L. (2022). Engagement in online learning: Student attitudes and behavior during COVID-19. *Frontiers in Education*, 7(851019), 1–16. DOI: 10.3389/feduc.2022.851019

Holmes, M. R., Tracy, E. M., Painter, L. L., Oestreich, T., & Park, H. (2015). Moving from flipcharts to the flipped classroom: Using technology-driven teaching methods to promote active learning in foundation and advanced masters social work courses. *Clinical Social Work Journal*, 43(2), 215–224. DOI: 10.1007/s10615-015-0521-x

Homer, B. D., Plass, J. L., & Blake, L. (2008). The effects of video on cognitive load and social presence in multimedia-learning. *Computers in Human Behavior*, 24(3), 786–797. DOI: 10.1016/j.chb.2007.02.009

Hong, Y., Saab, N., & Admiraal, W. (2024). Approaches and game elements used to tailor digital gamification for learning: A systematic literature review. *Computers & Education*, 212, 105000. DOI: 10.1016/j.compedu.2024.105000

Horvitz, B. S., Beach, A. L., Anderson, M. L., & Xia, J. (2015). Examination of faculty self-efficacy related to online teaching. *Innovative Higher Education*, 40(4), 305–316. DOI: 10.1007/s10755-014-9316-1

Hosny, S., Ghaly, M., AlSheikh, M. H., Shehata, M. H., Salem, A. H., & Atwa, H. (2021). Developing, validating, and implementing a tool for measuring the readiness of medical teachers for online teaching post-COVID-19: A multicenter study. *Advances in Medical Education and Practice*, 12(755), 755–768. Advance online publication. DOI: 10.2147/AMEP.S317029 PMID: 34285628

Hossen, M. K., & Uddin, M. S. (2023). Attention monitoring of students during online classes using XGBoost classifier. *Computers and Education: Artificial Intelligence*, 100191, 100191. Advance online publication. DOI: 10.1016/j.caeai.2023.100191

Howard, P. (2019). Re-visioning teacher education for sustainability in Atlantic Canada. In *Environmental and sustainability education in teacher education: Canadian perspectives* (pp. 179–191). Springer International Publishing. DOI: 10.1007/978-3-030-25016-4_11

Hrastinski, S. (2009). A theory of online learning as online participation. *Computers & Education*, 52(1), 78–82. DOI: 10.1016/j.compedu.2008.06.009

Hrastinski, S. (2019). What do we mean by blended learning? *TechTrends*, 63(5), 564–569. DOI: 10.1007/s11528-019-00375-5

Hrastinski, S. (2021). Student-student online collaboration: A critical review of theoretical approaches. *International Review of Research in Open and Distributed Learning*, 22(2), 19–37.

Hsia, L. H., Huang, I., & Hwang, G. J. (2016). Effects of different online peer-feedback approaches on students' performance skills, motivation and self-efficacy in a dance course. *Computers & Education*, 96, 55–71. DOI: 10.1016/j.compedu.2016.02.004

Hsu, T. C., & Liang, Y. S. (2021). Simultaneously improving computational thinking and foreign language learning: Interdisciplinary media with plugged and unplugged approaches. *Journal of Educational Computing Research*, 59(6), 1184–1207. DOI: 10.1177/0735633121992480

Huang, A. Y. Q., Lu, O. H. T., & Yang, S. J. H. (2023). Effects of artificial Intelligence–Enabled personalized recommendations on learners' learning engagement, motivation, and outcomes in a flipped classroom. *Computers & Education*, 194, 104684. Advance online publication. DOI: 10.1016/j.compedu.2022.104684

Huberman, A. (Host). (2023, October 29). Mental health toolkit: Tools to bolster your mood and mental health [Audio podast episode]. In *Huberman Lab*. https://www.hubermanlab.com/episode/mental-health-toolkit-tools-to-bolster-your-mood-mental-health?timestamp=240

Huda, N., Wahyuni, T. S., & Fauziyah, F. D. (2021). *Students' perceptions of online mathematics learning and its relationship towards their achievement*. Atlantis Press., DOI: 10.2991/assehr.k.210421.077

Hughey, J. (2020). Individual Personalized Learning. *Educational Considerations*, 46(2). Advance online publication. DOI: 10.4148/0146-9282.2237

Humpherys, S. L., Bakir, N., & Babb, J. (2022). Experiential learning to foster tacit knowledge through a role play, business simulation. *Journal of Education for Business*, 97(2), 119–125. DOI: 10.1080/08832323.2021.1896461

Hung, H. T. (2017). Design-based research: Redesign of an English language course using a flipped classroom approach. *TESOL Quarterly*, 51(1), 180–192. DOI: 10.1002/tesq.328

Hu, P., & Zhang, J. (2017). A pathway to learner autonomy: A self-determination theory perspective. *Asia Pacific Education Review*, 18(1), 147–157. DOI: 10.1007/s12564-016-9468-z

Hu, S. (2008). Reinventing undergraduate education: Engaging college students in research and creative activities. *ASHE Higher Education Report*, 33(4), 1–103. DOI: 10.1002/aehe.3304

Hutchins, N. M., Biswas, G., Maróti, M., Lédeczi, Á., Grover, S., Wolf, R., Blair, K. P., Chin, D., Conlin, L., Basu, S., & McElhaney, K. (2020). C2STEM: A system for synergistic learning of physics and computational thinking. *Journal of Science Education and Technology*, 29(1), 83–100. DOI: 10.1007/s10956-019-09804-9

Hwu, S.-L. (2023). Developing SAMM: A Model for Measuring Sustained Attention in Asynchronous Online Learning. *Sustainability (Basel)*, 15(12), 9337. DOI: 10.3390/su15129337

Hyunjin, J. K., Yiren, K., & Tirotta-Esposito, R. (2023). Promoting diversity, equity, and inclusion: An examination of diversity-infused faculty professional development programs. *Journal of Higher Education Theory and Practice*, 23(11), 138–153. DOI: 10.33423/jhetp.v23i11.6224

Ilioudi, C., Giannakos, M. N., & Chorianopoulos, K. (2013). Investigating differences among the commonly used video lecture styles. In WAVe 2013 the Workshop on Analytics on video-based learning (pp. 21e26).

Im, H., & Lee, Y. L. (2021). A study of the relationship between learning flow and learning burnout in college online classes. *Journal of Digital Convergence*, 19(6), 39–46. DOI: 10.14400/JDC.2021.19.6.039

Ingkavara, T., Panjaburee, P., Srisawasdi, N., & Sajjapanroj, S. (2022). The use of a personalized learning approach to implementing self-regulated online learning. *Computers and Education: Artificial Intelligence*, 3, 100086. DOI: 10.1016/j.caeai.2022.100086

Ingram, D. (2012). College students' sense of belonging: Dimensions and correlates (Publication No. 28168034) [Doctoral dissertation, Stanford University]. ProQuest Dissertation and Theses Global. https://purl.stanford.edu/rd771tq2209

Iversen, O. S., Smith, R. C., & Dindler, C. (2018, August). From computational thinking to computational empowerment: a 21st century PD agenda. In *Proceedings of the 15th participatory design conference: Full papers-Volume 1* (pp. 1-11).

İzmirli, S., & Akyüz, H. İ. (2017). Examining synchronous virtual classroom software. *Journal of Theory and Practice in Education*, 13(4). Advance online publication. DOI: 10.17244/eku.347815

Jackson, L. (2016). Globalization and education. In Oxford research encyclopedia of education. DOI: 10.1093/acrefore/9780190264093.013.52

Jackson, K. T., Richardson, S., & Breen, J. M. (2022). Enacting a diversity, equity, inclusion, and justice emphasis in graduate and professional leadership education. *New Directions for Student Leadership*, 2022(176), 75–87. DOI: 10.1002/yd.20532 PMID: 36565141

Jacob, M. (2023). Active cognitive tasks- Synthesizing frameworks for active learning online. In Gowers, I., & Garnham, W. (Eds.), *Active learning in higher education: Theoretical considerations and perspectives* (1st ed., pp. 5–11). Routledge., https://www.taylorfrancis.com/chapters/edit/10.4324/9781003360032-6/active-cognitive-tasks-synthesising-frameworks-active-learning-online-mary-jacob DOI: 10.4324/9781003360032-6

Jaggars, S. S., & Bailey, T. (2010). *Effectiveness of fully online courses for college students: Response to a Department of Education meta-analysis.* Community College Research Center, Teachers College, Columbia University.

James, A. (2021). Play in research? Yes, it is "proper" practice. *Journal of Play in Adulthood*, 3(1), 9–30. DOI: 10.5920/jpa.864

Jarvis, P. (2010). *Adult education and lifelong learning: Theory and practice* (4th ed.). Routledge.

Jennings, C. L. (2020). Enhancing social presence in online courses: Facilitation strategies and best practices. In Thornburg, A., Abernathy, D., & Ceglie, R. (Eds.), *Handbook of research on developing engaging online courses* (pp. 259–276). IGI Global., DOI: 10.4018/978-1-7998-2132-8.ch015

Jensen, J. L., Kummer, T. A., & Godoy, P. D. D. M. (2015). Improvements from a flipped classroom may simply be the fruits of active learning. *CBE Life Sciences Education*, 14(1), 1–12. DOI: 10.1187/cbe.14-08-0129 PMID: 25699543

Jeremic, Z., Milikic, N., Jovanovic, J., Brkovic, M., & Radulovic, F. (2012). Using online presence to improve online collaborative learning. [iJET]. *International Journal of Emerging Technologies in Learning*, 7(S1), 7. DOI: 10.3991/ijet.v7iS1.1918

Jiang, D., Chen, O., Yong, H., & Kalyuga, S. (2023). Improving English language skills through learning Mathematic contents: From the expertise reversal effect perspective. *The British Journal of Educational Psychology*, 93(S2), 386–401. DOI: 10.1111/bjep.12596 PMID: 36990799

Jie, C. Y., & Ali, N. M. (2021). COVID-19: What are the challenges of online learning? A literature review. *International Journal of Advanced Research in Future Ready Learning and Education*, 23(1), 23–29. DOI: 10.37934/frle.23.1.2329

Johnson, D., & Samora, D. (2016). The potential transformation of higher education through computer-based adaptive learning systems. *Global Education Journal, 2016*(1).

Johnson, D. W., & Johnson, R. T. (2009). *Cooperation and Competition: Theory and Research*. Interaction Book Company.

Johnson, D. W., Johnson, R. T., & Smith, K. A. (1998). Cooperative learning returns to college: What evidence is there that it works? *Change*, 30(4), 26–35. DOI: 10.1080/00091389809602629

Johnson, K. R., Hewapathirana, G. I., & Bowen, M. M. (2019). Faculty development for online teaching. In *Handbook of research on virtual training and mentoring of online instructors* (pp. 40–55). IGI Global.

Johnson, L., Adams Becker, S., Cummins, M., Estrada, V., Freeman, A., & Hall, C. (2020). *NMC horizon report: 2020 higher education edition*. The New Media Consortium.

Johnston, V., & Martelli, C. D. (2017). Flipped learning: Student perceptions and achievement in teacher education. *Teacher Education and Practice*, 30(4).

Joiner, B. (2019). Leadership Agility for organizational agility. *Journal of Creating Value*, 5(2), 139–149. DOI: 10.1177/2394964319868321

Jonassen, D. H., & Hung, W. (2015). All problems are not equal: Implications for problem-based learning. In Walker, A., & Leary, H. (Eds.), *Essential readings in problem-based learning* (pp. 17–41). Purdue University Press. DOI: 10.2307/j.ctt6wq6fh.7

Jones, S. (2020). Computers and technology in Montessori Schools. *Montessori For Today*. https://montessorifortoday.com/computers-and-technology-in-montessori-schools/

Joshi, R., & Jaffer, S. (2024). Impact of organizational culture on job stress and well-being among higher education faculty. *Educational Administration: Theory and Practice*, 30(5), 13975–13985. DOI: 10.53555/kuey.v30i5.6170

Josifović-Elezović, S. (2022). Students' perceptions of the flipped classroom approach in tertiary EFL education:Aa case study from banja luka. *Folia Linguistica et Litteraria (Online)*, XIII(40), 351–373. DOI: 10.31902/fll.40.2022.18

Jump, M., & Schedlbauer, M. (2020). Effective practices for online teaching. *Proceedings of the 51st ACM Technical Symposium on Computer Science Education*. DOI: 10.1145/3328778.3372534

Junus, K., Santoso, H. B., Putra, P. O. H., Gandhi, A., & Siswantining, T. (2021). Lecturer readiness for online classes during the pandemic: A survey research. *Education Sciences*, 11(3), 139. DOI: 10.3390/educsci11030139

Kaiser, L., McKenna, K., Lopes, T., & Zarestky, J. (2023). Strategies for supporting adult working learners in the online learning environment. *New Directions for Adult and Continuing Education*, 2023(179), 53–65. DOI: 10.1002/ace.20502

Kalelioğlu, F., Atan, A., & Çetin, Ç. (2016). Experiences of instructors and learners in a virtual classroom environment. *Mersin University Journal of the Faculty of Education*, 12(2), 555–568.

Kaliisa, R., & Picard, M. (2017). A systematic review on mobile learning in higher education: The African perspective. *Turkish Online Journal of Educational Technology-TOJET*, 16(1), 1–18.

Kalir, R., & Garcia, A. (2021). Joining the 'great conversation'–the fundamental role of annotation in academic society. Impact of Social Sciences Blog. https://blogs.lse.ac.uk/impactofsocialsciences/

Kalir, J. H., Morales, E., Fleerackers, A., & Alperin, J. P. (2020). When I saw my peers annotating student perceptions of social annotation for learning in multiple courses. *Information and Learning Science*, 121(4), 207–230. DOI: 10.1108/ILS-12-2019-0128

Kalyuga, S. (2023). *Task Complexity, Learner Expertise, and Instructional Goals in Managing Instructional Guidance*. Copyright and Other Legal Notices, 122.

Kamel, S. (2014). Education in the Middle East: Challenges and opportunities. Business and education in the Middle East, 99-130.

Kang, M., & Im, T. (2020). Blended learning in Korea: Issues and challenges. *The Asia-Pacific Education Researcher*, 19(1), 1–11.

Kangwa, D., Xiulan, W., Msambwa Msafiri, M., & Fute, A. (2024). Enhanced learning engagement through teaching presence in online distance education. *Distance Education*, •••, 1–18. DOI: 10.1080/01587919.2024.2347998

Kara, N., Cubukcuoglu, B., & Elci, A. (2020). Using social media to support teaching and learning in higher education: An analysis of personal narratives.

Kariou, A., Koutsimani, P., Montgomery, A., & Lainidi, O. (2021). Emotional labor and burnout among teachers: A systematic review. *International Journal of Environmental Research and Public Health*, 18(23), 12760. DOI: 10.3390/ijerph182312760 PMID: 34886485

Karpicke, J. D., & Roediger, H. L.III. (2008). The critical importance of retrieval for learning. *Science*, 319(5865), 966–968. DOI: 10.1126/science.1152408 PMID: 18276894

Kaya, S. (2011). *Sanal sınıf yönetiminde görev alacak öğretim elemanlarının eğitim gereksinimlerinin belirlenmesi* [Identifying the educational needs of instructors commissioned in the virtual classroom management] [Doctoral dissertation]. Anadolu University, Eskişehir. Available from the Council of Higher Education, National Dissertation Center, Dissertation ID: 286819.

Kebritchi, M., Lipschuetz, A., & Santiague, L. (2017). Issues and challenges for teaching successful online courses in higher education: A literature review. *Journal of Educational Technology Systems*, 46(1), 4–29. DOI: 10.1177/0047239516661713

Keengwe, J., Onchwari, G., & Onchwari, J. (2009). Thechnology and students learning: Towards a learner-centered teaching model. *AACE Review*, 17(1), 11–22.

Kelly, B. (2019). Motivating adults to learn mathematics in the workplace: A trade union approach. *International Journal of Lifelong Education*, 38(2), 132–147. DOI: 10.1080/02601370.2018.1555190

Kelly, B., Devlin, M., Giffin, T., & Smith, L. (2021). Family learning online during lockdown in the UK. *Adults Learning Mathematics: An International Journal*, 16(1), 20–35.

Khafifah, K. A., Hasanah, U., & Zulfa, V. (2023). Hubungan antara stres akademik dengan academic performance pada santri Madrasah Aliyah Pondok Pesantren Al-Hamid [The relationship between academic stress and academic performance of students of Madrasah Aliyah, Al-Hamid Islamic Boarding School] [Jurnal Kesejahteraan Keluarga dan Pendidikan]. *JKKP*, 10(1), 27–37. DOI: 10.21009/JKKP.101.03

Khan, A., Egbue, O., Palkie, B., & Madden, J. (2017). Active learning: Engaging students to maximize learning in an online course. *Electronic Journal of e-Learning*, 15(2), 107–115.

Khayat, M., Hafezi, F., Asgari, P., & Talebzadeh Shoushtari, M. (2021). Comparison of the effectiveness of flipped classroom and traditional teaching method on the components of self-determination and class perception among University students. *Journal of Advances in Medical Education & Professionalism*, 9(4), 230–237. DOI: 10.30476/jamp.2021.89793.1385 PMID: 34692861

Khudhair, A. A., Khudhair, M. A., Jaber, M. M., Awreed, Y. J., Ali, M. H., AL-Hameed, M., Jassim, M., Malik, R., Alkhayyat, A., & Hameed, A. (2023). Impact on Higher Education and College Students in Dijlah University after COVID through E-learning. *Computer-Aided Design and Applications*, •••, 104–115. DOI: 10.14733/cadaps.2023.S12.104-115

Kilpatrick, W. H. (1918). The project method. The use of the purposeful act in the educative process. Teachers College, Columbia University. 525 West 120th Street. New York City DOI: 10.1177/016146811801900404

Kim, D., Wortham, S., Borowiec, K., Yatsu, D. K., Ha, S., Carroll, S., Wang, L., & Kim, J. (2021). Formative education online: Teaching the whole person during the global COVID-19 pandemic. *AERA Open*, 7, 23328584211015229. DOI: 10.1177/23328584211015229

Kim, H. S., & Oh, E. G. (2018). Scaffolding argumentation in asynchronous online discussion: Using students' perceptions to refine a design framework. *International Journal of Online Pedagogy and Course Design*, 8(2), 29–43. DOI: 10.4018/IJOPCD.2018040103

Kim, J., Park, H., Jang, M., & Nam, H. (2017). Exploring flipped classroom effects on second language learners' cognitive processing. *Foreign Language Annals*, 50(2), 260–284. DOI: 10.1111/flan.12260

Kim, J., Singh, S., Thiessen, E. D., & Fisher, A. V. (2020). A hidden Markov model for analyzing eye-tracking of moving objects. *Behavior Research Methods*, 52(3), 1225–1243. DOI: 10.3758/s13428-019-01313-2 PMID: 31898297

Kim, S. H. (2022). Structural relationships among course organization, student engagement and perceived learning outcome in online learning. *Journal of Learner-Centered Curriculum Education*, 22(21), 81–96. DOI: 10.22251/jlcci.2022.22.21.81

Kim, S. Y., & Martin, F. (2023). Validation of the Faculty Readiness to Teaching Online (FRTO) scale. *Journal of Applied Research in Higher Education*, 23(3). Advance online publication. DOI: 10.1108/JARHE-03-2023-0108

Kim, S., & Lee, Y. (2023). Global access to education through online open elective courses: A review. *The Journal of Educational Research*, 10(4), 345–359.

King, A. (1993). From sage on the stage to guide on the side. *College Teaching*, 41(1), 30–35. DOI: 10.1080/87567555.1993.9926781

King, C. G., Guyette, R. W.Jr, & Piotrowski, C. (2009). Online exams and cheating: An empirical analysis of business students' views. *The Journal of Educators Online*, 6(1), n1. https://files.eric.ed.gov/fulltext/EJ904058.pdf. DOI: 10.9743/JEO.2009.1.5

Kızılcık, H. H., & Türüdü, A. S. D. (2022). Humanising online teaching through care-centred pedagogies. *Australasian Journal of Educational Technology*, 38(4), 143–159. DOI: 10.14742/ajet.7872

Kleinknecht, M., & Gröschner, A. (2016). Fostering preservice teachers' noticing with structured video feedback: Results of an online and video-based intervention study. *Teaching and Teacher Education*, 59, 45–56. DOI: 10.1016/j.tate.2016.05.020

Knowles, M. Andragogy in Action, Malcolm S. Knowles and Associates. 1st ed. Jossey-Bass; 1984.

Knowles, M. (1975). *Self-directed learning: A guide for learners and teachers*. The Adult Education Company.

Kobasa, S. C. (1979). Stressful life events, personality, and health: An inquiry into hardiness. *Journal of Personality and Social Psychology*, 37(1), 1–11. DOI: 10.1037/0022-3514.37.1.1 PMID: 458548

Koehler, M. J., & Mishra, P. (2008). Introducing TPCK. In AACTE Committee on Innovation and Technology. (Ed.), Handbook of technological pedagogical content knowledge (TPCK). New York: Routledge

Kohli, H., Wampole, D., & Kohli, A. (2021). Impact of online education on student learning during the pandemic. *Studies in Learning and Teaching*, 2(2), 1–11. DOI: 10.46627/silet.v2i2.65

Kokoç, M., Ilgaz, H., & Altun, A. (2020). Effects of sustained attention and video lecture types on learning performances. *Educational Technology Research and Development*, 68(6), 3015–3039. DOI: 10.1007/s11423-020-09829-7

Komives, S. R., & Sowcik, M. (2020). How Academic Disciplines Approach Leadership Development. *New Directions for Student Leadership*, 2020(165). Advance online publication. DOI: 10.1002/yd.20365 PMID: 32187868

Kopish, M., & Marques, W. (2020). Leveraging technology to promote global citizenship in teacher education in the United States and Brazil. *Research in Social Sciences and Technology*, 5(1), 45–69. DOI: 10.46303/ressat.05.01.3

Kostenius, C., & Alerby, E. (2020). Room for interpersonal relationships in online educational spaces–a philosophical discussion. *International journal of qualitative studies on health and well-being, 15*(sup1), 1689603.

Kovich, M. K., Simpson, V. L., Foli, K. J., Hass, Z., & Phillips, R. G. (2022). Application of the PERMA model of well-being in undergraduate students. *International Journal of Community Well-being*, 6(1), 1–20. DOI: 10.1007/s42413-022-00184-4 PMID: 36320595

Kraatz, E., Nagpal, M., Lin, T., Hsieh, M., Ha, S. Y., Kim, S., & Shin, S. (2020). Teacher scaffolding of social and intellectual collaboration in small groups: A comparative case study. *Frontiers in Psychology*, 11, 587058. Advance online publication. DOI: 10.3389/fpsyg.2020.587058 PMID: 33240179

Krackhardt, D. (1999). The ties that torture: Simmelian tie analysis in organizations. *Research in the Sociology of Organizations*, 16, 183–210.

Kreijns, K., Xu, K., & Weidlich, J. (2022). Social presence: Conceptualization and measurement. *Educational Psychology Review*, 34(1), 139–170. DOI: 10.1007/s10648-021-09623-8 PMID: 34177204

Kremenova, I., & Gajdos, M. (2019). Decentralized networks: The future internet. *Mobile Networks and Applications*, 24(6), 2016–2023. DOI: 10.1007/s11036-018-01211-5

Kropiewnicki, M. I., & Shapiro, J. P. (2001). *Female Leadership and the Ethic of Care: Three Case Studies*.

Kruger, J., Wirtz, D., Van Boven, L., & Altermatt, T. W. (2004). The effort heuristic. *Journal of Experimental Social Psychology*, 40(1), 91–98. DOI: 10.1016/S0022-1031(03)00065-9

Kuh, G. D. (2016). Making learning meaningful: Engaging students in ways that matter to them. *New Directions for Teaching and Learning*, 145(145), 49–56. DOI: 10.1002/tl.20174

Kukulska-Hulme, A. (2012). How should the higher education workforce adapt to advancements in technology for teaching and learning? *The Internet and Higher Education*, 15(4), 247–254. DOI: 10.1016/j.iheduc.2011.12.002

Kumalasari, D., & Akmal, S. Z. (2021). Less stress, more satisfied in online learning during the COVID-19 pandemic: The moderating role of academic resilience. *Psychological Research on Urban Society*, 4(1), 36–44. DOI: 10.7454/proust.v4i1.115

Kumar, A., Krishnamurthi, R., Bhatia, S., Kaushik, K., Ahuja, N. J., Nayyar, A., & Masud, M. (2021). Blended learning tools and practices: A comprehensive analysis. *IEEE Access : Practical Innovations, Open Solutions*, 9, 85151–85197. DOI: 10.1109/ACCESS.2021.3085844

Kumar, B., Swee, M. L., & Suneja, M. (2020). Leadership training programs in graduate medical education: A systematic review. *BMC Medical Education*, 20(1), 1–10. DOI: 10.1186/s12909-020-02089-2 PMID: 32487056

Kumi-Yeboah, A., & Amponsah, S. (2023). An exploratory study of instructors' perceptions on inclusion of culturally responsive pedagogy in online education. *British Journal of Educational Technology*, 54(4), 878–897. DOI: 10.1111/bjet.13299

Kumi-Yeboah, A., Kim, Y., Sallar, A. M., & Kiramba, L. K. (2020). Exploring the use of digital technologies from the perspective of diverse learners in online learning environments. *Online Learning : the Official Journal of the Online Learning Consortium*, 24(4), 42–63. DOI: 10.24059/olj.v24i4.2323

Kundu, A., & Bej, T. (2021). COVID-19 response: Students' readiness for shifting classes online. *Corporate Governance (Bradford)*, 21(6), 1250–1270. DOI: 10.1108/CG-09-2020-0377

Kuntz, J. R. C., Kuntz, J. R., Elenkov, D., & Nabirukhina, A. (2013). Characterizing ethical cases: A cross-cultural investigation of individual differences, organizational climate, and leadership on ethical decision-making. *Journal of Business Ethics*, 113(2), 317–331. DOI: 10.1007/s10551-012-1306-6

Kutsyuruba, B., Walker, K. D., Stasel, R. S., & Makhamreh, M. A. (2019). Developing resilience and promoting well-being in early career teaching. *Canadian Journal of Education/Revue canadienne de l'éducation,* 42(1), 285-321.

Kwon, J., & Woo, H. (2018). The Impact of Flipped Learning on Cooperative and Competitive Mindsets. *Sustainability (Basel)*, 10(1), 79. Advance online publication. DOI: 10.3390/su10010079

Kyungbin, K., Daehoon, H., Eun-Jun, B., & Armstrong, S. (2010). Feelings of isolation and coping mechanism in online learning environments: A case study of Asian international students. *International Journal of Learning*, 17(2), 343–355.

Lacroix, P. (2019). Big data privacy and ethical challenges. Big Data, Big Challenges: A Healthcare Perspective: Background, Issues, Solutions and Research Directions, 101-111.

Lage, M. J., Platt, G. J., & Treglia, M. (2000). Inverting the classroom: A gateway to creating an inclusive learning environment. *The Journal of Economic Education*, 31(1), 30–34. DOI: 10.1080/00220480009596759

Låg, T., & Sæle, R. G. (2019). Does the flipped classroom improve student learning and satisfaction? A systematic review and meta-analysis. *AERA Open*, 5(3), 2332858419870489. Advance online publication. DOI: 10.1177/2332858419870489

Lakshmi, Y. V. (2021). eLearning Readiness of Higher Education Faculty Members. *Indian Journal of Educational Technology*, 3(2). https://ssrn.com/abstract=3970655

Lammers, W. J., & Gillaspy, J. A.Jr. (2013). Brief measure of student-instructor rapport predicts student success in online courses. *International Journal for the Scholarship of Teaching and Learning*, 7(2), 16. DOI: 10.20429/ijsotl.2013.070216

Lam, R. (2017). Enacting feedback utilization from a task-specific perspective. *Curriculum Journal*, 28(2), 266–282. DOI: 10.1080/09585176.2016.1187185

Landrum, B., Bannister, J., Garza, G., & Rhame, S. (2021). A class of one: Students' satisfaction with online learning. *Journal of Education for Business*, 96(2), 82–88. DOI: 10.1080/08832323.2020.1757592

Lange, C., Gorbunova, A., Shmeleva, E., & Costley, J. (2023). The relationship between instructional scaffolding strategies and maintained situational interest. *Interactive Learning Environments*, 31(10), 6640–6651. DOI: 10.1080/10494820.2022.2042314

Larsen, D. P., Butler, A. C., & Roediger, H. L.III. (2013). Comparative effects of test-enhanced learning and self-explanation on long-term retention. *Medical Education*, 47(7), 674–682. DOI: 10.1111/medu.12141 PMID: 23746156

Larsen, J., & Liljedahl, P. (2022). Building thinking classrooms online: From practice to theory and back again. *Adults Learning Mathematics: An International Journal*, 16(1), 36–52.

Lateh, H., & Raman, A. (2005). Distance Learning and Educational Technology in Malaysia. In *Encyclopedia of Distance Learning* (pp. 641–653). IGI Global. DOI: 10.4018/978-1-59140-555-9.ch092

Lave, J., & Wenger, E. (1991). *Situated Learning: Legitimate Peripheral Participation*. Cambridge University Press. DOI: 10.1017/CBO9780511815355

Lawrence, K. (2013). Developing leaders in a VUCA environment. *UNC Executive Development*, 2013, 1–15.

Lawson, A. P., Mayer, R. E., Adamo-Villani, N., Benes, B., Lei, X., & Cheng, J. (2021). Recognizing the emotional state of human and virtual instructors. *Computers in Human Behavior*, 114, 106554. DOI: 10.1016/j.chb.2020.106554

Lazarevic, B., Fuller, J., & Cain, J. (2023). Facilitating community of inquiry through video-enhanced online instruction: What are learners' impressions? *TechTrends*, 67(4), 611–625. DOI: 10.1007/s11528-023-00864-8

Learning Ecosystems and Leadership. (2021). The hidden support from social capital to implementing PBL in diverse contexts globally. https://www.wise-qatar.org/hidden-support-social-capital-implementing-pbl-sarojani-mohammed/

Learning, P. B. (2022). Use of Technology with Problem-Based Learning in Higher Education.

Leary, H., Dopp, C., Turley, C., Cheney, M., Simmons, Z., Graham, C. R., & Hatch, R. (2020). Professional development for online teaching: A literature review. *Online Learning : the Official Journal of the Online Learning Consortium*, 24(4). Advance online publication. DOI: 10.24059/olj.v24i4.2198

Leather, M., Harper, N. J., & Obee, P. (2020). A pedagogy of play: Reasons to be playful in postsecondary education. *Journal of Experiential Education*, 44(3), 208–226. DOI: 10.1177/1053825920959684

Lee, A. B. C. (2020) *Open University Malaysia (OUM): The Path Travelled (2000 – 2020) & The Way Forward (2021 – 2030) - Issues, Challenges, Opportunities.* Master's thesis, Open University Malaysia (OUM).

Lee, D., Huh, Y., Lin, C. Y., & Reigeluth, C. M. (2018). Technology functions for personalized learning in learner-centered schools. *Educational Technology Research and Development*, 66(5), 1269–1302. DOI: 10.1007/s11423-018-9615-9

Lee, E., & Hannafin, M. J. (2016). A design framework for enhancing engagement in student-centered learning: Own it, learn it, and share it. *Educational Technology Research and Development*, 64(4), 707–734. DOI: 10.1007/s11423-015-9422-5

Lee, G., & Wallace, A. (2018). Flipped Learning in the English as a Foreign Language Classroom: Outcomes and Perceptions. *TESOL Quarterly*, 52(1), 62–84. DOI: 10.1002/tesq.372

Lee, I., Grover, S., Martin, F., Pillai, S., & Malyn-Smith, J. (2020). Computational thinking from a disciplinary perspective: Integrating computational thinking in K-12 science, technology, engineering, and mathematics education. *Journal of Science Education and Technology*, 29(1), 1–8. DOI: 10.1007/s10956-019-09803-w

Lee, J. W. (2020). The roles of online instructional facilitators and student performance of online class activity. *Journal of Asian Finance Economics and Business*, 7(8), 723–733. DOI: 10.13106/jafeb.2020.vol7.no8.723

Lee, J., Soleimani, F., Irish, I., Hosmer, J., Soylu, M. Y., Finkelberg, R., & Chatterjee, S. (2022). Predicting cognitive presence in at-scale online learning: MOOC and for-credit online course environments. *Online Learning : the Official Journal of the Online Learning Consortium*, 26(1), 58–79. DOI: 10.24059/olj.v26i1.3060

Lee, K. (2017). Rethinking the accessibility of online higher education: A historical review. *The Internet and Higher Education*, 33, 15–23. DOI: 10.1016/j.iheduc.2017.01.001

Leger, K. A., Charles, S. T., & Almeida, D. M. (2020). Positive emotions experienced on days of stress are associated with less same-day and next-day negative emotion. *Affective Science*, 1(1), 20–27. DOI: 10.1007/s42761-019-00001-w PMID: 34113848

Leibold, N., & Schwarz, L. (2015). The art of giving online feedback. *The Journal of Effective Teaching*, 15(1), 34–46.

Leo. (2023). Unlocking your child's potential: understanding the zone of proximal development. https://psychologily.com/zone-of-proximal-development/

Leonard, J., Buss, A., Gamboa, R., Mitchell, M., Fashola, O. S., Hubert, T., & Almughyirah, S. (2016). Using robotics and game design to enhance children's self-efficacy, STEM attitudes, and computational thinking skills. *Journal of Science Education and Technology*, 25(6), 860–876. DOI: 10.1007/s10956-016-9628-2

Leonard, J., Petta, K., & Porter, C. (2016). A fresh look at graduate programs in teacher leadership in the United States. In *Teacher Leadership and Professional Development* (pp. 29–44). Routledge.

Levykh, M. G. (2008). The affective establishment and maintenance of Vygotsky's zone of proximal development. *Educational Theory*, 58(1), 83–101. DOI: 10.1111/j.1741-5446.2007.00277.x

Liao, Y., & Chang, C. C. (2022). Personalized learning environments and their impact on student engagement. *Journal of Educational Technology Systems*, 50(3), 273–294.

Lichtenberger-Majzikné, K., & Fischer, A. (2017). The role of feedback in developing reflective competence. *Practice and Theory in Systems of Education*, 12(3), 119–127. DOI: 10.1515/ptse-2017-0012

Li, L. (2022). Reskilling and upskilling the future-ready workforce for Industry 4.0 and beyond. *Information Systems Frontiers*, 1–16. PMID: 35855776

Lim Abdullah, M. R. T., Hussin, Z., & Zakaria, A. R. (2013). MLearning scaffolding model for undergraduate English language learning: Bridging formal and informal learning. *The Turkish Online Journal of Educational Technology*, 12(2), 217–233.

Lim, E. L., Murugesan, R. K., & Balakrishnan, S. (2024). Leveraging machine learning techniques for student's attention detection: A review. *IAES International Journal of Artificial Intelligence*, 13(2), 1195–1195. DOI: 10.11591/ijai.v13.i2.pp1195-1205

Lim, J. (2022). Impact of instructors' online teaching readiness on satisfaction in the emergency online teaching context. *Education and Information Technologies*, •••, 1–18. DOI: 10.1007/s10639-022-11241-y PMID: 36247026

Lim, J., & Richardson, J. C. (2021). Predictive effects of undergraduate students' perceptions of social, cognitive, and teaching presence on affective learning outcomes according to disciplines. *Computers & Education*, 161, 104063. Advance online publication. DOI: 10.1016/j.compedu.2020.104063

Lin, C.-H., Wu, W.-H., & Lee, T.-N. (2022). Using an Online Learning Platform to Show Students' Achievements and Attention in the Video Lecture and Online Practice Learning Environments. *Journal of Educational Technology & Society*, 25(1), 155–165. https://www.jstor.org/stable/48647037

Lindsay, G. W. (2020). Attention in psychology, neuroscience, and machine learning. *Frontiers in Computational Neuroscience*, 14(29), 29. Advance online publication. DOI: 10.3389/fncom.2020.00029 PMID: 32372937

Ling, X., Yang, J., Liang, J., Zhu, H., & Sun, H. (2022). A Deep-Learning Based Method for Analysis of Students' Attention in Offline Class. *Electronics (Basel)*, 11(17), 2663–2663. DOI: 10.3390/electronics11172663

Lin, H.-C., & Hwang, G.-J. (2019). Research trends of flipped classroom studies for medical courses: A review of journal publications from 2008 to 2017 based on the technology-enhanced learning model. *Interactive Learning Environments*, 27(8), 1011–1027. DOI: 10.1080/10494820.2018.1467462

Lin, X., Tang, W., Ma, W., Liu, Y., & Ding, F. (2023). The impact of media diversity and cognitive style on learning experience in programming video lecture: A brainwave analysis. *Education and Information Technologies*, 28(8), 10617–10637. DOI: 10.1007/s10639-023-11608-9

Lipson, S. K., Zhou, S., Abelson, S., Heinze, J., Jirsa, M., Morigney, J., Patterson, A., Singh, M., & Eisenberg, D. (2022). Trends in college student mental health and help-seeking by race/ethnicity: Findings from the National Healthy Minds study, 2013-2021. *Journal of Affective Disorders*, 306(1), 138–147. DOI: 10.1016/j.jad.2022.03.038 PMID: 35307411

Li, R., Lund, A., & Nordstein, A. (2023). The link between flipped and active learning: A scoping review. *Teaching in Higher Education*, 28(8), 1–35. DOI: 10.1080/13562517.2021.1943655

Liu, H. P., Perera, S. M., & Klein, J. W. (2017). Using model-based learning to promote computational thinking education. *Emerging research, practice, and policy on computational thinking*, 153-172.

Liu, C. H. (2008). *A Vygotskyan educational psycho-semiotic perspective of interpsychology in classroom teaching and teacher socialization: Theories, instrument, and interpretive analyses* [Unpublished doctoral dissertation]. University of Adelaide., https://hekyll.services.adelaide.edu.au/dspace/bitstream/2440/69483/8/02whole.pdf

Liu, J. (2020). Perceptions of student engagement with online mathematics learning: A systematic review of literature. *Journal of Online Learning Research*, 6(1), 1–22. DOI: 10.59495/jolr.2020.001

Liu, K., & Jirigela, W. (2024). Research on innovative music teaching: To stimulate students' interest in learning. *International Journal of New Developments in Education*, 6(1), 26–32. DOI: 10.25236/IJNDE.2024.060105

Liu, N.-H., Chiang, C.-Y., & Chu, H.-C. (2013). Recognizing the Degree of Human Attention Using EEG Signals from Mobile Sensors. *Sensors (Basel)*, 13(8), 10273–10286. DOI: 10.3390/s130810273 PMID: 23939584

Liu, Z., Zhang, N., Peng, X., Liu, S., & Yang, Z. (2023). Students' social-cognitive engagement in online discussions. *Journal of Educational Technology & Society*, 26(1), 1–15. DOI: 10.30191/ETS.202301_26(1).0001

Li, W., & Wang, W. (2024). The impact of teaching presence on students' online learning experience: Evidence from 334 Chinese universities during the pandemic. *Frontiers in Psychology*, 15, 1291341. DOI: 10.3389/fpsyg.2024.1291341 PMID: 38947911

Li, Y., Hu, F., & He, X. (2021). How to make students happy during periods of online learning: The effect of playfulness on university students' study outcomes. *Frontiers in Psychology*, 12, 12. DOI: 10.3389/fpsyg.2021.753568 PMID: 34690899

Li, Y., Schoenfeld, A. H., diSessa, A. A., Graesser, A. C., Benson, L. C., English, L. D., & Duschl, R. A. (2020). Computational thinking is more about thinking than computing. *Journal for STEM Education Research*, 3(1), 1–18. DOI: 10.1007/s41979-020-00030-2 PMID: 32838129

Lizzio, A., Wilson, K., & Simons, R. (2002). University students' perceptions of the learning environment and academic outcomes: Implications for theory and practice. *Studies in Higher Education*, 27(1), 27–52. DOI: 10.1080/03075070120099359

Lo, C. K. (2023). What is the impact of ChatGPT on education? A rapid review of literature. *Education Sciences*, 13(4), 410. DOI: 10.3390/educsci13040410

Lo, C. K., & Hew, K. F. (2023). A review of integrating AI-based chatbots into flipped learning: New possibilities and challenges. *Frontiers in Education*, 8, 1175715. DOI: 10.3389/feduc.2023.1175715

Lockwood, J., & Mooney, A. (2017). Computational Thinking in Education: Where does it fit? A systematic literary review. *arXiv preprint arXiv:1703.07659*.

Lodi, M., & Martini, S. (2021). Computational thinking, between Papert and Wing. *Science & Education*, 30(4), 883–908. DOI: 10.1007/s11191-021-00202-5

Londoño-Velasco, E., Montoya-Cobo, E., García, A., Bolaños-Martinez, I., Bolaños-Martinez, I., Osorio-Roa, D. M., & Isaza Gómez, G. D. (2021). Percepción de estudiantes frente a procesos de enseñanza-aprendizaje durante pandemia por la covid-19. *Educ. Educ.*, 24(2), 199–217. DOI: 10.5294/edu.2021.24.2.2

Long, T., Cummins, J., & Waugh, M. (2017). Use of the flipped classroom in higher education: Instructors' perspectives. *Journal of Computing in Higher Education*, 29(2), 179–200. DOI: 10.1007/s12528-016-9119-8

Lorente, L. M. L., Arrabal, A. A., & Pulido-Montes, C. (2020). The right to education and ICT during COVID-19: An international perspective. *Sustainability (Basel)*, 12(21), 9091. DOI: 10.3390/su12219091

Lotrecchiano, G. R., McDonald, P. L., Lyons, L., Long, T., & Zajicek-Farber, M. (2013). Blended learning: Strengths, challenges, and lessons learned in an interprofessional training program. *Maternal and Child Health Journal*, 17(9), 1725–1734. DOI: 10.1007/s10995-012-1175-8 PMID: 23291875

Lowenthal, P., Borup, J., West, R., & Archambault, L. (2020). Thinking beyond zoom: Using asynchronous video to maintain connection and engagement during the COVID-19 pandemic. *Journal of Technology and Teacher Education*, 28(2), 383–391.

Lu, H., & Smiles, R. (2022). The Role of Collaborative Learning in the Online Education. *International Journal of Economics, Business and Management Research*. Vol. 6, No.06; 2022. ISSN: 2456-7760

Lubker, J. R., & Petrusa, E. R. (2022). Utilizing co-curricular learning tools to foster leadership development in graduate and professional schools: Examples and lessons learned. *New Directions for Student Leadership*, 2022(176), 53–64. DOI: 10.1002/yd.20530 PMID: 36565143

Lundin, M., Rensfeldt, A. B., Hillman, T., Lanzt-Andersson, A., & Peterson, L. (2018). Higher education dominance and siloed knowledge: A systematic review of flipped classroom research. *International Journal of Educational Technology in Higher Education*, 15(1), 20. DOI: 10.1186/s41239-018-0101-6

Lupac, P. (2018). *Beyond the digital divide: Contextualizing the information society*. Emerald Publishing Limited. DOI: 10.1108/9781787565470

Lussier, J. (2020). Reciprocity, Exchange, and Indebtedness in Noddings's Concept of Care. *Philosophy of Education*, (2020), 134-47.

Lu, Y., Hong, X., & Xiao, L. (2022). Toward high-quality adult online learning: A systematic review of empirical studies. *Sustainability (Basel)*, 14(4), 2257. DOI: 10.3390/su14042257

Ma, W. W. K. (2022). Effective learning through project-based learning: collaboration, community, design, and technology. In: Tso, A.W.B., Chan, A.Ck., Chan, W.W.L., Sidorko, P.E., Ma, W.W.K. (eds) *Digital Communication and Learning. Educational Communications and Technology Yearbook*. Springer, Singapore. DOI: 10.1007/978-981-16-8329-9_17

Ma, C. (2021). Smart city and cyber-security; technologies used, leading challenges and future recommendations. *Energy Reports*, 7, 7999–8012. DOI: 10.1016/j.egyr.2021.08.124

Machalek, R., & Martin, M. W. (2015). Sociobiology and Sociology: A new synthesis. Editor(s): James D. Wright, *International Encyclopedia of the Social & Behavioral Sciences* (Second Edition), Elsevier, 2015, pp. 892-898. ISBN 9780080970875. DOI: 10.1016/B978-0-08-097086-8.32010-4

MacKenzie, A., Bacalja, A., Annamali, D., Panaretou, A., Girme, P., Cutajar, M., Abegglen, S., Evens, M., Neuhaus, F., Wilson, K., Psarikidou, K., & Gourlay, L. (2022). Dissolving the dichotomies between online and campus-based teaching: A collective response to the manifesto for teaching online (Bayne et al. 2020). *Postdigital Science and Education*, 4(2), 271–329. DOI: 10.1007/s42438-021-00259-z

Mackworth, N. H. (1948). The Breakdown of Vigilance during Prolonged Visual Search. *The Quarterly Journal of Experimental Psychology*, 1(1), 6–21. DOI: 10.1080/17470214808416738

Madda, M. J. (2023). Why schools should focus on social capital development – not just skills. https://www.edsurge.com/news/2023-10-16-why-schools-should-focus-on-social-capital-development-not-just-skills

Maghsudi, S., Lan, A., Xu, J., & van Der Schaar, M. (2021). Personalized education in the artificial intelligence era: What to expect next. *IEEE Signal Processing Magazine*, 38(3), 37–50. DOI: 10.1109/MSP.2021.3055032

Major, J., Tait-McCutcheon, S. L., Averill, R., Gilbert, A., Knewstubb, B., Mortlock, A., & Jones, L. (2020). Pedagogical innovation in higher education: Defining what we mean. [IJITLHE]. *International Journal of Innovative Teaching and Learning in Higher Education*, 1(3), 1–18. DOI: 10.4018/IJITLHE.2020070101

Maloch, B. (2002). Scaffolding student talk: One teacher's role in literature discussion groups. *Reading Research Quarterly*, 37(1), 94–112. DOI: 10.1598/RRQ.37.1.4

Mandernach, B. J., Hudson, S., & Wise, S. (2013). Where has the time gone? Faculty activities and time commitments in the online classroom. *The Journal of Educators Online*, 10(2), 1–15. https://www.learn-techlib.org/p/114366/. DOI: 10.9743/JEO.2013.2.2

Mandhana, D. M., & Caruso, V. (2023). Inducing flow in class activities to promote student engagement. *Communication Education*, 72(4), 348–366. DOI: 10.1080/03634523.2022.2158353

Maphosa, V. (2021). Teachers' perspectives on remote-based teaching and learning in the COVID-19 era: Rethinking technology availability and suitability in Zimbabwe. *European Journal of Interactive Multimedia and Education*, 2(1), e02105. DOI: 10.30935/ejimed/9684

Marcos Pardo, P. J., González Gálvez, N., & Vaquero Cristobal, R. (2023). Jigsaw Puzzle technique vs. traditional group work: Academic performance and satisfaction of the university students. *Cultura, Ciencia y Deporte*, 18(58), 69–79. DOI: 10.12800/ccd.v18i58.2034

Margolis, H., & McCabe, P. P. (2003). Self-efficacy: A key to improving the motivation of struggling learners. *Preventing School Failure*, 47(4), 162–169. DOI: 10.1080/10459880309603362

Maria, M., Shahbodin, F., & Pee, N. C. (2018). Malaysian higher education system towards industry 4.0–current trends overview. In *AIP Conference Proceedings* (Vol. 2016, No. 1). AIP Publishing.

Marienko, M., Nosenko, Y., & Shyshkina, M. (2020). Personalization of learning using adaptive technologies and augmented reality. *arXiv preprint arXiv:2011.05802*. DOI: 10.31812/123456789/4418

Martin, D. (2020) Providing students with multimodal feedback experiences. *Journal of Curriculum, Teaching, Learning and Leadership in Education, 5*(7). https://digitalcommons.unomaha.edu/ctlle/vol5/iss1/2

Martin, F., Parker, M. A., & Ndoye, A. (2011). *Measuring success in a synchronous virtual classroom*. Student satisfaction and learning outcomes in E-Learning: An introduction to empirical research. Edt (Sean B. Eom., & J.B. Arbaugh), USA: IGI Global. DOI: 10.4018/978-1-60960-615-2.ch011

Martin, F., Budhrani, K., & Wang, C. (2019). Examining faculty perception of their readiness to teach online. *Online Learning : the Official Journal of the Online Learning Consortium*, 23(3), 97–119. DOI: 10.24059/olj.v23i3.1555

Martin, F., & Parker, M. A. (2014). Use of synchronous virtual classrooms: Why, Who, and How? *Journal of Online Learning and Teaching*, 10(2), 192–210.

Martin, F., Polly, D., & Ritzhaupt, A. D. (2022). Global trends in online education: Pedagogical strategies for the digital classroom. *The International Review of Research in Open and Distributed Learning*, 23(3), 1–26.

Martin, F., Wang, C., Jokiaho, A., May, B., & Grübmeyer, S. (2019). Examining Faculty Readiness to Teach Online: *A Comparison of US and German Educators. European Journal of Open. Distance and E-Learning*, 22(1), 53–69. DOI: 10.2478/eurodl-2019-0004

Martin, F., Wang, C., & Sadaf, A. (2020). Facilitation matters: Instructor perception of helpfulness of facilitation strategies in online courses. *Online Learning : the Official Journal of the Online Learning Consortium*, 24(1), 28–49. DOI: 10.24059/olj.v24i1.1980

Mattingly, V., & Kraiger, K. (2019). Can emotional intelligence be trained? A meta-analytical investigation. *Human Resource Management Review*, 29(2), 140–155. https://www.sciencedirect.com/science/article/abs/pii/S1053482218301840. DOI: 10.1016/j.hrmr.2018.03.002

Matud, M. P., Díaz, A., Bethencourt, J. M., & Ibáñez, I. (2020). Stress and psychological distress in emerging adulthood: A gender analysis. *Journal of Clinical Medicine*, 9(9), 2859. Advance online publication. DOI: 10.3390/jcm9092859 PMID: 32899622

Mavo Navarro, J. C., & McGrath, B. M. (2022). Strategies for effective online teaching and learning: Practices and techniques with a proven track of success in online education. In *Handbook of Research on Future of Work and Education* (pp. 495–510). IGI Global.

Mayer, R. E. (2001). *Multimedia Learning*. DOI: 10.1017/CBO9781139164603

Mayer, R. E. (2021). Evidence-Based Principles for How to Design Effective Instructional Videos. *Journal of Applied Research in Memory and Cognition*, 10(2), 229–240. DOI: 10.1016/j.jarmac.2021.03.007

Mayer, R. E., & Massa, L. J. (2003). Three Facets of Visual and Verbal Learners: Cognitive Ability, Cognitive Style, and Learning Preference. *Journal of Educational Psychology*, 95(4), 833–846. DOI: 10.1037/0022-0663.95.4.833

Maynard, P. L., Rohrer, J. E., & Fulton, L. (2015). Health-related quality of life among online university students. *Journal of Primary Care & Community Health*, 6(1), 48–53. DOI: 10.1177/2150131914545517 PMID: 25117557

Mazzetti, G., Paolucci, A., Guglielmi, D., & Vannini, I. (2020). The impact of learning strategies and future orientation on academic success: The moderating role of academic self-efficacy among Italian undergraduate students. *Education Sciences*, 10(5), 134. DOI: 10.3390/educsci10050134

Mc Kay, M., Davis, M., & Fanning, P. (2009). *Messages: The communication skills workbook* (3rd ed.). New Harbinger Publications, Inc.

McAlvage, K., & Rice, M. (2018). Access and Accessibility in Online Learning: Issues in higher Education and K-12 Contexts. *OLC Research Centre for Digital Learning & Leadership*. https://eric.ed.gov/?id=ED593920

McBain, B., Drew, A., James, C., Phelan, L., Harris, K. M., & Archer, J. (2016). Student experience of oral communication assessment tasks online from a multi-disciplinary trial. *Education + Training*, 58(2), 134–149. www.emeraldinsight.com/0040-0912.htm. DOI: 10.1108/ET-10-2014-0124

McCallum, F. (2021). Teachers' wellbeing during times of change and disruption. In *Wellbeing and Resilience Education* (pp. 183-208). Routledge.

McCarthy, J. (2017). Enhancing feedback in higher education: Students' attitudes towards online and in-class formative assessment feedback models. *Active Learning in Higher Education*, 18(2), 127–141. DOI: 10.1177/1469787417707615

Mccloskey, A. (2012). Caring in professional development projects for mathematics teachers: An example of stimulation and harmonizing. *For the Learning of Mathematics*, 32(3), 28–33.

McHaney, R. (2023). *The new digital shoreline: How Web 2.0 and millennials are revolutionizing higher education*. Taylor & Francis. DOI: 10.4324/9781003447979

McKeithan, G. K., Rivera, M. O., Mann, L. E., & Mann, L. B. (2021). Strategies to promote meaningful student engagement in online settings. *Journal of Education and Training Studies*, 9(4), 1–11. DOI: 10.11114/jets.v9i4.5135

McLeod, S. (2024). Vygotsky's theory of cognitive development. https://www.simplypsychology.org/vygotsky.html

McLeod, S. (2024, February 1). *Constructivism learning theory & philosophy of education*. https://www.simplypsychology.org/constructivism.html

McLoughlin, C. (2002). Learner support in distance and networked learning environments: Ten dimensions for successful design. *Distance Education*, 23(2), 149–162. DOI: 10.1080/0158791022000009178

McNamee, A., Mercurio, M., & Peloso, J. M. (2007). Who cares about caring in early childhood teacher education programs? *Journal of Early Childhood Teacher Education*, 28(3), 277–288. DOI: 10.1080/10901020701555580

McNiff, J., & Aicher, T. (2017). Understanding the challenges and opportunities associated with online learning: A scaffolding theory approach. *Sport Management Education Journal*, 11(1), 13–23. DOI: 10.1123/smej.2016-0007

Means, B., Bakia, M., & Murphy, R. (2014). *Learning online: What research tells us about whether, when and how*. Routledge. DOI: 10.4324/9780203095959

Mega, C., Ronconi, L., & De Beni, R. (2014). What makes a good student? How emotions, self-regulated learning, and motivation contribute to academic achievement. *Journal of Educational Psychology*, 106(1), 121–131. DOI: 10.1037/a0033546

Meng, N., Dong, Y., Roehrs, D., & Luan, L. (2023). Tackle implementation challenges in project-based learning: a survey study of PBL e-learning platforms. https://link.springer.com/article/10.1007/s11423-023-10202-7

Merchant, Z., Goetz, E. T., Cifuentes, L., Keeney-Kennicutt, W., & Davis, T. J. (2014). Effectiveness of virtual reality-based instruction on students' learning outcomes in K-12 and higher education: A meta-analysis. *Computers & Education*, 70, 29–40. DOI: 10.1016/j.compedu.2013.07.033

Merriam, S. B., & Baumgartner, L. M. (2020). *Learning in adulthood: A comprehensive guide*. John Wiley & Sons.

Merrill, M. D. (2002). First principles of instruction. *Educational Technology Research and Development*, 50(3), 43–59. DOI: 10.1007/BF02505024

Mesquita, C., Nazar, B. P., Pinna, C. M. S., Rabelo, B., Serra-Pinheiro, M. A., Sergeant, J., & Mattos, P. (2016). How can Continuous Performance Test help to assess inattention when mood and ADHD symptoms coexist? *Psychiatry Research*, 243, 326–330. DOI: 10.1016/j.psychres.2016.06.054 PMID: 27434202

Messick, S. (1984). The nature of cognitive styles: Problems and promise in educational practice. *Educational Psychologist*, 19(2), 59–74. DOI: 10.1080/00461528409529283

Meyer, A., Rose, D. H., & Gordon, D. (2014). *Universal design for learning: Theory and practice*. CAST Professional Publishing.

Meyer, K. A., & Jones, S. J. (2013). Do students experience flow conditions online? *Online Learning : the Official Journal of the Online Learning Consortium*, 17(3), 137–148. DOI: 10.24059/olj.v17i3.339

Mezirow, J. (1995). Transformation theory of adult learning. In Welton, M. (Ed.), *In defense of the lifeworld: Critical perspectives on adult learning* (pp. 37–90). State University of New York Press.

Mezirow, J. (1997). Transformative learning: Theory to practice. *New Directions for Adult and Continuing Education*, 1997(74), 5–12. DOI: 10.1002/ace.7401

Miao, C., Humphrey, R. H., & Qian, S. (2017). A meta-analysis of emotional intelligence and work attitudes. *Journal of Occupational and Organizational Psychology*, 90(2), 177–202. https://bpspsychub.onlinelibrary.wiley.com/doi/abs/10.1111/joop.12167. DOI: 10.1111/joop.12167

Miao, J., Chang, J., & Ma, L. (2022). Teacher-student interaction, student-student interaction and social presence: Their impacts on learning engagement in online learning environments. *The Journal of Genetic Psychology*, 183(6), 514–526. DOI: 10.1080/00221325.2022.2094211 PMID: 35815529

Miller, L. D., Soh, L. K., Chiriacescu, V., Ingraham, E., Shell, D. F., Ramsay, S., & Hazley, M. P. (2013, October). *Improving learning of computational thinking using creative thinking exercises in CS-1 computer science courses. In 2013 ieee frontiers in education conference (fie)*. IEEE.

Mills, J. (1996). Virtual classroom management and communicative writing pedagogy. *Paper presented at theEuropean Writing Conferences, pp:1-19*. Barcelona, Spain, October 23-25.

Misanchuk, M., & Anderson, T. (2001). *Building Community in an Online Learning Environment: Communication*. Cooperation and Collaboration.

Mishan, F. (2022). Language learning materials in the digital era. In *The Routledge Handbook of materials development for language teaching* (pp. 17–29). Routledge. DOI: 10.4324/b22783-3

Mishra, L., Gupta, T., & Shreee, A. (2020). Online teaching-learning in higher education during lockdown period of COVID-19 pandemic. *International Journal of Educational Research Open*, 1, 100012. DOI: 10.1016/j.ijedro.2020.100012 PMID: 35059663

MIT OCW - MIT OpenCourseWare. https://ocw.mit.edu/

Mitchell, M. M., & Poutiatine, M. I. (2001). Finding an experiential approach in graduate leadership curricula. *Journal of Experiential Education*, 24(3), 179–185. DOI: 10.1177/105382590102400309

Mohamed, H., & Lamia, M. (2018). Implementing flipped classroom that used an intelligent tutoring system into learning process. *Computers & Education*, 124, 62–76. DOI: 10.1016/j.compedu.2018.05.011

Mohammed, A. B., Maqableh, M., Qasim, D., & AlJawazneh, F. (2024). Exploring the Factors Influencing Academic Learning Performance Using Online Learning Systems. *Heliyon*, 10(11), e32584–e32584. DOI: 10.1016/j.heliyon.2024.e32584 PMID: 38912470

Moller, S., Stearns, E., Mickelson, R., Bottia, M., & Banerjee, N. (2014). Is academic engagement the panacea for achievement in mathematics across racial and ethnic groups? Assessing the role of teacher culture. *Social Forces*, 92(4), 1513–1544. DOI: 10.1093/sf/sou018

Moll, L. C. (2013). *L. S. Vygotsky and education*. Taylor and Francis Group. DOI: 10.4324/9780203156773

Mont'Alverne. C., Badrinathan, S., Ross Arguesdas, A., Toff, B., Fletcher, R., & Nielsen, R. (2022). The trust gas: how and why news on digital platforms is viewed more skeptically versus news in general. https://ora.ox.ac.uk/objects/uuid:42cc0bd8-f737-4a79-947f-e528e8116926

Montiel, H., & Gomez-Zermeño, M. G. (2021). Educational challenges for computational thinking in k–12 education: A systematic literature review of "scratch" as an innovative programming tool. *Computers*, 10(6), 69. DOI: 10.3390/computers10060069

MOOCs - Massive Open Online Courses. https://onlinelearningconsortium.org/

Moore, M. G. (2013). The theory of transactional distance. In *Handbook of distance education* (pp. 84–103). Routledge. DOI: 10.4324/9780203803738.ch5

Moore, M. L. (2020). *Qualitative Exploration of Instructional Designers' Use of Microlearning for Formal Workplace Training*. Capella University.

Morales, E., Kalir, J. H., Fleerackers, A., & Alperin, J. P. (2022). Using social annotation to construct knowledge with others: A case study across undergraduate courses. *F1000 Research*, 11, 235. Advance online publication. DOI: 10.12688/f1000research.109525.1 PMID: 35388338

Morawo, A., Sun, C., & Lowden, M. (2020). Enhancing engagement during live virtual learning using interactive quizzes. *Medical Education*, 54(12), 1188. DOI: 10.1111/medu.14253 PMID: 32438462

Morrison, L., & Jacobsen, M. (2023). The role of feedback in building teaching presence and student self-regulation in online learning. *Social Sciences & Humanities Open*, 7(1), 100503. DOI: 10.1016/j.ssaho.2023.100503

Morris, R., Perry, T., & Wardle, L. (2021). Formative assessment and feedback for learning in higher education: A systematic review. *Review of Education*, 9(3), e3292. Advance online publication. DOI: 10.1002/rev3.3292

Mosher, C. J., Morton, A., Tarbet, A., & Palaganas, J. C. (2023). Factors of engagement in synchronous online learning conversations and distance debriefing: A realist synthesis review. *Simulation in Healthcare*, 18(2), 126–134. DOI: 10.1097/SIH.0000000000000650 PMID: 35470345

Mrazek, M. D., Phillips, D. T., Franklin, M. S., Broadway, J. M., & Schooler, J. W. (2013). Young and restless: Validation of the Mind-Wandering Questionnaire (MWQ) reveals disruptive impact of mind-wandering for youth. *Frontiers in Psychology*, 4(560). Advance online publication. DOI: 10.3389/fpsyg.2013.00560 PMID: 23986739

Msekelwa, P. Z. (2023). Beyond The Borders Global Collaboration in Open Distance Education through Virtual Exchanges. *Journal of Knowledge Learning and Science Technology ISSN: 2959-6386 (online)*, 2(2), 1-13.

Muir, T., Milthorpe, N., Stone, C., Dyment, J., Freeman, E., & Hopwood, B. (2021). Challenging and supporting pre-service teachers in a fully online mathematics education course. Journal of Open. *Flexible and Distance Learning*, 24(1), 4–16.

Mulcare, D., & Shwedel, A. (2017). Transforming Bloom's taxonomy into classroom practice: A practical yet comprehensive approach to promote critical reading and student participation. *Journal of Political Science Education*, 13(2), 121–137. DOI: 10.1080/15512169.2016.1211017

Mullen, C. A., & Eadens, D. W. (2018). "Quality leadership matters": A research-based survey of graduate programming. *Journal of Research on Leadership Education*, 13(2), 162–200. DOI: 10.1177/1942775117739415

Mund, P. (2016). Kobasa concept of hardiness. *International Research Journal of Engineering, IT & Scientific Research*, 2(1), 34–40. https://sloap.org/journals/index.php/irjeis/article/view/243

Murphy, K. L., & Cifuentes, L. (2001). Using Web tools, collaborating, and learning online. *Distance Education*, 22(2), 285-305.

Mu, S., Cui, M., Wang, X. J., Qiao, J. X., & Tang, D. M. (2019). Learners' attention preferences of information in online learning. *Interactive Technology and Smart Education*, 16(3), 186–203. DOI: 10.1108/ITSE-10-2018-0090

Nachowitz, M. (2018). Scaffolding progressive online discourse for literary knowledge building. *Online Learning : the Official Journal of the Online Learning Consortium*, 22(3), 133–156. DOI: 10.24059/olj.v22i3.1261

Nahas, E. (2022). *Impact Of Personalized Learning*. https://elearningindustry.com/impact-of-personalized-learning

Naidu, S. (2008). Enabling time, pace, and place independence. In *Handbook of Research on Educational Communications and Technology* (pp. 259–268). Routledge.

National Center for Education Statistics. (2022). *Number and percentage of students enrolled in degree-granting postsecondary institutions, by distance education participation, location of student, level of enrollment, and control and level of institution: Fall 2020 and fall 2021*. https://nces.ed.gov/programs/digest/d22/tables/dt22_311.15.asp

National Center for Education Statistics. (2024). *Characteristics of postsecondary faculty. Condition of Education*. U.S. Department of Education, Institute of Education Sciences. https://nces.ed.gov/programs/coe/indicator/csc

National Center for Faculty Development and Diversity. (n.d.). https://www.ncfdd.org/home

Nave, L. (2021). Universal design for learning: UDL in online environments: The WHAT of learning. *Journal of Developmental Education*, 44(2), 30–32.

Nazempour, R., & Darabi, H. (2023). Personalized learning in virtual learning environments using students' behavior analysis. *Education Sciences*, 13(5), 457. DOI: 10.3390/educsci13050457

Ndukwe, , I. GDaniel, , B. K. (2020). Teaching analytics, value and tools for teacher data literacy: A systematic and tripartite approach. *International Journal of Educational Technology in Higher Education*, 17, 1–31.

Neha, J. (2020). *Online Learning Vs Traditional Learning*. https://www.evelynlearning.com/online-learning-vs-traditional-learning/

Nepali, S. (2021). The impact of academic stress on the academic performance of CBSE higher secondary students, with special reference to Ernakulam district. *Quest Journals,* 9(8), 88–94. https://www.questjournals.org/jrhss/papers/vol9-issue8/Ser-3/N09088894.pdf

Nevgi, A., Virtanen, P., & Niemi, H. (2006). Supporting students to develop collaborative learning skills in technology-based environments. *British Journal of Educational Technology*, 37(6), 937–947. DOI: 10.1111/j.1467-8535.2006.00671.x

Newman, N. (2022). Overview and key findings of the 2022 digital news report. https://reutersinstitute.politics.ox.ac.uk/digital-news-report/2022/dnr-executive-summary

Nguyen, L. Q. (2022). Learners' satisfaction of courses on Coursera as a massive open online course platform: A case study. *Frontiers in Education*, 7, 1086170. Advance online publication. DOI: 10.3389/feduc.2022.1086170

Nicholas, G., Bell, C., Coombe, R., Welch, J. R., Noble, B., Anderson, J., & Watkins, J. (2010). Intellectual property issues in heritage management: Part 2: Legal dimensions, ethical considerations, and collaborative research practices. *Heritage Management*, 3(1), 117–147. DOI: 10.1179/hma.2010.3.1.117

Nicolaides, A., Lim, A., Herr, N., & Barefield, T. (Eds.). (2024). *Reimagining Adult Education as World Building: Creating Learning Ecologies for Transformation*. Taylor & Francis. DOI: 10.4324/9781003371359

Nicol, D. J., & Macfarlane-Dick, D. (2020). Formative assessment and self-regulated learning: A model and seven principles of good feedback practice. *Studies in Higher Education*, 31(2), 199–218. DOI: 10.1080/03075070600572090

Nieves, L. H., Moya, E. C., & Soldado, R. M. (2019). A MOOC on universal design for learning designed based on the UDL paradigm. *Australasian Journal of Educational Technology*, 35(6), 30–47. DOI: 10.14742/ajet.5532

Nkomo, L. M., Daniel, B. K., & Butson, R. J. (2021). Synthesis of student engagement with digital technologies: A systematic review of the literature. *International Journal of Educational Technology in Higher Education*, 18, 1–26. PMID: 34778529

Noddings, N. (1986). *Caring: A feminine approach to ethics and moral education.*

Noddings, N. (1992). *The challenge to care in schools: an alternative approach to education.*

Noddings, N. (2002). Educating moral people: A caring alternative to character education. Teachers College Press, PO Box 20, Williston, VT 05495-0020

Noddings, N. (2007). Caring as relation and virtue in teaching. *Working virtue: Virtue ethics and contemporary moral problems*, 41-60.

Noddings, N. (2013). *Caring: A relational approach to ethics and moral education* (updated). Berkeley, CA and Los Angeles: University of California Press (Original work published 1984).

Noddings, N. (2019). Concepts of care in teacher education. In *Oxford Research Encyclopedia of Education*. DOI: 10.1093/acrefore/9780190264093.013.371

Noddings, N. (1988). An ethic of caring and its implications for instructional arrangements. *American Journal of Education*, 96(2), 215–230. DOI: 10.1086/443894

Noddings, N. (1995). Teaching themes of care. *Phi Delta Kappan*, 76, 675–675.

Noddings, N. (1999). Caring and competence. *Teachers College Record*, 100(5), 205–220. DOI: 10.1177/016146819910000509

Noddings, N. (2006). Educational leaders as caring teachers. *School Leadership & Management*, 26(4), 339–345. DOI: 10.1080/13632430600886848

Noddings, N. (2012). The caring relation in teaching. *Oxford Review of Education*, 38(6), 771–781. DOI: 10.1080/03054985.2012.745047

Noddings, N. (2012). The language of care ethics. *Knowledge Quest*, 40(5), 52.

Nokes-Malach, T. J., Richey, J. E., & Gadgil, S. (2015). When is it better to learn together? Insights from research on collaborative learning. *Educational Psychology Review*, 27(4), 645–656. DOI: 10.1007/s10648-015-9312-8

Nordin, N., & Norman, H. (2018). Cross-culture learning via massive open online courses for higher education. [Malaysian Journal of Education]. *Jurnal Pendidikan Malaysia*, 43(1), 35–39. DOI: 10.17576/JPEN-2018-43.01-05

Norman, P. D., & Zoncita, D. (2024). Elaborating the Efficacy of Outdoor Arts-based Cooperative Learning Experiences on the Latino Immigrant Students' Engagement, and Academic & Social Success in ESL-STEAM Education. *Available atSSRN 4757518*.

Normore, A. H., & Issa Lahera, A. (2019). The evolution of educational leadership preparation programmes. *Journal of Educational Administration and History*, 51(1), 27–42. DOI: 10.1080/00220620.2018.1513914

Novak, G. M. (2011). Just-in-time teaching. *New Directions for Teaching and Learning*, 2011(128), 63–73. DOI: 10.1002/tl.469

Nussbaum, E. M., Hartley, K., Sinatra, G. M., Reynolds, R. E., & Bendixen, L. D. (2004). Personality interactions and scaffolding in on-line discussions. *Journal of Educational Computing Research*, 30(1-2), 113–137. DOI: 10.2190/H8P4-QJUF-JXME-6JD8

Nworie, J. (2021, May 19). *Beyond COVID-19: What's next for online teaching and learning in higher education?* https://er.educause.edu/articles/2021/5/beyond-covid-19-whats-next-for-online-teaching-and-learning-in-higher-education

O'Brien, T. J. (2016). *Looking for development in leadership development: Impacts of experiential and constructivist methods on graduate students and graduate schools*. Harvard University.

O'Dowd, R. (2016). Learning from the past and looking to the future of online intercultural exchange. In *Online Intercultural Exchange* (pp. 273–294). Routledge. DOI: 10.4324/9781315678931

O'Dowd, R. (2021). Virtual exchange: Moving forward into the next decade. *Computer Assisted Language Learning*, 34(3), 209–224. DOI: 10.1080/09588221.2021.1902201

O'Flaherty, J., & Costabile, M. (2020). Using a science simulation-based learning tool to develop students' active learning, self-confidence, and critical thinking in academic writing. *Nurse Education in Practice*, 47, 102839. Advance online publication. DOI: 10.1016/j.nepr.2020.102839 PMID: 32943173

O'Flaherty, J., & Phillips, C. (2015). The use of flipped classrooms in higher education: A scoping review. *The Internet and Higher Education*, 25, 85–95. DOI: 10.1016/j.iheduc.2015.02.002

O'Keefe, L., Rafferty, J., Gunder, A., & Vignare, K. (2020). *Delivering High-Quality Instruction Online in Response to COVID-19: Faculty Playbook*. Online Learning Consortium.

O'Shea, S., Stone, C., & Delahunty, J. (2015). "I 'feel'like I am at university even though I am online." Exploring how students narrate their engagement with higher education institutions in an online learning environment. *Distance Education*, 36(1), 41–58. DOI: 10.1080/01587919.2015.1019970

OECD. (2023a). PISA 2022 results (volume I): The state of learning and equity in education. *OECD Publishing.* https://doi.org/DOI: 10.1787/53f23881-en

OECD. (2023b). *OECD skills outlook 2023: Learning for a more resilient future.* OECD Publishing., DOI: 10.1787/28a2ea09-

Oh, C. S., Bailenson, J. N., & Welch, G. F. (2018). A systematic review of social presence: Definition, antecedents, and implications. *Frontiers in Robotics and AI*, 5, 409295. DOI: 10.3389/frobt.2018.00114 PMID: 33500993

Okai-Ugbaje, S., Ardzejewska, K., & Imran, A. (2017). A systematic review of mobile learning adoption in higher education: The African perspective. *i-manager's Journal on Mobile Applications & Technologies*, 4(2), 1-13

Oliver, B. (2019). *Making micro-credentials work for learners, employers, and providers.*

Olusegun, S. (2015). Constructivism learning theory: A paradigm for teaching and learning. *Journal of Research & Method in Education*, 5(6), 66–70. DOI: 10.9790/7388- 05616670

Onah, D. F., Pang, E. L., Sinclair, J. E., & Uhomoibhi, J. (2021). An innovative MOOC platform: The implications of self-directed learning abilities to improve motivation in learning and to support self-regulation. *The International Journal of Information and Learning Technology*, 38(3), 283–298. DOI: 10.1108/IJILT-03-2020-0040

Oncu, S., & Cakir, H. (2011). Research in online learning environments: Priorities and methodologies. *Computers & Education*, 57(1), 1098–1108. DOI: 10.1016/j.compedu.2010.12.009

Ong, S. G. T., & Quek, G. C. L. (2023). Enhancing teacher-student interactions and student online engagement in an online learning environment. *Learning Environments Research*, 26(3), 681–707. DOI: 10.1007/s10984-022-09447-5 PMID: 36685638

Oppenheimer, M., LaVan, H., & Martin, W. F. (2015). A framework for understanding ethical and efficiency issues in pharmaceutical intellectual property litigation. *Journal of Business Ethics*, 132(3), 505–524. DOI: 10.1007/s10551-014-2365-7

Orr, M. T. (2011). Pipeline to preparation to advancement: Graduates' experiences in, through, and beyond leadership preparation. *Educational Administration Quarterly*, 47(1), 114–172. DOI: 10.1177/0011000010378612

Ottenbreit-Leftwich, A., Liao, J. Y.-C., Sadik, O., & Ertmer, P. (2018). Evolution of teachers' technology integration knowledge, beliefs, and practices: How can we support beginning teachers use of technology? *Journal of Research on Technology in Education*, 50(4), 282–304. DOI: 10.1080/15391523.2018.1487350

Otto, F., Kling, N., Schumann, C.-A., & Tittmann, C. (2023). A conceptual approach to an AI-based adaptive study support system for individualized higher education. *International Journal of Advanced Corporate Learning*, 16(2), 69–80. DOI: 10.3991/ijac.v16i2.35699

Owens, A. D., & Hite, R. L. (2022). Enhancing student communication competencies in STEM using virtual global collaboration project-based learning. *Research in Science & Technological Education*, 40(1), 76–102. DOI: 10.1080/02635143.2020.1778663

Owens, L. M., & Ennis, C. D. (2005). The ethic of care in teaching: An overview of supportive literature. *Quest*, 57(4), 392–425. DOI: 10.1080/00336297.2005.10491864

Owusu-Agyeman, Y. (2021). Experiences and perceptions of academics about student engagement in higher education. *Policy Futures in Education*, 20(6), 661–680. DOI: 10.1177/14782103211053718

Oxford Dictionary. Lexicon.com

Ozogul, G., Zhu, M., & Phillips, T. M. (2022). Perceived and actual cognitive presence: A case study of an intentionally-designed asynchronous online course. *Online Learning : the Official Journal of the Online Learning Consortium*, 26(1), 38–57. DOI: 10.24059/olj.v26i1.3051

Pajares, F. (2012). Motivational role of self-efficacy beliefs in self-regulated learning. In *Motivation and self-regulated learning* (pp. 111–139). Routledge.

Palaming, A. (2022). Online instructional strategies. *EPRA International Journal of Multidisciplinary Research* (IJMR).Published online 2022:176-179.

Paliwal, M., & Singh, A. (2021). Teacher readiness for online teaching-learning during COVID– 19 outbreak: A study of Indian institutions of higher education. *Interactive Technology and Smart Education*, 18(3), 403–421. Advance online publication. DOI: 10.1108/ITSE-07-2020-0118

Palloff, R. M., & Pratt, K. (2011). *The excellent online instructor: Strategies for professional development*. Jossey-Bass.

Palvia, S., Aeron, P., Gupta, P., Mahapatra, D., Parida, R., Rosner, R., & Sindhi, S. (2018). Online education: Worldwide status, challenges, trends, and implications. *Journal of Global Information Technology Management*, 21(4), 233–241. DOI: 10.1080/1097198X.2018.1542262

Papadakis, S. (2020). Evaluating a teaching intervention for teaching STEM and programming concepts through the creation of a weather-forecast app for smart mobile devices. In *Handbook of research on tools for teaching computational thinking in P-12 education* (pp. 31–53). IGI Global. DOI: 10.4018/978-1-7998-4576-8.ch002

Parambil, M. M. A., Alhammadi, A. M. A., Alnajjar, F., Trabelsi, Z., Ali, L., & Swavaf, M. (2023). Visualizing Student Attention in Smart Classrooms: A Preliminary Study. *2023 15th International Conference on Innovations in Information Technology, IIT 2023*. IEEE. DOI: 10.1109/IIT59782.2023.10366478

Parker, C., Kennedy-Behr, A., Wright, S., & Brown, T. (2022). Does the self-reported playfulness of older adults influence their wellbeing? An exploratory study. *Scandinavian Journal of Occupational Therapy*, 30(1), 86–97. DOI: 10.1080/11038128.2022.2145993 PMID: 36409561

Parker, K. R., Lenhart, A., & Moore, M. (2021). How students' choice of online elective courses influences engagement and learning outcomes. *Distance Education*, 42(2), 153–170.

Pascoe, M. C., Hetrick, S. E., & Parker, A. G. (2019). The impact of stress on students in secondary school and higher education. *International Journal of Adolescence and Youth*, 25(1), 104–112. DOI: 10.1080/02673843.2019.1596823

Passi, D. (2023). *Why Personalized Learning is the Future of eLearning: Benefits and Impacts*. https://www.kytewayelearning.com/article/personalized-learning-in-elearning

Patiar, A., Kensbock, S., Benckendorff, P., Robinson, R., Richardson, S., Wang, Y., & Lee, A. (2021). Hospitality students' acquisition of knowledge and skills through a virtual field trip experience. *Journal of Hospitality & Tourism Education*, 33(1), 14–28. DOI: 10.1080/10963758.2020.1726768

Pattemore, C. (2021). Ten ways to build and preserve better boundaries. *PsychCentral,* https://psychcentral.com/lib/10-way-to-build-and-preserve-better-boundaries#types

Patterson, M. B. (2020). PIAAC numeracy skills and home use among adult English learners. *Adult Literacy Education*, 2(1), 22–40. DOI: 10.35847/MPatterson.2.1.22

Paudel, P. (2021). Online education: Benefits, challenges and strategies during and after COVID-19 in higher education. [IJonSE]. *International Journal on Studies in Education*, 3(2), 70–85. DOI: 10.46328/ijonse.32

Paul, A. R., Aldiab, A., Chattopadhyaya, S., Hossain, A., Tasneem, Z., Haque, N., & Alam, F. (2021). Impact of COVID-19 on Online Education in Developing Countries–An Overview. *International Journal of Engineering Education*, 37(6), 1489–1510.

PBLworks. https://www.pblworks.org/

Pedrosa-de-Jesus, H., Moreira, A. C., da Silva Lopes, B., Guerra, C., & Watts, M. (2018). Assessment and Feedback. In *Academic Growth in Higher Education* (pp. 200–216). BRILL. DOI: 10.1163/9789004389342_016

Pekrun, R., Goetz, T., Frenzel, A. C., Barchfeld, P., & Perry, R. P. (2011). Measuring emotions in students' learning and performance: The Achievement Emotions Questionnaire (AEQ). *Contemporary Educational Psychology*, 36(1), 36–48. DOI: 10.1016/j.cedpsych.2010.10.002

Pekrun, R., Goetz, T., Titz, W., & Perry, R. P. (2002). Academic emotions in students' self-regulated learning and achievement: A program of qualitative and quantitative research. *Educational Psychologist*, 37(2), 91–105. DOI: 10.1207/S15326985EP3702_4

Pellas, N. (2014). The influence of computer self-efficacy, metacognitive self-regulation, and self-esteem on student engagement in online learning programs: Evidence from the virtual world of Second Life. *Computers in Human Behavior*, 35, 157–170. DOI: 10.1016/j.chb.2014.02.048

Pellerin, L. A. (2005). Applying Baumrind's parenting typology to high schools: Toward a middle-range theory of authoritative socialization. *Social Science Research*, 34(2), 283–303. DOI: 10.1016/j.ssresearch.2004.02.003

Peng, H., Ma, S., & Spector, J. M. (2019). Personalized adaptive learning: An emerging pedagogical approach enabled by a smart learning environment. *Smart Learning Environments*, 6(1), 1–14. DOI: 10.1186/s40561-019-0089-y

Pepin, B. (2014). Using the construct of the didactic contract to understand student transition into university mathematics education. *Policy Futures in Education*, 12(5), 646–658. DOI: 10.2304/pfie.2014.12.5.646

Perez, S. (2023). Integrating student voice in social capital development. https://edstrategy.org/integrating-student-voice-in-social-capital-development/

Perkins, M. Y. (2021). Beyond the building: Unleashing leadership potential in the graduate classroom. *Teaching Theology and Religion*, 24(2), 93–106. DOI: 10.1111/teth.12586

Perrigino, M. B., & Raveendhran, R. (2020). Managing remote workers during quarantine: Insights from organizational research on boundary management. *Behavioral Science & Policy*, 6(2), 87–94. DOI: 10.1177/237946152000600211

Persaud, C. (2024, May 15). *Bloom's taxonomy: The ultimate guide.* https://tophat.com/blog/blooms-taxonomy/

Pesare, E., Roselli, T., Corriero, N., & Rossano, V. (2016). Game-based learning and gamification to promote engagement and motivation in medical learning contexts. *Smart Learning Environments*, 3(1), 1–21. DOI: 10.1186/s40561-016-0028-0

Petersen, G. B., Stenberdt, V., Mayer, R. E., & Makransky, G. (2023). Collaborative generative learning activities in immersive virtual reality increase learning. *Computers & Education*, 207, 104931. DOI: 10.1016/j.compedu.2023.104931

Pew Research Center. (2022). *Public trust in government: 1958-2022.* https://www.pewresearch.org/ politics/2022/06/06/public-trust-in-government-1958-2022/

Pham, N. M. T. (2023). *The effects of question prompt-based scaffolding and social presence enhancement on students' argumentation and ill-structured problem-solving.* [Doctoral dissertation, University of Missouri-Columbia]. https://core.ac.uk/reader/578762458

Phan, D., & Coxhead, I. (2014). Education in Southeast Asia: Investments, achievements, and returns. In Routledge Handbook of Southeast Asian Economics (pp. 245-269). Routledge.

Phan, T. T. N., & Dang, L. T. T. (2017). Teacher Readiness for Online Teaching: A Critical Review*. *International Journal on Open and Distance E-Learning*, 3(1). https://www.ijodel.com/index.php/ijodel/article/view/18

Phiriepa, A., Mapaling, C., Matlakala, F. K., & Tsabedze, W. F. (2023). COVID-19 and online learning: A scoping review of the challenges faced by students in higher institutions during lockdown. *e-Bangi. Journal of Social Sciences and Humanities*, 20(4), 68–80. DOI: 10.17576/ebangi.2023.2004.23

Piaget, J. (1954). *The Construction of Reality in the Child.* Basic Books. DOI: 10.1037/11168-000

Picciano, A. G., Seaman, J., & Allen, I. E. (2010). Educational transformation through online learning: To be or not to be. *Online Learning : the Official Journal of the Online Learning Consortium*, 14(4), 17–35. DOI: 10.24059/olj.v14i4.147

Piotrowski, M. (2010). *What is an E-Learning platform? In: Learning management system technologies and software solutions for online teach-ing: tools and applications,* pp. 20–36; 2010. DOI: 10.4018/978-1-61520-853-1.ch002

Plass, J. L., & Hovey, C. M. (2021). The emotional design principle in multimedia learning. In Mayer, R. E., & Fiorella, L. (Eds.), *The Cambridge handbook of multimedia learning* (pp. 324–336). Cambridge University Press. DOI: 10.1017/9781108894333.034

Pokhrel, S., & Chhetri, R. (2021). A literature review on impact of COVID-19 Pandemic on teaching and learning. *Higher Education for the Future*, 8(1), 133–141. DOI: 10.1177/2347631120983481

Pollak, M., & Ebner, M. (2019). The missing link to computational thinking. *Future Internet*, 11(12), 263. DOI: 10.3390/fi11120263

Pollock, L., Mouza, C., Guidry, K. R., & Pusecker, K. (2019, February). Infusing computational thinking across disciplines: Reflections & lessons learned. In *Proceedings of the 50th ACM Technical Symposium on Computer Science Education* (pp. 435-441). DOI: 10.1145/3287324.3287469

Popescu, E., Tătucu, M., & Dobromirescu, V. (2021). Students' well-being in online education in Covid-19 context. *International Journal of Education and Research*, 9(2), 1–10. https://www.ijern.com/journal/2021/February-2021/01.pdf

Presley, R., Cumberland, D. M., & Rose, K. (2023). A comparison of cognitive and social presence in online graduate courses: Asynchronous vs. synchronous modalities. *Online Learning : the Official Journal of the Online Learning Consortium*, 27(2), 245–264. DOI: 10.24059/olj.v27i2.3046

Prestridge, S., & Tondeur, J. (2015). Exploring elements that support teachers engagement in online professional development. *Education Sciences*, 5(3), 199–219. DOI: 10.3390/educsci5030199

Prilop, C. N., Weber, K. E., Prins, F. J., & Kleinknecht, M. (2021). Connecting feedback to self-efficacy: Receiving and providing peer feedback in teacher education. *Studies in Educational Evaluation*, 70, 101062. DOI: 10.1016/j.stueduc.2021.101062

Prodgers, L., Travis, E., & Pownall, M. (2023). "It's hard to feel a part of something when you've never met people": Defining "learning community" in an online era. *Higher Education*, 85(6), 1219–1234. DOI: 10.1007/s10734-022-00886-w PMID: 35919398

Protopsaltis, S., & Baum, S. (2019). Does online education live up to its promise? A look at the evidence and implications for federal policy. Center for Educational Policy Evaluation, 1-50.

Psotka, J. (2022). Exemplary online education: For whom online learning can work better. *Interactive Learning Environments*, 30(2), 199–201. DOI: 10.1080/10494820.2022.2031065

Psycharis, S., Kalovrektis, K., Sakellaridi, E., Korres, K., & Mastorodimos, D. (2018). Unfolding the curriculum: physical computing, computational thinking and computational experiment in STEM's transdisciplinary approach. *European Journal of Engineering and Technology Research*, 19-24.

Psycharis, S. (2018). STEAM in education: A literature review on the role of computational thinking, engineering epistemology and computational science. computational steam pedagogy (CSP). *Scientific Culture*, 4(2), 51–72.

Pulimood, S. M., Pearson, K., & Bates, D. C. (2016, February). A study on the impact of multidisciplinary collaboration on computational thinking. In *Proceedings of the 47th ACM technical symposium on computing science education* (pp. 30-35). DOI: 10.1145/2839509.2844636

Pulver, C. J. (2020). Active reading to understand a problem. Introduction to professional and public writing. https://rwu.pressbooks.pub/wtng225/chapter/active-close-reading/

Pumptow, M., & Brahm, T. (2021). Students' digital media self-efficacy and its importance for higher education institutions: Development and validation of a survey instrument. *Technology. Knowledge and Learning*, 26(3), 555–575. DOI: 10.1007/s10758-020-09463-5

Puntambekar, S. (2022). Distributed scaffolding: Scaffolding students in classroom environments. *Educational Psychology Review*, 34(1), 451–472. DOI: 10.1007/s10648-021-09636-3

Pushpalatha, K., Sheela, A. J., Kumar, S. D., & Gokila, S. (2022). Effective methodology to improve teaching-learning process and teacher education in online classes. [IJHS]. *International Journal of Health Sciences*, •••, 8289–8295. DOI: 10.53730/ijhs.v6nS3.7840

Putnam, C., O'Donnell, J., & Bertozzi, N. (2010, June). *Scaffolding and fading within and across a six-semester CDIO design sequence* [Paper presentation]. The Proceedings of the 6th International CDIO Conference, Montreal, Canada.

Putnam, R. D. (2000). *Bowling Alone: The Collapse and Revival of American Community*. Simon & Schuster.

Qin, H. (2019). Teaching computational thinking through bioinformatics to biology students. In *Proceedings of the 40th ACM technical symposium on Computer science education* (pp. 188-191).

Quamar, M. M., Al-Ramadan, B., Khan, K., Shafiullah, M., & El Ferik, S. (2023). Advancements and applications of drone-integrated geographic information system technology—A review. *Remote Sensing (Basel)*, 15(20), 5039. DOI: 10.3390/rs15205039

Quigley, C. F., & Hall, A. H. (2016). Taking care: Understanding the roles of caregiver and being cared for in a kindergarten classroom. *Journal of Early Childhood Research*, 14(2), 181–195. DOI: 10.1177/1476718X14548783

Raaj, S. (2024). EDUCATION, RESEARCH AND INNOVATION IN INDIA: THE SHIFTING PARADIGMS. *Journal of Higher Education Theory and Practice*, 24(1), 75.

Rabia, A., & Hazza, M. (2017). Undergraduate Arab International Students' Adjustment to US Universities. *International Journal of Higher Education*, 6(1), 131–139. DOI: 10.5430/ijhe.v6n1p131

Rabin, C. (2021). Care ethics in online teaching. *Studying Teacher Education*, 17(1), 38–56. DOI: 10.1080/17425964.2021.1902801

Raes, A., Detienne, L., Windey, I., & Depaepe, F. (2019). A systematic literature review on synchronous hybrid learning: Gaps identified. *Learning Environments Research*, 23(23), 269–290. Advance online publication. DOI: 10.1007/s10984-019-09303-z

Rafi, M., JianMing, Z., & Ahmad, K. (2019). Technology integration for students' information and digital literacy education in academic libraries. *Information Discovery and Delivery*, 47(4), 203–217. DOI: 10.1108/IDD-07-2019-0049

Rahimi, R. A., & Oh, G. S. (2024). Rethinking the role of educators in the 21st century: navigating globalization, technology, and pandemics. Journal of Marketing Analytics, 1-16.

Rahma, H., Leng, C. O., & Mashedi, R. (2020). Innovative educational practice for impactful teaching strategies through scaffolding method. *Asian Journal of University Education*, 16(4), 53–60. DOI: 10.24191/ajue.v16i4.11952

Rajaram, K. (2021). *Evidence-based teaching for the 21st-century classroom and beyond*. Springer Singapore. DOI: 10.1007/978-981-33-6804-0

Rajaram, K. (2023). Future of learning: Teaching and learning strategies. In *Learning Intelligence: Innovative and Digital Transformative Learning Strategies: Cultural and Social Engineering Perspectives* (pp. 3–53). Springer Nature Singapore. DOI: 10.1007/978-981-19-9201-8_1

Randall, L., & Zundel, P. (2012). Students' perceptions of the effectiveness of assessment feedback as a learning tool in an introductory problem-solving course. *The Canadian Journal for the Scholarship of Teaching and Learning*, 3(1). Advance online publication. DOI: 10.5206/cjsotl-rcacea.2012.1.3

Ransdell, S. (2013). Meaningful posts and online learning in Blackboard across four cohorts of adult learners. *Computers in Human Behavior*, 29(6), 2730–2732. DOI: 10.1016/j.chb.2013.07.021

Rao, , K. (2021). Inclusive instructional design: Applying UDL to online learning. *The Journal of Applied Instructional Design*, 10(1), 83–97.

Rao, K., Torres, C., & Smith, S. J. (2021). Digital tools and UDL-based instructional strategies to support students with disabilities online. *Journal of Special Education Technology*, 36(2), 105–112. DOI: 10.1177/0162643421998327

Rasheed, R. A., Kamsin, A., & Abdullah, N. A. (2020). Students and teachers' challenges of using technology in blended learning environments. *Proceedings of the 2020 the 3rd International Conference on Computers in Management and Business*. DOI: 10.1145/3383845.3383875

Ray, S., & Sikdar, D. (2023). Learning Motivation Scale (LMS): Development and validation with prospective-teachers in West Bengal, India. *Asian Journal of Education and Social Studies*.

Reagans, R., & McEvily, B. (2003). Network structure and knowledge transfer: The transfer problem revisited. *Administrative Science Quarterly*, 48, 240–267. DOI: 10.2307/3556658

Reagans, R., & Zuckerman, E. W. (2001). Networks, diversity and productivity: The social capital of corporate R&D teams. *Organization Science*, 12(4), 502–517. DOI: 10.1287/orsc.12.4.502.10637

Redmer, A., & Dannath, J. (2020). The influence of number sense on financial literacy: Implications for numeracy education. *Journal of Financial Literacy and Education*, 12(1), 68–85.

Rees Lewis, D. G., Gerber, E. M., Carlson, S. E., & Easterday, M. W. (2019). Opportunities for educational innovations in authentic project-based learning: Understanding instructor perceived challenges to design for adoption. *Educational Technology Research and Development*, 67(4), 953–982. DOI: 10.1007/s11423-019-09673-4

Reich, J., Buttimer, C. J., & Murray, J. (2021). The digital divide and the challenges of online learning during the COVID-19 pandemic. *Education Policy Analysis Archives*, 29(110), 1–28.

Rejeb, A., Rejeb, K., Simske, S., & Treiblmaier, H. (2021). Humanitarian drones: A review and research agenda. *Internet of Things : Engineering Cyber Physical Human Systems*, 16, 100434. DOI: 10.1016/j.iot.2021.100434

Resei, C., Friedl, C., & Zur, A. (2018). MOOCs and entrepreneurship education-contributions, opportunities and gaps. *International Entrepreneurship Review*, 4(3), 151.

Resta, P., & Laferriere, T. (2015). Digital equity and intercultural education. *Education and Information Technologies*, 20(4), 743–756. DOI: 10.1007/s10639-015-9419-z

Revadekar, A., Oak, S., Gadekar, A., & Bide, P. (2020, December 1). *Gauging attention of students in an e-learning environment*. IEEE Xplore. DOI: 10.1109/CICT51604.2020.9312048

Rezaei, A. R. (2020). Groupwork in active learning classrooms: Recommendations for users. *Journal of Learning Spaces*, 9(2), 1–21.

Riccio, C. A., & Reynolds, C. R. (2006). Continuous Performance Tests Are Sensitive to ADHD in Adults but Lack Specificity. *Annals of the New York Academy of Sciences*, 931(1), 113–139. DOI: 10.1111/j.1749-6632.2001.tb05776.x PMID: 11462737

Rice, L. (2009). Playful learning. *The Journal for Education in the Built Environment*, 4(2), 94–108. DOI: 10.11120/jebe.2009.04020094

Richardson, J. C., Castellanos Reyes, D., Janakiraman, S., & Duha, M. S. U. (2023). The process of developing a digital repository for online teaching using design-based research. *TechTrends*, 67(2), 217–230. DOI: 10.1007/s11528-022-00795-w PMID: 36258921

Riegnell, J., & Bulthuis, S. (2022). *Successful Adult Learning Principles*.

Rikard, L. G. (2009). The significance of teacher caring in physical education. *Journal of Physical Education, Recreation & Dance*, 80(7), 4–5. DOI: 10.1080/07303084.2009.10598348

Rizvi, F. (2019). Global interconnectivity and its ethical challenges in education. *Asia Pacific Education Review*, 20(2), 315–326. DOI: 10.1007/s12564-019-09596-y

Roach, T. (2014). Student perceptions toward flipped learning: New methods to increase interaction and active learning in economics. *International Review of Economics Education*, 17, 74–84. DOI: 10.1016/j.iree.2014.08.003

Robertson, I., Cooper, C., Sarkar, M., & Curran, T. (2015). Resilience training in the workplace from 2003 to 2014: A systematic review. *Journal of Occupational and Organizational Psychology*, 88(3), 533–562. DOI: 10.1111/joop.12120

Robinson, H., Al-Freih, M., & Kilgore, W. (2020). Designing with care: Towards a care-centered model for online learning design. *The International Journal of Information and Learning Technology*, 37(3), 99–108. DOI: 10.1108/IJILT-10-2019-0098

Robison, M. K., Diede, N. T., Nicosia, J., Ball, B. H., & Bugg, J. M. (2022). A multimodal analysis of sustained attention in younger and older adults. *Psychology and Aging*, 37(3), 307–325. DOI: 10.1037/pag0000687 PMID: 35446084

Rockquemore, K. A. (2015). How to listen less. *Inside Higher Ed*.https://www.insidehighered.com/advice/2015/11/04/setting-boundaries-when-it-comes-students-emotional-disclosures-essay

Roddy, C., Amiet, D. L., Chung, J., Holt, C., Shaw, L., McKenzie, S., Garivaldis, F., Lodge, J. M., & Mundy, M. E. (2017, November). Applying best practice online learning, teaching, and support to intensive online environments: An integrative review. *Frontiers in Education*, 2, 59. DOI: 10.3389/feduc.2017.00059

Rodríguez-Hernández, C. F., & Rincon-Flores, E. G. (2023). Comparative study between delivery modalities in higher education during emergency remote teaching due to COVID-19. *Frontiers in Education*, 8, 1179330. Advance online publication. DOI: 10.3389/feduc.2023.1179330

Rodríguez-Muñoz, A., Antino, M., Ruíz-Zorrilla, P., & Ortega, E. (2021). Positive emotions, engagement, and objective academic performance: A weekly diary study. *Learning and Individual Differences*, 92, 102087. Advance online publication. DOI: 10.1016/j.lindif.2021.102087

Rodzalan, S. A., Noor, N. N. M., Arif, L. S. M., & Saat, M. M. (2020). Factors influencing the improvement of students' critical thinking and problem-solving skill: An industrial training intervention. *International Journal of Emerging Technologies in Learning*, 15(22), 134–145. DOI: 10.3991/ijet.v15i22.16303

Roehler, L. R., & Cantlon, D. J. (1997). Scaffolding: A powerful tool in social constructivist classrooms. In K. Hogan & M. Pressley, M. (Eds.), *Scaffolding student learning: Instructional approaches & issues* (pp. 6–42). Brookline Books.

Rohrer, J. E., Cole, L. J., & Schulze, F. W. (2012). Cigarettes and self-rated health among online university students. *Journal of Immigrant and Minority Health*, 14(3), 502–505. DOI: 10.1007/s10903-011-9564-4 PMID: 22207447

Romero-Hall, E. (2021). Current initiatives, barriers, and opportunities for networked learning in Latin America. *Educational Technology Research and Development*, 69(4), 2267–2283. DOI: 10.1007/s11423-021-09965-8 PMID: 33584078

Romero, M., Lepage, A., & Lille, B. (2017). Computational thinking development through creative programming in higher education. *International Journal of Educational Technology in Higher Education*, 14(1), 1–15. DOI: 10.1186/s41239-017-0080-z

Root, B., & Bhala, P. (2020). Tailoring online learning: How adaptive learning systems impact student achievement in mathematics. *Journal of Educational Technology Systems*, 49(2), 215–238. DOI: 10.1177/0047239518816260

Rosati-Peterson, G. L., Piro, J. S., Straub, C., & O'Callaghan, C. (2021). A nonverbal immediacy treatment with pre-service teachers using mixed reality simulations. *Cogent Education*, 8(1), 1882114. DOI: 10.1080/2331186X.2021.1882114

Rose, E. (2017). Beyond social presence: Facelessness and the ethics of asynchronous online education. *McGill Journal of Education*, 52(1), 17–32. DOI: 10.7202/1040802ar

Roski, M., Walkowiak, M., & Nehring, A. (2021). Universal design for learning: The more, the better? *Education Sciences*, 11(4), 164. DOI: 10.3390/educsci11040164

Roth, J. A. (2019). *Making the struggle productive: Conceptualizing the role and impact of the mathematics teacher in episodes of productive struggle* [Doctoral dissertation, Kennesaw State University]. https://digitalcommons.kennesaw.edu/seceddoc_etd/16/?utm_source=digitalcommons.kennesaw.edu%2Fseceddoc_etd%2F16&utm_medium=PDF&utm_campaign=PDFCoverPages

Roth, K. B., & Szlyk, H. S. (2022). Hotline use in the United States: Results from the collaborative psychiatric epidemiology surveys. *Administration and Policy in Mental Health*, 48(3), 564–578. DOI: 10.1007/s10488-020-01089-0 PMID: 33057932

Rothstein, R., Lee, Y., Berger, E. J., Rhoads, J., & Deboer, J. (2023). Collaborative engagement and help-seeking behaviors in engineering asynchronous online discussions. *International Journal of Engineering Education*, 39(1), 189–207.

Roy, G., Babu, R., Abul Kalam, M., Yasmin, N., Zafar, T., & Nath, S. R. (2021). Response, readiness and challenges of online teaching amid COVID-19 pandemic: the case of higher education in Bangladesh. *Educational and Developmental Psychologist*, 1-11. https://doi.org/DOI: 10.1080/20590776.2021.1997066

Rufai, M. M., Alebiosu, S. O., & Adeakin, O. A. S. (2015). Conceptual model for virtual classroom management. *International Journal of Computer Science* [IJCSEIT]. *Engineering and Information Technology*, 5(1), 27–32. PMID: 26029735

Ruiz, G., Mintzer, J., & Leipzig, M. (2006). The Impact of e-Learning in Medical Education. *Academic Medicine*, 31(3), 207–212. DOI: 10.1097/00001888-200603000-00002 PMID: 16501260

Rummel, N., & Spada, H. (2005). Learning to collaborate: An instructional approach to promoting collaborative problem-solving in computer-mediated settings. *Journal of the Learning Sciences*, 14(2), 201–241. DOI: 10.1207/s15327809jls1402_2

Ryan, T. (2021). Designing video feedback to support the socioemotional aspects of online learning. *Educational Technology Research and Development*, 69(1), 137–140. DOI: 10.1007/s11423-020-09918-7 PMID: 33456286

S. Aruna, Maturi, S., Kotha, V., & K. Swarna. (2024). Leveraging AI for Student Attention Estimation. *CRC Press EBooks*, 15–21. DOI: 10.1201/9781003470939-3

Sachdeva, A. K. (1996). Use of effective feedback to facilitate adult learning. *Journal of Cancer Education: The Official Journal of the American Association for Cancer Education*, 11(2). Advance online publication. DOI: 10.1080/08858199609528405 PMID: 8793652

Sadaf, A., Kim, S. Y., & Wang, Y. (2021). A comparison of cognitive presence, learning, satisfaction, and academic performance in case-based and non-case-based online discussions. *American Journal of Distance Education*, 35(3), 214–227. DOI: 10.1080/08923647.2021.1888667

Sadaf, A., Wu, T., & Martin, F. (2021). Cognitive presence in online learning: A systematic review of empirical research from 2000 to 2019. *Computers and Education Open*, 2, 10050. DOI: 10.1016/j.caeo.2021.100050

Sadri, G. (1996). A Study of Agentic Self-Efficacy and Agentic Competence Across Britain and the USA. *Journal of Management Development*, 15(1), 51–61. DOI: 10.1108/02621719610107818

Sagna, S., & Vaccaro, A. (2023). "I Didn't Just Do It for Myself": Exploring the Roles of Family in Adult Learner Persistence. *The Journal of Continuing Higher Education*, 71(2), 168–182. DOI: 10.1080/07377363.2021.2023989

Şahin, M., & Kurban, C. F. (2016). Flipped learning: A transformative approach designed to meet the needs of today's knowledge economies and societies. In *The Flipped Approach to Higher Education* (pp. 15–24). Emerald Group Publishing Limited., DOI: 10.1108/978-1-78635-744-120161006

Sahu, P., Kumar, M., Sahu, D., & Chauhan, S. (2024). A correlational study between the level of academic performance and the level of academic stress among young adults. *Revista Review Index Journal of Multidisciplinary*, 4(2), 8–16. DOI: 10.31305/rrijm2024.v04.n02.002

Saini, M. A., & Corrente, S. (2024). Educating for change: A meta-analysis of education programs for separating and divorcing parents. *Family Court Review*, 62(3), 512–541. DOI: 10.1111/fcre.12801

Salas-Pilco, S. Z., Yang, Y., & Zhang, Z. (2022). Student engagement in online learning in Latin American higher education during the COVID-19 pandemic: A systematic review. *British Journal of Educational Technology*, 53(3), 593–619. DOI: 10.1111/bjet.13190 PMID: 35600418

Saleem, A. N., Noori, N. M., & Ozdamli, F. (2022). Gamification applications in E-learning: A literature review. *Technology. Knowledge and Learning*, 27(1), 139–159. DOI: 10.1007/s10758-020-09487-x

Saleem, F., AlNasrallah, W., Malik, M. I., & Rehman, S. U. (2022). Factors Affecting the Quality of Online Learning During COVID-19: Evidence From a Developing Economy. *Frontiers in Education*, 7, 847571. Advance online publication. DOI: 10.3389/feduc.2022.847571

Salimi, N., Gere, B., Talley, W. B., & Irioogbe, B. (2021). College students' mental health challenges: Concerns and considerations in the COVID-19 pandemic. *Journal of College Student Psychotherapy*, 37(1), 39–51. DOI: 10.1080/87568225.2021.1890298

Salmon, G. (2021). *E-tivities: The key to active online learning* (2nd ed.). Routledge.

Sammel, A., Townend, G., & Kanasa, H. (2018). Hidden Expectations Behind the Promise of the Flipped Classroom. *College Teaching*, 66(2), 49–59. DOI: 10.1080/87567555.2016.1189392

Sanchez, E., van Oostendorp, H., Fijnheer, J. D., & Lavoue, E. (2020). Gamification. In *Encyclopedia of Education and Information Technologies* (pp. 816–827). Springer International Publishing. DOI: 10.1007/978-3-030-10576-1_38

Sanders, M. (2022). *Creating inclusive and engaging online courses: A teaching guide*. Edward Elgar Publishing. DOI: 10.4337/9781800888883

Sanmugam, M., Zaid, N. M., Abdullah, Z., Aris, B., Mohamed, H., & van der Meijden, H. (2016, December). The impacts of infusing game elements and gamification in learning. In *2016 IEEE 8th International Conference on Engineering Education (ICEED)* (pp. 131-136). IEEE. DOI: 10.1109/ICEED.2016.7856058

Santiago, P., & Cerna, L. (2020). Strength through diversity: education for inclusive societies. *EDU/EDPC(2019)11/REV2*, Organization for Economic Co-operation and Development. https://www.oecd.org/education/strength-through-diversity/Design-and-Implementation-Plan.pdf

Sari, F. M., & Oktaviani, L. (2021). Undergraduate students' views on the use of online learning platform during COVID-19 pandemic. [Shute]. *Teknosastik*, 19(1), 41–47. DOI: 10.33365/ts.v19i1.896

Saritepeci, M. (2020). Developing computational thinking skills of high school students: Design-based learning activities and programming tasks. *The Asia-Pacific Education Researcher*, 29(1), 35–54. DOI: 10.1007/s40299-019-00480-2

Sarter, M., Givens, B., & Bruno, J. P. (2001). The cognitive neuroscience of sustained attention: Where top-down meets bottom-up. *Brain Research. Brain Research Reviews*, 35(2), 146–160. DOI: 10.1016/S0165-0173(01)00044-3 PMID: 11336780

Sauter, M., Wagner, T., Hirzle, T., Rukzio, E., & Huckauf, A. (2023). Where are my students looking at? Using Gaze Synchronicity to Facilitate Online Learning. *Journal of Vision (Charlottesville, Va.)*, 23(9), 5538–5538. DOI: 10.1167/jov.23.9.5538

Sawyer, R. K. (2005). Analyzing collaborative discourse. In Sawyer, R. K. (Ed.), *The Cambridge handbook of learning sciences* (pp. 187–204). Cambridge University Press. DOI: 10.1017/CBO9780511816833.013

Saykili, A. (2018). Distance education: Definitions, generations and key concepts and future directions. *International Journal of Contemporary Educational Research*, 5(1), 2–17.

Scherer, K. R. (2009). The dynamic architecture of emotion: Evidence for the component process model. *Cognition and Emotion*, 23(7), 1307–1351. DOI: 10.1080/02699930902928969

Scherer, R., Howard, S. K., Tondeur, J., & Siddiq, F. (2021). Profiling teachers' readiness for online teaching and learning in higher education: Who's ready? *Computers in Human Behavior*, 118, 106675. DOI: 10.1016/j.chb.2020.106675

Scherer, R., Siddiq, F., Howard, S. K., & Tondeur, J. (2022). The more experienced, the better prepared? New evidence on the relation between teachers' experience and their readiness for online teaching and learning. *Computers in Human Behavior*, 139, 1–14. DOI: 10.1016/j.chb.2022.10753

Scherer, R., Siddiq, F., Howard, S. K., & Tondeur, J. (2023). Gender divides in teachers' readiness for online teaching and learning in higher education: Do women and men consider themselves equally prepared? *Computers & Education*, 199, 104774. DOI: 10.1016/j.compedu.2023.104774

Schmidt, S. M. P., & Ralph, D. L. (2016). The flipped classroom: A twist on teaching. *Contemporary Issues in Education Research*, 9(1), 1–6. DOI: 10.19030/cier.v9i1.9544

Schneider, C. (2016). Using scaffolding techniques for legal research instruction. *Legal Info. Rev.*, 2, 61–80.

Schunk, D. H. (1989). Self-efficacy and achievement behaviors. *Educational Psychology Review*, 1(3), 173–208. DOI: 10.1007/BF01320134

Schunk, D. H. (1990). Goal setting and self-efficacy during self-regulated learning. *Educational Psychologist*, 25(1), 71–86. DOI: 10.1207/s15326985ep2501_6

Schunk, D. H. (2012). *Learning theories: An educational perspective* (6th ed.). Pearson Education, Inc.

Schunk, D. H., & DiBenedetto, M. K. (2022). Academic self-efficacy. In *Handbook of positive psychology in schools* (pp. 268–282). Routledge. DOI: 10.4324/9781003013778-21

Scott, L. A., Thoma, C. A., Puglia, L., Temple, P., & D'Aguilar, A. (2017). Implementing a UDL framework: A study of current personnel preparation practices. *Intellectual and Developmental Disabilities*, 55(1), 25–36. DOI: 10.1352/1934-9556-55.1.25 PMID: 28181884

Searson, M., Hancock, M., Soheil, N., & Shepherd, G. (2015). Digital citizenship within global contexts. *Education and Information Technologies*, 20(4), 729–741. DOI: 10.1007/s10639-015-9426-0

Seckman, C. (2018). Impact of interactive video communication versus text-based feedback on teaching, social, and cognitive presence in online learning communities. *Nurse Educator*, 43(1), 18–22. DOI: 10.1097/NNE.0000000000000448 PMID: 28858951

Segundo, S. M. T., Díaz, E. Z. G., Vizuete, O. M. Z., & Chávez, E. E. O. (2022). Analysis of Artificial Intelligence Applied in Virtual Learning Environments in Higher Education for Ecuador. *Frontiers in Artificial Intelligence and Applications*, 363. Advance online publication. DOI: 10.3233/FAIA220563

Seligman, M. E. (2011). *Flourish: A visionary new understanding of happiness and wellbeing*. Simon and Schuster.

Selvaraj, A. M., & Azman, H. (2020). Reframing the effectiveness of feedback in improving teaching and learning achievement. [IJERE]. *International Journal of Evaluation and Research in Education*, 9(4), 1055. DOI: 10.11591/ijere.v9i4.20654

Sewandono, R. E., Thoyib, A., Hadiwidjojo, D., & Rofiq, A. (2022). Performance expectancy of E-learning on higher institutions of education under uncertain conditions: Indonesia context. *Education and Information Technologies*. Advance online publication. DOI: 10.1007/s10639-022-11074-9 PMID: 36247027

Shakespeare, W. (n.d.). *Sonnet 33: Full many a glorious morning have I seen*. https://www.poetryfoundation.org/poems/45093/sonnet-33-full-many-a-glorious-morning-have-i-seen

Sharma, A., & Singh, B. (2022). Measuring Impact of E-commerce on Small Scale Business: A Systematic Review. *Journal of Corporate Governance and International Business Law*, 5(1).

Sharma, P., & Hannafin, M. J. (2022). Scaffolding in technology-enhanced learning environments. *Interactive Learning Environments*, 15(1), 27–46. DOI: 10.1080/10494820600996972

Shaw, E. (2005). Assessing and scaffolding collaborative learning in online discussions. In Looi, C. K., McCalla, G. I., Bredeweg, B., & Breuker, J. (Eds.), *AIED* (pp. 587–594). IOS Press., https://www.researchgate.net/publication/221297731_Assessing_and_Scaffolding_Collaborative_Learning_in_Online_Discussions

Shea, P. (2019). A study of student' sense of learning community in online environments. *Online Learning: The Official Journal of the Online Learning Consortium*, 10(1), 35–44. DOI: 10.24059/olj.v10i1.1774

Shea, P., & Bidjerano, T. (2009). Community of inquiry as a theoretical framework to foster "epistemic engagement" and "cognitive presence" in online education. *Computers & Education*, 52(3), 543–553. DOI: 10.1016/j.compedu.2008.10.007

Shea, P., Pickett, A., & Li, C. S. (2005). Increasing access to higher education: A study of the diffusion of online teaching among 913 college faculty. *International Review of Research in Open and Distance Learning*, 6(2), 1–27. DOI: 10.19173/irrodl.v6i2.238

Shee, M. Y., & Lip, S. T. (2022). Online learning motivation during Covid-19 pandemic: The role of learning environment, student self-efficacy and learner-instructor interaction. [MJLI]. *Malaysian Journal of Learning and Instruction*, 19(2), 213–249.

Shernoff, D. J., Sinha, S., Bressler, D. M., & Ginsburg, L. (2017). Assessing teacher education and professional development needs for the implementation of integrated approaches to STEM education. *International Journal of STEM Education*, 4(1), 1–16. DOI: 10.1186/s40594-017-0068-1 PMID: 30631669

Shevalier, R., & McKenzie, B. A. (2012). Culturally responsive teaching as an ethics- and care-based approach to urban education. *Urban Education*, 47(6), 1086–1105. DOI: 10.1177/0042085912441483

Shonfeld, M., Cotnam-Kappel, M., Judge, M., Ng, C. Y., Ntebutse, J. G., Williamson-Leadley, S., & Yildiz, M. N. (2021). Learning in digital environments: A model for cross-cultural alignment. *Educational Technology Research and Development*, 69(4), 1–20. DOI: 10.1007/s11423-021-09967-6 PMID: 33654347

Siebrits, A., & van de Heyde, V. (2019). Towards the sustainable development goals in Africa: The African space-education ecosystem for sustainability and the role of educational technologies. In *Embedding Space in African Society: The United Nations Sustainable Development Goals 2030 Supported by Space Applications* (pp. 127–180). Springer International Publishing. DOI: 10.1007/978-3-030-06040-4_10

Siemens, G. (2005). Connectivism: A learning theory for the digital age. *International Journal of Instructional Technology and Distance Learning*, 2(1), 3–10.

Siergiejczyk, G. (2020). Virtual international exchange as a high-impact learning tool for more inclusive, equitable and diverse classrooms. *European Journal of Open. Distance and E-Learning*, 23(1), 1–17. DOI: 10.2478/eurodl-2020-0001

Simen, J. H., & Meyer, T. (2021). Leadership education in professional and graduate schools. *New Directions for Student Leadership*, 2021(171), 113–122. DOI: 10.1002/yd.20461 PMID: 34658177

Singh Dubey, R., Paul, J., & Tewari, V. (2022). The soft skills gap: A bottleneck in the talent supply in emerging economies. *International Journal of Human Resource Management*, 33(13), 2630–2661. DOI: 10.1080/09585192.2020.1871399

Singh, B. (2023). Blockchain Technology in Renovating Healthcare: Legal and Future Perspectives. In *Revolutionizing Healthcare Through Artificial Intelligence and Internet of Things Applications* (pp. 177-186). IGI Global.

Singh, B. (2024). Evolutionary Global Neuroscience for Cognition and Brain Health: Strengthening Innovation in Brain Science. In *Biomedical Research Developments for Improved Healthcare* (pp. 246-272). IGI Global.

Singh, B., Kaunert, C., & Vig, K. (2024). Reinventing Influence of Artificial Intelligence (AI) on Digital Consumer Lensing Transforming Consumer Recommendation Model: Exploring Stimulus Artificial Intelligence on Consumer Shopping Decisions. In *AI Impacts in Digital Consumer Behavior* (pp. 141-169). IGI Global.

Singh, B. (2023). Federated Learning for Envision Future Trajectory Smart Transport System for Climate Preservation and Smart Green Planet: Insights into Global Governance and SDG-9 (Industry, Innovation and Infrastructure). *National Journal of Environmental Law*, 6(2), 6–17.

Singh, B. (2023). Tele-Health Monitoring Lensing Deep Neural Learning Structure: Ambient Patient Wellness via Wearable Devices for Real-Time Alerts and Interventions. *Indian Journal of Health and Medical Law*, 6(2), 12–16.

Singh, B. (2023). Unleashing Alternative Dispute Resolution (ADR) in Resolving Complex Legal-Technical Issues Arising in Cyberspace Lensing E-Commerce and Intellectual Property: Proliferation of E-Commerce Digital Economy. *Revista Brasileira de Alternative Dispute Resolution-Brazilian Journal of Alternative Dispute Resolution-RBADR*, 5(10), 81–105. DOI: 10.52028/rbadr.v5i10.ART04.Ind

Singh, B. (2024). Cherish Growth, Advancement and Tax Structure: Addressing Social and Economic Prospects. *Journal of Taxation and Regulatory Framework*, 7(1), 7–10.

Singh, B. (2024). Evolutionary Global Neuroscience for Cognition and Brain Health: Strengthening Innovation in Brain Science. In Prabhakar, P. (Ed.), *Biomedical Research Developments for Improved Healthcare* (pp. 246–272). IGI Global., DOI: 10.4018/979-8-3693-1922-2.ch012

Singh, B. (2024). Green Infrastructure in Real Estate Landscapes: Pillars of Sustainable Development and Vision for Tomorrow. *National Journal of Real Estate Law*, 7(1), 4–8.

Singh, B. (2024). Legal Dynamics Lensing Metaverse Crafted for Videogame Industry and E-Sports: Phenomenological Exploration Catalyst Complexity and Future. *Journal of Intellectual Property Rights Law*, 7(1), 8–14.

Singh, B. (2024). Social Cognition of Incarcerated Women and Children: Addressing Exposure to Infectious Diseases and Legal Outcomes. In Reddy, K. (Ed.), *Principles and Clinical Interventions in Social Cognition* (pp. 236–251). IGI Global., DOI: 10.4018/979-8-3693-1265-0.ch014

Singh, B., Jain, V., Kaunert, C., Dutta, P. K., & Singh, G. (2024). Privacy Matters: Espousing Blockchain and Artificial Intelligence (AI) for Consumer Data Protection on E-Commerce Platforms in Ethical Marketing. In Saluja, S., Nayyar, V., Rojhe, K., & Sharma, S. (Eds.), *Ethical Marketing Through Data Governance Standards and Effective Technology* (pp. 167–184). IGI Global., DOI: 10.4018/979-8-3693-2215-4.ch015

Singh, B., & Kaunert, C. (2024). Computational Thinking for Innovative Solutions and Problem-Solving Techniques: Transforming Conventional Education to Futuristic Interdisciplinary Higher Education. In Fonkam, M., & Vajjhala, N. (Eds.), *Revolutionizing Curricula Through Computational Thinking, Logic, and Problem Solving* (pp. 60–82). IGI Global., DOI: 10.4018/979-8-3693-1974-1.ch004

Singh, B., & Kaunert, C. (2024). Harnessing Sustainable Agriculture Through Climate-Smart Technologies: Artificial Intelligence for Climate Preservation and Futuristic Trends. In Kannan, H., Rodriguez, R., Paprika, Z., & Ade-Ibijola, A. (Eds.), *Exploring Ethical Dimensions of Environmental Sustainability and Use of AI* (pp. 214–239). IGI Global., DOI: 10.4018/979-8-3693-0892-9.ch011

Singh, B., & Kaunert, C. (2024). Integration of Cutting-Edge Technologies such as Internet of Things (IoT) and 5G in Health Monitoring Systems: A Comprehensive Legal Analysis and Futuristic Outcomes. *GLS Law Journal*, 6(1), 13–20. DOI: 10.69974/glslawjournal.v6i1.123

Singh, B., & Kaunert, C. (2024). Revealing Green Finance Mobilization: Harnessing FinTech and Blockchain Innovations to Surmount Barriers and Foster New Investment Avenues. In Jafar, S., Rodriguez, R., Kannan, H., Akhtar, S., & Plugmann, P. (Eds.), *Harnessing Blockchain-Digital Twin Fusion for Sustainable Investments* (pp. 265–286). IGI Global., DOI: 10.4018/979-8-3693-1878-2.ch011

Singh, B., & Kaunert, C. (2024). Salvaging Responsible Consumption and Production of Food in the Hospitality Industry: Harnessing Machine Learning and Deep Learning for Zero Food Waste. In Singh, A., Tyagi, P., & Garg, A. (Eds.), *Sustainable Disposal Methods of Food Wastes in Hospitality Operations* (pp. 176–192). IGI Global., DOI: 10.4018/979-8-3693-2181-2.ch012

Singh, J., Singh, L., & Matthees, B. (2022). Establishing social, cognitive, and teaching presence in online learning: A panacea in COVID-19 pandemic, post vaccine and post pandemic times. *Journal of Educational Technology Systems*, 51(1), 28–45. DOI: 10.1177/00472395221095169

Singh, J., Steele, K., & Singh, L. (2021). Combining the best of online and face-to-face learning: Hybrid and blended learning approach for COVID-19, post vaccine, & post-pandemic world. *Journal of Educational Technology Systems*, 50(2), 140–171. DOI: 10.1177/00472395211047865

Singh, M., Adebayo, S. O., Saini, M., & Singh, J. (2021). Indian government E-learning initiatives in response to COVID-19 crisis: A case study on online learning in Indian higher education system. *Education and Information Technologies*, 26(6), 7569–7607. DOI: 10.1007/s10639-021-10585-1 PMID: 34177350

Singh, S. V., & Hiran, K. K. (2022). The impact of AI on teaching and learning in higher education technology. *Journal of Higher Education Theory and Practice*, 12(13), 135–148. https://nabpress.com/higher-education-theory-and-practice

Singh, V., & Thurman, A. (2019). How many ways can we define online learning? A systematic literature review of definitions of online learning (1988-2018). *American Journal of Distance Education*, 33(4), 289–306. DOI: 10.1080/08923647.2019.1663082

Sinha, B., Roberts, D. P., & Jane, C. (2022). Effective strategies for using asynchronous online discussion forums in educational curriculums. *American International Journal of Business Management*, 5(7), 87–98.

Sırakaya, M., Alsancak Sırakaya, D., & Korkmaz, Ö. (2020). The impact of STEM attitude and thinking style on computational thinking determined via structural equation modeling. *Journal of Science Education and Technology*, 29(4), 561–572. DOI: 10.1007/s10956-020-09836-6

Siti Subaryani Zainol, Suhaili Mohd. Hussin, Maisarah Syazwani Othman & Nur Hazrini Mohd Zahari. (2021). Challenges of Online Learning Faced by The B40 Income Parents In Malaysia. *International Journal of Education and Pedagogy.*, 3(2).

Skenderi, F., & Skenderi, L. (2023). Fostering Innovation in Higher Education: Transforming Teaching for Tomorrow. *Knowledge-International Journal*, 60(2), 251–255.

Skulmowski, A., & Xu, K. M. (2021). Understanding cognitive load in digital and online learning: A new perspective on extraneous cognitive load. *Educational Psychology Review*, 34(1), 171–196. DOI: 10.1007/s10648-021-09624-7

Smagorinsky, P. (2018). Deconflating the ZPD and instructional scaffolding: Retranslating and reconceiving the zone of proximal development as the zone of next development. *Learning, Culture and Social Interaction*, 16, 70–75. DOI: 10.1016/j.lcsi.2017.10.009

Smith, C., & Costello, T. J. (2020). The individual's role in maintaining a positive climate. *Currents in Pharmacy Teaching & Learning*, 12(5), 496–498. DOI: 10.1016/j.cptl.2020.01.006 PMID: 32336443

Smith, S. M., & Cardaciotto, L. A. (2011). Is active learning like broccoli? Student perceptions of active learning in large lecture classes. *The Journal of Scholarship of Teaching and Learning*, 11(1), 53–61.

Smith, Y. M., & Crowe, A. R. (2017). Nurse educator perceptions of the importance of relationship in online teaching and learning. *Journal of Professional Nursing*, 33(1), 11–19. DOI: 10.1016/j.profnurs.2016.06.004 PMID: 28131143

Smole, V. (2001). School Leadership-Balancing Power With Caring. *American Secondary Education*, 29(4), 56.

Smylie, M. A., Murphy, J., & Louis, K. S. (2016). Caring school leadership: A multidisciplinary, cross-occupational model. *American Journal of Education*, 123(1), 1–35. DOI: 10.1086/688166

Sohrabi, B., & Iraj, H. (2016). Implementing flipped classroom using digital media: A comparison of two demographically different groups perceptions. *Computers in Human Behavior*, 60, 514–524. DOI: 10.1016/j.chb.2016.02.056

Souheyla, B. (2021). Zoom sessions in distant learning: Algerian EFL students' perceptions and attitudes. *Arab World English Journal*, 264–280.

Spender, J. C. (1996). Organizational knowledge, learning, and memory: Three concepts in search of a theory. *Journal of Organizational Change Management*, 9(1), 63–78. DOI: 10.1108/09534819610156813

Spinks, M. L., Metzler, M., Kluge, S., Langdon, J., Gurvitch, R., Smitherman, M., Esmat, T., Bhattacharya, S., Carruth, L., Crowther, K., Denton, R., Edwards, O. V., Shrikhande, M., & Strong-Green, A. (2023). "This Wasn't Pedagogy, It Was Panicgogy": Perspectives of the Challenges Faced by Students and Instructors during the Emergency Transition to Remote Learning Due to COVID-19. *College Teaching*, 71(4), 227–243. DOI: 10.1080/87567555.2021.2018395

Stapp, A., & Prior, L. (2018). The impact of physically active brain breaks on college students' activity levels and perceptions. *Journal of Physical Activity Research*, 3(1), 60–67. DOI: 10.12691/jpar-3-1-10

Statti, A., & Torres, K. M. (2020). Digital literacy: The need for technology integration and its impact on learning and engagement in community school environments. *Peabody Journal of Education*, 95(1), 90–100. DOI: 10.1080/0161956X.2019.1702426

Steen-Utheim, A. T., & Foldnes, N. (2018). A qualitative investigation of student engagement in a flipped classroom. *Teaching in Higher Education*, 23(3), 307–324. DOI: 10.1080/13562517.2017.1379481

Steinel, N., Palmer, G. C., Nowicki, E., Lee, E., Nelson, E., Whiteley, M., & Lee, M. W. (2019). Integration of microbiology, pharmacology, immunology, and infectious disease using active teaching and self-directed learning. *Medical Science Educator*, 29(1), 315–324. DOI: 10.1007/s40670-018-00689-8 PMID: 34457482

Stephen, J. S., & Rockinson-Szapkiw, A. (2022). Promoting online student persistence: Strategies to promote online learning self-efficacy. In *Academic Self-efficacy in Education: Nature, Assessment, and Research* (pp. 161–176). Springer Singapore. DOI: 10.1007/978-981-16-8240-7_10

Sternberg, R. J. (1988). Mental Self-Government: A Theory of Intellectual Styles and Their Development. *Human Development*, 31(4), 197–224. DOI: 10.1159/000275810

Stewart, O. G. (2023). Understanding what works in humanizing higher education online courses: Connecting through videos, feedback, multimodal assignments, and social media. *Issues and Trends in Learning Technologies*, 11(2), 2–26.

Stickney, L. T., Bento, R. F., Aggarwal, A., & Adlakha, V. (2019). Online higher education: Faculty satisfaction and its antecedents. *Journal of Management Education*, 43(5), 509–542. DOI: 10.1177/1052562919845022

Stoddard, J. (2009). Toward a virtual field trip model for social studies. *Contemporary Issues in Technology & Teacher Education*, 9(4), 412–438.

Stone, C., & Springer, M. (2019). Interactivity and collaboration: How professional development changes the way faculty teach. *Journal of Interactive Online Learning*, 17(3), 233–249.

Stradomska, M. (2022). Visual Thinking (VT) in Educational Issues. *Innovative Teaching Methods. Project Management*, 39-54.

Strayer, J. F. (2012). How learning in an inverted classroom influences cooperation, innovation and task orientation. *Learning Environments Research*, 15(2), 171–193. DOI: 10.1007/s10984-012-9108-4

Streit, M., Levin, M., & Harris, A. (2024, August 8–10). *A qualitative analysis of faculty perceptions: Using asynchronous video exchanges and video feedback in A fully online classroom*. [Conference presentation]. APA 2024 Convention, Seattle, WA, United States.

Streit, M., Levin, M., Harris, A., & Watters, Y. (2023, August 4–6). *Using asynchronous video exchanges to promote faculty presence in the online classroom*. [Conference presentation]. APA 2023 Convention, Washington, D.C., United States.

Strijbos, J. W., & Wichmann, A. (2018). Promoting learning by leveraging the collaborative nature of formative peer assessment with instructional scaffolds. *European Journal of Psychology of Education*, 33(1), 1–9. DOI: 10.1007/s10212-017-0353-x

Strobel, J., & van Barneveld, A. (2009). When is PBL more effective? A meta-synthesis of meta-analyses comparing PBL to conventional classrooms. *The Interdisciplinary Journal of Problem-Based Learning*, 3(1), 44–58. DOI: 10.7771/1541-5015.1046

Su Kim, L. (2003). Multiple identities in a multicultural world: A Malaysian perspective. *Journal of Language, Identity, and Education*, 2(3), 137–158. DOI: 10.1207/S15327701JLIE0203_1

Sumardani, D., & Lin, C.-H. (2023). Cognitive processes during virtual reality learning: A study of brain wave. *Education and Information Technologies*, 28(11), 14877–14896. DOI: 10.1007/s10639-023-11788-4

Sun, G., Cui, T., Yong, J., Shen, J., & Chen, S. (2015, May). Drawing micro learning into MOOC: Using fragmented pieces of time to enable effective entire course learning experiences. In *2015 IEEE 19th International Conference on Computer Supported Cooperative Work in Design (CSCWD)* (pp. 308-313). IEEE.

Sun, A., & Chen, X. (2016). Online education and its effective practice: A research review. *Journal of Information Technology Education*, 15, 15. DOI: 10.28945/3502

Sun, C., Hwang, G., Yin, Z., Wang, Z., & Wang, Z. (2023). Trends and issues of social annotation in education: A systematic review from 2000 to 2020. *Journal of Computer Assisted Learning*, 39(2), 329–350. DOI: 10.1111/jcal.12764

Suwastini, N. K. A., Ersani, N. P. D., Padmadewi, N. N., & Artini, L. P. (2021). Schemes of scaffolding in online education. *Retorika: Jurnal Ilmu Bahasa*, 7(1), 10–18. DOI: 10.22225/jr.7.1.2941.10-18

Svensson, L., & Wihlborg, M. (2010). Internationalizing the content of higher education: The need for a curriculum perspective. *Higher Education*, 60(6), 595–613. DOI: 10.1007/s10734-010-9318-6

Swan, J. A., Newell, S., Scarbrough, H., & Hislop, D. (1999). Knowledge management and innovation: Networks and networking. *Journal of Knowledge Management*, 3(4), 262–275. DOI: 10.1108/13673279910304014

Swan, K., Garrison, D. R., & Richardson, J. C. (2009). A constructivist approach to online learning: The community of inquiry framework. In *Information technology and constructivism in higher education: Progressive learning frameworks* (pp. 43–57). IGI global. DOI: 10.4018/978-1-60566-654-9.ch004

Sweller, J. (2020). Cognitive load theory and educational technology. *Educational Technology Research and Development*, 68(1), 1–16. Advance online publication. DOI: 10.1007/s11423-019-09701-3

Sweller, J., van Merrienboer, J. J. G., & Paas, F. G. W. C. (1998). Cognitive Architecture and Instructional Design. *Educational Psychology Review*, 10(3), 251–296. DOI: 10.1023/A:1022193728205

Szobonya, P., & Roche, C. M. (2023). Virtual Exchange Experiences Energized by an Educational Technology Paradigm Shift. In *Handbook of Research on Current Trends in Cybersecurity and Educational Technology* (pp. 267–297). IGI Global. DOI: 10.4018/978-1-6684-6092-4.ch016

Szpunar, K. K., Moulton, S. T., & Schacter, D. L. (2013). Mind wandering and education: From the classroom to online learning. *Frontiers in Psychology*, 4. Advance online publication. DOI: 10.3389/fpsyg.2013.00495 PMID: 23914183

Taber, K. S. (2018). Scaffolding learning: Principles for effective teaching and the design of classroom resources. In Abend, A. (Ed.), *Effective teaching and learning: Perspectives, strategies, and implementation* (pp. 1–43). Nova.

Taber, K. S. (2018). Scaffolding students' learning: Strategies to promote active engagement. *Learning and Instruction*, 54(1), 39–47.

Talbert, R., & Bergmann, J. (2017). *Flipped learning : A guide for higher education faculty* (1st ed.). Stylus Publishing, LLC.

Tansey, T. N., Smedema, S. M., Umucu, E., Iwanaga, K., Wu, J., Cardoso, E. D., & Strauser, D. R. (2018). Assessing college life adjustment of students with disabilities: Application of the PERMA framework. *Rehabilitation Counseling Bulletin*, 61(3), 131–142. DOI: 10.1177/0034355217702136

Tareen, H., & Haand, M. T. (2020). A case study of UiTM post-graduate students' perceptions on online learning: Benefits challenges. *International Journal of Advanced Research and Publications*, 4(6), 86–94.

Tawwab, N. G. (2021). *Set boundaries, find peace: A guide to reclaiming yourself.* Penguin.

Taylor, C., & Burke da Silva, K. (2014). An analysis of the effectiveness of feedback to students on assessed work. *Higher Education Research & Development*, 33(4), 794–806. DOI: 10.1080/07294360.2013.863840

Taylor, C., Dewsbury, B., & Brame, C. (2022). Technology, equity, and inclusion in the virtual education space. In *Technologies in Biomedical and Life Sciences Education: Approaches and Evidence of Efficacy for Learning* (pp. 35–60). Springer International Publishing. DOI: 10.1007/978-3-030-95633-2_2

Tayyib, N. A., Ramaiah, P., Alshmemri, M. S., Alsolami, F. J., Lind-say, G. M., Alsulami, S. A., & Asfour, H. I. (2020). Faculty members' readiness implementing e-learning in higher education Saudi Universities: A cross-sectional study. *Indian Journal of Science and Technology*, 13(25), 2558–2564. DOI: 10.17485/IJST/v13i25.828

Tedre, M., & Denning, P. J. (2016, November). The long quest for computational thinking. In *Proceedings of the 16th Koli Calling international conference on computing education research* (pp. 120-129).

Tempelaar, D., Rienties, B., & Nguyen, Q. (2020). Subjective data, objective data and the role of bias in predictive modelling: Lessons from a dispositional learning analytics application. *PLoS One*, 15(6), e0233977. DOI: 10.1371/journal.pone.0233977 PMID: 32530954

The Community of Inquiry. (2024). *The Community of Inquiry: About the framework.* The Community of Inquiry. https://www.thecommunityofinquiry.org/coi

The Healthy Minds Network. *Healthy mind study—Student survey.* https://healthymindsnetwork.org/hms/

The history of distance learning. (2024). Oxford Learning College. https://www.oxfordcollege.ac/news/history-of-distance-learning/

TheoryHub. (n.d.). Social capital theory. https://open.ncl.ac.uk/academic-theories/45/social-capital-theory/#:~:text=Social%20Capital%20Theory%2C%20a%20multifaceted,James%20Coleman%2C%20and%20Robert%20Putnam

Thomas, J. W. (2000). *A Review of Research on Project-Based Learning*. The Autodesk Foundation.

Thomas, R. A., West, R. E., & Borup, J. (2017). An analysis of instructor social presence in online text and asynchronous video feedback comments. *The Internet and Higher Education*, 33, 61–73. DOI: 10.1016/j.iheduc.2017.01.003

Thompson, G. (2023, December 21). *Understanding the causes of World War I*. https://www.worldhistory.org.uk/world-war-i-causes

Thomson, A. M., Smith-Tolken, A. R., Naidoo, A. V., & Bringle, R. G. (2011). Service learning and community engagement: A comparison of three national contexts. *Voluntas*, 22(2), 214–237. DOI: 10.1007/s11266-010-9133-9

Tidmand, L. (2021). Building positive emotions and playfulness. In Kern, M. L., & Wehmeyer, M. L. (Eds.), *The Palgrave handbook of positive education* (pp. 421–440). Springer., DOI: 10.1007/978-3-030-64537-3_17

Tolcher, K., Cauble, M., & Downs, A. (2022). Evaluating the effects of gratitude interventions on college student well-being. *Journal of American College Health*, 72(5), 1321–1325. DOI: 10.1080/07448481.2022.2076096 PMID: 35623017

Tomas, L., Evans, N., Doyle, T., & Skamp, K. (2019). Are first year students ready for a flipped classroom? A case for a flipped learning continuum. *International Journal of Educational Technology in Higher Education*, 16(1), 1–22. DOI: 10.1186/s41239-019-0135-4

Tomkins, L., & Simpson, P. (2015). Caring leadership: A Heideggerian perspective. *Organization Studies*, 36(8), 1013–1031. DOI: 10.1177/0170840615580008

Tony, B. (2016). *Teaching in a Digital Age*. BC campus. DOI: 10.14288/1.0224023

Toprak, E., Ozkanal, B., Kaya, S., & Aydin, S. (2007). What do learners and instructors of online learning environments think about ethics in e-learning? A case study from Anadolu University. In European Association of Distance Teaching Universities Conference.

Torres Vega, M., Liaskos, C., Abadal, S., Papapetrou, E., Jain, A., Mouhouche, B., & Famaey, J. (2020). Immersive interconnected virtual and augmented reality: A 5G and IoT perspective. *Journal of Network and Systems Management*, 28(4), 796–826. DOI: 10.1007/s10922-020-09545-w

Tout, K. (2020). Augmented and virtual reality in mathematics education: Current status and future trends. *Journal of Virtual Worlds Research*, 13(1), 1–25. DOI: 10.4101/jvwr.2020.13.1.1

Tran, V. D. (2019). Does cooperative learning increase students' motivation in learning? *International Journal of Higher Education*, 8(5), 12–20. DOI: 10.5430/ijhe.v8n5p12

Trede, F., Bowles, W., & Bridges, D. (2013). Developing intercultural competence and global citizenship through international experiences: Academics' perceptions. *Intercultural Education*, 24(5), 442–455. DOI: 10.1080/14675986.2013.825578

Trello. https://trello.com/

Trieu, E., & Abeyta, A. (2023). Finding meaning in education bolsters academic self-efficacy. *International Journal of Applied Positive Psychology*, 8(2), 1–21. DOI: 10.1007/s41042-023-00095-5

Trout, M. (2010). Social skills in action: An ethic of care in social studies student teaching supervision. Advancing social studies education through self-study methodology: *The power, promise, and use of self-study in social studies education*, 119-137.

Trout, I. Y., & Alsandor, D. J. (2020). Graduate student well-being: Learning and living in the US during the COVID-19 pandemic. *International Journal of Multidisciplinary Perspectives in Higher Education*, 5(1), 150–155. DOI: 10.32674/jimphe.v5i1.2576

Trout, M. (2008). The supervision dance: Learning to lead and follow a student teacher. *New Educator*, 4(3), 252–265. DOI: 10.1080/15476880802234649

Tsai, C.-L., Ku, H.-Y., & Campbell, A. (2021). Impacts of course activities on student perceptions of engagement and learning online. *Distance Education*, 42(1), 106–125. DOI: 10.1080/01587919.2020.1869525

Tshuma, L. S. & Chasokela, D. (2024). The Rise of Online Learning and the Technological Revolution in Higher Education. In M. Kayyali & B. Christiansen (Eds.), *Insights into International Higher Education Leadership and the Skills Gap* (pp. 447-470). IGI Global. https://doi.org/10.4018/979-8-3693-3443-0.ch017

Tsortanidou, X., Daradoumis, T., & Barberá, E. (2019). Connecting moments of creativity, computational thinking, collaboration and new media literacy skills. *Information and Learning Science*, 120(11/12), 704–722. DOI: 10.1108/ILS-05-2019-0042

Tucker, S. Y. (2020). Instructor perceptions of feedback and the best practices: A pilot study. *American Communication Journal, 22*(1). 1–9. https://www.ac-journal.org/wp-content/uploads/2020/11/Instructor-Perceptions-of-Feedback-and-the-Best-Practices-A-Pilot-Study.pdf

Tuckwiller, E., Fox, H., Ball, K., & St. Louis, J. (2024). More than just a "nod" to care: Expanding Nel Noddings' ethics of care framework to sustain educator resilience. *Leadership and Policy in Schools*, ●●●, 1–18. DOI: 10.1080/15700763.2024.2311249

Turan, Z., & Goktas, Y. (2015). A new approach in higher education: The students' views on flipped classroom method. *Journal of Higher Education and Science*, 5(2), 156. DOI: 10.5961/jhes.2015.118

Turkel, M. C. (2014). Leading from the heart: Caring, love, peace, and values guiding leadership. *Nursing Science Quarterly*, 27(2), 172–177. DOI: 10.1177/0894318414522663 PMID: 24740954

Turk, M., Heddy, B. C., & Danielson, R. W. (2022). Teaching and social presences supporting basic needs satisfaction in online learning environments: How can presences and basic needs happily meet online? *Computers & Education*, 180, 104432. DOI: 10.1016/j.compedu.2022.104432

Tyner, A., & Petrilli, M. J. (2018). The case for holding students accountable: How extrinsic motivation gets kids to work harder and learn more. *Education Next*, 18(3), 26–32. https://www.educationnext.org/wp-content/uploads/2022/01/ednext_xviii_3_tyner_petrilli.pdf

Tzimas, D., & Demetriadis, S. (2021). Ethical issues in learning analytics: A review of the field. *Educational Technology Research and Development*, 69(2), 1101–1133. DOI: 10.1007/s11423-021-09977-4

Ulger, K. (2018). The effect of problem-based learning on the creative thinking and critical thinking disposition of students in visual arts education. *The Interdisciplinary Journal of Problem-Based Learning*, 12(1). Advance online publication. DOI: 10.7771/1541-5015.1649

Ulla, M. B., & Espique, F. P. (2022). Hybrid Teaching and the Hybridization of Education: Thai University Teachers' Perspectives, Practices, Challenges. *Journal of Interactive Media in Education*, 2022(1), 9. DOI: 10.5334/jime.758

University of Massachusetts Amherst. (2023). *How to set boundaries.* https://www.umass.edu/studentsuccess/march-how-to-set-boundaries

Uzondu, I. C. (2021). Innovative trends and advances in education and communication in Africa. *AMAMIHE Journal of Applied Philosophy, 19*(3).

Uzondu, I. C. (2021). Innovative trends and advances in education and communication in Africa. *AMAMIHE Journal of Applied Philosophy,* 19(3), 120–134.

Valovičová, Ľ., Ondruška, J., Zelenický, Ľ., Chytrý, V., & Medová, J. (2020). Enhancing computational thinking through interdisciplinary STEAM activities using tablets. *Mathematics,* 8(12), 2128. DOI: 10.3390/math8122128

Van Boxtel, J. M., & Sugita, T. (2022). Exploring the implementation of lesson-level UDL principles through an observation protocol. *International Journal of Inclusive Education,* 26(4), 348–364. DOI: 10.1080/13603116.2019.1655596

Van der Hijden, P., & Martin, M. (2023). *Short courses, micro-credentials, and flexible learning pathways: A blueprint for policy development and action.* International Institute for Educational Planning.

Van der Kleij, F. (2022). Reimagining classroom assessment and feedback to meet learner needs. *Research Conference 2022: Reimagining Assessment: Proceedings and Program.* DOI: 10.37517/978-1-74286-685-7-5

Van der Kleij, F. M., & Lipnevich, A. A. (2021). Student perceptions of assessment feedback: A critical scoping review and call for research. *Educational Assessment, Evaluation and Accountability,* 33(2), 345–373. DOI: 10.1007/s11092-020-09331-x

Van Dinther, M., Dochy, F., & Segers, M. (2011). Factors affecting students' self-efficacy in higher education. *Educational Research Review,* 6(2), 95–108. DOI: 10.1016/j.edurev.2010.10.003

Van Laer, S., & Elen, J. (2023). An instrumentalized framework for supporting learners' self-regulation in blended learning environments. In *Learning, Design, and Technology: An International Compendium of Theory, Research, Practice, and Policy* (pp. 575–612). Springer International Publishing. DOI: 10.1007/978-3-319-17461-7_121

Vanoostveen, R., Desjardins, F., & Bullock, S. (2019). Professional development learning environments (PDLEs) embedded in a collaborative online learning environment (COLE): Moving towards a new conception of online professional learning. *Education and Information Technologies,* 24(2), 1863–1900. DOI: 10.1007/s10639-018-9686-6

Varela, J. L., Magnante, A. T., Miskey, H. M., Ord, A. S., Eldridge, A., & Shura, R. D. (2024). A systematic review of the utility of continuous performance tests among adults with ADHD. *The Clinical Neuropsychologist*, 38(7), 1–62. DOI: 10.1080/13854046.2024.2315740 PMID: 38424025

Vassilakopoulou, P., & Hustad, E. (2023). Bridging digital divides: A literature review and research agenda for information systems research. *Information Systems Frontiers*, 25(3), 955–969. DOI: 10.1007/s10796-020-10096-3 PMID: 33424421

Vaughan, N. D., Cleveland-Innes, M., & Garrison, D. R. (2013). *Teaching in Blended Learning Environments: Creating and Sustaining Communities of Inquiry*. Athabasca University Press. DOI: 10.15215/aupress/9781927356470.01

Veletsianos, G., & Kimmons, R. (2020). What is online learning? The past, present, and future of online education. *Learning and Instruction*, 2(4), 7–16.

Venter, C. M. (2005). Analyze this: Using taxonomies to scaffold students' legal thinking and writing skills. *Mercer Law Review*, 57(2), 621–644.

Ventura, M., Salanova, M., & Llorens, S. (2015). Professional self-efficacy as a predictor of burnout and engagement: The role of challenge and hindrance demands. *The Journal of Psychology*, 149(3), 277–302. DOI: 10.1080/00223980.2013.876380 PMID: 25590343

Verpoorten, D., Glahn, C., Kravcik, M., Ternier, S., & Specht, M. (2009). Personalisation of Learning in Virtual Learning Environments. In Lecture notes in computer science (pp. 52–66). DOI: 10.1007/978-3-642-04636-0_7

Vieira, C., Magana, A. J., Roy, A., & Falk, M. (2021). Providing students with agency to self-scaffold in a computational science and engineering course. *Journal of Computing in Higher Education*, 33(2), 328–366. DOI: 10.1007/s12528-020-09267-7

Vita, G. D. (2001). Learning styles, culture and inclusive instruction in the multicultural classroom: A business and management perspective. *Innovations in Education and Teaching International*, 38(2), 165–174. DOI: 10.1080/14703290110035437

Vlachopoulos, D., & Makri, A. (2019). Online communication and interaction in distance higher education: A framework study of good practice. *International Review of Education*, 65(4), 605–632. DOI: 10.1007/s11159-019-09792-3

Vu, P., Fredrickson, S., & Moore, C. (Eds.). (2016). *Handbook of research on innovative pedagogies and technologies for online learning in higher education*. IGI Global.

Vygotsky, L. S. (1978). *Mind in society: The development of higher psychological processes*. Harvard University Press.

Vygotsky, L. S. (1978). *Mind in Society: the Development of Higher Psychological Processes*. Harvard University Press.

Vyletel, B., Voichoski, E., Lipson, S., & Heinze, J. (2023). *Exploring faculty burnout through the 2022-23 HMS faculty/staff survey.* https://www.apa.org/ed/precollege/psychology-teacher-network/introductory-psychology/faculty-burnout-survey

Wager, T. D., Jonides, J., & Reading, S. (2004). Neuroimaging studies of shifting attention: A meta-analysis. *NeuroImage*, 22(4), 1679–1693. DOI: 10.1016/j.neuroimage.2004.03.052 PMID: 15275924

Wai-Cook, M. S. S. (2021). Students' perceptions of interactions from instructor presence, cognitive presence, and social presence in online lessons. *International Journal of TESOL Studies*, 3(1), 134–161.

Waks, L. J. (2019). Massive open online courses and the future of higher education. *Contemporary Technologies in Education: Maximizing Student Engagement, Motivation, and Learning*, 183-213.

Waldow, J. L., & AuCoin, D. (2021). Computer to community. In Fudge, T., & Ferebee, S. (Eds.), *Curriculum development and online instruction for the 21st century* (pp. 1–19). IGI Global., DOI: 10.4018/978-1-7998-7653-3.ch001

Wang, C. H., Shannon, D. M., & Ross, M. E. (2013). Students' characteristics, self-regulated learning, technology self-efficacy, and course outcomes in online learning. *Distance Education*, 34(3), 302–323. DOI: 10.1080/01587919.2013.835779

Wang, C., Shen, J., & Chao, J. (2022). Integrating computational thinking in STEM education: A literature review. *International Journal of Science and Mathematics Education*, 20(8), 1949–1972. DOI: 10.1007/s10763-021-10227-5

Wang, S. (2024). Problems with students' mental health in the context of online learning. *Transactions on Social Science. Education and Humanities Research*, 5, 44–48. DOI: 10.62051/2r8w5b08

Wang, T. (2017). Overcoming barriers to 'flip': Building teacher's capacity for the adoption of flipped classroom in Hong Kong secondary schools. *Research and Practice in Technology Enhanced Learning*, 12(1), 6–17. DOI: 10.1186/s41039-017-0047-7 PMID: 30613255

Wang, X., Zhang, L., & He, T.-C. (2022). Learning Performance Prediction-Based Personalized Feedback in Online Learning via Machine Learning. *Sustainability (Basel)*, 14(13), 7654–7654. DOI: 10.3390/su14137654

Wang, Y., Cao, Y., Gong, S., Wang, Z., Li, N., & Ai, L. (2022). Interaction and learning engagement in online learning: The mediating roles of online learning self-efficacy and academic emotions. *Learning and Individual Differences*, 94, 102128. DOI: 10.1016/j.lindif.2022.102128

Wang, Y., Stein, D., & Shen, S. (2021). Students' and teachers' perceived teaching presence in online courses. *Distance Education*, 42(3), 373–390. DOI: 10.1080/01587919.2021.1956304

Warner, J. (2024). In student-centered classrooms, the instructor must come first. *Inside Higher Ed.* https://www.insidehighered.com/opinion/blogs/just-visiting/2024/07/18/student-centered-teaching-should-consider-instructors-first?utm_source=Inside+Higher+Ed&utm_campaign=91db10faf5-DNU_2021_COPY_02&utm_medium=email&utm_term=0_1fcbc04421-91db10faf5-236162669&mc_cid=91db10faf5&mc_eid=a4ce5578c6

Watson, S., Sullivan, D. P., & Watson, K. (2023). Teaching presence in asynchronous online classes: It's not just a façade. *Online Learning : the Official Journal of the Online Learning Consortium*, 27(2), 288–303. https://files.eric.ed.gov/fulltext/EJ1392861.pdf. DOI: 10.24059/olj.v27i2.3231

Waytz, A. (2019). *The power of human*. W.W. Norton & Co.

Wedege, T. (2020). The role of adult numeracy in sustainable development goals. *ZDM Mathematics Education*, 52(3), 413–425. DOI: 10.1007/s11858-019-01083-1

Weems-Landingham, V., & Paternite, J. B. (2021). Using asynchronous discussions to improve online student success. *College Teaching*, 71(3), 195–196. DOI: 10.1080/87567555.2021.2008295

Wegerif, R. (1998). The social dimension of asynchronous learning networks. *Online Learning : the Official Journal of the Online Learning Consortium*, 2(1), 34–49. DOI: 10.24059/olj.v2i1.1928

Weintrop, D., Beheshti, E., Horn, M., Orton, K., Jona, K., Trouille, L., & Wilensky, U. (2016). Defining computational thinking for mathematics and science classrooms. *Journal of Science Education and Technology*, 25(1), 127–147. DOI: 10.1007/s10956-015-9581-5

Wekerle, C., Daumiller, M., & Kollar, I. (2022). Using digital technology to promote higher education learning: The importance of different learning activities and their relations to learning outcomes. *Journal of Research on Technology in Education*, 54(1), 1–17. DOI: 10.1080/15391523.2020.1799455

Weru, N. (2023). The role of instructors support and feedback on the performance of online and distance learning. *International Journal of Online and Distance Learning*, 4(1), 35–46. DOI: 10.47604/ijodl.2001

Whiteside, A., Dikkers, A. L., & Lewis, S. (2014, May 19). *The power of social presence for learning*. https://er.educause.edu/articles/2014/5/the-power-of-social-presence-for-learning

Whiteside, A. L., Dikkers, A. G., & Swan, K. (Eds.). (2023). *Social presence in online learning: Multiple perspectives on practice and research*. Taylor & Francis.

Wikoff, N. (2022). Numeracy and financial wellbeing during the COVID-19 pandemic. *Numeracy*, 15(1), 4. Advance online publication. DOI: 10.5038/1936-4660.15.1.1399

Wiliam, D. (2010). The role of formative assessment in effective learning environments. In *Educational Research and Innovation* (pp. 135–159). OECD.

Wiliam, D., & Thompson, M. (2017). Integrating assessment with instruction: What will it take to make it work? *The Future of Assessment*, 2(3), 53–83. DOI: 10.4324/9781315086545-3

Williams, K. H., Childers, C., & Kemp, E. (2013). Stimulating and enhancing student learning through positive emotions. *Journal of Teaching in Travel & Tourism*, 13(3), 209–227. DOI: 10.1080/15313220.2013.813320

Williams, K. M., Stafford, R. E., Corliss, S. B., & Reilly, E. D. (2018). Examining student characteristics, goals, and engagement in Massive Open Online Courses. *Computers & Education*, 126, 433–442. DOI: 10.1016/j.compedu.2018.08.014

Williams, P. G., Rau, H. K., Suchy, Y., Thorgusen, S. R., & Smith, T. W. (2017). On the validity of self-report assessment of cognitive abilities: Attentional control scale associations with cognitive performance, emotional adjustment, and personality. *Psychological Assessment*, 29(5), 519–530. DOI: 10.1037/pas0000361 PMID: 27504900

Williams, S. A. S., Conyers, A., & Garcia, F. (2018). Practical applications of ecological consultation in higher education: Diversity and inclusion initiatives. *Public Administration Quarterly*, 42(2), 183–212. https://paq.spaef.org/. DOI: 10.1177/073491491804200204

Willmann, R., Zebedin, G., & Miksche, D. (2020). Technical setup of an inverted virtual classroom. *2020 IEEE Global Engineering Education Conference (EDUCON)*, pp. 931-936. 27–30 April, 2020, Porto, Portugal

Wills, S., & Grimes, R. (2020). Developing relationships in an online environment. *The European Conference on Language Learning 2020: Official Conference Proceedings*. DOI: 10.22492/issn.2188-112X.2020.8

Wilson, K. (2023). What does it mean to do teaching? A qualitative study of resistance to flipped learning in a higher education context. *Teaching in Higher Education*, 28(3), 473–486. DOI: 10.1080/13562517.2020.1822312

Wilton, M., Gonzalez-Nino, E., McPartlan, P., Terner, Z., Christoffersen, R. E., & Rothman, J. H. (2019). Improving academic performance, belonging, and retention through increasing structure of an introductory biology course. *CBE Life Sciences Education*, 18(4), ar53. Advance online publication. DOI: 10.1187/cbe.18-08-0155 PMID: 31675276

Witherspoon, N., & Arnold, B. M. (2010). Pastoral care: Notions of caring and the Black female principal. *The Journal of Negro Education*, 79(3), 220–232.

Witkowski, P. L., & Cornell, T. (2015). An investigation into student engagement in higher education classrooms. *InSight: A Journal of Scholarly Teaching, 10*, 56–67. DOI: 10.46504/10201505wi

Wlodarczyk, J. R., Alicuben, E. T., Hawley, L., Sullivan, M., Ault, G. T., & Inaba, K. (2021). Development and emergency implementation of an online surgical education curriculum for a General Surgery program during a global pandemic: The University of Southern California experience. *the American Journal of Surgery, 221*(5), 962–972. DOI: 10.1016/j.amjsurg.2020.08.045

Wong, J., Baars, M., Davis, D., Van Der Zee, T., Houben, G. J., & Paas, F. (2019). Supporting self-regulated learning in online learning environments and MOOCs: A systematic review. *International Journal of Human-Computer Interaction*, 35(4-5), 356–373. DOI: 10.1080/10447318.2018.1543084

Wong, J., Baars, M., He, M., Koning, B. B., & Paas, F. (2021). Facilitating goal setting and planning to enhance online self-regulation of learning. *Computers in Human Behavior*, 124, 106913. Advance online publication. DOI: 10.1016/j.chb.2021.106913

Wood, A., Symons, K., Falisse, J. B., Gray, H., & Mkony, A. (2021). Can lecture capture contribute to the development of a Community of Inquiry in online learning? *Distance Education*, 42(1), 126–144. DOI: 10.1080/01587919.2020.1869521

Wood, D., Bruner, J. S., & Ross, G. (1976). The role of tutoring in problem solving. *Journal of Child Psychology and Psychiatry, and Allied Disciplines*, 17(2), 89–100. DOI: 10.1111/j.1469-7610.1976.tb00381.x PMID: 932126

Wu, R., & Yu, Z. (2022). Exploring the effects of achievement emotions on online learning outcomes: A systematic review. *Frontiers in Psychology*, 13, 977931. Advance online publication. DOI: 10.3389/fpsyg.2022.977931 PMID: 36160514

Wynants, S., & Dennis, J. (2018). Professional development in an online context: Opportunities and challenges from the voices of college faculty. *The Journal of Educators Online*, 15(1). Advance online publication. DOI: 10.9743/JEO2018.15.1.2

Wyrick, A. (2022). How to define boundaries with your students – and stick to them. *Harvard Business Publishing,* https://hbsp.harvard.edu/inspiring-minds/how-to-define-boundaries-with-your-students-and-stick-to-them

Xia, X., & Li, X. (2022). Artificial Intelligence for higher education development and teaching skills. *Wireless Communications and Mobile Computing*, •••, 1–10. DOI: 10.1155/2022/7537764

Xia, Y. (2023). Service-Learning Practices and Reflections in the Perspective of Nel Noddings' Theory of Caring Education: The "Care for the Elderly" Service-Learning Program as an Example. *Journal of Contemporary Educational Research*, 7(10), 25–32. DOI: 10.26689/jcer.v7i10.5479

Xun, G. E., & Land, S. M. (2004). A conceptual framework for scaffolding ill-structured problem-solving processes using question prompts and peer interactions. *Educational Technology Research and Development*, 52(2), 5–22. DOI: 10.1007/BF02504836

Yackle, K., Schwarz, L. A., Kam, K., Sorokin, J. M., Huguenard, J. R., Feldman, J. L., Luo, L., & Krasnow, M. A. (2017). Breathing control center neurons that promote arousal in mice. *Science*, 355(6332), 1411–1415. DOI: 10.1126/science.aai7984 PMID: 28360327

Yadav, A., Mayfield, C., Zhou, N., Hambrusch, S., & Korb, J. T. (2024). Computational thinking in elementary and secondary teacher education. [TOCE]. *ACM Transactions on Computing Education*, 14(1), 1–16. DOI: 10.1145/2576872

Yang, C. (2021). Online teaching self-efficacy, social-emotional learning (SEL) competencies, and compassion fatigue among educators during the COVID-19 pandemic. *School Psychology Review*, 50(4), 505–518. DOI: 10.1080/2372966X.2021.1903815

Yang, Q.-F., Lin, C.-J., & Hwang, G.-J. (2021). Research focuses and findings of flipping mathematics classes: A review of journal publications based on the technology-enhanced learning model. *Interactive Learning Environments*, 29(6), 905–938. DOI: 10.1080/10494820.2019.1637351

Yang, X. (2023). A historical review of collaborative learning and cooperative learning. *TechTrends*, 67(4), 718–728. DOI: 10.1007/s11528-022-00823-9 PMID: 36711122

Yan, X., Peng, P., & Liu, Y. (2024). Optimal Design Feature of Computer-Assisted Reading Instruction for Students with Reading Difficulties? A Bayesian Network Meta-Analysis. *Computers in Human Behavior*, 152, 108062. Advance online publication. DOI: 10.1016/j.chb.2023.108062

Yan, Z., Chiu, M. M., & Ko, P. Y. (2020). Effects of self-assessment diaries on academic achievement, self-regulation, and motivation. *Assessment in Education: Principles, Policy & Practice*, 27(5), 562–583. DOI: 10.1080/0969594X.2020.1827221

Yao, Y., Wang, P., Jiang, Y., Li, Q., & Li, Y. (2022). Innovative Online learning strategies for the successful construction of student Self-awareness during the COVID-19 pandemic: Merging TAM with TPB. *Journal of Innovation & Knowledge*, 7(4), 100252. DOI: 10.1016/j.jik.2022.100252

Yeap, C. F., Suhaimi, N., & Nasir, M. K. M. (2021). Issues, challenges, and suggestions for empowering technical vocational education and training education during the COVID-19 Pandemic in Malaysia. *Creative Education*, 12(8), 1818–1839. DOI: 10.4236/ce.2021.128138

Yildirim, Y., Arslan, E. A., Yildirim, K., & Bisen, I. (2021). Reimagining education with artificial intelligence. *Eurasian. The Journal of Higher Education*, 4(4), 32–46. DOI: 10.31039/ejohe.2021.4.52

Yilmaz Ince, E., & Koc, M. (2021). The consequences of robotics programming education on computational thinking skills: An intervention of the Young Engineer's Workshop (YEW). *Computer Applications in Engineering Education*, 29(1), 191–208. DOI: 10.1002/cae.22321

Yılmaz, Ş., & Sarı, İ. (2010). Php Gd Kütüphanesi Kullanılarak Etkileşimli Uygulama Geliştirme [Interactive Application Development Using Php GD Library]. G. T. Yamamoto, U. Demiray, & M. Kesim (Ed), Türkiye'de e-Öğrenme: Gelişmeler ve Uygulamalar içinde [e-Learning in Turkey: Developments and Applications] (185-200). Denizli.

Yilmaz, R. (2016). Knowledge sharing behaviors in e-learning community: Exploring the role of academic self-efficacy and sense of community. *Computers in Human Behavior*, 63, 373–382. DOI: 10.1016/j.chb.2016.05.055

Yılmazsoy, B., Özdinç, F., & Kahraman, M. (2018). Investigating student opinions about classroom management in a virtual classroom. *Trakya Üniversitesi Eğitim Fakültesi Dergisi*, 8(3), 513–525.

You, J., & Yang, J. (2021). Engaging students with instructional videos: Perspectives from faculty and instructional designers. *Quarterly Review of Distance Education*, 22(3), 1–10.

Yu, Q. (2022). Factors Influencing Online Learning Satisfaction. *Frontiers in Psychology*, 13, 852360. Advance online publication. DOI: 10.3389/fpsyg.2022.852360 PMID: 35496260

Yusoff, N. S., Rashid, M. F., & Halim, N. A. (2022). The Impact of Covid-19 Pandemic Towards Socioeconomic Wellbeing of Rural Community in Malaysia. [). IOP Publishing.]. *IOP Conference Series. Earth and Environmental Science*, 1064(1), 012054. DOI: 10.1088/1755-1315/1064/1/012054

Zahra, A., Waheed, Z., Fatima, T., & Khong, K. W. (2024). Leveraging Technology for Environmental Awareness: Insights from Experimental Research with Middle School Students in Malaysia. *RMLE Online: Research in Middle Level Education*, 47(4), 1–17. DOI: 10.1080/19404476.2024.2322046

Zain, F. M., & Sailin, S. N. (2020). Students' experience with flipped learning approach in higher education. *Universal Journal of Educational Research*, 8(10), 4946–4958. DOI: 10.13189/ujer.2020.081067

Zakharova, I., & Jarke, J. (2022). Educational technologies as matters of care. *Learning, Media and Technology*, 47(1), 95–108. DOI: 10.1080/17439884.2021.2018605

Zalaznick, M. (2023). How ChatGPT can actually be a force for good rather than a boon for cheaters. https://districtadministration.com/chatgpt-impact-schools-teaching-cheating-writing/

Zamiri, M., & Esmaeili, A. (2024). Methods and Technologies for Supporting Knowledge Sharing within Learning Communities: A Systematic Literature Review. *Administrative Sciences*, 14(1), 17. DOI: 10.3390/admsci14010017

Zawacki-Richter, O., Baecker, E., & Vogt, S. (2009). Review of distance education research (2000 to 2008): Analysis of research areas, methods, and authorship patterns. *International Review of Research in Open and Distance Learning*, 10(6), 21–50. DOI: 10.19173/irrodl.v10i6.741

Zgheib, G., Al Daia, R., & Serhan, M. (2023). A contextual approach for exploring faculty readiness to teach online. *Heliyon*, 9(10), e20491. Advance online publication. DOI: 10.1016/j.heliyon.2023.e20491 PMID: 37867860

Zhai, X. M. (2022). ChatGPT user experience: implications for education. *SSRN*: https://ssrn.com/abstract=4312418 or DOI: 10.2139/ssrn.4312418

Zhang, J., & Cui, Q. (2018). Collaborative learning in higher nursing education: A systematic review. *Journal of Professional Nursing*, 34(5), 378–388. DOI: 10.1016/j.profnurs.2018.07.007 PMID: 30243695

Zhang, L.-F. (2002). Thinking Styles: Their relationships with modes of thinking and academic performance. *Educational Psychology*, 22(3), 331–348. DOI: 10.1080/01443410220138557

Zhang, S., Gao, Q., Wen, Y., Li, M., & Wang, Q. (2021). Automatically detecting cognitive engagement beyond behavioral indicators: A case of online professional learning community. *Journal of Educational Technology & Society*, 24(2), 58–72.

Zhao, L., Dixon, R., Dousay, T., & Carr-Chellman, A. (2022). Outsourced Professional Development for Online Instructors: Recommendations from research. *ELearn, 2022*(4). DOI: 10.1145/3532688.3529094

Zhao, H., Liu, X., & Xu, Y. (2022). Innovative teaching methods and technology in mathematics education. *Educational Technology Research and Development*, 70(3), 659–678. DOI: 10.1007/s11423-022-10071-0

Zheng, F., Khan, N. A., & Hussain, S. (2020). The COVID-19 pandemic and digital higher education: Exploring the impact of proactive personality on social capital through internet self-efficacy and online interaction quality. *Children and Youth Services Review*, 119, 105694. DOI: 10.1016/j.childyouth.2020.105694

Zheng, L., Long, M., Zhong, L., & Gyasi, J. F. (2022). The effectiveness of technology-facilitated personalized learning on learning achievements and learning perceptions: A meta-analysis. *Education and Information Technologies*, 27(8), 11807–11830. DOI: 10.1007/s10639-022-11092-7

Zhu, M., Bonk, C. J., & Doo, M. Y. (2020). Self-directed learning in MOOCs: Exploring the relationships among motivation, self-monitoring, and self-management. *Educational Technology Research and Development*, 68(5), 2073–2093. DOI: 10.1007/s11423-020-09747-8

Zhu, Q., & Jesiek, B. K. (2020). Practicing engineering ethics in the global context: A comparative study of expert and novice approaches to cross-cultural ethical situations. *Science and Engineering Ethics*, 26(4), 2097–2120. DOI: 10.1007/s11948-019-00154-8 PMID: 31721025

Zhu, X., Chen, B., Avadhanam, R. M., Shui, H., & Zhang, R. Z. (2020). Reading and connecting: Using social annotation in online classes. *Information and Learning Science*, 121(5/6), 261–271. DOI: 10.1108/ILS-04-2020-0117

Zhu, Y., Zhang, J. H., Au, W., & Yates, G. (2020). University students' online learning attitudes and continuous intention to undertake online courses: A self-regulated learning perspective. *Educational Technology Research and Development*, 68(3), 1485–1519. DOI: 10.1007/s11423-020-09753-w

Zint, M., Michel, J. O., Valentine, T., & Collins, S. (2024). *Collaborating with Students to Advance Climate Change Education at the University of Michigan*. Insights and Recommendations.

About the Contributors

Lori Doyle works as Associate Professor of Education at Concordia University Irvine and serves as Director of the Master of Arts in Educational Leadership Programs in Social Emotional Learning, Character, and Ethics and Cognition, Motivation, and Development. She is Subject Matter Expert for multiple courses in both programs and has worked on extensive curriculum development projects for the university. Working as an instructor keeps her mindful of relevant and changing trends in adult education. Lori also serves as the Assistant Director of the Servant Leadership Institute and oversees framework integration and faculty support. Her areas of research interest are adult education, Biblical contexts, leadership, and faculty mental health.

Tanya Tarbutton works at Concordia University Irvine where she serves as the Senior Director of Master of Arts in Education Degree Programs, Educational Administration Practicum Coordinator and Associate Professor of Education. Prior to this Dr. Tarbutton enjoyed her role as Director of MAED, Educational Administration emphasis. She has worked as a supervisor and instructor at several higher education institutions in Southern California, mentoring and supporting new administrators and teachers. Her work expands to include participating on Academic Advisory Boards focused on transformational change, presenting at international conferences and being invited to present at UNESCO's Commission on the Status of Women Conference. Before switching to higher education, Dr. Tarbutton worked as a site based school administrator, resource teacher and general education teacher. She brings a unique perspective grounded in more than 25 years of career experience.

***

Vishnu Achutha Menon is an independent journalist, writer, researcher, and an Indian percussionist. He is a recipient of the Junior Scholarship the Ministry of Culture awarded. His research interests are film studies, verbal & nonverbal communication, south Asian performances, Natyasastra, media studies, media analysis techniques, Laban Movement Analysis, and Ethnomusicology.

Khalid Alharbi holds a Master's degree from Ohio University and a PhD from Georgetown University. He is currently an Assistant Professor at Al-Jouf University. During his time at Georgetown, he worked as an Online Programs Associate at the Center for New Designs in Learning and Scholarship (CNDLS), where he contributed to a range of initiatives at the intersection of higher education innovation and new technologies.

Linda C. Ashar, J.D., is a passionate advocate of education and continuous learning. As an Associate Professor at American Public University System, she teaches diverse undergraduate and graduate courses, spanning business, law, artificial intelligence, crisis management, and ethics. Holding a Juris Doctor from the University of Akron School of Law, her legal expertise spans 30+ years of practice in Ohio and federal courts. She also holds a Master of Arts in Special Education and Bachelor of English. Dr. Ashar is a recipient of the Dr. Wallace E. Boston School of Business Award for Teaching Excellence and Co-editor of The International Journal of Open Educational Resources.

Linda Ashar is an associate professor at American Public University System and recipient of the Dr. Wallace E. Boston School of Business Award for Excellence in Teaching. Her teaching encompasses undergraduate and graduate courses in business, law, artificial intelligence, crisis management, and ethics. Dr. Ashar is Co-editor of The International Journal of Open Educational Resources, an Independent Online APPQMR Facilitator and QM Peer Reviewer. She obtained her J.D. from the University of Akron School of Law, M.A. in Special Education from Kent State University, and B.A. in English from Muskingum University. She regularly publishes and podcasts on current issues.

Guruprasad B G is a dedicated and experienced educator with over 14 of experience in the field of commerce and management. I began my Career as a lecturer in UG. I quickly rose through the ranks and become an assistant professor and Principal and then a Principal at Surana Evening College.

Patcha Bhujanga Rao is a highly accomplished professional with over two decades of experience in Human Resources, Legal, and Soft Skills. He has an impressive academic background, holding degrees like M.Com., DCFA., M.Phil., Ph.D, MBA (HR), M.Sc (Psychology), and LL.B. His diverse qualifications equip him with a comprehensive understanding of various disciplines, which enables him to excel in his roles. Dr. Patcha Bhujanga Rao is currently serving as a Professor at Jain Deemed-to-be University in Bengaluru. He has made significant contributions to the academic realm, particularly in the field of Human Resources. His profound expertise in HR management has been instrumental in guiding and mentoring the next generation of professionals. Dr. Rao has equipped them with essential skills and knowledge to thrive in their careers. His passion for imparting knowledge, coupled with his extensive experience, has enabled him to shape talent and drive positive change in countless professional trajectories. Beyond his expertise in HR, Dr. Patcha Bhujanga Rao is also well-versed in Soft Skills. He recognizes the paramount importance of effective communication, leadership, and interpersonal abilities in today's professional landscape. His dedication to enhancing these skills among students and professionals alike has been invaluable, fostering personal and professional development. Dr. Rao's unwavering dedication, expertise, and commitment to excellence have earned him widespread respect and admiration in the realms of HR and Soft Skills. He stands as a beacon of inspiration for aspiring professionals, embodying the values of continuous learning, mentorship, and leadership in the pursuit of professional success.

Doris Chasokela is a senior lecturer at the National University of Science and Technology, Faculty of Science and Technology Education, Department of Technical and Engineering Education. She holds a Doctor of Education, Master of Engineering in Electrical Systems Control and Information Technology, Bachelor of Education in Electrical and Electronics Engineering, Diploma in Technical and Vocational Education, Certificate in Automobile Electrics & Electronics and a Class One Skilled Worker in Automobile Electrics. She has 11 years' experience in higher education. Her interests are higher education, engineering education, artificial intelligence, control, e learning.

Deepak D, an academician of two years old, with teaching experience in the areas of taxation, accounting, and IFRS. He has expertise in academic publishing, research content writing, coaching, teaching, editing, and analytical abilities. He possesses a PhD from JAIN (Deemed To Be University) in the School of Commerce. He has participated in a number of FDPs, workshops, seminars, and conferences. He as published more than 10 research paper in different UGC Care journal, web of science, Scopus.

Zhuqing Ding is the Assistant Director for Online Programs at the Center for New Designs in Learning and Scholarship at Georgetown University. She has over 10 years of experience advancing technology-enhanced education through learning design, media design, and technology implementation. She is currently pursuing her doctoral degree in Human and Organizational Learning at George Washington University. Her research interests are in online teaching readiness and embodied and artistic learning.

Seyfullah Gökoğlu is a researcher and faculty member at Bartın University, Türkiye. With MA and PhD degrees in computer education and instructional technologies, Dr. Gökoğlu focuses on empirical studies in virtual reality, online learning, programming education, and educational technology. He applies critical theories like constructivism, experiential learning, and social learning to his research. Dr. Gökoğlu is also interested in emerging research paradigms, including topic modeling, sentiment analysis, and meta-analysis. Dr. Gökoğlu's studies also cover integrating artificial intelligence technologies into educational processes in the axis of human-computer interaction. His dedication to advancing the field is reflected in his publications in leading journals in the instructional technology field, such as Computers & Education, Journal of Educational Computing Research, The International Review of Research in Open and Distributed Learning, and Online Information Review.

Carrie Grimes is an Assistant Professor at Vanderbilt University's Peabody College of Education and Human Development, in the department of Leadership, Policy, and Organizations. She directs the master's program in Independent School Leadership and teaches leadership courses online at the master's and doctoral level.

Nazifah Binti Hamidun is a senior lecturer at the Languages & General Studies Department, Faculty of Business & Communication, UniMAP. She holds a doctoral degree in TESOL from Universiti Sains Malaysia (USM). She earned both degree and master degree in education at Universiti Utara Malaysia (UUM). She collaborates closely with Perlis State teachers and had produced an English literacy module for schools to promote learning and literacy. Her main research interests are in the area of TESL, curriculum and pedagogy.

Aida Shakila Ishak is a Senior Lecturer at the Faculty of Business & Communication, Universiti Malaysia Perlis. Her area of expertise is counseling psychology and her sub-field expertise is related to drug abuse. She has served in the field of Education since 2019 until now. After being awarded a Doctor of Philosophy Degree from Universiti Malaysia Perlis, she actively continued to contribute in terms of scholarly writing, namely papers in national and international journals.

Christian Kaunert is Professor of International Security at Dublin City University, Ireland. He is also Professor of Policing and Security, as well as Director of the International Centre for Policing and Security at the University of South

Wales. In addition, he is Jean Monnet Chair, Director of the Jean Monnet Centre of Excellence and Director of the Jean Monnet Network on EU Counter-Terrorism (www.eucter.net).

Servet Kılıç provides training as a lecturer in the Department of Computer Technologies at Ordu University on programming, three-dimensional object design, educational robotics applications, testing and automation, and graphic analysis. In the field of computer education and educational technologies, he conducts studies as an associate professor on topics such as educaetional technologies, distance education, teacher education, programming, robotics, virtual education technologies, STEM, and artificial intelligence technologies.

Mary Lannon is a professor of graduate public safety at Purdue University Global. Dr. Lannon has over 11 years of experience in higher education and worked for 12 years in public safety communications. Dr. Lannon's research interests include emergency preparedness and response, online teaching and learning, and research ethics.

Youmei Liu received her Doctor of Education in Curriculum and Instruction focusing on instructional technology in 2003 from the College of Education at the University of Houston (UH). She has been serving as a Director of Assessment and Accreditation Services since 2011. Before assuming this position, she worked as an educational production specialist and an instructional designer. She is also an adjunct faculty at the Jack J. Valenti School of Communications at UH, and has been teaching Information and Communication Technology course for over 20 years. Dr. Liu functioned as a conference chair for the Society of International Chinese Educational Technology (SICET) and the Chinese American Educational Research and Development Association (CAERDA) in the US. She has rich research experience and has numerous publications in the areas of quality course design, innovative use of educational technology, distance education and mobile learning, cross-cultural communication, and social capital development in e-learning and social media platforms.

Lunisani Mpofu is a is a lecturer at the National University of Science and Technology, Faculty of Science and Technology Education, Department of Science, Mathematics Technology Education. He holds a B Comm Accounting a B Compt Honours, MSc finance and Investment and Postgraduate diploma in higher education. His research interests are in higher education, Performance measurement and accounting for climatic change.

Rocío Rodríguez Padín is a professor at the Faculty of Education Sciences at the Universidade da Coruña, where she teaches in the Department of Pedagogy and Didactics. Rocío is known for her dedication and creativity in the educational field. Her innovative and dynamic approach has made her an inspiring figure for her students and colleagues. Through her work, she fosters an environment of collaboration, respect, and motivation in the teaching-learning process, positively impacting the formation of new generations. In addition, Rocío is the author of various publications and research works in the field of education, with a special interest in the development of pedagogical methodologies that enhance integral learning. Her commitment to promoting quality education and her dedication to improving learning experiences make her a leader in her field.

Audra Pickett has worked in various education roles for over 23 years. She began her education journey as a sixth-grade teacher and transitioned to higher education teaching in 2010. In 2015, Dr. Pickett began her online higher education professional career. She's served in roles such as in-person and online instructor, concurrent enrollment coordinator, professional development specialist, and curriculum revisions manager. She returned to K-12 in 2023 as an elementary instructional facilitator. In this role, Dr. Pickett is actualizing her dream as a support for teachers and administrators. She also teaches online for the American College of Education in the Teaching & Learning department. She has a Bachelor's in Elementary Education, a Master's in Curriculum Development & Instruction, a graduate certificate in Post-secondary Reading & Learning, and a Doctorate in Leadership. In her free time, Dr. Pickett enjoys taking advantage of the Colorado outdoors, and spending time with family, friends, and her dog, Manchester.

Usha Prabhu holds four Master degrees- MA, M. Phil, MBA, UGC- NET, Ph.D. She has more than 22 Years of teaching experience at the graduate and post-graduate levels. She was one of the member in the syllabus revision committee for the PG- MBA at Bangalore University. She is currently a Faculty at Jain (Deemed-to be University, Bangalore Karnataka, India. She co-authored the book- Organization Behaviour for PG Students.

Nurul Naimah Rose is a Senior Lecturer at Universiti Malaysia Perlis (UniMAP), Malaysia. She has a strong academic background, having earned her Bachelor's degree in Human Sciences and a Master's degree in Guidance and Counselling from International Islamic University Malaysia (IIUM). Her academic journey reached its pinnacle with a PhD in Counselling from Universiti Sains Malaysia (USM), where she specialized in counselling interventions for individuals with psychological distress. Her areas of expertise include psychological counselling, teaching, and learning. She is recognized for her engaging teaching style and her dedication to student success. Throughout her career, she has actively contributed to research projects in collaboration with the community. Her work has been published in various books, book chapters, and both local and international journals and conferences.

Bhupinder Singh working as Professor at Sharda University, India. Also, Honorary Professor in University of South Wales UK and Santo Tomas University Tunja, Colombia. His areas of publications as Smart Healthcare, Medicines, fuzzy logics, artificial intelligence, robotics, machine learning, deep learning, federated learning, IoT, PV Glasses, metaverse and many more. He has 3 books, 139 paper publications, 163 paper presentations in international/national conferences and seminars, participated in more than 40 workshops/FDP's/QIP's, 25 courses from international universities of repute, organized more than 59 events with international and national academicians and industry people's, editor-in-chief and co-editor in journals, developed new courses. He has given talks at international universities, resource person in international conferences such as in Nanyang Technological University Singapore, Tashkent State University of Law Uzbekistan; KIMEP University Kazakhstan, All'ah meh Tabatabi University Iran, the Iranian Association of International Criminal law, Iran and Hague Center for International Law and Investment, The Netherlands, Northumbria University Newcastle UK,

Vah Seliskar has more than nineteen years of experience in higher education, and is a Professor within the Graduate Public Safety Programs at Purdue University Global. Dr. Vah Seliskar's research interests include restorative justice, restorative practices in K-12 and higher education, restorative practices in the workplace, subjectivity in qualitative research, and best practices in online learning, teaching, and mentoring.

David Alan White is a Professor of Criminal Justice at Purdue University Global. He graduated with a Ph.D. from Northcentral University. He also earned an M.S. in Criminal Justice Studies from American International College and an M.P.A. from Florida Gulf Coast University. He was a law enforcement officer for over twenty-five years.

Index

A

Access and Accessibility 109, 113, 126, 130
active learning 16, 29, 48, 65, 84, 85, 88, 98, 116, 117, 123, 133, 134, 135, 136, 137, 138, 139, 140, 141, 143, 146, 147, 151, 152, 153, 154, 157, 158, 159, 160, 161, 163, 164, 175, 200, 209, 210, 236, 250, 291, 296, 342, 405, 407, 413, 420, 447, 457, 495, 518
active reading 133, 136, 150, 151, 152, 153, 164
Adobe Connect 415, 416, 423, 424, 425, 426, 438
adult learning 20, 171, 172, 174, 185, 186, 188, 190, 192, 414
AI Technology 195, 202, 212, 215, 216, 217, 218, 221, 227
Asynchronous learning 71, 90, 282, 338, 499
Asynchronous Video Exchange 448

B

Best Practices 14, 33, 37, 41, 50, 51, 65, 73, 74, 75, 76, 86, 89, 90, 115, 126, 175, 183, 187, 219, 229, 230, 235, 238, 246, 332, 342, 381, 394, 403, 407, 409, 443, 445, 446, 448, 453, 457, 472, 474, 476, 477, 491, 504, 519
BigBlueButton 415, 423, 425, 426, 438
Bloom's taxonomy 134, 141, 142, 144, 153, 325, 326, 327, 331, 332, 335, 336
Burnout 6, 10, 21, 33, 74, 77, 96, 104, 262, 271, 369, 370, 374, 375, 378, 387, 389, 390, 391, 397

C

care theory 167, 168, 169, 171, 172, 173, 175, 177, 178, 179, 180, 181, 182, 183, 184
Civic Responsibility 149, 182, 206, 228
Code of Conduct 378, 379, 383, 387, 391
Cognitive load theory 4, 140, 157, 284, 285, 287, 302, 303, 305, 309
Cognitive Presence 111, 112, 127, 205, 206, 227, 250, 313, 314, 318, 321, 324, 331, 332, 336, 337, 339, 340, 443, 444, 445, 446, 455, 456, 457, 458, 459, 460, 462, 463, 464, 466, 467, 468, 469
Collaborative Learning 12, 59, 65, 73, 78, 79, 81, 88, 100, 105, 109, 122, 125, 127, 130, 138, 141, 143, 146, 147, 149, 157, 163, 200, 202, 207, 210, 316, 317, 327, 328, 330, 337, 338, 339, 344, 350, 351, 352, 355, 359, 397, 474
Community Engagement 70, 195, 198, 206, 210, 211, 228, 462, 502
Community of Inquiry 111, 112, 127, 131, 200, 201, 205, 226, 313, 314, 318, 332, 333, 334, 337, 338, 340, 443, 444, 445, 448, 458, 460, 463, 464, 467
constructivism 131, 137, 140, 141, 150, 151, 157, 164, 185, 200, 226, 316, 317, 318, 332, 334, 335, 340

D

digital divide 43, 52, 55, 66, 72, 81, 82, 83, 89, 95, 215, 220, 476, 477, 495, 516
digital transformation 63, 124, 253, 254, 256, 274
Diverse Learners 48, 55, 98, 208, 241, 401, 501

E

educational psychology 37, 94, 95, 103, 106, 130, 137, 160, 163, 190, 192, 284, 303, 306, 307, 309, 311, 336
Educational Technologies 30, 103, 107, 194, 258, 341, 407
E-Learning 29, 61, 69, 70, 84, 92, 95, 98, 102, 103, 105, 119, 122, 124, 125, 127, 128, 129, 131, 189, 198, 223, 224, 249, 266, 273, 274, 275, 276, 277, 278, 279, 280, 282, 283, 285, 287, 288, 289, 290, 291, 292, 293,

294, 295, 296, 297, 298, 299, 300, 301, 304, 305, 308, 309, 311, 441, 473, 474, 475, 502
Electa 415, 423, 434, 435

F

Facilitated Discourse 468
faculty development 98, 253, 254, 256, 258, 259, 266, 267, 271, 375, 390
Faculty Engagement 6
Faculty online teaching readiness 254, 255, 256, 257, 260, 263, 264, 265, 266, 268, 269
Faculty Presence 31, 443, 444, 461, 467, 468
flipped learning 133, 134, 135, 137, 138, 139, 140, 141, 143, 144, 145, 146, 147, 153, 154, 157, 158, 159, 161, 162, 163, 164, 165, 166, 299
Formative Assessment 88, 95, 129, 341, 357, 358, 359, 401, 413, 414, 475, 494, 495

G

global citizenship 43, 50, 51, 58, 59, 60, 63, 65, 70, 72
global collaboration 41, 43, 44, 45, 46, 53, 58, 67, 72, 344
Global education 55, 65, 72

H

HEIs 497, 498, 499, 500, 501, 503, 504, 505, 506, 507, 508, 517
higher education 2, 3, 5, 6, 7, 14, 18, 20, 21, 28, 31, 32, 33, 35, 37, 38, 51, 52, 61, 63, 64, 65, 66, 67, 68, 69, 70, 71, 73, 74, 75, 76, 77, 79, 81, 87, 88, 90, 91, 92, 93, 94, 96, 97, 98, 99, 100, 101, 102, 103, 104, 105, 106, 109, 111, 114, 118, 127, 128, 129, 130, 131, 134, 135, 138, 140, 144, 145, 147, 149, 153, 154, 155, 158, 159, 160, 161, 163, 164, 165, 166, 168, 185, 186, 187, 188, 189, 192, 226, 230, 231, 240, 242, 246, 247, 248, 249, 250, 251, 253, 254, 256, 257, 258, 262, 264, 269, 271, 273, 274, 275, 276, 281, 303, 304, 305, 309, 313, 316, 317, 328, 333, 334, 336, 339, 341, 342, 366, 393, 400, 402, 410, 411, 412, 413, 414, 415, 416, 440, 441, 462, 463, 466, 467, 493, 494, 495, 497, 498, 500, 501, 502, 503, 504, 506, 507, 508, 512, 513, 516, 517, 518, 519, 521, 522, 523
Humanized Communication 468

I

Inclusive practices 111, 195, 393
Innovative pedagogy 63, 498
Institutional Policy 379, 380, 381, 382, 391
Instructional Strategies 95, 102, 111, 175, 192, 288, 299, 301, 321, 342, 402, 407, 408, 474, 476, 501
Interactive learning 44, 58, 61, 73, 81, 84, 106, 144, 154, 163, 166, 239, 259, 271, 272, 303, 334, 345, 346, 395, 406, 408, 413, 426, 436, 455, 458, 460, 461, 495
Interactive Tools 122, 230, 344, 347, 348, 352, 355, 356, 357, 360, 396

J

jigsaw 133, 136, 147, 148, 149, 150, 159, 163

K

Kahoot 116, 233, 396, 415, 423, 437, 438

L

language barriers 42, 45, 49, 72, 83, 84, 139
Learning Styles 41, 47, 58, 84, 87, 90, 94, 105, 121, 123, 149, 215, 228, 231, 235, 239, 277, 278, 280, 304, 343, 345, 348, 395, 396, 398, 405, 408, 442, 503
Lev Vygotsky 199

M

Martin Seligman 2, 7, 39
Massive Open Online Courses (MOOCs) 42, 55, 71, 105, 130, 197, 224, 277, 278, 280, 281, 282, 283, 300, 311
Microsoft Teams 59, 80, 95, 118, 396, 397, 415, 423, 429, 430, 438, 504
Moodle 80, 115, 122, 152, 197, 395, 396, 403, 415, 416, 423, 426, 427, 431, 438, 504, 515
multicultural education 72, 95
Multimodal Feedback 465, 468

O

Online Collaborative Learning Theory 109
online education 3, 8, 9, 11, 12, 14, 15, 17, 19, 26, 31, 36, 41, 42, 43, 44, 47, 48, 49, 50, 51, 52, 53, 54, 55, 56, 57, 58, 60, 61, 64, 66, 67, 68, 70, 75, 76, 89, 90, 96, 101, 110, 112, 114, 119, 123, 126, 127, 128, 130, 136, 155, 157, 172, 174, 184, 192, 197, 202, 205, 231, 237, 249, 254, 255, 256, 263, 266, 267, 269, 271, 273, 278, 282, 296, 314, 316, 319, 337, 341, 342, 348, 361, 371, 374, 376, 393, 394, 395, 396, 397, 402, 403, 404, 408, 409, 413, 426, 436, 461, 464, 472, 474, 475, 477, 478, 495, 496, 504
Online Engagement 75, 116, 466
online instruction 21, 38, 76, 77, 89, 90, 106, 172, 174, 175, 186, 333, 394, 406, 408, 410, 411, 464, 476, 503
online instructors 2, 13, 23, 73, 74, 75, 76, 77, 78, 81, 86, 87, 89, 90, 91, 98, 107, 167, 168, 172, 173, 174, 402, 403, 414
Online Learning 1, 2, 4, 8, 9, 10, 11, 12, 13, 14, 15, 16, 17, 18, 21, 22, 28, 29, 30, 31, 32, 33, 34, 35, 36, 37, 38, 39, 42, 43, 44, 48, 49, 50, 51, 55, 56, 58, 59, 61, 63, 65, 67, 69, 70, 71, 72, 74, 75, 77, 78, 79, 80, 81, 82, 83, 84, 85, 86, 87, 90, 91, 92, 95, 96, 97, 98, 100, 101, 102, 103, 104, 105, 106, 109, 110, 111, 112, 113, 114, 115, 116, 117, 118, 119, 120, 121, 122, 123, 126, 127, 129, 130, 131, 132, 151, 156, 167, 168, 172, 173, 174, 175, 177, 183, 185, 186, 189, 190, 192, 193, 194, 197, 200, 201, 202, 203, 218, 226, 227, 228, 229, 230, 231, 232, 246, 249, 250, 255, 259, 260, 262, 266, 269, 275, 276, 277, 278, 279, 280, 281, 282, 283, 289, 290, 292, 295, 297, 298, 301, 302, 306, 307, 308, 309, 310, 311, 333, 334, 335, 336, 337, 338, 339, 342, 345, 347, 348, 350, 351, 358, 360, 361, 362, 364, 366, 367, 393, 395, 396, 399, 405, 408, 409, 410, 412, 413, 415, 416, 421, 426, 439, 441, 442, 443, 444, 446, 451, 452, 454, 455, 460, 462, 463, 464, 465, 466, 467, 468, 469, 473, 477, 493, 494, 495, 496, 499, 503, 504, 515, 516
Online Learning Community 11, 91, 110, 111, 120, 121, 122, 126, 202, 203, 228, 395, 503
Online Open Elective Courses 394, 471, 472, 473, 474, 494
Online Platforms 4, 61, 81, 82, 89, 107, 197, 211, 300, 343, 344, 345, 357, 406, 472, 473, 474
online teaching 37, 51, 52, 75, 76, 80, 84, 86, 91, 96, 97, 98, 103, 105, 113, 128, 154, 172, 184, 185, 189, 192, 230, 232, 249, 250, 253, 254, 255, 256, 257, 258, 259, 260, 261, 262, 263, 264, 265, 266, 267, 268, 269, 270, 271, 272, 273, 274, 275, 276, 304, 336, 396, 402, 403, 404, 408, 409, 410, 412, 413, 434, 435, 438, 439, 441, 446, 447, 459, 472, 474, 476, 482, 491
online teaching readiness 253, 254, 255, 256, 257, 258, 260, 262, 263, 264, 265, 266, 267, 268, 269, 270, 273, 274, 275

P

Personalized Learning 41, 47, 48, 52, 58, 60, 62, 65, 71, 78, 80, 92, 96, 99, 111, 124, 125, 126, 128, 129, 130, 131,

155, 156, 215, 221, 250, 283, 296, 298, 300, 341, 343, 347, 348, 351, 353, 354, 358, 393, 395, 406, 408, 409, 473, 477, 494, 515, 516
Playful Pedagogy 1, 2, 18, 19, 20, 21, 28
Positive Academic Culture 6, 15, 16, 17
Positive emotions 1, 2, 7, 8, 9, 10, 14, 17, 19, 21, 23, 32, 34, 36, 37, 38, 39
Positive Psychology 1, 2, 7, 10, 29, 30, 37, 39, 103
Professional development 49, 58, 71, 74, 75, 76, 77, 78, 86, 91, 103, 113, 132, 157, 173, 176, 185, 188, 190, 234, 242, 246, 249, 260, 263, 279, 280, 281, 364, 393, 396, 402, 403, 404, 406, 407, 408, 409, 410, 412, 413, 414, 476, 477, 495, 496, 504
Project-based Learning 47, 67, 195, 196, 197, 198, 199, 200, 202, 204, 205, 212, 213, 216, 219, 221, 222, 224, 225, 226, 227, 228, 404, 405, 409, 463, 493, 511

R

Remediation 235, 378, 379, 387, 391
Remote Classroom 314

S

self-efficacy 37, 73, 74, 75, 76, 77, 78, 79, 80, 81, 86, 90, 91, 93, 97, 98, 99, 100, 101, 103, 104, 105, 106, 107, 153, 260, 262, 264, 275, 342, 345, 346, 348, 349, 350, 351, 360, 369, 411, 451, 520
Self-Regulation 5, 38, 77, 78, 79, 92, 100, 101, 104, 105, 106, 154, 155, 176, 181, 298, 319, 341, 344, 345, 347, 353, 354, 358, 360, 361, 397, 400, 446, 465
Social Capital 106, 195, 198, 199, 201, 202, 203, 204, 205, 207, 208, 209, 210, 211, 212, 216, 218, 219, 220, 221, 222, 224, 225, 226, 227, 228, 365
Social Presence 12, 33, 111, 112, 127, 130, 132, 192, 201, 205, 206, 250, 306, 314, 316, 318, 319, 322, 324, 328, 336, 337, 338, 340, 444, 445, 451, 452, 453, 455, 458, 459, 460, 462, 463, 465, 467, 469
Societal Impact 60, 217, 228
Student-centered Learning 20, 84, 85, 99, 136, 137, 145, 196, 211, 212, 221, 228, 407
Student engagement 1, 2, 8, 15, 16, 17, 21, 33, 34, 35, 38, 52, 69, 71, 76, 80, 81, 85, 86, 88, 89, 90, 91, 92, 97, 100, 101, 102, 111, 129, 130, 135, 137, 150, 151, 155, 156, 160, 165, 229, 230, 231, 235, 236, 239, 291, 297, 298, 299, 301, 304, 341, 342, 348, 357, 359, 360, 366, 395, 404, 405, 408, 409, 411, 437, 445, 455, 460, 461, 463, 471, 472, 474, 475, 476, 477, 480, 482, 483, 484, 485, 487, 488, 489, 490, 491, 493, 494, 516
Student Support 106, 111, 228, 502, 513
Student Voice 208, 225, 228
synchronous learning 94, 174

T

Teaching Presence 94, 111, 112, 127, 200, 205, 206, 259, 261, 263, 271, 315, 318, 319, 322, 324, 330, 331, 338, 340, 444, 446, 447, 448, 449, 450, 455, 458, 459, 460, 461, 462, 463, 464, 465, 466, 467, 468, 469
Technological advancements 51, 175, 298, 393, 408
technology-enhanced learning 72, 98, 163, 166, 495
traditional education 123, 202, 279
Transactional Distance 443, 444, 465, 469

V

Virtual classroom 44, 90, 91, 93, 174, 186, 316, 415, 416, 417, 418, 419, 420, 421, 422, 423, 425, 434, 435, 436, 438, 439, 440, 441, 442, 443, 444
virtual exchange 43, 44, 50, 64, 67, 70, 72, 463
Virtual Mathematics Education 344